# Assistive Technology Research, Practice, and Theory

Boaventura DaCosta
*Solers Research Group, USA*

Soonhwa Seok
*Korea University, South Korea*

A volume in the Advances in Medical Technologies and Clinical Practice (AMTCP) Book Series

| | |
|---|---|
| Managing Director: | Lindsay Johnston |
| Production Manager: | Jennifer Yoder |
| Publishing Systems Analyst: | Adrienne Freeland |
| Development Editor: | Allyson Gard |
| Acquisitions Editor: | Kayla Wolfe |
| Typesetter: | John Crodian |
| Cover Design: | Jason Mull |

Published in the United States of America by
Medical Information Science Reference (an imprint of IGI Global)
701 E. Chocolate Avenue
Hershey PA 17033
Tel: 717-533-8845
Fax: 717-533-8661
E-mail: cust@igi-global.com
Web site: http://www.igi-global.com



Library of Congress Cataloging-in-Publication Data

Assistive technology research, practice, and theory / Boaventura DaCosta and Soonhwa Seok, editors.
pages cm
Includes bibliographical references and index.
Summary: "This book presents cutting-edge research in the field of assistive technologies, including both theoretical frameworks and empirical research to benefit individuals with motor and cognitive disabilities"-- Provided by publisher.
ISBN 978-1-4666-5015-2 (hardcover) -- ISBN 978-1-4666-5016-9 (ebook) -- ISBN 978-1-4666-5017-6 (print & perpetual access) 1. Self-help devices for people with disabilities. 2. Assistive computer technology. I. DaCosta, Boaventura. II. Seok, Soonhwa, 1970-
HV1569.5.A85 2014
681'.761--dc23
2013037508

This book is published in the IGI Global book series Advances in Medical Technologies and Clinical Practice (AMTCP) (ISSN: 2327-9354; eISSN: 2327-9370)

British Cataloguing in Publication Data
A Cataloguing in Publication record for this book is available from the British Library.

All work contributed to this book is new, previously-unpublished material. The views expressed in this book are those of the authors, but not necessarily of the publisher.

For electronic access to this publication, please contact: eresources@igi-global.com.

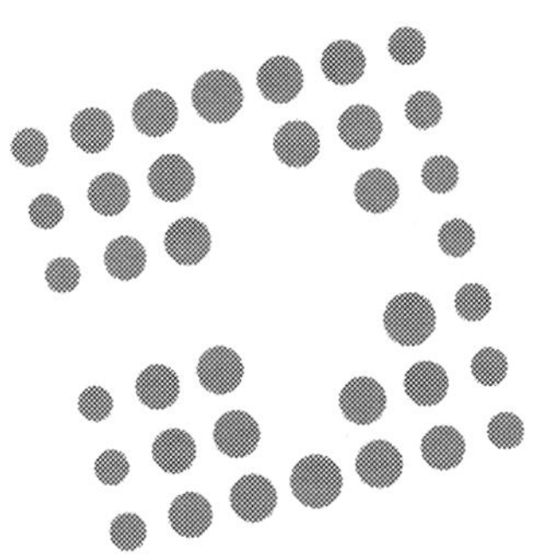

# Advances in Medical Technologies and Clinical Practice (AMTCP) Book Series

ISSN: 2327-9354
EISSN: 2327-9370

## Mission

Medical technological innovation continues to provide avenues of research for faster and safer diagnosis and treatments for patients. Practitioners must stay up to date with these latest advancements to provide the best care for nursing and clinical practices.

The **Advances in Medical Technologies and Clinical Practice (AMTCP) Book Series** brings together the most recent research on the latest technology used in areas of nursing informatics, clinical technology, biomedicine, diagnostic technologies, and more. Researchers, students, and practitioners in this field will benefit from this fundamental coverage on the use of technology in clinical practices.

## Coverage

- Biomedical Applications
- Clinical Data Mining
- Clinical High-Performance Computing
- Clinical Studies
- Diagnostic Technologies
- E-Health
- Medical Imaging
- Neural Engineering
- Nursing Informatics
- Patient-Centered Care

IGI Global is currently accepting manuscripts for publication within this series. To submit a proposal for a volume in this series, please contact our Acquisition Editors at Acquisitions@igi-global.com or visit: http://www.igi-global.com/publish/.

The Advances in Medical Technologies and Clinical Practice (AMTCP) Book Series (ISSN 2327-9354) is published by IGI Global, 701 E. Chocolate Avenue, Hershey, PA 17033-1240, USA, www.igi-global.com. This series is composed of titles available for purchase individually; each title is edited to be contextually exclusive from any other title within the series. For pricing and ordering information please visit http://www.igi-global.com/book-series/advances-medical-technologies-clinical-practice/73682. Postmaster: Send all address changes to above address. 

## Titles in this Series

*For a list of additional titles in this series, please visit: www.igi-global.com*

*Assistive Technology Research, Practice, and Theory*
Boaventura DaCosta (Solers Research Group, USA) and Soonhwa Seok (Korea University, South Korea)
Medical Information Science Reference • copyright 2014 • 282pp • H/C (ISBN: 9781466650152) • US $200.00 (our price)

*Assistive Technologies and Computer Access for Motor Disabilities*
Georgios Kouroupetroglou (University of Athens, Greece)
Medical Information Science Reference • copyright 2014 • 351pp • H/C (ISBN: 9781466644380) • US $200.00 (our price)

*Disability Informatics and Web Accessibility for Motor Limitations*
Georgios Kouroupetroglou (University of Athens, Greece)
Medical Information Science Reference • copyright 2014 • 443pp • H/C (ISBN: 9781466644427) • US $200.00 (our price)

*Medical Advancements in Aging and Regenerative Technologies Clinical Tools and Applications*
Andriani Daskalaki (Max Planck Institute for Molecular Genetics, Germany)
Medical Information Science Reference • copyright 2013 • 333pp • H/C (ISBN: 9781466625068) • US $245.00 (our price)

*E-Health, Assistive Technologies and Applications for Assisted Living Challenges and Solutions*
Carsten Röcker (RWTH Aachen University, Germany) and Martina Ziefle (RWTH Aachen University, Germany)
Medical Information Science Reference • copyright 2011 • 392pp • H/C (ISBN: 9781609604691) • US $245.00 (our price)

*Evidence-Based Practice in Nursing Informatics Concepts and Applications*
Andrew Cashin (Southern Cross University, Australia) and Robyn Cook (Sidra Medical & Research Center, Qatar)
Medical Information Science Reference • copyright 2011 • 320pp • H/C (ISBN: 9781609600341) • US $245.00 (our price)

*Biomedical Diagnostics and Clinical Technologies Applying High-Performance Cluster and Grid Computing*
Manuela Pereira (University of Beira Interior, Portugal) and Mario Freire (University of Beira Interior, Portugal)
Medical Information Science Reference • copyright 2011 • 396pp • H/C (ISBN: 9781605662800) • US $245.00 (our price)

## Editorial Advisory Board



## List of Reviewers

# Table of Contents

**Chapter 6**
Technology and Disability Laws, Regulations, and Rights ........ 75
*Carolyn Kinsell, Solers Research Group, USA*

**Section 2**
**Software, Devices, and Games**

**Chapter 7**
The Changing Face of Assistive Technology: From PC to Mobile to Cloud Computing ........ 90
*James R. Stachowiak, University of Iowa, USA*

**Chapter 8**
A Step toward Assistive Technology Evidence-Based Practices: Latent Dimensions of Information and Communication Technology ........ 99
*Boaventura DaCosta, Solers Research Group, USA*
*Soohnwa Seok, Korea University, South Korea*

**Chapter 9**
A Phatic Approach to Assistive and Augmentative Communications Vocabularies ........ 127
*Benjamin Slotznick, Point-and-Read, Inc., USA*

**Chapter 10**
Social Skills Development for Children with Autism Spectrum Disorders through the Use of Interactive Storytelling Games ........ 144
*Sukun Jin, Konkuk University, South Korea*
*Boaventura DaCosta, Solers Research Group, USA*
*Soohnwa Seok, Korea University, South Korea*

**Chapter 11**
Simulation Games as Interventions in the Promotion of Social Skills Development among Children with Autism Spectrum Disorders ........ 160
*Carolyn Kinsell, Solers Research Group, USA*
*Boaventura DaCosta, Solers Research Group, USA*
*Angelique Nasah, Solers Research Group, USA*

**Section 3**
**Implementation, Assessment, and Evaluation**

**Chapter 12**
From Barriers to Beginnings: New Media as Assistive Technology ........ 183
*Aubry Threlkeld, Harvard University, USA*

**Chapter 13**
Teacher Education and Principles of Effective Assistive Technology Implementation .................... 192
*Jennifer Courduff, Azusa Pacific University, USA*
*Amy Duncan, Claremont Graduate University, USA & California State University – San Bernardino, USA*
*Joanne Gilbreath, Azusa Pacific University, USA*

**Chapter 14**
Engaging in Play through Assistive Technology: Closing Gaps in Research and Practice for Infants and Toddlers with Disabilities........................................................................................................ 207
*Fiona S. Baker, Emirates College for Advanced Education, UAE*

**Chapter 15**
Creating Protective Barriers for Students with Disabilities in E-Learning Environments ................ 222
*Bob Barrett, American Public University, USA*

**Chapter 16**
Assistive Technology and Distance Learning: Making Content Accessible...................................... 233
*Kathleen Bastedo, University of Central Florida, USA*
*Jessica Vargas, Rollins College, USA*

**Chapter 17**
A 15 Factor and 157 Item Checklist for Assessing Website Usability and Accessibility .................. 252
*Carolyn Kinsell, Solers Research Group, USA*
*Boaventura DaCosta, Solers Research Group, USA*

**Compilation of References** ........................................................................................................ 277

**About the Contributors** ............................................................................................................. 306

**Index**........................................................................................................................................... 311

# Detailed Table of Contents



In this chapter, the challenges in accommodating the variety of students in today's diverse learning environments are presented along with the difficulties all students face in learning, not only those with disabilities. The authors present the case that Universal Design for Learning (UDL) can be successfully applied in helping reduce many of the barriers commonly found to access and learning. The authors explore the strides made in creating content that brain-based research supports as a way for not only motivating students to learn, but at the same time provide those with disabilities a means in which to learn that fits their specific needs. Namely, in this chapter, the authors examine and describe UDL to include its history, the framework, and the application of its principles, along with related laws and regulations at the federal level.



In this chapter, the authors discuss how the Universal Design for Learning framework provides guidelines that can be leveraged to help educators consider where and how assistive features and technology can be utilized to increase flexibility and choice for students. Ways in which teachers can use the assistive features of commonplace technology tools and software for classroom-based lessons are presented that can give students multiple means of representation, expression, action, and engagement. This is accomplished by presenting three vignettes that illustrate how computer applications and Web-based tools can be used to support diverse students, including students with learning disabilities and struggling learners. Namely, the case studies highlight ways in which educators can use a Web-based book builder that has built-in assistive supports, digital graphic organizer software, and an interactive whiteboard application on a tablet computer.

In this chapter, the author focuses on reading skills and explicitly presents the case for mainstreaming text-to-speech software for students with reading difficulties in the educational environment through the use of a socio-constructivist approach. The author contends that a purely functional approach for students with assessed specific reading disabilities limits the delivery of text-to-speech software outreach and use. This is because, despite increased consumer involvement with attendant potential to increase student participation and use, the target population of students with reading disabilities is typically defined in the context of human function. By transitioning to a socio-constructivist approach, the author presents the case that there is greater potential to assist a larger number of students.



In this chapter, the author discusses the challenges that today's students face while providing solutions and recommendations from the perspective of Assistive Technology (AT). The author begins the chapter by providing a brief overview, defining AT; he helps to put the state of writing skills in context by presenting what recent U.S. and international writing assessment results indicate; he continues with a discussion focused on the characteristics of struggling writers; finally, he explains how AT can be used effectively to help these students improve and manage the complex and interdependent task of creating prose, story in particular. Key examples of AT services discussed include self-regulated strategy development and mnemonic strategies. The author also reviews his own research focused on story writing and how integral AT is to helping struggling writers. Finally, the need for students' pre-requisite practice with AT is also emphasized.



In this chapter, the authors focus on ecological perspectives surrounding the design of self-determination-enhanced Problem-Based Learning (PBL). The authors present a PBL conceptual framework that can be leveraged in the implementation of the skills needed for the 21st-century, specifically self-determination for students with disabilities in inclusive settings. The framework is built upon an extensive research synthesis of the principles behind PBL instructional design with an emphasis on special education. Findings of the research synthesis revealed the relationships between self-determination learning and PBL. A collaborative learning model—SHARE: Structure, Hypothesis, Analysis, Research, and Evaluation—is proposed as a positive intervention in implementing PBL. Overall, the research synthesis points to a trend whereby technology-enhanced PBL is practiced with students with disabilities in inclusive settings and teacher education programs.

In this chapter, the author offers a broad overview of federal civil rights laws that ensure equal opportunity and fair treatment to people with disabilities. Although great strides have been made to make information about federal civil rights laws and regulations transparent and freely available to everyone, particularly with the ease of information dissemination on the Internet, the abundance of information available today can also be overwhelming. This is especially true given the complexity of some of these laws and regulations and the subtle differences in the manner in which states operate programs and offer services. Since some of these laws and regulations bring with them a wide range of rights and services, some of which translate to entitlements in the form of assistive technology services and devices, it is imperative that those with disabilities, their family members, and individuals who support people with disabilities become familiar with these various laws and regulations.



In this chapter, the author presents the powerful effect Assistive Technology (AT) has had on people with disabilities, particularly in the areas of reading, writing, communicating, and accessing information. The author notes that one of the roadblocks for use has always been the expense of AT. Advancements in computing and mobile technology, however, are making some technology more readily available, accessible, and cost-effective for people with disabilities. Using this line of thinking, the author presents accessible technologies, discussed in terms of mobile, personal computer, and cloud computing, that have or are quickly becoming part of the mainstream and every day, but which have already shown, or have the potential, to be incredibly helpful to those with disabilities, in particular those who have visual and hearing impairments.



In this chapter, the authors discuss the importance of Assistive Technology (AT) but from the perspective of Information and Communication Technology (ICT) and the need for validation research that contributes to AT evidence-based practices. The authors present the findings of a study aimed to identify latent dimensions of ICT that can serve as the basis for the eventual development of a standardized instrument for ICT assessment and selection in the context of AT. The ICT preferences and practices of 1,258 postsecondary students across 7 major universities were examined. A confirmatory factor analysis within the framework of structure equation modeling revealed the 5 latent dimensions: communicating, socializing, downloading and sharing, gaming, and learning. These dimensions, examined in the context of age, gender, and income, further revealed that these demographics, as sole determinants of ICT usage, are not supported. Noteworthy findings were also found with regard to participants' preferences for ICT to include a tendency to text over all other technologies.

**Chapter 9**
A Phatic Approach to Assistive and Augmentative Communications Vocabularies .......................... 127
*Benjamin Slotznick, Point-and-Read, Inc., USA*

In this chapter, the author presents the tools being developed to help remedy the challenges facing users of Augmentative Communications (AAC) systems and the "phatic" approach on which these tools are based. Namely, the author explains these users sometimes have difficulty participating in conversation outside of a script they already know, repairing a derailed conversation, or engaging in the quick and varied banter demanded of many social situations. Although the intent of this chapter is not to advocate for the replacement of standard AAC vocabularies, it does show how phatic vocabularies, through the use of tools and devices, can be successfully used to enhance a user's language development, particularly social language and social development, by creating vocabularies that encourage a user to engage in social settings.

**Chapter 10**
Social Skills Development for Children with Autism Spectrum Disorders through the Use of Interactive Storytelling Games .......................................................................................... 144
*Sukun Jin, Konkuk University, South Korea*
*Boaventura DaCosta, Solers Research Group, USA*
*Soohnwa Seok, Korea University, South Korea*

In this chapter, the authors discuss the potential that video games have in assisting children with autism spectrum disorders in the development of social skills. The importance of storytelling is discussed in the context of video games in part based on the role story plays in human development from early childhood. There is research to suggest, for instance, that storytelling in video games can be beneficial because it can be used to help players identify with characters and their goals, creating a greater sense of immersion, positive feelings, and more physiological arousal. The authors articulate that the use of computers and video games, combined with more traditional storytelling, may serve as hopeful tools for motivating and engaging students as well as promoting learning. The authors also propose a conceptual model that may be used to guide such an effort.

**Chapter 11**
Simulation Games as Interventions in the Promotion of Social Skills Development among Children with Autism Spectrum Disorders .......................................................................................... 160
*Carolyn Kinsell, Solers Research Group, USA*
*Boaventura DaCosta, Solers Research Group, USA*
*Angelique Nasah, Solers Research Group, USA*

In this chapter, the authors discuss use of video games in promoting social skills development for children with autism spectrum disorders, building upon the line of thinking in chapter 10 but narrowing the focus from the general application of video games to that of simulation-based games. The authors present the characteristics of this video game genre that help make this technology particularly attractive in education, especially as an intervention for social skills development. The authors also discuss the pivotal storytelling component contributing to the successful development of simulation-based games in an instructional context. This includes a discussion on the importance of immersion and motivation. This chapter is intended to be viewed as a call for researchers and practitioners who see potential in game technology to push for practical examples that can be shared as to how such games can be used to help mitigate the many challenges experienced by these children.

**Section 3**
**Implementation, Assessment, and Evaluation**

**Chapter 12**
From Barriers to Beginnings: New Media as Assistive Technology ................................................ 183
*Aubry Threlkeld, Harvard University, USA*

In this chapter, the author introduces the shifting and dynamic barriers that make the implementation of new media a challenge, while at the same time illuminating convergences between the goal of new media and Assistive Technology (AT). While the author explicitly concentrates on opportunities within the classroom, educators can also employ the guidelines outlined generally in out-of-school contexts. Barriers discussed by the author include electronic curb cuts and aggressive Internet filters. After discussing such barriers, solutions, including some classroom protocols and a list of resources, are shared to help educators evaluate new media as well as in the integration of new and old media as AT.

**Chapter 13**
Teacher Education and Principles of Effective Assistive Technology Implementation ..................... 192
*Jennifer Courduff, Azusa Pacific University, USA*
*Amy Duncan, Claremont Graduate University, USA & California State University – San Bernardino, USA*
*Joanne Gilbreath, Azusa Pacific University, USA*

In this chapter, the authors maintain that effective implementation of Assistive Technology (AT) is transformative for educator practice and student learning outcomes. Educators who embrace this effort are faced with a set of challenges that are not found in typical technology integration efforts, and in order to successfully and deeply integrate technology into instruction and learning, a change in pedagogy must be made. The authors, therefore, identify the unaddressed perspectives that impede technology implementation in diverse learning environments. First, a brief discussion on special education law and AT is provided. Next, foundations of AT and effective implementation strategies at the classroom level are discussed. The process by which educators can be supported in integrating technology tools into learning tasks is reviewed. This includes the presentation of a matrix that connects student-learning tasks with technology tools common to every classroom. Systemic implementation issues and strategies for success are also shared.

**Chapter 14**
Engaging in Play through Assistive Technology: Closing Gaps in Research and Practice for Infants and Toddlers with Disabilities............................................................................................................ 207
*Fiona S. Baker, Emirates College for Advanced Education, UAE*

In this chapter, the author discusses the challenges facing those who wish to effectively implement Assistive Technology (AT) but from the perspective of infants and toddlers. This chapter first discusses the importance of play and then draws attention to some issues and tensions that limit play and AT in early intervention for infants and toddlers with special needs. The criticality of exploring the potential of play for infants and toddlers with disabilities is then discussed by presenting research on the subject and offering practice-based suggestions. The author makes submission for some easily applied practical solutions for providers and parents and discusses some of the tensions that currently limit the provision of AT and services for infants and toddlers. Finally, thoughts are presented for the future of AT through research, early intervention play-based practices, and on-going education and development of early intervention providers and parents of infants and toddlers with special needs.

**Chapter 15**
Creating Protective Barriers for Students with Disabilities in E-Learning Environments ............... 222
*Bob Barrett, American Public University, USA*

In this chapter, the author presents two disparaging barriers facing people with disabilities: difficulties endured in securing permanent employment and obstacles in obtaining a quality education. In presenting barriers to employment, the significance of culture is discussed. This includes a discussion on the values and assumptions held by organizations and the societal changes that must occur if people with disabilities are to be given the same opportunities toward employment as those without disabilities. In presenting the barriers to education, the important role that academic institutions play in preparing people with disabilities for the workforce is discussed. This discussion is followed by the challenges facing not only learners with disabilities but also the challenges facing educational professionals in today's technologically rich online learning environment. This chapter ends by the author discussing the creation of strategies to erode the barriers commonly found in course design and how to empower students with disabilities with strategic tools.

**Chapter 16**
Assistive Technology and Distance Learning: Making Content Accessible...................................... 233
*Kathleen Bastedo, University of Central Florida, USA*
*Jessica Vargas, Rollins College, USA*

In this chapter, the authors focus exclusively on online learning, specifically distance learning courses and the benefits they can provide to people with disabilities. Through the exploration of current research and trends, the authors review Learning Management Systems (LMS), learner interaction styles and tools, and methods to design accessible course materials. The authors provide educators with not only a working vocabulary but also strategies and implementation methods for ensuring accessible content in online learning. Specifically, the authors investigate the types of interactions in distance learning, identify the distance learner and their technological needs, distinguish between two classifications of LMS (i.e., open vs. closed or proprietary), recognize the features of learning managements systems that incorporate accessible design, identify the laws related to accessibility of distance learning materials in K-12 and higher education, and most importantly, offer accessibility best practices to the creation of distance learning course materials.

**Chapter 17**
A 15 Factor and 157 Item Checklist for Assessing Website Usability and Accessibility ................. 252
*Carolyn Kinsell, Solers Research Group, USA*
*Boaventura DaCosta, Solers Research Group, USA*

In this chapter, the authors offer a checklist comprised of 15 factors and 157 items rooted in cognitive psychology, instructional design, computer science, but most importantly, human-computer interface study. The authors contend that instruments to help assess and measure the usability of websites are vital in ensuring that websites not only meet their intended purpose but are also usable and accessible. The checklist offered in this chapter has been extensively used and matured over a number of years in assessing the usability and accessibility of website design for clients in the private and public sectors as well as government. Although the checklist should in no way be considered exhaustive, it should be viewed as a practical starting point, which can be augmented to meet the specific needs of companies, organizations, and individuals in their website assessment efforts.

# Foreword

The goal of the editors in designing this book was based on the strong belief that learning environments in which students with disabilities learn and thrive have been significantly enhanced by the collective efforts of policy makers, researchers, and practitioners in the field of Assistive Technology (AT). Supportive policies are in place, and educators have a sense of direction as to what needs to be done to continue strengthening the impact of AT in schools. Parents understand the benefits of technology for their children who struggle with learning. They are informed advocates for their children and are much more sophisticated in their perspectives on the potential of technology to not only improve learning environments but also to also make a qualitative difference in the lives of their children as they mature into independent contributors to society.

These changes in e-learning environments are also driven by advancements in technology. However, these improvements are not solely the result of the commercial sector. The emergence of evidence-based practices and increased educational leadership at all levels in education serve to inform the growing industry that undergirds AT. Teachers are better prepared to sense the technology needs of students. Building administrators are demonstrating that as instructional leaders they must also be the source of leadership in moving the application of technology forward as a resource essential to learning and teaching for all learners. Community leaders serving on local boards of education bring to their role personal experience in technology that is not only recent but also often central to their professional and personal lives. State and federal agencies have played a pivotal role in changing the landscape of e-learning environments for all learners. In many ways the policies of these agencies are ahead of their times and/or too ambitious for today's economy.

Clearly, great strides have been made in recent years in positioning schools to meet the needs of student's disabilities. Take for example the possibilities of AT in enriching the lives of these individuals. First defined in the U.S. through the Individuals with Disabilities Education Act of 1990 (Public Law 101-476) and later modified in the Individuals with Disabilities Education Improvement Act (Public Law 108-446) to address the exclusion of surgically implanted medical devices, AT is defined in terms of both devices and services. This is important in that AT should not only be viewed in the context of devices that promote greater independence by enabling individuals with disabilities to achieve their learning potential but also to perform everyday tasks that they otherwise would not be able to accomplish. Assistive technology should also be viewed in the context of services that directly assist individuals with disabilities in sustaining and furthering their utilization of technology as a major contributor to their quality of life.

Providing an optimistic context in introducing the work of contributing authors to this book is not intended to imply that the challenges have been met in maximizing the potential of AT for the benefit of all learners. That is certainly not the case. However, lessons have been learned over the past decade and the learning environments experienced in the schools have changed. The circumstances are such that the publication of this book is very timely. In a field changing so dramatically as AT, no one author has the breadth of experience and perspective to address the lessons learned, the evolvement of the growing knowledge base, evidence-based practices, and policy needs. Considerable effort was invested in recruiting authors to the team whose expertise was complimentary of other authors on the team and whose collective knowledge and experience address the focus of the book at this time in the evolution of AT. Although AT is positioned as an integral part of the knowledge base and holds a significant place in the professional literature on instructional technology and special education, much more work remains to be done in theory development, research, and practice.

While the challenges of the future may appear to be daunting, it is important to point out that there is no better time than currently to be involved in moving forward to strengthen e-learning environments and increase preparation for independent living through technology. The knowledge base is substantial, advancements in technology remain to be employed through technological advancements, and industry is well positioned to expand research and development to yield AT devices and services not currently available. Technologies, such as mobile devices and social media, as well as features, such as text-to-speech, have created opportunities and afforded access to content that not long ago would have been beyond the reach of people with disabilities without specialized and sometimes cost prohibitive assistive devices. That is no longer the case. There is every reason to believe that the horizon for AT is bright.

*Assistive Technology Research, Practice, and Theory*, by Boaventura DaCosta and Soonhwa Seok, is an important contribution for those who are interested in the present and future of AT. More importantly, it represents a significant resource for those who are interested in what is possible in supporting individuals with disabilities in K-12 and higher education as well in the communities where their contributions to society will occur. Unlike other books focused almost exclusively on cutting-edge technology or limited to specific applications in the classroom, this book offers a broader perspective through the transdisciplinary perspectives of the authors currently involved in different facets of AT and who collectively build on their expertise to share visions for the future. This is a highly integrated book that provides theoretical frameworks, empirical research findings, and evidence-based practices that will guide the future. This book addresses trends and issues related to AT in the context of what is available to drive research, practices, policies, and emerging technologies for the future.

As you read through these chapters, I encourage you to reflect upon the insights they offer as well as consider the recommendations provided by the authors. With this said, at the core of special education is individualized instruction. Thus, I also encourage you to challenge the ideas presented in this book and determine what works in your specific situation. Most importantly, share your experiences with others. It is only through steady questioning and exploration that we can truly help those with special needs and promote the field of AT.

*Edward Meyen*
*University of Kansas, USA*

**Edward Meyen** *is a professor in special education. During his career at the University of Kansas, he has served in a number of leadership roles in administration while continuing his teaching. In 2001, he and a small group of colleagues from across the campus founded the eLearning Design Lab, which is basically a partnership between a telecommunication center and the Center for Research on Learning. The lab is focused on research and development in e-learning at the post-secondary and K-12 levels with a particular emphasis on students with disabilities. It is self-supporting through grants and contracts and employs a large number of students. Since 2001, 24 PhD and numerous Master and undergraduate degrees have been earned by students while working in the lab. He is actively involved in a wide variety of research and development projects that are focused on online instruction.*

# Preface

Our world has witnessed extraordinary technological advancements impacting almost every field of human endeavor. Now more than ever, practical and empirically grounded research focused on education and technology is needed if we are to better understand the world, ourselves, and how we can advance. The field of Assistive Technology (AT) has come a long way since the term "universal design" was first coined and linear perspectives were at the forefront of assisting those with disabilities. Specialized software and devices once synonymous with AT are now commonplace. The unprecedented advancements in mobile computing, coupled with legislation and the collective movement towards inclusive settings, for example, makes it no better time than today to strive for AT equity in terms of universal implementation.

This book is a realization of a yearlong collaborative endeavor by professionals, practitioners, and researchers from both academia and industry in the U.S. and abroad dedicated to the advancement and promotion of AT in the everyday through enriching the lives of those with special needs. Those who contributed their time and expertise to this publication have been leaders and positive influences in the ever-changing technology and education landscape. These individuals come from a diverse set of disciplines to include computer science, curriculum and instruction, game development, human performance, industrial and operations engineering, instructional design, law, medicine, occupational therapy, special education, and social work to name only a few. Providing a transdisciplinary perspective, this book provides relevant theoretical frameworks, the latest empirical research findings, and the practical application of AT, setting this publication apart from other works providing insights into AT. Namely, this book addresses trends and issues related to AT, presenting the latest practices based on what is available to date with regard to research and emergent technologies. This book is intended for educational professionals and practitioners as well as researchers involved in special education along with other fields which benefit from AT.

## SECTION ONE: THEORIES, CONCEPTS, AND LAWS

This book is comprised of 17 chapters presented in three sections. "Section 1: Theories, Concepts, and Laws" serves as scaffolding for the remainder of this book, by introducing theories, concepts, and laws either discussed or mentioned in many of the chapters. This book begins with a discussion of Universal Design for Learning (UDL)—an educational framework founded on research in the learning sciences to include cognitive neuroscience—intended to help guide in the development of educational content accommodating individual learning differences (Rose & Meyer, 2002). In fact, UDL is so important in the context of this book that 2 chapters have been dedicated to its coverage.

In chapter 1, the challenges in accommodating the variety of students in today's diverse learning environments are presented along with the difficulties *all* students face in learning, not only those with disabilities. The authors present the case that Universal Design for Learning (UDL) can be successfully applied in helping reduce many of the barriers commonly found to access and learning. The authors explore the strides made in creating content that brain-based research supports as a way for not only motivating students to learn, but at the same time provide those with disabilities a means in which to learn that fits *their* specific needs. Namely, in this chapter, the authors examine and describe UDL to include its history, the framework, and the application of its principles, along with related laws and regulations at the federal level.

This line of thinking is continued in Chapter 2. Bryant, Rao, and Ok discuss how the UDL framework provides guidelines that can be leveraged to help educators consider where and how assistive features and technology can be utilized to increase flexibility and choice for students. The authors describe ways in which teachers can use the assistive features of commonplace technology tools and software for classroom-based lessons to give students multiple means of representation, expression, action, and engagement. Specifically, the authors provide three vignettes that illustrate how computer applications and Web-based tools can be used to support diverse students, including students with learning disabilities and struggling learners.

Bryant, Rao, and Ok maintain that with an awareness of the assistive features of various applications, educators can apply UDL principles to lessons by integrating technology in thoughtful and deliberate ways into instruction and assessment. Furthermore, the authors describe how teachers can consider UDL principles during the lesson design and implementation process and can proactively provide options and enable support features through the technologies they use in their lessons and classes. The case studies highlight ways in which educators can use a Web-based book builder that has built-in assistive supports, digital graphic organizer software, and an interactive whiteboard application on a tablet computer.

Finally, Bryant, Rao, and Ok submit that most intervention research on learning disabilities has focused on reading, writing, and mathematics, with reading garnering the most attention. Text-to-speech is one example of an AT feature that has become ubiquitous on various devices. Therefore, it should not come as a surprise that the next three chapters touch upon these kinds of skills.

For example, in Chapter 3, Baker focuses on reading skills and explicitly presents the case for mainstreaming text-to-speech software for students with reading difficulties in the educational environment through the use of a socio-constructivist approach. The author contends that a purely functional approach for students with assessed specific reading disabilities limits the delivery of text-to-speech software outreach and use. This is because, despite increased consumer involvement with attendant potential to increase student participation and use, the target population of students with reading disabilities is typically defined in the context of human function. By transitioning to a socio-constructivist approach, the author presents the case that there is greater potential to assist a larger number of students.

The focus moves to writing skills in Chapter 4, where Dunn discusses the challenges that today's students face while providing solutions and recommendations from the perspective of Assistive Technology (AT). The author begins the chapter by providing a brief overview, defining AT; he helps to put the state of writing skills in context by presenting what recent U.S. and international writing assessment results indicate; he continues with a discussion focused on the characteristics of struggling writers; finally, he explains how AT can be used effectively to help these students improve and manage the complex and interdependent task of creating prose, story in particular. Key examples of AT services discussed include self-regulated strategy development and mnemonic strategies. The author also reviews his own research focused on story writing and how integral AT is to helping struggling writers. Finally, the need for students' pre-requisite practice with AT is also emphasized.

While in Chapter 5, Seok, DaCosta, and Kim focus on ecological perspectives surrounding the design of self-determination-enhanced Problem-Based Learning (PBL). The authors present a PBL conceptual framework that can be leveraged in the implementation of the skills needed for the 21st century, specifically self-determination for students with disabilities in inclusive settings. The framework is built upon an extensive research synthesis of the principles behind PBL instructional design with an emphasis on special education. Findings of the research synthesis revealed the relationships between self-determination learning and PBL.

A collaborative learning model—SHARE: Structure, Hypothesis, Analysis, Research, and Evaluation—is proposed as a positive intervention in implementing PBL. Overall, the research synthesis points to a trend whereby technology-enhanced PBL is practiced with students with disabilities in inclusive settings and teacher education programs (Brown, 2005; Raskind & Bryant, 2002; Wehmeyer, 1999). In addition to the recommendation to use the SHARE learning model as a positive intervention, the authors propose that educator quality is essential in designing and implementing self-determination-enhanced PBL, as can be implemented using the proposed PBL conceptual framework. Educators, educational policymakers, and researchers involved in inclusive education practices will find that this chapter has far-reaching implications in the context of problem solving, as 21st century learning skills become increasingly vital in today's society.

Finally, this section of the book concludes with chapter 6, in which Kinsell offers a broad overview of federal civil rights laws that ensure equal opportunity and fair treatment to people with disabilities. Although great strides have been made to make information about federal civil rights laws and regulations transparent and freely available to everyone, particularly with the ease of information dissemination on the Internet, the abundance of information available today can also be overwhelming. This is especially true given the complexity of some of these laws and regulations and the subtle differences in the manner in which states operate programs and offer services. Since some of these laws and regulations bring with them a wide range of rights and services, some of which translate to entitlements in the form of assistive technology services and devices, it is imperative that those with disabilities, their family members, and individuals who support people with disabilities become familiar with these various laws and regulations.

Although this chapter does not cover all laws and regulations, such as the Higher Education Opportunity Act of 2008 (briefly discussed in chapter 1 in the context of UDL), much of the legislation presented by the author is either discussed or presented in the chapters found in this book. Most notably are the Americans with Disabilities Act and the Individuals with Disabilities Education Act, which are referenced in almost all of the chapters. This chapter should therefore be used as a reference in not only learning more about the specific laws and regulations but also in finding additional resources to the respective governing office, agency, or outside organization in order to obtain the latest up-to-date information.

## SECTION 2: SOFTWARE, DEVICES, AND GAMES

In the second section of this book, "Section 2: Software, Devices, and Games," the emphasis moves away from theories, concepts, and laws to focus on the AT itself. As the title implies, this section of the book focuses specifically on software, devices, and games. As previously stated, text-to-speech is one example of a once synonymous AT feature that has become ubiquitous across various devices, most notably mobile technology (e.g., smartphones, tablets, and eReaders). Technology now considered everyday forms of communication, such as email, instant messaging, and texting, have made a huge impact on the lives of those with certain disabilities. Even video games now hold the interest of educators and researchers, as potential interventions in teaching children with certain neurodevelopmental disorders.

Chapter 7 begins the discussion with Stachowiak presenting the effect Assistive Technology (AT) has had on people with disabilities, particularly in the areas of reading, writing, communicating, and accessing information. The author notes that one of the roadblocks for use has always been the expense of AT. Advancements in computing and mobile technology, however, are making some technology more readily available, accessible, and cost-effective for people with disabilities. Using this line of thinking, the author presents *accessible technologies*, discussed in terms of mobile, personal computer, and cloud computing, that have or are quickly becoming part of the mainstream and every day, but which have already shown, or have the potential, to be incredibly helpful to those with disabilities, in particular those who have visual and hearing impairments. Take for example, computer operating systems, to include Microsoft Windows® and Apple Mac OS®, which continue to be feature rich with AT capabilities, such as the ability to magnify the screen for reading and in the entering of text, or the mobile movement of smartphones, eReaders, and tablets, that have also been changing the way people with disabilities access information. The capabilities of these devices combined with the immediate availability, affordability, and ease of use, has been making the world more accessible for people with disabilities, and with mobile devices increasingly becoming a necessity for most, this trend is anticipated to only continue.

In Chapter 8, the discussion of AT continues, but from the perspective of Information and Communication Technology (ICT) and the need for validation research that contributes to AT evidence-based practices. The authors present the findings of a study aimed to identify latent dimensions of ICT that can serve as the basis for the eventual development of a standardized instrument for ICT assessment and selection in the context of AT. The ICT preferences and practices of 1,258 postsecondary students across 7 major universities were examined. A confirmatory factor analysis within the framework of structure equation modeling revealed the 5 latent dimensions: communicating, socializing, downloading and sharing, gaming, and learning. These dimensions, examined in the context of age, gender, and income, further revealed that these demographics, as sole determinants of ICT usage, are not supported. Noteworthy findings were also found with regard to participants' preferences for ICT to include a tendency to text over all other technologies.

As with the Nasah et al. (2010) study, claims that students are much more adept at all things digital are not borne out of the findings in this chapter, but instead the findings call into question the overarching suppositions made about young people and their technological prowess, to include the belief that young people are more interested in using technology for social networking and personal reasons (Keen, 2007). At the same time, DaCosta and Seok point out that there is no denying the significance of ICT in modern society. The latent dimensions of ICT fleshed out in this chapter, accordingly, provide a reference point in which to begin examining the ICT preferences and practices of those with special needs, and more importantly, may lead to the eventual development of a standardized instrument for ICT assessment and selection in the context of AT.

An extension of a chapter found in the book, *Handbook of Research on Human Cognition and Assistive Technology: Design, Accessibility, and Transdisciplinary Perspectives* by Seok, Meyen, and DaCosta (2010), chapter 9 continues the discussion on communication-related AT with Slotznick presenting the tools being developed to help remedy the challenges facing users of Augmentative Communications (AAC) systems and the "phatic" approach on which these tools are based. Namely, the author explains these users sometimes have difficulty participating in conversation outside of a script they already know, repairing a derailed conversation, or engaging in the quick and varied banter demanded of many social situations. Although the intent of this chapter is not to advocate for the replacement of standard AAC vocabularies, it does show how phatic vocabularies, through the use of tools and devices, can be successfully used to enhance a user's language development, particularly social language and social development, by creating vocabularies that encourage a user to engage in social settings.

In the last 2 chapters found in this section of the book, the benefits of video games, specifically simulation-based games, are presented, and how this genre of game, when coupled with the element of storytelling, may be effectively used as an intervention in helping children with Autism Spectrum Disorders (ASD), who have trouble with everyday social situations and/or communication difficulties not seen with neurotypical children. It has been suggested that game technology can be successfully used to aid in social skills development among those with special needs (Griffiths, 2002). In the context of these 2 chapters, such technology has been used in social skills development for children and adolescents with ASD, along with other developmental challenges (Gaylord-Ross, Haring, Breen, & Pitts-Conway, 1984; Grandin, 2012; McElroy, 2011; Porter, 1995; Tartaro & Cassell, 2006), to include helping children with limited vocal speech acquisition (Horn, Jones, & Hamlett, 1991), disabilities in spatial ability development (Masendorf, 1993), problem-solving (Hollingsworth & Woodward, 1993), and mathematics (Okolo, 1992).

In chapter 10, Jin, DaCosta, and Seok discuss the potential that video games have in assisting children with ASD in the development of social skills. The importance of storytelling is discussed in the context of video games in part based on the role story plays in human development from early childhood (Eisenberg, 1985; Fivush, 1994). There is research to suggest, for instance, that storytelling in video games can be beneficial because it can be used to help players identify with characters and their goals, creating a greater sense of immersion, positive feelings, and more physiological arousal. Furthermore, when the content is specific and targeted, these games are well suited for promoting acquisition, maintenance, and generalization of skills and knowledge. The authors articulate that findings such as these hold immense promise in the context of improving social skills for children with ASD. Thus, the use of computers and video games, combined with more traditional storytelling, may serve as hopeful tools for motivating and engaging students as well as promoting learning. The authors expound upon this line of reasoning and explore the use of interactive storytelling games as an effective intervention in social skills development for children with ASD, proposing a conceptual model that may be used to guide such an effort.

In chapter 11, Kinsell, DaCosta, and Nasah continue the discussion on the use of video games in promoting social skills development for children with ASD, building upon the work of Jin, DaCosta, and Seok in chapter 10, but narrowing the focus from the general application of video games to that of simulation-based games. The authors present the characteristics of this video game genre that help make this technology particularly attractive in education, especially as an intervention for social skills development. The authors also discuss the pivotal storytelling component contributing to the successful development of simulation-based games in an instructional context. This includes a discussion on the importance of immersion and motivation.

Although these 2 chapters only begin to scratch the surface as to the potential benefits and challenges of leveraging video games in helping children with special needs, the discussions presented by Jin, DaCosta, and Seok and Kinsell, DaCosta, and Nasah should be viewed as a call for researchers and practitioners who see potential in game technology. There are many factors that must be taken into consideration when leveraging such technology, and learning how to use these factors together is imperative if game technologies, such as simulation-based games, are to be effective in helping children with ASD develop needed social skills. Researchers and practitioners should, therefore, push for practical examples that can be shared as to how such games can be used to help mitigate the many challenges experienced by these children. It is through such investigation that the authors argue the manner in which this technology can present greater possibilities in promoting the generalization of social skills among children with ASD and other disabling conditions.

## SECTION 3: IMPLEMENTATION, ASSESSMENT, AND EVALUATION

Finally, "Section 3: Implementation, Assessment, and Evaluation" focuses on the challenges in the implementation, assessment, and evaluation of AT for those with disabilities of all ages, both in and out of the classroom. Namely, in the chapters that follow, common barriers experienced by professionals, educators, as well as students with disabilities are discussed, such as difficulties endured in securing permanent employment, obstacles (i.e., physical and virtual) in accessing quality education, and limited opportunities offered to those seeking quality AT interventions for infants and toddlers. More importantly, solutions are offered in mitigating such barriers by providing strategies and best practices in the implementation, assessment, and evaluation of AT for students with disabilities both in and out of the classroom.

In chapter 12, Threlkeld introduces the shifting and dynamic barriers that make the implementation of new media a challenge, while at the same time illuminating convergences between the goal of new media and Assistive Technology (AT). While the author explicitly concentrates on opportunities within the classroom, educators can also employ the guidelines outlined generally in out-of-school contexts. Barriers discussed by the author include electronic curb cuts and aggressive Internet filters. After discussing such barriers, solutions, including some classroom protocols and a list of resources, are shared to help educators evaluate new media as well as in the integration of new and old media as AT.

The discussion on the challenges facing educators who wish to effectively implement AT continues in chapter 13. Courduff, Duncan, and Gilbreath maintain that effective implementation of AT is transformative for educator practice and student learning outcomes. Educators who embrace this effort are faced with a set of challenges that are not found in typical technology integration efforts, and in order to successfully and deeply integrate technology into instruction and learning, a change in pedagogy must be made. The authors, therefore, identify the unaddressed perspectives that impede technology implementation in diverse learning environments, contending that when this unique set of perspectives is addressed, strategies for effective practice can emerge.

Courduff, Duncan, and Gilbreath first provide a brief discussion on special education law and AT to help frame the chapter. Next, foundations of AT and effective implementation strategies at the classroom level are discussed. The process by which educators can be supported in integrating technology tools into learning tasks is reviewed. This includes the presentation of a matrix that connects student-learning tasks with technology tools common to every classroom. The importance of making emotional connections and providing time to practice and share in an environment where failure is seen as an opportunity for growth is also discussed. Finally, systemic implementation issues and strategies for success are shared.

In Chapter 14, Baker discusses the challenges facing those who wish to effectively implement Assistive Technology (AT) but from the perspective of infants and toddlers. This chapter first discusses the importance of play and then draws attention to some issues and tensions that limit play and AT in early intervention for infants and toddlers with special needs. The criticality of exploring the potential of play for infants and toddlers with disabilities is then discussed by presenting research on the subject and offering practice-based suggestions. The author makes submission for some easily applied practical solutions for providers and parents and discusses some of the tensions that currently limit the provision of AT and services for infants and toddlers. Finally, thoughts are presented for the future of AT through research, early intervention play-based practices, and on-going education and development of early intervention providers and parents of infants and toddlers with special needs.

In the remaining 3 chapters of this book, barriers to implementing AT are further discussed, but in the context of online learning. In chapter 15, Barrett claims 2 of the most disparaging barriers facing people with disabilities are difficulties endured in securing permanent employment and obstacles in obtaining a quality education. In presenting barriers to employment, the significance of culture is discussed. This includes a discussion on the values and assumptions held by organizations and the societal changes that must occur if people with disabilities are to be given the same opportunities toward employment as those without disabilities. In presenting the barriers to education, the important role that academic institutions play in preparing people with disabilities for the workforce is discussed. This discussion is followed by the challenges facing not only learners with disability but also the challenges facing educational professionals in today's technologically rich online learning environment. This chapter ends with the author discussing the creation of strategies to erode the barriers commonly found in course design and how to empower students with disabilities with strategic tools. This chapter serves as a catalyst in the facilitation of discussion between professionals in industry and academia in how to work together in what should be a symbiotic relationship in assisting those with disabilities in not only accessing a quality education but at the same time being prepared for meeting the employment needs and demands of the business community.

In chapter 16, Bastedo and Vargas focus exclusively on online learning, specifically distance learning courses and the benefits they can provide to people with disabilities. Through the exploration of current research and trends, the authors review Learning Management Systems (LMS), learner interaction styles and tools, and methods to design accessible course materials. The authors provide educators with not only a working vocabulary but also strategies and implementation methods for ensuring accessible content in online learning. Specifically, the authors investigate the types of interactions in distance learning, identify the distance learner and their technological needs, distinguish between two classifications of LMS (i.e., open vs. closed or proprietary), recognize the features of learning managements systems that incorporate accessible design, identify the laws related to accessibility of distance learning materials in K-12 and higher education, and most importantly, offer accessibility best practices to the creation of distance learning course materials.

Finally, this book ends with chapter 17, in which Kinsell and DaCosta offer a checklist comprised of 15 factors and 157 items rooted in cognitive psychology, instructional design, computer science, but most importantly, human-computer interface study. The checklist can be used to guide researchers and practitioners in assessing the usability and accessibility of website design. The authors explain that although academic researchers have long advocated the importance of assessing the effectiveness of websites (Law, Qi, & Buhalis, 2010), with numerous approaches published (Law & Bai, 2006; Tullis & Stetson, 2004; Evans & King, 1999; Lu & Yeung, 1998; Stern, 2002; Stout, 1997) and efforts made to help improve the overall quality of websites (Law & Bai, 2006), website assessment is still a very much ill-defined practice, conducted by some and largely ignored by most.

The authors contend that instruments to help assess and measure the usability of websites are vital in ensuring that websites not only meet their intended purpose but are also usable and accessible. The checklist offered in this chapter has been extensively used and matured over a number of years in assessing the usability and accessibility of website design for clients in the private and public sectors, as well as government. Although the checklist should in no way be considered exhaustive, it should be viewed as a practical starting point, which can be augmented to meet the specific needs of companies, organizations, and individuals in their website assessment efforts.

We conclude by acknowledging our gratitude to have been afforded the opportunity to have assembled such a diverse collection of chapters into a single work. Although the benefits of technology for people with disabilities are widely recognized, much more needs to be done. It is our hope that this book is a step forward in advancing the field of AT and that it serves as a positive influence towards improving the lives of those with disabilities.

*Boaventura DaCosta*
*Solers Research Group, USA*

*Soohnwa Seok*
*Korea University, Korea*

## REFERENCES

Brown, M. (2005). Access granted: Achieving technological equity in the 21st century. In D. Edyburn, K. Higgins, & R. Boone (Eds.), *Handbook of special education technology research and practice* (pp. 105–118). Whitefish Bay, WI: Knowledge by Design.

Eisenberg, A. R. (1985). Learning to describe past experiences in conversation. *Discourse Processes*, *8*, 177–208. doi:10.1080/01638538509544613

Evans, J. R., & King, V. E. (1999). Business-to-business marketing and the world wide web: Planning, managing, and assessing websites. *Industrial Marketing Management*, *28*(4), 343–358. doi:10.1016/S0019-8501(98)00013-3

Fivush, R. (1994). Constructing narrative, emotion, and self in parent-child conversations about the past. In U. Neisser, & R. Fivush (Eds.), *The remembering self: Construction and accuracy in the self-narrative* (pp. 136–157). Cambridge, UK: Cambridge University Press. doi:10.1017/CBO9780511752858.009

Gaylord-Ross, R. J., Haring, T. G., Breen, C., & Pitts-Conway, V. (1984). The training and generalization of social interaction skills with autistic youth. *Journal of Applied Behavior Analysis*, *17*, 229. doi:10.1901/jaba.1984.17-229 PMID:6735954

Grandin, T. (2012). What's the big deal about video games? *Autism Asperger's Digest*. Retrieved from http://autismdigest.com/whats-the-big-deal-about-video-games/

Griffiths, M. D. (2002). The educational benefits of videogames. *Education for Health*, *20*(3), 47–51.

Hollingsworth, M., & Woodward, J. (1993). Integrated learning: Explicit strategies and their role in problem solving instruction for students with learning disabilities. *Exceptional Children*, *59*, 444–445. PMID:8440301

Horn, E., Jones, H. A., & Hamlett, C. (1991). An investigation of the feasibility of a video game system for developing scanning and selection skills. *Journal for the Association for People with Severe Handicaps*, *16*, 108–115.

Keen, A. (2007). *The cult of the amateur: How today's Internet is killing our culture*. London: Broadway Business.

Law, R., & Bai, B. (2006). Website development and evaluations in tourism: A retrospective analysis. In M. Hitz, M. Sigala, & J. Murphy (Eds.), *Information and communication technologies in tourism* (pp. 1–12). New York: Springer-Wien. doi:10.1007/3-211-32710-X_1

Law, R., Qi, S., & Buhalis, D. (2010). Progress in tourism management: A review of website evaluation in tourism research. *Tourism Management*, *31*, 297–313. doi:10.1016/j.tourman.2009.11.007

Lu, M., & Yeung, W. L. (1998). A framework for effective commercial web application development. *Electronic Networking Applications and Policy*, *8*(2), 166–173. doi:10.1108/10662249810211638

Masendorf, F. (1993). Training of learning disabled children's spatial abilities by computer games. *Zeitschrift fur Padagogische Psychologie*, *7*, 209–213.

McElroy, J. (2011). Asperger's expert recommends L.A. Noire as teaching tool. *Jostiq*. Retrieved from http://www.joystiq.com/2011/05/24/aspergers-expert-recommends-l-a-noire-as-teaching-tool/

Nasah, A., DaCosta, B., Kinsell, C., & Seok, S. (2010). The digital literacy debate: An investigation of digital propensity and information and communication technology. *Educational Technology Research and Development*, *58*(5), 531–555. doi:10.1007/s11423-010-9151-8

Okolo, C. (1992). The effect of computer-assisted instruction format and initial attitude on the arithmetic facts proficiency and continuing motivation of students with learning disabilities. *Exceptionality*, *3*, 195–211. doi:10.1080/09362839209524815

Porter, D. B. (1995). Computer games: Paradigms of opportunity. *Behavior Research Methods, Instruments, & Computers*, *27*(2), 229–234. doi:10.3758/BF03204737

Raskind, M., & Bryant, B. R. (2002). *Functional evaluation for assistive technology*. Austin, TX: Psycho-Educational Services.

Rose, D. H., & Meyer, A. (2002). *Teaching every student in the digital age: Universal design for learning*. Alexandria, VA: ASCD.

Seok, S., Meyen, E., & DaCosta, B. (Eds.). (2010). *Handbook of research on human cognition and assistive technology: Design, accessibility and transdisciplinary perspectives*. Hershey, PA: IGI Global. doi:10.4018/978-1-61520-817-3

Stern, J. (2002). *Web metrics: Proven methods for measuring web site success*. New York, NY: Wiley Publishing.

Stout, R. (1997). *Web site stats: Tracking hits and analyzing traffic*. Berkeley, CA: Osborne/McGraw-Hill.

Tartaro, A., & Cassell, J. (2006). *Authorable virtual peers for autism spectrum disorders*. Paper presented at the Combined Workshop on Language-Enabled Educational Technology and Development and Evaluation for Robust Spoken Dialogue Systems at the 11th European conference on Artificial Intelligence (ECA 106). Riva del Garda, Italy.

Tullis, T. S., & Stetson, J. N. (2004). *A comparison of questionnaires for assessing website usability*. Retrieved from http://home.comcast.net/~tomtullis/publications/UPA2004TullisStetson.pdf

Wehmeyer, M. L. (1999). Assistive technology and students with mental retardation: Utilization and barriers. *Journal of Special Education Technology*, *12*(1), 48–58.

# Acknowledgment

We first would like to thank the chapter authors for their contributions to this edited book. They were an inspiration to us as we carried out our research. Sincere gratitude is extended to our editorial review board for their wisdom. This work is a reflection of their vision in guiding our efforts. Finally, we are grateful to all of the reviewers. Those listed in this text and those who asked to remain anonymous, who donated their time, expertise, and support in making this publication possible. Thank you.

*Boaventura DaCosta*
*Solers Research Group, USA*

*Soohnwa Seok*
*Korea University, South Korea*

# Section 1
# Theories, Concepts, and Laws

*Section 1 serves as scaffolding for the remainder of this book by introducing theories, concepts, and laws either discussed or mentioned in many of the chapters. Chapters 1 and 2 are dedicated to a discussion on Universal Design for Learning (UDL), an educational framework founded on research in the learning sciences, intended to help guide in the development of educational content accommodating individual learning differences. Whereas chapter 1 serves as a primer on UDL, including a brief history, an introduction to the framework, the application of its principles, and a discussion by the authors on the related laws and regulations at the federal level, in chapter 2, the authors present how the UDL framework provides guidelines that can be leveraged to help educators consider where and how assistive features and technology can be utilized to increase flexibility and choice for students. This is accomplished through the presentation of three vignettes that illustrate how computer applications and Web-based tools can be used to support diverse students, including students with learning disabilities and struggling learners.*

*Chapters 3, 4, and 5 focus on reading, writing, and 21st century skills, as it has been suggested that most intervention research today on learning disabilities has focused on these skills, with reading garnering the most attention. Chapter 3 focuses predominately on reading skills where the author explicitly presents the case for mainstreaming text-to-speech software for students with reading difficulties in the educational environment, through the use of a socio-constructivist approach. Chapter 4 centers specifically on writing skills, in which the author discusses the challenges that today's students face while providing solutions and recommendations from the perspective of assistive technology. While in chapter 5, the authors discuss the ecological perspectives surrounding the design of self-determination-enhanced Problem-Based Learning (PBL) by presenting a PBL conceptual framework that can be leveraged in the implementation of the skills needed for the 21st century, specifically self-determination for students with disabilities in inclusive settings.*

*Finally, this section of the book concludes with chapter 6, in which the author presents a broad overview of federal civil rights laws that ensure equal opportunity and fair treatment to people with disabilities. Although this chapter does not cover all laws and regulations, much of the legislation introduced is either discussed or presented in the chapters found in this book. This chapter should, therefore, be used as a reference in not only learning more about the specific laws and regulations but also in finding additional resources to the respective governing office, agency, or outside organization in order to obtain the latest up-to-date information.*

# Chapter 1
# Universal Design for Learning in Today's Diverse Educational Environments

**Kathleen Bastedo**
*University of Central Florida, USA*

**Jessica Vargas**
*Rollins College, USA*

## ABSTRACT

*Learning can be difficult for a myriad of reasons and not just for those with disabilities and for those dedicated to teaching in its many forms. It can be next to impossible to accommodate the variety of students encountered in today's diverse learning environments. This is where the principle of Universal Design for Learning (UDL) can be successfully applied. This chapter explores the strides made in creating content that brain-based research supports as a way for not only motivating students to learn, but also for allowing those with disabilities a way to learn that meets their specific needs. Although there is no one surefire way to design learning that teaches everyone, UDL is a stepping-stone to that pursuit. If implemented to its fullest potential, it can be a panacea to reducing many barriers to access and learning.*

## INTRODUCTION

In the 1970s, Ron Mace, an architect, product designer, and educator, created a design foundation which he coined universal design (NCSU, 2008). Most people are familiar with the application of universal design principles (e.g., curb cuts, automatic door openers, ramps) even if they are not familiar with the actual term. The main function of universal design is to "simplify life for everyone by making products, communications, and the built environment more usable by as many people as possible at little or no extra cost" (CEC, 2005, p. xi). Its features generally benefit other users as well. For example, a curb cut designed for individuals in wheelchairs also benefits people using rolling computer bags, individuals pushing shopping carts, or children on tricycles.

DOI: 10.4018/978-1-4666-5015-2.ch001

In addition, universal design has spawned other principles since its inception, including Universal Design for Learning (UDL).

## Objectives

The objectives of this chapter are:

- Examine and describe UDL
- Demonstrate knowledge regarding the history, the frameworks, and the application of the principles of UDL
- Learn how to apply the basic principles of UDL to the learning environment
- Identify the laws related to UDL

## DEFINITION OF UNIVERSAL DESIGN FOR LEARNING

Students attending school today (K-12 and higher education) are learners with diverse backgrounds; some are obvious (e.g., different cultures, different languages, some have disabilities), while some are not so obvious (e.g., variety of learning styles, various abilities). Dr. David Rose, a developmental neuropsychologist and educator, co-founded the Center for Applied Special Technology (CAST, 2012a) in 1984. He recognized the importance of these learner differences. The concept of UDL grew out of Dr. Rose's frustration of working with students with disabilities in a "one-size-fits-all" assessment environment. This environment was limited and was not designed to meet their needs nor the needs of a diverse culture of students (Rappolt-Schlichtmann, 2012, p. 3). Universal Design for Learning was designed to provide "a blueprint for creating instructional goals, methods, materials, and assessments that work for everyone – not a single, one-size-fits-all solution but rather flexible approaches that can be customized and adjusted for individual needs" (CAST, 2012b). It also provides students with "an environment where instruction is flexible, equitable, and accessible every day of the school year" (CEC, 2005, p. 2).

Although UDL minimizes the need for assistive technology (AT), it does not completely eliminate it. One of the big differences between AT and UDL is that UDL is not added as a reaction to a need. It is incorporated into a classroom or online course during the design or planning stages. Although UDL cannot solve every issue, it provides a solid foundation for all students to start at the same level and more importantly, before a student ever enters a classroom (whether a physical or virtual space). Specific accessibility issues may need to be addressed on an individual basis, but overall, fewer accommodations will need to be made when UDL principles are applied from the start. As in the case of universal design, UDL benefits others as well. For example, using closed captioning for videos also helps improve comprehension for students with English as a second language, and provides access to information in a quiet environment, such as a library when headphones are not available.

## THE THREE PRINCIPLES OF UNIVERSAL DESIGN FOR LEARNING

The UDL concept is based on research in the fields of neuroscience, cognitive psychology, and the learning sciences; and results of this research helped in the creation of the UDL Guidelines. These guidelines "can assist anyone who plans lessons/units of study or develops curricula (goals, methods, materials, and assessments) to reduce barriers, as well as optimize levels of challenge and support, to meet the needs of all learners from the start" (National Center on UDL, 2011a). These guidelines also help instructors develop curriculum that not only assists a variety of different students, but also provides an opportunity for designing learning activities that can play to a student's particular strength. The three principles are:

1. Multiple means of representation,
2. Multiple means of action and expression, and
3. Multiple means of engagement (CAST, 2012b).

If properly utilized, these principles allow student engagement to remain high and students to excel. Although little research has been done to determine if data supports this method, the preliminary findings have shown some promise that is theoretically sound (Roberts, Park, Brown, & Cook, 2011). Refer to Figure 1 for a breakdown of each of the three primary brain networks of UDL.

Practical classroom examples for each of the UDL networks are provided. Many of the examples can be applied in either the face-to-face environment or in the online setting.

## Provide Multiple Means of Representation

This first principle affects the recognition networks of the brain, essentially – *the what of learning* (CAST, 2012b) – which is accomplished through perception and comprehension of the learning material. Utilizing this concept helps to decrease barriers to learning for those with learning disabilities, for those with sensory disabilities, and for those individuals who may have difficulty learning due to cultural differences. Essentially, this principle requires the designer to organize information in a meaningful way by showing the same learning concept in a variety of formats. For example, provide students with the opportunity to read a passage online to prepare for class or pair this material with a video that demonstrates that same information medium. For those that prefer reading, the first format would have more than sufficed. Yet the second, the video, may clarify the concept for a learner who prefers an audio/visual approach. Take that same video and provide closed captioning and it not only becomes accessible for students with hearing impairments, but other students can turn on the captioning if they prefer to, thus enabling further absorption of the learning material. This approach asks that the instructor consider the learners first and in a way that they may better receive and translate information that works best for them. The following are

*Figure 1. Three primary brain networks of UDL. © 2012, CAST. Used with permission. All rights reserved.*

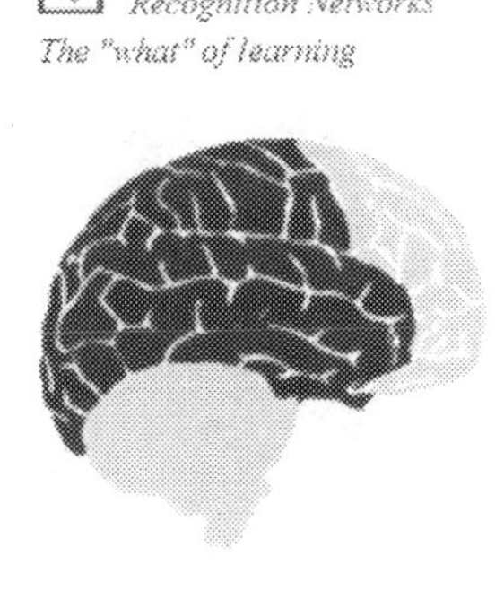
Recognition Networks
The "what" of learning
How we gather facts and categorize what we see, hear, and read. Identifying letters, words, or an author's style are recognition tasks.
Present information and content in different ways

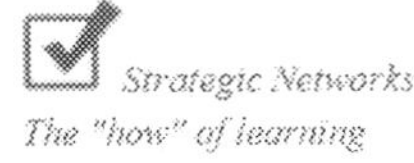
Strategic Networks
The "how" of learning

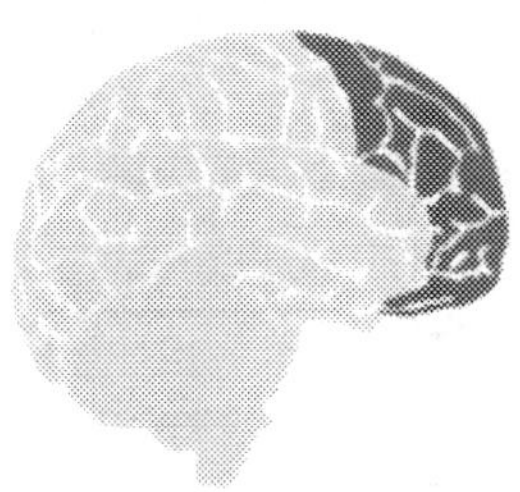
Planning and performing tasks. How we organize and express our ideas. Writing an essay or solving a math problem are strategic tasks.
Differentiate the ways that students can express what they know

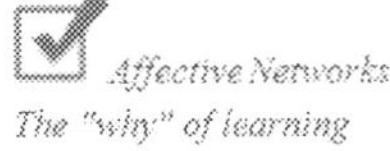
Affective Networks
The "why" of learning

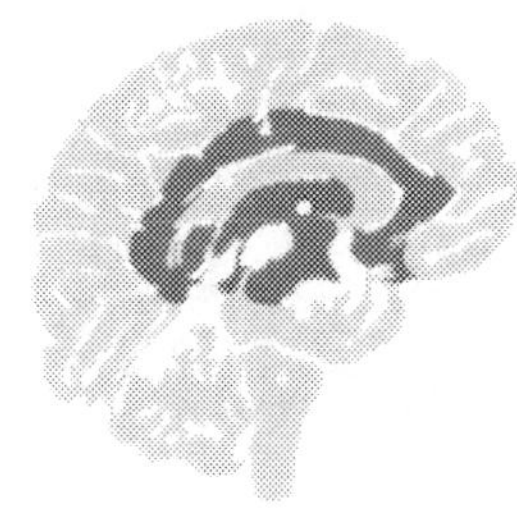
How learners get engaged and stay motivated. How they are challenged, excited, or interested. These are affective dimensions
Stimulate interest and motivation for learning

more examples of tactics that can be utilized to increase student comprehension:

*Highlight important material with a different-colored background container:* Sometimes students miss information because the use of text can be overwhelming (consider how individuals are now engaged with multiple types of technology). Breaking up text by using text boxes and using a different color background will demonstrate to readers that the information in those boxes is of the utmost importance. Be sure to use the WebAIM: Color Contrast Checker (refer to Table 1 for more information) to ensure that low-vision or color-blind students can still see the content.

*Break up content by adding some white space and meaningful media elements:* In the online environment, users should only have to scroll one to two times per screen, three at the most, or essentially three to five pages in Microsoft Word® to remain engaged with the content. As the human eye grows tired, readers are more likely to miss important material. Including white space will help make the page less overwhelming and less confusing. Adding appropriate visual elements (e.g., pictures) will provide learners with the ability to recall information more easily as they associate the picture to the content.

*Provide audio/visuals for hard-to-grasp concepts*: It perhaps cannot be stressed enough that today's learners have been confronted by multiple means of engagement with the advent of technology. Therefore, reading material may be enough to explain a concept to most students, but that is rarely the case. Similar to the example in the introduction to this chapter, adding a short, instructive video can further illustrate to students how something works by providing a visual means of action. One added benefit is that a learner can stop, start, and review a video multiple times until they are able to absorb the information.

*Provide graphical and narrative organizers to help supply background information and present a plan for learning:* These tools, also known as "advanced organizers," are known for the ability to assist students to recall previously-learned information which helps them create a frame of reference as they learn new content (for more information see Additional Reading section).

## Provide Multiple Means of Action and Expression

This second principle directly relates to the strategic networks in the brain. This means it requires physical action on the part of the learner. It also relates to the learning activities and assessments that students encounter in a course – *the how of learning* (CAST, 2012b). This method allows the learner to express what they know by performing a variety of tasks. As the educational researchers at CAST (2012b) have pointed out, there is no one means of action and expression that is optimal for all learners because of the wide variety in access limitations learners may have; for reasons such as a lack of motor skills or the existence of speech/language barriers. Since there is no one preferred method, some instructors may offer students a choice in how they are allowed to create their assignments (e.g., turn in a paper, create a video project, or build a website). Although this is a great opportunity for students to choose a format that they may excel in, this may prove taxing on the instructor if they are unequipped to handle the grading of such a variety of assignments. Planning ahead and the utilization of learning rubrics can assist in limiting the amount of work this approach entails. Although providing rubrics would be ideal, this may not be a practical solution for some instructors; therefore, they could select a variety of different outputs for students to use throughout the semester, but only one method per assignment/activity. For traditional writing assignments and assessments, instructors can assign a final project that either incorporates learner choice or utilizes a different output mechanism (e.g., develop a 30-second commercial, create a vocal mash-up).

*Table 1. Online resources*

| Title | URL | Description |
|---|---|---|
| AHEAD | http://www.ahead.org | The Association on Higher Education and Disability is a professional association dedicated to ensuring that all individuals with disabilities have access to postsecondary education. |
| Center for Applied Special Technology (CAST) | http://www.cast.org | Started in 1984, this organization uses research and development to expand learning opportunities through the utilization of UDL principles. |
| Center for Universal Design | http://www.ncsu.edu/ncsu/design/cud/index.htm | From North Carolina State University, the Center for Universal Design provides information, technical assistance, and research for accessible design in commercial, residential, and product design. |
| Council for Exceptional Children (CEC) | http://www.sped.org | An international professional organization dedicated to ensuring the success of those with disabilities by advocating for policy change and setting professional standards. |
| DO-IT | https://www.washington.edu/doit | This organization focuses on assisting individuals with disabilities that are interested in focusing a career in STEM-related (Science, Technology, Engineering, and Mathematics) fields. |
| National Consortium for Universal Design for Learning | http://www.cast.org/pd/consortium | A virtual community dedicated to sharing and developing practices to help all students especially those with disabilities. |
| NIMAS Center | http://aim.cast.org | The Individuals with Disabilities Education Act established the National Instructional Materials Accessibility Standards (NIMAS), which ensures that individuals with print disabilities receive learning materials in a format that the individual can consume. |
| Rehabilitation and Engineering Assistive Technology Society of North America (RESNA) | http://www.resna.org | An organization of dedicated professionals and engineers devoted to discovering methods to improve AT through engineering. |
| Toolkit for Universal Design for Learning | http://www.osepideasthatwork.org/UDL/intro.asp | Developed by the U.S. Department of Education in 2006, the toolkit was designed to improve student outcomes for students with disabilities. |
| WebAIM | http://www.webaim.org | Since 1999, WebAIM at Utah State University is a nonprofit organization within the Center for Persons with Disabilities. They have been providing web accessibility training. It is quintessentially the source for designing accessible online materials. |
| WebAIM Color Contrast Checker | http://www.webaim.org/resources/contrastchecker | Allows a person to determine if the colors used for background and text are discernible for those with vision disabilities. |

The benefits to supplying students with these types of choices provides them with the ability to use the knowledge they gained from previously completed assignments and apply that knowledge to a larger, more work-intensive final project. The list of particular types of projects can be indeed as long and as varied as one's brain would allow, but keep a few of the following strategies in mind:

*Provide application-based learning opportunities*: Learning can be enhanced by allowing students to build real-world skills that not only cater to their individual learning needs, but also make them more competitive upon graduation (e.g., submit an art piece for an art show, create an article for a local newspaper, build a Microsoft PowerPoint® slideshow to create or present a final project). The key here is that students are learning to manipulate the tools necessary to help them become more successful. The variety of opportunities provided also allows those that have physical limitations the ability to participate in a format more conducive to their learning preference and abilities.

*Provide various self-assessment strategies:* If students are offered the opportunity to gauge their own progress, a faculty member can pinpoint if an intervention is required. Also, if there is an opportunity to view other students' work, learners will quickly understand if their own work is meeting the same expectations (e.g., peer reviews, self-test where answers are provided once completed, reflection activities).

*Provide multiple opportunities for students to communicate with you:* Although it may seem misplaced, this approach coincides with the decision to allow students to build or construct their responses to learning activities. This method benefits everyone including students with disabilities. Students select and begin communication with the instructor or with other students via a method that best fits their learning style and comfort level (e.g., email, instant messaging, message boards, physical and online office hours). Limiting the means of communication can prove problematic, since employing one method may preclude some students from participating in the activity.

## Provide Multiple Means of Engagement

The third and final principle refers to a concern that affects all classroom design: maintaining engagement and motivation for student success. This principle applies to the affective network or – *the why of learning* (CAST, 2012b). Motivation studies have yet to indicate a single method for ensuring successful completion of any given task. However, there are some reasons why individuals respond to some motivational strategies over others. Some factors may include the following:

1. The way the brain responds (e.g., neurology),
2. Culturally-generated factors (e.g., a social emphasis to fit in with one's peers can lead to behavioral issues in the classroom when a student is not readily accepted into a particular group),
3. Personal relevance or competition (e.g. the need to obtain an 'A' in every class), or
4. A meaningful reward system (e.g., grades alone may be meaningless to some students).

Keep in mind that what works for one student may not work for others. For example, some students prefer spontaneity (e.g., the course material for the day may be changed to include an immediate relevance to the world around them), while others may prefer a strict course schedule that never changes regardless of topic (e.g., students read before class on Monday, they receive a recap in class followed by that day's lecture and finish with a learning activity until an exam is given; the cycle continues until the end of the semester). Though it may seem difficult to reach all students, the goal is to provide enough variety so that students can become engaged with the learning opportunities offered in class. The goal of acquiring learner attention and eliciting and maintaining engagement is of utmost importance in every class design. The following strategies provide several approaches that can be utilized to improve student engagement:

*Allow students the opportunity to choose assignments:* As mentioned before, classroom design and administrative limitations may prevent students from actually choosing their own assignments; however, allowing opportunities for learners to choose an assignment heightens learner engagement. This method allows students to become more invested in the given tasks, hence increasing the chances that students will become more successful in the classroom.

*Provide authentic tasks directly related to content:* This particular method coincides with an approach under the multiple means of action and expression: provide application-based learning opportunities. This approach is beneficial because it increases opportunities for learner engagement and improves student comprehension while providing students with a more rewarding experience in the course or class (e.g., submit an article to a journal, apply for a grant, help students upload a project to You Tube™ or iTunesU®). This approach is also important where concepts can be hard to learn unless students are given the opportunity to experience them (e.g., a demonstration of static electricity clarifies how atoms and electrical charges work or conducting an experiment to test a hypothesis).

*Provide students with the means of submitting components of a larger project to encourage reflection:* All too often instructors assign students a large project that is due at a particular point in the class (e.g., often these projects are due at or near the end of the class). However, some students will use this as an opportunity to wait until the last minute to begin the assignment. This behavior often results in mediocre outcomes or unfinished projects. To better prepare students for success, break up projects into smaller increments. This provides the instructor with the opportunity to assess student progress and furnish useful feedback to the student prior to the due date of the final project. This technique will help students not only learn to self-manage their own projects, but it will also allow students the ability to reflect upon what they are producing. When given the opportunity to improve scores, students can influence the outcome of their grade to some degree. Also, implementing a peer review will let students see how they stand among their peers. Meanwhile, the instructor can point out some of the more creative, innovative work thus encouraging students to compete with each other for recognition.

*Encourage learning communities to form:* In distance courses it has become a point of conversation whether or not the engagement between learner and instructor is truly achieved as well in the face-to-face counterpart. With learning tools such as discussion boards, students are granted an opportunity to have continued conversation in the online environment where discussion was only limited to a particular time and physical location in the class. Students who are not outspoken in class may feel more comfortable in the online medium. Once these learning communities form, students can assist each other as they prepare for classroom activities and assessments.

## LATEST DEVELOPMENTS, TRENDS, AND ISSUES

It cannot be overstated: UDL itself is not a passing trend. Though UDL has been in existence for many years it has only just been gaining in momentum. One reason is that the language related to UDL has been added to several public laws over the past few years such as the Assistive Technology Act of 1998 as amended in 2004 (DOE, 2004a), the reauthorization of the Individuals with Disabilities Education Act (IDEA) in 2004 (DOE, 2004b), and the Higher Education Opportunity Act (HEOA) as amended in 2008 (DOE, 2008). The Higher Education Opportunity Act also requires that the principles of UDL should be incorporated into the curriculum as it is created (for face-to-face and online environments).The law not only includes access for students with disabilities, but also addresses students with English as a second language (DOE, 2008). In addition, the National Center on Universal Design for Learning provides a website (refer to Table 1) with information related to UDL laws and activities happening at the state level. For example, in 2010, Maryland became the first state in the union to sign the Universal Design for Learning bill into law (National Center on UDL, 2011b).

The trend's increase is also in part due to educators and others who are looking for meaningful ways to change the current educational processes. According to James E. Zull, Professor of Biology and Biochemistry at Case Western Reserve University, there must be a change in the way teaching is approached. Educators must "focus more on individuals, their differences, and how they change, rather than focus on the group" (Zull, 2011, p. 1).

By examining current research regarding UDL, educators should learn "to develop strategies that will allow students to succeed in classrooms that contain a diverse mix of abilities, cultures, and languages" (Sousa & Tomlinson, 2011, p. 1). Teaching does not have to become more difficult for instructors in order to apply these principles; however, instructors must begin to teach "different" (Sousa, & Tomlinson, 2011, p. 3). The authors, David A. Sousa, and Carol Ann Tomlinson, provide a tips page at the end of each chapter in their book, *Differentiation and the Brain*. These pages are available for instructors to download and use in their classrooms in order to assist them to enhance their teaching strategies. "What the field of UDL needs now is a robust, varied, active, and interdisciplinary field of research..." (Rose & Meyer, 2006, p. 230). The CAST website (www.cast.org) can be a foothold to that endeavor. The following list provides a variety of ways to become involved and learn more about CAST and UDL:

- Universal Design for Learning fellows program
- Professional development opportunities
- National UDL Consortium Newsletter
- Free UDL online modules
- A newly-formed exchange program of UDL learning tools used to obtain or share ideas with others
- Free iPad™ apps for download

## RESOURCES FOR UNIVERSAL DESIGN FOR LEARNING

There are also other available resources designed to provide the latest information regarding implementation of UDL principles. Simple searches yield many results, but finding meaningful organizations can take some time. A few of the more recognizable professional organizations and research sites related to UDL are provided in Table 1.

## CONCLUSION

Universal Design for Learning provides a foundation to render equal access to learning for everyone, but only if it is implemented. Today's instructors can use this information to make a difference. Instructors should make a pledge to review the latest research and trends especially to research those individuals who study cognitive neuroscience and how the brain learns. Instructors should consider incorporating UDL principles into their teaching style but should begin slowly to ensure success. As Rose and Meyer (2006) point out, "we do harm to both our students and our culture by not setting higher goals and by not providing a much richer and more varied means of achieving them, means that are as varied as our students" (p. 233). The following suggestions from Sousa and Tomlinson (2011) can be applied to help instructors begin implementing these principles and enhance learning styles:

- Take time to observe students' behavior online and in the face-to-face environment.
- Take notes on how students are working (e.g., Are they finishing projects in a timely fashion? Are they asking a lot of questions about various assignments?)

- Ask students for their input (e.g., Are they interested in the subject matter?)
- Break out of the silo mentality and ask co-workers if they are interested in exploring various ways to change the learning environment.
- Start small. Select one element in the classroom and determine how this activity can be made more flexible (p. 183).

For more information related to UDL, visit the CAST website (www.cast.org). This website contains an abundance of UDL-related information, ideas, suggestions, and games designed to help instructors get started.

Universal Design for Learning provides a blueprint for creating materials that anyone regardless of ability can access. By reducing barriers, it can allow for those who were once denied the ability to learn in a way that works best for them to contribute in meaningful ways. Although it cannot solve all issues and concerns, it enables professionals with a starting point beginning that long process towards ensuring access to all. As more information becomes available, educational professionals will be able to better meet the challenge of teaching diverse learners. Universal Design for Learning applied to the curriculum can engage all students, provide depth to learning, and encourage students to achieve in ways they never did before, thus realizing most instructors' dreams of creating lifelong learners.

## REFERENCES

CAST. (2012a). *About CAST: Staff: David H. Rose*. Retrieved from http://www.cast.org/about/staff/drose.html

CAST. (2012b). *About UDL: What is universal design for learning?* Retrieved from http://www.cast.org/udl

Council for Exceptional Children (CEC). (2005). Universal design for learning: A guide for teachers and education professionals. Arlington, VA: Pearson: Merrill Prentice Hall.

National Center on Universal Design for Learning. (2011a). *National center for universal design on learning*. Retrieved from http://www.udlcenter.org/aboutudl/udlguidelines

National Center on Universal Design for Learning. (2011b). References to UDL in public policy, 2010. *UDL Bill – Maryland, 2010*. Retrieved from http://www.udlcenter.org/advocacy/referencestoUDL

North Carolina State University (NCSU). (2008). About the center: Ronald L. Mace. *The Center for Universal Design*. Retrieved from http://www.ncsu.edu/www/ncsu/design/sod5/cud/about_us/usronmace.htm

Rappolt-Schlichtmann, G., Daley, S., & Rose, L. T. (2012). *A research reader in universal design for learning*. Cambridge, MA: Harvard Education Press.

Roberts, K. D., Park, H. J., Brown, S., & Cook, B. (2011). Universal design for instruction in postsecondary education: A systematic review of empirically based articles. *Journal of Postsecondary Education and Disability*, *24*(1), 5–15.

Rose, D. H., & Meyer, A. (Eds.). (2006). *A practical reader in universal design for learning*. Cambridge, MA: Harvard Education Press.

Sousa, D. A., & Tomlinson, C. A. (2011). *Differentiation and the brain: How neuroscience supports the learner-friendly classroom*. Bloomington, IN: Solution Tree Press.

U.S. Department of Education. (2004a). *Assistive technology act of 1998 as amended in 2004*. Retrieved from http://www.gpo.gov/fdsys/pkg/PLAW-108publ364/html/PLAW-108publ364.htm

U.S. Department of Education. (2004b). *Individuals with disabilities education act, section 602(35)*. Retrieved from http://idea.ed.gov/explore/view/p/%2Croot%2Cstatute%2CI%2CA%2C602%2C

U.S. Department of Education. (2008). *Higher education opportunity act - 2008, public law 110-315*. Retrieved from http://www.gpo.gov/fdsys/pkg/PLAW-110publ315/html/PLAW-110publ315.htm

Zull, J. E. (2011). *From brain to mind: Using neuroscience to guide change in education*. Sterling, VA: Stylus Publishing, LLC.

Sousa, D. A., & Tomlinson, C. A. (2011). *Differentiation and the brain: How neuroscience supports the learner-friendly classroom*. Bloomington: In Solution Tree Press.

Vargas, J. (2013). *On track: Ensuring student success with advanced organizers*. Retrieved from http://social.rollins.edu/wpsites/cooltools/2013/03/12/on-track-ensuring-student-success-with-advanced-organizers/

Zull, J. E. (2011). *From brain to mind: Using neuroscience to guide change in education*. Sterling, VA: Stylus Publishing, LLC.

## ADDITIONAL READING

Burghstahler, S. E., & Cory, R. C. (Eds.). (2008). *Universal design in higher education: From principles to practice*. Cambridge, MA: Harvard Education Press.

Council for Exceptional Children (CEC). (2005). Universal Design for Learning: A guide for teachers and education professionals. Arlington, VA: Pearson: Merrill Prentice Hall.

Rappolt-Schlichtmann, G., Daley, S., & Rose, L. T. (2012). *A research reader in Universal Design for Learning*. Cambridge, MA: Harvard Education Press.

Rose, D. H., & Meyer, A. (Eds.). (2006). *A practical reader in Universal Design for Learning*. Cambridge, MA: Harvard Education Press.

## KEY TERMS AND DEFINITIONS

**Affective:** Causing emotion or feeling.

**Brain-Based Research:** Using principles based on solid scientific research to enhance teaching and learning.

**Closed-Captioning:** When the user has the ability to turn the captions on and off.

**Neuropsychology:** The branch of psychology that explores language, memory, and perception.

**Rubrics:** A set of standards and criteria designed to provide directions to students for what is expected in an assignment.

**Universal Design:** Creating all products and the environment to be accessible to as wide a range of individuals as possible regardless of age or ability.

**Universal Design for Learning:** A set of principles that can be used to design curriculum, providing a flexible approach to learning instead of a one-size-fits-all mentality.

# Chapter 2
# Universal Design for Learning and Assistive Technology:
## Promising Developments

**Brian R. Bryant**
*University of Texas – Austin, USA*

**Kavita Rao**
*University of Hawai'i – Mānoa, USA*

**Min Wook Ok**
*The University of Texas – Austin, USA*

## ABSTRACT

*Universal Design for Learning (UDL) has become a popular and effective way to help all students access what is taught in the classroom. Modeled after universal design, which enabled people with disabilities to access multiple physical environments, UDL provides access to the curriculum via three guiding principles: (a) multiple means of representation, (b) multiple means of expression, and (c) multiple means of engagement. This chapter looks at UDL and Assistive Technology (AT) for students who have specific Learning Disabilities (LD). Further, the authors examine AT research that has been conducted with students who have LD in reading, writing, and mathematics, and they provide case studies wherein UDL and AT are used to enhance accessibility in U.S. schools, specifically Grades 1 and 6 as well as high school.*

## INTRODUCTION

Universal Design for Learning (UDL) has gained popularity in the past decade as a framework for designing curriculum and instruction that is accessible to diverse learners, including students who have learning disabilities (LD). The concept of universal design (UD) comes from the work of Ron Mace in the 1980s. The original focus was on proactively reducing environmental barriers and providing increased access to the physical environment (Center for Universal Design, 2010). In the past two decades, researchers and educators have begun to apply the principles of UDL

DOI: 10.4018/978-1-4666-5015-2.ch002

to curriculum and instruction, modifying the original principles and applying them to learning environments (Rose, Harbour, Johnston, Daley, & Abarbanell, 2006). The UDL principles focus on designing flexible curriculum and instructional environments that provide a range of options for the learner and reduce barriers to accessing the curriculum. The three UDL principles involve providing:

1. Multiple means of representation,
2. Multiple means of expression, and
3. Multiple means of engagement.

Each of the three principles has three additional guidelines associated with it, defining how multiple options and choices can be built into curriculum and instruction (National Center on Universal Design for Learning, 2010).

Technology plays a key role in universally designed curriculum by naturally providing flexibility and customization. Digital media inherently supports the development of flexible curricula, allowing information to be represented in various ways. For example, digital text can easily be modified to meet different needs and preferences. No longer immutably set on the page in printed format, text can be digitized and converted and listened to or modified visually to suit an individual's needs and preferences. In this way, digital text can be made accessible to an individual who has a visual impairment or an individual with LD who may have trouble reading. The modified text can also be helpful to individuals who are learning the language of instruction (such as English language learners) and those whose comprehension of text is enhanced if they can review it in multiple formats (e.g., listening and reading at the same time.) Once the domain of assistive technology (AT) devices, these flexible features are now readily available on the technology tools (e.g., laptops, tablets, smartphones) that are accessed daily.

This chapter looks at UDL and AT for students who have specific LD. Further, we examine AT research that has been conducted with students who have LD in reading, writing, and mathematics, and we provide case studies wherein UDL and AT are used to enhance accessibility in U.S. schools, specifically Grades 1 and 6 as well as high school.

## ASSISTIVE TECHNOLOGY DEVICES AND SERVICES IN UNIVERSAL DESIGN FOR LEARNING

Although UDL lessons can reduce barriers, increase access, and build in supports for a range of learners, accommodations may still need to be made for individual learners who have specific needs. Such accommodations often include the use of AT devices and services. Years ago, an International Business Machine (IBM) training program for AT stated, "For people without disabilities, technology makes things easier. For people with disabilities, technology makes things possible" (1991, p. 2). In this case, "things possible" means having access to the general education curriculum.

The role of AT and UDL has been discussed at length by, among others, Rose et al. (2006), Edyburn (2010), and Bryant, Bryant, and Ok (in press). Edyburn correctly argued that UDL is not AT, but he also noted that AT and UDL may co-exist, and there is a possibility that UDL may pre-empt the need for certain AT devices, depending on the student and the lesson. Many times, the technology used during instruction is helpful technology for students without disabilities, yet AT for students with disabilities (Bryant & Bryant, 2011). In this section, AT and UDL are explored further by presenting an overview of AT and discussing how research has validated its use for students with LD.

### Defining Assistive Technology

Interestingly, AT is not defined in U. S. legislation. Assistive technology devices and AT services are defined, both in the Technology-Related Assistance for People with Disabilities (better known as the Tech Act of 1988) and the Individuals with Education Disabilities Improvement Act of 2004. For purposes of this discussion, AT can be thought of as a combination of AT devices and services that are intended to enhance the skills of people with disabilities in a variety of contexts of interaction, for example, at school, in the home, at the workplace, and in recreation.

In examining our definition, it is critical to recognize that "people with disabilities" compose a diverse group of individuals, all of whom have different types and degrees of challenges posed by their individual conditions. When we say, "people with cerebral palsy," for example, we recognize that cerebral palsy is itself a heterogeneous condition that manifests in different ways in different individuals (e.g., speaking challenges, motor challenges), and people may have mild, moderate, or severe disabilities that present different levels of challenges. We also recognize that people have multi-faceted lifestyles that usually include combinations of the classroom, a work environment, social venues, home environments, and so forth. Thus, when we think of AT, we think in terms, not of the disability category, but by the challenges faced as a person interacts with his or her various contexts and a myriad of people (Bryant & Bryant, 2011). When we think of AT and UDL, this is particularly important, because it is impossible to create a lesson or a plan that incorporates and/or accounts for every challenge that will be faced by students. That said, we address AT devices and AT services as they generally pertain to students in a classroom environment. We will do so using definitions provided in the Individuals with Disabilities Education Improvement Act (IDEIA), because they are similar to those provided in the Tech Act but are particularly suited to students with disabilities.

## Assistive Technology Device

Previously, we mentioned that in some UDL classrooms, technology can be helpful for students without disabilities, yet assistive for students with disabilities. Consider, for example, the use of computer-assisted instruction (CAI) as part of a universally designed science class. For students without disabilities, the videos and narratives explain many of the same scientific terms and concepts that are discussed in a textbook. For a student who does not have a disability, the CAI is helpful because animations and illustrations explain visually and verbally how, for instance, radiant heat and energy from the sun can be harnessed to produce solar energy. For a student with a reading LD, the same CAI becomes an AT device, because the information is now accessible in a way that a text version, as is, would make the content inaccessible. The point is that UDL may incorporate technology devices that are both helpful and assistive, which reduces the need for additional AT devices, but this is both student- and context-specific. It is important to keep this in mind when reading the vignettes later in this chapter.

## Assistive Technology Service

Assistive technology services play a valuable role in service delivery for many reasons. With regard to AT's role in UDL, we pay particular attention to the coordination and training and technical assistance portions of the definition.

In today's diverse classroom, it is highly likely that students with disabilities, especially those with LD, will be accessing the general education curriculum, as required by IDEIA 2004. Typically, a special educator is providing support services of some kind, both to the student and the teacher. This may take the form of a co-teaching arrangement (Friend, 2008a, 2008b), or possibly the special educator will serve in a consultancy role. In either case, the special educator's role with regard to AT use in the classroom is to coordinate with the general educator how AT can best be used by the student to access instruction. Over time, general educators will gain experience and expertise as more of their students with disabilities use AT devices in their classroom. For now, this is rarely the case, so special educators work with their general education colleagues to integrate AT devices into the universally designed lesson.

As part of the coordination, special educators may provide training in AT to their general education colleagues. Or, if the special educator is not an expert in AT, it may be necessary to call upon the services of an AT specialist to provide training to both teachers.

## RESEARCH ON ASSISTIVE TECHNOLOGY AND LEARNING DISABILITIES

Problems of students with specific LD can be manifested in one or more of the following areas: Listening, speaking, reading, writing, mathematics, and reasoning (National Joint Committee on Learning Disabilities, 1994). Most intervention research in LD has focused on reading, mathematics, and writing; with reading garnering the most attention, followed by mathematics and writing. Two selected studies in each area are briefly reviewed in Table 1. The studies provide examples of how AT can be used successfully to help students with LD meet disability-related academic challenges.

## BUILT-IN ASSISTIVE TECHNOLOGY SUPPORTS ON COMMONLY-USED TECHNOLOGY DEVICES

Desktop and laptop computers, tablet computers and smartphones are commonplace devices that we use regularly. In this chapter, we address how these technologies can be integrated into instruction to support diverse learners.

Many of today's software applications, "apps" (software on mobile devices), and web-based tools have built-in features and supports that used to be the domain of specialized assistive devices. Examples of built-in features that provide assistive support functions include: (a) text-to-speech; (b) options for modifying visual formats, such as size, color, contrast and spacing; (c) speech input; and (d) multimedia tools. Some interactive educational Web 2.0 sites also provide assistive support features that can be integrated into curriculum and instruction.

Text-to-speech is one example of an AT feature that has become ubiquitous on our various devices. For example, the Macintosh® operating system (Mac OSX ® v. 6 and above) has a built-in text-to-speech generator that creates an audio file of text that is selected on screen. The user can select a paragraph on a website, an email message, or a document and, with a click of the mouse, convert it into a format that can be played back on the computer or transferred to an MP3 player or smartphone. If a user wants a feature that is unavailable in the built-in text-to-speech generator, several inexpensive software options are available on the market to purchase and install on the computer. Specialized software offers additional options for text-to-speech, allowing the user to change parameters such as the voice, pitch and rate of the speech playback. E-reader devices and apps for the tablet computer also provide text-to-speech playback.

The multimodal options built into our digital devices and software are another way to provide assistive supports through commonplace technologies. Text, audio and video can be created quickly and embedded in documents and presentations, providing multiple ways of representing and expressing information. Teachers can create multimodal resources to explain concepts. Students can express themselves using a combination of text, audio and video. These multimodal tools can be incorporated into lessons as scaffolds and as alternative means of demonstrating knowledge. For example, for students with LD may find it useful to write a report using visuals and record a

*Table 1. Sample of AT research in reading, mathematics, and writing*

| Citation | Participants | Purpose | Experimental Design | Results |
|---|---|---|---|---|
| **Reading** | | | | |
| Twyman & Tindal (2006) | *Experimental group:*<br>*N* = 12<br>*Disability*: All LD<br>*Grade*: 11-12th<br>*Ethnicity*: 11 White, 1 Hispanic<br>*Control group:*<br>*N* = 12<br>*Disability*: All LD<br>*Grade*: 11-12th<br>*Ethnicity*: 10 White, 2 Hispanic | Improve the comprehension and problem-solving skills of students with disabilities in social studies using a conceptually framed, computer-adapted history text | Quasi-experimental | No statistically significant interaction effects for comprehension, vocabulary, or problem-solving, but effect sizes of.73 (vocabulary),.67 (comprehension), and.84 (problem-solving) |
| Kim et al. (2006) | *Experimental group:*<br>*N* = 16<br>*Disability/Difficulties*: 13 reading disabilities, 3 reading difficulties<br>*Gender*: 12 male, 4 female<br>*Gender*: 6-8th<br>*Ethnicity*: 4 African American, 7 Hispanic, 5 European American<br>*Control group:*<br>*N* = 18<br>*Disability/Difficulties*: 15 reading disabilities, 3 reading difficulties<br>*Grade*: 6-8th<br>*Gender*: 9 male, 9 female<br>*Ethnicity*: 3 African American, 5 Hispanic, 10 European American | Examine the effects of the Computer-Assisted Collaborative Strategic Reading | Quasi-experimental | Statistically significant differences favored experimental condition on the distal measure; (proximal effect sizes =.50-1.18 and.87-1.18) specifically on the measure that assessed students' ability to generate questions about their reading |
| **Mathematics** | | | | |
| Bryant et al. (2013) | *N* = 6<br>*Disability*: All LD<br>*Grade*: 4th<br>*Gender*: 4 male, 3 female<br>*Ethnicity*: 1 European American, 5 Hispanic | Compare the effectiveness of teacher-directed instruction, technology-based instruction, and a combination of teacher-direct and technology-based instruction | Alternating treatment, single case design | Visual and quantitative analysis showed mixed results across the six students, with teacher-directed instruction, on average, slightly ahead of the other approaches when looking at individual student data, yet combination approach slightly ahead when looking at averages across students |
| Seo & Bryant (2012) | *N* = 4<br>*Difficulties*: Mathematics (2 students: additional reading difficulty)<br>*Grade*: 2nd-3rd<br>*Gender*: 3 males, 1 female<br>*Ethnicity*: 2 Hispanic, 1 African American, 1 White | Examine the effects of CAI on math performance | Multiple-probe across subject, single case design | Increasing trends from baseline from 0% for three of the four students to 16%, 16%, 27%, and 22% for students 1 to 4; maintenance showed continuing high levels of accuracy (i.e., above 70%) for the 3-to 6-week follow-up phase; the lowest score 75%, highest 100% |
| **Writing** | | | | |
| Silió & Barbetta (2010) | *N* = 6<br>*Disability/Difficulties*: All LD & English language learners<br>*Grade*: 5th<br>*Gender*: All males<br>*Ethnicity*: All Hispanic | Examine the effects of using word prediction and text-to-speech, alone or in combination, on narrative writing abilities | Multiple baseline across subjects, single case design | Overall, average results across the intervention phases for both cohorts, showed a stronger effect for the word prediction alone with Microsoft Word® and in combination with text-to-speech with Word® for both groups |

*continued on following page*

*Table 1. Continued*

| Citation | Participants | Purpose | Experimental Design | Results |
|---|---|---|---|---|
| MacArthur, Graham, Haynes, & DeLaPaz (1996) | *N* = 27<br>*Disability*: All LD<br>*Grade*: 6-7th<br>*Gender*: 16 males, 11 females<br>*Ethnicity*: 13 White, 7 African American, 6 Hispanic, 1 Asian America | Examine the effects of spelling checkers on the performance of students with severe LD | Quasi-experimental | On average, 81.5% of misspellings were corrected when the intended spelling was presented and the percentage increased to 83.5% when the intended word was first in the list of corrections. However, based on the severity of the misspelling, no suggestions might be offered or suggestions might not include the intended spelling; in these cases, only 24.7% of the spelling errors were corrected, no change was made 30% of the time and another spelling was typed 48% of the time. |

narration of their ideas. This can be a precursor to writing a report or an alternate form of assessing student knowledge.

With an awareness of what assistive features are available in various devices, software, and web-based tools, teachers can integrate various instructional technologies into lesson planning to provide increased choice and flexibility to meet the needs of diverse learners. The UDL framework provides guidelines that can help teachers consider where and how assistive features of technology can be utilized to increase flexibility and choice for students. In the next section, we describe ways in which teachers use the assistive features of commonplace technology tools and software for classroom-based lessons to give students multiple means of representation, expression and action and engagement. Within each case study, we provide a model for how instructional practices can be mapped to specific principles and guidelines of the UDL framework.

## SCHOOL-BASED CASE STUDIES

This section contains three vignettes that illustrate how computer applications and web-based tools can be used to support diverse students, including students with LD and struggling learners. With an awareness of the *assistive features* of various applications, a teacher can apply UDL principles to lessons by integrating technology in thoughtful and deliberate ways into instruction and assessment. We describe how teachers can consider UDL principles during the lesson design and implementation process and can proactively provide options and enable support features through the technologies they use in their lessons and classes. The case studies highlight ways in which teachers can use the following technologies: (a) a web-based book builder that has built-in assistive supports, (b) digital graphic organizer software, and (c) an interactive whiteboard app on a tablet computer.

### First Grade: Creating a Classroom Book in UDL Book Builder™

*This scenario illustrates the use of the UDL Book Builder™, web-based tool that builds in assistive supports and instructional scaffolds.*

Each year, Ms. R implements an integrated unit about zoo animals, addressing language learning, literacy, science, and art skills for her first grade class. She begins the unit by reading various books about animals each day during circle time, immersing the children in both fiction and non-fiction depictions of animals. As part of science lessons, the students discuss the habitats and characteristics of each animal and categorize and organize their information. After several weeks of learning about the animals, they take a trip to the local zoo.

## Traditional Lesson

As a culmination of this integrated unit, Ms. R has each child pick an animal and draw it. With the help of Ms. R and her educational assistant (EA), students write sentences about their animal. Ms. R makes a classroom *big book*, placing photos of each child's illustration, the sentences written by the child and zoo photos of the child near the selected animal. This *Animals Book* becomes a beloved classroom artifact for the children. Ms. R places the book on a table near the classroom entrance and the children often flip through it and show it to their parents when they visit the classroom.

## Universal Design for Learning and Technology-Enhanced Lesson

Every year, parents admire the classroom book and tell Ms. R that they would like to have a copy of it to keep for their child. Ms. R has thought about transforming the book into a digital format, pasting the children's illustrations into a document and typing in their sentences as captions. As she explores ways to create a digital version of the book, she discovers UDL Book Builder™ (Center for Applied Special Technology [CAST], 2013), a web-based tool that can be accessed at http://bookbuilder.cast.org. Developed by CAST, UDL Book Builder™ is an online authoring environment with built-in reading supports and various AT tools.

The UDL Book Builder™ authoring environment allows Ms. R to upload digital photos, type in text, and add audio files. Ms. R is excited about the AT tools built into the environment because they provide specific reading supports that some of her students require. The sentences she types are automatically read aloud by the computer through the built-in text-to-speech option. As the computer reads back the words, each word is individually highlighted, a helpful support for students that reinforces their word recognition skills. The UDL Book Builder™ has a "Text Help" feature that provides a floating toolbar with support features (such as a translator and playback features). The UDL Book Builder™ also provides supports for literacy processes, such as reading comprehension. The authoring environment provides several animated characters (known as "coaches") that can be customized to ask specific questions related to each page in the book. For example, questions can reinforce new vocabulary and to predict and extend presented concepts. Ms. R likes the fact that she can create a glossary within the book, with specific words linked to a visual online dictionary. Best of all, once the book is finalized, Ms. R can click "share" and send the link to anyone's email address, thus sharing the book with parents via a click of the mouse.

This year, instead of creating the classroom book in the traditional way, Ms. R takes photos of each child's animal illustration and uploads it to UDL Book Builder™. Over the next few days, she and her EA work with the students on the classroom computer to help them type in sentences about their animal. The educators provide as much support as the child needs during the writing process. Some children are eager to type on their own, while others look to Ms. R and the EA for help with word selection, spelling, usage, and so forth. Each child gets one page in the online book. After completing a draft of the book, Ms. R and her EA spend some time after school to come up with some questions for the animated coaches to ask on each page. They make sure the animated coaches say the name of the child whose page it is. On this first try, they decide not to record audio; but they like the fact that they can record each child reading the sentences if they wish to extend the project further.

*Table 2. Universal design for learning connections: Making a classroom book in udl Book Builder™*

| **Multiple Means of Representation** |
|---|
| **1. Provide options for perception** |
| Universal Design for Learning Book Builder™ authoring environment offers options for customization of display, auditory and visual information (1.1, 1.2, 1.3) |
| **2. Provide options for language, mathematical expressions, and symbols** |
| • Embeds options to clarify vocabulary, including linked glossary (2.1)<br>• Supports decoding of text, through text-to-speech, digital text, and human voice recording (2.3)<br>• Promotes understanding across languages, by embedding visual, non-linguistic supports for vocabulary clarification (2.4)<br>• Digital translation tools embedded (2.4)<br>• Illustrates concepts through multiple media (2.5) |
| **3. Provide options for comprehension** |
| • Activates background knowledge (3.1)<br>• Highlights previously learned skills (3.2)<br>• Provides interactive models that guide exploration (3.3)<br>• Incorporates opportunities for review and practice (3.4) |
| **Multiple Means of Action and Expression** |
| **4. Provide options for physical action** |
| • Alternate means of composition (4.1)<br>• Text-to-speech can be enabled on the computer (or added on with literacy support software) if needed (4.2)<br>• As needed, students can be provided with AT tools for accessing the computer (e.g., alternate keyboards, text-to-speech software) (4.2) |
| **5. Provide options for expression and communication** |
| • Students compose using multiple media (5.1)<br>• Universal Design for Learning Book Builder™ environment provides multiple tools for composition (5.2)<br>• Environments provides scaffolds (e.g., coaches help with reading comprehension and can be used as appropriate) (5.3) |
| **6. Provide options for executive functions** |
| • Provides models and examples for students (6.1)<br>• Embeds "stop and think" prompts (6.2)<br>• Embeds coaches and mentors to model thinking process (6.2)<br>• Embeds questions to guide self-monitoring and reflection (6.4) |
| **Multiple Means of Engagement** |
| **7. Provide options for recruiting interest** |
| • Provides choices (e.g., color, design, graphics) (7.1)<br>• Activity is authentic and communicates to real audiences (7.2)<br>• Allows for active participation (7.2)<br>• Varies social demands on students by providing appropriate levels of support (7.3) |
| **8. Provide options for sustaining effort and persistence** |
| • Emphasizes process and effort (8.2)<br>• Provides a range of demands, and a range of possible resources, allows all learners to find challenges that are optimally motivating (8.2)<br>• Project emphasizes the importance of practice and effort (8.4) |
| **9. Provide options for self-regulation** |
| Project builds in various levels of mentorship (9.1) |

For the next few days, children look at their book in delight on the classroom computer. Ms. R gives each child a chance to click through the book, pointing out features, such as the coaches and the glossary words. Most children go to the page they created and delightedly read their words and check to see what their animated coach asks. They then proceed to the pages made by their classmates to see what their peers have written and answer the questions asked by the coaches on those pages. Parents who have computers report that their children eagerly show them the book at home. Ms. R encourages parents to sit with the children at home and have them go through the whole book and answer the coaches' questions as a reinforcement of what they are learning in class. Ms. R and her EA agree that the project is a success as they watch students using the assistive features of UDL Book Builder™ to reinforce their reading skills as they revisit the classroom book several times throughout the year.

Table 2 illustrates how various components of this instructional strategy map to UDL principles. The table provides details on the specific guidelines and checkpoints associated with the UDL framework. An overview of the UDL principles, guidelines and their related checkpoints can be found on this one page overview (http://www.udlcenter.org/sites/udlcenter.org/files/updateguidelines2_0.pdf.) For detailed descriptions of each checkpoint (e.g., 1.2, 3.1, 5.2) listed in Table 2, go to the National Center for UDL website at http://www.udlcenter.org/aboutudl/udlguidelines.

## Sixth Grade: Using a Graphic Organizer to Support the Writing Process

This scenario describes how a teacher combines instructional strategies with assistive features within digital graphic organizer software to provide supports for writing and expression.

Each year, Ms. C's sixth grade class visits the Museum of Natural History and students write a short report on the field trip in the class sessions following the trip. Because she has only one digital camera to use in the classroom, Ms. C and her EA strategically take pictures during the field trip, making sure to document all the key areas that the students visit in the museum. She makes sure she takes at least one picture of each child sometime during the museum tour.

### Traditional Lesson

In the days following the museum visit, Ms. C puts the pictures on the classroom computer and projects the pictures onto a screen. The class discusses together what they see in the pictures, and they discuss the exhibits depicted in each photo. The discussion results in a lively class discussion as children call out what they remember from the tour guide's description. Following whole class discussion, Ms. C asks each student to write an essay about the field trip. She provides a clear structure for the essay, directing students to describe at least three artifacts they saw during the field trip. The photos and class discussion serve as scaffolds for the students who struggle with generating ideas when asked to write.

Ms. C notes that the students who tend to have trouble with idea generation continue to struggle when asked to draft their essays, despite the class discussion that preceded the writing activity. One student, Anna, who has taken notes during the class discussion, is able to write down a few sentences based on her notes. Jack, who has a reading and writing LD, does not write anything on paper, but is able to tell the EA about three things he saw and why he remembers them in particular.

### Universal Design for Learning and Technology-Enhanced Lesson

Ms. C decides to use the multimodal tools built into digital graphic organizer software as part of the first stage of the writing process. She knows that graphic organizers provide a good pre-writing tool, allowing students to brainstorm their thoughts and organize their ideas before trying to compose sentences about their ideas. She feels that using a digital graphic organizer will support the needs of the diverse students in the class, providing specific assistive supports and varied levels of challenges for different students (see Table 3).

Ms. C uses Kidspiration® (Inspiration, 2013) graphic organizer software to enhance her traditional lesson activity of discussing photos of the field. Using the classroom computer, she launches Kidspiration® and projects a blank visual web on the screen. Kidspiration® can be used to create a visual web, also known as a "concept map" or "mindmap." Ms. C also displays a slide show of photos from the field trip, asking students to call

*Table 3. Universal design for learning connections: using a graphic organizer as pre-writing tool*

| Multiple Means of Representation |
|---|
| **1. Provide options for perception** |
| • Students can customize the display of information; font sizes and contrast can be changed to accommodate student needs (1.1)<br>• For students who struggle with generating handwritten text, drafting on the computer provides keyboarding supports (1.1) |
| **2. Provide options for language, mathematical expressions, and symbols** |
| • Teacher models how to express key concepts (and generate text) using images/symbols; students use images to categorize information as a pre-writing strategy (2.1)<br>• Process makes the structure of a written report explicit (2.2)<br>• Students can use digital translation tools on the computer to translate key words in their organizers; visual representation of concepts and photos as prompts also provide visual, non-linguistic supports (2.4)<br>• Students make use of multiple media (e.g., images, audio and text) as part of writing process (2.5) |
| **3. Provide options for comprehension** |
| • Photos provide link to students' background knowledge as they begin writing; Students are given options to take or download relevant photos (3.1)<br>• Process provides students practice with using outlines and graphic organizers to emphasize key ideas and relationships (3.2)<br>• Teacher provides modeling on how to begin generating and organizing ideas in this environment; the project provides options for organizing information visually and seeing how a visual web can be easily transformed into a textual outline (3.3) |
| **Multiple Means of Action and Expression** |
| **4. Provide options for physical action** |
| • Text-to-speech can be enabled on the computer (or added on with literacy support software) if needed (4.2)<br>• As needed, students can be provided with AT tools for accessing the computer (e.g., alternate keyboards) (4.2) |
| **5. Provide options for expression and communication** |
| • Students use multimodal means of expressing what they know (e.g., photos, text, audio) and get a better understanding of how written expression can be developed in conjunction with images (5.1)<br>• Introduces students to outlining tools and methods that can be used for various other purposes and in other subject areas for writing (5.2)<br>• Students have flexibility in how they express themselves; teachers can guide students to address particular skills that a student might need to work on (e.g., organization, generating more writing) (5.3) |
| **6. Provide options for executive functions** |
| Photos help students plan and organize steps explicit for students before they begin drafting their writing (6.2) |
| **Multiple Means of Engagement** |
| **7. Provide options for recruiting interest** |
| • Provides students choices on several facets (e.g., level of challenge, tools used for info gathering and production, color, design and graphics and sequencing of info) (7.1)<br>• Allows students to make sense of complex ideas in creative ways (7.2)<br>• Project provides a structure and routine for writing (7.3) |
| **8. Provide options for sustaining effort and persistence** |
| • Long-term (writing) goals broken into short-term objectives (8.1)<br>• Varied levels of challenge built into the writing process; teacher differentiates the degree of difficulty or complexity of the core activity for students (8.2)<br>• Provides a range of demands, and a range of possible resources, allows all learners to find challenges that are optimally motivating (8.2)<br>• Project emphasizes the importance of practice and effort (8.4) |

out what they see in the photos. As students excitedly describe what they see, Ms. C asks them to categorize each artifact. As they generate names for categories and decide which artifact should go under each category, Ms. C creates a visual web, inputs their ideas, and models how information can be categorized and organized. To the student's great delight, she also inserts some of the photos into visual web and types in text to accompany the photos.

Because Jack is so excited to describe what he saw in the dinosaur exhibit, Ms. C asks him to come up to the computer and record an audio clip of what he has to say. In Kidspiration®, students simply click a button to record their voices, and they can place the audio clip near the related photo or text. Ms. C invites others to come up and record short audio clips related to the words she has typed on the visual web. Several eager students record sentences and practice saying the words that are written on screen. When they are done, the students see a completed graphic organizer with accompanying text, photos, and audio that they generated, categorized, and organized in the visual web.

During this lesson, Ms. C models several processes for the students:

1. Brainstorming,
2. Categorizing and organizing information,
3. Using visuals as prompts for writing, and
4. Practicing oral expression as a part of the writing process.

She shows students how they can transform the visual web into a written outline with a click of a button, a feature within this graphic organizer software. The students also learn how to use the graphic organizer software as they watch Ms. C model its features during the whole class activity. After the class discusses the photos and what they learned on their field trip, Ms. C asks them to begin writing their individual reports about the field trip.

Ms. C projects the visual web generated by the whole class on screen as a resource for them to use as they write. For Jack and Anna, Ms. C copies the digital graphic organizer generated by the class and places the file on two computers in the back of the classroom. Ms. C circulates around the room, helping various students with their writing. At one computer station, Jack works with the EA to record his thoughts into the graphic organizer. He finds he has a lot to say about each of the photos on the graphic organizer. The EA helps Jack transcribe what he has recorded into a text document. Jack is engaged in this process of typing in the words he has recorded and begins to write his report in this way. When Ms. C stops by to see how Jack is doing, he excitedly shows her all that he has typed.

At the other computer station, Anna chooses not to record her voice on the computer, but is intensely engaged with categorizing the remaining photos from the field trip and adding captions to each one. She carefully chooses categories for each photo and labels each picture with a descriptive sentence. Anna uses the outline feature of the graphic organizer to transform the visual web into a text outline. Ms. C shows her how the text she has written for each photo provides much of the content for her report. Ms. C works with Anna to flesh out her paragraphs, write topic sentences, and create transitions and connections between the text she has generated. In this way, Anna generates a greater volume of writing than she would if faced with a blank page of paper and starts to understand how to organize her thoughts into a report.

## High School Ninth Grade: Interactive Whiteboard App and Mathematics

This scenario illustrates how a teacher creatively uses an interactive whiteboard app on a mobile tablet computer to provide multimodal supports for students.

Mr. S teaches Algebra 1 classes to ninth graders. To teach concepts, Mr. S follows an instructional routine of introducing a new concept, modeling problem-solving, and giving students multiple opportunities to practice problem-solving independently in class.

### Traditional Lesson

Mr. S is starting a unit on solving systems of linear equations. In this unit, he will teach three methods for solving systems of equations: by addition, by graphing, and by substitution. Mr. S starts with an overview of what the students will learn in the unit and introduces the first new concept, solving systems of equation by addition. He models the steps used to solve systems of equations by addition on the board, using examples from the textbook. After modeling several examples to the whole class, he gives students a worksheet to complete. Mr. S asks them to solve equations using the steps he has shown them, and he walks around the class as students work independently, checks for understanding, and provides corrective feedback as needed. When a majority of students have completed the problems, Mr. S has student volunteers go to the board and write their problem solving steps. The class discusses whether the answer is correct and Mr. S asks students to check and, if need be, correct their steps on their worksheets. At the end of the class, Mr. S hands out a homework worksheet with similar practice problems for students to complete for independent practice.

## Universal Design for Learning and Technology-Enhanced Lesson

Mr. S knows that many of the students in his class struggle with understanding new mathematical concepts when they are first introduced. For some students, the classroom routine of completing a worksheet causes them to disengage and do the bare minimum required to get through the class period. At the start of this new unit on solving systems of equations, Mr. S decides to engage reluctant students by giving them opportunities to express their understanding of mathematical concepts in an alternate way. He knows that the students are more engaged using technology, so he devises a creative way to use the pool of tablet computers that the school has purchased.

Mr. S recently read about "interactive whiteboard apps," software that can be downloaded to the tablet computers and be used to create short video tutorials. Examples of interactive whiteboard apps are Educreations® (Educreations, 2012), ShowMe® (ShowMe, 2012), and ScreenChomp® (TechSmith, 2013). These apps allow the user to draw or write on the screen, narrate, and capture the action in video format. He likes the fact that the interactive whiteboard app provides a relatively quick and easy way to create multimedia by bringing together handwritten text, images, and audio narration. Mr. S designs a culminating activity for the unit on solving equations by using the interactive whiteboard app to model critical skills for his students and to give students the opportunity to express what they know (see Table 4).

Using the interactive whiteboard app, Educreations®, on his tablet computer, Mr. S creates several short video tutorials that demonstrate the steps of the mathematical concepts as he does in class. Each 2- to 3-minute segment video tutorial is focused and depicts the step-by-step process of solving systems of equations. He creates tutorials with multiple examples of solving systems of equation by addition method. All the video tutorials are stored on the interactive whiteboard app's website, which students can access at school or at home on any tablet, laptop, or desktop computer. As students work on the problems independently in class, Mr. S encourages them to use the tablets and watch the short video tutorials if they forget a step. Students also are able to watch the video tutorials at home while doing their homework problems. The tutorials provide opportunities for his students to review new concepts *just in time* when they need a reminder of how to solve a problem.

In addition to creating these tutorials as a multimedia resource for students, Mr. S has another objective. He wants students to use this multimodal method to express what they know. His tutorials serve as a model for videos that he wants his students to create once they have practiced the various ways of solving systems of equations. To make the activity more authentic, Mr. S provides students with an audience for their tutorials; that they will share their work with peers who will

*Table 4. Universal design for learning connections: Interactive whiteboard application and mathematics*

| Multiple Means of Representation |
|---|
| **1. Provide options for perception** |
| Project builds options for students to articulate skills and knowledge in alternative ways, both auditory and visual (1.2, 1.3) |
| **2. Provide options for language, mathematical expressions, and symbols** |
| • Provides opportunities for students to articulate concepts related to mathematical notation and symbols in multimodal ways (2.3)<br>• Teacher models problem solving through multiple media formats (2.5)<br>• Students represent solutions through multiple media formats (2.5) |
| **3. Provide options for comprehension** |
| • Teacher-made and student-made video tutorials link to prior knowledge (3.1)<br>• Process of creating content for tutorials helps focus on big ideas and critical features (3.2)<br>• Provides interactive models for acquisition of mathematical knowledge/skills (3.3)<br>• Process includes practice and articulation of sequential (3.3)<br>• Provides opportunities for review and practice (3.4) |
| **Multiple Means of Action and Expression** |
| **4. Provide options for physical action** |
| Use of tablets provides alternatives to written formats of worksheets (4.1, 4.2) |
| **5. Provide options for expression and communication** |
| • Process gives students options to compose in multiple media including video, audio, and image formats (5.1)<br>• Teacher-created tutorials provide just in time support for students (5.3)<br>• Process of creating tutorials provides opportunities to practice and build fluency with skills (5.3) |
| **6. Provide options for executive functions** |
| • Project builds in models and scaffolds (6.1)<br>• Rubric provides guidelines, breaks down larger goal, and provides criteria for self reflection and scoring (6.2, 6.4) |
| **Multiple Means of Engagement** |
| **7. Provide options for recruiting interest** |
| • Students have autonomy to create videos (e.g., using different color, audio, image; selecting problems as a group; using graphic organizers) (7.1)<br>• Students can choose to review teacher-created videos as needed (7.1)<br>• Process invites students to personalize information, participate actively and communicate to real audiences (7.2) |
| **8. Provide options for sustaining effort and persistence** |
| • Student-made tutorials are viewed by others, creating a sense of purpose and motivation for students (8.1)<br>• Process builds in varied levels of acceptable performance and emphasizes process and effort (8.2)<br>• Students worked in collaborative pairs with clear goals and expectations (8.3)<br>• Teacher and peers provide timely and specific feedback on student-made tutorials (8.4)<br>• Teacher provides feedback emphasizing students' effort, improvement and achieving a standard (8.4) |
| **9. Provide options for self-regulation** |
| Teacher provides a rubric elevating the frequency of self-reflections and self-reflection during creating videos (9.1, 9.3) |

assess whether their described steps to solving the equation are clear and correct. Mr. S intends to use this activity as a formative assessment of his students' understanding of solving systems of equations by various methods. The process of creating the tutorials gives students multiple opportunities to practice and articulate what they know, providing a built-in way to review concepts prior to the required unit quiz. Mr. S creates a grading rubric that students will use to assess each other's projects. The rubric clearly states expectations for the tutorials, including criteria for working together as a pair, information that should be included in each tutorial, and organization of the information presented.

Mr. S reserves the school's set of tablet computers for the 2-week span when the students will use them, downloads the Educreations® app onto each tablet, and provides a tablet to each student pair. Because the students have seen and used his video tutorials, they have a model for the tutorials' format. Mr. S gives them time in class to experiment with the app, draw pictures, and record their voices in an unstructured way before they start creating their actual tutorials. It takes the students little time to learn how to use the interactive whiteboard app's features, and they are enthusiastic about being able to record and express themselves in this alternate way.

Mr. S assigns each pair an equation to solve and asks them to create three tutorials, one for each method of solving equations. Over the course of the next few days, each pair plans out the steps for the solutions, writes out their plan, and decides what each individual will do and say while recording on the app. The rubric notes that each person in the pair should play an active role in the tutorial, and students have the freedom to make their own choices about what role(s) they play.

Students enjoy using the features of the interactive whiteboard app and have fun with the choices they can make as they create their tutorials (e.g., choosing different colors, recording sound/ voices, drawing and writing on the screen). The activity combines a structured purpose along with choice and self-direction, allowing each pair to integrate creativity and personality into the video tutorials. All the videos are available on the interactive whiteboard app's website. Mr. S provides specific feedback to each group on their tutorials, and each pair assesses another pair of peers. Mr. S is pleased with the end results and notes that the video tutorials he has created, when combined with the student-created projects, gives his students a way to practice skills and articulate their understanding of mathematical concepts in a manner that increases their motivation and engagement in learning. Mr. S also notes that his students who have LD did not require additional assistive devices; using the app to demonstrate knowledge provided assistive supports that those students could use to successfully complete their projects.

## CONCLUSION

Universal Design for Learning has shown great promise as a way to allow students from diverse backgrounds and needs, including students with LD, to access quality instruction. In this chapter, we examined the characteristics of UDL and ways in which AT can play a role in making instruction accessible. Especially in inclusive settings, where teachers are charged with meeting the needs of students receiving special education services as well as meeting the needs of general education students. In such an environment, there is a need to design curriculum and instruction that addresses a broader range of student abilities.

The UDL framework provides useful principles and guidelines for the proactive design of lessons that include choice and flexibility; and technology plays a key role in providing these flexible options for students. Specifically, technology that can be helpful for teaching all students can also serve as AT to those with disabilities. Using technology to promote access makes good sense, and we provided several case studies to help demonstrate our call for instructional equity.

## ACKNOWLEDGMENT

The authors would like to thank Mr. Naohito Miura for his permission to base one of the case studies on his creative use of interactive whiteboard apps in his mathematics classes.

## REFERENCES


Bryant, B. R., Ok, M. W., Kang, E. Y., Kim, M. K., Lang, R., Bryant, D. P., & Pfannestiel, K. (2013). A multi-dimensional comparison of mathematics interventions for 4th grade students with learning disabilities. *Submitted for peer review*.

Bryant, D. P., & Bryant, B. R. (2011). *Assistive technology for people with disabilities* (2nd ed.). Boston: Allyn & Bacon/Pearson.

Bryant, D. P., Bryant, B. R., & Ok, M. W. (2013). *Assistive technology for students with learning disabilities*. New York: Springer Publishing.

Center for Applied Special Technology (CAST). (2013). *UDL book builder*. Retrieved from http://bookbuilder.cast.org

Center for Universal Design. (2010). *Ronald L. Mace*. Retrieved from http://www.ncsu.edu/project/design-projects/udi/center-for-universal-design/ron-mace

Educreations. (2012). *Educreations*. Retrieved from http://www.educreations.com

Edyburn, D. L. (2010). Would you recognize universal design for learning if you saw it? Ten propositions for new directions for the second decade of UDL. *Learning Disability Quarterly*, *33*(1), 33–41.

Friend, M. (2008a). *Co-teach! A handbook for creating and sustaining successful classroom partnerships in inclusive schools*. Greensboro, NC: MFI.

Friend, M. (2008b). Co-teaching: A simple solution that isn't simple after all. *Journal of Curriculum and Instruction*, *2*(2), 9–19. doi:10.3776/joci.2008.v2n2p9-19

Individuals with Disabilities Education Improvement Act of 2004. Pub. L. No. 108-446.

Inspiration Software Inc. (2013). *Kidspiration*. Retrieved from http://www.inspiration.com/Kidspiration

International Business Machines. (1991). *Technology and persons with disabilities*. Atlanta, GA: IBM Support Programs.

Kim, A., Vaughn, S., Klingner, J. K., Woodruff, A. L., Reutebuch, C. K., & Kouzekanani, K. (2006). Improving the reading comprehension of middle school students with disabilities through computer-assisted collaborative strategic reading. *Remedial and Special Education*, *27*, 235–249. doi:10.1177/07419325060270040401

MacArthur, C. A., Graham, S., Haynes, J. B., & DeLaPaz, S. (1996). Spelling checkers and students with learning disabilities: Performance comparisons and impact on spelling. *Special Education Technology*, *30*(1), 35–57. doi:10.1177/002246699603000103

National Center on Universal Design for Learning. (2010). *UDL guidelines*. Retrieved from http://www.udlcenter.org/aboutudl/udlguidelines

National Joint Committee on Learning Disabilities (Ed.). (1994). *Collective perspectives on issues affecting learning disabilities*. Austin, TX: PRO-ED.

Rose, D. H., Harbour, W. S., Johnston, C. S., Daley, S. G., & Abarbanell, L. (2006). Universal design for learning in postsecondary education: Reflections on principles and their application. *Journal of Postsecondary Education and Disability*, *19*(2), 135–151.

Seo, Y., & Bryant, D. (2012). Multimedia CAI program for students with mathematical difficulties. *Remedial and Special Education*, *33*(4), 217–225. doi:10.1177/0741932510383322

ShowMe. (2012). *Showme*. Retrieved from http://www.showme.com

Silió, M., & Barbetta, P. (2010). The effects of word prediction and text-to-speech technologies on the narrative writing skills of Hispanic students with specific learning disabilities. *Journal of Special Education Technology*, *25*(4), 17–32.

Technology-Related Assistance for People with Disabilities. (1988). Catalog No. 850. (senate rpt. 100-438). Washington, DC: U.S. Government Printing Office.

TechSmith. (2013). *ScreenChomp*. Retrieved from http://www.techsmith.com/labs.html

Twyman, T., & Tindal, G. (2006). Using a computer-adapted conceptually based history text to increase comprehension and problem-solving skills of students with disabilities. *Journal of Special Education Technology*, *21*(2), 5–16.

## ADDITIONAL READING

Dell, A. G., Newton, D. A., & Petroff, J. G. (2011). *Assistive technology in the classroom, enhancing the school experience of students with disabilities* (2nd ed.). Upper Saddle River, NJ: Pearson.

Gordon, D. T., Gravel, J. W., & Schifter, L. A. (2009). *A policy reader in universal design for learning*. Cambridge, MA: Harvard Education Press.

Hitchcock, C., & Stahl, K. (2007). Assistive technology, universal design, universal design for learning: Improved learning opportunities. *Journal of Special Education Technology*, *18*(4), 45–52.

Ralabate, P., Hehir, T., Dodd, E., Grindal, T., Vue, G., & Eidelman, H. et al. (2012). *Universal design for learning: Initiatives on the move: Understanding the impact of the Race to the Top and ARRA funding on the promotion of universal design for learning*. Wakefield, MA: National Center on Universal Design for Learning.

Rose, D., & Vue, G. (2010). 2020's learning landscape: A retrospective on dyslexia. *Perspectives on Language and Literacy*, *36*(1), 33–37.

Tegmark-Chita, M., Gravel, J. W., & Serpa, M., deL. B., Domings, Y., & Rose, D. H. (2012). Using the Universal Design for Learning framework to support culturally diverse learners. *Journal of Education*, *192*(1), 17–22.

# Chapter 3
# Text-to-Speech Software as Assistive and Mainstream Technology:
## Transitioning from a Functional to a Socio-Constructivist Approach

**Fiona S. Baker**
*Emirates College for Advanced Education, UAE*

## ABSTRACT

*This chapter presents the case for mainstreaming text-to-speech software for students with reading difficulties in the educational environment through a socio-constructivist approach. Socio-constructivism guides this chapter and communicates its purpose. The argument presented is that a purely functional approach that serves only students with reading disabilities such as dyslexia, confines the delivery of text-to-speech software to a select population, which results in limited outreach and use. Further, despite increased consumer involvement in assistive technology delivery with its potential to increase student participation, the target population is defined by professionals and based on human function rather than determined by a self-assessment of individual need, and may be further negatively impacted by human, contextual, and technological factors. By transitioning to a socio-constructivist approach, there is greater potential to assist a larger number of students who may otherwise not have the opportunity to explore text-to-speech software's potential and throughout their educational career may continue to experience difficulties in reading.*

DOI: 10.4018/978-1-4666-5015-2.ch003

## INTRODUCTION

Although many students are motivated and intrinsically interested in their studies, those experiencing reading difficulties may find studies challenging and frustrating. For these students, such reading difficulties continue throughout their academic careers. Without an effective support system in place, and the awareness of specific accommodations that can support them, students who struggle with reading may be at risk of underachieving, or worse yet, dropping out of school altogether. Accommodations designed to support these students do not need to be costly, but should be readily available for students to explore and use. Text-to-speech software for example, represents a viable and cost effective opportunity to improve and remediate for deficits in reading among students and should be an option for a larger number of students to potentially benefit from its use.

Commonly viewed as an assistive technology (AT), text-to-speech software is now supported by a growing research body for its use with those with low levels of literacy and English as second language (ESL) learners. Traditionally speaking, AT recommendations have been made by determining the functional limitation of a disability and how it hinders the individual's performance within a defined setting. Through a socio-constructivist approach, text-to-speech's potential to capture a wider audience of students who struggle to read will occur, with a greater number of students having the opportunity to experience its research-based benefits in meeting their study needs and achieving their reading goals.

### The Purpose of this Chapter

This chapter presents the case for transitioning from a functional to a socio-constructivist approach for the delivery of text-to-speech software. It is argued that a functional approach to delivering text-to-speech software as AT limits its outreach and use. This is in contrast to a socio-constructivist model, which has great potential to extend it. First, the benefits of text-to-speech software are discussed in the context of language literacy with regard to students with learning disabilities, ESL learners with low literacy levels, non-English speaking students with diverse language learning needs, and international students who lack the needed academic reading skills to attend postsecondary institutions. The challenges in applying the use of the functional approach are then discussed to include the myriad of factors that should be taken into consideration, that are not only complex in and of themselves, but are typically intertwined with one another. The benefits of taking a socio-constructivist approach to text-to-speech software delivery are then argued to increase outreach, and hence, increase the potential of text-to-speech software in serving a larger student population for whom there is a "good fit."

To support the argument of the delivery of text-to-speech software using a socio-constructivist approach in favor of making recommendations based on functional limitations, this chapter draws upon a multi-disciplinary research base focused on learning environments, education and technology, learning disabilities, ESL, literacy, occupational therapy, dyslexia, and special education.

## LANGUAGE LITERACY AND THE BENEFITS OF TEXT-TO-SPEECH SOFTWARE

### Students with Learning Disabilities

Text-to-speech software has historically been used to support students with specific reading disabilities (Balajthy, 2005; Kanitkar, Ochoa, & Handel, n.d.). The text-to-speech software features combined with electronic study tools have been found to motivate students to read and comprehend, while improving their overall study skills (Shaw, Madaus, & Dukes, 2010). A number of studies (e.g., Brinckerhoff & Banerjee, 2011; Elkind,

1998; Elkind, Black, & Murray, 1996; Elkind, Cohen, & Murray, 1993) have shown that text-to-speech software can motivate and assist students with specific reading disabilities in both reading and comprehension, while at the same time, also improving their study skills.

Take for example Borgh and Dickson (1992), who found that text-to-speech software improved student skills in various content areas and improved academic performance. Wise, Olson, Ring, & Johnson (1997), found that phonics instruction paired with a computerized reader, made significant improvements in decoding. Chiang and Jacob (2009) found that text-to-speech software has the ability to not only assist in reading, but also improve academic performance, self-perception, and functional task performance. Lewandowski and Montali (1996) found that an optical character recognition pen increased student motivation to read. Similar findings were found by Higgins and Raskind (2005), in researching the Quicktionary Reading Pen II® with 30 students who had learning disabilities in grades 4-12. In their study, it was found that these students experienced increased enjoyment and improved reading scores. Elkind, Black, and Murray (1996) found that for students with reading disabilities, the use of text-to-speech software made reading less tiring and less stressful. Finally, Sorrell, Bell, and Mccallum's (2007) study of elementary students in the context of text-to-speech software use, found that overall reading rate and comprehension increased.

## English as Second Language Learners with Low Literacy Levels

In addition to text-to-speech software being used with students with reading disabilities, benefits have also been experienced with ESL students and those who have shown low literacy levels. This is also important in the context of academic achievement. For instance, Klingner, Artiles, and Méndez Barletta (2006) reported that non-native English speaking students tend to exhibit lower academic achievement (particularly in literacy) than their non-English language counterparts. This includes similar negative trends also being observed in other educational outcomes, to include grade repetitions and school dropout (Abedi, Lord, Hofstetter, & Baker, 2000; Zehler et al., 2003). It has been questioned, however, as to how many of these ESL learners are aware of the benefits of text-to-speech software, and if they are, whether they have had the opportunity to explore it.

In U.S. schools, educators continue to be challenged, as demands for accountability continue to increase. Particularly under legislation, such as the No Child Left Behind Act, which requires that students from all language, cultural, and economic backgrounds, reach the same high level of academic achievement as native-English speaking students (U.S. Department of Education, n.d.). But, at the same time, this population of ESL learners continues to be underserved (Ruiz-de-Velasco, Fix, & Clewell, 2000). Challenges facing schools continue as low reading levels are present at admission and may persist well into postsecondary studies. In fact, according to Thevenot (2012), many students who drop out of college started their college careers with serious deficits in reading, writing, and mathematics.

## Non-English Speaking Students with Diverse Language Learning Needs

Another group of struggling learners is non-native English speaking students who are recent immigrants or long-term U.S. resident ESL learners. This is a population which continues to steadily rise in numbers. Take for instance the figures provided in 1995 by Fitzgerald, who reported that in California approximately 50% of students spoke a language other than English as their primary language, with the prediction that by 2030 the percentage would increase to approximately 70%. Also consider predictions by the Federal Interagency Forum on Child and Family Statistics (2000), who reported that the number of children whose first language is not English more than doubled from 1979 to 1995, rising from 1.3 million to 2.4 million. Such figures help illustrate the importance of helping this student population.

It is important to note that while some non-native English speaking students are assessed and placed into ESL courses prior to starting their academic studies at college; some students have language skills above the level of these courses. However, these students do not have fully-developed English literacy. Further compounding matters, these students all have diverse language learning needs and progress at different rates as they acquire, in the context of academics, language proficiency (Cummins, 2000). In addition, although it may appear that intermediate-level learners understand grade-level academic texts, they still require contextual support to completely comprehend academic content and the use of literacy skills. Researchers, for instance, have found that content lessons do not always necessarily allow time for interaction, or for students to practice the presented information (Short & Echevarria, 1999).

There is a compelling body of research on computer-assisted instruction which addresses reading in elementary school settings for non-native English speaking students. Studies within this body, for instance, have shown that Spanish-dominant, computer-using ESL students have improved their academic performance, significantly improving their English skills (Knox & Anderson-Inman, 2001). While only one example, such research contributes to validation in the use of text-to-speech software as an important intervention for non-native English speaking students in learning to read and in the comprehension of grade-level content-area curriculum. Furthermore, such research also provides support for the use of text-to-speech software for all non-native English speaking students in the classroom. Finally, it also fuels support for how specific features can successfully contribute to important aspects of the reading and learning process for all English language learners, regardless of their ability level or educational background.

Text-to-speech software can address a non-native English speaking student's need for comprehensible input because the text is tracked visually as the student reads. Furthermore, targeted words can be played back as often as necessary to facilitate learning. Text-to-speech also promotes active manipulation of text to foster use of comprehension strategies and can assist in making content instruction accessible (Hernandez, 2003) through software targeted for reading and study skills. Often students need support in phonics and assistance with decoding (Clay, 1993). By reading text aloud, for example, text-to-speech software also supports this process, while at the same time, elevating vocabulary and increasing reading fluency through explicit instruction and the abundance of practice (Ramirez, 1986).

For non-native English speaking students, research has also shown the potential of text-to-speech software to provide linguistic and academic support (Leung, 1996; Root, 1994). Drezek (2007), for instance, studied 10 adults who were able to develop their reading comprehension along with confidence, overcome their avoidance behaviors, and experience overall pleasure from reading. D'Silva (2005) used text-to-speech software to enhance reading performance for Canadian ESL students. Findings from the D'Silva study showed that young adults spent more of their time reading and making meaning from texts. Furthermore, text-to-speech software has also been studied with non-native English speaking audiences with learning disabilities. For instance, Chiang and Liu (2011), in investigating 15 participants in a Taiwanese high school, studied the effectiveness of text-to-speech software with ESL/dyslexic students. Findings of their study showed that students experienced an immediate impact on their word recognition and also made reading, writing, spelling, and pronouncing easier. Furthermore, their participants reported an increase in comprehending more in class while also experiencing benefits in learning and student life.

### International Students Who Lack Academic Reading Skills

Adding to the non-native English speaking students are international students who may also lack academic reading skills. McMurtrie (2012) reported double-digit growth in the number of students arriving from China along with steady growth from Saudi Arabia. Xueqin (2011) also reported the trend that many countries have been sending underprepared students to postsecondary education in the U.S.. China in particular, has been known to have coaching industries with services that teach a variety of less-than-educational methods intended to inflate the proficiency scores of students. The result is that these students are placed into postsecondary programs without the needed prerequisite language proficiency. These low level readers not only face language learning challenges, but at the same time, encounter unfamiliar academic materials (Fraser, 2007). Kitao, Kitao, Headrick Miller, Carpenter, and Rinner (1995) and Kitao, Yoshida, and Yoshida (1986) found that an increasing number of international students are at risk of not acquiring literacy skills. A lack of proficiency in reading impedes growth and academic achievement, leads to frustration, and is a challenge in postsecondary environments (Fraser, 2007). This issue of language literacy is crucial in regard to policy and practice, given that these students are the fastest growing subgroup in the U.S. educational system (Slavin & Cheung, 2003).

## CHALLENGES IN THE USE OF THE FUNCTIONAL APPROACH

Student service providers are often required to make decisions about AT to address the needs of learners identified as having a disability (Zabala, 2000). Yet, all too often, an in-depth needs analysis from the student perspective is lacking, not to mention that adequate monitoring and follow-up is not carried out to ensure meaningful academic and socially valid outcomes. The result is that the benefits of the AT are often analyzed and assessed from the perspective of whether the technology can remediate and compensate for the disability itself, rather than meet human *needs* over time. That is, in the functional approach, decisions on the provision of AT services are based on factors related to human *function*, and the focus is on the problem the individual has in functioning within his or her environment. The outcome is that as technology continues to advance, experiences and benefits expressed by students in enabling and empowering aspects of personal, social and academic life over time, remain largely unexplored.

### Factors that Should be Taken into Consideration

This commonly used approach does not work particularly well, as there are many individualized factors that should be taken into consideration when making decisions about the nature of the AT services to be provided. These are factors that can be rather involved and interact with one another in complex ways. Take for example the following factors:

- **Motivation**: Theories associated with learning and research into motivation for learning suggest that motivation is vital. Motivational theory, for instance, relates to both social constructivism and symbolic interaction (Williams, Burden & Lanvers, 2002). Lepper and Chabay (1985), even go so far as to say that motivation can often influence achievement more than cognitive factors.
- **Attitudes and Personal Perceptions**: Personal perceptions play a significant role in exploring response strategies and in making decisions about what to accept. For instance, depending on the individual, there may or may not be a perceived need

for AT. Some may not think that a problem exists, and thus may not be open to exploring such an option. Then there are those who perceive their current AT as sufficient, dismissing the opportunity to explore the adoption of new technology.

- **Learning Control and Feedback**: It has been suggested that total learner control of one's own learning is only beneficial if appropriate learning strategies are in place and the learner knows how to use them (Steinberg, 1997). In addition, feedback about performance enhances the potential benefits of learner control. Feedback will also assist a computer-mediated environment in which the AT alone may not enhance performance, but feedback in use of the technology may. Steinberg, Baskin, and Hofer (1986) found that when students had a computer tool in their learning environment, it was not the tool itself, but instead the tool along with feedback that affected performance.
- **Learner Intelligences, Learning Styles, and Preference**: Learners preferentially take in and process information in different ways (e.g., sight, hearing, reflecting and acting, reasoning logically, analyzing and visualizing). The theory of multiple intelligences, for instance, states that there are at least seven different abilities of learning, and therefore, "seven intelligences" which include visual, auditory and tactile/kinesthetic modalities (Gardner, 1983; Lazear, 1991). An understanding of these intelligences may help in better understanding the relationship between learner and application, especially in the complex text-to-speech software planning process for the use of AT.

While these factors only begin to scratch the surface of the variables that should be taken into consideration when making decisions about the nature of AT services to be provided to students, these factors help illustrate the complexity of selecting AT. These factors along with the challenges discussed thus far in this chapter, also illustrate the need for a socio-constructivist approach to text-to-speech software delivery and use, as in effect, such complexities constrain the delivery of text-to-speech software for what is already a professionally "pre-selected" and "defined" population of students. It stands to reason that while the complexities that constrain use within this population should be researched and practice should aim to minimize the factors that impact negatively on text-to-speech use for this population, at the same time, given the number of human and contextual factors that may impact negatively on use, it is crucial to capture a wider audience and hence overall, increase the potential for text-to-speech software to enhance the lives of struggling readers.

## THE SOCIO-CONSTRUCTIVIST APPROACH

Socio-constructivists believe that knowledge is constructed rather than transmitted from social interactions found within specific cultural contexts (Jonassen, 1996). Socio-constructivists place emphasis on the learners' intentions, experiences, and meta-cognitive strategies in constructing knowledge by assimilating data and by modifying their understanding from the discovery of new information. Socio-constructivists believe that learners bring with them feelings, ideas, and beliefs that are based on learner's observations and experiences (Nolan, 2006). Furthermore, these learners are provided with opportunities to reconstruct concepts, schema, and other cognitive structures that are based on to their interpretations of new information and experiences. Most importantly, social constructivism not only acknowledges the uniqueness and complexity of the learner, but goes one step further, and encourages, utilizes and rewards it as an essential element of the learning experience (Wertsch, 1997).

Instruction is, therefore, viewed as being concerned with experiences in contexts that are structured to make extrapolation possible. According to Kuhn (2000), knowledge is believed to be assembled within individual social and symbolic systems where the human experience is a vital part of developing self in multifaceted and telling relationships. So it should not come as a surprise that the contemporary constructivist theory of learning recognizes that individuals are active agents in their learning, so students should be involved as part of the decision making process. What this also means is that socio-constructivists embrace the belief that educators should be assessing student abilities to construct knowledge. Advocates, consequently, suggest that educators should first and foremost consider the knowledge and experiences students bring with them to the learning task.

Starting with the learner's knowledge and understandings can assist in filling-in the gaps necessary to address a situation or solve a specific problem. In their environment, learners rely on their individual characteristics as well as making sense of their experiences in many varied ways. That is, following the socio-constructivist line of thinking, each learner has his or her own unique and individual characteristics; and because of this, each learner as a unique entity is central to the interpretative paradigm in text-to-speech software use. Following this school of thought, it is once again reiterated that each case should be considered for its unique and individual characteristics, so user perspectives are central to the interpretative paradigm in researching such software. This is in stark contrast to making AT recommendations by determining the functional limitation of a disability and researching how the limitation hinders the learner's performance within a defined setting.

## Text-to-Speech Software in a Socio-Constructivist Environment

It is regrettable that not all students will automatically take to text-to-speech software recommended by professionals through a functional approach. In addition, students may not be aware of the text-to-speech software and its potential benefits and in some cases, students may be struggling with reading, but not self-identifying. In a socio-constructivist environment, text-to-speech software commonly used to help an individual compensate for a disability in one area might be used creatively, alone or in conjunction with other technologies, to meet an individual's needs in another area of disability or weakness, so the scope provided for exploration in a socio-constructivist model to meet student needs in a purposeful and meaningful way to the individual, are greatly enhanced. Experimentation in practice, research, and a creative approach to each student's unique needs is crucial.

Educators need to provide as many opportunities and choices as possible to all students and allow text-to-speech software to be simply one more strategy available for learners to explore, manipulate, and make their own. If professionals have a repertoire and menu of strategies available to students, then individual learners can explore what works best and develop their sense of selves as readers in a socio-constructivist environment. From a socio-constructivist point of view, this is likely the most important thing professionals can do:

- Make sure that students believe in their ability to read,
- Make sure they understand the complex process of reading, and
- Make sure that they are in a position to know what to ask for to make themselves strong readers.

For an educator taking a socio-constructivist approach, this means to provide choices and options for the student rather than coercing him/her into any set method of remediation and accommodation. It means assisting the student to become confident and proactive in their engagement of reading and to gain insights into their own reading process so they can understand and work with their strengths and weaknesses. By empowering the student, it also means that the student becomes a self-advocate and regulates their own learning through an educator's support and guidance. Ideally, the student should be in a position to purposefully explore the tools available and closely monitor progress as he or she adjusts to, and adapts to changing circumstances.

When students are provided with the choice to use text-to-speech software in a socio-constructivist learning environment, there is acknowledgement that they may well be the individuals best able to make a decision as to what works best under what conditions. This approach may also foster better continued life use, and reap more benefits than those captured by a functional model. As Anderson-Inman and Horney (1998) point out, AT should be "a ubiquitous and effective option for all students, not an accommodation for a select few" (p. 157). In Parr's (2011) study, for example, students demonstrated they were capable of participating in decision making and taking part in instructional, contextual, and task-related demands. Student choice and ownership became increasingly important to students and afforded them the opportunity to develop self-advocacy and self-efficacy with some viewing it as a life-long tool. What is important is that potential users have the benefit of being exposed to text-to-speech software use in an interactive and responsive manner, in a way that is not imposed, but simply as an invitation to learn more. As Parr suggests, students are capable of making a decision about the use of text-to-speech software and when they do, so it becomes a support of choice, differentiation and self-advocacy.

Parr's (2011) research concluded that text-to-speech software should not be limited to students assessed with reading disabilities, but rather that text-to-speech software should be a mainstream technology for all. This notion puts a whole new perspective on the scope of text-to-speech software as a technology with use for a wider audience than for those identified and assessed through a functional approach. For Parr's notion to occur, a socio-constructivist approach should be taken. This requires that students start to be in charge of their own learning, continually trying new ways, monitoring how they worked and then adjusting accordingly. In a socio-constructivist approach, there will be a shift in education to be more student focused, which in itself requires additional skills, focus and a change in the role of student and teacher. It places the student at the centre of his own learning and improves learning and engagement. In today's technological world, it means that educators will provide learning experiences which require the development of technological literacies, so students are adept in using appropriate technology and are critical in its uses and understanding of what technology means. Among the technological tools at a student's disposal will be text-to-speech software. This approach recognizes and values the importance of placing the student at the center of learning and allows the student to make his or her own decisions with text-to-speech software as a potential tool to naturally explore reading within his or her context.

## CONCLUSION

As text-to-speech continues to technologically evolve with more and more enhancements to text-to-speech software becoming available, there should be continued research into student uptake and use of this software in educational contexts worldwide. Practice in educational institutions should transition from a purely functional based approach to a socio-constructivist approach, accompanied by on-going monitoring of uptake and evaluation of use, especially from the student perspective. While developing the software itself and consistently researching factors that impact text-to-speech use are valid, given the constraints identified, what will reap greater benefits is to focus on increasing student use by opening up the potential of the technology to a wider audience through a socio-constructivist approach. For as long as a purely functional based approach is taken, efforts are likely to be limited by student numbers and often thwarted by factors affecting text-to-speech take-up. Should efforts however, be re-directed toward a socio-constructivist approach to learning, text-to-speech's true potential will likely open up with the student at the centre of his/her own progress in reading with the teacher as facilitator and guide.

## REFERENCES

Abedi, J., Lord, C., Hofstetter, C., & Baker, E. (2000). Impact of accommodation strategies on English language learners' test performance. *Educational Measurement: Issues and Practice*, *19*(3), 16–26. doi:10.1111/j.1745-3992.2000.tb00034.x

Anderson-Inman, L., & Horney, M. A. (1998). Transforming text for at-risk readers. In D. Reinking, L. Labbo, M. McKenna, & R. Kieffler (Eds.), *Handbook of literacy and technology: Transformations in a post-typographical world* (pp. 15–44). Mahwah, NJ: Lawrence Erlbaum Associates.

Balajthy, E. (2005). Text-to-speech software for struggling readers. *Reading Online*, *8*(4), 1–9.

Borgh, K., & Dickson, W. (1992). The effects on children are writing of adding speech synthesis to a word processor. *Journal of Research in Computing in Education*, *24*(4), 533–544.

Brinckerhoff, L., & Banerjee, M. (2011). Brochure on college students with learning disabilities. *Association on Higher Education and Disability (AHEAD)*. Retrieved from http://www.ahead.org/

Chiang, H., & Jacob, K. (2009). Effect of computer-based instruction on students' self-perception and functional task performance. *Disability and Rehabilitation. Assistive Technology*, *4*(2), 106–118. doi:10.1080/17483100802613693 PMID:19253099

Chiang, H., & Liu, C. (2011). Evaluation of the benefits of assistive reading software: Perceptions of high school students with learning disabilities. *Assistive Technology*, *23*(4), 199–204. doi:10.1080/10400435.2011.614673 PMID:22256668

Clay, M. (1993). *Reading recovery in English and other languages.* Paper presented at the West Coast Literacy Conference. Palm Springs, CA.

Cummins, J. (2000). *Language, power and pedagogy: Bilingual children in the crossfire*. Clevedon, UK: Multilingual Matters.

D'Silva, R. (2005). *Promoting reading skills of young adult EAL learners through voice recognition software*. (Masters dissertation). University of British Columbia, Vancouver, Canada.

Drezek, J. (2007). *Adult ESOL reading comprehension and text-to-speech software*. (Masters dissertation). University of Texas, Arlington, TX. Retrieved from dspace.uta.edu/bitstream/handle/10106/23/umi-uta-1661.pdf?sequence=1

Elkind, J. (1998). *Computer reading machines for poor readers*. Los Angeles, CA: Lexia Institute.

Elkind, J., Black, M., & Murray, C. (1996). Computer-based compensation of adult reading disabilities. *Annals of Dyslexia*, *46*, 159–186. doi:10.1007/BF02648175

Elkind, J., Cohen, K., & Murray, C. (1993). Using computer-based readers to improve reading comprehension of students with dyslexia. *Annals of Dyslexia*, *43*, 238–259. doi:10.1007/BF02928184

Federal Interagency Forum on Child and Family Statistics. (2000). *America's children: Key national indicators of well-being*. Washington, DC: Federal Interagency Forum on Child and Family Statistics.

Fitzgerald, J. (1995). English-as-a-second-language reading instruction in the United States: A research review. *Journal of Reading Behavior*, *27*(2), 115–152.

Fraser, C. (2007). Reading rate in L1 Mandarin Chinese and L2 English across five reading tasks. *Modern Language Journal*, *91*(3), 372–394. doi:10.1111/j.1540-4781.2007.00587.x

Gardner, R. C. (1983). *Frames of mind: The theory of multiple intelligences*. New York: Basic Books.

Hernandez, A. (2003). *Making content instruction accessible for English language learners: Reaching the highest level of English*. Retrieved from http://www.reading.org

Higgins, E. L., & Raskind, M. H. (2005). The compensatory effectiveness of the Quicktionary Reading Pen II on the reading comprehension of students with learning disabilities. *Journal of Special Education Technology*, *20*(1), 31–40.

Jonassen, D. H. (1996). *Handbook of research for educational communications and technology*. New York: Macmillan.

Kanitkar, A. S., Ochoa, T. A., & Handel, M. L. (n.d.). *Kurzweil: A computer-supported reading tool for students with learning*. Retrieved from http://www.kurzweiledu.com/files/kurzweil-white-paper-report-from-indiana-university.pdf

Kitao, K., Kitao, S. K., Headrick Miller, J., Carpenter, J. W., & Rinner, C. (1995). *Culture and communication*. Kyoto, Japan: Yamaguchi Shoten.

Kitao, K., Yoshida, S., & Yoshida, H. (1986). Daigakusei no eigo dokkairyoku no mondaiten--Gotou noruikei to genin. *Chubu Chiku Eigo Kyoiku Gakkai Kiyo*, *15*, 8–13.

Klingner, J. K., Artiles, A., & Méndez Barletta, L. (2006). English language learners who struggle with reading: Language acquisition or LD? *Journal of Learning Disabilities*, *39*(2), 108–128. doi:10.1177/00222194060390020101 PMID:16583792

Knox, C., & Anderson-Inman, L. (2001). Migrant ESL high school students succeed using networked laptops. *Learning and Leading with Technology*, *28*(5), 1–53.

Kuhn, D. (2000). Metacognitive development. *Current Directions in Psychological Science*, *9*(5), 178–181. doi:10.1111/1467-8721.00088

Lazear, D. (1991). *Seven ways of knowing: Teaching for multiple intelligences*. Retrieved from http://pss.uvm:edu/pss162/learningstyles.html

Lepper, M. R., & Chabay, R. W. (1985). Intrinsic motivation and instruction: Conflicting views on the role of motivational processes in computer-based education. *Educational Psychologist*, *20*, 217–231. doi:10.1207/s15326985ep2004_6

Leung, B. P. (1996). Quality assessment practices in a diverse society. *Teaching Exceptional Children*, *28*(3), 42–45.

Lewandowski, L., & Montali, J. (1996). Bimodal reading: Benefits of a talking computer for average and less skilled readers. *Journal of Learning Disabilities*, *29*, 271–279. doi:10.1177/002221949602900305 PMID:8732888

McMurtrie, B. (2012, November). China continues to drive foreign-student growth in the United States. *The Chronicle of Higher Education*. Retrieved from http://chronicle.com/article/China-Continues-to-Drive/135700/

Nolan, J. (2006). The influence of ASCII on the construction of internet-based knowledge. In J. Weiss, J. Nolan, J. Hunsinger, & P. Trifonas (Eds.), *International handbook of virtual learning environments* (pp. 207–220). Dordrecht, The Netherlands: Springer. doi:10.1007/978-1-4020-3803-7_7

Parr, M. (2011). *The voice of text-to-speech technology: One possible solution for struggling readers, what works?* Retrieved from http://www.edu.gov.on.ca/eng/literacynumeracy/inspire/research/whatWorks.html

Ramirez, S. (1986). The effects of Suggestopedia in teaching English vocabulary to Spanish dominant Chicano third graders. *The Elementary School Journal*, *86*, 325–333. doi:10.1086/461453

Root, C. (1994). *A guide to learning disabilities for the ESL classroom practitioner*. Retrieved from http://www.ldonline.org/article/8765/

Ruiz-de-Velasco, J., Fix, M., & Clewell, B. (2000, December). *Overlooked and underserved: Immigrant students in U.S. secondary schools*. Washington, DC: The Urban Institute.

Shaw, S. Madaus, J., & Dukes, L. (2010). Preparing students with disabilities for college success: A practical guide for transition planning. Baltimore, MD: Brookes.

Short, D., & Echevarria, J. (1999). *The sheltered instructional observation protocol*. Washington, DC: Center for Applied Linguistics.

Slavin, R., & Cheung, A. (2003). *Effective programs for English language learners: A best-evidence synthesis*. Baltimore, MD: Johns Hopkins University, CRESPAR.

Sorrell, C., Bell, S., & McCallum, R. (2007). Reading rate and comprehension as a function of computerized versus traditional presentation mode: A preliminary study. *Journal of Special Education Technology*, *22*(1), 1–12.

Steinberg, E. R. (1977). Cognition and learner control: A literature review. *Journal of Computer-Based Instruction*, *16*(4), 117–121.

Steinberg, E. R., Baskin, A. B., & Hofer, L. (1986). Organizational/memory tools: A technique for improving problem solving skills. *Journal of Educational Computing Research*, *2*(2), 169–187. doi:10.2190/QNF3-NM3V-FRTE-17B3

Thevenot, B. (2012, February). Most community college students never graduate. *The Texas Tribune*. Retrieved from http://www.texastribune.org/texas-education/higher-education/most-community-college-students-never-graduate/

U.S. Department of Education. (n.d.). *No child left behind: Elementary and secondary education act (ESEA)*. Retrieved from http://www2.ed.gov/nclb/landing.jhtml

Wertsch, J. V. (1997). *Vygotsky and the formation of the mind*. Cambridge, MA: Harvard University Press.

Williams, M. D., Burden, R. L., & Lanvers, U. (2002). French is the language of love and stuff: Student perceptions of issues related to motivation in learning a foreign language. *British Educational Research Journal*, *28*(4), 503–528. doi:10.1080/0141192022000005805

Wise, B. K., Olson, R. K., Ring, J., & Johnson, M. C. (1997). Interactive computer support for improving phonological skills in remedial reading. In J. Metsala, & L. Ehri (Eds.), *Word recognition in beginning literacy*. Mahwah, NJ: Lawrence Erlbaum Inc.

Xueqin, J. (2011, November). Selecting the right Chinese students. *The Chronicle of Higher education*. Retrieved from http://chronicle.com/article/Selecting-the-Right-Chinese/129621/

Zabala, J. S. (2000). Setting the stage for success: Building success through effective selection and use of assistive technology systems. *LD Online*. Retrieved from http://www.ldonline.org/article/5874/

Zehler, A. M., Fleischman, H. L., Hopstock, P. J., Stephenson, T. G., Pendzick, M. L., & Sapru, S. (2003). Descriptive study of services to LEP students and LEP students with disabilities: Vol. I. *Research report*. Arlington, VA: Development Associates, Inc.

## ADDITIONAL READING

Ajzen, I. (1991). The Theory of Planned Behavior. *Organizational Behavior and Human Decision Processes*, *50*, 179–211. doi:10.1016/0749-5978(91)90020-T

Ajzen, I. (1998). *Attitudes, person and behaviour*. Chicago, Illinois: The Dorsey Press.

Ajzen, I., & Fishbein, M. (1980). *Understanding attitudes and predicting social behavior*. Englewood Cliffs, NJ: Prentice Hall.

Armitage, C. J., & Conner, M. (2001). Efficacy of the Theory of Planned Behaviour: A meta-analytic review. *The British Journal of Social Psychology*, *40*, 471–499. doi:10.1348/014466601164939 PMID:11795063

Bandura, A. (1977). Self-efficacy: Toward a unifying theory of behavioral change. *Psychological Review*, *84*, 191–215. doi:10.1037/0033-295X.84.2.191 PMID:847061

Bandura, A. (1982). Self-efficacy mechanism in human agency. *The American Psychologist*, *37*, 122–147. doi:10.1037/0003-066X.37.2.122

Bean, J., & Metzner, B. (1985). A conceptual model of nontraditional undergraduate student attrition. *Review of Educational Research*, *55*, 485–650. doi:10.3102/00346543055004485

Beigel, A. R. (2000). *Assistive technology assessment: More than the device. Intervention in school and clinic*. New York: Pro-Ed Inc.

Brosnan, M. (2004). *A longitudinal study of computer usage: 6 months*. Retrieved from http://ltsnpsy.york.ac.uk/LTSNCiPAAbstracts/CIP96CD/BROSNAN/XHTML/PAPEHTM

Burden, R. L. (2005). *Dyslexia and self-concept: Seeking a dyslexic identity*. New York: Wiley.

Bynum, H., & Rogers, J. (1987). The use and effectiveness of assistive devices possessed by patients seen in home care. *The Occupational Therapy Journal of Research*, *7*, 181–191.

Carswell, A., McColl, M. A., Baptiste, S., Law, M., & Pollock, N. (2004). The Canadian Occupational Performance Measure: A research and clinical literature review. *Canadian Journal of Occupational Therapy*, *71*(4), 210–223. doi:10.1177/000841740407100406 PMID:15586853

Cook, A. M., & Hussey, S. M. (2008). *Assistive technologies: Principles and practice*. St. Louis, MO: Mosby-Yearbook.

Curry, L. (1987). *Integrating concepts of cognitive or learning style: A review with attention to psychometric standards*. Ottawa, ON: Canadian College of Health Service Executives.

Cushman, L. A., & Scherer, M. J. (1996). Measuring outcomes of assistive technology use through mixed methods. *Archives of Physical Medicine and Rehabilitation*, *75*, 726–727.

Davis, F. (1986). *A technology acceptance model for empirically testing new end-user information systems: Theory and results* (Doctoral dissertation, Sloan School of Management: MIT, 1986).

Davis, F. (1989). Perceived usefulness, perceived ease of use, and user acceptance of information technology. *Management Information Systems Quarterly*, *13*(3), 319–340. doi:10.2307/249008

Davis, F. D., Bagozzi, R. P., & Warshaw, P. R. (1989). User acceptance of computer technology: A comparison of two theoretical models. *Management Science*, *35*, 982–1003. doi:10.1287/mnsc.35.8.982

Demos, G. D. (1965). *Controlled physical classroom environments and their effect upon elementary school children (windowless classroom study). Riverside County*. CA: Palm Springs School District.

Denscombe, M. (2003). *The good research guide: For small-scale social research projects*. Maidenhead, England: The Open University Press.

Dewey, J. (1916). *Democracy and Education. An introduction to the philosophy of education* (1966th ed.). New York: Free Press.

Dunn, R., & Dunn, K. (1978). *Teaching students through their individual learning styles: A practical approach*. Reston, VA: Reston Publishing.

Felder, R. M., & Silverman, L. K. (1988). Learning styles and teaching styles in engineering education. *English Education*, *78*(7), 674–681.

Feuerstein, R. (1980). *Instrumental enrichment*. Baltimore, MD: University Park Press.

Fishbein, M., & Ajzen, I. (1975). *Belief, attitude, intention and behavior: An introduction to theory and research*. MA: Addison Wesley.

Fostnot, C. T. (1996). *Constructivism: Theory, perspectives, and practice*. New York: Teachers' College Press.

Garber, S. L., & Gregorio, T. L. (1990). Upper extremity assistive devices: Assessment of use by spinal cord-injured patients with quadriplegia. *The American Journal of Occupational Therapy.*, *44*(2), 12–131. doi:10.5014/ajot.44.2.126 PMID:2178440

Gardner, R. C. (1985). *Social psychology and second language learning: The role of attitude and motivation*. London: Edward Arnold.

Garner, J. B., & Campbell, P. H. (1987). Technology for persons with severe disabilities: Practical and ethical considerations. *The Journal of Special Education*, *21*, 122–132. doi:10.1177/002246698702100310

Gitlin, L. N. (1994). *Technology and self-care: What can social science research contribute to an understanding of technology use and aging?* Paper presented at Conference on Research Issues Related to Self-Care and Aging and the Administration on Aging, Washington, D.C., May 26-27.

Glanz, K., Lewis, F. M., & Rimer, B. K. (1997). *Health behavior and health education: Theory, research and practice*. San Francisco: Jossey-Bass Inc.

Godin, G., & Kok, G. (1996). The theory of planned behavior: A review of its applications to health-related behaviors. *American Journal of Health Promotion*, *11*(2), 87–98. doi:10.4278/0890-1171-11.2.87 PMID:10163601

Goetzfried, L. L., & Hannafin, M. J. (1985). The effects of embedded CAI Instructional control strategies on the learning and application of mathematics rules. *American Educational Research Journal*, *22*(2), 273–278. doi:10.3102/00028312022002273

Grant, R., & Wong, S. (2003). Barriers to literacy for language-minority learners: An argument for change in the literacy education profession. *Journal of Adolescent & Adult Literacy*, *46*(5), 386–394. doi:10.1598/JAAL.46.5.2

Halpain, D. R., Glover, J. A., & Harvey, A. L. (1985). Differential effects of higher and lower order questions. *Journal of Educational Psychology*, *73*, 736–744.

Hecker, L., Burns, L., Elkind, J., Elkind, K., & Katz, L. (2002). Benefits of assistive reading software for students with attention disorders. *Annals of Dyslexia*, *52*, 244–272. doi:10.1007/s11881-002-0015-8

Hess, R., & Miura, I. (1985). Gender differences in enrollment in computer camps and classes. *Sex Roles*, *13*, 193–203. doi:10.1007/BF00287910

Hill, T., Smith, N. D., & Mann, M. F. (1987). Role of efficacy expectations in predicting the decisions to use advanced technologies: The case of computers. *The Journal of Applied Psychology*, *72*, 307–313. doi:10.1037/0021-9010.72.2.307

Horowitz, P., & Otto, D. (1973). *The teaching effectiveness of an alternative teaching facility*. Washington DC. (ERIC Document Reproduction Service No. ED083242).

Huffman, H. B., Jernstedt, G. C., Reed, V. A., Reber, E. S., Burns, M. B., Oostenink, R. J., & Williams, M. T. (2003). Optimizing the design of computer classrooms: The physical environment. *Educational Technology*, *43*(4), 9–13.

Janssen Reinen, I., & Plomp, T. (1993). Some gender issues in educational computer use: Results of an international comparative survey. *Computers & Education*, *20*(4), 353–365. doi:10.1016/0360-1315(93)90014-A

Jarrow, J. E. (April, 1992a). *The Impact of Section 504 on postsecondary education*. Columbus, OH: Association on Higher Education and Disability.

Jarrow, J. E. (April, 1992b). *Title by title: The ADA's impact on postsecondary education*. Columbus, OH: Association on Higher Education and Disability.

Jay, T. (1981). Computerphobia: What to do about it. *Educational Technology*, *21*, 47–48.

Jernstedt, G. C. (1982). Active learning increases educational effectiveness and efficiency. *T.H.E. Journal*, *9*, 97–100.

Jonassen, D. H. (1991a). Objectivism vs. constructivism: Do we need a new philosophical paradigm? *Educational Technology Research and Development*, *39*(3), 5–14. doi:10.1007/BF02296434

Jonassen, D. H. (1991b). Evaluating constructivist learning. *Educational Technology*, *31*(9), 28–33.

Jonassen, D. H. (1997). Instructional design models for well-structured and illstructured problem-solving learning outcomes. *Educational Technology Research and Development*, *45*(1), 65–94. doi:10.1007/BF02299613

Jonassen, D. H. (1999). *Computers as mind tools for schools. Engaging critical thinking. Instructional technology & training series*. San Francisco, CA: Pfeiffer.

Jordan, E., & Stroup, D. (1982). The behavioral antecedents of computer fear. *Journal of Data Education*, *22*, 7–8.

Keefe, B., Scherer, M. J., & McKee, B. G. (1996). MainePOINT: Outcomes of teaching American sign language via distance learning. *Technology and Disability*, *5*(4), 319–326. doi:10.1016/S1055-4181(96)00178-1

Keefe, J. W. (1979). Learning style: An overview. In NASSP (Eds.), Student learning styles: Diagnosing and prescribing programs (pp. 1-17). Reston, VA: National Association of Secondary School Principals.

Knirk, F. G. (1997). *Instructional facilities for the information age*. Washington D.C. (ERIC Document Reproduction Service No. ED296734).

Kolb, D. (1984). *Experiential learning: Experience as the source of learning and development*. Englewood Cliffs, NJ: Prentice-Hall.

Kozulin, A. (1998). *Psychological tools: A sociocultural approach to education*. Cambridge, MA: Harvard University Press.

Lee, Y., & Vail, C. (2005). Computer based reading instruction for young children with disabilities. *Journal of Special Education Technology*, *20*, 5–18.

Leong, C. (1995). Effects of on-line reading and simultaneous DECtalk aiding in helping below-average and poor readers comprehend and summarize text. *Learning Disability Quarterly*, *78*, 101–115. doi:10.2307/1511198

Levine, T., & Donitsa-Schmidt, S. (1995). Computer experience, gender and classroom environment in computer-supported writing classes. *Journal of Educational Computing Research*, *13*, 337–357. doi:10.2190/DR9Y-PXFJ-JRWL-CFD8

Lewis, A. (2002). Accessing children's views about inclusion and integration. *Support for Learning*, *17*, 110–116.

Lewis, A. (2004). And when did you last see your father? Exploring the views of children with learning difficulties/disabilities. *British Journal of Special Education*, *31*, 4–10. doi:10.1111/j.0952-3383.2004.00319.x

Lewis, A., & Porter, J. (2004). Interview methods and children with learning disabilities. *British Journal of Learning Disabilities*, *32*, 191–197. doi:10.1111/j.1468-3156.2004.00313.x

Lincoln, Y. S., & Guba, E. G. (1985). *Naturalistic inquiry*. Thousand Oaks, CA: Sage.

Lindamood, P. (1994). Issues in researching the link between phonological awareness, learning disabilities, and spelling. In G. R. Lyon (Ed.), *Frames of reference for the assessment of learning disabilities*. Baltimore, MD: Paul H. Brookes Publishing.

Lindsay, G. (2003). Inclusive education: A critical perspective. *British Journal of Special Education*, *17*(1), 23–31.

Linkowski, D. (1971). A scale to measure acceptance of disability. *Rehabilitation Counseling Bulletin*, *14*(4), 236–244.

Linkowski, D. C. (1969). *ETS Test Collection Database Online 2005*. Retrieved from http://www.ets.org/testcoll/index.html

Meier, S. (1985). Computer aversion. *Computers in Human Behavior*, *1*, 171–179. doi:10.1016/0747-5632(85)90030-5

Menter, I., Elliot, D., Hulme, M., Lewin, J., & Lowden, K. (2011). *A guide to practitioner research in education*. London: Sage Publications.

Mercer, C. D., Jordan, L., Allsopp, D. H., & Mercer, A. R. (1996). Learning disabilities definitions and criteria used by state Education departments. *Learning Disability Quarterly*, *19*, 217–232. doi:10.2307/1511208

Merrill, M. D. (1980). Learner control in computer-based learning. *Computers & Education*, *4*, 77–95. doi:10.1016/0360-1315(80)90010-X

Mertens, D. (2000). *Research and inequality*. New York: Taylor and Francis.

Mertens, D. M., & Wang, Z. (1998). Attitudes toward computers of pre-service teachers of hearing impaired students. *American Annals of the Deaf*, *133*(1), 40–42. doi:10.1353/aad.2012.0719

Middlemas, B. (1991). Information technology for students with Learning Difficulties: Some experiences at Brookland Technical College. In *O. Boyd-Barrett & E. Scanlon, Computers and Learning*. MA: Addison Wesley.

Montali, J., & Lewandowski, L. (1996). Bimodal reading: Benefits of a talking computer for average and less skilled readers. *Journal of Learning Disabilities*, *29*(3), 271–279. doi:10.1177/002221949602900305 PMID:8732888

Myers, I. (1978). *Myers-Briggs Type Indicator*. Palo Alto, CA: Consulting Psychologists Press.

NCIHD. (2000, April). *National reading panel reports combination of teaching phonics, word sounds, giving feedback on oral reading most effective way to teach reading*. Retrieved from http://www.nichd.nih.gov/new/releases/nrp.htm

Olson, R., Foltz, G., & Wise, B. (1985). *Reading instruction and remediation with the aid of computer speech*. Boston, MA: Oral Presentation, Meeting of the Society for Computers in Psychology.

Olson, R. K. (1985). Disabled reading processes and cognitive profiles. In D. Gray, & J. Kavanagh (Eds.), *Biobehavioral measures of dyslexia* (pp. 215–244). Parkton, MD: York Press.

Olson, R. K., & Wise, B. (1987). Computer speech in reading instruction. In D. Reinking (Ed.), *Reading and computers: Issues for theory and practice* (pp. 156–177). New York: Teachers College Press.

Philips, B., & Zhao, H. (1993). Predictors of assistive technology abandonment. *Assistive Technology*, (5): 36–45. doi:10.1080/10400435.1993.10132205 PMID:10171664

Raskind, M., & Higgins, E. (1999). Speaking to read: The effects of speech recognition technology on the reading and spelling performances of children with learning disabilities. *Annals of Dyslexia*, *49*, 251–281. doi:10.1007/s11881-999-0026-9

Reichmann, S. W., & Grasha, A. F. (1974). A rational approach to developing and assessing the construct validity of a student learning style scale instrument. *The Journal of Psychology*, *87*, 213–223. doi:10.1080/00223980.1974.9915693

Rigney, J. W. (1978). Learning strategies: A theoretical perspective. In H. F. O'Neil Jr., (Ed.), *Learning strategies* (pp. 165–205). New York: Academic Press.

Rogers, C. R., & Freiberg, H. J. (1994). *Freedom to learn*. Columbus, OH: Merrill/Macmillan.

Rogers, J. C., & Holm, M. B. (1993). AT device use in participants with rheumatic disease: A literature review. *The American Journal of Occupational Therapy.*, *46*(2), 120–127. doi:10.5014/ajot.46.2.120

Rogoff, B. (1990). *Apprenticeship in thinking: Cognitive development in social context*. New York: Oxford University Press.

Rohe, W., & Patterson, A. H. (1974). The effects of varied levels of resources and density on behavior in a day care center. In D. H. Carson (Ed.), *Man-environment interactions: Evaluations and applications* (pp. 476–489). Washington, DC: Environmental Design Research Association.

Romiszowski, A. J. (1981). *Designing instructional systems: Decision making in course planning and curriculum design. London: Kogan Page*. York: Springer-Verlay.

Sadler-Smith, E., & Smith, P. J. (2004). Strategies for accommodating individual styles and preferences in flexible learning programs. *British Journal of Educational Technology*, *35*(4), 395–412. doi:10.1111/j.0007-1013.2004.00399.x

Scherer, M. (2000). *Living in the state of stuck. How assistive technology impacts the lives of people with disabilities*. Cambridge, MA: Brookline Books.

Scherer, M. J. (1991). Matching person and technology. New York: Webster.

Scherer, M. J. (1996a). Introduction to outcomes measurement. *Technology and Disability*, *5*, 283–284. doi:10.1016/S1055-4181(96)00174-4

Scherer, M. J. (1996b). *Living in the state of stuck: How technology impacts people with disabilities*. Cambridge, MA: Brookline Books.

Scherer, M. J. (1996c). Outcomes of assistive technology use on quality of life. *Disability and Rehabilitation*, *18*(9), 439–448. doi:10.3109/09638289609165907 PMID:8877302

Schettino, A. P., & Borden, R. J. (1976). Sex differences in response to naturalistic crowding: Affective reactions in group size and group density. *Personality and Social Psychology Bulletin*, *2*(1), 67–70. doi:10.1177/014616727600200115

Schloss, P. J., Wisniewski, L. A., & Cartwright, G. P. (1988). The differential effect of learner control and feedback on college students' performance on CAI modules. *Journal of Educational Computing Research*, *4*(2), 141–150. doi:10.2190/XJYY-TX9V-DHGQ-5Q50

Schneiderman, H. (1987). *Designing the user interface: Strategies for effective human computer interaction*. Reading, MA: Addision-Wesley Publishing Service. doi:10.1145/25065.950626

Smith, C. B., & Sensenbaugh, R. (1992). *Helping children overcome reading difficulties*. Retrieved from http://www.kidsource.com/kidsource/content2/overcome.reading.html

Steinberg, E. R. (1977). Review of student control in computer-assisted instruction. *Journal of Computer-Based Instruction*, *3*(3), 84–90.

Sutton, R. E. (1998). *Equity issues in educational computer use*. Paper presented at the New Zealand Computers in Education Society, New Plymouth, New York.

Sweet, A., & Snow, C. (2003). *Rethinking reading comprehension*. NY: The Guilford Press.

Tennyson, R. D., Robert, D., & Rothen, W. (1979). Management of computer-based instruction: design of an adaptive control strategy. *Journal of Computer-Based Instruction*, *5*(3), 63–71.

Terrell, S. (2002). Learning style as a predictor of success in a limited residency doctoral program. *The Internet and Higher Education*, *5*(4), 345–352. doi:10.1016/S1096-7516(02)00128-8

Tinto, V. (1993). *Leaving college: Rethinking the causes and cures of student attrition*. Chicago: University of Chicago Press.

Todman, J., & Dick, G. (1994). Primary children and teacher's attitudes to computers. *Computers & Education*, *20*(2), 199–203. doi:10.1016/0360-1315(93)90088-Z

Todman, J., & Monaghan, E. (1995). Qualitative differences in computer experience, Computer anxiety and student's use of computers: A path model. *Computers in Human Behavior*, *10*(4), 529–539. doi:10.1016/0747-5632(94)90045-0

Triphonas, P. (Ed.), *The pedagogy of difference*. New York: Routledge.

Wells, G. (1999). *Dialogic inquiry: Towards a sociocultural practice and theory of education*. Cambridge: Cambridge University Press. doi:10.1017/CBO9780511605895

Witkin, H. A. (1954). *Personality through perception*. Westport, CT: Greenwood.

Zabala, J. (1996). *SETTing the stage for success: Building success through effective use of assistive technology*. Proceedings of the Southeast Augmentative Communication Conference. Birmingham, AL, United Cerebral Palsy of Greater Birmingham

Zabala, J. (1998). *Get SETT for successful inclusion and transition LD online*. Retrieved from http://www.online.org/ld_indepth/technology/zabalaSETT1.html

# Chapter 4
# Helping Struggling Writers:
## Assistive Technology as Part of Intervention Programming

**Michael Dunn**
*Washington State University – Vancouver, USA*

## ABSTRACT

*Assistive Technology (AT), in the domain of special education, is defined as both tools and services. This chapter provides a description of this definition, what recent national and international writing assessment results indicate, what the characteristics of struggling writers are, and how AT can help these children improve and manage the complex and interdependent task of creating prose, story writing in particular. Key examples of AT services are Self-Regulated Strategy Development (SRSD: a step-by-step process for teaching a student a strategy) and mnemonic strategies (the use of keywords to help a child retain the steps in managing a task such as story writing). In the context of writing, AT can range from a pencil grip to a complete computer system with writing-assistance software. Furthermore, the author reviews his own research studies about story writing and how integral AT is to helping these children. Finally, the need for students' pre-requisite practice with AT is emphasized.*

## INTRODUCTION

Writing can be a challenging task. Generating story ideas, organizing them into a sequential timeline, applying spelling, grammar and punctuation, while writing the outline and draft texts are the key challenges for children who struggle with story writing (Troia, 2009). Recent assessments of children's writing skills have documented the extent of the issue. The most recent National Assessment of Educational Progress (NAEP; 2012) for writing indicated that as few as 25% of students in public schools can write at a proficient level or higher. This number is even lower for children from diverse backgrounds such as low-income families or English language learners.

To address the needs of struggling writers, educational researchers have developed evidence-based practices to help these children improve their story-writing skills (Graham & Harris, 2005;

DOI: 10.4018/978-1-4666-5015-2.ch004

Reid & Lienemann, 2006). These practices can be considered as assistive technologies (AT). The Individuals with Disabilities Education Improvement Act (IDEIA; 2004) defines AT as any service or device to help children in the learning process. An example of each is mnemonic-strategy instruction (as a service; Scruggs & Mastropieri, 1990) and word-prediction software (as a device; Batorowicz, Missiuna, & Pollock, 2012). A mnemonic strategy is a key word for which each letter represents a sequential part of the step-by-step process to manage a task (e.g., POW = Plan, Organize, and Write). In the context of writing, AT could be a variety of items from a pencil grip to a sophisticated computer system with writing-assistance software.

The objectives of this chapter are to:

1. Define AT from the perspective of special education;
2. Review students' performance on writing assessments (e.g., NAEP, 2012);
3. Describe how the writing process breaks down for struggling writers;
4. Describe mnemonic-strategy instruction and how teaching struggling writers a step-by-step process can help them better manage writing tasks; and
5. Describe AT components that can supplement mnemonic-strategy instruction and help struggling writers better manage story writing.

## BACKGROUND

### The Challenges of Struggling Writers

Writing may be considered the most difficult core academic skill to master as compared to reading and math (Klassen & Welton, 2009). In reading a text, one must decode the prose, but it has already been planned, organized, and generated. This applies to math as well; the text (i.e., the math question) has already been provided. In writing, both encoding and decoding are required. To help children manage academics and a core skill such as writing, teachers can provide children with AT.

The IDEIA (2004) defines AT as both a device and a service. The most common definition cited for AT is "any item, piece of equipment, or product system, whether acquired commercially off the shelf, modified, or customized, that is used to increase, maintain, or improve functional capabilities of a child with a disability" (see Sec. 300.5). Examples can include a wide range of tools such as pencil grip, smartphones, digital tablets (e.g., iPads®), and computers. An AT service is an activity that directly assists a child with a disability in the selection, acquisition, or use of an AT device. The process of a teacher providing instruction to a child to improve a skill using a pencil grip could be one example. The growing prevalence of AT (especially tools such as tablets and smartphones) in the general population has prompted assessment organizations to include devices such as laptops for students to type their text on a keyboard.

National and state assessments indicate that many children struggle with writing. In 2012, the NAEP released its most recent eighth and 12th-grade results. They indicated that only 25% of students can write at a proficient level or higher. The assessment required students to use computers to type their story products. Other regional assessment (e.g., Washington State [2012] as well as Ontario [Canada]) 2011-2012 results indicated that as few as 60% of students could write at a benchmark level. The 25% versus 60% score differences could be attributed to the format of each test. The Education Quality and Accountability Office (EQAO; 2013) writing tests included having students write a report (e.g., what happened at the park), an announcement of an event (e.g., an upcoming visitor to the class), and composing a letter. The children did these activities across 3-5 school days and for no more than 1-2 hours per day. Spelling, grammar, and punctuation were specific items for students to address. Multiple choice questions were also part of the assessment; students answered questions such as what was the best order of sentences to make a paragraph, choose the best opening sentence, etc. The Washington State writing assessment required students to compose a narrative story and type their text into a web browser. They were provided up to one school day to work on this task. The NAEP assessment had three types of writing tasks: to explain, persuade, and convey experience (real or imagined). There were 22 different writing tasks. Students were randomly assigned to two of the tasks and had 30 minutes to complete each. The NAEP had the lowest proficiency score (25%) as compared to the regional assessments (40%) described. The NAEP's use of laptops for the entire writing process may have accounted for the difference as compared to the regional assessments, but the nature of the writing task could account for students' overall lack of performance on these types of assessments.

As a process, writing can pose a challenge for students in a variety of ways. First and foremost is the high correlation between good writers and good readers (Shanahan, 2006; Shaywitz, 2003). If a student is not regularly reading other authors' published texts, the child will not see and hear what good writing looks and sounds like. Lacking this foundation will often impact their writing. In terms of the process of writing, struggling writers often have difficulty generating ideas (Donovan & Smolkin, 2006). This may stem back to a lack of reading others' stories, narrowing down a concept to focus on about their own life experiences, or lacking ideas of what one can write about and how to develop it. Once a decision is made about a story topic, students then face the challenge of noting their ideas for a story web or outline with words and phrases. Spelling and word choice are often an issue for struggling writers (Saddler, Behforooz, & Asaro, 2008). Once these issues have been managed to make a first draft, the next challenge is to arrange them into a story sequence and fill in any remaining gaps. The next step, writing the second draft, requires more sentence creation (e.g., spelling, syntax, and grammar) to add details to the outline and craft a more elaborate text. At that point, the mental energies of a struggling writer have been largely exhausted leaving few resources for making edits for subsequent drafts and writing a final copy (Berninger et al., 2008). The lack of reading experience further impairs the editing process as struggling writers often do not know what or how to edit. The result of the writing activity is often a brief series of poorly-connected ideas that lack a coherent story line.

## A Step-By-Step Learning Process for Story Writing

To address the needs of struggling writers, a step-by-step learning process is needed. One of the most-often cited means to do this is an AT process called "mnemonic strategy instruction" (Graham & Perrin, 2007; Saddler, Moran, Graham, & Harris, 2004). Specifically, the term "mnemonic" refers to a learning technique that helps one to translate information into acronyms (e.g., POW: Plan, Organize, and Write; Saddler, Moran, Graham, & Harris, 2004), short phrases, auditory, visual, or kinesthetic forms, which the human brain may find easier to retain (Masrtropieri & Scruggs, 2002). There is no one specific mnemonic for writing given the many different types of text genres (e.g., persuasive essays, letters, and stories). Even for story writing, educational researchers have created various examples. There is, however, a widely-accepted means to teach a mnemonic strategy such as the process for story writing called "self-regulated strategy development" (SRSD) that was developed by Harris and Graham (1985).

There are six suggested SRSD steps (Graham & Harris, 2005; Harris, Graham, Mason, & Friedlander, 2008). First, teachers may review past written story products of the student and administer assessments of background knowledge about writing. In the Rhodes (1993) writing-interest questionnaires, children state their feelings about writing, who they view as a good writer, why, and what a good writer should do. The teacher can then later address the child's concerns or frustration as intervention programming unfolds. The second SRSD component is to develop background knowledge. This is the point when the teacher begins to dialogue with the student about story writing, what it entails, and how mnemonic strategy instruction could help the child. They could review some of the students' past story products and compare them to a published story or example texts of a more proficient student writer. Comparing and contrasting could help the struggling writer see where improvements could be made. In the third SRSD step, the teacher presents the mnemonic strategy to be taught to the child (e.g., POW; Saddler et al., 2004). While the acronym itself refers to the type of task, it is the phrases represented by each letter that provide the sequential step-by-step process to help the student improve. The fourth SRSD step has the teacher discuss the strategy, attain the student's commitment to learning and using it, the teacher's modeling of the strategy with verbalization of all thoughts in working through the sequential steps, and the student's memorizing the strategy's steps to develop automaticity of use. In the fifth step, the teacher provides guided practice as the student begins to apply the strategy on their own. The sixth and final SRSD step is the student's independent use of the strategy. The power of mnemonic strategy instruction for the improvement of weak skills is the combination of academic strategies with procedural instructions. The intended result is the student's ability to self-regulate (i.e., better self-manage) the completion of a task such as story writing. The SRSD process provides a type of AT for students to manage a task such as story writing.

The research base for SRSD is large (e.g., Graham & Harris, 2003), and many of these studies have focused on mnemonic strategies for writing. Mason, Kubina, and Taft (2011), for instance, employed SRSD with middle school students. Student participants employed two mnemonic strategies: the *Plan*, *Organize* and *Write* (POW; Saddler et al., 2004), and *Topic* sentence, *Reasons* (three or more), *Examine*, and *Ending* (TREE; Graham & Harris, 2005). The 16 participants improved their performance from baseline to intervention phases. Like other single subject design studies, the authors assessed the average length of participants' texts during pre- and then post-intervention for *number of words written* (NWW). The participants had lower NWW scores during the intervention phase, which the authors attributed to participants' focusing on writing more text. This does not always result in a text of improved quality (Graham, Harris, & Mason, 2005; Harris, Graham, & Mason, 2006). By focusing on story content, children may devote less attention to quality, as appeared to be the case in Mason et al.'s study.

Graham and Harris (1989) created the *WWW, W=2, H=2* cue questions to help struggling writers better include key content in a narrative story. Each 'W' and 'H' represents a question for what should be included in a story: Who? Where? When? What do the characters do? What do the other characters do? How does the story end? How do the characters feel? There is evidence that the WWW, W=2, H=2 cue questions are effective when used by struggling writers. Saddler et al. (2004) concluded that when six struggling writers used the WWW, W=2, H=2 cue questions, the children's stories had improved elaborate story content. Students' progress over time (referred to as "progress monitoring" [PM]) was assessed by reviewing stories the children wrote every few sessions. This type of assessment where the task reflects a typical activity that students would do in a classroom is defined as curriculum-based measurement (CBM; Deno, 2003). The students' scores doubled that of their baseline performance when they used all seven WWW, W=2, H=2 cue questions. As an alternative to writing words for the WWW, W=2, H=2 cue questions during planning,

Danko-McGhee and Slutsky (2007) suggested that students illustrate their story ideas in order to visualize their story's content. Using art media to note story ideas would help alleviate students' mental energies typically devoted to spelling and phrasing so that more of their focus could be on idea generation and organization.

## The Case for Art Media in Making Story Plans

Offering the AT service of noting ideas in a visual form to writers who struggle with encoding text can help them produce more elaborate prose. Using symbols rather than print can make the idea generation process more meaningful because of the visual meaning of the images. Eisner (1994) commented that children are more likely to problem solve with a task that is meaningful to them. "One of the ways to increase relevance and transfer is to help students see…the variety of forms of representation through which meanings can be construed by the student" (p. 84). Illustrating ideas with art provides a means to make the story planning process more representational or even concrete, as opposed to abstract letters and words, which can encourage more use of all of the five senses in this process (Hurwitz & Day, 2001; Klepsch & Logie, 1982). Kirby and Kuykendall (1991) suggested that illustrating "slows the act of seeing, allowing time for new insights to develop" (p. 105). These new ideas can then prompt more questions and thoughts, which can facilitate even more elaborate story ideas (Blecher & Jafee, 1998). The National Center for Learning Disabilities (2011) advocates children's use of art to develop confidence in self-expression. Art provides a means for these children to demonstrate their story ideas without being overwhelmed with composing text at the outset of the writing process. Moss (2011) commented that students who have a learning disability often have an affinity for the arts. Struggling writers' creating an artistic representation of their idea(s) will result in their having a meaningful and unique product.

In a summer arts-based/integrated-curriculum program, Dunn and Finley (2008) offered an arts-based mnemonic with typically achieving second- to seventh-grade students. The children improved by using art to illustrate story-component ideas. The *Ask*, *Reflect*, *Text* (ART) mnemonic strategy was based on Calkins (1986) and Graves (1983) as well as Ernst (1993) and Olshanky's (1994) artists' workshop. This strategy included three sequential components: (a) the children would *A*sk themselves the WWW, W=2, H=2 cue questions for what they would like to include as story content; (b) as students *R*eflect on their answers, they would illustrate their ideas with art media (e.g., markers, watercolor paints, or play-doh®); and (c) the children then use their aesthetic story plan to generate their *T*ext while having access to writing-assistance software (i.e., CoWriter:SOLO®). Table 1 lists some other AT

*Table 1. Assistive technology tools (task types), and example data that each can provide*

| Assistive Technology | Example types of PM/CBM Data |
|---|---|
| Language Arts and Math: SuccessMaker® (reading and math practice) | Average level, percentage correct, time needed for each target level |
| Reading: Read Naturally® (improve oral reading fluency) | E.g., average number of words used to retell the story, words read correctly per minute |
| Writing: Microsoft Word® (text encoding software) | Number of words written, characters, paragraphs, length of editing session |
| Dragon Naturally Speaking®, iDictate®, SpeakWrite® (speech-to-text software) | Within Word®, number of words written, characters, paragraphs, length of editing session |
| Dynamic Indicators of Basic Early Literacy Skills (DIBELS, 2013; letter and reading decoding as well as comprehension activities for assessment) | Reading percentile scores |
| AIMSweb® (reading, writing, and math assessment) | Reading, writing, math progress-monitoring data |

examples and describes their possible uses for both task types and assessment (e.g., PM, CBM data).

In employing the ART mnemonic strategy steps, the children wrote more elaborate stories. These results reflect those of other writing-intervention researchers such as MacArthur and Philippakos (2010), who included the WWW, W=2, H=2 cue questions within a larger mnemonic.

This author has completed other writing-intervention studies with the ART mnemonic strategy using single subject design methodology (Kennedy, 2005). All of these studies included participants in grades two to four, when story writing becomes an integral part of the literacy curriculum. The spring 2010 study (Dunn, in press b) for three participants with learning disabilities included goals and objectives for writing. In all of these projects, the participants demonstrated improvement with story content in using ART; however, there was only small improvement in story quality.

A follow-up study during fall 2010 (Dunn, 2012) employed a reversal single subject design study (Kennedy, 2005): progress-monitoring assessments during intervention sessions with art media then some sessions without these materials, and student interviews. The resulting data documented how the four 4th-grade (two Caucasian, two of Hispanic descent, but with native-like fluency in English) struggling writers' stories differed between the intervention phase when they applied ART versus the baseline phase. When art tools were not provided during the reversal portion of the intervention phase, two students decreased in story content and two students continued with the same level of scores. After the re-introduction of art tools, the data illustrated that the two students, who had decreased in story content, returned to their levels prior to the removal of art tools. Like the previously described studies, story quality changed little, if any.

To explore how to help struggling writers improve story quality, this author designed and completed a randomized control trial study (Dunn, in press a), to compare three groups: (a) children using ART; (b) children using *Think-Talk-Text* (T3; Katahira, 2012; Traweek, 1993) where struggling writers verbalized aloud their story ideas in lieu of illustrating them; and (c) a control group, who only participated in general education classroom writing instruction. The results indicated that the T3 group had a large and the highest effect size as compared to the ART and control groups for story quality. The data indicated that the practice of students' saying their story plan aloud before writing helped them produce more elaborate texts.

Illustrating story ideas and verbalizing them aloud could help both story content and quality. Hayes and Flower's (1980) writing model includes an oral component: idea generation (voicing story ideas), translation (putting oral language into written text), reviewing (the writer reads the composition to classmates), and revising (for a book publication at the end of the school year; Berninger, 2009). Vygotsky (1986) too suggested that self-talk can help struggling writers manage the idea-generation process.

To help kindergarten students in a low income and racially diverse community improve in literacy skills, Traweek (1993), with Dr. Ginger Berninger at the University of Washington, created the *What I think, I can say, I can write* (or T3) mnemonic strategy, a type of AT service. The components included: what I *think*, I can *tell* to others (i.e., verbalize aloud), and then write as *text* (Katahira, 2012). Once Traweek scribed each child's ideas, the students made illustrations to represent their story content. By the end of that school year, most of the children were reading at an average level or above, except for one who was below average. This verbalizing of story ideas aloud helped the children improve their story's content.

## The Need for Strategy Instruction

There are three main issues for struggling writers:

1. The promise and limitations that new technologies can offer,
2. The continued need to learn strategies in tandem with using technologies to manage story writing, and
3. Being able to manage assessments to demonstrate improvement in writing skills.

While much has changed for struggling writers over time in terms of strategies and technology, their underlying needs and challenges remain.

The general population, especially those of school age, has welcomed the large growth, popularity, and prominence of technology. While the medium for storytelling is changing from the pen-and-paper era to that of keyboarding and apps, the content of what story writing is remains largely the same, but technology has made the means to manage producing text easier. This is a welcome development for struggling writers. In lieu of struggling with spelling, word-prediction software offers word choices to students from which they can choose the desired word or select from suggestions to rephrase part of a sentence (e.g., Word's® editing capabilities). Writing-assistance software (e.g., Naturally Speaking®) can type the text for the student. The limitations that struggling writers demonstrate (e.g., generate story ideas, develop a storyline, manage grammar, syntax) still remain. No one technology tool has yet to make the story-writing process effortless. The concurrent process of ideas, word choice, and story progression remain.

While technology tools continue to be more plentiful and refined, the need for strategy instruction remains because children need to learn with a teacher's instruction how to manage complex tasks. Writing is a prime example. To date, the idea of using technology tools in tandem with teaching struggling writers mnemonic strategies has been minimal in the writing research literature. Beginning in 2006, this author offered struggling writers keyboarding on a computer with the option of CoWriter:SOLO® writing-assistance software. As this author observed the children trying CoWriter:SOLO®, he observed that the students found it somewhat complicated to use. The process of typing a letter and reviewing the word choices that appeared even when the computer read them aloud seemed more complicated than writing in Word® and allowing that software to offer suggested edits. During discussions with other writing researchers, this author discovered that they preferred pencil and paper while teaching and practicing mnemonic strategies for writing. However, since 2006, technology has progressed and become more prevalently used by people of all ages. The NAEP writing assessment in 2012 was a computer-based assessment in its entirety. There is a growing general practice, inferred in the new Common Core State Standards (2012), that the need for cursive writing as a skill is not needed for writing tasks.

In a series of single subject design research projects from 2008 to 2011, this author focused on paper and pencil as a means for children's writing instruction. Technology in those studies focused solely on being a service as opposed to also using a computer-type tool. The students demonstrated good progress with story content (e.g., who, when where, what happened?), but story quality lagged in comparison; some participants made no improvement. These projects had teacher-student ratios to help the intervention specialist have more interaction. In all of the studies, only a few children were disinterested in the activities.

One disinterested student surfaced during the spring 2010 project (Dunn, 2012). A fourth-grade student, Tadeo, who had a learning disability in writing, had become indifferent about doing the writing-practice exercises (e.g., spelling practice, sentence creation, sentence combining) by the mid-point of the study. The intervention specialist informed this author about this. This author provided a laptop with Microsoft PowerPoint® software for Tadeo to make a slideshow with pictures and phrases. In doing so, he met this portion of the aims of project in terms of writing short phrases and spelling words. Technology software helped to maintain Tadeo's attention and facilitate his story-writing improvement. His story content and quality scores demonstrated this as his story content remained at the highest score (7/7) and his story quality score improved from 4 to 5/7. Because the story quality of many students in this author's research projects up to that time were only maintaining or improving little in story quality, he decided to add to the components of ART based on Traweek's (1993) findings that saying a story aloud before writing could help improve story quality, as discussed earlier.

During fall 2010 (Dunn, in press a), this author's randomized control trial project had three groups of four children: an ART group, a group that employed ART but also said their story aloud while planning (Reflecting), and a control group that remained in the general education classroom's writing program. The students' writing assessments consisted of writing a story about a cartoon picture (10 minutes to plan, 15 minutes to write). There were four assessments during baseline, none during the four sessions of Training for groups A and B, and one probe every three days during the intervention (practice) phase. The results indicated that the students who read their story plans aloud before writing had the largest effect sizes for story quality.

The fall 2010 results rendered the author's creation of a new mnemonic strategy, which included iPads® and drawing apps as AT for students to use in creating their illustrated story plan. The focus mnemonic strategy was *STORY*: *S*tart thinking about WWW, W=2, H=2 questions, *T*hink about your answers and illustrate them, *O*rganize and say your story aloud, *R*evise your text's ideas and write it on paper, and *Y*ou can make edits and read it to others. The key difference from ART was that STORY had the children say their story text aloud during or just after planning, but before they actually wrote their text. Although they had other art media (e.g., paints, markers) as options, the students preferred to use the iPad® drawing apps (e.g., Doodle Buddy®) at almost every opportunity. Figure 1 provides Baco's (Dunn, under review) example from using the STORY mnemonic strategy.

The fall 2012 study's results demonstrated that the children did improve in story content and quality; their level of progress for each skill had a positive trend, but their scores declined slightly in the last eight sessions. The students may have either plateaued in ability or lost some motivation as time passed. Since the focus of the project was writing, which is the area of weakness for these students, it is understandable that they would have difficulty maintaining their motivation. Writing

*Figure 1. Baco's (Dunn, under review) STORY mnemonic strategy product (November 26, 2012). "They are having a party and the four dogs are at the party. They are having fun and ate a big biscuit cake and they got presents. They had the party at the beach in the day and they got their instruments and made some music. They saw the swimmers swim to the finish line and the four dogs are happy."*

is a complex skill requiring a number of processes to work together simultaneously; long-term intervention (e.g., a few months) may be needed to see consistent improvement. Ongoing personal reading and discussion with others about the text's content should facilitate writing improvement.

## Solutions and Recommendations

The first AT step to improving writing skills is children's regular reading of published texts (Shaywitz, 2003). The increase in computer-type tools will likely provide for more opportunities for this in the future given the rise in tablets and eReaders, which can function as audiobooks that are now available and used by the general population. These tools are very helpful in aiding students to hear the text being read by a proficient reader. Reading along with a proficient reader and doing this multiple times can significantly increase a student's reading fluency. In the process, comprehension can improve, which can provide for a better understanding of a text's story structure and elaborate text.

Voice-to-text software (e.g., SIRI®) offers AT possibilities in terms of encoding text. The availability, reliability, and acceptance of this type of tool is becoming more prevalent. Many smartphones now have this type of feature, and apps for tablets and laptops/desktops exist as well. A practical challenge is how to manage all students in a given general education class voicing aloud their story texts at the same time. Dispersing students to various parts of the school could be one way to address this. In doing so, children will have the opportunity to compose text, review their work, seek feedback from others, and work to improve their writing abilities. This will represent a key component of the larger realm that helps support literacy instruction and skills improvement.

Students' growth with academics is part of a life-experience process that occurs both in and outside of school. While evidence-based instruction during language arts and integrated-curriculum activities across the school day play a key role in students' academic growth, educational experiences and practice outside of school do so as well. Parents/guardians, family, and friends can all help children practice these skills and develop general knowledge abilities through reading of books with children, discussing their contents, and modeling reading for different purposes both in and outside of the home. Visits to the local public library and trips to museums, for instance, all help to improve a child's life experiences, vocabulary, and general knowledge. If the percentage of proficient writers is to exceed 25% (e.g., NAEP, 2012), then a holistic perspective to writing skills practice and development is necessary.

# FUTURE RESEARCH DIRECTIONS

There are two directions in terms of writing instruction that are developing, in this author's opinion. First, keyboarding is becoming the prime method for encoding text given its inferred prominence in the 2013 Common Core State Standards (i.e., exclusion of handwriting as a needed skill after first grade). Second, NAEP's (2012) exclusive use of laptop computers for students to compose text is also an indicator of a future direction for writing. With only 25% of students being at the proficient level of ability, students may benefit from more keyboarding practice to make this component less of a challenge for students in the next NAEP writing assessment.

Future research for writing should explore students' comparative abilities to compose texts in handwriting versus using keyboards versus voice-activation software. This author would suspect that verbalizing story texts could produce the highest level of content and quality given there is no need for using the visual-integration process as in handwriting (i.e., brain messages to arm, hand, and then fingers) to produce text on the page.

## CONCLUSION

Assistive technology offers children, including those who struggle with writing, alternative means to manage very complex and interdependent processes. Although no one computer-type tool will provide for all of the teaching for a student or means to encode text, the complimentary AT service component of SRSD and mnemonic strategy instruction can help make text composition a manageable task for struggling writers. Use of computers is the trend as the only means to complete writing tasks. It will be imperative for children to have access to AT (both tools and services) so as to have the familiarity and fluency with keyboarding and produce the best final text product that is possible. While planning and idea generation are key components to writing, it is the final text that is given all of the prominence in terms of a score. Thanks to AT, children have a means to produce better and improved-quality texts.

## REFERENCES


Batorowicz, B., Missiuna, C. A., & Pollock, N. A. (2012). Technology supporting written productivity in children with learning disabilities: A critical review. *Canadian Journal of Occupational Therapy*, *79*(4), 211–224. doi:10.2182/cjot.2012.79.4.3 PMID:23210371

Berninger, V. (2009). Highlights of programmatic, interdisciplinary research on writing. *Learning Disabilities Research & Practice*, *24*, 68–79. doi:10.1111/j.1540-5826.2009.00281.x PMID:19644563

Berninger, V., Richards, T., Stock, P., Abbott, R., Trivedi, P., Altemeier, L., & Hayes, J. R. (2008, Summer). From idea generation to idea expression in written composition: Expressing thought in language by hand. *British Journal of Educational Psychology: Monograph.*

Blecher, S., & Jaffee, K. (1998). *Weaving in the arts: Widening the learning circle*. Portsmouth, NH: Heinemann.

Calkins, L. M. (1986). *The art of teaching writing*. Portsmouth, NH: Heinemann.

Common Core State Standards. (2012). *Implementing the common core state standards*. Retrieved from http://www.corestandards.org/

Danko-McGhee, K., & Slutsky, R. (2007). *Impact of early art experiences on literacy development*. Reston, VA: National Art Education Association.

Deno, S. L. (2003). Developments in curriculum-based measurement. *The Journal of Special Education*, *37*(3), 184–192. doi:10.1177/00224669030370030801

DIBELS. (2013). *Dynamic indicators of basic early literacy skills*. Eugene, OR: University of Oregon. Retrieved from https://dibels.uoregon.edu/

Donovan, C. A., & Smolkin, L. B. (2006). Children's understanding of genre and writing development. In C. A. MacArthur, S. Graham, & J. Fitzgerald (Eds.), *Handbook of writing instruction* (pp. 131–143). New York: The Guilford Press.

Dunn, M., & Finley, S. (2008). Thirsty thinkers: A workshop for artists and writers. *Journal of Reading Education*, *33*(2), 28–36.

Dunn, M. W. (2012). Response to intervention: Employing a mnemonic strategy with art media to help struggling writers. *Journal of International Education and Leadership*, *2*(3), 1–12.

Dunn, M. W. (2013a). Comparing two story-writing mnemonic strategies: A randomized control trial study. *International Journal of Special Education.*

Dunn, M. W. (2013b). *Using art media during pre-writing: Helping students with dysgraphia manage idea generation before encoding text.* Manuscript submitted for publication.

Dunn, M. W. (2013c). *Students at-risk of having dysgraphia: Applying assistive technology tools to help with pre-writing*. Manuscript under review.

Education Quality and Accountability Office. (2013). *Ontario student achievement: EQAO's provincial elementary school report: Results of the 2011-2012 assessments of reading, writing and mathematics, primary division (grades 1-3) and junior division (grades 4-6)*. Retrieved from http://www.eqao.com/ProvincialReport/ProvincialReport.aspx?Lang=E&yr=12&cat=e

Eisner, E. (1994). *Cognition and curriculum reconsidered*. New York: Teachers College Press.

Ernst, K. (1993). *Picture learning*. Portsmouth, NH: Heinemann.

Graham, S., & Harris, K. R. (1989). A component analysis of cognitive strategy instruction: Effects on learning disabled students' compositions and self-efficacy. *Journal of Educational Psychology*, *81*, 353–361. doi:10.1037/0022-0663.81.3.353

Graham, S., & Harris, K. R. (2003). Students with learning disabilities and the process of writing: A meta-analysis of SRSD studies. In H. L. Swanson, K. R. Harris, & S. Graham (Eds.), *Handbook of learning disabilities* (pp. 323–344). New York: The Guilford Press.

Graham, S., & Harris, K. R. (2005). *Writing better: Effective strategies for teaching students with learning difficulties*. Baltimore, MD: Paul H. Brookes Publishing Co.

Graham, S., Harris, K. R., & Mason, L. (2005). Improving the writing performance, knowledge, and motivation of struggling young writers: The effects of self-regulated strategy development. *Contemporary Educational Psychology*, *30*, 207–241. doi:10.1016/j.cedpsych.2004.08.001

Graham, S., & Perin, D. (2007). A meta-analysis of writing instruction for adolescent students. *Journal of Educational Psychology*, *99*, 445–476. doi:10.1037/0022-0663.99.3.445

Graves, D. (1983). *Writing: Teachers & children at work*. Portsmouth, NH: Heinemann.

Harris, K., & Graham, S. (1985). Improving learning disabled students' composition skills: Self-control strategy training. *Learning Disability Quarterly*, *8*(1), 27–36. doi:10.2307/1510905

Harris, K. R., Graham, S., & Mason, L. (2006). Improving the writing, knowledge, and motivation of struggling young writers: Effects of self-regulated strategy development with and without peer support. *American Educational Research Journal*, *43*, 295–340. doi:10.3102/00028312043002295

Harris, K. R., Graham, S., Mason, L., & Friedlander, B. (2008). *Powerful writing strategies for all students*. Baltimore, MD: Brookes.

Hayes, J. R., & Flower, L. S. (1980). Identifying the organization of writing processes. In L. W. Gregg, & E. R. Steinbert (Eds.), *Cognitive processes in writing* (pp. 3–30). Hillsdale, NJ: Lawrence Erlbaum Associates.

Hurwitz, A., & Day, M. (2001). *Children and their art: Methods for the elementary school*. Belmont, CA: Wadsworth Group/Thomson Learning.

IDEIA. (2004). *Individuals with disabilities education improvement act of 2004*. Pub. L. No. 108-446, 118 Stat. 2647.

Katahira, J. (2012). *Note writing in the primary classroom*. Retrieved from http://www.readwritethink.org/classroom-resources/lesson-plans/note-writing-primary-classroom-285.html

Kennedy, C. H. (2005). *Single-case designs for educational research*. Boston: Allyn and Bacon.

Kirby, D., & Kuykendall, C. (1991). *Mind matters: Teaching for thinking*. Portsmouth, NH: Boynton/Cook.

Klassen, R. M., & Welton, C. (2009). Self-efficacy and procrastination in the writing of students with learning disabilities. In G. A. Troia (Ed.), *Instruction and assessment for struggling writers* (pp. 51–74). New York: The Guilford Press.

Klepsch, M., & Logie, L. (1982). *Children draw and tell: An introduction to the projective uses of children's human figure drawings*. New York: Brunner/Mazel Publishers.

MacArthur, C., & Philippakos, Z. (2010). Instruction in a strategy for compare-contrast writing. *Exceptional Children*, *76*(4), 438–456.

Mason, L. H., Kubina, R. M., & Taft, R. J. (2011). Developing quick writing skills of middle school students with disabilities. *The Journal of Special Education*, *44*(4), 205–220. doi:10.1177/0022466909350780

Masrtropieri, M., & Scruggs, T. (2002). *Effective instruction for special education*. Austin, TX: Pro-Ed.

Moss, P. (2001). *Art and learning disabilities*. Retrieved from http://www.ldonline.org/article/5628/

National Assessment of Educational Progress. (2012). *NAEP writing assessment*. Retrieved from http://nces.ed.gov/nationsreportcard/writing/

National Center for Learning Disabilities. (2011). *Learning disabilities and the arts*. Retrieved from http://www.ncld.org/in-the-home/parenting-issues/play-enrichment-aamp-holidays/learning-disabilities-and-the-arts

Olshansky, B. (1994). Making writing a work of art: Image-making within the writing process. *Language Arts*, *71*, 350–357.

Reid, R., & Lienemann, T. (2006). *Strategy instruction for students with learning disabilities*. New York: The Gilford Press.

Rhodes, L. K. (1993). *Literacy assessment: A handbook of instruments*. Portsmouth, NH: Heinemann.

Saddler, B., Behforooz, B., & Asaro, K. (2008). The effects of sentence-combining instruction on the writing of fourth-grade students with writing difficulties. *The Journal of Special Education*, *42*(2), 79–90. doi:10.1177/0022466907310371

Saddler, B., Moran, S., Graham, S., & Harris, K. R. (2004). Preventing writing difficulties: The effects of planning strategy instruction on the writing performance of struggling writers. *Exceptionality*, *12*, 13–17. doi:10.1207/s15327035ex1201_2

Scruggs, T., & Mastropieri, M. (1990). The case for mnemonic instruction: From laboratory research to classroom applications. *The Journal of Special Education*, *24*(1), 7–32. doi:10.1177/002246699002400102

Shanahan, T. (2006). Relations among oral language, reading, and writing development. In C. A. MacArthur, S. Graham, & J. Fitzgerald (Eds.), *Handbook of writing instruction* (pp. 171–183). New York: The Guilford Press.

Shaywitz, S. (2003). *Overcoming dyslexia: A new and complete science-based program for reading problems at any level*. New York: Knopf.

Traweek, D. (1993). *Teacher and learner variables in early literacy instruction: Treatment, evaluation and ethnographic studies*. (Ph.D. Dissertation). University of Washington, Seattle, WA.

Troia, G. A. (Ed.). (2009). *Instruction and assessment for struggling writers*. New York: The Guilford Press.

Vygotsky, L. (1986). *Thought and language*. Cambridge, MA: The MIT Press.

## ADDITIONAL READING

Bloser, Z. (2001). *Handwriting research and resources: A guide to curriculum planning*. Columbus, OH: Zaner-Bloser.

Fayol, M., Amargot, D. A., & Berninger, V. (Eds.). (2012). *Translation of thought to written text while composing: Advancing theory, knowledge, methods, and applications*. New York: Psychology Press/Taylor Francis Group/Routledge.

Harris, K. R., Graham, S., Mason, L., & Friedlander, B. (2008). *Powerful writing strategies for all students*. Baltimore, MD: Brookes.

MacArthur, C. A., Graham, S., & Fitzgerald, J. (Eds.). (2006). *Handbook of writing instruction*. New York: The Guilford Press.

Nagin, C. (2006). *Because writing matters: Improving student writing in our schools*. San Francisco, CA: John Wiley & Sons.

Washington. (2012). *Measurements of student progress*. Retrieved from http://www.k12.wa.us/assessment/statetesting/MSP.aspx

Wong, B., & Butler, D. (Eds.). (2012). *Learning about LD* (4th ed.). Maryland Heights, MO: Elsevier/Academic Press.

# Chapter 5
# Ecological Perspectives Surrounding the Design of Self-Determination-Enhanced Problem-Based Learning as a Formative Intervention for Students with Disabilities in Inclusive Settings

**Soohnwa Seok**
*Korea University, South Korea*

**Boaventura DaCosta**
*Solers Research Group, USA*

**Woo Kim**
*Ja Hae Special School, Korea*

## ABSTRACT

*This transdisciplinary chapter focuses on ecological perspectives surrounding the design of self-determination-enhanced Problem-Based Learning (PBL). The chapter presents a PBL conceptual framework that can be leveraged in implementation of the skills needed for the 21st-century, specifically self-determination for students with disabilities in inclusive settings. The framework is built upon an extensive research synthesis of the principles behind PBL instructional design with an emphasis on special education. The research synthesis revealed the relationships between self-determination learning and PBL. A collaborative learning model—SHARE: Structure, Hypothesis, Analysis, Research, and Evaluation—was subsequently designed as a positive intervention in implementing PBL. In brief, technology and teacher education constitute the essence of quality self-determination-enhanced PBL practices. Educators, educational policymakers, and researchers involved in inclusive education practices will find this chapter of particular interest as 21st-century learning skills are becoming increasingly vital in today's society.*

DOI: 10.4018/978-1-4666-5015-2.ch005

## INTRODUCTION

Estimates show that over 9% of students ages 6 to 21 in the U.S. were placed in special education between 2003 and 2004 (Turnbull, Turnbull, & Wehmeyer, 2007; U.S. Department of Education, n.d.). These students were classified as follows: learning disabilities (47.4%), speech or language impairments (18.7%), intellectual disabilities (9.6%), emotional disturbance (8.0%), multiple disabilities (2.2%), hearing impairments (1.2%), orthopedic impairments (1.1%), other health impairments (7.5%), autism (2.3%), visual impairments (0.43%), traumatic brain injury (0.37%), developmental delay (1.09%), and deaf-blindness (0.03%; U.S. Department of Education, n.d.).

Today, most students with these disabilities are placed in inclusive settings in keeping with the mandates of the No Child Left Behind Act (Lenz & Deshler, 2004; U.S. Department of Education, 2002) and the Individuals with Disabilities Education Act (IDEA; Turnbull, Turnbull, & Wehmeyer, 2007; Vaughn, Bos, & Schumm, 2007). However, the placement of students with diverse abilities in inclusive classrooms poses challenges to general and special education teachers as well as students with disabilities (Lambe, 2007).

The idea behind inclusion is fundamentally simple: inclusion is based on the premise that all children (with and without disabilities) should be allowed to learn together in the general classroom. Despite its simple premise and the apparent benefits and fairness of this principle, its practice creates a number of challenges for students with disabilities, whose special needs often require both support and accommodations if they are to succeed along with their peers without disabilities in the general education setting.

Unfortunately, specific curricula or learning models have not been developed for students with disabilities in inclusive settings. The practice of inclusion has altered how teachers, schools, and educational systems think about the needs of students, including prompting educators to reexamine their pedagogy and the instructional design of their learning content to meet the needs of students with special needs in their classrooms. To be successfully implemented, inclusion requires a community that offers collective assistance from students, families, educators, and community members (Wood, 2006). Examples of community support include positive behavioral supports, assistive technology, individualized instruction for both individuals and groups, and collaboration and communication. When part of instructional strategies, these supports yield positive results, including effective transitions between settings, as well as positive behavior, and social and academic outcomes (Bryant, Smith, & Bryant, 2008; Salend, 2005).

To date, numerous studies have explored inclusive pedagogy and instructional practices such as inclusion, legal issues, and Universal Design for Learning (Rose & Meyer, 2002; Sailor & Skrtic, 2009; Wood, 2006). However, little attention has been paid to how advanced learning skills, such as 21st-century skills, can best be taught to all students in inclusive settings, in particular, students with disabilities, for whom these critical skills pose special challenges.

The Partnership for 21st-Century Skills (2004) and Ravitz (2008) named the following as 21st-century skills:

1. Creativity and innovation;
2. Critical thinking and problem-solving;
3. Communication and collaboration;
4. Information literacy;
5. Media literacy;
6. Information, communication, and technology literacy;
7. Flexibility and adaptability;
8. Initiative and self-direction;
9. Social and cross-cultural skills;
10. Productivity and accountability; and
11. Leadership and responsibility.

These complex skills are problematic for many students with learning, academic, communication, perceptual, motor, and social-emotional disabilities (Salend, 2005). Furthermore, traditional teaching approaches are inadequate for teaching them. Instead, what is required are constructivist approaches, which presume that humans generate knowledge and meaning from interactions between their experiences and their ideas. Such approaches have been found to enhance students' content knowledge, problem-solving, and higher thinking skills by having students examine and solve problems through collaboration and active engagement with a focus on self-determination in their own learning (Hmelo-Silver, 2004; Park & Ertmer, 2008). As explored in the following, this is an area where problem-based learning (PBL) can play a significant role because it includes specific academic, social, and behavioral goals (Cote, 2007; Ochoa & Robinson, 2005).

## Self-Determination-Enhanced Problem-Based Learning an Important Intervention

Problem-based learning is defined as a constructivist learning approach that starts with problems, not lectures, for the purpose of helping students to learn and/or enhance the skills of self-direction, critical thinking, collaboration, and self-determination structured within systematic exploration (Hmelo-Silver, 2004; Mills, 2006; Park & Ertmer, 2008). Self-determination is important for all students, but particularly for students with disabilities, whose needs tend to make them dependent on others for many life decisions. Thus, self-determination is one of the most requisite skills for students with disabilities and is commonly an intervention in inclusive settings (Turnbull, Turnbull, & Wehmeyer, 2007).

Self-determination skills afford students with disabilities numerous benefits. For example, such skills:

1. Provide them access to academic and social support from their peers;
2. Give them responsibility for and ownership of their own learning; and
3. Allows them to engage in the general education curriculum and in transitioning to different settings.

In addition, self-determination skills enhance students' general knowledge and skills by allowing them to participate in the planning, performance, and evaluation of their own learning (Agran, Wehmeyer, Cavin, & Palmer, 2008; Carter & Kennedy, 2006; Palmer, Wehmeyer, Gipson, & Agran, 2004; Wehmeyer & Palmer, 2003; Wehmeyer & Schwartz, 1997). As such, self-determination is a core skill of PBL for all students.

When considering the skills and knowledge students with disabilities need to acquire within a standards-based curriculum, the practice of PBL as an intervention in inclusive settings becomes essential and critical (Carter & Kennedy, 2006). Not surprisingly, PBL and learning self-determination overlap in several areas. Thus, self-determination-enhanced PBL is an important intervention, particularly for students with disabilities in inclusive settings. Regrettably, little research on PBL and self-determination enhanced PBL has been conducted with students with disabilities in inclusive settings.

## The Purpose of this Chapter

This chapter presents the benefits of self-determination-enhanced PBL and its potential contribution to teaching students with disabilities advanced learning skills, including the 21st-century skills discussed earlier. Specifically, the chapter presents the findings of an extensive research synthesis that investigated the relations between PBL and self-determination and how they can be utilized to teach advanced learning skills to students with disabilities in inclusive settings.

Seeing a self-determination-enhanced PBL process as an important instructional design for students with disabilities, this chapter proposes a self-determination-enhanced PBL-based conceptual framework. In addition, a collaborative learning model that fosters problem-solving and self-determination is discussed, called SHARE: Structure, Hypothesis, Analysis, Research, and Evaluation.

Problem-based learning and self-determination can be used formatively and ecologically as interventions for students with disabilities in inclusive settings as a way to help them acquire the skills needed to succeed in the 21st-century. That is, PBL and self-determination can be a natural, long-lasting intervention. The problem-based learning conceptual model depicted in Figure 1 is based on the design principles of PBL focusing on self-determination supported by empirical research built around the following three research questions:

1. What is the potential efficacy and feasibility of PBL for students with disabilities?
2. What are the issues surrounding PBL and what related strategies/tactics can be developed to address these issues?
3. How can PBL be rapidly and cost-effectively implemented to support the 21st-century learning skills of students with disabilities in inclusive settings?

To pursue answers to these questions, an extensive literature review was performed that focused on:

1. Overlap between PBL and existing instructional practices for students with disabilities in inclusive settings;
2. Variables that make PBL more effective than other approaches; and
3. Instructional design components of PBL, including learning and teaching objects.

*Figure 1. Problem-based learning conceptual framework*

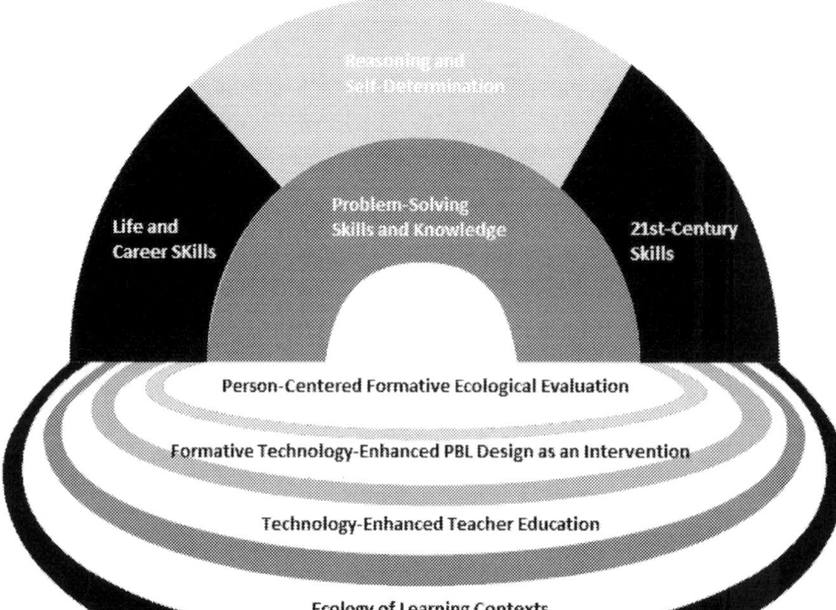

This chapter has implications for educators, policymakers, stakeholders, and researchers involved in inclusive education who are interested in PBL and self-determination and its benefits and utilization with students with disabilities in inclusive settings.

## MATERIALS AND METHODS

The research synthesis presented here was conducted using a four-phased approach to answer the three underlying research questions. First, to arrive at a comprehensive synthesis of the literature on PBL as a means of teaching students with disabilities, studies were drawn from a variety of sources, including published articles, books, reports, and dissertations, between 2002 and 2009. The earliest publication was Leven, Hibbard, and Rock's (2002) "Using Problem-Based Learning as a Tool for Learning to Teach Students With Special Needs." Several data-collection approaches were employed, including electronic databases (e.g., ERIC, WilsonWeb) and online sources (e.g., Google Scholar™). The terms "special education" and "problem-based learning" were used as descriptors. Since little research on PBL in special education has been conducted, few articles were found using these descriptors. In addition, the final review consisted of even fewer studies because the search was further filtered using the topics of "disabilities" and "inclusion." Second, the selected articles were divided into two groups: teacher education and PBL implementation focused on the learning of students with disabilities. Third, overlaps between PBL and existing instructional practices and the variables and instructional design components of PBL were discussed, based on the synthesis of the research to support the answers to the underlying questions and the conclusion of the research. Finally, the conclusion was developed based on the three aforementioned phases.

## RESULTS

### Overlap between Problem-Based Learning and Self-Determination

The skills involved in learning are nested in the learning processes of PBL and self-determination. Thus, the definitions and design principles of both PBL and self-determination stress learning and cognition and the sequences associated with making critical decisions at the individual and group levels while students interact with learning objects within the context (Butler, 2008; Ochoa & Robinson, 2005). Problem-based learning is a team-based learning process that encompasses intellectual and cognitive exploration in a search for answers. The design technique (similar to human cognitive processing) is attributed to individual and collective analysis of problems and investigation in a context sequenced in team-based synthesis and evaluation (Albanese & Mitchell, 1993; Engel, 1991; Mills, 2006).

Similar to the design process of PBL, Wehmeyer and his colleagues (i.e., Agran, Blanchard, & Wehmeyer, 2000; Mithaug, Wehmeyer, Agran, Martin, & Palmer, 1998; Wehmeyer, Palmer, Agran, Mithaug, & Martin, 2000) developed and conducted research on the Self-Determined Learning Model of Instruction (SDLMI) for students with disabilities in inclusive settings. The SDLMI is based on a three-stage, self-controlled problem-solving model: Stage I: Establishing a goal; Stage II: Planning actions to achieve the goal; and Stage III: Evaluating plans, achievements, and the problem-solving process. Overall, their research efforts led to promising results (Turnbull, Turnbull, & Wehmeyer, 2007).

There are two primary areas of overlap between PBL and self-determined learning (SDL) for students with disabilities: (a) both PBL and SDL implement problem-solving strategies (Agran, Blanchard, Wehmeyer, & Hughes, 2002; Savoie

& Hughes, 1994); and (b) the goals of PBL and SDL for students are congruent, as detailed below.

Problem-solving refers to cognitive processing oriented toward reaching a goal when no method of solving the presenting problem is immediately clear (Mayer & Wittrock, 2006). Thus, students must be active problem solvers in both the PBL and SDL processes. Problem-solving, as a cognitive process, represents facts and concepts. Students need to acknowledge the problems and information in order to design the problem-solving process. In addition, problem-solving involves planning, executing, and monitoring strategies and procedures for solving problems by using cognition (Runco, 2003). By using the above processes, effective problem solvers can change the problematic context by using metacognition and transforming their belief systems (Lovett, 2002).

Congruent goals are purported to:

1. Enhance the skills of constructing and structuring practical knowledge to solve authentic problems in context by practicing acquisition, retention, and use of knowledge;
2. Augment the reasoning process necessary to make a critical decision; for example, reasoning is necessary to complete a sequence of an operation in medical school;
3. Strengthen self-directed skills to pursue the goals in a critical context; and
4. Enhance the motivation for learning; for example, students reach a level of autonomy and seek answers while solving problems (Barrows, 1986; Norman & Schmidt, 1992; Wehmeyer et al., 2000).

In sum, although implementation of PBL practices for students with disabilities is limited, self-determination skills are utilized as one of the PBL practices in special education, and PBL and SDL overlap in terms of problem-solving and an orientation toward 21st-century learning skills.

## Variables that Make Problem-Based Learning Work Effectively

Certain variables are manipulated by curriculum designers (Elrod, Coleman, & Medley, 2005) to help enhance various educational interactions, adding to the overall learning experience. The learning experience, to include PBL, consists of interactions between students, teachers, and learning objects (Seok, 2008a, 2008b). Problem-based learning is implemented to facilitate interactions between learning objects and students in the learning process. As a result, PBL enhances students' autonomy and reasoning skills. This means that the degree of students' decision-making, students' free inquiry, students' self-direction, teacher quality, and feasibility of PBL are critical variables in designing self-determination-enhanced PBL (Barrows, 1986).

Most of the articles analyzed as part of the research synthesis focused on the importance of teacher education in integrating teaching objects, such as hypermedia, computer technology, and software. Only a few articles discussed students' learning in the process of PBL (Azevedo & Cromley, 2004; Ochoa & Robinson, 2005; Van den Bossche, Gijselaers, Segers, & Kirschner, 2006).

Problem-based learning has had a long history in medical education starting in the 1960s, but is now used in many other disciplines as well (Camp, 1996; Hmelo-Silver, 2004). The technology-enhanced PBL pedagogy increasingly used in the digital age is vastly different from the non-technology-implemented PBL of the 1960s. Technology-implemented PBL primarily augments meaningful learning experiments (Cote, 2007; Park & Ertmer, 2008). That is, in the PBL process, students can conduct research to solve problems and gather information using the Internet or integrate technology such as spreadsheets, multimedia, and organization tools (e.g., Inspiration® and computerized concept mapping tools; Ertmer, Lehman, Park, Cramer, & Grove, 2003;

Jonassen, Howland, Moore, & Marra, 2003; Sage, 2000). Thus, technology-enhanced PBL augments the so-called 21st-century learning skills using self-determination, which is particularly critical for students with disabilities.

## Computer Technology, Hypermedia, and Concept Mapping

For the sake of simplicity, technology called out in the literature as part of the research synthesis has been categorized into three major areas:

1. Computer technology,
2. Hypermedia, and
3. Concept mapping. Each of these areas is discussed in the following.

*Computer technology:* Computer technology includes the Internet, computer-supported learning modules (Ochoa & Robinson, 2005), software (Cote, 2007), and games (Kinsell, 2010). A plethora of research has shown that computer-enhanced problem-solving strategies boost students' problem-solving skills (Brown, 2005; Park & Ertmer, 2008; Raskind & Bryant, 2002; Wehmeyer, 1999). Computer technology provides students with authentic learning experiences of real-life skills through risk-free simulations or games so that students can be prepared for adulthood. Further, engagement in the learning process augments students' ownership of their learning (Cote, 2007; Kinsell, 2010; Taylor, 2005; Williams, Hemstreet, Liu, & Smith, 1998).

*Hypermedia:* Refers to the non-linear intertwining (linking) of text and graphics, audio and video, to create information. A great deal of research has been conducted on hypermedia implementation, showing that hypermedia is an indispensable learning tool in today's information society (Gilbert & Driscoll, 2002). For example, hypermedia provides students with ill-structured complex learning contexts, presenting multiple layers of non-linear information. Students develop self-determination skills by controlling the ill-structured context and selecting the information they need to learn. As such, the ill-structured nature of hypermedia facilitates students' meta-cognitive skills; namely, the skills of learning how to learn (Aleven & Koedinger, 2002; Azevedo & Cromley, 2004).

*Computerized concept mapping:* Also commonly referred to as concept- or mind-mapping software, it can be used to visually depict relationships between concepts, ideas, and other information. Numerous studies evaluating learning and assessing critical thinking have shown the effectiveness of using concept maps in PBL (Daley, Shaw, Balistrieri, Glasenapp, & Piacentine, 1999; Gijbels, Dochy, Van den Bossche, & Segers, 2005). Specifically, concept maps were found to empower students' metacognitive skills and thinking processes by connecting theories and problems in an authentic context (Mok, Whitehill, & Dodd, 2008; Novak & Gowin, 1984).

## A Proposed Model of Problem-Based Learning

### Problem Design

Consider the following two brief examples as ways to think about the problem design in order to address the variables discussed earlier, the degree of students':

1. Decision-making,
2. Free inquiry, and
3. Self-direction.

The first case deals with a medical school classroom in 1992, in which the following scenario was presented to make an authentic situation: "A 55-year-old woman lies crawling on the floor in obvious pain. The pain emerges in waves and extends from the right lumbar region to the right side of the groin and the front of the right leg" (Norman & Schmidt, 1992, p. 557). The second case takes place in an inclusive educational setting, where students with mild disabilities are analyzing a problem scenario using a video clip on how to add and multiply when shopping in stores.

While these two cases on the surface appear to be drastically different in terms of the complexity of the problems at hand – one dealing with a medical dilemma and the other focused on simple arithmetic – in reality, in both situations, students were tasked to solve problems with their own reasoning and autonomy using critical thinking and self-determination.

Effectively designed problems such as these explicitly and implicitly enhance students' learning experience in an authentic context. First and foremost, such problems facilitate the general goals and augment the benefits of PBL (Cote, 2007); namely, the skill of critical thinking and analysis, and autonomy: the skill of self-directed learning and self-determination (Schmidt, 1999; Soppe, Schmidt, & Bruysten, 2005; Van Berkel & Schmidt, 2001). Research has indicated that authentic problems relevant to their everyday experiences improve students' learning and, ultimately, their quality of life (Soppe, Schmidt, & Bruysten, 2005). Thus, the design and use of effective problems is critical in this context. Enhancing student reasoning and autonomy is a critical element of effective educational problem-solving (Des Marchais, 1999; Jacobs, Dolmans, Wolfhagen, & Scherpbier, 2003; Soppe et al., 2005).

When cognitive, academic, physical, and behavioral diversity in inclusive settings along with individualized curricula are considered, individual students' cognitive and academic ability and their motivation are the critical variables. However, this is further dependent on a number of additional factors, including the structure, familiarity, intricacy, complexity, and difficulty of the problem at hand.

In short, problems posed within an educational context should stimulate students' intellectual curiosity and motivation and support their learning preference and intellectual ability, while taking into consideration the cognitive load they impose on students. That is, care should be taken in proposing problems that are beneficial in the context of intellectual curiosity and motivation, while at the same time not overloading the finite amount of working memory one possesses (see DaCosta & Seok [2010] for a discussion on managing cognitive load in the design of assistive technology for those with learning disabilities). Thus, the appropriate amount of cognitive load and motivation augments the degree of students' decision-making, free inquiry, self-direction, and engagement in the learning process (adapted from Bransford, Brown, & Cocking, 2000). These skills can be addressed under the rubric of self-determination in inclusive settings.

In the next section, the general sequence in the PBL process, called the SHARE learning model, is presented. Based on the review of the research discussed earlier, the construct of the SHARE learning model is self-determination, and it can be implemented in the inclusive setting (see Figure 2).

## The SHARE Learning Model

As depicted in Figure 2, the SHARE learning model is comprised of five phases: Phase I: Structure, Phase II: Hypothesis, Phase III: Analysis, Phase IV: Research, and Phase V: Evaluation, Formatively and Ecologically. Each phase is discussed in the following.

*Phase I:* Structure. Students recognize and acknowledge the problem presented in the context. They pay attention to, acknowledge, and organize terms, concepts, and problems. They recall and retrieve information and knowledge related to the problem and the context from their long- and short-term memories. As such, they develop the organic structure of solving problems by defining the nature of the problem and contexts (Barrows, 1986; Mills, 2006; Soppe et al., 2005).

*Phase II:* Hypothesis. Students formulate research hypotheses and elaborate on them to construct sequences to systematize the tasks that must be undertaken to solve a given problem. Students

*Figure 2. The SHARE learning model*

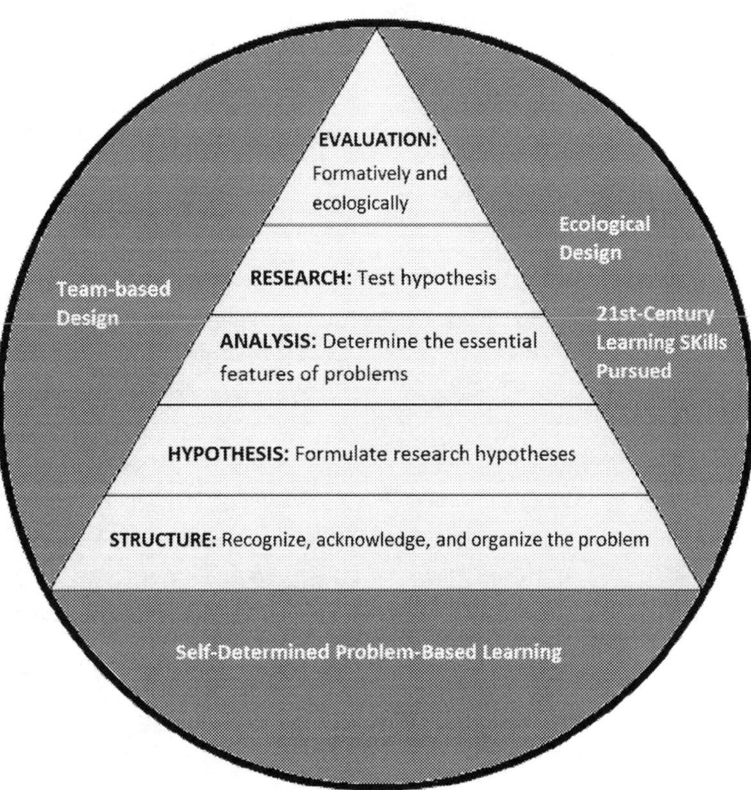


also design frameworks for completing the tasks and develop their own theories for conducting in-depth research and justifying their hypotheses.

*Phase III:* Analysis. Through brainstorming, students determine the essential features of the contextual problems and the relationship between the problems and the context. They also develop descriptions and scenarios, using possible explanation and interpretations of the problems (Mills, 2006). Students retrieve information stored in memory to analyze the problems.

*Phase IV:* Research. Students conduct their own research to test their hypotheses. Students consult books, articles, and websites and discuss in group or individual settings. In the process, they acquire knowledge on the topic or subject matter under consideration.

*Phase V:* Evaluation, Formatively and Ecologically. Students synthesize what they have explored and discovered to reach conclusions. They then incorporate and apply the newly learned information as knowledge about the problem and the context. Students also define new concepts through the ongoing formative process, reformulating their hypotheses if necessary.

## Ecological Context Design

Finally, this chapter turns to ecological context design. Students, teachers, and problems are the three common elements in all contexts of PBL ecology, whether well structured or not (Barrows, 1986; Mok, Whitehill, & Dodd, 2008). The purpose of ecological PBL design is to enhance interactions between these elements to achieve the goal of problem-solving. As a result, an ecological design for a PBL context is student-centered and team-based problem-solving (Bryant, Seok, & Bryant, 2010). *Student-centered* means that students have more ownership in using self-determination skills in the learning experience than the teacher does. That is, students are actively involved in planning and implementing problem-solving, whereas teachers serve as facilitators. For example, students develop hypotheses, test them, and make their own decisions with the teacher's support.

The ecological design for PBL is also *team-based*, taking a time-interrupted case approach (Reinking & Bradley, 2008). That is, teachers or peers can break students' cognitive equilibrium and boost their metacognitive abilities by providing feedback or scaffolding. This facilitates data-based decision-making on students' progress, learning behavior, and attitudes because the ecology of PBL consists of person-centered, ongoing inquiries in an individual and collective constructive learning community (Bryant, Smith, & Bryant, 2008; Bryant, Seok, & Bryant, 2010).

## DISCUSSION

Against the background of the previous sections, each of the research questions proposed earlier in the chapter is next revisited.

### Research Question 1: What is the Potential Efficacy and Feasibility of Problem-Based Learning for Students with Disabilities?

The potential efficacy and feasibility of PBL for students with disabilities is positive and promising. Two reasons support this conclusion.

First, the analysis and review of the literature revealed an overlap of self-determination with PBL and special education practices of inclusive settings. Self-determination is predominantly employed with students with disabilities in inclusive settings aligned with the No Child Left Behind Act and IDEA (Wehmeyer et al., 2000; Wehmeyer, Abery, Mithaug, & Stancliffee, 2003). A major goal of self-determination is to acquire problem-solving skills.

Second, an ecological design is employed in designing functional evaluations and individualized education programs. Both seek the best match between learning experiences and students' learning characteristics to compensate for their disabilities (Zabala, 1996). The ecological design is viable in inclusive settings. Therefore, the self-determination-enhanced PBL empowered by the SHARE model can be successfully used to enhance skills and knowledge in the academic, social, and emotional domains for students with disabilities in inclusive settings.

### Research Question 2: What are the Corresponding Issues Surrounding Problem-Based Learning and What Related Strategies/Tactics can be Developed to Address the Issues?

The research synthesis surrounding effective variables and instructional design components revealed three critical issues related to efficacy and feasibility of PBL implementation:

1. How to enhance interactions between students, objects, and teachers;
2. How to structure the class; for example, the degree of free inquiry and self-direction for students in inclusive settings; and
3. How to use cognitive load theory to create the best match between students' cognitive load, motivation, and inquiry preference.

In addition, there are also issues related to:

1. Teacher education, whereby teachers can acquire 21$^{st}$-century learning skills, share their visions with their colleagues, and implement them in the classroom; and
2. Integration of learning objects that best match students in ill- or well-structured contexts.

In summary, major issues encompass the design of problems and context, matching learning objects to students, and designing teacher education to acquire 21st-century learning skills. The SHARE model is, therefore, recommended as a positive intervention in inclusive settings to resolve the aforementioned issues.

### Research Question 3: How can Problem-Based Learning be Rapidly and Cost-Effectively Implemented to Support Students with Disabilities Learning 21st-Century Skills in Inclusive Settings?

Finally, the findings on ecological content design and specific learning and teaching objects in PBL indicate that technology-enhanced PBL is effective and viable. Technology implementation stresses the use of instructional or assistive technology in the PBL process. Specifically, the technology:

1. Enhances students' self-directional skills, critical thinking skills, engagement, and motivation;
2. Supports students' cognitive load; and
3. Facilitates the acquisition of 21st-century skills for students and teachers alike.

For example, the Internet is increasingly ubiquitous in classrooms, which can facilitate rapid and cost-effective computer use in the PBL process.

### Self-Determination-Enhanced Problem-Based Learning as an Intervention and Formative Design Experiment

If implemented properly (i.e., a good match between students and problems using formative, ongoing interventions), PBL can be a viable solution to the challenge of access to the traditional curriculum encountered by many students with disabilities, as suggested in the PBL conceptual framework and the SHARE learning model (see Figures 1 & 2).

The rationale for this conclusion is simple: the approach is nested in design, research, test, and evaluation of what students are learning in a structured context. Further, both students and their teachers can manipulate and formulate learning and its process, if necessary, as constructivists (Bannan, 2007; Reinking & Bradley, 2008). In addition, the design principles of the self-determination-enhanced PBL are person-centered, problem-solving, goal-oriented, formative-experimental, constructivist, and ecological, which facilitates acquisition of 21st-century learning skills for students with disabilities, making them more successful and competitive in the global marketplace.

## CONCLUSION

The research synthesis presented here has pointed to a trend whereby technology-enhanced PBL is practiced with students with disabilities in inclusive settings and teacher education programs (Brown, 2005; Raskind & Bryant, 2002; Wehmeyer, 1999). In addition to use of the SHARE learning model as a positive intervention, it is suggested that teacher quality is essential in designing and implementing self-determination-enhanced PBL as can be implemented using the proposed PBL conceptual framework.

The findings of the research synthesis revealed that teacher education programs utilizing technology-enhanced PBL address the importance of: (a) having higher expectations for students to develop reasoning skills to structure their knowledge and apply it in their daily lives; (b) instructional strategies that enhance students' communication skills, self-determination skills, and collaboration that align individual strengths and mutual supports; and (c) teachers having the knowledge and skills to construct person-centered ecological supports in their infrastructure. Technology-enhanced PBL can evolve into a system that values the beliefs underlying PBL and meets the demands of the 21st-century digital society as implied in the proposed PBL conceptual framework and the SHARE learning model. All in all, the conclusions presented here emphasize a need for teachers who can implement 21st-century skills in their classrooms.

In light of these findings and conclusions, the following criteria for self-determination-enhanced PBL expertise are recommended:

1. Skills and knowledge that entail the capacity to inquire, collect, interpret, assess, and apply problems in context as collective learning experiences to real life.
2. The ability to provide scaffolding and feedback, to include motivation (Azevedo, Cromley, Winters, Moos, & Greene, 2006; Norman & Schmidt, 1992; Park & Ertmer, 2008; Uzuntiryake & Geban, 2005). Scaffolding enhances metacognitive skills by breaking students' knowledge equilibrium and building new knowledge through teachers' questions or supports or peers' interactions (Choi, Land, & Turgeon, 2005; Raymond, 2008).
3. A pedagogical belief in student-centered constructivism and its implementation. Students acquire and build their knowledge effectively when the class structure is student-centered.
4. Civic professionalism emphasizing collaboration, professional development, and participating in reciprocal research aligned with stakeholders (Sailor & Skrtic, 2009).

In conclusion, the potential efficacy and feasibility of PBL in inclusive settings is promising. Self-determination-enhanced PBL practices will be beneficial for all students by utilizing the 21st-century learning skills and technology learning objects empowered by quality teachers. Hence, the stance that PBL as a formative intervention for students with disabilities in inclusive settings is very feasible.

## ACKNOWLEDGMENT

This study was made possible with funds granted by the National Research Foundation in Korea under the title "Development and Validation of Functional, Ecological, and Matching Evaluation Instrument for Assistive Technology and Students With Disabilities at the Elementary and Secondary Levels by Applying Multidimensional Scaling," number B00078.

## REFERENCES

Agran, M., Blanchard, C., & Wehmeyer, M. (2000). Promoting transition goals and self-directed learning model of instruction. *Education and Training in Mental Retardation and Developmental Disabilities*, *35*, 351–364.

Agran, M., Blanchard, C., Wehmeyer, M., & Hughes, C. (2002). Increasing the problem-solving skills of students with developmental disabilities participating in general education. *Remedial and Special Education*, *23*(5), 279–288. doi:10.1177/074193250202300503 01

Agran, M., Wehmeyer, M. L., Cavin, M., & Palmer, S. (2008). Promoting student active classroom participation skills through instruction to promote self-regulated learning and self-determination. *Career Development for Exceptional Individuals*, *31*(2), 106–114. doi:10.1177/0885728808317656

Albanese, M. A., & Mitchell, S. (1993). Problem based learning: A review of literature on its outcomes and implementation issues. *Medicine*, *68*(1), 52–81. PMID:8447896

Aleven, V., & Koedinger, K. (2002). An effective metacognitive strategy: Learning by doing and explaining with a computer-based cognitive tutor. *Cognitive Science*, *26*(2), 147–181. doi:10.1207/s15516709cog2602_1

Azevedo, R., & Cromley, J. G. (2004). Does training on self-regulated learning facilitate students' learning with hypermedia? *Journal of Educational Psychology*, *96*(3), 523–535. doi:10.1037/0022-0663.96.3.523

Azevedo, R., Cromley, J. G., Winters, F. I., Moos, D. C., & Greene, J. A. (2006). Using computers as metacognitive tools to foster students' self-regulated learning. *Technology, Instruction, Cognition, and Learning Journal*, *3*, 97–104.

Bannan, B. (2007). The integrative learning design framework: An illustrated example from the domain of instructional technology. In T. Plomp, & N. Nieveen (Eds.), *An introduction to educational research* (pp. 53–73). Dordrecht, The Netherlands: SLO.

Barrows, H. (1986). A taxonomy of problem-based learning methods. *Medical Education*, *20*(6), 481–486. doi:10.1111/j.1365-2923.1986.tb01386.x PMID:3796328

Beck, R. J. (2009). *What are learning objects?* Milwaukee, WI: University of Wisconsin-Milwaukee, Center for International Education. Retrieved from http://www4.uwm.edu/cie/learning_objects.cfm?gid=56

Bransford, J. D., Brown, A. L., & Cocking, R. R. (Eds.). (2000). How people learn: Brain, mind, experience, and school: Expanded ed. Washington, DC: National Academies Press.

Brown, M. (2005). Access granted: Achieving technological equity in the 21st century. In D. Edyburn, K. Higgins, & R. Boone (Eds.), *Handbook of special education technology research and practice* (pp. 105–118). Whitefish Bay, WI: Knowledge by Design.

Bryant, B., Seok, S., & Bryant, D. (2010). Assistive technology solutions for individuals with learning problems: Conducting assessments using the functional evaluation for assistive technology (FEAT). In S. Seok, E. Meyen, & B. DaCosta (Eds.), *Handbook of research on human cognition and assistive technology: Design, accessibility and transdisciplinary perspectives* (pp. 264–284). Hershey, PA: IGI Global. doi:10.4018/978-1-61520-817-3.ch018

Bryant, D. P., Smith, D. D., & Bryant, B. R. (2008). *Teaching students with special needs in inclusive classrooms*. Boston: Allyn and Bacon.

Butler, D. (2008). Promoting authentic inquiry in the sciences: Challenges faced in redefining university students' scientific epistemology. *Inquiry in Education: Overcoming Barriers to Successful Implementation*, *2*, 301–324.

Camp, G. (1996). *Problem based learning: A paradigm shift or a passing fad?* Retrieved from http://www.med-ed-online.org/f0000003.htm

Carter, E., & Kennedy, C. (2006). Promoting access to the general curriculum using peer support strategies. *Research and Practice for Persons with Severe Disabilities*, *31*, 284–292.

Choi, I., Land, S. M., & Turgeon, A. J. (2005). Scaffolding peer-questioning strategies to facilitate metacognition during online small group discussion. *Instructional Science*, *33*, 483–511. doi:10.1007/s11251-005-1277-4

Cote, D. (2007). Problem-based learning software for students with disabilities. *Intervention in School and Clinic*, *43*(29), 29–37. doi:10.1177/10534512070430010401

DaCosta, B., & Seok, S. (2010). Managing cognitive load in the design of assistive technology for those with learning disabilities. In S. Seok, E. Meyen, & B. DaCosta (Eds.), *Handbook of research on human cognition and assistive technology: Design, accessibility and transdisciplinary perspectives* (pp. 21–42). Hershey, PA: IGI Global. doi:10.4018/978-1-61520-817-3.ch002

Daley, B. J., Shaw, C. R., Balistrieri, T., Glasenapp, K., & Piacentine, L. (1999). Conceptual maps: A strategy to teach and evaluate critical thinking. *The Journal of Nursing Education*, *38*, 42–47. PMID:9921788

Des Marchais, J. E. (1999). A Delphi technique to identify and evaluate criteria for construction of PBL problems. *Medical Education*, *33*, 504–508. doi:10.1046/j.1365-2923.1999.00377.x PMID:10354334

Elrod, G. F., Coleman, A. M., & Medley, M. B. (2005). The use of problem-based learning in rural special education preservice training programs. *Rural Special Education Quarterly*, *24*(2), 28–32.

Engel, J. (1991). Not just a method but a way of learning. In D. Bould, & G. Felletti (Eds.), *The challenge of problem-based learning* (pp. 21–31). New York, NY: St. Martin's Press.

Ertmer, P. A., Lehman, J., Park, S. H., Cramer, J., & Grove, K. (2003, June). Barriers to teachers' adoption and use of technology in the problem-based learning. In *Proceedings of Association for the Advancement of Computing in Education (AACE) Society for Information Technology and Teacher Education (SITE) International Conference,* (pp. 1761-1766). Washington, DC: AACE.

Gijbels, D., Dochy, F., Van den Bossche, P., & Segers, M. (2005). Effects of problem-based learning: A meta-analysis from the angle of assessment. *Review of Educational Research*, *75*, 27–61. doi:10.3102/00346543075001027

Gilbert, J. N., & Driscoll, P. M. (2002). Collaborative knowledge building: A case study. *Educational Technology Research and Development*, *50*(1), 59–79. doi:10.1007/BF02504961

Hmelo-Silver, C. E. (2004). Problem-based learning: What and how do students learn? *Educational Psychology Review*, *16*, 235–266. doi:10.1023/B:EDPR.0000034022.16470.f3

Jacobs, A. E. J. P., Dolmans, D. H. J. M., Wolfhagen, I. H. A. P., & Scherpbier, A. J. J. A. (2003). Validation of a short questionnaire to assess the degree of complexity and structuredness of PBL problems. *Medical Education*, *37*, 1001–1007. doi:10.1046/j.1365-2923.2003.01630.x PMID:14629413

Jonassen, D., Howland, J., Moore, J., & Marra, R. (2003). *Learning to solve problems with technology: A constructivist perspective* (2nd ed.). Upper Saddle River, NJ: Merrill Prentice Hall.

Kinsell, C. (2010). Investigating assistive technologies using computers to simulate basic curriculum for individuals with cognitive impairments. In S. Seok, E. Meyen, & B. DaCosta (Eds.), *Handbook of research on human cognition and assistive technology: Design, accessibility and transdisciplinary perspectives* (pp. 61–74). Hershey, PA: IGI Global. doi:10.4018/978-1-61520-817-3.ch004

Lambe, J. (2007). Student teachers, special educational needs and inclusion education: Reviewing the potential for problem based e-learning pedagogy to support practice. *Journal of Education for Teaching*, *33*(3), 359–377. doi:10.1080/02607470701450551

Lenz, K. B., & Deshler, D. D. (2004). *Teaching content to all*. Boston, MA: Pearson.

Leven, B., Hibbard, K., & Rock, T. (2002). Using problem-based learning as a tool for learning to teach students with special needs. *Teacher Education and Special Education*, *25*, 278–290. doi:10.1177/088840640202500307

Lovett, M. C. (2002). Problem-solving. In D. Medin (Ed.), *Stevens' handbook of experimental psychology: Memory and cognitive processes* (3rd ed., pp. 317–326). New York, NY: Wiley. doi:10.1002/0471214426.pas0208

Mayer, R. E., & Wittrock, M. C. (2006). Problem-solving. In P. Alexander, & P. Winne (Eds.), *Handbook of educational psychology* (2nd ed., pp. 287–303). Hill Side, NJ: Erlbaum.

Mills, D. (2006). *Problem based learning*. Retrieved from http://www.c-sap.bham.ac.uk/resources/project_reports/ShowOverview.asp?id=4

Mithaug, D. E., Wehmeyer, M., Agran, M., Martin, J. E., & Palmer, S. (1998). The self-determined learning model of teaching: Engaging students to solve their learning problems. In M. Wehmeyer, & D. J. Sands (Eds.), *Making it happen: Student involvement in educational planning* (pp. 299–328). Baltimore, MD: Paul H. Brookes.

Mok, C. K. F., Whitehill, T. L., & Dodd, B. J. (2008). Problem-based learning, critical thinking and concept mapping in speech-language pathology education: A review. *International Journal of Speech-Language Pathology*, *10*(6), 438–448. doi:10.1080/17549500802277492 PMID:20840023

Norman, G. R., & Schmidt, H. G. (1992). The psychological basis of problem-based learning: A review of the evidence. *Academic Medicine*, *67*(9), 557–565. doi:10.1097/00001888-199209000-00002 PMID:1520409

Novak, J. D., & Gowin, D. B. (1984). *Learning how to learn*. Cambridge, UK: Cambridge University Press. doi:10.1017/CBO9781139173469

Ochoa, T. A., & Robinson, J. M. (2005). Revisiting group consensus: Collaborative learning dynamics during a problem-based learning activity in education. *Teacher Education and Special Education*, *28*(1), 10–20. doi:10.1177/088840640502800102

Palmer, S., Wehmeyer, M. L., Gipson, K., & Agran, M. (2004). Promoting access to the general curriculum for students with intellectual disabilities by teaching self-determination skills. *Exceptional Children*, *70*, 427–439.

Park, S. H., & Ertmer, P. A. (2008). Examining barriers in technology-enhanced problem-based learning: Using a performance support systems approach. *British Journal of Educational Technology*, *39*(4), 631–643. doi:10.1111/j.1467-8535.2008.00858.x

Partnership for 21st Century Skills. (2004). *Framework for 21st century skills*. Retrieved from http://www.21stcenturyskills.org

Raskind, M., & Bryant, B. R. (2002). *Functional evaluation for assistive technology*. Austin, TX: Psycho-Educational Services.

Ravitz, J. (2008). *Project-based learning as a catalyst*. Paper presented at the annual meeting of the American Educational Research Association. New York, NY.

Raymond, E. B. (2008). *Learners with mild disabilities: A characteristics approach* (3rd ed.). San Francisco, CA: Pearson.

Reinking, D., & Bradley, B. A. (2008). *Formative and design experiments*. New York, NY: Teachers College Press.

Rose, D. H., & Meyer, A. (2002). *Teaching every student in the digital age: Universal design for learning*. Alexandria, VA: Association for Supervision & Curriculum Development.

Runco, M. A. (2003). *Critical creative processes*. Creskill, NJ: Hampton Press.

Sage, S. M. (2000). A natural fit: Problem-based learning and technology standards. *Learning and Leading with Technology*, *28*(1), 6–12.

Sailor, W., & Skrtic, T. M. (2009). Policy. In T. M. Skrtic, C. M. Gary, & E. M. Horn (Eds.), *Taking stock of special education policy & practice: A retrospective commentary* (pp. 409–422). Denver, CO: Love Publishing Company.

Salend, S. J. (2005). Creating inclusive classrooms: Effective and reflective practices for all students (5th ed.). Columbus, OH: Pearson: Merrill/ Prentice Hall.

Savoie, J. M., & Hughes, A. S. (1994). Problem-based learning as classroom solution. *Educational Leadership*, *52*(3), 54–60.

Schmidt, H. G. (1999). *Testing a causal model of problem-based learning*. Paper presented at the annual meeting of the American Educational Research Association. Montreal, Canada.

Seok, S. (2008a). Teaching aspects of e-learning. *International Journal on E-Learning*, *7*(4), 725–741.

Seok, S. (2008b). Maximizing web accessibility through user-centered interface design. In C. Calero, C. C. Munoz, A. M. Moraga, & P. Mario (Eds.), *Handbook of research on web information systems quality* (pp. 206–219). Hershey, PA: IGI Global. doi:10.4018/978-1-59904-847-5.ch012

Soppe, M., Schmidt, H. G., & Bruysten, R. (2005). Influence of problem familiarity on learning in a problem-based course. *Instructional Science*, *33*, 271–281. doi:10.1007/s11251-004-7688-9

Taylor, A. (2005). What employers look for: The skills debate and the fit with youth perceptions. *Journal of Education and Work*, *18*, 201–218. doi:10.1080/13639080500085984

Turnbull, A., Turnbull, R., & Wehmeyer, M. L. (2007). Exceptional lives: Special education in today's schools (5th ed.). Columbus, OH: Pearson: Merrill/Prentice Hall.

U.S. Department of Education. (2002)... *Public Law*, 107–110. Retrieved from http://www.ed.gov

U.S. Department of Education, Office of Special Education Programs. (n.d.). *IDEA data*. Retrieved from http://www.ideadata.org

Uzuntiryake, E., & Geban, O. (2005). Effect of conceptual change approach accompanied with concept mapping on understanding of solution concepts. *Instructional Science*, *33*, 311–339. doi:10.1007/s11251-005-2812-z

Van Berkel, H., & Schmidt, H. G. (2001). Motivation to commit oneself as a determinant of achievement in problem-based learning. *Higher Education*, *40*, 231–242. doi:10.1023/A:1004022116365

Van den Bossche, P., Gijselaers, W., Segers, M., & Kirschner, P. A. (2006). Social and cognitive factors driving teamwork in collaborative learning environments: Team learning beliefs & behaviors. *Small Group Research*, *37*(5), 490–521. doi:10.1177/1046496406292938

Vaughn, S., Bos, C. S., & Schumm, J. S. (2007). *Teaching students who are exceptional, diverse, and at risk in the general education classroom*. Boston, MA: Allyn & Bacon.

Wehmeyer, M. L. (1999). Assistive technology and students with mental retardation: Utilization and barriers. *Journal of Special Education Technology*, *12*(1), 48–58.

Wehmeyer, M. L., Abery, B., Mithaug, D. E., & Stancliffee, R. J. (2003). *Theory in self -determination: Foundations for educational practice*. Springfield, IL: Thomas.

Wehmeyer, M. L., & Palmer, S. B. (2003). Adult outcomes for students with cognitive disabilities three years after high school: The impact of self-determination. *Education and Training in Developmental Disabilities*, *38*, 131–144.

Wehmeyer, M. L., Palmer, S. B., Agran, M., Mithaug, D. E., & Martin, J. (2000). Promoting causal agency: The self-determined learning model of instruction. *Exceptional Children*, *66*, 439–453.

Wehmeyer, M. L., & Schwartz, M. (1997). Self-determination and positive adult outcomes: A follow-up study of youth with mental retardation or learning disabilities. *Exceptional Children*, *63*, 245–255.

Williams, D., Hemstreet, S., Liu, M., & Smith, V. (1998). Examining how middle school students use problem-based learning software. In T. Ottmann & I. Tomek (Eds.), *Proceedings of ED-MEDIA/ ED-TELECOM 98,* (pp. 1550-1556). Charlottesville, VA: Association for the Advancement of Computing in Education.

Wood, J. W. (2006). *Teaching students in inclusive settings: Adapting and accommodating instruction* (5th ed.). Upper Saddle River, NJ: Pearson/ Merrill Prentice Hall.

Zabala, J. S. (1996). Setting the stage for success: Building success through effective use of assistive technology. In *Proceedings of the Southeast Augmentative Communication Conference* (pp. 129-187). Birmingham, AL: United Cerebral Palsy of Greater Birmingham. Retrieved from http://www.joyzabala.com

## ADDITIONAL READING

Azevedo, R., Cromley, J. G., Winters, F. I., Moos, D. C., & Greene, J. A. (2006). Using computers as metacognitive tools to foster students' self-regulated learning. *Technology, Instruction, Cognition, and Learning Journal*, *3*, 97–104.

Barrows, H. (1986). A taxonomy of problem-based learning methods. *Medical Education*, *20*(6), 481–486. doi:10.1111/j.1365-2923.1986.tb01386.x PMID:3796328

Bryant, B., Seok, S., & Bryant, D. (2010). Assistive technology solutions for individuals with learning problems: Conducting assessments using the functional evaluation for assistive technology (FEAT). In S. Seok, E. Meyen, & B. DaCosta (Eds.), *Handbook of research on human cognition and assistive technology: Design, accessibility and transdisciplinary perspectives* (pp. 264–284). New York, NY: IGI Global. doi:10.4018/978-1-61520-817-3.ch018

Butler, D. (2008). Promoting authentic inquiry in the sciences: Challenges faced in redefining university students' scientific epistemology. *Inquiry in Education: Overcoming Barriers to Successful Implementation*, *2*, 301–324.

Choi, I., Land, S. M., & Turgeon, A. J. (2005). Scaffolding peer-questioning strategies to facilitate metacognition during online small group discussion. *Instructional Science*, *33*, 483–511. doi:10.1007/s11251-005-1277-4

Cote, D. (2007). Problem-based learning software for students with disabilities. *Intervention in School and Clinic*, *43*(29), 29–37. doi:10.1177/10534512070430010401

DaCosta, B., & Seok, S. (2010). Managing cognitive load in the design of assistive technology for those with learning disabilities. In S. Seok, E. Meyen, & B. DaCosta (Eds.), *Handbook of research on human cognition and assistive technology: Design, accessibility and transdisciplinary perspectives* (pp. 21–42). Hershey, PA: IGI Global. doi:10.4018/978-1-61520-817-3.ch002

Gijbels, D., Dochy, F., Van den Bossche, P., & Segers, M. (2005). Effects of problem-based learning: A meta-analysis from the angle of assessment. *Review of Educational Research*, *75*, 27–61. doi:10.3102/00346543075001027

Gilbert, J. N., & Driscoll, P. M. (2002). Collaborative knowledge building: A case study. *Educational Technology Research and Development*, *50*(1), 59–79. doi:10.1007/BF02504961

Kinsell, C. (2010). Investigating assistive technologies using computers to simulate basic curriculum for individuals with cognitive impairments. In S. Seok, E. Meyen, & B. DaCosta (Eds.), *Handbook of research on human cognition and assistive technology: Design, accessibility and transdisciplinary perspectives* (pp. 61–74). New York, NY: IGI Global. doi:10.4018/978-1-61520-817-3.ch004

Leven, B., Hibbard, K., & Rock, T. (2002). Using problem-based learning as a tool for learning to teach students with special needs. *Teacher Education and Special Education*, *25*, 278–290. doi:10.1177/088840640202500307

Novak, J. D., & Gowin, D. B. (1984). *Learning how to learn*. Cambridge, UK: Cambridge University Press. doi:10.1017/CBO9781139173469

Ochoa, T. A., & Robinson, J. M. (2005). Revisiting group consensus: Collaborative learning dynamics during a problem-based learning activity in education. *Teacher Education and Special Education*, *28*(1), 10–20. doi:10.1177/088840640502800102

Park, S. H., & Ertmer, P. A. (2008). Examining barriers in technology-enhanced problem-based learning: Using a performance support systems approach. *British Journal of Educational Technology*, *39*(4), 631–643. doi:10.1111/j.1467-8535.2008.00858.x

Savoie, J. M., & Hughes, A. S. (1994). Problem-based learning as classroom solution. *Educational Leadership*, *52*(3), 54–60.

Seok, S. (2008a). Teaching aspects of e-learning. *International Journal on E-Learning*, *7*(4), 725–741.

Seok, S. (2008b). Maximizing web accessibility through user-centered interface design. In C. Calero, C. C. Munoz, A. M. Moraga, & P. Mario (Eds.), *Handbook of research on Web information systems quality* (pp. 206–219). Hershey, PA: IGI Global. doi:10.4018/978-1-59904-847-5.ch012

Wehmeyer, M. L. (1999). Assistive technology and students with mental retardation: Utilization and barriers. *Journal of Special Education Technology*, *12*(1), 48–58.

## KEY TERMS AND DEFINITIONS

**Computerized Concept Mapping:** Also commonly referred to as concept- or mind-mapping software, it can be used to visually depict relationships between concepts, ideas, and other information.

**Computer Technology:** The Internet, computer-supported learning modules (Ochoa & Robinson, 2005), software (Cote, 2007), and games (Kinsell, 2010).

**Hypermedia:** Refers to the non-linear intertwining (linking) of text and graphics, audio and video, to create information.

**Learning Objects:** Describes what a learner will be able to do in terms of knowledge and skills upon the completion of a unit of instruction. Beck (2009), for instance, describes a learning objective as a collection comprising content, practice, and assessment items.

**Problem-Based Learning:** A constructivist learning approach that starts with problems, not lectures, for the purpose of helping students to learn and/or enhance the skills of self-direction, critical thinking, collaboration, and self-determination structured within systematic exploration (Hmelo-Silver, 2004; Mills, 2006; Park & Ertmer, 2008).

**Problem-Solving:** Cognitive processing oriented toward reaching a goal when no clear method of solving the problem is provided (Mayer & Wittrock, 2006).

**Self-Determination:** An individual's own ability and desire to make decisions that impact the individual's future. It: (a) provides the person access to academic and social support from peers; (b) gives the person responsibility for and ownership of his or her own learning; and (c) allows the person to engage in the general education curriculum and in transitioning to different settings.

# Chapter 6
# Technology and Disability Laws, Regulations, and Rights

**Carolyn Kinsell**
*Solers Research Group, USA*

## ABSTRACT

*This chapter provides a broad overview of federal civil rights laws that ensure equal opportunity and fair treatment to people with disabilities. These laws and regulations bring with them a wide range of rights and services, some of which translate to entitlements in the form of assistive technology services and devices. It is therefore important that those with disabilities, their family members, and individuals who support people with disabilities become familiar with these various laws and regulations. In addition to discussing technology and disability laws, regulations, and rights, Website URLs of the respective governing office, agency, or outside organization have been included, allowing this chapter to serve not only as a primer but also as a reference as well.*

## INTRODUCTION

Although great strides have been made to make information about federal civil rights laws and regulations transparent and freely available to everyone, particularly with the ease of information dissemination on the Internet, the abundance of information available today can also be overwhelming. This is especially true given the complexity of some of these laws and regulations and the subtle differences in the manner in which states operate programs and offer services. These laws and regulations bring with them a wide range of rights and services, some of which translate to entitlements in the form of assistive technology (AT) services and devices. It is therefore important that those with disabilities, their family members, and individuals who support people with disabilities become familiar with these various laws and regulations.

This chapter provides a broad overview of federal civil rights laws that ensure equal opportunity and fair treatment to people with disabilities. As a

DOI: 10.4018/978-1-4666-5015-2.ch006

primer, this chapter offers a general understanding of these laws and regulations in non-expert terms, describing them in the context of their role in affording AT to those with special needs. It is important to note that although an attempt was made to make this chapter as comprehensive as possible, it is in no way exhaustive because federal laws and regulations are amended on a regular basis. The contents of this chapter, including the hyperlinks, may not necessarily address further changes in the law. (Even government websites are not always kept up-to-date on changes in the laws). Additional resources have therefore been included, providing website URLs of the governing office, agency, or outside organization to help ensure this chapter remains relevant with the latest up-to-date information and changes. In doing so, these additional resources also allow this chapter to serve as a reference guide. Those with disabilities, their family members, and individuals who support people with disabilities may wish to contact these resources directly in order to obtain the latest information, to find out what these laws and regulations offer, or to have questions and inquiries answered.

Finally, while every effort has been made to ensure the accuracy of the information provided herein, this chapter is intended to inform rather than advise. It is strongly recommended to consult with qualified individuals, groups, or organizations that specialize in these laws and regulations about particular situations and legal rights. If legal advice or other professional assistance is required, the services of a competent professional must be sought.

## LAWS AND REGULATIONS ON TECHNOLOGY AND DISABILITIES

A wide-range of laws and regulations exist to protect people with disabilities. Some of these laws and regulations, such as the Americans with Disabilities Act and the Individuals with Disabilities Education Act, are better known than others, such as the Carl D. Perkins Vocational and Technical Education Act Amendments of 1998. Although numerous laws and regulations exist, those found in this chapter were chosen for inclusion because they hold important relevance to those with special needs, particularly in the context of AT.

The laws and regulations found in this chapter are:

1. The Americans with Disabilities Act;
2. The Individuals with Disabilities Education Act;
3. Section 508 of the Rehabilitation Act;
4. The Assistive Technology Act of 1998;
5. The Carl D. Perkins Vocational and Technical Education Act Amendments of 1998; (f) the Fair Housing Act Amendments of 1988;
6. The Hearing Aid Compatibility Act of 1988;
7. The Television Decoder Circuitry Act of 1990, Section 3;
8. The Telecommunications Act of 1996;
9. Title III - Public Law 104-104 [47 USC 613]; and
10. The Workforce Investment Act of 1998. What follows is a discussion of each.

### Americans with Disabilities Act

The Americans with Disabilities Act (ADA; Public Law 101-336, 104 Stat. 327, 42 U.S.C. 12101-12213 and 47 U.S.C. 225 and 611) was passed by the 101st Congress on July 26, 1990. The purpose behind the Act is to "establish a clear and comprehensive prohibition of discrimination on the basis of disability" (Public Law 101-336, 1990, p. 1). The Americans with Disabilities Act defines the rules and regulations that govern the treatment of persons with disabilities by private and public organizations. Keywords such as, "equality of opportunity," "full participation," "independent living," and "economic self sufficiency" (Public Law 101-336, 1990, p. 3), help define the goals of the Act.

The Act covers 10 areas with 10 specific agencies that help define and govern rules and regulations:

1. Employment (Equal Employment Opportunity Commission [EEOC]);
2. Mobility by way of public transportation (Department of Transportation [DOT]);
3. The capability to receive and send information (Federal Communications Commission [FCC]);
4. Design criteria for accessibility, which includes telecommunications and information technology (IT; U.S. Access Board);
5. Education (Department of Education [EOD]);
6. Medical services (Health and Human Services [HHS]);
7. Labor rules and regulations (Department of Labor [DOL]);
8. Access to housing (Department of Housing and Urban Development);
9. Public access to parks and recreation (Department of Interior [DOI]); and
10. Agriculture (U.S. Department of Agriculture [USDA]; Public Law 101-336, 1990).

After the passage of a statute, ambiguities inevitably arise that must be interpreted by the courts to clarify language and delineate specific rules for the practical application of the law. Executive agencies also promulgate rules to further define the application of the regulations that they are charged with enforcing. An examples includes the context of AT, the Act (Title IV) updated in 2010 to clarify hearing, speech, and vision language. That is, clarification on the type of telecommunication devices made available under "Auxiliary Aids and Services" (U.S. Department of Justice: Americans with Disabilities Act, 2013; see Sec. 36.303). Devices include qualified interpreters for those who are hard of hearing or deaf or have a speech deficiency, and qualified readers for those who are blind or have impaired vision; to be specific, access to information based on the functionality of products and services offered. Examples include telephones using telecommunication relay services and speech-to-speech recognition, along with services provided by operators (e.g., communication assistants) to help complete the transaction of having a conversation (FCC, 2011b).

All-in-all, as vast as this Act is, it affords those with disabilities more freedoms due to the expansive capabilities of technology and those behind the ideas that get that technology into the mainstream. This removes roadblocks that often times would stop those with disabilities from performing even normal day-to-day activities. To illustrate the far reaching implications of the ADA, take for example, state and federal courts, which have been examining the requirement that documents filed with the courts be ADA compliant, so that they can be read by all people, particularly those visually impaired. This is something that was recently emphasized by the Supreme Court in its imposition in late 2012 of the new e-Filing system (The Florida Bar, 2012).

For additional information about the ADA, please visit the following resource:

**U.S. Department of Justice:** *Americans with Disabilities Act:* http://www.ada.gov/

## Individuals with Disabilities Education Act

Education is the cornerstone by which an individual can improve upon their skill sets, gain a new knowledge base, and obtain positive internal attitudes, such as a feeling of accomplishment based upon their learning activities. This can also lead to a significant increase in financial status, based on employability brought about through education. Although there are many with educational affordance, those with disabilities may find themselves at a disadvantage. Enacted by the 101st Congress as the Education for All Handicapped Children Act (Public Law 94-142) in 1975, the amendment of this Act, known as the Individuals with Disabilities Education Act (IDEA) took place in 1997, with a focus on improving results and successes of this program (U.S. Department of Education, 2006).

The initial requirement under this law is for states to provide a free and appropriate education (FAPE) to children with disabilities in environments that put these children into mainstream classes when possible (i.e., inclusion). As with any other federally funded program, participation requires that states develop and implement policies that support FAPE and adhere to the standards of these laws. Therefore, there should be consistency across states in the implementation of these standards, and the educational treatment of those with disabilities (U.S. Department of Education, 2010).

Based on amendments of 2004, the IDEA is now comprised of two parts, Part B and Part C. Part B addresses children from the ages of 3 to 21 years of age and focuses on the importance of including parents in the decision making process regarding their children's education (U.S. Department of Education, 2013a). Part C covers children from infancy through 2 years of age and measures and improves outcomes of these children to support the transition from preschool and kindergarten (U.S. Department of Education, 2013a).

The Individuals with Disabilities Education Act notes the Four Purposes of PL 94-142, as found in the U.S. Office of Special Education Programs (OSEP; U.S. Department of Education, 2013c):

- Providing FAPE and related services to children with disabilities
- Protecting the rights of children with disabilities and the rights of their parents
- Granting assistance to states that provide, or wish to provide, educational opportunities to children with disabilities
- Measuring effectiveness of the IDEA programs that are currently in place

For additional information about the IDEA, please visit the following resource:

**U.S. Department of Education:** http://idea.ed.gov/

## Section 508 of the Rehabilitation Act

The focus of the amended Authority 29 U.S.C. § 794dc, of Section 508 of the Rehabilitation Act of 1973, is on electronics and IT. This Amendment took place in 1998 when signed into law by President Clinton. Over the span of 25 years, this Amendment vastly improved the accessibility to federal agency information to disabled federal employees and for the general public with disabilities. This mandate does not require compliance from private entities (The Rehabilitation Act Amendments, 2013).

The goal of this Amendment is to ensure that those with disabilities are afforded the same access to information as people without disabilities (The Rehabilitation Act Amendments, 2013). Electronic and IT, as defined by the Electronic and Information Technology Accessibility Standards (2000) includes equipment that is used in the "creation, conversion, or duplication of data or information" (see section §1194.4). Specifically, equipment that is used to gain access to federally provided information includes telecommunications products, such as telephones, information kiosks and transaction machines, the Internet, multimedia, and office equipment, such as copiers and fax machines; whereas IT is equipment or systems that support the delivery of such information, to include computers and related equipment, software packages, firmware updates and related procedures, (support) services, and related resources. From the perspective of AT, those with disabilities will have the same access to federally provided information using such equipment as those without disabilities. However, mandates are often required in order for the accessibility to be acted upon by organizations, from the federal level to state agencies.

This section of the Authority also covers the enforcement guidelines of this law. It is important to the community (those with and without disabilities) to promote equality; and to achieve this equality is through mandates. According to the Rehabilitation Act Amendments (Section 508), under enforcement, there is a grace period in which the federal department or agency is able to incorporate the mandate into their procurement policies and directives allowing time for implementation. Following implementation of a mandate, agency evaluations in the form of interim and biennial reports provide a status on the extent of usability by those with disabilities and actions taken regarding individual complaints. These reports provide data from the Attorney General to the President and to Congress on effectiveness of these mandates.

For additional information about Section 508 of the Rehabilitation Act, please visit the following resources:

**The Rehabilitation Act Amendments (Section 508):** http://www.access-board.gov/sec508/guide/act.htm

**Electronic and Information Technology Accessibility Standards (Section 508):** http://www.access-board.gov/sec508/standards.htm

## Assistive Technology Act of 1998

The Assistive Technology Act of 1998 (Public Law 105-394 [29 USC 2201]) targets grant based programs within states to provide access to AT (devices) through consumer-oriented programs, protection and advocacy services to protect those trying to gain access to AT, and financial options for the disabled to purchase AT. Also known as the "Tech Act," passed by the 105th Congress, it creates rights for those with disabilities and their families under the protection and advocacy services instructed statues and provided by state agencies. This chapter addresses three programs found under the grant umbrella (National Dissemination Center for Children with Disabilities, 2012). Each of these is discussed in what follows:

The consumer-oriented programs include demonstration and information centers. The demonstration centers help to educate those with disabilities and their family members by providing physical contact and demonstration of equipment, while showing the unique features specific to each device. An information center provides those who work with or are involved with those with disabilities the opportunity to become educated in the latest AT, and the implementation of those technologies. Referral services are a type of consumer-oriented program evaluating the need of a person with a disability for an AT or service. States offer referral services, as do many universities, hospitals, and human resource departments of businesses (National Dissemination Center for Children with Disabilities, 2012).

The protection and advocacy programs (i.e., The Protection and Advocacy for Assistive Technology [PAAT], established in 1994 prior to the Tech Act) provide grant funds to states to hire full-time advocates to represent disabled people (or advocates to pursue implementation of programs for disabled people). These advocates help represent those with disabilities who have been overlooked or denied an assistive device or service (Consortium for Citizens with Disabilities, 2013). Examples include denial through a medical insurance claim or an inappropriately handled student in the educational system. Needless to say, state advocacy groups are paramount in removing barriers.

Finally, the third program entails funding support to those with disabilities to purchase AT. Through grants, federal and state programs can provide loans and other financial options at low interest rates specifically targeted to the purchase of an AT, as noted in the list of State Tech ACT

Projects found at the National Public Website on Assistive Technology (see Assistivetech.net, 2013).

A sampling of the types of programs offered by states receiving grant money can be found on this website (see Assistivetech.net, 2013) and includes but is not limited to the following:

- Advocacy and awareness activities
- Assistive tools to provide independence in the community
- Comprehensive online resource centers
- Device demonstrations for selection and educational training
- Technology partnerships to acquire AT devices and services
- Product search and referral
- Recycling programs
- Financial programs and funding sources

For additional information about the Assistive Technology Act of 1998, please visit the following resource:

**National Public Website on Assistive Technology:** http://assistivetech.net/webresources/stateTechActProjects.php

## Carl D. Perkins Vocational and Technical Education Act Amendments of 1998

The latest amendments to this Act took place under the Career and Technical Education Improvement Act of 2006 on August 12, 2006, which renames the Carl D. Perkins Vocational and Technical Education for the Future Act of 1998 (Public Law 105-332 Section 1 (b) [20 USC 2302]). This Act promotes career growth for students in secondary (i.e., high school) and post-secondary (i.e., college, graduate school) education, with an emphasis on technical areas (U.S. Department of Education, 2003, 2013b).

As outlined in McKeon (2006), there are seven key purposes of this Act. Descriptions of these purposes are as follows:

- For a person who is disabled, seeking an education does not mean lowered requirements to a level in which the education is meaningless. The disabled person can seek an education knowing that their educational materials and expectations of them as a student by the educational organizations meet standards and, in addition, offer challenging learning environments.
- The promotion of these programs is twofold. First, there is the integration of services and activities with academia/instruction. Second, when meeting standards at one educational level, these standards act as pre-requisites for even greater learning. In other words, secondary education lays the academic (and intellectual) foundation for the post-secondary track. This follows the basic model for educational growth and alignment with a career path found at educational institutions.
- In the curriculum of activities and services, state and local educational organizations have flexibility to build improvements into their curricula. This ensures that the person is receiving the best training available. In other words, the variety of programs available enable state and local educational organizations the flexibility to build improvements into their curriculum.
- State and local improvements, such as "best practices" type data is captured at a national level. The distribution of this data to state and local educational organizations serves as a reference for future improvements upon their educational programs, services, and activities.
- Within this Act, there is recognition of the value support staff, from teachers to ad-

ministrators, adding to the success of this Act. Therefore, the offering of technical assistance, such as professional development training, enhances skill sets and knowledge for these support positions.
- The Act encourages partnerships among educational institutions and local industry. This fosters an awareness in the academic environment of the knowledge, capabilities, and skill sets that are in demand in the business community, enabling them to build programs that will prepare students for entry into a competitive market.
- In turn, the strengths of this Act increases the likelihood of better employability and a better way of life for those with disabilities. This adds to the "competitiveness" and well-being of the country.

The intertwining of the seven purposes encourages or enables (through funding) organizations to be dynamic or progressive. Further allowing expansion and contraction of knowledge-based and skill set programs when and where needed at the state and local level. This empowers states to improve upon their offerings for their specific disabled populations.

For additional information about the Carl D. Perkins Vocational and Technical Education Act Amendments of 1998, please visit the following resource:

**U.S. Department of Education:** http://www2.ed.gov/policy/sectech/leg/perkins/index.html and http://www2.ed.gov/offices/OVAE/CTE/legis.html

## Fair Housing Act Amendments of 1988

The Fair Housing Act Amendments of 1988 (Public Law 100-430 [42 USC 3604]), approved on September 13, 1988, focuses on multifamily housing construction and accessibility requirements, which appended Title VIII of the Civil Rights Act of 1968 to include those with disabilities or with familial status. The Fair Housing Act became effective March 12, 1989 (U.S. Department of Housing and Urban Development, 2013, see section Statutory and Regulatory Background).

The Amendments focus on the design and construction of multi-family dwellings with three main requirements. They include:

1. Public use accessible areas,
2. Width of doors and passageways for accommodation of wheelchairs, and
3. Accessible routes, locations of switches and outlets, reinforced walls in bathrooms to support "grab bars," and maneuverability in kitchens and bathrooms for those in wheelchairs (U.S. Department of Housing and Urban Development, 2013, see section Statutory and Regulatory Background).

These "accessibility provisions" supported by Congress' intent in passing these provisions was to improve the quality of life for citizens with disabilities by providing enforceable standards of accessibility. Standardization of housing and construction design has removed barriers that previously limited disabled citizens' access to fair, affordable housing. Implementation of statutory accessibility models has minimized, if not eliminated, the need for costly modifications to houses, giving every person a meaningful choice of housing options. These standards have granted freedom to disabled people who may live where they choose, without having to endure obstacles to their mobility.

Other items covered under the Fair Housing Act in the context of those with disabilities include the rent or purchase of housing, mortgage loans, and modifications to the dwelling based on disability needs. However, the burden of modification is not one-sided. A property owner can request, under reasonable conditions, that restoration of the property is made to the state in which the person with disabilities first occupied the residence (U.S. Department of Housing and Urban Development, 2013, see section Statutory and Regulatory Background).

For additional information about the Fair Housing Act Amendments of 1988, please visit the following resource:

**U.S. Department of Housing and Urban Development:** http://portal.hud.gov/hudportal/HUD?src=/program_offices/fair_housing_equal_opp/disabilities/fhguidelines/fhefha1

## Hearing Aid Compatibility Act of 1988

The Federal Communications Commission is an executive agency regulating communications within the U.S. and oversees the Hearing Aid Compatibility Act of 1988 (HAC Act; Public Law 100-394 [47 USC 610 (b)]). The Hearing Aid Compatibility Act requires the design of "essential telephones" to include hearing aid capabilities. According to the National Association of the Deaf (2013), essential telephones are defined as "coin-operated telephones, telephones provided for emergency use, and other telephones frequently needed for use by persons using such hearing aids" (¶ 2). The Hearing Aid Compatibility Act of 1988 is exempted from wireless phones as an essential telephone. Originally, the growth and common use of wireless telecommunications industry was not foreseen and the FCC realized that amendments to the original HAC Act were essential. As a result, an amendment, passed by Congress in August 2003, reduced the exemption of digital wireless phones.

Having this Act in place may have advanced the telecommunications industry to improve upon sound quality for the hearing impaired that may not have otherwise occurred at all or as rapidly. However, according to Rocker & Allure (2009), there are still technical sound issues, such as noise management, that still need research and application to improve the wireless and hearing aid device compatibility.

For additional information about the HAC Act of 1988, please visit the following resource:

**National Association of the Deaf:** http://www.nad.org/issues/telephone-and-relay-services/hearing-aid-compatible-telephones

## The Television Decoder Circuitry Act of 1990, Section 3

Sec. 3, Section 303(u) of the Television Decoder Circuitry Act of 1990 is an amendment requiring that television devices with over a 13-inch picture screen have built-in circuitry to display closed captioning. The Act requires that specified television devices noted in the law either imported or manufactured in the U.S. contain the decoder circuitry (FCC, 2011b; Television Decoder Circuitry, 1990). Closed caption capability was required for all television sets manufactured beginning in 1991.

Sec 2 of the law outlines how closed captioning benefits those who are deaf and hearing impaired. Closed captioning is the showing of audio via text on the screen of a television program. Overall, this captioning, to be transmitted in English, assists "children with reading and other learning skills, and improve[s] literacy skills among adults" (Television Decoder Circuitry, 1990, p. 2). That is, this type of encoding not only benefits those with hearing loss but also those in learning the English language; a side benefit not typically shared with other AT devices.

Those taking advantage of closed captioning can expect to see more and more electronic devices that contain this capability, such as mobile devices supporting movies and TV programming. Any program that has closed captioning is noted by "cc" and can easily be turned on and off by use of a TV controller or the accessibility features on mobile devices.

For additional information about the Television Decoder Circuitry Act of 1990, Section 3, please visit the following resources:

**Federal Communications Commission:** http://www.fcc.gov/guides/closed-captioning

**Television Decoder Circuitry, Public Law 101-431 – Oct. 15, 1990:** http://transition.fcc.gov/Bureaus/OSEC/library/legislative_histories/1395.pdf

## Telecommunications Act of 1996

This Act (Title I - Public Law 104-104 [47 USC 255]), created in 1934 as the Federal Communications Act of 1934, was amended as the Telecommunications Act of 1996 to increase competition in the telecommunication industry. This Act covers the regulations for the "development of competitive markets" by defining Title I, Telecommunication Services; Title II, Broadcast Services; Title III, Cable Services; Title IV, Regulatory Reform; Title V, Obscenity and Violence; Title VI, Effect on Other Laws; and Title VII, Miscellaneous Provisions (U.S. Government Printing Office, 1996).

The regulations noted in these titles "affect telephone service – local and long distance, cable programming and other video services, broadcast services and services provided to schools" (FCC, 2011c, ¶ 2). The Federal Communications Commission's role is to "create fair rules" that will increase competition in this industry. However, there has been non-favorable receipt of the rules governing the competition by larger corporations (Consumer Union, 2001). One of the larger concerns with the requirement for "interconnectivity" (Thomas, 1996), which was not implemented on a large scale by corporations, hence decreasing the competitive collaboration.

For additional information about the Telecommunications Act of 1996, Section 3, please visit the following resources:

**Federal Communications Commission, Telecommunications Act of 1996:** http://transition.fcc.gov/telecom.html

**Telecommunications Act of 1996, 104th Congress Public Law, US:** http://www.gpo.gov/fdsys/pkg/PLAW-104publ104/html/PLAW-104publ104.htm

## Title III - Public Law 104-104 [47 USC 613]

As noted in the Telecommunications Act of 1996, Title III covers cable services with a focus for this topic on Section V, Sec. 613, and video programming accessibility. The regulation under this section of the Act is specific to videos. The common language found in these regulations is the use of "video description" and "video programming." Video description retrieved from the regulation is defined as the "insertion of audio narrated descriptions of a television program's key visual elements into natural pauses between the program's dialogue," (Cornell University Law School, 2013, see Title 47, p. 297), whereas the definition of "video programming" is the "programming by, or generally considered comparable to programming provided by a television broadcast station" (Cornell University Law School, 2013, see Title 47, p. 298). In the context of this chapter, it is the video description aspect of this law that is of particular interest.

Cornell University Law School (2013) provides a condensed version of the law outlining the rules set forth for closed captioning of videos and the parameters in which videos could be exempt for providers and distributors if there is an undue burden in the forms of difficulty or expense. Overall, the Act supports the use of closed captioning within videos under the right circumstances covered by the law.

For additional information about Title III - Public Law 104-104 [47 USC 613], please visit the following resource:

**Cornell University Law School:** http://www.law.cornell.edu/uscode/text/47/613

## Workforce Investment Act of 1998

According to the U.S. Department of Labor, Employment and Training Administration (2010), the Workforce Investment Act (WIA; Public Law 105-220), passed during the Clinton administration by Congress in 1998, was created to largely reform the U.S. job training system. Areas impacted by the Act include employment, training, and education programs. Purposed to streamline services to allow easy access to all people, the Act provides jobseekers with a system of different federally funded employment programs to help people find jobs or advance their careers.

Described as a framework, the system is based on the "One-stop" concept, comprising workforce career centers providing job training, education, and employment services in neighborhood locations. According to the Department of Labor (2010), centers are being built in over 95 percent of the states, with over 800 centers operating throughout the U.S. The Act encourages businesses to participate in local workforce development services, as the centers are intended to meet not only the needs of the jobseeker, but local businesses as well. Thus each center may provide different services specific to the local job market and the employment needs of the local community.

The Act is built upon the most successful elements found in previous federal legislation, and key components of the Act are based on local and state input, extensive research, and the evaluation of studies of successful training and employment advancements over the past decade. Title I of the Act is comprised of the following elements:

- Training and employment programs must be designed and managed at the local level where businesses and job seeker needs are best understood
- Jobseekers must have easy access to the employment, education, training, and information programs they need at a single location in their neighborhood
- Jobseekers should have control over their career development path in deciding the programs that best fit their needs and the organizations that will provide services
- Service providers will disseminate information about the success rate of their programs in preparing jobseekers for employment
- Business will be proactive, playing an active role through the dissemination of information and leadership, to ensure jobseekers are prepared for current and future employment

The Act is of significance to those with disabilities in that it is founded on the belief that all persons have the right to "core" employment and training related services. Specifically, Section 188 of the Act prohibits discrimination against qualified individuals with disabilities who are applicants, employees, and participants in the WIA Title I – financially assisted programs and activities, as well as programs that are part of the One-Stop workforce career centers.

For additional information about the WIA, please visit the following resource:

**The U.S. Department of Labor: Workforce Investment Act Laws and Regulations:** http://www.doleta.gov/usworkforce/wia/act.cfm

## CONCLUSION

While all of laws, regulations, and rights presented in this chapter are important to those with disabilities, their family members, and individuals who support people with disabilities, no single legislation stands alone addressing all the challenges and concerns of those with special needs. Instead, all of the legislation discussed in this chapter, *together*, has helped in the defense of civil rights, the enforcement of equal opportunity and fair treatment, the improvement of accessibility and mobility, and access to services. It is therefore important to understand these laws and regulations as a whole.

Fortunately, such understanding is becoming more and more possible. Although the amount of information available is still overwhelming, many government entities are requiring that their documentation be written in "plain language" along with meeting certain readability standards and guidelines, such as those outlined in the Federal Plain Language Guidelines, which are based on the premise that "citizens deserve clear communications from government" (Plainlanguage.gov, 2011, p. ii). Such requirements benefit all people, but specifically make information more accessible to people with limited education, learning disabilities, and mental deficiencies.

## REFERENCES

Assistivetech.net. (2013). *National public website on assistive technology: State tech ACT projects*. Retrieved from http://assistivetech.net/webresources/stateTechActProjects.php

Consortium for Citizens with Disabilities. (2013). *Protection and advocacy for assistive technology*. Retrieved from http://www.c-c-d.org/task_forces/tech_telecom/ATprotectadvoch.htm

Consumer Union. (2001). *Lessons from 1996 telecommunications act: Deregulation before meaningful competition spells consumer disaster*. Retrieved from http://www.consumersunion.org/telecom/lessondc201.htm

Cornell University Law School. (2013). *47 USC § 613 - Video programming accessibility*. Retrieved from http://www.law.cornell.edu/uscode/text/47/613

Electronic and Information Technology Accessibility Standards. (2000). *Section 508*. Retrieved from http://www.access-board.gov/sec508/standards.htm

Federal Communications Commission. (2011a). *Guide: Closed captioning*. Retrieved from http://www.fcc.gov/guides/closed-captioning

Federal Communications Commission. (2011b). *Guide: Speech-to-speech relay service*. Retrieved from http://www.fcc.gov/guides/speech-speech-relay-service

Federal Communications Commission. (2011c). *Telecommunications act of 1996*. Retrieved from http://transition.fcc.gov/telecom.html

Florida Bar. (2012, March). *E-fillings musts be ADA compliant*. Retrieved from http://www.floridabar.org/DIVCOM/JN/jnnews01.nsf/Articles/5ED3206D77DA1280852579AA004E0B17

Go track. (2012). *H.R. 4227 (112th), workforce investment act of 2012*. Retrieved from http://www.govtrack.us/congress/bills/112/hr4227#overview

McKeon, M. (2006). *Carl D. Perkins career and technical education improvement act of 2006, conference report*. Retrieved from http://www.gpo.gov/fdsys/pkg/CRPT-109hrpt597/pdf/CRPT-109hrpt597.pdf

National Association of the Deaf. (2013). *Hearing aid compatible telephones*. Retrieved from http://www.nad.org/issues/telephone-and-relay-services/hearing-aid-compatible-telephones

National Dissemination Center for Children with Disabilities. (2012). *Assistive technology act*. Retrieved from http://nichcy.org/laws/ata

Plainlanguage.gov. (2011). *Federal plain language guidelines*. Retrieved from http://www.plainlanguage.gov/howto/guidelines/bigdoc/fullbigdoc.pdf

Public Law 101-336. (1990). *Public law 101-336 – July26, 1990*. Retrieved from http://www.brockport.edu/~govdoc/SocPol/pl1013a.pdf

Recker, K., & Kalluri, S. (2009). The impact of new technology on phone use. *Hearing Review*, *16*(3), 16–20.

Rehabilitation Act Amendments. (2013). *Section 508*. Retrieved from http://www.access-board.gov/sec508/guide/act.htm

Television Decoder Circuitry. (1990). *Public law 101-431 – Oct. 15, 1990*. Retrieved from http://transition.fcc.gov/Bureaus/OSEC/library/legislative_histories/1395.pdf

Thomas, E. (1996). *Overview of the telecommunications act of 1996: Pros and cons for municipal provision of fiber optic utilities*. Retrieved from http://www.mrsc.org/subjects/legal/telecomm/thomas.aspx

U.S. Department of Education. (2003). *Carl D. Perkins career and technical education act of 2006*. Retrieved from http://www2.ed.gov/offices/OVAE/CTE/legis.html

U.S. Department of Education. (2006). *34 CFR parts 300 and 301, assistance to states for the education of children with disabilities and preschool grants for children with disabilities, final rule*. Retrieved from http://idea.ed.gov/download/finalregulations.html

U.S. Department of Education. (2010). *Free appropriate public education for students with disabilities: Requirements under section 504 of the rehabilitation act of 1973*. Retrieved from http://www2.ed.gov/about/offices/list/ocr/docs/edlite-FAPE504.html

U.S. Department of Education. (2013a). *Building the legacy: IDEA 2004*. Retrieved from http://idea.ed.gov/

U.S. Department of Education. (2013b). *Carl D. Perkins career and technical education act of 2006*. Retrieved from http://www2.ed.gov/policy/sectech/leg/perkins/index.html

U.S. Department of Education. (2013c). *Office of special education and rehabilitation services: Thirty-five years of progress in educating children with disabilities through IDEA*. Retrieved from http://www2.ed.gov/about/offices/list/osers/idea35/history/index.html

U.S. Department of Housing and Urban Development. (2013). *Adoption of final guidelines*. Retrieved from http://portal.hud.gov/hudportal/HUD?src=/program_offices/fair_housing_equal_opp/disabilities/fhguidelines/fhefha1

U.S. Department of Justice. Americans with Disabilities Act. (2013). *ADA home page: Information and technical assistance on the Americans with disability act*. Retrieved from http://www.ada.gov/

U.S. Department of Labor. Employment and Training Administration. (2010). *The plain English version of the workforce investment act of 1998*. Retrieved from http://www.doleta.gov/usworkforce/wia/Runningtext.cfm

U.S. Government Printing Office. (1996). *Telecommunications act, public law 104-104*. Retrieved from http://www.gpo.gov/fdsys/pkg/PLAW-104publ104/html/PLAW-104publ104.htm

## ADDITIONAL READING

Assistive Technology Laws. (n.d.). *Understanding the law & assistive technology*. Retrieved from http://www.fctd.info/resources/ATlaws_print.pdf

In addition to the resources found with each law and regulation, additional resources can be found here that may be of interest and value to those with disabilities, their family members, and individuals who support people with disabilities.

Microsoft Active Accessibility. (2013). *Windows*. Retrieved from http://msdn.microsoft.com/en-us/library/windows/desktop/dd373592(v=vs.85).aspx

U.S. Department of Justice. (2009). *A guide to disability rights laws*. Retrieved from http://www.ada.gov/cguide.htm

U.S. Equal Opportunity Commission. (2013). *Disability discrimination*. Retrieved from http://www.eeoc.gov/laws/types/disability.cfm

U.S. Government Printing Office. (2013). *Electronic code of Federal regulations*. Retrieved from http://www.ecfr.gov/cgi-bin/ECFR?page=browse

Word Wide Web Consortium. (2013). *Accessibility*. Retrieved from http://www.w3.org/standards/webdesign/accessibility

# Section 2
# Software, Devices, and Games

*In section 2 of this book, emphasis moves away from theories, concepts, and laws to more of a focus on the Assistive Technology (AT) itself, specifically software, devices, and games. Chapter 7 begins the discussion with the author presenting the powerful effect AT has had on people with disabilities, particularly in the areas of reading, writing, communicating, and accessing information. Accessible technologies are discussed by the author in terms of mobile, personal computer, and cloud computing, that have or are quickly becoming part of the mainstream and every day, but which have already shown, or have the potential, to be incredibly helpful to those with disabilities, in particular those who have visual and hearing impairments. In chapter 8, the discussion of AT continues, but from the perspective of Information and Communication Technology (ICT) and the need for validation research that contributes to AT evidence-based practices. Namely, the authors present the findings of a study aimed to identify a latent dimension of ICT that can serve as the basis for the eventual development of a standardized instrument for ICT assessment and selection in the context of AT. Chapter 9 continues the discussion on communication-related AT, with the author presenting the tools being developed to help remedy the challenges facing users of augmentative communications systems, and the "phatic" approach on which these tools are based.*

*In chapters 10 and 11, the benefits of video games, specifically simulation-based games, are presented, and how this genre of game, when coupled with the element of storytelling, may be effectively used as interventions in helping children with Autism Spectrum Disorders (ASD) who have trouble with everyday social situations and/or communication difficulties not seen with neurotypical children. In chapter 10, the authors discuss the potential that video games have in assisting children with ASD in the development of social skills. The importance of storytelling is discussed in the context of video games, in part based on the role story plays in human development from early childhood. In chapter 11, the authors continue the discussion on the use of video games in promoting social skills development for children with ASD, building upon the work of the authors in chapter 10, but narrowing the focus from the general application of video games to that of simulation-based games. The authors present the characteristics of this video game genre that help make this technology particularly attractive in education, especially as an intervention for social skills development. The authors also discuss the pivotal storytelling component contributing to the successful development of simulation-based games in an instructional context. This includes a discussion on the importance of immersion and motivation.*

*Although chapters 10 and 11 only begin to scratch the surface as to the potential benefits and challenges of leveraging video games in helping children with special needs, the discussions presented should be viewed as a call for researchers and practitioners who see potential in game technology, including simulation-based games, to not only expand the investigation of such technology and its use as educational and training interventions but also push for the specific investigation into how this technology presents greater possibilities in promoting the generalization of social skills among children with ASD and other disabling conditions.*

# Chapter 7
# The Changing Face of Assistive Technology:
## From PC to Mobile to Cloud Computing

**James R. Stachowiak**
*University of Iowa, USA*

## ABSTRACT

*Computer-based Assistive Technology (AT) has had a powerful effect on people with disabilities in the areas of reading, writing, communicating, and accessing information. One of the roadblocks for use has always been the expense of AT. Advancements in computing and mobile technology, however, are making some technology more readily available, accessible, and cost effective for people with disabilities. Computer operating systems, for example, now contain features to magnify screens for reading and in the entering of text. The mobile movement of smartphones, eReaders, and tablets has also been changing the way people with disabilities access information. The capabilities of these devices combined with the immediate availability, affordability, and ease of use, has been making the world more accessible for people with disabilities, and with mobile devices increasingly becoming a necessity for most, this trend is anticipated to only continue.*

## INTRODUCTION

Assistive technology (AT) has been around as long as people have been attempting to compensate for injuries or disabilities. It could be argued that the first time a stick was used as a crutch, the field of AT was born. Assistive technology began to gain momentum during war time with soldiers returning from battle with physical injuries and other impairments that required tools to help them compensate (Bryant & Bryant, 2003). Since then, many different types of tools have been developed to help people communicate, read, make their homes more accessible, travel, and so on. There will always be a need for AT to help people with

DOI: 10.4018/978-1-4666-5015-2.ch007

disabilities. However, as technology continues to evolve, and devices, such as e-readers and tablets continue to permeate everyday life, many technologies that were once solely available as AT are now commonly available as "accessible technology." Assistive technology is typically associated with individual use, whereas this new trend of accessible technology provides greater access to a wide range of people. This trend is most evident with technology that can be used to help those with visual and hearing impairments.

For example, prior to the proliferation of e-mail and text messaging, people with hearing impairments relied heavily on AT. Typical communication modes included sign language, text telephones (TTY), and relay services. Sign language creates a challenge for many in that it requires the learning of a new language, and so, very few people who do not have hearing impairments, are able to sign. It is estimated that between 100,000 and 500,000 Americans use sign language, and this predominately includes those who are deaf, hearing children of deaf parents, and fluent deaf signers (Wilcox & Peyton, 1999). Given this, it could be argued that sign language works very well for a small percentage of the population, but in terms of widespread use, it unfortunately falls short.

Consider next the TTY device, which connects to a telephone and allows the person who is hearing impaired to either type a message or view a message on a screen. This technology works well if both parties have a TTY device. However, when communicating with someone that does not have such a device, a relay service must be used. In such an instance, both parties would call the relay number, the caller with the TTY device would type a message, a relay operator would read the message to the caller without the device, this caller would then speak a message to the relay operator, who would then type the message to the other caller's TTY device. Although this device works well, it adds an extra step to the communication process, and in regard to the relay service, third-party involvement (i.e., an operator).

## E-Mail, Instant Messaging, and Text Messaging

With e-mail, instant messaging, and text messaging now part of everyday life, such complexities have been almost eliminated. People with hearing impairments now have immediate access to forms of communication that connect them more easily. Instead of purchasing a special device for their phone or communicating through a relay service, these individuals now have many of the same communication options as everyone else. To use e-mail, for example, a person only needs a computer and an Internet connection, and to use text messaging, a person only needs a smartphone with a text or data plan. Furthermore, since text messaging has become one of the most popular ways in which to communicate, smartphones with text plans are now affordable, readily available, and easy for almost anyone to use, including those with hearing impairments (Madar, 2012).

Although statistical data is not widely available on how accessible technology, such as e-mail, instant messaging, and text messaging have affected the use of certain traditional AT, the use of TTY, for instance, is now often referred to and viewed as a "legacy" device. This could be argued as the first example of how accessible technology has had a profound effect on providing greater access to people with disabilities. The rest of this chapter discusses this line of thinking, presenting accessible technologies that have or are quickly becoming part of the mainstream and every day, but which have already shown, or have the potential to be incredibly helpful to those with disabilities; in particular, those who have visual and hearing impairments. In doing so, this chapter is presented in terms of the three biggest areas of technological change in recent years: mobile, personal computer (PC), and cloud computing.

## ACCESSIBLE TECHNOLOGY

### Mobile Computing

It could be argued that the biggest area of recent technological advancement has been in the area of mobile computing. These devices, to include smartphones, e-readers, and tablets, along with their respective applications (apps), are so pervasive, affordable, and easy to obtain, that most everyone has access to at least one of these types of devices (Burgess, 2012). Today, there are a multitude of apps available that can be easily used to read, write, and access content. Furthermore, the method of delivery on mobile devices makes such apps very easy to obtain. Although apps created for mobile devices are often fairly limited in scope when compared to their PC software counterparts, they are at the same time also simpler to create and thus less expensive for consumers (Burgess, 2012). The benefit of these low cost apps for people with disabilities cannot be overstated, in that these apps (and even PC-based software) are a fraction of the cost of traditional AT (e.g., TTY devices). This is particularly the case with regard to reading and writing related apps and software (Hamilton, 2012).

In fact, one of the biggest areas of improvement has been in helping those with visual impairments. The integration of cameras, for example, on mobile devices has created a whole world of possibilities for helping people who are visually impaired. In that, it has allowed for the creation of apps in which the camera feature can be used to zoom in on objects or text to make things large enough to be seen. Apps are now also available that can help identify the denomination of US currency, for example. And perhaps the biggest advancement, and one that continues to improve with regard to camera technology, are apps which can be used to take a photo of text, and using optical character recognition (OCR), read the converted text aloud. Such apps can help those who are visually impaired have better access to a wide variety of resources, from restaurant menus, to signs, to text found in newspapers and books. Furthermore, many of these apps can be purchased for less than $20 USD. This is a stark contrast from traditional AT reading machines that not long ago would have easily cost thousands of dollars, such as the Kurzweil Reading Machine®.

### Reading Machines

The Kurzweil Reading Machine® was created in the 1970s by Ray Kurzweil in conjunction with the National Federation for the Blind. This machine quickly became popular because it had the capability to help people with many different types of disabilities access text. Without question, accessing printed text can be a challenge for many. For instance, those with physical disabilities may have difficulty turning pages in books; those with visual impairments might have difficulty seeing text; whereas those with learning disabilities might struggle with the decoding and processing of such text. And so the Kurzweil Reading Machine® was seen by many as a technological wonder. More importantly, what should be taken away from this discussion is that the Kurzweil Reading Machine® helps illustrate the importance of reading to those with visual impairments, and the need for AT dating back 40 years.

Regrettably, the original Kurzweil Reading Machine® was not very practical as it was the size of a small dishwasher, had a very robotic sounding voice, and cost $50,000 (Burton, 2006). As a result of the high cost, this technology was only accessible to organizations and individuals who could afford it. For example, the first person to purchase one of these machines was the American singer and song-writer, Stevie Wonder, who loved the opportunity to have access to printed material (Burton, 2006).

The subsequent evolution of reading machines showed to be more practical, in the form of software that could be run on most PCs and basically worked on the premise of paper-based text that was scanned into the computer. This brought the cost down considerably as compared to the early days of the Kurzweil Reading Machine®, but reading software was still expensive and the scanning method of getting the printed text into a digital format was difficult (Hodapp & Rachow, 2010). Consequently, the complex process coupled with high costs meant that software for reading text aloud was still very much a traditional AT, used primarily by people with disabilities, who had access or who could afford such software. This trend continued until recently, with the advent of the eReader and similar mobile devices.

## E-Readers and Tablets

E-readers allow a user to download books and other text for immediate access. These devices typically weigh less than traditional hardcover books, and at the time of this writing, the most popular e-readers (e.g., NOOK®, Kindle®) can store several hundred books. That is, the storage capability and portability benefits of these devices have made them instantly popular by those with and without disabilities. It could be said that e-readers have done for the print industry what MP3 players have done for the music industry.

E-readers have allowed people to access hundreds of books and other digital text resources at any time and from anywhere in a small and easily portable device. Tablets, such as the iPad® also have this capability, increasing the desire for digital text for people who have such devices. Development in such technology as a result of widespread popularity and use was a big breakthrough for people with disabilities. Because people are reading more and more on these devices, publishers are creating more and more printed material that is able to be purchased in a digital format. Thus, this printed material is readily available to people with disabilities, removing one of the barriers to those with visual impairments.

Manufactures of e-readers have shown an understanding for those with visual impairments. Consequently, manufactures have added some important features to these reading devices making them more accessible. First, there is the capability to adjust the size of text on the screen. One of the perks of digital text is that it can be manipulated to do just about anything, thus it is very easy to customize font size and other preferences for each individual user. Every eReader and tablet has a feature that will easily and instantaneously change the size of text to a size that can be easily viewed by the individual. The other area that has seen potential for access is having text read aloud. Many e-readers as well as tablets have a text-to-speech built-in feature (Lamb, 2010). Although these reading capabilities don't necessarily have the adjustability or customization options that are available in traditional AT, they are in fact standard features found in current technology, which shows how far reading technology, such as e-readers and tablets have come.

Another reason for the proliferation of read aloud technology now commonly found in e-readers and tablets is that it is more acceptable than ever for people to listen to text. Audio books are very popular and one of the tenants of Universal Design for Learning is in providing multiple means of representation of materials (Rose & Meyer, 2002). This concept basically allows people to choose how to best access text based on their strengths. For example, digital text in written form is best suited for those who are partial to visual modality that prefer reading and are not impaired to do so; whereas those who can more easily process in an auditory modality, or do have visual impairments, can listen to the spoken text on their devices (Rose & Meyer, 2002).

Speech recognition is another area that has seen considerable development in recent years, due to the desire for hands free texting. When speech recognition became first available, it required lots of training on the part of user. That is, the user would say one word at a time to the software or device, in order for the technology to recognize the word in the future, and even then, it was not very accurate. Advancements in technology, however, have taken speech recognition to the point where it has become very reliable and affordable. Unlike the costs associated with early versions of speech recognition technology, the best software at the time of this writing, for example, can be obtained for approximately $200 USD.

This type of capability has been a staple in traditional AT for people with physical disabilities. As previously noted, there has been a movement that has made speech recognition more readily available as a result of the text messaging boom. A big concern associated with text messaging is texting while driving. One solution has been to provide options for hands free texting, which includes speech recognition. The latest smartphone and tablet technology now commonly includes speech recognition, which is not only built-in, but also very accurate (Knight, 2012). The most recent Apple® mobile devices, for instance, include a microphone button directly on the keyboard, which activates speech recognition when pressed. The feature allows users to speak and compose texts, e-mails, and documents (Knight, 2012). And because it is on the main keyboard, it is pervasive and can be used within any app that runs on mobile devices. This is great, considering that historically, features found in one app or software product typically couldn't be shared in another.

Although this type of speech recognition on mobile devices is accurate, it does work slightly differently, than say, its PC software counterpart. At the time of this writing, because of the way mobile devices work, they are not yet powerful enough to run speech recognition themselves. So the user has to be connected to the Internet and the speech recognition must be activated. In addition, the speech must be recorded and sent to the appropriate online server for processing. On the positive side, this is speaker independent so no training is required and almost anyone can use it. On the negative side, text doesn't show up as dictated, so effective use requires speaking in short chunks, and reviewing the text, before moving on to the next sentence or chunk of information. Because this has become a mainstream feature found in many mobile devices, it is easy for people with disabilities to get access. The popularity of mobile devices also helps promote further research and development, which will undoubtedly help evolve speech recognition.

Mobile speech recognition apps are also widely available to run in conjunction with most standard computers today in order to compose documents. Because of the capabilities of cloud computing (to be discussed later in this chapter), a user can open a document in Google Doc™ on their computer and their mobile device at the same time, then using speech recognition on their smartphone or device, see what is spoken appear in the document. This is possible because the user is essentially collaborating on a document with him or herself. Also, using Google Chrome™, users can download a free extension called VoiceNote®, which acts much the same way as Apple's® speech recognition, thus giving users microphone free access to speech recognition on their computers.

All in all, accessible technology, such as e-readers and tablets, help illustrate how far things have evolved from the early days of the Kurzweil Reading Machine®. Technology that at one time would have only been available as traditional AT, is now readily available and accessible by almost everyone.

## PC Computing

### Software

Obviously, all this has been very beneficial to people with disabilities for several reasons, and with more and more digital materials becoming available every day, access to digital content by people with disabilities is anticipated to only grow. It is important to point out, however, that the availability of digital text is not restricted to e-readers and similar devices. That is, it is not just handheld devices that are adopting built-in reading technology, but instead text-to-speech has been a common staple found in many software applications for years now, that can be easily run on most PCs. However, the proliferation of e-readers and tablets has sparked an explosive interest in text-to-speech software and features.

For example, users can now download free software, such as Blio® and NOOK Study®, which provide access to purchased books in a digital form. These applications provide advanced features, such as text-to-speech that reads text aloud. Another software application is Read&Write® for Google Docs™. It is a Chrome™ browser extension that can be used with PCs, Macs®, or Chromebooks™. Read&Write® for Google Docs™ adds additional features to Google Docs™, making documents more accessible. Namely, it can read text aloud and does so while highlighting text. In doing so, the software provides reading access to anything found in Google Docs™. In addition, Google Docs™ itself also has a built-in feature that allows the user to upload any file that has text, including PDFs and Word® documents. What is most beneficial is that users can also upload images and have those images converted to text when applicable.

Take for example the case when a person with a visual impairment wants access to reading material, but only has the material in paper form, and a digital version is not available for download. Barring legal implications, such as copyright, the document could be scanned and uploaded to Google Docs™. There the scanned image can be converted to text. And using the Chrome™ browser extension of Read&Write® for Google Docs®, the text can be read aloud to the individual. This example helps illustrate the degree of access that people with disabilities now have at their disposal with regard to accessible technology. It is important to note that this type of software in itself may not provide the needed level of access for those with severe disabilities. However, for those with mild, high incidence learning, or reading disabilities, such accessible technology may be more than adequate.

## Operating Systems

The accessible technology trend can also be found with regard to operating systems (OS). For example, Microsoft® and Apple® have recognized, for some time now, the need to provide OS accessibility for people with disabilities. On PCs running Windows®, for instance, Microsoft® offers a magnifier with color contrast changes for people with visual impairments, enabling these individuals to better see what they are working on (Microsoft Accessibility, 2012). Microsoft® also offers a narrator which can read text aloud for people who are visually impaired. For people with disabilities who struggle with physical access, Microsoft® provides both an onscreen keyboard as well as speech recognition software throughout their OS (Microsoft Accessibility, 2012). Apple's Mac OS® provides similar tools for access including screen and cursor magnification, voice-over-screen reading, and text-to-speech software. Apple®, however, does not offer an onscreen keyboard as part of their OS.

It is important to point out that these features have greatly improved with each new release of Windows® and the Mac OS®. For many, however, such capabilities are not a complete substitute for traditional AT, and many, for instance, continue to use commercial magnifiers that physically overlay on monitors, or specialized, third-party speech recognition software. This is all well and good. However, one of the nice aspects of these built-in features is that people who use or need access to such capabilities, can do so from any computer that runs these OS, to include public computers found in libraries and other public places. These features also benefit those who use traditional AT, in the sense that if they do not have access to their preferred software or devices, they may still be able to access similar features from any computer running these OS. In addition, such capabilities may also provide a considerable cost savings as alternative accessibility technology to traditional, and more costly AT. This is particularly important to those who may not otherwise have access to such technology as a result of socioeconomic circumstance.

### Cloud Computing

Finally, attention is turned to the area of cloud computing, where growth is expected in the future with regard to accessible technology, helping those with disabilities. The "Cloud" has started to become a crucial part of the computing experience for many users, allowing the use of software that once was restricted to the computers in which they were installed (e.g., Microsoft Office®) as well as allowing users to access, edit, and share documents from almost anywhere (e.g., PCs, mobile devices) and anytime. The Cloud has allowed individuals to become more mobile in everyday computing, and consequently, it is argued in this chapter that cloud computing is the next evolutionary step in accessible technology that may show great promise in helping those with disabilities.

Cloud computing is anticipated to help those with disabilities in two ways. First, software and mobile app developers are now producing products that are accessible via the Cloud. Several publishers of reading and writing AT, for instance, have already created products in which text and other content can be saved in the Cloud and accessed on any computer with Internet access. Kurzweil®, for instance, has a cloud-based system called Firefly®, which users can access by logging in from any computer or mobile device. Although Firefly® is still limited, it does provide core aspects of being able to read and highlight text. While it doesn't have all of the features of the more well known Kurzweil 3000®, Cambium Learning™ is continuing to improve the product by adding capabilities with each release. Another example is that of Crick Software™, which has produced a cloud-based application for writing called Write Online®. With this product, students who need help through tools, such as word prediction or word bars can log into the system from any computer with Internet access and use these features. This makes it much easier for students to work on writing assignments both at school and at home, and is a great example of how the Cloud can be used to access technology from anywhere.

The second way in which cloud computing is anticipated to help those with disabilities is the concept that a user can log into a cloud-based system and have their computer adapt to their needs or preferences as opposed to what has been traditionally the other way around. There is a project currently underway that is developing this concept called the Global Public Inclusive Infrastructure (GPII). The GPII does not aim to create new AT, but instead an infrastructure for making their development, identification, delivery, and use easier, less expensive, and more effective (GPII, 2011). The GPII aims to create an automatic personalization of user interfaces, basically allowing the system to adapt to the user instead of the other way around (GPII, 2011). In using the GPII, users would have access to their desired AT from any computer, via the Cloud, making everything more accessible.

## CONCLUSION

The field of AT has come a long way from the days in which such technology was available to a limited few. Through accessible technology, those with disabilities have access to technology and capabilities that are now part of the everyday. The explosive growth and popularity of mobile devices, for example, has made access to digital text easier for those with visual impairments. Apps found on mobile devices are often simple to use, but most importantly, affordable as compared to traditional AT.

Given their widespread popularity, it is anticipated that such emerging accessible technology will continue in a multitude of mediums, to include cloud-based computing, under initiatives such as the GPII, that are anticipated to eventually allow people to configure computers to their needs and preferences, as well as in the remote access of online applications. All of these technological advancements are promising, having positive and far reaching implications for people with disabilities.

Finally, it is important to end this chapter on the note that while the accessible technology discussed can be considered a huge step forward towards helping those with disabilities, it is essential to understand that this technology is not a replacement for traditional AT. That is, while accessible technology can benefit many people with disabilities, there are still those that will require technology designed specifically for *their* special needs. For instance, the accessible technology presented in this chapter may help those with mild disabilities or high incidence disabilities, such as mild visual impairment or dyslexia. People with more moderate, severe, or multiple disabilities, for instance, may still require traditional AT that is specifically tailored for their special needs. It must, therefore, be made very clear that although there is a wealth of accessible technology now available, when working with people with disabilities, it is vital that each individual is evaluated using evidence-based practices, so that their needs are being properly met; whether through more common place accessible technology, or through more specialized, traditional AT.

## REFERENCES


Bryant, D. P., & Bryant, B. R. (2003). *Assistive technology for people with disabilities*. Boston: Allyn and Bacon.

Burgess, B. (2012). A new way to think about assistive technology. *The bookshare blog*. Retrieved from http://blog.bookshare.org/2012/03/08/a-new-way-to-think-about-assistive-technology/

Burton, D. (2006). Reading by hand: A review of the Kurzweil-national federation of the blind reader. *Access World*. Retrieved from http://www.afb.org/afbpress/pub.asp?DocID=aw070604

GPII. (2011). *Raising the floor*. Retrieved from http://www.gpii.net

Hamilton, P. (2012). Mobile devices as powerful assistive technology for all. *Supporting universal access and universal design for learning*. Retrieved from http://paulhami.edublogs.org/2012/05/17/mobile-devices-as-powerful-assistive-technology-for-all/

Hodapp, J. B., & Rachow, C. (2010). Impact of text-to-speech software on access to print: A longitudinal study. In S. Seok, E. L. Meyen, & B. DaCosta (Eds.), *Human cognition and assistive technology: Design, accessibility, and transdisciplinary perspectives* (pp. 199–219). Hershey, PA: IGI Global. doi:10.4018/978-1-61520-817-3.ch014

Knight, W. (2012). Where speech recognition is going. *MIT Technology Review*. Retrieved from http://www.technologyreview.com/news/427793/where-speech-recognition-is-going/

Lamb, P. (2010). Hidden opportunity: Mobile reading solutions for the blind. *Educational technology debate exploring ICT and learning in developing countries*. Retrieved from https://edutechdebate.org/assistive-technology/mobile-reading-solutions-for-the-blind/

Madar, K. (2012). Text messaging provide deaf with new means of communication. *The Daily Times*. Retrieved from http://www.daily-times.com/ci_20245436/text-messages-provide-deaf-new-means-communication

Microsoft Accessibility. (2012). *Microsoft accessibility*. Retrieved from http://www.microsoft.com/enable/products/windows7/

Rose, D. H., & Meyer, A. (2002). *Teaching every student in the digital age: Universal design for learning*. Alexandria, VA: ASCD.

(1988). Technology-Related Assistance for Individuals with Disabilities Act of 1988 (Tech Act). *Public Law*, 100–407.

Wilcox, S., & Peyton, J. K. (1999). American sign language as a foreign language. *ERIC Clearinghouse on Language and Linguistics Digest* (EDO-FL-89-01). (ERIC Document Reproduction Service No. ED309651).

## KEY TERMS AND DEFINITIONS

**Application:** Software developed for and run on mobile devices such as smartphones and tablets. These applications are also typically referred to as "apps."

**Assistive Technology (AT):** Any item, piece of equipment or product system whether acquired commercially off the shelf, modified or customized that is used to increase, maintain or improve the functional capabilities of people with disabilities (Tech Act, 1988).

**E-Reader:** Mobile device, such as the NOOK® or Kindle® that allows the user to download and read digital text.

**Mobile Device:** A device such as a smartphone, tablet, or eReader that gives the user computing power and Internet access while being easily portable.

**Optical Character Recognition (OCR):** The process of software recognizing text within an image. This can be done on either JPEGs or PDFs. This process allows text in these formats to be read aloud by computer software.

**Relay Service:** A service that allows TTY and non-TTY users to communicate with each other. Participants will call a relay service where an operator will read what the TTY user types to the non-TTY user and will type what the non-TTY user says to the TTY user.

**Screen Magnifier:** A software tool that increases the size of objects and text on a computer screen to a size that can be seen by a user with a visual impairment.

**Speech Recognition:** Software that turns spoken words into text.

**Text Telephone (TTY):** A home phone with a text typing and display option used primarily by the deaf community. This device connects to a home phone and allows users to type messages to other TTY users, or phone users through a relay service.

# Chapter 8
# A Step toward Assistive Technology Evidence-Based Practices:
## Latent Dimensions of Information and Communication Technology

**Boaventura DaCosta**
*Solers Research Group, USA*

**Soohnwa Seok**
*Korea University, South Korea*

## ABSTRACT

*In an attempt to meet the need for validation research that contributes to Assistive Technology (AT) evidence-based practices, this chapter presents the findings of a study aimed to identify latent dimensions of Information and Communication Technology (ICT) that can serve as the basis for the eventual development of a standardized instrument for ICT assessment and selection in the context of AT. The ICT preferences and practices of 1,258 postsecondary students across 7 major universities were examined. A confirmatory factor analysis within the framework of structure equation modeling revealed the 5 latent dimensions: communicating, socializing, downloading and sharing, gaming, and learning. These dimensions examined in the context of age, gender, and income, further reveal that these demographics, as sole determinants of ICT usage, are not supported. Noteworthy findings were also found with regard to participant's preferences for ICT, to include a tendency to text over all other technologies surveyed.*

DOI: 10.4018/978-1-4666-5015-2.ch008

## INTRODUCTION

The amount of information and communication technology (ICT) available today is astounding. Take smartphone ownership alone, which by 2013 is forecasted to surpass PCs as the most common way in which people will access online content (Whitney, 2011). In fact, it has been predicted that the number of smartphones and similar types of devices will surpass 1.82 billion, with 6.5 billion mobile connections projected by 2014 (Whitney, 2011). Explosive growth such as this has in part helped fuel a number of research interests, to include ICT preferences and practices, as well as identifying underlying factors that may be used in the proper selection of ICT (e.g., Nasah, DaCosta, Kinsell, & Seok, 2010). These are topics of particular importance, especially to those in special education who are involved in the evaluation and selection of assistive technology (AT). Unfortunately, research on the subject is inconclusive if not lacking, both generally and with regard to ICT in the context of AT.

### Information and Communication Technology and Young People

By and large, much of what can be found on ICT is based on anecdotal information, focused on today's young people. That is, those individuals considered to have been "born digital" (Palfrey & Gasser, 2008) into the late twentieth and early twenty-first centuries. Known by a number of monikers – the Millennial Generation (Howe & Strauss, 2000), the Net Generation (Tapscott, 1998), the Technological Generation (Monereo, 2004), Generation M (Roberts, Foehr, & Rideout, 2005), the Google Generation (Rowlands et al., 2008), and Digital Natives (Prensky, 2001a) – these young people have, undeniably, been the most investigated, marketed to, and captivating age bracket to date (Cone Inc., 2006). In fact, there is no refuting that their "contagious" nature (Hoover, 2009) has turned them into a lucrative industry. Books and countless articles have been written about them, and the U.S. television news magazine, 60 Minutes, broadcast a story entitled, The Age of the Millennials, depicting these young adults as ill-prepared for a demanding workplace. Fortune 500 companies, such as Merrill Lynch and Ernst & Young, have even gone as far as to hire consultants to help them better understand how to deal with this group of up-and-coming workers (Safer, 2007).

Yet, even with everything that has been published about these young people since the late twentieth century, our understanding of these youth is at best, muddled (Hoover, 2009). This lack of clarity partly stems from the fact that the wealth of commentary on the topic is mostly founded on opinions and subjective evidence, with scarce empirical findings to support the suppositions made about these individuals (StudentPOLL, 2010). Take, for example, the strongly argued and commonly cited theories of Howe and Strauss (2000). As commonsensical as their theories appear to be, some argue that their suppositions are founded on problematic research. As Hoover explains, the theories put forth by Howe and Strauss "were based on a hodgepodge of anecdotes, statistics, and pop-culture references, as well as on surveys of teachers and about 600 high-school seniors in Fairfax County, Va., which in 2007 became the first county in the nation to have a median household income of more than $100,000, about twice the national average" (¶ 9).

Also, take for example the equally commonly cited theories proposed by Prensky (2001a, 2001b), a proponent of game-based learning, who has suggested that today's students have spent their lives so immersed in a digital culture that it has fundamentally changed the way in which they process information. Although this is a compelling argument embraced by many, others, such as Pivec and Pivec (2008), have concluded that the majority of Prensky's publications are "mainly opinion papers, not peer-reviewed studies, and offer very little empirical research to support the claims" (p. 5). Some have even gone so far as to suggest that the digital native label is a "misleading and deceptive title that dissuades educators from looking at the intricacies of how individuals engage digital media" (Guo, Dobson, & Petrina, 2008, p. 237).

This overabundance of anecdotal information has made it difficult for educators, policy-makers, practitioners, and researchers alike to separate reality from conjecture, particularly as it applies to the suppositions made about young people and their propensity and application of ICT. To make matters worse, the empirical evidence that does exist is as varied as the opinions mentioned above. While some have found that young people make extensive use of personal technology and software for their private needs, intermingling such technologies with institutional or course tools and resources (e.g., Conole, Laat, Dillon, & Darby, 2006), others have found that young people make limited recreational use of social networking websites and have little knowledge about authoring tools, virtual worlds, web publishing, and other social technologies (e.g., Margaryan & Littlejohn, 2008). In fact, there is little research to suggest that young people want more technology integration in the educational setting (McWilliam, 2002), but instead are more interested in using technology for social networking and personal reasons (Keen, 2007).

Conflicting research findings, coupled with the wealth of largely opinionated rhetoric, has led some to caution that our understanding of young people's use of technology is anything but clear (Bennett, Maton, & Kervin, 2008), and that while it is important to remain mindful of the changing technological needs of young people, it is critical to avoid today's commonly used monikers and accompanying suppositions and instead focus on bettering our understanding of how technology is actually being used in contemporary society (Selwyn, 2009).

## Information and Communication Technology as Assistive Technology

This caution by Selwyn (2009) is important, particularly when discussing ICT in the context of AT, in that an excessively high rate of abandonment has been reported (Ebner, 2004; Johnston & Evans, 2005; Scherer & Craddock, 2002). There are numerous reasons cited for the abandonment of AT. Beigel (2000), for instance, has cited the lack of an appropriate match between the user and AT before purchase, and Betsy and Hongxin (1993) have pointed to the insufficient consideration of the user's preferences for and opinions about the AT selection choice.

Irrespective of the reasons, it has been argued that issues such as these could be resolved through proper evaluation of needs and functionalities prior to and during the use of AT. Take Hutinger (1999), for example, who has argued that an appropriate assessment along with individualized programming is one of the conditions needed in order to establish a comprehensive technological program for children with disabilities. Hutinger concludes that by conducting a proper evaluation, basing the assessment and selection of AT on the use of empirically supported findings (Margolis & Goodman, 1999; Graham & Warnie, 2012), the pitfalls common when technology is the primary factor driving selection, can be mitigated.

Unfortunately, in much the same way that there is a lack of clarity with regard to young people's use of technology from a general standpoint, the same can be argued with regard to the quality of AT, to include assessment (Judge, 2002), validation and reliability studies, standards, and guidelines (Seok, 2007a, 2007b). In other words, there is a lack of research on validation study focused on key factors and items, founded on sound empirical study, leading to empirically-based practices, which can be used to properly assess AT for the purposes of selection. Karmarkar et al. (2012), argues that this kind of research would help improve the quality of AT.

## The Purpose of this Chapter

In an attempt to meet the need for validation research, this chapter presents the findings of a study aimed to identify latent dimension of ICT. The present study is considered a *first step* toward the development of a standardized instrument that may be used in ICT assessment and selection that can be conducted in the context of AT.

As a result, the present study examined students' preferences for and the frequency with which they communicate, socialize, download and share content, play games, and learn online. Factors that were derived during a confirmatory factor analysis (CFA) within the framework of structure equation modeling (SEM) in the present study, that in addition to the need for validation research, stems from the need for empirical study investigating dimensions affecting ICT implementation in general settings (Bennett, Maton, & Kervin, 2008; Drent & Meelissen, 2008; Nasah et al., 2010). In addition, these factors were examined in the context of age, gender, and income, as it has been suggested that these may play a significant role in explaining why individuals use ICT to varying degrees (Kennedy, Krause, Judd, Churchward, & Gray, 2008; Kvavik, Caruso, & Morgan, 2004; Livingstone & Bober, 2004; see Selwyn, 2009).

This was accomplished by using an updated version of an index used by Nasah et al. (2010) to measure the frequency with which individuals use ICT in their daily lives and the level of importance they attach to these technologies (Henderson & Hirumi, 2005, as cited in Norman, 2008). The index was updated to reflect technologies that have gained popularity in recent years; a limitation of the index cited by Nasah et al.

South Korean postsecondary students were selected because of the country's high broadband penetration rate, as substantiated by a 2008 study, which found that 95% of households had a high-speed Internet connection (Anderson, 2009), thus providing a well-suited population from which to draw. These students were also chosen as a result of the recommendation put forth by Nasah et al. (2010), that their original questionnaire undergo additional reliability analysis with a more diverse sample.

# MATERIALS AND METHODS

## Participants

The present study was carried out in 2011 at seven major universities in the area surrounding Seoul, South Korea. The universities were traditional, academically-based institutions. Of the 1,400 post-secondary students who were randomly solicited for inclusion, 1,258 freely chose to participate.

The majority of the students were 19 to 29 years of age (86.6%, $n$ = 1,089), followed a distant second and third by those who reported age ranges of 30 to 39 (4%, $n$ = 50) and those exactly 18 years old (3.3%, $n$ = 41). Participants were almost equally split by gender, but in favor of females. That is, almost 51% reported being female ($n$ = 637), compared to 47% who reported being male ($n$ = 591).

The majority of households from which the students came had an annual family income of $40,000 or more, with approximately 36% of the participants reporting an annual income of $60,000 or more and almost 35% reporting an annual income of $40,000 to $59,999. Participants reported that these incomes supported 58% of households, which consisted of at least four people living in the home ($n$ = 728), followed by approximately 19% of households with five people or more ($n$ = 240), and almost 19% with three or more ($n$ = 233). Almost 45% of the participants also reported having two computers in the home ($n$ = 561), followed by approximately 32% who reported at least one ($n$ = 404). Less than 1% of the participants reported not having a computer ($n$ = 11) in the home at all.

With regard to academics, most of the participants reported their primary area of study was in education (22.9%, $n = 288$), followed by business (12.5%, $n = 157$) and medical and health services (7.9%, $n = 100$). Approximately 13% responded that their primary area of study was "other" ($n = 161$). Participant demographics are shown in Table 1.

## Materials

A 54-item questionnaire was developed to measure the frequency with which participants used ICT in their daily lives and the level of importance they attach to these technologies. The questionnaire was based on a 50-item digital propensity index used by Nasah et al. (2010) to measure how often people use various forms of communication technology in their everyday lives (Henderson & Hirumi, 2005, as cited in Norman, 2008). The questionnaire was augmented from the original index to include relevant and timely technology not available at the time the index had been created, such as the use of social networking websites. It was also expanded to include four additional items addressing the digital native propositions put forth by Prensky (2001a, 2001b).

Overall, the questionnaire investigated several ICTs, to include cell and smartphones; texting and two-way instant messaging; chat rooms; email; blogs; personal and social networking websites; single- and multiplayer- video games; online shopping and rating systems; and downloading and sharing, to include the download, streaming, and sharing of images, audio, and video.

The questionnaire was comprised of two parts. The first 48 items measured frequency and level of importance. The remaining 6 items were demographic in nature. With regard to the items measuring frequency and level of importance, responses were designed to the items in question. For example, participants chose from "not at all (never)," "1-5 times per day," "6-10 times per day," "11-15 times per day," or "more than 15 times per day" when asked the questions, "I use a cell or smartphone to send and receive calls" and "I communicate with others by texting." However, participants chose from the responses "not at all (never)," "weekly," "2-3 days per week," "daily," or "more than 3 times daily" when asked, "I communicate with others using email," "I communicate with others using instant messaging (IM)," "I communicate with others using chat rooms," "I communicate with others through social networking websites (e.g., My Space™, Facebook™, Twitter™)," "I update my website or personal web space (e.g., My Space™, Facebook™, Twitter™)," "I socialize with others online using email, instant messaging (IM), and/or chat rooms," and "I socialize with others online using social networking websites (e.g., My Space™, Facebook™, Twitter™)."

With regard to demographics, participants were asked their age, gender, number of people and computers in the home, family's annual income, and primary area of study (i.e., college major). Again, responses were designed to the item in question. For example, when asked, "I have the following number of computers in my home," participants chose from "none at all," "1," "2," "3," or "4 or more;" whereas when asked, "my family's annual gross income is," participants choose from "$0-19,999," "$20,000-39,999," "$40,000-59,999," "$60,000-99,999," or "$100,000 and over." The instrument was presented in Korean. All responses were self-reported.

## Procedure

Two hundred paper-based copies of the questionnaire were distributed to each of the seven universities. Ten undergraduate students were solicited and assigned to one or more of the universities and respective classrooms to administer the paper-and-pencil questionnaire to a sampling of students. Participants were instructed on the questionnaire to "give the answer that truly applies to you and not what you would like to be true, or what you

*Table 1. Participant demographics*

| Demographic | N | Levels | Frequency | Percent | Median Response |
|---|---|---|---|---|---|
| Respondent Age | 1,250 | 70 and over | 12 | 1.0 | 19-29 |
| | | 60-69 | 9 | .7 | |
| | | 50-59 | 28 | 2.2 | |
| | | 40-49 | 21 | 1.7 | |
| | | 30-39 | 50 | 4.0 | |
| | | 19-29 | 1,089 | 86.6 | |
| | | 18 | 41 | 3.3 | |
| | | Missing Responses | 8 | .6 | |
| Respondent Gender | 1,241 | Male | 591 | 47.0 | Female |
| | | Female | 637 | 50.6 | |
| | | Transgender | 13 | 1.0 | |
| | | Missing Response | 17 | 1.4 | |
| Number of Computers in the Home | 1,236 | None | 11 | .9 | 4 or more |
| | | 1 | 404 | 32.1 | |
| | | 2 | 561 | 44.6 | |
| | | 3 | 197 | 15.7 | |
| | | 4 or more | 63 | 5.0 | |
| | | Missing Response | 22 | 1.7 | |
| Number of People in the Home | 1,245 | 1 | 13 | 1.0 | 4 or more |
| | | 2 | 31 | 2.5 | |
| | | 3 | 233 | 18.5 | |
| | | 4 | 728 | 57.9 | |
| | | 5 or more | 240 | 19.1 | |
| | | Missing Response | 13 | 1.0 | |
| Family Annual Income | 1,223 | $0-$19,999 | 89 | 7.1 | $40,000- $59,999 |
| | | $20,000-$39,999 | 241 | 19.2 | |
| | | $40,000-$59,999 | 439 | 34.9 | |
| | | $60,000 and over | 454 | 36.1 | |
| | | Missing Response | 35 | 2.8 | |
| Primary Area of Study | 1,248 | Agriculture | 11 | .9 | Education |
| | | Architecture/Drafting | 74 | 5.9 | |
| | | Biological/Biomedical | 56 | 4.5 | |
| | | Business | 157 | 12.5 | |
| | | Journalism | 30 | 2.4 | |
| | | Computer Sciences/IT | 46 | 3.7 | |
| | | Culinary/Personal | 42 | 3.3 | |
| | | Education | 288 | 22.9 | |
| | | Engineering | 95 | 7.6 | |
| | | Legal | 44 | 3.5 | |
| | | Liberal Arts/Humanities | 9 | .7 | |
| | | Mechanic/Repair Tech | 17 | 1.4 | |
| | | Medical and Health | 100 | 7.9 | |
| | | Military | 1 | .1 | |
| | | Physical Science | 6 | .5 | |
| | | Political Science | 21 | 1.7 | |
| | | Psychology | 10 | .8 | |
| | | Transportation | 6 | .5 | |
| | | Visual/Performing Arts | 74 | 5.9 | |
| | | Other | 161 | 12.8 | |
| | | Missing Response | 10 | .8 | |

think others want to hear" and to "think about each statement by itself and indicate how true it is" and "not be influenced by your answers to other statements." Answers were recorded directly on the questionnaire by selecting the item's corresponding checkbox or by writing in the designated space. Items could be answered in any order or could be skipped altogether. Participants could withdraw from the study at any time. Permission to conduct the study was acquired from officials in the university system, and students consented to participate prior to receiving the questionnaire. Participants were 18 years of age or older, were not paid for their involvement, and were treated in accordance with the American Psychological Association's (APA) Ethics in Research with Human Participants (APA, 2002).

## RESULTS

For the sake of clarity, the results presented herein are organized and discussed in three parts:

1. First, latent factors of ICT are identified and questionnaire items are validated;
2. The influence of age, family income, and gender is discussed; and finally,
3. Participants' preferences and practices are presented.

First, in order to identify latent dimensions of ICT and to validate the items on the questionnaire, a statistical approach comprised of a CFA within the framework of SEM was selected. This approach was chosen because it is considered one of the most rigorous methodological approaches to testing the validity of factorial structures (Byrne, 2001, 2010) in the reduction of observable variables into a subset of latent variables through examination of covariation among the observed variables (Schreiber, Nora, Stage, Barlow, & King, 2006). The analysis of moment structures (AMOS) add-on module for the Statistical Package for the Social Sciences (SPSS) software application was used for its structural equation modeling, covariance structure modeling, and graphical interface capabilities.

Second, in order to investigate if age, family income, and/or gender influenced the use of ICT, items validated against the latent dimensions were correlated with these three demographic items. A statistical approach comprising a series of Spearman's Rho correlation coefficients was used to investigate age and family income, whereas a series of point-biserial correlation coefficients was used to investigate gender. The two tests were selected because of the ratio and nominal scale differences. Alpha level was set a priori at.05.

Finally, ICT preferences and practices of the participants were investigated. The inquiry was conducted and discussed through the reporting of descriptive statistics. Namely, the reporting of frequency responses for the items, comprising the first part of the questionnaire developed to measure frequency and level of importance, which were identify as the final items making up the latent dimensions of ICT.

### Identifying Latent Factors of Information and Communication Technology and Validating Items

The 48 items in the questionnaire measuring frequency and level of importance were logically divided into the seven conceptual factors – communicating, socializing, self-publicizing, downloading and sharing, gaming, learning, and digital native propositions – to stimulate and organize comprehensive item development. The organization was based on the work of Norman (2008), Nasah et al. (2010), and a research synthesis examining latent factors of digital propensity and ICT. Two items were removed from the analysis: one was a duplicate of a demographic item, the other made reference to technology using dated terms, potentially contributing to misunderstanding and possibly skewing the item responses. Furthermore,

24 participant responses were removed from the analysis because of missing data.

In the end, 46 items and a sample total of 1,234 responses were used in the SEM analysis with the AMOS graphic approach. The items and their corresponding factors are shown in Table 2.

Since the reliability coefficients and content validity had been established through factor analysis by Norman (2008) and Nasah et al. (2010) with regard to the digital propensity index, their exploratory factor analyses was adopted for the present study; the CFA was conducted to validate items for each factor based on the covariations and correlations between observed measures and latent dimensions. To ensure valid items for each factor, the CFA was conducted using the 46 items shown in Table 2, deleting items with low loadings and a high modification index (MI). Items were deleted until the remaining items had appropriate loadings and a good MI. For instance, with respect to the communicating factor, items 2, 3, 4, 5, 6, 7, and 13 were explored by CFA, whereas items 2, 4, and 13 were deleted due to low loadings. Similarly, for the factor socializing, items 9, 10, 11, 12, 17, and 19 were explored, whereas items 17 and 19 were deleted.

On the whole, all seven factors showed statistically significant indices of fit. Each factor comprised four items, as confirmed by CFA explorations and depicted in Figure 1: communicating ($\chi^2$ = 7.82, df = 2, $p$ =.02; CFI =.993; TLI =.980; RMSEA =.049); socializing ($\chi^2$ = 1.75, df = 2, $p$ =.41; CFI = 1.00; TLI = 1.00; RMSEA =.00); self-publicizing ($\chi^2$ = 9.94, df = 2, $p$ =.01; CFI =.991; TLI =.973; RMSEA =.057); downloading and sharing ($\chi^2$ = 7.90, df = 2, $p$ =.02; CFI =.992; TLI =.975; RMSEA =.049); gaming ($\chi^2$ = 8.60, df = 2, $p$ =.01; CFI =.997; TLI =.992; RMSEA =.052); learning ($\chi^2$ = 1.51, df = 2, $p$ =.47; CFI = 1.00; TLI = 1.00; RMSEA =.00); and digital native propositions ($\chi^2$ =.50, df = 2, $p$ =.78; CFI = 1.00; TLI = 1.00; RMSEA =.00).

The hypothesized and revised models were next developed based on the CFA results. Application of the SEM indicated that the hypothesized model had a good fit of complete covariance in data (CFI =.87; TLI =.85) and was an appropriate measure of error estimation in the sample (RMSEA =.058). The hypothesized model, with value of intercorrelations between factors, is depicted in Figure 2. The revised model, in which items 12, 15, 24, and 48 were deleted because of poor loadings and indices, is depicted in Figure 3.

With regard to the correlations between factors, communicating and downloading and sharing correlated at.699, downloading and sharing and learning correlated at.675, communicating and learning correlated at.655, self-publicizing correlated with downloading and sharing at.630, communicating and socializing correlated at.544, socializing and downloading and sharing correlated at.501, and communicating correlated with self-publicizing at.482. Digital native propositions showed a very low correlation with the other six factors. These correlations are listed in Table 3.

Finally, Table 4 shows the reliability estimates for the seven factors and selected items. Overall, as demonstrated, the questionnaire was found to be reliable (24 items; $\alpha$ =.84), with the factors communicating (4 items; $\alpha$ =.71), socializing (3 items; $\alpha$ =.77), gaming (4 items; $\alpha$ =.85), and learning (4 items; $\alpha$ =.71) shown to be acceptable. However, the factors self-publicizing (2 items; $\alpha$ =.51) and digital native propositions (3 items; $\alpha$ =.58) were found to be poor, whereas the factor downloading and sharing (4 items; $\alpha$ =.68) questionable.

Given these poor reliability estimates, the self-publicizing and digital native propositions factors were removed from the model, with the latent factors underlying the set of observed ICT implementations – communicating, socializing, downloading and sharing, gaming, and learning – comprising a total of 19 items. The finalized

*Table 2. Items measuring frequency and level of importance organized by factor*

| Factor | Items |
|---|---|
| Communicating | 2. I use a cell or smartphone to send and receive calls<br>3. I communicate with others by texting*<br>4. I communicate with others using email<br>5. I communicate with others using instant messaging (IM)*<br>6. I communicate with others using chat rooms*<br>7. I communicate with others through social networking websites (e.g., My Space™, Facebook™, Twitter™)*<br>13. When I am online, I can manage the following maximum number of conversations at the same time |
| Socializing | 9. I socialize with others online using email, instant messaging (IM), and/or chat rooms*<br>10. I socialize with others online using social networking websites (e.g., My Space™, Facebook™, Twitter™)*<br>11. I initially meet or arrange meetings with new people online (e.g., using email, instant messaging (IM), chat rooms, webcam, Skype™, WebEx™, online dating websites, social networking websites)*<br>12. I meet with people I know online (e.g., using email, instant messaging (IM), chat rooms, webcam, Skype™, WebEx™, online dating websites, social networking websites)*<br>17. I make online purchases<br>19. I contribute to online evaluation systems (e.g., star rating system) after making online purchases |
| Self-Publicizing | 1. In general, I prefer speaking to other people<br>14. I read or contribute to web blogs*<br>15. I go online to learn about topics that interest me*<br>16. I search online for information on products, entertainment, and personal reasons*<br>18. I review online evaluation systems (e.g., star rating system) before making online purchases<br>24. I share ideas, documents, information, and/or knowledge online*<br>25. I exchange jokes/humor using email, by texting, or the Internet<br>45. I prefer to be online on a regular basis through my mobile device, computer, or other Internet-ready device |
| Downloading and Sharing | 8. I update my web site or personal web space (e.g., My Space™, Facebook™, Twitter™)<br>20. I download music files from the Internet*<br>21. I download/view videos from the Internet (e.g., YouTube™)*<br>22. I download/view movies from the Internet (e.g., Netflix™, Hulu™)*<br>23. I share images/pictures online* |
| Gaming | 26. I play video games (can be any digital-based game)*<br>27. I play 1-2 player video games*<br>28. I play games requiring more than 2 players*<br>29. I participate in group games (e.g., massively multiplayer online role-playing games [MMORPGs])<br>30. I use handheld game devices (e.g., Nintendo DS®)<br>31. When playing video games, I customize (mod) the environment, characters, and/or scenes/levels within the game*<br>32. I have expertise in the following number of programming or scripting language (e.g., ASP, Java, Python, PHP) |
| Learning | 35. I typically take courses or training online*<br>38. I use the Internet to complete assignments for school*<br>39. I use email, instant messaging (IM), chat rooms, or other online means to communicate with the instructor and/or fellow classmates*<br>40. I find information to complete school tasks online*<br>41. I play video games that engage me in learning activities (educational games, game-based learning)<br>42. I prefer to complete multiple tasks (e.g., instant messaging (IM), alternative activities, watching TV) rather than one task at a time while I'm learning |
| Digital Native Propositions | 36. I prefer taking courses or training online rather than face-to-face<br>37. I prefer training and/or education that encourages me to communicate and learn with others rather learning by myself<br>43. I prefer training and/or education that allows me to randomly access various components of a lesson, rather than materials that steps me through a lesson one component at a time<br>44. I prefer training and/or educational materials that present graphics, rather than text first*<br>46. I prefer a hands-on approach to learning, such as learning by doing, than a traditional teacher-centered approach*<br>47. I prefer training and/or education that is play oriented, rather than work oriented*<br>48. I expect immediate feedback and/or results while learning and don't want to wait for the payoff* |

*Items chosen for final inclusion.

*Figure 1. Confirmatory factor analysis explorations*

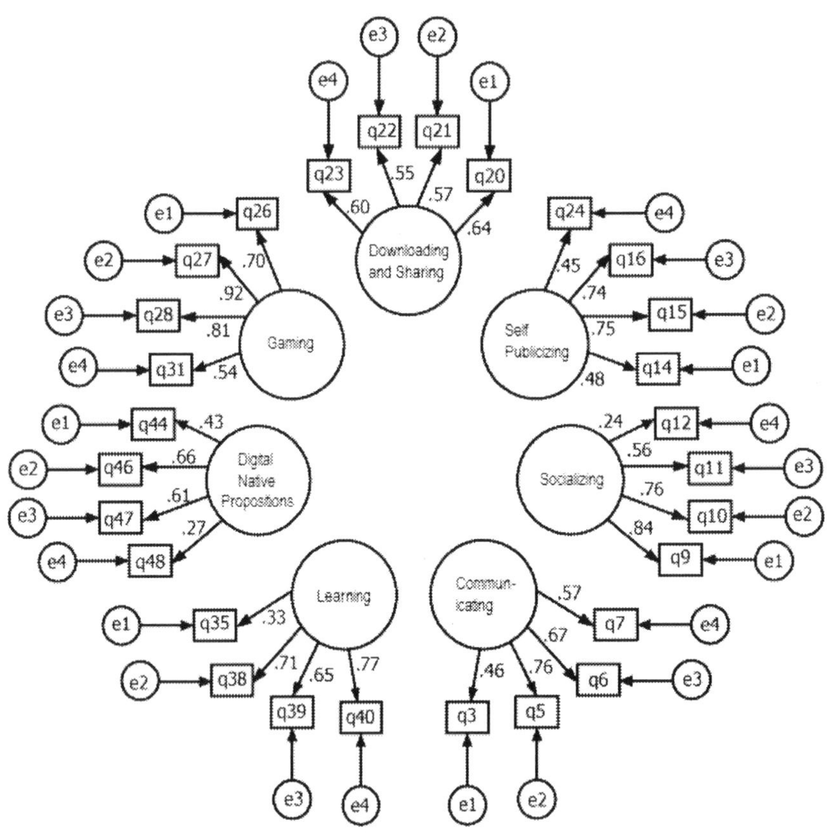


model, represented as an order-5 Venn diagram (diagram design originally devised by Branko Grünbaum [Wolfram Research, Inc., 2012]), is depicted in Figure 4.

## Influence of Age, Family Income, and Gender

To determine if there were statistically significant relationships among the latent factors and the demographics of age, family income, and gender, a series of Spearman's Rho and point-biserial correlation coefficients were computed. To interpret effect size, the Davis (1971) convention was adopted as follows:.70 or higher: very strong association,.50 to.69: substantial association,.30 to.49: moderate association,.10 to.29: low association, and.01 to.09: negligible association.

## Communicating

The Spearman's Rho test revealed statistically significant positive correlations with almost all of the items comprising the communicating factor and the age and family income demographics, as shown in Table 5. However, the associations were, at best, low (Davis, 1971). A low statistically significant correlation was found among all the items and age: texting ($r_s$ =.216, $p$ <.01), with age ($r_s^2$ =.047) accounting for almost 5% of the variability; instant messaging ($r_s$ =.127, $p$ <.01), with age ($r_s^2$ =.016) accounting for almost 2% of the variability; social networking websites ($r_s$ =.122, $p$ <.01), with age ($r_s^2$ =.015) also accounting for almost 2% of the variability; and chat rooms ($r_s$ =.116, $p$ <.01), with age ($r_s^2$ =.014) accounting for 1% of the variability.

*Figure 2. The hypothesized model: fit indices: $\chi^2$ = 1690.19, df = 329, p =.00; CFI =.87; TLI =.85; RMSEA =.058.*

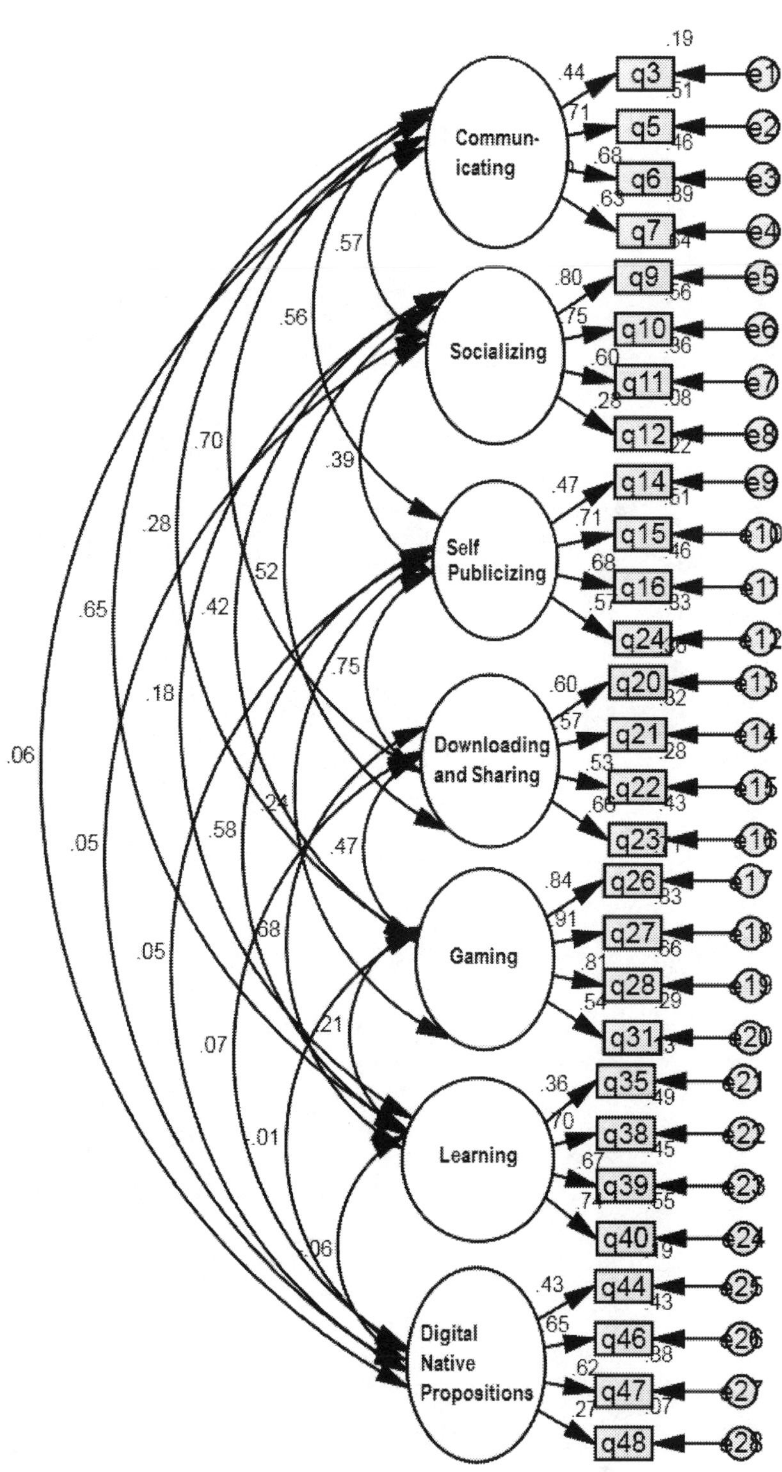

*Figure 3. The revised model: fit indices:* $\chi^2 = 992.68$, $df = 231$, $p = .00$; *CFI* $= .92$; *TLI* $= .90$; *RMSEA* $= .05$.

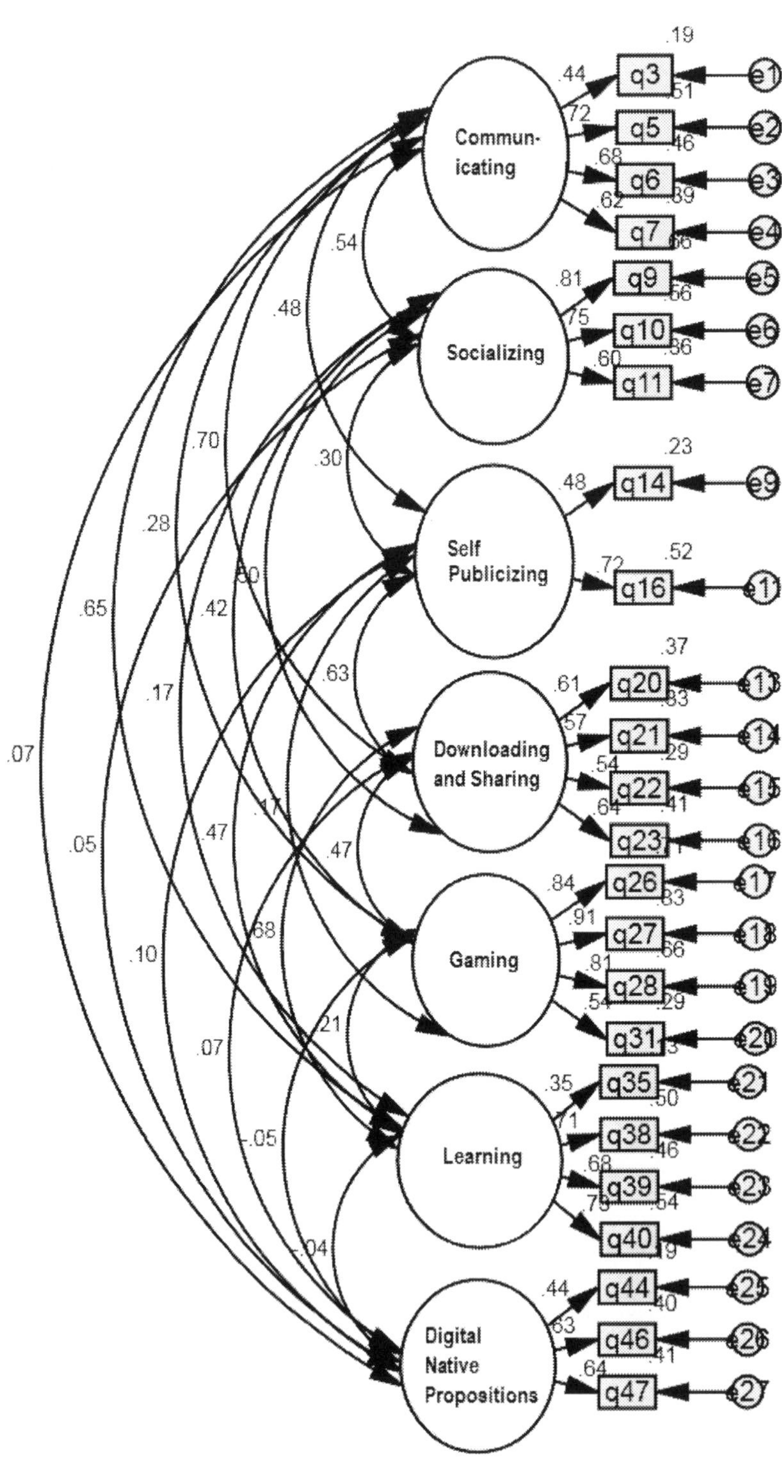

*Table 3. Correlations between factors*

| Factor/Factor | | Correlation |
|---|---|---|
| Communicating | Downloading and Sharing | .699 |
| Downloading and Sharing | Learning | .675 |
| Communicating | Learning | .655 |
| Self Publicizing | Downloading and Sharing | .630 |
| Communicating | Socializing | .544 |
| Socializing | Downloading and Sharing | .501 |
| Communicating | Self-Publicizing | .482 |
| Self-Publicizing | Learning | .472 |
| Downloading and Sharing | Gaming | .467 |
| Socializing | Gaming | .420 |
| Socializing | Self-Publicizing | .303 |
| Communicating | Gaming | .285 |
| Gaming | Learning | .212 |
| Self Publicizing | Gaming | .172 |
| Socializing | Learning | .166 |
| Self-Publicizing | Digital Native Propositions | .103 |
| Downloading and Sharing | Digital Native Propositions | .074 |
| Communicating | Digital Native Propositions | .069 |
| Socializing | Digital Native Propositions | .047 |
| Learning | Digital Native Propositions | -.041 |
| Gaming | Digital Native Propositions | -.047 |

A negligible statistical correlation was found among three of the four items and family income: chat rooms ($r_s$ =.091, $p$ <.01), with family income ($r_s^2$ =.008) accounting for almost 1% of the variability; instant messaging ($r_s$ =.086, $p$ <.01), with family income ($r_s^2$ =.007) accounting for almost 1% of the variability; and social networking websites ($r_s$ =.077, $p$ <.01), with family income ($r_s^2$ =.006) also accounting for almost 1% of the variability.

*Table 4. Factors, reliability, number, and selected items*

| Factor | Alpha | (N) of Items | Selected Item # |
|---|---|---|---|
| Questionnaire | .84 | 24 | All 24 items |
| Communicating | .71 | 4 | 3, 5, 6, 7 |
| Socializing | .77 | 3 | 9, 10, 11 |
| Self-Publicizing | .51 | 2 | 14, 16 |
| Downloading and Sharing | .68 | 4 | 20, 21, 22, 23 |
| Gaming | .85 | 4 | 26, 27, 28, 31 |
| Learning | .71 | 4 | 35, 38, 39, 40 |
| Digital Native Propositions | .58 | 3 | 44, 46, 47 |

*Figure 4. Latent factors underlying the set of observed ICT implementations*

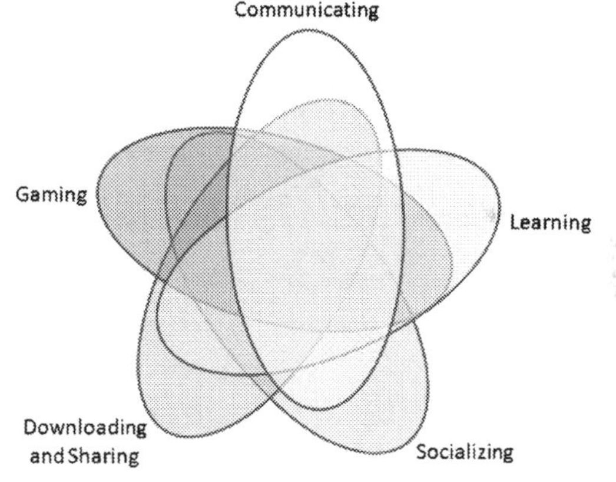


The correlation coefficients in Table 5 indicate that age had more impact on the items comprising communicating than family income, with texting having the strongest correlation. Even so, age only accounted for approximately 5% of the variability in texting, revealing that although statistically significant relationships were found between age and the various ICT as well as family income and the various ICT, the findings do not suggest any practical significance.

*Table 5. Correlation coefficients among communicating items and age/family annual income*

| | Communicate by texting | Communicate using instant messaging (IM) | Communicate using chat rooms | Communicate through social networking websites |
|---|---|---|---|---|
| Respondent Age | .216** | .127** | .116** | .122** |
| Family Annual Income | .040 | .086** | .091** | .077** |

**Correlation is significant at the.01 level.

The point-biserial test revealed a negligible statistically significant positive correlation between texting and gender ($r_{pb}$ =.091, $p$ <.01), as shown in Table 6, with gender ($r_{pb}^2$ =.008) accounting for almost 1% of the variability. While of interest from a theoretical standpoint, the findings have no real-world significance.

## Socializing

With regard to the socializing factor and the demographics of age and family income, the Spearman's Rho test revealed negligible statistically significant positive correlations between socializing through the use of social networking websites and age ($r_s$ =.081, $p$ <.01) and socializing using the various ICT and age ($r_s$ =.077, $p$ <.01). As shown in Table 7, age ($r_s^2$ =.007) accounted for almost 1% of the variability in socializing through the use of social networking websites. The same was true for age ($r_s^2$ =.006) and the variability in socializing using the various ICT.

All in all, the correlation coefficients shown in Table 7 indicate that age has a statistically significant impact on at least two of the three items comprising socializing, with social networking websites showing the strongest correlation. At the same time, however, age accounted for less than 1% of the variability among these items; these findings cannot be seen as having any practical value.

The results were no better for gender and socializing. The point-biserial test revealed a negligible statistically significant inverse correlation between socializing using the various ICT and gender ($r_{pb}$ = -.060, $p$ <.05). As shown in Table 8, gender ($r_{pb}^2$ =.004) accounted for less than 1%

*Table 6. Correlation coefficients among communicating items and gender*

| | Communicate by texting | Communicate using instant messaging (IM) | Communicate using chat rooms | Communicate through social networking websites |
|---|---|---|---|---|
| Respondent Gender | .091** | .023 | .017 | .045 |

**Correlation is significant at the.01 level.

*Table 7. Correlation coefficients among socializing items and age/family annual income*

| | Socialize using email, instant messaging (im), and/or chat rooms | Socialize online using social networking websites | Initially meet or arrange meetings with new people online |
|---|---|---|---|
| Respondent Age | .077** | .081** | .046 |
| Family Annual Income | .007 | .029 | -.038 |

**Correlation is significant at the.01 level.

*Table 8. Correlation coefficients among socializing items and gender*

| | Socialize using email, instant messaging (im), and/or chat rooms | Socialize online using social networking websites | Initially meet or arrange meetings with new people online |
|---|---|---|---|
| Respondent Gender | -.060* | -.009 | -.028 |

*Correlation is significant at the.05 level.

of the variability. These findings suggest that gender had very little impact on the use of ICT in socializing.

## Downloading and Sharing

The Spearman's Rho test revealed statistically significant positive correlations with almost all of items comprising the downloading and sharing factor. However, the associations were low, at best. As shown in Table 9, there was a low statistically significant correlation between the download/view of videos and age ($r_s$ =.187, $p$ <.01), the download of music and age ($r_s$ =.170, $p$ <.01), the download/view of videos and family income ($r_s$ =.119, $p$ <.01), and the download/view of movies and age ($r_s$ =.104, $p$ <.01). Specifically, age ($r_s^2$ =.035) accounted for almost 4% of the variability in the download/view of videos, age ($r_s^2$ =.029) accounted for almost 3% of the variability in the download of music, family income ($r_s^2$ =.014) accounted for 1% of the variability in the download/view of videos, and age ($r_s^2$ =.011) accounted for 1% of variability in the download/view of movies.

At the same time, negligible statistically significant correlations were found between the sharing of images/pictures and age ($r_s$ =.095, $p$ <.01) and the download/view of movies and family income ($r_s$ =.069, $p$ <.05). Age ($r_s^2$ =.009) accounted for almost 1% of the variability in the sharing of images/pictures, whereas family income ($r_s^2$ =.005) accounted for almost 1% of the variability in the download of movies.

Once again, the correlation coefficients indicate that age had more impact on the items comprising downloading and sharing than family income, with the download/view of videos showing the strongest correlation. Given their weak associations, though, these findings cannot be viewed as practically significant, suggesting that age and family income does not have any real-world impact on the download, viewing, and/or sharing of content from the Internet.

The point-biserial test revealed statistically significant positive and inverse correlations between the sharing of images/pictures and gender as well as the download of videos and gender. As shown in Table 10, all the associations were negligible: sharing images/pictures ($r_{pb}$=.068, $p$<.05), with gender ($r_{pb}^2$ =.005) accounting for almost 1% of the variability and download/view of videos ($r_{pb}$= -.080, $p$<.01), with gender ($r_{pb}^2$=.006) also accounting for almost 1% of the variability. Despite

*Table 9. Correlation coefficients among downloading and sharing items and age/family annual income*

| | Download music files from the Internet | Download/view videos from the Internet | Download/view movies from the Internet | I share images/ pictures online |
|---|---|---|---|---|
| Respondent Age | .170** | .187** | .104** | .095** |
| Family Annual Income | -.005 | .119** | .069* | -.026 |

**Correlation is significant at the.01 level. *Correlation is significant at the.05 level.

*Table 10. Correlation coefficients among downloading and sharing items and gender*

| | Download music files from the Internet | Download/view videos from the Internet | Download/view movies from the Internet | I share images/ pictures online |
|---|---|---|---|---|
| Respondent Gender | .017 | -.080** | -.045 | .068* |

**Correlation is significant at the.01 level. *Correlation is significant at the.05 level.

statistically significant findings, gender does not appear to practically impact the downloading, viewing, and/or sharing of content from the Internet.

## Gaming

Statistically significant positive and inverse correlations were found between the gaming factor and the demographics of age and family income. Associations were low, however, as shown in Table 11. There was a low statistically significant positive correlation between customizing the game and age ($r_s$ =.133, $p$ <.01), with age ($r_s^2$ =.018) accounting for almost 2% of the variability, a low statistically significant inverse correlation between customizing the game and family income ($r_s$ = -.131, $p$ <.01), with family income ($r_s^2$ =.017) also accounting for almost 2% of the variability, and a negligible statistically significant inverse correlation between 2+ player games and family income ($r_s$ = -.057, $p$ <.05), with family income ($r_s^2$ =.003) accounting for less than 1% of the variability.

The correlation coefficients shown in Table 11 indicate that customizing the game environment had the strongest correlation among the items. However, family income produced inverse correlations and both age and family income accounted for less than 1% of the variability among the items. Thus, neither demographic showed to have a practical impact.

The point-biserial test revealed statistically significant inverse correlations between all of the items comprising the gaming factor and gender. However, as shown in Table 12, the associations were again low at best. Specifically, there was a low correlation between 2+ player games and gender ($r_{pb}$ = -.182, $p$ <.01), with gender ($r_{pb}^2$ =.033) accounting for 3% of the variability; play video games and gender ($r_{pb}$ = -.176, $p$ <.01), with gender ($r_{pb}^2$ =.031) accounting for 3% of the variability; 1-2 player games and gender ($r_{pb}$ = -.173, $p$ <.01), with gender ($r_{pb}^2$ =.030) also accounting for 3% of the variability; and a negligible correlation between customizing the game and gender ($r_{pb}$ = -.080, $p$ <.01), with gender ($r_{pb}^2$ =.006) accounting for almost 1% of the variability. Although statistically significant correlations were found, gender did not have a practical impact on the items comprising the gaming factor.

## Learning

The Spearman's Rho test revealed statistically significant positive correlations with almost all

*Table 11. Correlation coefficients among the gaming items and age/family annual income*

| | Play video games | Play 1-2 player video games | Play games requiring 2+ players | Customize (mod) the environment, characters, and/or scenes/levels |
|---|---|---|---|---|
| Respondent Age | .001 | .043 | .016 | .133** |
| Family Annual Income | -.050 | -.038 | -.057* | -.131** |

**Correlation is significant at the.01 level. *Correlation is significant at the.05 level.

*Table 12. Correlation coefficients among gaming items and gender*

| | Play video games | Play 1-2 player video games | Play games requiring more than 2 players | Customize (mod) the environment, characters, and/or scenes/levels |
|---|---|---|---|---|
| Respondent Gender | -.176** | -.173** | -.182** | -.080** |

**Correlation is significant at the.01 level. *Correlation is significant at the.05 level.

of the items comprising the learning factor and the demographics of age and family income, as shown in Table 13. However, associations were once again, at most, low. There was a low statistically significant correlation between using the Internet to complete school work and age ($r_s$ =.161, $p$ <.01), with age ($r_s^2$ =.026) accounting for almost 3% of the variability; finding information online and family income ($r_s$ =.126, $p$ <.01), with family income ($r_s^2$ =.016) accounting for almost 2% of the variability; finding information online and age ($r_s$ =.124, $p$ <.01), with age ($r_s^2$ =.015) also accounting for 2% of the variability; using the Internet to complete school work and family income ($r_s$ =.118, $p$ <.01), with family income ($r_s^2$ =.014) accounting for 1% of the variability; using various ICT to communicate with instructors/classmates and age ($r_s$ =.116, $p$ <.01), with age ($r_s^2$ =.013) accounting for 1% of the variability; and using various ICT to communicate with instructors/classmates and family income ($r_s$ =.113, $p$ <.01), with family income ($r_s^2$ =.013) also accounting for 1% of the variability.

The correlation coefficients shown in Table 13 indicate that both age and family income influence learning. Using the Internet to complete school work and age showed the strongest correlation. However, age only accounted for approximately 3% of the variance. So, as with the aforementioned findings, although statistically significant, the findings are not practically relevant.

Finally, there was no practically significant difference between gender and the items comprising the learning factor. The point-biserial test revealed a negligible statistically significant positive correlation between finding information online and gender ($r_{pb}$ =.069, $p$ <.01), as shown in Table 14, with gender ($r_{pb}^2$ =.005) accounting for less than 1% of the variability.

## Preferences and Practices

Finally, the ICT preferences and practices of the participants are discussed. The descriptive statistics are organized by the aforementioned latent dimensions.

### Communicating

Participants preferred communicating by texting over instant messaging, chat rooms, and social networking websites. As shown in Table 15,

*Table 13. Correlation coefficients among the learning items and age/family annual income*

| | Typically take courses or training online | Use the Internet to complete assignments for school work | Use email, instant messaging (IM), chat rooms, or other online means to communicate with the instructor and/or fellow classmates | Find information to complete school tasks online |
|---|---|---|---|---|
| Respondent Age | .050 | .161** | .116** | .124** |
| Family Annual Income | .034 | .118** | .113** | .126** |

**Correlation is significant at the.01 level.

*Table 14. Correlation coefficients among learning items and gender*

| | Typically take courses or training online | Use the Internet to complete assignments for school work | Use email, instant messaging (IM), chat rooms, or other online means to communicate with the instructor and/or fellow classmates | Find information to complete school tasks online |
|---|---|---|---|---|
| Respondent Gender | .011 | .012 | .036 | .069* |

*Correlation is significant at the.05 level.

almost 40% ($n$ = 490) of participants reported that they text more than 15 times per day in comparison to almost 23% ($n$ = 281) who used instant messaging, almost 10% ($n$ = 119) who used chat rooms, and almost 11% ($n$ = 135) who used social networking websites more than three times daily. Overall, almost 98% ($n$ = 1,203) of the participants reported that they text, and almost 82% ($n$ = 1,009) reported that they used instant messaging in comparison to 66% ($n$ = 808) of participants who reported that they communicated using social networking websites.

## Socializing

Surprisingly, participants socialized little online. As shown in Table 16, a majority reported that they did not socialize with others using email, instant messaging, chat rooms (61%, $n$ = 757), or social networking websites (60%, $n$=737). Furthermore, the majority (71%, $n$ = 872) also did not meet or arrange meetings with new people online.

*Table 15. Communicating preferences and practices*

| Item | Levels | Frequency | Percent | Median Response |
|---|---|---|---|---|
| I communicate with others by texting | Not at all<br>1-5 times per day<br>6-10 times per day<br>11-15 times per day<br>More than 15 times per day | 31<br>230<br>248<br>235<br>490 | 2.5<br>18.6<br>20.1<br>19.0<br>39.7 | 11-15 times per day |
| I communicate with others using instant messaging (IM) | Not at all<br>Weekly<br>2-3 days per week<br>Daily<br>More than 3 times daily | 225<br>236<br>271<br>221<br>281 | 18.2<br>19.1<br>22.0<br>17.9<br>22.8 | 2-3 days per week |
| I communicate with others using chat rooms | Not at all<br>Weekly<br>2-3 days per week<br>Daily<br>More than 3 times daily | 459<br>253<br>252<br>151<br>119 | 37.2<br>20.5<br>20.4<br>12.2<br>9.6 | Weekly |
| I communicate with others through social networking websites (e.g., My Space™, Facebook™, Twitter™) | Not at all<br>Weekly<br>2-3 days per week<br>Daily<br>More than 3 times daily | 426<br>249<br>264<br>160<br>135 | 34.5<br>20.2<br>21.4<br>13.0<br>10.9 | Weekly |

*Table 16. Socializing preferences and practices*

| Item | Levels | Frequency | Percent | Median Response |
|---|---|---|---|---|
| I socialize with others online using email, instant messaging (IM), and/or chat rooms | Not at all<br>Weekly<br>2-3 days per week<br>Daily<br>More than 3 times daily | 757<br>218<br>136<br>85<br>38 | 61.3<br>17.7<br>11.0<br>6.9<br>3.1 | Not at all |
| I socialize with others online using social networking websites (e.g., My Space™, Facebook™, Twitter™) | Not at all<br>Weekly<br>2-3 days per week<br>Daily<br>More than 3 times daily | 737<br>219<br>152<br>89<br>36 | 59.7<br>17.7<br>12.3<br>7.2<br>2.9 | Not at all |
| I initially meet or arrange meetings with new people online (e.g., using email, instant messaging (IM), chat rooms, webcam, Skype™, WebEx™, online dating websites, social networking websites) | Never<br>Monthly<br>Weekly<br>Daily<br>More than 3 times daily | 872<br>228<br>89<br>20<br>25 | 70.7<br>18.5<br>7.2<br>1.6<br>2.0 | Weekly |

## Downloading and Sharing

With regard to downloading and sharing of content online, participants did download and/or view music, videos, and movies, while also sharing images. As shown in Table 17, almost 49% ($n$ = 598) of the participants reported that they downloaded music on a monthly basis; the same was true for almost 32% ($n$ = 391) who downloaded and viewed videos, and almost 44% ($n$ = 538) who downloaded and viewed movies. Furthermore, approximately 32% ($n$ = 388) of the participants reported that they shared images on a monthly basis. Overall, almost 88% ($n$ = 1,083) of the participants downloaded music, almost 85% (n = 1,043) downloaded and viewed videos, almost 78% ($n$ = 959) downloaded and viewed movies, and almost 77% ($n$ = 945) shared images from a monthly basis to more than three times per day.

## Gaming

Gaming also fared poorly alongside socializing among the participants. As shown in Table 18, an almost 64% ($n$ = 782) majority reported that they did not play video games, regardless of title, genre, or platform. A similar percentage reported that they did not play 1-2 (68%, $n$ = 843) and 2+ (63%, $n$ = 777) video games or customize the game environment (57%, $n$ = 703).

## Learning

Finally, participants appeared to have a preference for learning online. As shown in Table 19, although almost 38% ($n$ = 463) of the participants reported that they typically did not take courses or training online, approximately 35% ($n$ = 437) reported that they took between 1 and 5 courses per year, with the remaining percentage (27%, $n$ = 334) taking 6 to 20 or more per year. Thirty-one percent of the participants equally reported that they used the Internet to complete assignments for school on a weekly basis ($n$ = 383) and 2-3 days per week ($n$ = 382). Further, approximately 42% ($n$ = 515) reported that they used email, instant messaging, chat rooms, or other online means to communicate with the instructor and/or fellow classmates on at least a weekly basis, with 36% ($n$ = 442) reporting that they do so more frequently. Finally, almost 40% ($n$ = 486) of the participants reported that they used the Internet to find infor-

*Table 17. Downloading and sharing preferences and practices*

| Item | Levels | Frequency | Percent | Median Response |
|---|---|---|---|---|
| I download music files from the Internet | Never<br>Monthly<br>Weekly<br>Daily<br>More than 3 times daily | 151<br>598<br>278<br>140<br>67 | 12.2<br>48.5<br>22.5<br>11.3<br>5.4 | Monthly |
| I download/view videos from the Internet (e.g., YouTube™) | Never<br>Monthly<br>Weekly<br>Daily<br>More than 3 times daily | 191<br>391<br>335<br>227<br>90 | 15.5<br>31.7<br>27.1<br>18.4<br>7.3 | Monthly |
| I download/view movies from the Internet (e.g., Netflix™, Hulu™) | Never<br>Monthly<br>Weekly<br>Daily<br>More than 3 times daily | 275<br>538<br>290<br>92<br>39 | 22.3<br>43.6<br>23.5<br>7.5<br>3.2 | Monthly |
| I share images/pictures online | Never<br>Monthly<br>Weekly<br>Daily<br>More than 3 times daily | 289<br>388<br>303<br>165<br>89 | 23.4<br>31.4<br>24.6<br>13.4<br>7.2 | Monthly |

*Table 18. Gaming preferences and practices*

| Item | Levels | Frequency | Percent | Median Response |
|---|---|---|---|---|
| I play video games (can be any digital-based game) | Not at all<br>Weekly<br>2-3 days per week<br>Daily<br>More than 3 times per day | 782<br>225<br>114<br>93<br>20 | 63.4<br>18.2<br>9.2<br>7.5<br>1.6 | Not at all |
| I play 1-2 player video games | Not at all<br>Weekly<br>2-3 days per week<br>Daily<br>More than 3 times per day | 843<br>213<br>89<br>69<br>20 | 68.3<br>17.3<br>7.2<br>5.6<br>1.6 | Not at all |
| I play games requiring more than 2 players | Not at all<br>Weekly<br>2-3 days per week<br>Daily<br>More than 3 times per day | 777<br>241<br>118<br>71<br>27 | 63.0<br>19.5<br>9.6<br>5.8<br>2.2 | Not at all |
| When playing video games, I customize (mod) the environment, characters, and/or scenes/levels within the game | Not at all<br>Once only<br>More than once<br>Once during a session<br>Three or more times during a session | 703<br>155<br>267<br>82<br>27 | 57.0<br>12.6<br>21.6<br>6.6<br>2.2 | Not at all |

*Table 19. Learning preferences and practices*

| Item | Levels | Frequency | Percent | Median Response |
|---|---|---|---|---|
| I typically take courses or training online | Not at all<br>1-5 times per year<br>6-10 times per year<br>11-20 times per year<br>More than 20 times per year | 463<br>437<br>155<br>92<br>87 | 37.5<br>35.4<br>12.6<br>7.5<br>7.1 | 1-5 Times per year |
| I use the Internet to complete assignments for school | Not at all<br>Weekly<br>2-3 days per week<br>Daily<br>More than 3 times per day | 107<br>383<br>382<br>229<br>133 | 8.7<br>31.0<br>31.0<br>18.6<br>10.8 | 2-3 days per week |
| I use email, instant messaging (IM), chat rooms, or other online means to communicate with the instructor and/or fellow classmates | Not at all<br>Weekly<br>2-3 days per week<br>Daily<br>More than 3 times per day | 277<br>515<br>254<br>148<br>40 | 22.4<br>41.7<br>20.6<br>12.0<br>3.2 | Weekly |
| I find information to complete school tasks online | Not at all<br>Weekly<br>2-3 days per week<br>Daily<br>More than 3 times daily | 114<br>486<br>311<br>228<br>95 | 9.2<br>39.4<br>25.2<br>18.5<br>7.7 | 2-3 days per week |

mation for completing school assignments on a weekly basis, with approximately 51% ($n = 634$) reporting that they did so more often.

## DISCUSSION

The subsequent discussion is also organized in three parts:

1. First, the identified latent factors of ICT and associated validated items are discussed;
2. The influence of age, family income and gender is discussed; and finally,
3. Participants' preferences and practices are discussed.

### Identifying Latent Factors of Information and Communication Technology and Validating Items

The CFA within the framework of SEM analysis revealed a model comprising the latent factors of communicating, socializing, downloading and sharing, gaming, and learning; dimensions that mirror a subset of those reported by Nasah et al. (2010). That is, the factors reported by Nasah et al. – digital communications, ICT-facilitated social/economic activities, online media activities, gaming, and ICT-facilitated learning activities – closely match those teased out in the present study. This is an important finding, providing more weight to these dimensions in that they appear to be consistent across studies.

Given the findings of Nasah et al. (2010) and the results of the present study, backed by further investigation and research, these latent factors may lead to a reliable model for defining the activities comprising ICT and the eventual design and development of a formal instrument that can be used in the assessment and selection of AT to ensure quality of AT.

### Influence of Age, Family Income, and Gender

Findings also revealed that from a real-world standpoint, age, gender, and income, although statistically significant, were by themselves not valid indicators of ICT usage. This finding was shared by Nasah et al. (2010), who reported that individually these demographics as sole determinants of ICT use are not supported, but appear to have some role in ICT usage as a whole. Nasah et al. reported that age, gender, and socioeconomic status together account for approximately 30% of digital propensity index score, with age and gender combined accounting for approximately 15%. A finding that is at least partially at odds with those who have suggested that these demographics may play a significant role in explaining why individuals use ICT to varying degrees (Kennedy et al., 2008; Kvavik, Caruso, & Morgan, 2004; Livingstone & Bober, 2004; see Selwyn, 2009). Therefore, we reemphasize the recommendations put forth by Nasah et al.: that those involved in ICT integration consider these demographics carefully when planning such technology use for today's students, especially in the assessment and selection of AT, and that these demographics not account for the major share of the decision-making paradigm.

## Preferences and Practices

Finally, in terms of ICT preferences and practices, participants favored communicating by texting over other technologies, to include instant messaging, chat rooms, and, most surprising, social networking websites. Given the perceived global popularity of these websites, such as Facebook™ and Twitter™, it was anticipated that this means of communication would have ranked high. Instead, almost 98% of the participants reported that they text on a regular basis in comparison to 66%, who reported the use of social networking websites.

Participants were also found to socialize very little, at least not with the technologies investigated as part of the socializing factor. The majority reported that they did not socialize with others using email, instant messaging, chat rooms, or social networking websites; a finding in agreement with those who found that young people made limited recreational use of social networking websites (e.g., Margaryan & Littlejohn, 2008), and in contrast to those who found young people making extensive use of personal technology for their private needs (e.g., Conole et al., 2006). Furthermore, the majority were not interested in meeting or arranging meetings with new people online.

Participants did, however, download music, download and stream videos and movies, and share images on at least a monthly basis, with some reporting that they engaged in such activities more than three times per day.

Gaming fared poorly alongside socializing. Overall, only approximately 37% of the participants reported that they play video games. This is a surprising finding and in stark contrast to the supposition that the stereotypical game player is an adolescent male or that young adults want game-based learning. It is in even starker contrast when considering that video game addiction appears to be so severe in South Korea that the country has been described "as the world's most intense gaming culture" and that as much as "one-eighth of the population between the ages of nine and thirty-nine either is addicted to these games or has a compulsion that borders on addiction" (Brown & Vaughan, 2009, p. 177) and that Internet addiction treatment centers have opened to handle the influx of reported addiction cases (Brown & Vaughan, 2009). Overall, the low percentage of game players may suggest that our perceptions of youth and video game play may not be accurate, prompting the need for further study.

While a majority of the participants reported that they took at least 1 to 5 online courses per year and used the Internet to complete school assignments, they also reported that they used technologies, such as email, instant messaging, chat rooms, or other online means, to communicate with the instructor and/or fellow classmates on at least a weekly basis. It is unknown, however, as to whether participants chose to do so by their own accord or were required to do so as part of course requirements.

## Limitations

The findings presented here must be viewed in light of the present study's limitations. First, although a diverse sampling was sought by conducting the study across seven universities, the sampled population was restricted to postsecondary students. More importantly, however, although the sampled population focused on students who are perceived to be grossly involved in ICT, the present study and the latent dimensions presented herein should be examined with a sample of individuals with special needs most benefiting from ICT as AT.

The questionnaire was administered via paper-and-pencil as opposed to digitally through a mobile app or a website. The paper-and-pencil venue may have discouraged those with a high digital propensity from participating. A limitation also noted by Nasah et al. (2010), with the difference that they administered their index online, thus arguing that the online venue may have discouraged those with a low digital propensity from participating.

Further, environmental factors may have posed limitations. For example, it is unknown if outside influences affected participant responses and if participants responded to the questionnaire in the manner instructed. This is a problematic issue when using survey instruments in general; in that participants may have reported what they felt were the socially desirable responses or what they felt others wanted to hear (Nasah et al., 2010).

## CONCLUSION

As with the Nasah et al. (2010) study, claims that students are much more adept at all things digital are not borne out of the findings presented herein. Instead, the findings call into question the overarching suppositions made about young people and their technological prowess, to include the belief that young people, for instance, are more interested in using technology for social networking and personal reasons (Keen, 2007).

At the same time, however, there is no denying the significance of ICT in modern society. The extraordinary technological advancements in the area of mobile computing alone have the potential of benefiting a multitude of areas to include helping those with special needs. The latent dimensions of ICT – communicating, socializing, downloading and sharing, gaming, and learning – provide a reference point in which to begin examining the ICT preferences and practices of those with special needs. But more importantly, may lead to the eventual development of a standardized instrument for ICT assessment and selection in the context of AT.

## REFERENCES

American Psychological Association. (2002). Ethical principles of psychologists and code of conduct. *APA Online*. Retrieved from http://www.apa.org/ethics/code/code-1992.aspx

Anderson, N. (2009). US 20th in broadband penetration, trails S. Korea, Estonia. *ARS*. Retrieved from http://arstechnica.com/tech-policy/news/2009/06/us-20th-in-broadband-penetration-trails-s-korea-estonia.ars

Beigel, A. R. (2000). Assistive technology assessment: More than the device. *Intervention in School and Clinic*, *35*(4), 237–243. doi:10.1177/105345120003500407

Bennett, S., Maton, K., & Kervin, L. (2008). The digital natives debate: A critical review of the evidence. *British Journal of Educational Technology*, *39*(5), 775–786. doi:10.1111/j.1467-8535.2007.00793.x

Betsy, P., & Hongxin, Z. (1993). Predictors of assistive technology abandonment. *Assistive Technology*, *5*(1), 36–45. doi:10.1080/10400435.1993.10132205 PMID:10171664

Brown, S., & Vaughan, C. (2009). *Play: How it shapes the brain, opens the imagination, and invigorates the soul*. New York, NY: Avery.

Byrne, B. M. (2001). Structural equation modeling with AMOS, EQS, and LISREL: Comparative approaches to testing for the factorial validity of a measuring instrument. *International Journal of Testing*, *1*(1), 55–86. doi:10.1207/S15327574IJT0101_4

Byrne, B. M. (2010). *Structural equation modeling with AMOS: Basic concepts, applications, and programming* (2nd ed.). New York, NY: Routledge.

Cone Inc. in collaboration with AMP Agency. (2006). *The 2006 Cone millennial cause study: The millennial generation: Pro-social and empowered to change the world*. Retrieved from http://www.greenbook.org/Content/AMP/Cause_AMPlified.pdf

Conole, G., Laat, M. D., Dillon, T., & Darby, J. (2006). JISC LXP student experiences of technologies: Final report. *Joint Information Systems Committee*. Retrieved from http://www.jisc.ac.uk/media/documents/programmes/elearningpedagogy/lxpprojectfinalreportdec06.pdf

DaCosta, B., Kinsell, C., & Nasah, A. (2011). Millennials are digital natives? An investigation into digital propensity and age. In S. P. Ferris (Ed.), *Teaching, learning, and the net generation: Concepts and tools for reaching digital learners* (pp. 90–106). Hershey, PA: IGI Global. doi:10.4018/978-1-61350-347-8.ch006

DaCosta, B., Kinsell, C., & Nasah, A. (2013). Millennials are digital natives? An investigation into digital propensity and age. In Information Resources Management Association (Ed.), Digital literacy: Concepts, methodologies, tools, and applications (Vol. 1, pp. 103-119). Hershey, PA: IGI Global.

DaCosta, B., Nasah, A., Kinsell, C., & Seok, S. (2011). Digital propensity: An investigation of video game and information and communication technology practices. In P. Felicia (Ed.), *Handbook of research on improving learning and motivation through educational games: Multidisciplinary approaches* (pp. 1148–1173). Hershey, PA: IGI Global. doi:10.4018/978-1-60960-495-0.ch052

Davis, J. A. (1971). *Elementary survey analysis*. Englewood, NJ: Prentice Hall.

Drent, M., & Meelissen, M. (2008). Which factors obstruct or stimulate teacher educators to use ICT innovatively? *Computers & Education*, *51*, 187–199. doi:10.1016/j.compedu.2007.05.001

Ebner, I. (2004). *Abandonment of assistive technology*. Retrieved from http://www.florida-ese.org/atcomp/_PDF/MATR%20Abandon%20of%20Assistive%20Technology.pdf

ed.gov. (n.d.). *Building the legacy: IDEA 2004*. Retrieved from http://idea.ed.gov/

Graham, R., & Warnie, R. (2012). Levelling the playing field: Assistive technology, special education, and a Canadian perspective. *American International Journal of Contemporary Research*, *1*(2), 6–15.

Guo, R. X., Dobson, T., & Petrina, S. (2008). Digital natives, digital immigrants: An analysis of age and ICT competency in teacher education. *Journal of Educational Computing Research*, *38*(3), 235–254. doi:10.2190/EC.38.3.a

Hoover, E. (2009, October 11). The millennial muddle: How stereotyping students became a thriving industry and a bundle of contradictions. *The Chronicle of Higher Education*. Retrieved from http://chronicle.com/article/The-Millennial-Muddle-How/48772/

Howe, N., & Strauss, W. (2000). *Millennials rising: The next great generation*. New York, NY: Vintage Books.

Hutinger, P. L. (1996). Computer applications in programs for young children with disabilities: Recurring themes. *Focus on Autism and Other Developmental Disabilities*, *11*(2), 105–114. doi:10.1177/108835769601100206

Johnston, S. S., & Evans, J. (2005). Considering response efficiency as a strategy to prevent assistive technology abandonment. *Journal of Special Education Technology*, *20*(3), 45–50.

Judge, S. (2002). Family-centered assistive technology assessment and intervention practices for early intervention. *Infants and Young Children*, *15*(1), 60–68. doi:10.1097/00001163-200207000-00009

Karmarkar, A. M., Dicianno, B., Graham, J. E., Cooper, R., Kelleher, A., & Cooper, R. A. (2012). Factors associated with provision of wheelchairs in older adults. *Assistive Technology*, *24*(3), 155–167. doi:10.1080/10400435.2012.659795 PMID:23033733

Keen, A. (2007). *The cult of the amateur: How today's Internet is killing our culture*. London, UK: Broadway Business.

Kennedy, G., Krause, K.-L., Judd, T., Churchward, A., & Gray, K. (2008). First year students' experiences with technology: Are they really digital natives? *Australasian Journal of Educational Technology*, *24*(1), 108–122.

Kvavik, R. B., Caruso, J. B., & Morgan, G. (2004). *ECAR study of students and information technology, 2004: Convenience, connection, and control*. Retrieved from http://net.educause.edu/ir/library/pdf/ers0405/rs/ers0405w.pdf

Livingstone, S., & Bober, M. (2004). Taking up online opportunities? Children's use of the internet for education, communication and participation. *E-learning*, *1*(3), 395–419. doi:10.2304/elea.2004.1.3.5

Margaryan, A., & Littlejohn, A. (2008). *Are digital natives a myth or reality? Students' use of technologies for learning*. Unpublished manuscript.

Margolis, L., & Goodman, S. (1999). *Assistive technology services for students: What are these?* Washington, DC: Assistive Technology Funding & System Change Project.

McWilliam, E. L. (2002). Against professional development. *Educational Philosophy and Theory*, *34*(3), 289–300. doi:10.1080/00131850220150246

Monereo, C. (2004). The virtual construction of the mind: The role of educational psychology. *Interactive Educational Multimedia*, *9*, 32–47.

Nasah, A., DaCosta, B., Kinsell, C., & Seok, S. (2010). The digital literacy debate: An investigation of digital propensity and information and communication technology. *Educational Technology Research and Development*, *58*(5), 531–555. doi:10.1007/s11423-010-9151-8

Norman, D. K. (2008). *Predicting the performance of interpreting instruction based on digital propensity index score in text and graphic formats*. (Unpublished dissertation). University of Central Florida, Orlando, FL.

Palfrey, J., & Gasser, U. (2008). *Born digital: Understanding the first generation of digital natives*. New York, NY: Basic Books.

Pivec, M., & Pivec, P. (2008). *Games in schools: Executive summary*. Retrieved from http://www.paulpivec.com/Games_in_Schools.pdf

Prensky, M. (2001a). Digital natives, digital immigrants. *Horizon*, *9*, 1–6.

Prensky, M. (2001b). Digital natives, digital immigrants, part II: Do they really think differently? *Horizon*, *9*, 1–6.

Roberts, D. F., Foehr, U. G., & Rideout, V. (2005). *Generation M: Media in the lives of 8-18 year-olds*. Retrieved from http://www.kff.org/entmedia/upload/Generation-M-Media-in-the-Lives-of-8-18-Year-olds-Report.pdf

Rowlands, I., Nicholas, D., Williams, P., Huntington, P., Fieldhouse, M., & Gunter, B. et al. (2008). The Google generation: The information behaviour of the researcher of the future. *Aslib Proceedings*, *60*(4), 290–310. doi:10.1108/00012530810887953

Safer, M. (2007, May 25). The millennials are coming. *60 Minutes*. Retrieved from http://www.cbsnews.com/stories/2007/11/08/60minutes/main3475200.shtml

Scherer, M. J., & Craddock, G. (2002). Matching person and technology (MPT) assessment process. *Technology and Disability*, *14*, 125–131.

Schreiber, J. B., Nora, A., Stage, F. K., Barlow, E. A., & King, J. (2006). Reporting structural equation modeling and confirmatory factor analysis results: A review. *The Journal of Educational Research*, *99*(6), 323–337. doi:10.3200/JOER.99.6.323-338

Selwyn, N. (2009). *The digital native - Myth and reality*. Paper presented at the CILIP (Chartered Institute of Library and Information Professionals) London Seminar Series. London, UK. Retrieved from http://www.scribd.com/doc/9775892/Digital-Native

Seok, S. (2007a). Item validation of online post-secondary courses: Rating the proximity between similarity and dissimilarity among item pairs (validation study series I – multidimensional scaling). *Educational Technology Research and Development*, *57*(5), 665–684. doi:10.1007/s11423-007-9072-3

Seok, S. (2007b). Standards, accreditations, benchmarks in distance education. *Quarterly Review of Distance Education*, *8*(4), 387–398.

Seok, S., & DaCosta, B. (2013). Development and standardization of an assistive technology questionnaire using factor analyses: Eight factors consisting of 67 items related to assistive technology practices. *Assistive Technology*. doi:10.1080/10400435.2013.778917

Student, P. O. L. L. (2010). Research dispels millennial theories: Millennials appear more like than different from their parents' generation. *The CollegeBoard*. Retrieved from http://professionals.collegeboard.com/data-reports-research/trends/studentpoll/millennial

Tapscott, D. (1998). *Growing up digital: The rise of the net generation*. New York, NY: McGraw-Hill Companies.

Whitney, L. (2011). Smartphones to dominate PCs in Gartner forecast. *CNET News*. Retrieved from http://news.cnet.com/8301-1001_3-10434760-92.html

Wolfram Research, Inc. (2012). *Wolfram MathWord: Venn diagram*. Retrieved from http://mathworld.wolfram.com/VennDiagram.html

## ADDITIONAL READING

Arthanat, S., Bauer, S. M., Lenker, J. A., Nochajski, S. M., & Wu, Y. W. B. (2007). Conceptualization and measurement of assistive technology usability. *Disability and Rehabilitation. Assistive Technology*, *2*(4), 235–248. doi:10.1080/17483100701343665 PMID:19263540

Batavia, A. I., & Hammer, G. S. (1990). Toward the development of consumer-based criteria for the evaluation of assistive devices. *Journal of Rehabilitation Research*, *27*(4), 425–436. doi:10.1682/JRRD.1990.10.0425 PMID:2089152

Bennett, S., Maton, K., & Kervin, L. (2008). The digital native debate: A critical review of the evidence. *British Journal of Educational Technology*, *39*(5), 775–786. doi:10.1111/j.1467-8535.2007.00793.x

Bernd, T., Van Der Pijl, D., & De Witte, L. P. (2009). Existing models and instruments for the selection of assistive technology in rehabilitation practice. *Scandinavian Journal of Occupational Therapy*, *16*, 146–158. doi:10.1080/11038120802449362 PMID:18846479

DaCosta, B., Kinsell, C., & Nasah, A. (2011). Millennials are digital natives?: An investigation into digital propensity and age. In S. P. Ferris (Ed.), *Teaching, learning, and the Net Generation: Concepts and tools for reaching digital learners* (pp. 90–106). Hershey, PA: IGI Global. doi:10.4018/978-1-61350-347-8.ch006

Demers, L., Weiss-Lambrou, R., & Ska, B. (2000). Item analysis of the Quebec User Evaluation of Satisfaction with Assistive Technology (QUEST). *Assistive Technology*, *12*, 96–105. doi:10.1080/10400435.2000.10132015 PMID:11508406

Ebner, I. (2004). *Abandonment of assistive technology*. Retrieved from http://www.florida-ese.org/atcomp/_PDF/MATR%20Abandon%20of%20Assistive%20Technology.pdf

Emiliani, P. L. (2006). Assistive technology (AT) versus mainstream technology (MST), The research perspective. *Technology and Disability*, *18*, 19–29.

Fuhrer, M. J., Jutai, J. W., Scherer, M. J., & Deruyter, F. (2003). A framework for the conceptual modelling of assistive technology device outcomes. *Disability and Rehabilitation*, *25*, 1243–1251. doi:10.1080/09638280310001596207 PMID:14617441

Gelderblom, G. J., & de Witte, L. P. (2002). The assessment of assistive technology outcomes, effects and costs. *Technology and Disability*, *14*, 91–94.

Hoover, E. (2009, Oct. 11). The millennial muddle. How stereotyping students became a thriving industry and a bundle of contradictions. *The Chronicle of Higher Education*. Retrieved from http://chronicle.com/article/The-Millennial-Muddle-How/48772/

Howe, N., & Strauss, W. (2000). *Millennials rising: The next great generation*. New York, NY: Vintage Books.

Lenker, J. A., & Paquet, V. L. (2003). A review of conceptual models for assistive technology outcomes research and practice. *Assistive Technology*, *15*, 1–15. doi:10.1080/10400435.2003.10131885 PMID:14760977

Lenker, J. A., Scherer, M. J., Fuhrer, M. J., Jutai, J. W., & DeRuyter, F. (2005). Psychometric and administrative properties of measures used in assistive technology device outcomes research. *Assistive Technology*, *17*, 7–22. doi:10.1080/10400435.2005.10132092 PMID:16121642

Nasah, A., DaCosta, B., Kinsell, C., & Seok, S. (2010). The digital literacy debate: An investigation of digital propensity and information and communication technology. *Educational Technology Research and Development*, *58*(5), 531–555. doi:10.1007/s11423-010-9151-8

Prensky, M. (2001a). Digital natives, digital immigrants. *Horizon*, *9*, 1–6. Retrieved from http://www.marcprensky.com/writing/default.asp

Prensky, M. (2001b). Digital natives, digital immigrants, part II: Do they really think differently? *Horizon*, *9*, 1–6. Retrieved from http://www.marcprensky.com/writing/default.asp

Scherer, M., Jutai, J., Fuhrer, M., Demers, L., & Deruyter, F. (2007). A framework for modelling the selection of assistive technology devices (ATDs). *Disability and Rehabilitation. Assistive Technology*, *2*(1), 1–8. doi:10.1080/17483100600845414 PMID:19263548

Scherer, M., Sax, C., Vanbiervliet, A., Cushman, L. A., & Scherer, J. V. (2005). Predictors of assistive technology use: The importance of personal and psychosocial factors. *Disability and Rehabilitation*, *27*(21), 1321–1331. doi:10.1080/09638280500164800 PMID:16298935

Seok, S., & DaCosta, B. (in press). Development and standardization of an assistive technology questionnaire using factor analyses: Eight factors consisting of 67 items related to assistive technology practices. *Assistive Technology*.

Wessel, R., de Witte, L., Andrich, R., Ferrario, M., Persson, J., & Oberg, B. et al. (2000). IPPA, a user-centred approach to assess effectiveness of assistive technology provision. *Technology and Disability*, *13*, 105–115.

## KEY TERMS AND DEFINITIONS

**Assistive Technology Device:** "Any item, piece of equipment or product system, whether acquired commercially off the shelf, modified, or customized, that is used to increase, maintain, or improve the functional capabilities of children [(individuals)] with disabilities." (ED.GOV, n.d.).

**Information & Communication Technology (ICT):** Any digital product that can be used to store, retrieve, manipulate, transmit, or receive electronic information, such as mobile devices, email, two-way instant messaging, chat rooms, blogs, personal web pages, and so on (DaCosta, Kinsell, & Nasah, 2011, 2013; DaCosta, Nasah, Kinsell, & Seok, 2011).

**Quality of Assistive Technology:** The degree to which AT implementation, or providing AT devices or services, produces the intended, or better than intended outcomes or benefits (Seok & DaCosta, in press).

# Chapter 9
# A Phatic Approach to Assistive and Augmentative Communications Vocabularies

**Benjamin Slotznick**
*Point-and-Read, Inc., USA*

## ABSTRACT

*Users of Assistive and Augmentative Communications (AAC) systems sometimes have difficulty: (a) participating in conversation outside of a script they already know, (b) repairing a derailed conversation, or (c) engaging in the quick and varied banter demanded of many social situations. This chapter presents tools being developed to remedy these challenges, and the "phatic" approach on which they are based. In contrast to most AAC vocabularies, phatic vocabularies are characterized by providing a variety of expressions for the same meme. In addition, vocabularies developed via a phatic approach may use language to convey gesture, affirmation, or emotive support as much as or more than to convey wants, needs, or narrative. The intent of this chapter is not to argue for the replacement of standard AAC vocabularies, but instead to show how phatic vocabularies, through the use of tools, can be successfully used to enhance a user's language development, particularly social language and social development, by creating vocabularies that encourage a user to engage in social settings.*

DOI: 10.4018/978-1-4666-5015-2.ch009

## INTRODUCTION

This chapter is an extension of (and motivated by) the work conducted by this author on developing a computer interface through which non-literate users of assistive and augmentative communications (AAC) devices and software would be able to use instant messaging over the Internet (Slotznick, 2010). In 2008-2009, a small collaborative research grant, from the National Center for Technology Innovation, funded a pilot study which investigated the efficacy of AAC interfaces (see Slotznick, Hershberger, & Higginbotham, 2009). Specifically, the study involved observing how people who require AAC devices were able to use the Point-and-Chat™ software: a custom developed instant messaging (IM) application developed for users of AAC devices.

Findings of the study revealed that instant messaging conversations using the software degraded, could not be salvaged, and ended abruptly. This was in contrast to scripted, face-to-face conversations conducted during the same study. The reasons for why the instant messaging conversations faired poorly (in comparison to the scripted face-to-face conversations) were out of the scope of the pilot study. However, the most obvious conclusion was that the software lacked the needed vocabularies or interfaces for successful online interaction. These findings sparked a line of questioning (e.g., "What vocabularies or interfaces are needed?" and "How do these differ from regular vocabularies?") that lead to the "phatic" approach described in this chapter and the subsequent evolution of the Point-and-Chat™ software.

The phatic approach discussed in this chapter is significant because it takes into consideration gaps in narrative content (including scripted content) that are filled with small talk, chit-chat, chatter, and other phatic elements. It accepts that people engage in conversations even when they don't have anything to say (e.g., sometimes for only entertainment purposes because humans like to listen to language). It recognizes that in many cases traditional AAC vocabularies and interfaces are not good at engaging in free-form chatter in part because of their strengths. It acknowledges that many conversations are not scripted. It realizes that continuing an unscripted conversation has much in common with finding a way to get a derailed conversation back on track. Finally, it even concedes that much of social conversation is in fact, phatic.

More importantly, however, for the reason that the words used in chit-chat may not be the crux of the social content being conveyed, this approach helps identify social interactions which have similar phatic components, even if the vocabularies and emotions are different. This enables one interface to be developed for a class of interactions. In taking this approach, users of AAC devices and software (referred to as "AAC users" or "users" throughout the remainder of this chapter) can learn one interface that provides channeled improvisation rather than many scripts. The primary benefit of such an approach is that it facilitates developing phatic vocabularies and interfaces which allow users to engage in a wider range of social interactions and ultimately in the development of increased social skills.

## BACKGROUND

### Phatic Communication

In 1923, Bronislaw Malinowski coined the term, "phatic" communication, to refer to speech that is used to express or create an atmosphere of shared feeling, goodwill, or sociability rather than to impart information. Many have equated the term with small talk, but this chapter takes a broader view. In this chapter, the term "phatic" communication is extended to include not only speech, but also facial expressions and body gestures, along with non-speech vocalizations and utterances. From this perspective, phatic communication is so instinctual and pervasive that it underpins all conversation. In fact, people seldom consciously notice it, unless it is absent.

To better understand the notion of phatic communication, consider some concrete examples. When speaking face-to-face with someone and telling them something pleasant, the listener will nod, smile, and exhibit other gestures of affirmation and positive feedback. The listener, from time to time, will utter reinforcing vocalizations such as "uh huh," actual words, such as "yeah," and even full phrases, such as "for sure." However, if the story being told relates unpleasant information, the listener is likely to shake his or her head back and forth in a "no" gesture, as well as utter vocalizations, such as "uh oh," words, such as "bummer," or phrases, such as "no way!"

In all of these examples the listener is engaged in phatic communication. That is, the listener is communicating an essential phatic message: "We are in a conversation," "I am listening," "I understand what you are saying," "I echo and affirm the emotive content of your message," and "I want you to continue." In this message, the exact position of the mouth, stance of the body, vocalization, or word phrase does not matter so long as it is within an appropriate range of response.

In fact, during face-to-face conversations, many AAC users will use gestures and non-speech vocalizations as part of their communication repertoire. However, this might only be intelligible to those who know them well. For conversations that are not face-to-face, gestures are not communicable, and without the gestures, the non-speech vocalizations are severely degraded. As listeners, this is so instinctual that people do it automatically. When speaking, it is so pervasive among listeners that it is not consciously noticed.

Consider another example to help solidify this discussion point, by examining communication over the telephone where the visual component of the interaction is missing. A listener will still say, "uh huh," "yeah," or "for sure." Again, this is so pervasive that a speaker will not consciously notice it until it stops. When it does cease, the speaker is likely to say, "Are you still there?" If there is no response the speaker is likely to hang up the phone and end the call.

Such a scenario is not restricted to telephone conversations, but instead can occur in face-to-face conversations as well. If a listener appears to be looking all over the place except at the speaker, crossing his or her arms, and nervously jiggling legs or feet, the speaker is likely to conclude that the listener is not interested in the conversation, perhaps not even listening. In many social scenarios, the speaker is again likely to end the conversation. In other scenarios the speaker will take offense. For example, if the speaker is a boss, teacher, or a parent, and talking to a subordinate, such as an employee, student, or child, the listener's phatic message might be conveying not only lack of interest, but also defiance. In such a scenario the speaker is likely to say something to reassert control, such as, "*You* listen here, buddy!"

Consider now traditional text messaging over a cell phone, or instant messaging over the Internet. One can neither see nor hear the other person in the text conversation. One must rely upon text alone to send content or respond phatically. (Parenthetically, in addition to text, users may add graphics such as emoticons. Emoticons were originally alphanumeric combinations which suggested a face, often on its side. For example **:-)** suggests a smiling face, whereas **:-(** suggests a frowning face, and **;-P** suggests a winking face with a tongue hanging out.) Not surprisingly, in such text conversations the unspoken rules for continuing conversations still apply and phatic vocalizations such as "uh huh" and "mmm…" are still frequently used, but spelled out.

It should be noted that "talking about the weather," or other specific topics of small talk, have not been purposely mentioned. The rationale for this is simple: although this chapter touches upon some of this type of communication, by and large, this chapter focuses on basic and pervasive aspects of social communication.

## Characteristics of Phatic Communication

A general understanding of phatic communication is incomplete without a discussion encapsulating its major features. It is useful to separate and list these characteristics, and juxtapose the phatic aspects with narrative content. In doing so, it is helpful to refer to the concept of a "meme," which is an idea or element of social behavior passed on through generations in a culture, especially by imitation.

*Phatic speech may use a variety of expressions or gestures to convey the same content or meme:* "Uh huh," "yup," "yeah," and "right" may all be used by one person as affirmative phatic responses within the course of a conversation. This is because what is being conveyed is so general and basic, it often does not matter which expression is chosen so long as it is within a fairly large acceptable set. This set, however, may vary depending on age, culture, or social setting.

*Using a variety of expressions for the same meme is normative (if not instinctive):* This is the case because it shows that the listener is actually listening. Consider this common theme from situation comedies or comic strips: A husband is watching TV and his wife asks him several questions, to which he mechanically replies, "Yes." It is obvious to all that he is not really listening. At which point his wife asks if she can go shopping and spend a lot of money, to which he again replies, "Yes."

*Phatic responses express an emotive rapport:* Consequently a speaker will expect to hear a range of emotion in a listener's phatic responses, rather than a bland narrative tone (the previous section applies as well.)

*Phatic responses do not interrupt conversation flow:* Certainly there are exceptions; when the speaker may wait for a phatic response. For example, a speaker may expect a strong reaction to a punch line of a joke or a juicy piece of gossip. However, phatic responses are usually given during the conversation flow, either *sotto voce*, while the speaker is talking, or in the short pauses between phrases and sentences. This is because a phatic response is usually not part of a dialogue, but rather the active listening accompaniment to the speaker's monologue.

This is obfuscated by film, theater, and novels, where the scripted conversations are perceived as highly interactive, but distinct lines of dialogue. Instead, many real-life conversations are serial monologues. One person gets to tell his or her story (for example, "Here's what I did at work today"), while the other is an active listener. Then it is the next person's turn to talk. Being a good, active, and attentive listener while another tells his or her story is designed to engender reciprocity when it is the listener's turn to do the same.

*In a group context, there may be one speaker, and several (or many) listeners who simultaneously give phatic responses*: Such a group context reinforces the previous points: a variety of expressions will be used as phatic responses and they will all be delivered within the conversation flow.

Interestingly, in the context of one-on-one conversations, one could say that half of the conversation is phatic. In the context of group conversations, one might say that more than half is phatic. This is not to say that half of all content is phatic, but is meant to remind us of how pervasive and important phatic communication is.

## ASSISTIVE AND AUGMENTATIVE COMMUNICATIONS INTERFACES

With the discussion of phatic communication complete, attention is turned next to AAC interfaces. It is important to understand that traditional AAC interfaces strive for breadth and depth of vocabulary. They do this in a number of ways.

One type of such interface uses many symbols per word. For literate users, an AAC interface may be based on putting letters on buttons found on the device that can be pressed by users in order to spell out words. (Notice that since letters are symbols, this maps several keystrokes into one word, though shortcuts may map several keystrokes into a phrase.) This may be reduced by spelling and word predication. The semantic compaction of MinSpeak® used in Prentke-Romich® devices reduces the number of keystrokes per word, for instance, but still requires several symbols (one to three) per word.

Another type of interface uses one symbol per word (or phrase). For literate users this may involve having one word per button and use word prediction to reduce the number of strokes to find the right word. For less literate (and non-literate) users this involves having one icon per button and one word or phrase per button. Word prediction and dynamic screens may be used to reduce the number of strokes to find the right word.

Traditional AAC interfaces can allow users to have a broad and precise vocabulary, but it takes a long time to say anything, limiting expert users to approximately 30 words per minute. In contrast, a person who does not use assistive technology to speak will usually speak at 120 to 150 words per minute. This can cause difficulties when quick responses are important, so many traditional interfaces have one page of *quick fires* that give access to several (or even a dozen) words like "yes," "no," and "stop."

In contrast, a phatic approach can use one symbol to represent a whole class of words or phrases which give a similar emotive feedback, because it doesn't really matter which word or phrase is used.[1]

Here is a recapitulation of some of the differences between a traditional approach to AAC interfaces and a phatic one:

- Phatic speech will use a variety of expressions or gestures to convey the same meme. In contrast, much of traditional AAC is picture based, with a unique icon for each meme. This is intended to accommodate poor readers, but it also means that vocabularies tend to be designed with a unique expression for each meme.
- Phatic speech giving the listener's *two cents* must be quick so it will not disrupt the speaker's conversational rhythm; so phatic speech will trade a large precise vocabulary for rapid access. In contrast, much of traditional AAC strives for a breadth and depth of vocabulary rather than quick fluidity. The process of drill-down to find the right word may allow more precise articulation of thought, but tends to limit expert users to about 30 words per minute. A traditional AAC approach might provide some one-word quick responses, but because screen *real estate* is precious, it doesn't provide a rich set of varied phatic responses.
- Phatic speech strives for empathy, so it gains power from the specific emotive qualities of recorded real speech. In contrast, much of traditional AAC strives for the ability to say anything and everything using the power of synthetic text-to-speech voices, thereby sacrificing inflection and emotion.

These differences are important to understand, in that they point out the strengths in using a phatic AAC interface over that of a traditional one. These differences are so important, in fact, that the remainder of this chapter is dedicated to examining phatic AAC interfaces and their implementation.

## Phatic Assistive and Augmentative Communications Interfaces

First, the implementation of phatic vocabulary (and interface) for pre-adolescents is discussed. The Fat Cat Snappy Chat® application will be used to facilitate the discussion. This software is designed for a pre-teen to engage in phatic conversation as an active listener or to just participate in social conversations as *one of the gang*. It is called this because the icons are drawings of fat cats (as opposed to the stick figures of SymbolStix®, for instance) and because it uses a variety of colloquialisms and slang geared towards pre-teen social vocabularies. The Fat Cat Snappy Chat® software is a member of a family of AAC mobile apps designed for the Apple iOS® and Google Android™ platforms to be run on smartphones, handheld computing devices, and tablets. The entire series of apps is given the alliterative and rhyming appellation of Fat Cat Phatic Chat®, all emerging from the initial work conducted with the Point-and-Chat™ software.

Figure 1 depicts a screen shot of the Home page of Fat Cat Snappy Chat®. It has a grid of 20 buttons, 4 columns of 5 rows each. The left-most and right-most columns show icons of cute orange cats. The two columns in the middle comprised of buttons have words in them. Each word is next to an icon which gives an indication of its meaning. For example, the top button of the second column from the left includes the word "Yes." It is adjacent to an icon of a cat head nodding up and down, the

*Figure 1. Fat Cat Snappy Chat® Home page*

gesture for approval. The two buttons in one of these pairs have the same background color (e.g., for the pair of "Yes" buttons, it is green). This background color for a pair helps distinguish the buttons from other pairs of buttons on the page.

When the user taps on one of the buttons with text, the device says that text aloud. (The app currently uses a recorded human voice, but could be coded for a speech engine with synthesized text-to-speech as well.) The word buttons on this page can be used as quick fires and consist of common short responses: "Yes," "No," "Maybe," "Don't know," and "What?!;" plus common ways to start, continue, or end a conversation: "Hi," "What's up?," "Tell me more," "Bye," and "STOP!" The word buttons on the Home page can be used as quick fires.

Consider the buttons with icons. The column of buttons on the left accesses phatic categories used for active listening, whereas the column of buttons on the right access conversation starters, continuers, and stoppers. (It is important to note that these latter buttons address some topics usually considered as small talk.)

The phatic features of the app only become evident when a user taps on one of the cat icons; for example, the button with the cat nodding (top button of left-most column). Figure 2 depicts a screen shot of this new page. The left-most column remains the same as on the Home page, providing access to other phatic pages. The rest of the page consists of buttons with text. The text in each button is a word or phrase consistent with nodding your head in affirmation while listening to someone speak. In other words, the nodding cat is the icon representing the gestural meaning of all of the different word buttons on that page or the one-to-many mapping.

Words and phrases are chosen from those a pre-teen might use. But they are also chosen (and voiced) so that they can be concatenated in any order, and still seem appropriate. Some affirmative phrases, such as "You sure told off that bully," would be good for some situations, but

*Figure 2. Fat Cat Snappy Chat® Yes page*

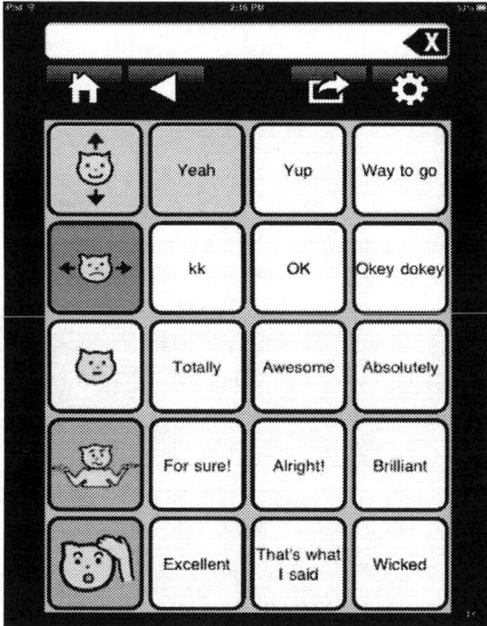


wrong for others. They are just *too* specific; that is, geared to a specific conversation topic. For that reason, they are not used. Remember that the AAC user is not telling the story, only adding appropriate responses. This means that he or she does not have to give the best possible or most precise response; only an appropriate one.

A user knows this is the Yes (or Affirmation) page, because the background color for the text button next to the nodding cat icon has the same background color as the nodding cat icon. That is, the background of the button with the word "Yeah" is colored the same green as the background of the button with the nodding cat. (Other icons have different background colors as well. For example the cat shaking its head back and forth has a red background color.) The rest of the buttons on the Yes page are colored a lighter version of this green.

This page has enough word choices to provide reasonable variation, and enough so that different users will have different favorites. However, there are only three columns of words; so many users will be able to remember the location of their favorite phrase. Nonetheless, because variation is important, semi-randomization of choice is useful. Consequently, it does not matter if a user is not literate or has difficulty reading the buttons. The one icon of the nodding cat represents all of these choices.

Users can not only concatenate two buttons within one phatic category, but also across categories, the same way that a listener's facial expressions would change during the telling of a story. Suppose a speaker was regaling a few friends with the following gossip: "I just saw Joe kissing his best friend's girl." The speaker is probably expecting his audience to be both surprised and also feeling that this was not a good thing that happened.

A Fat Cat Snappy Chat® user might tap the icon of the surprised cat (bottom left button). This would navigate to the What?! page (depicted in Figure 3). The user might then tap on one of the word buttons, such as "Oh my God!" The user could follow this up by tapping the icon of the

*Figure 3. Fat Cat Snappy Chat® What?! page*

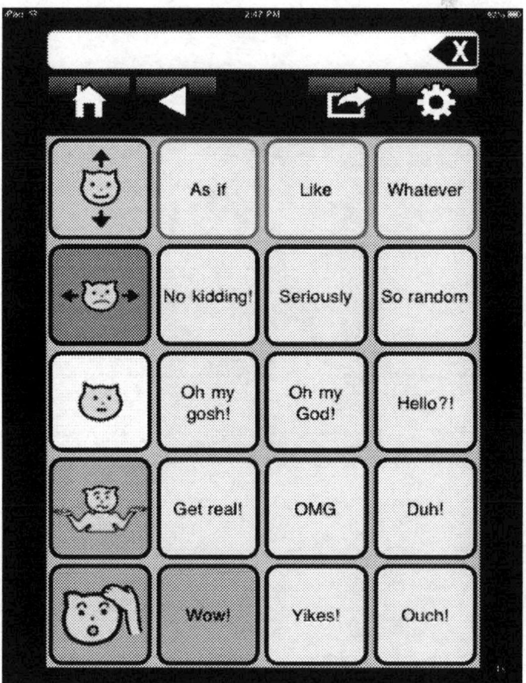

cat shaking its head, which would open the No page (depicted in Figure 4). The user might then tap the "Gag me with a spoon" button (shown in the lower right hand corner of Figure 4).

This example shows how a user who taps 4 buttons in 4 seconds can very quickly produce a rich appropriate utterance, "Oh my God! Gag me with a spoon." As the story continues, the user can continue to quickly respond in the conversation flow with varied supportive and emotively correct responses.

The five phatic response categories which the left-most column addresses are:

- Nodding the head, "Yes," or positive reinforcement
- Shaking the head, "No," or affirming a negative situation
- A straight face, "Maybe," or neutral response
- Shrugging shoulders, "Don't know," or puzzlement
- Surprised expression, "What?!," or surprise, exclamation, or intensification

*Figure 4. Fat Cat Snappy Chat® No page*

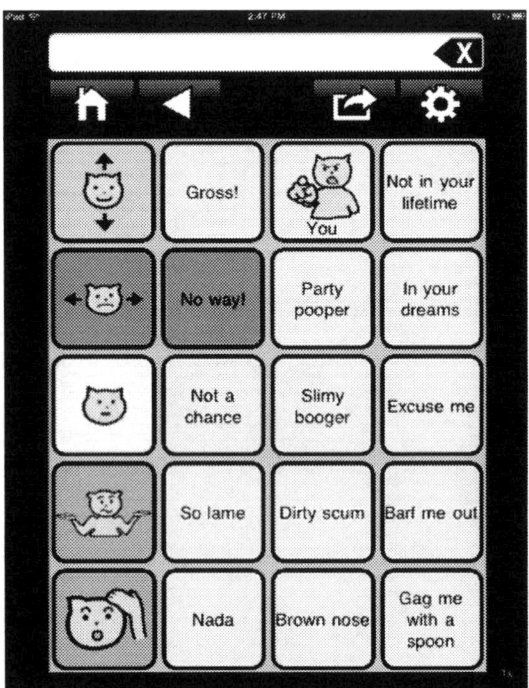


Consider again the Fat Cat Snappy Chat® interface by looking at the column on the right on the Home page, depicted in Figure 1. Each button in this column navigates to a page that replicates the right-most column and shows fifteen other buttons with responses appropriate to the icon. These are conversation starters, continuers, and stoppers. Figure 5 shows the page that would appear after tapping the "What's up?" button. While these phrases may be considered small talk, notice that they are still chosen to be not overly specific as to a particular situation, and hence able to be concatenated.

The Fat Cat Snappy Chat® interface allows the user to be an active listener (left-side categories) as well as start a conversation or invite others into it (right-side categories) all within the conversa-

*Figure 5. Fat Cat Snappy Chat® What's Up page*

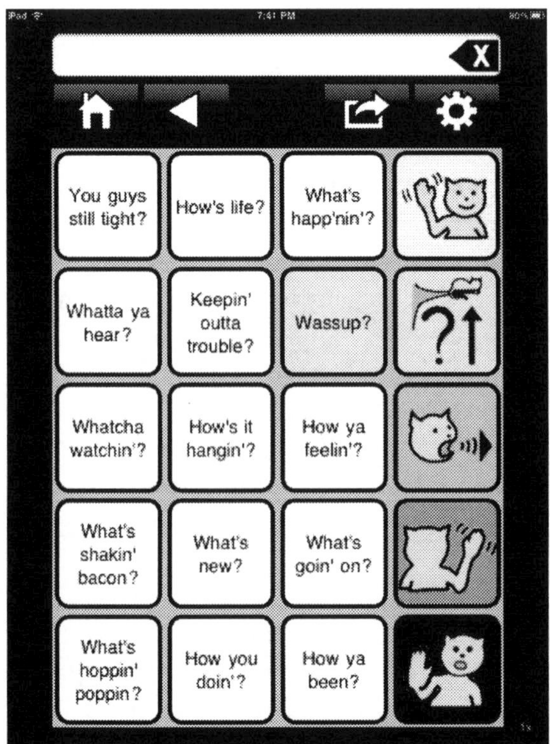

tion flow. When the user is ready to narrate his or her own story, or express wants and needs, the user must switch to an interface with a different or more complete vocabulary.

Several comments are in order. One would hope that when an AAC user is able to be a good active and engaged listener – responding phatically in the conversation flow rather than interrupting or delaying it – then he or she would be considered part of the social group. That has value in itself. But also, one would hope that when the AAC user is considered part of the social group, that other members of the group would be good listeners when it is the AAC user's turn to speak or when the AAC user has something substantive to say. At the same time, because traditional AAC interfaces may make it difficult to respond within the conversation flow, one wonders if that fact subconsciously trains many AAC users not to speak and not to be part of the social conversation.

## An Interface for "Hanging Out" with Friends for Social Conversation

There is another important use for a phatic interface like Fat Cat Snappy Chat®. It allows the user to just *hang out* and spend time with his or her friends, even if the AAC user feels no need to be the main speaker or no desire to say anything substantive. Indeed, for some *passive* activities, everyone in the room is reacting phatically. Consider what is happening when a group of people watch television together and *talk back* to the television or exchange commentary amongst them.

Fat Cat Snappy Chat® uses a vocabulary appropriate for a pre-teen, including colloquial expressions and slang. As an AAC user ages or the vocabulary of his or her social set changes, it is easy to imagine substituting different words and phrases, but keeping the interface the same. Alternatively, instead of these cat icons, the interface could substitute illustrations (e.g., pictures of people instead of cats) more appropriate for the age or social group. As long as the illustrations show the same gestures, the AAC user will not have to re-learn how to use the app.

## Extending a Phatic Interface to Similar Social Situations

This brings up an important point mentioned earlier. With a vocabulary and interface like Fat Cat Snappy Chat®, the phatic content (i.e., "We are in a conversation") is more important than the actual words used. Consequently, the interface can be re-used and extended to similar social situations by substituting similar, but different, illustrations and a different vocabulary. This amplifies the power of the interface, because the user does not have to learn a new one. Consider the following example: an interface for verbal accent games.

Sometimes kids (or adults for that matter) talk with a pretend accent as a form of fantasy play, social word play, or verbal sparring. Take for example, the September 19th parody holiday, International Talk like a Pirate Day, on which pirate aficionados talk to each other in pirate lingo (yes, this is actually an unofficial holiday); or the more well-known, St. Patrick's Day, in which many of Irish (and non-Irish) ancestry talk in the thickest brogue they can muster. Figure 6 shows the Home page of Fat Cat Pirate Chat®, designed to allow AAC users to participate in a fun *talk like a pirate* conversation. Notice that the cats have the same facial and body gestures as Fat Cat Snappy Chat®. The words are different and the voice is different, but the phatic (or emotive) content is the same. Someone who knows how to use Fat Cat Snappy Chat® can use Fat Cat Pirate Chat® without additional training. Because most of the cat icons are wearing pirate hats, even a non-literate user will not confuse the Fat Cat Pirate Chat® app with its Fat Cat Snappy Chat® counterpart.

*Figure 6. Fat Cat Pirate Chat® Home page*

## Another Use for a Phatic Approach: Recovering From a Failing Conversation

The previous discussion focused on how a phatic interface can be used to help AAC users participate in and continue conversations: both regular and fanciful. Now consider one of the original issues that prompted this inquiry: how to recover a conversation that is failing. One way that a conversation can fail is if it gets off script and the listener has nothing to say. Another way conversations can fail is when the listener does not understand the speaker. Perhaps the speaker spoke too fast, or the listener did not quite hear the words, or the listener did not understand the particular words spoken.

Traditional AAC interfaces often have at least two buttons to help recover a conversation. For instance, these buttons typically use the phrases like, "I don't understand" and "Please repeat." This is fine if it works the first or second time. Otherwise, it is likely to stop the conversation, because a speaker may not be able to think of a new way in which to explain the same thing.

An alternative phatic approach is to try to keep the conversation going, while at the same time trying to *repair* or recover it. Figure 7 depicts a screen shot of the Home page of Fat Cat Chat Repair®. As can be seen in the figure, this app is similar to that of Fat Cat Snappy Chat®, with the exception that expressions and gestures of the cat icons are different. The Fat Cat Chat Repair® interface has a grid of 20 buttons in 4 columns and 5 rows. On the Home page, the outer columns show buttons with cat icons, and the inner columns show buttons with words or word phrases. Tapping a button with text will say the text. Tapping on a button with an icon will show a new page.

The categories represented by the buttons (and icons) in the right-most column of Figure 7 focus on repairing or re-directing the conversation. They are:

- "Slow down"
- "Repeat" or say it again
- "Don't understand" (which is different than the "Don't know" of Fat Cat Snappy Chat®)
- "Change subject" of the conversation
- "That's it!," end the conversation

Tapping on an icon will bring up a new page with 15 different ways to express the sentiment. This is an attempt to turn repeated requests for clarification into a conversation rather than a demand or request.

To recover a conversation, the three most useful categories are "Slow down," "Repeat," and "Don't understand." Of these, the "Repeat" category is perhaps most important. Consider the page which appears when the "Repeat" icon button is tapped (see Figure 8). Notice that the text buttons do not just request repetition, but suggest different ways in which a thought can be expressed. Examples

*Figure 7. Fat Cat Chat Repair® Home page*

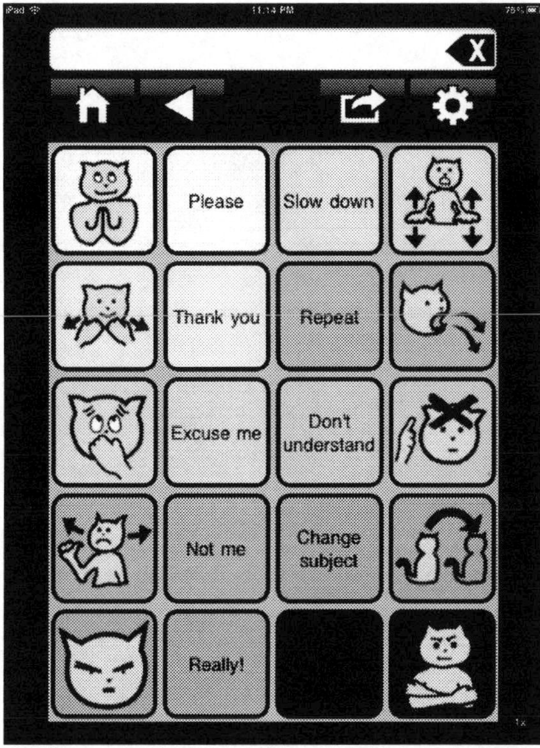


*Figure 8. Fat Cat Chat Repair® Repeat page*

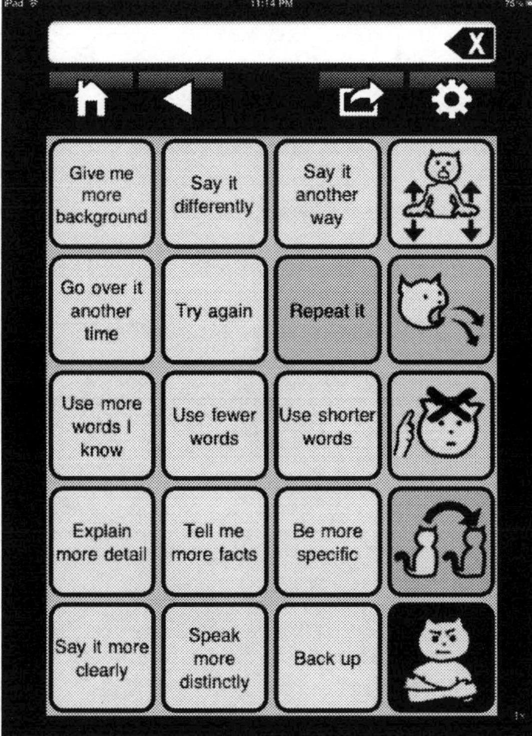


include, "Use more words I know," "Use shorter words," and "Be more specific." The intent is to help the speaker stop and think and then re-phrase what was said in a way that is more understandable to the listener. Again, the interface does not require that the AAC user is literate, but rather that a semi-randomization of choice will accomplish the variation in request.

The categories in the left-most column of Figure 7 help to keep the conversation going (while attempts are being made to repair it) by adding expressions of politeness, emphasis or excuse:

- "Please" and other imprecations
- "Thank you"
- "Excuse me" and other apologies
- "Not me" and other excuses which do not admit guilt
- "Really!" and other intensifiers

The first three expressions ("Please," "Thank you," and "Excuse me") allow the user to ask for help (such as politely asking the other person to slow down or repeat). An apology or imprecation can precede the request. An imprecation or thank you can follow it. Sometimes a conversation may break down because of something the user said or did, even if the user does not know what it is. The "Not me" category is intended to prevent a blame game or defuse an impasse in a light manner.

There are times when a conversation on a particular topic cannot be recovered, but the user wants to continue conversing. This may occur when the user does not understand the topic, but it can also occur when the user does not want to talk about a specific subject. In that case, the user can invoke the "Change subject" category. However, sometimes efforts to change the topic are unsuccessful. In such a case, the user may have to end the conversation using phrases in the "That's it!" (end the conversation) category.

The discussion thus far helps illustrate how software can be successfully used to facilitate a conversation or even recover one. The discussion thus far also addresses the initial concerns that were originally proposed by Slotznick, Hershberger, and Higginbotham (2009). However, in the course of developing a phatic approach to social chat and conversation repair, a broader application of this methodology became evident.

## A Simple Phatic Interface for Reception Line Situations and Social Queues

One value of at least considering a phatic approach is that it makes a vocabulary designer step back and consider the social context of a conversational situation. If participation in the social interaction is one of the primary messages being conveyed, then the vocabulary chosen can be more general, with the situation itself supplying the specifics. Using the vocabulary becomes less scripted and more improvisational (even if limited). In addition, a user can learn the interface rather than a script and re-use the interface when the situation reoccurs. Just as importantly, it helps "abstract" the situation and helps the vocabulary designer compare the social situation with others, so that even if the vocabularies are very different, the interface may be reused.

Consider the example of an AAC user going through a reception line at a wedding or other celebration. The AAC user has just participated and shared in an important life event with those who are celebrating the occasion and waiting in line to greet guests such as the AAC user. Part of sharing that event is validating that sharing by going through the reception line, standing in front of a celebrant, saying something congratulatory to the celebrant, moving on to the next celebrant, and repeating the same or similar. Many times, the people going through the reception line do not know the celebrants well (e.g., third cousin, once removed). Nonetheless, it is still important for social purposes and the pleasure of being one of the "family" to give congratulations, and engage in limited conversation. Keep in mind that the same goes for an AAC user who is the celebrant or host of a celebration. This person is faced with the same social task, having to accept congratulations both when people arrive and then again when they leave.

Now consider the example of the AAC user attending a funeral, and giving condolences to a mourner. While the words and emotions are different than at a celebration, the process is similar, and the conversations with the mourners are just as short and just as generalized. The same holds true in circumstances in which the AAC user is the mourner, and must accept such condolences.

Although these two examples could not be any more different in their purpose, these social settings involve similar constructs. There is a line or queue. One must go through the queue in order to exchange appropriate words, so that going through the queue is an important part of the social experience. Standing in such a social queue is far different than queuing up to pay for groceries at the food market, or buy tickets at the movie theater.

Certain cultural events also involve social queues. Consider going trick-or-treating at Halloween. The conversations are short and stylized, often with and at the house of someone that the trick-or-treater does not know. Figure 9 shows a screen shot for Fat Cat Spooky Chat®, designed for trick-or-treating. It is a one-page, two column, 10 button interface. The top four buttons are generalized phrases for a trick-or-treater to say. They can be said in any order. (This is the most phatic part of the interface, even though each button has its own icon.) Furthermore, they do not all have to be used. It is important to point out that the next four buttons ("Yes," "No," "Please," and "Thank you") allow the user to answer simple questions, such as "Do you want some candy?" or "Would you like another piece?" The bottom two buttons are partly customizable. One question frequently asked of a trick-or-treater is "What are you dressed as?" The answer is customizable, though it is likely to be changed only once a year. The "Help"

*Figure 9. Fat Cat Spooky Chat®*

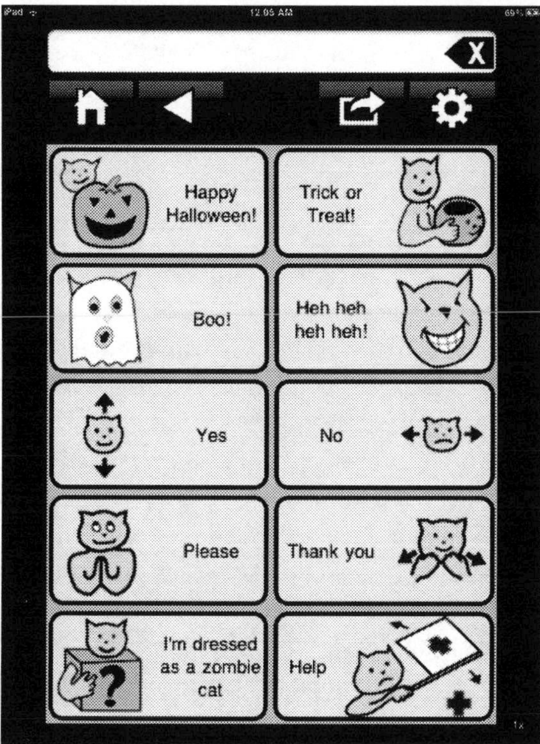


*Figure 10. Fat Cat Santa Chat®*

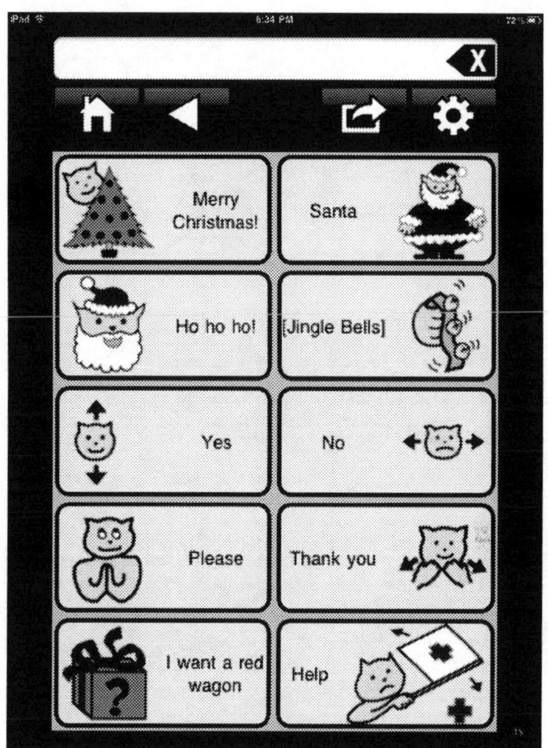


button allows a parent to add contact information in case a child gets lost.

Notice that a similar interface can be used for a reception line at a celebration or a funeral. There would be the four top buttons with general congratulations or condolences. The same simple answers ("Yes," "No," "Please" and "Thank you") for small talk questions. The bottom two buttons can remain customizable. For a funeral one might be a special memory ("Uncle Joe used to take me fishing.") The other might be an answer to the question "Who are you?" with a possible answer, "I'm cousin Bob, Emma's son." Vocabularies for these social queues are modeled in Fat Cat Celebration Chat®, Fat Cat Condolences®, and Fat Cat Welcome Chat®.

Similar vocabularies and interfaces can be created for other reception-line-type interactions. One example is talking to a department store Santa Claus (see Figure 10 for a screen shot of Fat Cat Santa Chat®). Here the editable answer provides a response to the question: "What do you want for Christmas?" Another example is talking to the shopping mall Easter Bunny (addressed by Fat Cat Bunny Chat®).

These aforementioned examples explore the phatic components of social settings that incorporate reception lines. They demonstrate how a phatic approach to AAC vocabulary design and interface construction can be very robust in the face of minor situational variation in contrast to a highly scripted approach. Though the above examples involve a variety of scenarios, there are undoubtedly more social settings or conversation situations that involve a social queue. Or for which this interface can be adapted.

All in all, social queues are relatively frequent, even though each instance may occur infrequently. Halloween, Christmas, and Easter each occur only once a year. However, a year may hold several celebrations or funerals. Taken together, many people must cope with a reception line event almost every other month (and for some, even more often). If an AAC user has to learn a new script for each event, or re-learn an old script, this is a significant cognitive burden. However, if the user can learn a standard reception line interface with error-free improvisation, then each of these social events becomes much more manageable and enjoyable.

## A Simple Phatic Interface for Run-Around Role-Play Games

Other interactions that involve phatic elements are some of the games that children play. So attention is turned next in this chapter to one of the most common and elementary games played by pre-adolescent boys: *run-around*. The role playing in these *let's pretend* type of games certainly requires narrative elements. However, the games are often played by groups of children in which the major narrative elements are dictated by a few group leaders. Consequently, it is important to explore how the utterances of the rest of the group (or otherwise called "followers") have a more phatic quality, so that for an AAC user, a phatic interface for a run-around game may support greater social interaction and increased enjoyment.

Most pre-adolescent boys play run-around games, even before they can talk. The essence of the game is very simple: you run around and scream. When boys get a little older and play in groups, a social construct or pretend world is built around these games. This is when the pretend role-play begins. The games are then called names like "cops and robbers," "space wars," or even "pirates," and typically often depend upon what is the latest, most popular action movie or television show. But the essence remains, running around and yelling, with the addition of sound effects for the weapons and explosions of the pretend battles (starting with "bang, bang"). And players pretend to die, with long drawn-out death screams. In these games, there is something generic about the running commentary. It must perform one of several functions and be appropriate for the pretend world. It does not have to be more specific than that. In this sense a run-around game can make use of a phatic-like interface. The underlying communication is that "We are yelling and playing run-around together." Consider Figure 11, a screen shot for Fat Cat Pirate Action®.

Before going further, it is important to point out that girls can certainly play run-around games too. However, as this author has been well advised by his daughters, girls' pretend games tend to be quite different. Namely, unlike the games of boys, girls typically refrain from yelling and using sound effects, and participants don't pretend to die.

Fat Cat Pirate Action® is designed for a handheld AAC device such as an iPod Touch® that can be held in one hand. Why? If a child has to use two hands to hold the device while running around,

*Figure 11. Fat Cat Pirate Action®*

the child is more likely to fall and get hurt. By holding the device in one hand, the child can also pretend that the device is a pretend weapon (e.g., pistol or sword; remember we're dealing with boys here). The interface is designed to need only one screen for the same reason.

Each row is a separate phatic category (and has a common background color). The five categories are:

- Yelling, and "go-here-go-there" commentary
- Things to say to teammates (most or all of whom are pretend)
- Things to say to opponents (most or all of whom are also pretend)
- Battle narration
- Sound effects for weapons and explosions

*Figure 12. Fat Cat Police Action®*

Even though each button has a separate icon, the narrative thrust of the game is supported by randomly picking from an appropriate row. (The exception may be picking the death scream, though if tapped mistakenly, it can be considered merely a painful, but superficial wound.)

The mechanics of the game are relatively simple: one of the players will point in a direction, say something appropriate, and run yelling in that direction (buttons in the top row; see Figure 11). Then the player will point in another direction, say something appropriate and run yelling in that new direction. There are pauses in the running in which the pretend battle occurs, during which a player pretends to coordinate action among teammates (buttons in the second row), challenge opponents (third row), or employ pretend weapons with varying sound effects (fifth row). The fourth row of buttons contains battle narration (e.g., "Got ya!") because even though these are battle games, one player can't touch or hurt another. Every once in a while, a player has to admit that "Ya got me!" and sometimes pretends to die. Even the smallest most junior player gets to take center stage when he pretends to die aloud, lingering, with a dramatic death.

While run-around games are a lot of fun – both in playing for these children and as a spectator (e.g., wheelchair bound AAC users, for instance who can't run around, can still join in the yelling part of the game from the sidelines) – these games also allow modeling of important social skills:

- Teamwork, leading, following, and helping the fallen
- Confrontation, group, individual, and limitation of actual violence
- Dealing with injury and death

It is important to note that it is straightforward to modify the Fat Cat Pirate Action® interface to model any other run-around game (see for example Fat Cat Police Action® in Figure 12). The key design constraint is to keep the phatic functionality of each row, but change the words and sound effects to reflect the pretend world of the new game. For example, it's easy to imagine how the interface for sea-faring pirates can be changed to space pirates. Phrases appropriate to space ships replace those used for sailing ships. Sound effects for light-sabers and ray guns substitute for those of cutlasses and pistols. In fact, Fat Cat Pirate Action® includes a setting that makes such a switch, and Fat Cat Police Action® can switch to space police or SWAT team.

If real voices are needed (as opposed to synthesized speech), then a voice or accent that is consistent with this pretend world, can be adapted into the app. Furthermore, the icons can be changed so that the pretend world and roles being played can be ascertained at a glance. Sometimes it is hard to illustrate a particular phrase used in pretend game play. In such a case, a phrase can be chosen with a similar function that can be illustrated. Remember that the action and commentary is not all encompassing, just sufficient. A player can also act out the pretend world narrations spoken by playmates.

## CONCLUSION

In short, a phatic vocabulary is not a substitute for a traditional narrative AAC vocabulary. At the same time, conversation is a social enterprise. If a person does not have the tools to deliver empathy, he or she may not receive it from others. If a person cannot be a good listener, others may be unwilling to listen to the person.

This chapter has presented how only a few phatic AAC interfaces and vocabularies allow a user to more fully participate in social conversation, whether listening actively, hanging out with friends, attending celebrations and funerals, going trick-or-treat, visiting Santa or the Easter Bunny, or playing run-around games, such as pirates or police. Much more applied research is needed, however; particularly given the advent of mobile technology and smart devices and the new world of possibilities such devices have created in furthering the study and application of phatic communication.

## REFERENCES

Malinowski, B. (1923). The problem of meaning in primitive language. In C. K. Ogden, & I. A. Richards (Eds.), *The meaning of meaning* (pp. 146–152). London: Routledge.

Slotznick, B. (2010). Point-and-Chat®: Instant messaging for AAC users. In S. Seok, E. Meyen, & B. DaCosta (Eds.), *Handbook of research on human cognition and assistive technology: Design, accessibility and transdisciplinary perspectives* (pp. 169–175). Hershey, PA: IGI Global. doi:10.4018/978-1-61520-817-3.ch011

Slotznick, B., Hershberger, D., & Higginbotham, J. (2009). *Point-and-chat instant messaging software for augmentative/alternative communications users*. Retrieved from http://www.nationaltechcenter.org/documents/point_and_chat_final_report.pdf

## ADDITIONAL READING

For additional information on phatic communication and the Fat Cat Chat® series of apps from Point-and-Read, Inc., please visit http://www.fatcatchat.net/.

## KEY TERMS AND DEFINITIONS

**Meme:** An idea or element of social behavior passed on through generations in a culture, especially by imitation.

**Phatic:** A type of communication that refers to speech that is used to express or create an atmosphere of shared feeling, goodwill, or sociability rather than to impart information (Malinowski, 1923).

**Social Queue:** A reception-line type situation at a social event or cultural setting, which requires the participants to go through the queue to meet pre-designated people, and exchange a few words with them that are appropriate to the setting.

## ENDNOTES

1 Aspects of this one-to-many mapping are patent pending. U.S. Patent Application Publication No. 2011\0184746 (Slotznick, 2010); automated method of recognizing inputted information items and selecting information items.

# Chapter 10
# Social Skills Development for Children with Autism Spectrum Disorders through the Use of Interactive Storytelling Games

**Sukun Jin**
*Konkuk University, South Korea*

**Boaventura DaCosta**
*Solers Research Group, USA*

**Soohnwa Seok**
*Korea University, South Korea*

## ABSTRACT

*Storytelling is an intricate part of the human psyche and hence, human history. From childhood, stories play an important role in human development, in that, for instance, humans automatically construct a storyline so that they can associate information. There is research to suggest that storytelling in video games can be beneficial because it can be used to help players identify with characters and their goals, creating a greater sense of immersion, positive feelings, and more physiological arousal. Furthermore, when the content is specific and targeted, these games are well suited for promoting acquisition, maintenance, and generalization of skills and knowledge. Findings such as these hold immense promise in the context of improving social skills for children with Autism Spectrum Disorders (ASD). Thus, the use of computers and video games, combined with more traditional storytelling, may serve as hopeful tools for motivating and engaging students as well as promoting learning. This chapter expounds upon this line of reasoning and explores the use of interactive storytelling games as an effective intervention in social skills development for children with ASD.*

DOI: 10.4018/978-1-4666-5015-2.ch010

## INTRODUCTION

For centuries, storytelling has been the most universal way in which to pass on information. Sarbin (1986) defined story as a "symbolized account of actions of human beings that has temporal dimension" (p. 3). That story is composed of a beginning, middle, and an end. It is held together by recognizable patterns of events otherwise known as plots and central to these plots is human predicaments and attempts at resolution. The role of narration has been shown to have a significant impact on human cognition and affect (Schneider, Lang, Shin, & Bradley, 2004). So it should come as no surprise that story plays an important role in human development. In fact, it has been proposed that humans automatically construct a storyline so that they can connect pieces of information (Sarbin, 1986).

Moreover, it has been suggested that the importance of story begins in childhood (Eisenberg, 1985; Fivush, 1994). According to Chatzara, Karagiannidis, and Stamatis (2012), storytelling is a well-established educational method for children (Robin, 2006; Valkanova & Watts, 2007; Yuksel, Robin, & McNeil, 2011). For example, early research on the subject has suggested that children, by identifying with heroes or good characters in a story, can psychologically learn how the act of being good is rewarding (Bettelheim, 1976). Such findings are of particular significance for children with autism spectrum disorders (ASD), in that the act of storytelling may be an effective way by which to help improve their social skills.

Autism spectrum disorders affects individuals in varying degrees of severity (Chatzara, Karagiannidis, & Stamatis, 2012), from classical autism to higher functioning, Asperger syndrome. A neurodevelopmental disorder with biological origins, the major characteristics of ASD include a qualitative impairment in social interactions and communication and a restricted or stereotypes pattern of activities, interests, and behaviors (Laushey & Heflin, 2000). Unlike most neurotypical children, who acquire social skills mostly by observation and imitation, it has been argued that these skills need to be taught directly and purposefully to children with ASD because these skills do not come naturally to them (Chatzara, Karagiannidis, & Stamatis, 2012). The need for explicit instruction coupled with the unique characteristics and learning styles of children with ASD makes storytelling a promising educational tool for this population of learners (Gray & Garand, 1993; More, 2008).

Story can be delivered using a variety of options, such as text, images, sounds, and multimedia, to include animation and video (Chatzara, Karagiannidis, & Stamatis, 2012). This is of particular interest for working with individuals with ASD, who tend to be attracted to technology (Heo, 2009; Tartaro & Cassell, 2007), presumably because it offers a predictable and controlled environment free of distracting social stimuli (Chatzara, Karagiannidis, & Stamatis, 2012), which are known to be challenging. In fact, there is research to suggest that computers and video games can be used to effectively improve the social skills of children with ASD (Barakova, Gillessen, & Feijs, 2009; Bernard-Optiz, Sriram, & Nakhoda-Sapuan, 2001; Gal et al., 2009). Thus, children with ASD have been known to not only show a great deal of interest in computers but have also been known to interact successfully with them (Demarest, 2000). This includes being able to successfully use computer software. Such software can also be malleable, adaptable to the special needs of children, to include the development of special hardware solutions and devices (Chatzara, Karagiannidis, & Stamatis, 2012). Thus, the union of story and computers hold great promise as part of educational interventions for learners with ASD, serving as potential catalysts in increasing the odds for learning and helping these learners gain independence (Mesibov, Shea, & Schopler, 2004).

## The Purpose of this Chapter

Taking into consideration the importance of stories in the course of human development, beginning in early childhood, including the benefits that stories bring to the educational process for different learners, as well as the positive role that computers and games can play in enriching the lives of children with ASD, this chapter presents an argument for combining the major features of the two by developing and using interactive storytelling games as educational tools to help improve the social skills of children with ASD.

As such, the chapter should be viewed as an introduction to the empirically supported benefits of interactive storytelling games in helping those with special needs, including students with ASD and related social-cognitive disorders, given the lifelong consequences that deficits in social interaction and communication impairments can have on a person's life, including personal relationships, education, and employment (Webb, Miller, Pierce, Strawser, & Jones, 2004).

The purpose of this chapter is also to encourage further investigation of the benefits of storytelling and to promote the development of interactive storytelling games. Thus, a conceptual model is provided at the end of the chapter that may help guide such efforts. This chapter is anticipated to be of particular importance to educators, educational policymakers, researchers, and game developers who seek new interventions in assisting children with special needs, but wish to mitigate certain factors, such as costs by leveraging existing technology (e.g., PCs, mobile devices).

## BACKGROUND

This chapter is presented in the following parts:

1. Prevalence of ASD through a cursory overview of the disorders and distinct characteristics, to serve as scaffolding for the chapter;
2. Empirical support for the use of story as a learning intervention;
3. The benefits and concerns of the use of storytelling in contemporary video games;
4. Social skills training for children with ASD using computer technology;
5. The technology preferences of children with ASD, along with the implications of the development of interactive storytelling games; and finally,
6. A conceptual model that may help in the design and development of such games.

## PREVALENCE AND CHARACTERISTICS OF AUTISM SPECTRUM DISORDERS

The growing prevalence of ASD in recent years has made it the third most common developmental spectrum of disabilities, outranking Down syndrome, for example (Dunlap & Bunton-Pierce, 1999; Fombonne, 2003; Prior, 2003). According to the Diagnostic and Statistical Manual (DSM), ASD includes to a range of pervasive developmental disorders comprising autism, Asperger syndrome, and pervasive developmental disorder not otherwise specified. Further, ASD is generally considered to demonstrate the following characteristics: atypical language and social development; repetitive and stereotypical activities, interests, and behaviors; need for structure and predictability; sensory and movement disorders; and a range of intellectual functioning.

In general, individuals with ASD are introverted, communicating or interacting very little with their peers, presumably because they do not know how (Welton, Vakil, & Carasea, 2004). Further, they have difficulty understanding what others are feeling and taking others' point of view, having to be explicitly taught human interaction skills that neurotypical children acquire on their own (Tartaro & Cassell, 2007).

Due to the shifting nature of and the many nuances involved in interpersonal relations, and given the need of individuals with ASD for just the opposite, it is no wonder that teaching and learning these skills is challenging. The matter is made even more difficult by the tremendous range of abilities and needs of individuals with ASD. For example, some lack functional language altogether, while others have a highly sophisticated vocabulary, but are able to express more than they can comprehend (Brill, 1994).

Although such challenges can be daunting, storytelling has shown promise as a universal teaching medium and may be able to aid those with ASD in regard to social skills development.

## STORYTELLING IN LEARNING

Many consider storytelling the original form of teaching (Pedersen, 1995). Thus, storytelling is the most widely used instructional strategy for teaching and enhancing the literacy skills of all students (Maier & Fisher, 2007) by using simple storylines to help learners make sense of the complex world around them (Bruner, 1990; Sadik, 2008; van Gils, 2005). There is considerable research to support the benefits of digitally-based storytelling in learning.

Kulla-Abbot and Polman (2008), while following the writing progress of seventh graders during an entire school year, found that storytelling using editing software helped engage students and inspired them to expand their creativity, allowing them to express their ideas in different ways. Similarly, while involved in "research-based practice" to adapt the British Broadcasting Corporation (BBC) model of digital storytelling practice (see Meadows, 2003) for community media projects, Burgess (2006) found that storytelling increased creativity. Further, Sadik (2008) found that overall learners performed well, meeting many of the pedagogical and technical attributes of digital storytelling, whereas despite concerns raised by teachers, the teachers in the study believed that digital storytelling could increase learners' understanding of curricular content, noting that they would be willing to include storytelling as part of their curriculum.

Examining the effects of the digital storytelling experience on preservice teachers' self-efficacy with regard to educational technology, Heo (2009) found that participants' technology competency and openness to change with regard to educational technology improved as a result of the storytelling. Meadows (2003), while working on the same digital storytelling community project as Burgess (2006), found that participants engaged more with the content when using multimedia software. As a result of examining pre- and inservice teachers' integration of digital storytelling technologies into education, Li (2007) found that the participants developed useful and flexible learning skills. Finally, Tsou, Wang, and Tzeng (2006) developed a multimedia storytelling website to study how web-based technology can be used to overcome challenges experienced by English foreign language (EFL) teachers. These researchers noted that the quality of subjects' teaching and learning improved along with their enjoyment of the program.

All in all, in these examples, the use of storytelling was a positive experience, resulting in an increase in learner engagement, enjoyment, and, in some instances, an increase in learning outcome on the part of teachers and students alike. The research outlined above, however, included neurotypical learners within the general education setting. It is important to point out that positive results have also been reported for learners with ADS as well, although the body of research examining storytelling for this group of learners is not as complete.

For instance, Losh and Capps (2003) examined the narrative abilities of high-functioning children with autism or Asperger syndrome alongside neurotypical children. The researchers found that when compared to the neurotypical group, the high-functioning group performed well, producing narratives comparable in length and content. However, these learners exhibited difficulty when incorporating more sophisticated characteristics used by the neurotypical learners. The high-functioning group also had difficulty inferring and building on underlying causal relationships with regard to story. Finally, Losh and Capps reported that the narrative abilities of these students were associated with performance on measures of emotional understanding, instead of other theories and factors, such as theory of mind or verbal IQ.

Finally, Sansosti, Powell-Smith, and Kincaid (2004), in conducting a research synthesis into the use of social stories found that incorporating storytelling had positive intervention effects for children with ASD. However, they caution that much more research is needed, proposing that further research be conducted on the use of storytelling with computers for effective learning.

Fortunately, storytelling has shown promise in this area as well. In particular, when used as narrative in video games.

## STORYTELLING IN VIDEO GAMES

Game developers have been successfully weaving storytelling into video games for some time. Unfortunately, benefits have been traditionally overshadowed by all the attention paid to the negative effects of video games on youth. That is, for several decades, the effects of these games have been a social concern in both the U.S. and other countries (Kirsh, 2002; Schneider et al., 2004). Some research even suggests that violent video games influence aggressive behavior, aggressive affect, aggressive cognition, and physiological arousal (Kirsh, 2002). However, research also suggests that the use of storytelling in video games can be positive (Schneider et al., 2004).

It has been argued that when storytelling is incorporated correctly, it makes game players feel they are part of the game (Laurel, 1993). Thus, research has suggested that when a story is present, game players identify with the characters and their goals, have a greater sense of immersion, feel more positive, and show more physiological arousal compared to non-story-based games (Schneider et al., 2004). It is this feeling of immersion that is vital in the successful use of storytelling in gaming. As a result, game designers are putting a lot of effort into making games more immersive.

The underlying premise is that the feeling of being immersed within the game results in greater enjoyment and positive attitudes towards game play. This feeling of being immersed within the virtual gaming environment is called "sense of presence" (Witmer & Singer, 1998). Witmer and Singer (1998) define this presence as "the subjective experience of being in one place or environment, even when one is physically situated in another" (p. 225). They further note that when applied to virtual environments, presence specifically refers to "experiencing the computer-generated environment rather than the actual physical locale" (p. 225).

It is believed that a sense of presence can be created in gaming by incorporating specific technologies such as display size, graphic resolution quality, and sound quality (Schneider et al., 2004). However, it has been suggested that the degree of immersion obtained by game players in video games varies considerably from individual to individual. That is, the degree of immersion is dependent on the game player's ability, desire, and motivation to temporarily suspend belief and believe he or she is truly a part of the game (Brown, 1999). Motivation is, therefore, vital in successfully helping game players feel as if they are immersed within the game.

It is this motivational element that has been credited as one of the reasons why video games are so popular. Specifically, it is argued that there is a motivational appeal to participate in learning through these types of games as opposed to the traditional classroom setting. Ricci, Salas, and Cannon-Bowers (1996) defined motivation as "the direction, intensity, and persistence of attentional effort invested by the trainee toward training" (p. 297). Further, they have indicated that specific properties associated with gaming have also been associated with motivation of individuals to participate in gaming, such as active participation, competition, and the challenge of uncertain outcomes within novel training.

While such findings are promising, it is important to note that not all research results with regard to the use of storytelling in video games are positive. First, some studies suggest that while human arousal may increase due to the use of advanced technology and storytelling, possibly through motivation and ultimately through the feeling of being immersed within the game, this may not influence specific performance and retention as previously expected. That is, motivation and immersion in game play does not necessarily mean better transfer of performance from the game to the real world. Second, longevity has been noted as a concern; specifically, it is uncertain how long the effects from motivation last. What is known is that short-term persistence is evident (Morris, Handcock, & Shirkey, 2004). Lastly, it has been suggested that gaming can be more effective if very specific content is targeted (Randel, Morris, Wetzel, & Whitehill, 1992). That is, the more specific the learning content, the greater the potential for transfer of performance of the learned skills and knowledge to the real world. This is an extremely important issue in the use of video games as learning tools, particularly in the context of social skill training for children with ASD, for whom generalization and maintenance of skills and knowledge is very challenging.

## SOCIAL SKILLS TRAINING FOR LEARNERS WITH AUTISM SPECTRUM DISORDERS USING COMPUTER AND GAME TECHNOLOGY

Historically, the focus of research in special education has been on developing interventions that foster and improve academic, behavioral, social, and emotional performance (Odom et al., 2005). Among these, social skills have typically received the least attention as most neurotypical children generally pick up such behaviors by observation and imitation. However, as mentioned earlier, this is not the case for children with ASD, who require direct instruction to learn what comes naturally to their nondisabled peers. Unfortunately, due to the range of abilities of individuals with ASD and the myriad of social skills nuances, there are no universally accepted strategies for improving their social skills.

At the core of special education is individualization (Dishion, McCord, & Poulin, 1999; Fenstermacher, Olympia, & Sheridan, 2006) with an emphasis on generalization and maintenance. As mentioned earlier, it is generalization and maintenance that pose the biggest challenge for children with ASD, who require that generalization and subsequent maintenance be deliberately incorporated into the educational approach (Haring, 1992).

The use of technology in social skills programming has great potential as it meets some of the underlying challenges related to the need of students with ASD for individualized and direct instruction (Thompson et al., 2010). In that, for example, from a general computer software point of view, such software can be customized to meet the needs of the individual learner. In addition, software can be designed to permit errors in a controlled, secure, and safe environment free from distractions from the outside world, thereby addressing some of the sensory challenges many students with ASD experience. A similar argument of benefits can be made for video games. In that these games can engage learners, model desired behaviors, and promote problem solving (Thompson et al., 2010). In addition to these benefits, video games have been found to enhance language skills as well as promoting social and emotional development (Weil & Pascal, 1990).

All in all, technology, such as computers can help support interactions between children; in particular, video games have been found to be effective in promoting social skills due to the individualized and targeted instruction they can offer.

## TECHNOLOGY PREFERENCE OF LEARNERS WITH AUTISM SPECTRUM DISORDERS

Due to their unique needs, the technology used to display and mediate interactions with video games (educational or otherwise) for neurotypical children cannot automatically be transferred to children with ASD (Rees, 2010). In instructional design, user preferences and needs must govern content and interaction parameters (Rees, 2010). For instance, to be effective for learners with ASD, instruction must include structure, familiarity, and predictability (Tutt, Powell, & Thornton, 2006). In addition, because they are strong visual learners (Rao & Gagie, 2006), to be effective, interventions for students with ASD must cater to this learning style, rather than relying on the auditory modality, which is prevalent in traditional instruction. Indeed, visual presentation of complex information enhances retrieval of memories or active engagement.

While some of the fundamental characteristics are known, such as a preference for structure, predictability, visual presentation of materials, and so on, to date, few studies have provided clarity on the technology preference of students with ASD. Further, of the research that does exist, findings are limited and methodological concerns limit generalizations. For example, Rees (2010) points to three empirically based studies that suffered from the limitations:

1. Parents or caregivers had responded on behalf of their children with ASD,
2. The surveyed populations were not chosen at random,
3. Results were aggregated based on a wide range of ages, and
4. The reported preferences were governed by access to commercially available software.

However, despite these concerns, findings from available research are still of interest. For instance, Lehman (1998) surveyed parents and caregivers of children with ASD and their neurotypical peers to evaluate their preferences for gaming software. The findings revealed that the use of text and audio information, to include fidelity of visual detail (e.g., animation), was more important to children with ASD than their neurotypical counterparts. Those in the ASD group also preferred educational software that permitted faster responses, even though they sometimes demonstrate impairments in motor planning (that is, difficulty in coordinating movements with intentions; Rinehart et al., 2006).

In another study, Shane and Albert (2008), while investigating families with at least one child with ASD under the age of 18, found that 89% of participants reported a preference for animated programs as opposed to media with more realistic human characters. Putnam and Chong (2008), on the other hand, in surveying parents or caregivers of children with ASD under the age of 18 years, found that respondents expressed interest in mobile devices and voice-activated devices, as well as for software that permitted users to set their own color and sound preferences. In this study,

20% of respondents also expressed interest in educational games.

While findings such as these are promising, much more research is needed in order to understand the user preferences and needs of children with ASD, if technology-based interventions, such as interactive storytelling games, are to be effective. More important, such games need to be developed using evidence-based approaches and effective practices, which is an area that is only now just emerging as a means in which to help learners with ASD.

## TOWARD THE DEVELOPMENT OF INTERACTIVE STORYTELLING GAMES

To qualify as an evidence-based practice (an important consideration in today's schools), an intervention must undergo multiple and iterative trials that show effectiveness through outcome evaluations. As such, evidence-based practice is likely to be effective in changing target behavior if implemented with integrity (Maxwell, 2004).

To benefit from such an approach, the conceptual model that follows is built upon a design-based theoretical foundation. According to Anderson and Shattuck (2012), design research, which came into being in the early 21st century, is a practical research methodology because it fills the gap between theoretical research and educational practices. As a result, it is a commonly used methodology in learning science (Brown, 1992).

The proposed conceptual model presented in this chapter is design-based because it meets the following criteria:

1. The intervention has been tested in a real-life educational context (Anderson & Shattuck, 2012);
2. The research design and the tests it has undergone are clear and focused (Brown, 1992; Mingfong, Yam San, & Ek Ming, 2010);
3. It uses mixed methodology (i.e., a combination of quantitative and qualitative approaches; Maxcy, 2003);
4. Iterative interventions have been conducted;
5. It involves collaboration between key personnel (e.g., participating teachers and researchers; Kuhne & Quigley, 1997); and
6. Evaluation is the major principle of the design.

The aim behind the model is to enable developers of interactive storytelling games to ecologically implement the theories that are the foundation of the research and to subsequently generalize learning, instructional methodologies, the process of the research design, and new theories for educational innovation. Thus, the model involves learning and teaching through research and systematic design of learning strategies (Collins, 1992).

As depicted in Figure 1, the conceptual model is comprised of key effective practices reported in the literature on ASD:

1. Interventions pursuing Universal Design for Learning (UDL) fitting the unique needs of learners,
2. Interventions using an individualized approach,
3. Interventions building on the modality (e.g., visual) strength of children with ASD, and
4. Interventions presented in familiar and natural environments.

In the development of interactive storytelling games, educators, educational policymakers, researchers, and game developers should consider these factors. For instance, a major focus should be individualization, to include individualized option tools, and the instructional content that should take into consideration evidence-based best practice, including observations, interviews, and multiple case studies. That is, the intervention should cater to the specific needs of the learner. It should build upon the visual strengths of the

*Figure 1. Conceptual model for the development of interactive storytelling games*

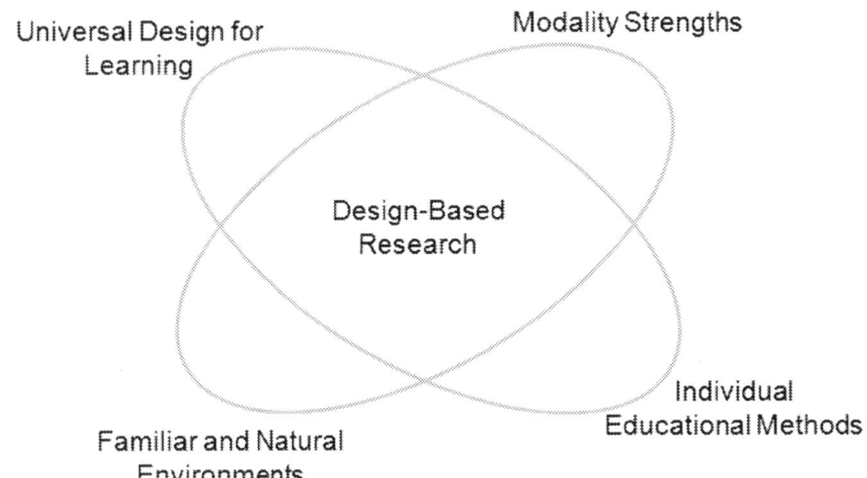


learner, such as the ability to change the game background or the individual characteristics of avatars, such as skin color and clothing. Auditory strategies could also be included, such as the control of background music or recording of the learner's voice. Furthermore, the intervention should include characteristics that are familiar and natural to the learner, to include visual, auditory, and psycho-motor approaches to learning. Finally, the learner's personal educational experiences could be incorporated into the game as a narrative component, as well as other types of educational materials.

At the same time, the intervention should be based on UDL in the underlying pedagogy and graphical interface to give all learners the same opportunity to learn (CAST, 2012). Rather than an argument for a "one-size-fits-all" solution, the intent here is to offer flexible interventions that can be adapted to individual needs and specific learning situations (CAST, 2012).

The conceptual model proposed here should be viewed as *work in progress* and should be expanded and refined based on empirically supported findings and lessons learned from the evaluation of interactive storytelling games. Furthermore, it should be examined in the context of human cognition to include other learning paradigms, such as multimedia learning theory (see DaCosta & Seok, 2010a, 2010b) and the management of cognitive load (see DaCosta & Seok, 2010c), as these may show promise in assisting learners with special needs.

## CONCLUSION

Storytelling is an intricate part of the human psyche and, therefore, human history. From childhood, stories play an important role in human development. Stories are found everywhere, on television, in movies, and recently in video games. Research suggests that storytelling in games can be beneficial (Schneider et al., 2004). For example, sense of presence is vital in the successful coupling of storytelling and gaming. That is, the game player must feel a sense of immersion, which is achieved through motivation. But most important, when educational content is specific and targeted, video games can be a well suited and effective tool for promoting skills and knowledge that are transferable from the instructional setting to the functional setting.

Such findings hold great promise in the context of assisting children with ASD in enhancing their social skills. However, much more study is needed. Specifically, future research must determine the best combinations of media and interface elements that facilitate and support the learning of children with ASD, including the use of video games, digital storytelling, and other emerging technologies.

## ACKNOWLEDGMENT

This work was made possible with funds granted by the National Research Foundation in Korea under the title "Development and Validation of Functional, Ecological, and Matching Evaluation Instrument for Assistive Technology and Students With Disabilities at the Elementary and Secondary Levels by Applying Multidimensional Scaling," number B00078.

## REFERENCES

Anderson, T., & Shattuck, J. (2012). Design-based research: A decade of progress in education research? *Educational Research*, *41*(1), 16–25.

Barakova, E., Gillessen, J., & Feijs, L. (2009). Social training of autistic children with interactive intelligent agents. *Journal of Integrative Neuroscience*, *8*(1), 23–34. doi:10.1142/S0219635209002046 PMID:19412978

Bernard-Optiz, V., Sriram, N., & Nakhoda-Sapuan, S. (2001). Enhancing social problem solving in children with autism and normal children through computer-assisted instruction. *Journal of Autism and Developmental Disorders*, *31*(4), 377–384. doi:10.1023/A:1010660502130 PMID:11569584

Bettelheim, B. (1976). *The uses of enchantment: The meaning and importance of fairy tales*. New York, NY: Knopf.

Brill, M. T. (1994). *Keys to parenting the child with autism* (2nd ed.). Hauppauge, NJ: Barron's Educational Series, Inc.

Brown, A. (1992). Design experiments: Theoretical and methodological challenges in creating complex interventions in classroom settings. *Journal of the Learning Sciences*, *2*(2), 141–178. doi:10.1207/s15327809jls0202_2

Brown, A. H. (1999). Simulated classrooms and artificial students: The potential effects of new technologies on teacher education. *Journal of Research on Computing in Education*, *32*(2), 307–318.

Bruner, J. (1990). *Acts of meaning: Four lectures on mind and culture*. Cambridge, MA: Harvard University Press.

Burgess, J. E. (2006). Hearing ordinary voices: Cultural studies, vernacular creativity and digital storytelling. *Continuum: Journal of Media and Cultural Studies*, *20*(2), 201–214. doi:10.1080/10304310600641737

CAST. (2012). *About UDL*. Retrieved from http://www.cast.org/udl/

Chatzara, K., Karagiannidis, C., & Stamatis, D. (2012, September). *Structural learning through digital storytelling for people with autism*. Paper presented at the 8th Hellenic Conference on ICT in Education (HCICTE 2012). Volos, Greece.

Collins, A. (1992). Toward a design science of education. In E. Scanlon, & T. O'Shea (Eds.), *New directions in educational technology* (pp. 15–22). New York, NY: Springer-Verlag. doi:10.1007/978-3-642-77750-9_2

DaCosta, B., & Seok, S. (2010a). Human cognition in the design of assistive technology for those with learning disabilities. In S. Seok, E. Meyen, & B. DaCosta (Eds.), *Handbook of research on human cognition and assistive technology: Design, accessibility and transdisciplinary perspectives* (pp. 1–20). Hershey, PA: IGI Global. doi:10.4018/978-1-61520-817-3.ch001

DaCosta, B., & Seok, S. (2010b). Managing cognitive load in the design of assistive technology for those with learning disabilities. In S. Seok, E. Meyen, & B. DaCosta (Eds.), *Handbook of research on human cognition and assistive technology: Design, accessibility and transdisciplinary perspectives* (pp. 21–42). Hershey, PA: IGI Global. doi:10.4018/978-1-61520-817-3.ch002

DaCosta, B., & Seok, S. (2010c). Multimedia design of assistive technology for those with learning disabilities. In S. Seok, E. Meyen, & B. DaCosta (Eds.), *Handbook of research on human cognition and assistive technology: Design, accessibility and transdisciplinary perspectives* (pp. 43–60). Hershey, PA: IGI Global. doi:10.4018/978-1-61520-817-3.ch003

Demarest, K. (2000). *Video games - What are they good for?* Retrieved from http://www.lessontutor.com/kd3.html

Dishion, T. J., McCord, J., & Poulin, F. (1999). When interventions harm: Peer groups and problem behavior. *The American Psychologist*, *54*(9), 755–764. doi:10.1037/0003-066X.54.9.755 PMID:10510665

Dunlap, G., & Bunton-Pierce, M. (1999). *Autism and autism spectrum disorder (ASD)* (Accession No. ED436068). Washington, DC: Office of Special Education and Rehabilitative Services (Ed.). Retrieved from http://search.ebscohost.com

Eisenberg, A. R. (1985). Learning to describe past experiences in conversation. *Discourse Processes*, *8*, 177–208. doi:10.1080/01638538509544613

Fenstermacher, K., Olympia, D., & Sheridan, S. M. (2006). Effectiveness of a computer-facilitated, interactive social skills training program for boys with attention deficit hyperactivity disorder. *School Psychology Quarterly*, *21*(2), 197–224. doi:10.1521/scpq.2006.21.2.197

Fivush, R. (1994). Constructing narrative, emotion, and self in parent-child conversations about the past. In U. Neisser, & R. Fivush (Eds.), *The remembering self: Construction and accuracy in the self-narrative* (pp. 136–157). Cambridge, UK: Cambridge University Press. doi:10.1017/CBO9780511752858.009

Fombonne, E. (2003). Epidemiological surveys of autism and other pervasive developmental disorders: An update. *Journal of Autism and Developmental Disorders*, *33*(4), 365–382. doi:10.1023/A:1025054610557 PMID:12959416

Gal, E., Bauminger, N., Goren-Bar, D., Pianesi, F., Stock, O., & Zancanaro, M. et al. (2009). Enhancing social communication of children with high-functioning autism through a co-located interface. *Artificial Intelligence and Society*, *24*(1), 75–84.

Gray, C. A., & Garand, J. D. (1993). Social stories: Improving responses of students with autism with accurate social information. *Focus on Autistic Behavior*, *8*(1), 1–10.

Haring, T. G. (1992). The context of social competence: Relations, relationships, and generalization. In S. L. Odom, S. R. McConnell, & M. A. McEvoy (Eds.), *Social competence of young children with disabilities: Issues and strategies for intervention* (pp. 307–320). Baltimore, MD: Paul H Brookes Publishing Co.

Heo, M. (2009). Digital storytelling: An empirical study of the impact of digital storytelling on pre-service teachers' self-efficacy and dispositions towards educational technology. *Journal of Educational Multimedia and Hypermedia*, *18*(4), 405–428.

Kirsh, S. J. (2002). The effects of violent video games on adolescents: The overlooked influence of development. *Aggression and Violent Behavior*, *8*, 377–389. doi:10.1016/S1359-1789(02)00056-3

Kuhne, G. W., & Quigley, A. B. (1997). Understanding and using action research in practice settings. In A. B. Quigley, & G. W. Kuhne (Eds.), *Creating practical knowledge: Posing problems, solving problems, and improving daily practice* (pp. 23–40). San Francisco, CA: Jossey-Bass. doi:10.1002/ace.7302

Kulla-Abbott, T., & Polman, J. L. (2008). Engaging student voice and fulfilling curriculum goals with digital storytelling. *Technology, Humanities. Education & Narrative*, *5*, 38–60.

Laurel, B. (1993). *Computers and theatre*. Reading, MA: Addison-Wesley.

Laushey, K. M., & Heflin, L. J. (2000). Enhancing social skills of kindergarten children with autism through the training of multiple peers as tutors. *Journal of Autism and Developmental Disorders*, *30*(3), 183–193. doi:10.1023/A:1005558101038 PMID:11055455

Lehman, J. F. (1998). *A feature-based comparison of software preferences in typically developing children versus children with autism spectrum disorders*. Retrieved from http://www.cs.cmu.edu/~jef/survey.html

Li, L. (2007). Digital storytelling: Bridging traditional and digital literacy's. In T. Bastiaens & S. Carliner (Eds.), *Proceedings of World Conference on E-Learning in Corporate, Government, Healthcare, and Higher Education 2007* (pp. 6201-6206). Chesapeake, VA: AACE.

Losh, M., & Capps, L. (2003). Narrative ability in high-functioning children with autism or Asperger's Syndrome. *Journal of Autism and Developmental Disorders*, *33*(3), 239–251. doi:10.1023/A:1024446215446 PMID:12908827

Maier, R. B., & Fisher, M. (2007). Strategies for digital storytelling via tabletop video: Building decision making skills in middle school students in marginalized communities. *Journal of Educational Technology Systems*, *35*(2), 175–192. doi:10.2190/5T21-43G4-4415-4MW5

Maxcy, S. J. (2003). Pragmatic threads in mixed methods research in the social sciences: The search for multiple modes of inquiry and the end of the philosophy of formalism. In A. Tashakkori, & C. Teddlike (Eds.), *Handbook of mixed methods in social and behavioral research* (pp. 51–89). Thousand Oaks, CA: Sage.

Maxwell, J. A. (2004). Reemergent scientism, postmodernism, and dialogue across differences. *Qualitative Inquiry*, *10*(1), 35–41. doi:10.1177/1077800403259492

Meadows, D. (2003). Digital storytelling: Research-based practice in new media. *Visual Communication*, *2*, 189–193. doi:10.1177/1470357203002002004

Mesibov, G. B., Shea, V., & Schopler, E. (2004). *The TEACCH approach to autism spectrum disorders*. New York, NY: Kluwer Academic/Plenum Publishers. doi:10.1007/978-0-306-48647-0

Mingfong, J., Yam San, C., & Ek Ming, T. (2010). Unpacking the design process in design-based research. In *Proceedings of the 9th International Conference of the Learning Sciences* (Vol. 2). Chicago: International Society of the Learning Science.

More, C. (2008). Digital stories targeting social skills for children with disabilities multidimensional learning. *Intervention in School and Clinic*, *43*(3), 168–177. doi:10.1177/1053451207312919

Morris, C. S., Handcock, P. A., & Shirkey, E, C. (2004). Motivational effects of adding context relevant stress in PC-based game training. *Military Psychology*, *16*(2), 135–147. doi:10.1207/S15327876MP1602_4

Odom, S. L., Brantlinger, E., Gersten, R., Horner, R., Thompson, B., & Harris, K. (2005). Research in special education: Scientific methods and evidence-based practices. *Exceptional Children, 71*(2), 137–148.

Pedersen, E. (1995). Storytelling and the art of teaching. *English Teaching Forum, 33*(1).

Prior, M. (2003). Is there an increase in the prevalence of autism spectrum disorders? *Journal of Paediatrics and Child Health, 39*(2), 81–82. doi:10.1046/j.1440-1754.2003.00097.x PMID:12603792

Putnam, C., & Chong, L. (2008). Software and technologies designed for people with autism: What do users want? In *Proceedings from Assets '08: The 10th International ACM SIGACCESS Conference on Computers and Accessibility*. Nova Scotia, Canada: ACM.

Randel, J. M., Morris, B. A., Wetzel, C. D., & Whitehill, B. V. (1992). The effectiveness of games for educational purposes: A review of recent research. *Simulation & Gaming, 23*(3), 261–276. doi:10.1177/1046878192233001

Rao, S. M., & Gagie, B. (2006). Learning through seeing and doing: Visual supports for children with autism. *Teaching Exceptional Children, 38*(6), 26–33.

Rees, D. (2010). *Designing learning games for children with autism spectrum disorder: Considering media and technology when creating the game world*. Retrieved from http://diannereessdsuassignments.weebly.com/uploads/6/3/9/0/6390810/literature_review.pdf

Ricci, K, E., Salas, E., & Cannon-Bowers, J. A. (1996). Do computer-based games facilitate knowledge acquisition and retention? *Military Psychology, 8*(4), 295–307. doi:10.1207/s15327876mp0804_3

Rinehart, N. J., Bellgrove, M. A., Tonge, B. J., Brereton, A. V., Howells-Rankin, D., & Bradshaw, J. L. (2006). An examination of movement kinematics in young people with high-functioning autism and Asperger's disorder: Further evidence for a motor planning deficit. *Journal of Autism and Developmental Disorders, 36*(6), 757–767. doi:10.1007/s10803-006-0118-x PMID:16865551

Robin, B. (2006). The educational uses of digital storytelling. In C. Crawford et al. (Eds.), *Proceedings of Society for Information Technology and Teacher Education International Conference 2006* (pp. 709-716). Chesapeake, VA: AACE.

Sadik, A. (2008). Digital storytelling: A meaningful technology-integrated approach for engaged students learning. *Educational Technology Research and Development, 56*, 487–506. doi:10.1007/s11423-008-9091-8

Sansosti, F. J., Powell-Smith, K. A., & Kincaid, D. (2004). A research synthesis of social story interventions for children with autism spectrum disorders. *Focus on Autism and Other Developmental Disabilities, 19*(4), 194–204. doi:10.1177/10883576040190040101

Sarbin, T. R. (1986). *Narrative psychology: The storied nature of human conduct*. New York, NY: Praege.

Schneider, E. F., Lang, A., Shin, M., & Bradley, S. D. (2004). Death with a story: How story impacts emotional, motivational, and physiological responses to first-person shooter video games. *Human Communication Research, 30*(3), 361–375.

Shane, H. C., & Albert, P. D. (2008). Electronic screen media for persons with autism spectrum disorders: Results of a survey. *Journal of Autism and Developmental Disorders, 38*(8), 1499–1508. doi:10.1007/s10803-007-0527-5 PMID:18293074

Tartaro, A., & Cassell, J. (2007). Using virtual peer technology as an intervention for children with autism. In J. Lazar (Ed.), *Universal Usability: Designing Computer Interfaces for Diverse User Populations* (pp. 231–262). West Sussex, UK: Academic Press.

Thompson, D., Baranowski, T., Buday, R., Baranowski, J., Thompson, V., Jago, R., & Griffith, M. J. (2010). Serious video games for health: How behavioral science guided the development of a serious video game. *Simulation & Gaming*, *41*(4), 587–606. doi:10.1177/1046878108328087 PMID:20711522

Tsou, W., Wang, W., & Tzeng, Y. (2006). Applying a multimedia storytelling website in foreign language learning. *Computers & Education*, *47*, 17–28. doi:10.1016/j.compedu.2004.08.013

Tutt, R., Powell, S., & Thornton, M. (2006). Educational approaches in autism: What we know about what we do. *Educational Psychology in Practice*, *22*(1), 69–81. doi:10.1080/02667360500512452

Valkanova, Y., & Watts, M. (2007). Digital story telling in a science classroom: Reflective self-learning (RSL) in action. *Early Child Development and Care*, *177*(6-7), 793–807. doi:10.1080/03004430701437252

van Gils, F. (2005). Potential applications of digital storytelling in education. In *Proceedings of 3rd Twente Student Conference on IT*. Enschede, The Netherlands: University of Twente.

Webb, B. J., Miller, S. P., Pierce, T. B., Strawser, S., & Jones, W. P. (2004). Effects of social skill instruction for high-functioning adolescents with autism spectrum disorders. *Focus on Autism and Other Developmental Disabilities*, *19*(1), 53–62. doi:10.1177/10883576040190010701

Weil, F., & Pascal, M. (1990). The place of verbal games in the framework of in-patient group psychotherapy with adolescents. *Journal of Group Psychotherapy, Psychodrama and Sociometry*, *43*(3), 128–138.

Welton, E., Vakil, S., & Carasea, C. (2004). Strategies for increasing positive social interactions in children with autism: A case study. *Teaching Exceptional Children*, *37*, 40–46.

Witmer, B. G., & Singer, M. J. (1998). Measuring presence in virtual environments: A presence questionnaire. *Presence (Cambridge, Mass.)*, *7*(3), 225–240. doi:10.1162/105474698565686

Yuksel, P., Robin, B., & McNeil, S. (2011). Educational uses of digital storytelling around the world. In M. Koehler & P. Mishra (Eds.), *Proceedings of Society for Information Technology & Teacher Education International Conference 2011* (pp. 1264-1271). Chesapeake, VA: AACE.

## ADDITIONAL READING

Anderson, T., & Shattuck, J. (2012). Design-based research: A decade of progress in education research? *Educational Research*, *41*(1), 16–25.

Barakova, E., Gillessen, J., & Feijs, L. (2009). Social training of autistic children with interactive intelligent agents. *Journal of Integrative Neuroscience*, *8*(1), 23–34. doi:10.1142/S0219635209002046 PMID:19412978

Bettelheim, B. (1976). *The uses of enchantment: The meaning and importance of fairy tales*. New York, NY: Knopf.

Chatzara, K., Karagiannidis, C., & Stamatis, D. (2012, September). Structural learning through digital storytelling for people with autism. *Paper presented at the 8th Hellenic Conference on ICT in Education* (HCICTE 2012), Volos, Greece.

DaCosta, B., & Seok, S. (2010a). Human cognition in the design of assistive technology for those with learning disabilities. In S. Seok, E. Meyen, & B. DaCosta (Eds.), *Handbook of research on human cognition and assistive technology: Design, accessibility and transdisciplinary perspectives* (pp. 1–20). Hershey, PA: IGI Global. doi:10.4018/978-1-61520-817-3.ch001

DaCosta, B., & Seok, S. (2010b). Managing cognitive load in the design of assistive technology for those with learning disabilities. In S. Seok, E. Meyen, & B. DaCosta (Eds.), *Handbook of research on human cognition and assistive technology: Design, accessibility and transdisciplinary perspectives* (pp. 21–42). Hershey, PA: IGI Global. doi:10.4018/978-1-61520-817-3.ch002

DaCosta, B., & Seok, S. (2010c). Multimedia design of assistive technology for those with learning disabilities. In S. Seok, E. Meyen, & B. DaCosta (Eds.), *Handbook of research on human cognition and assistive technology: Design, accessibility and transdisciplinary perspectives* (pp. 43–60). Hershey, PA: IGI Global. doi:10.4018/978-1-61520-817-3.ch003

Dunlap, G., & Bunton-Pierce, M. (1999). *Autism and autism spectrum disorder (ASD)* (Accession No. ED436068). Washington, DC: Office of Special Education and Rehabilitative Services (Ed.). Retrieved from http://search.ebscohost.com

Kulla-Abbott, T., & Polman, J. L. (2008). Engaging student voice and fulfilling curriculum goals with digital storytelling. *Technology, Humanities. Education & Narrative*, *5*, 38–60.

Meadows, D. (2003). Digital storytelling: Research-based practice in new media. *Visual Communication*, *2*, 189–193. doi:10.1177/1470357203002002004

Mingfong, J., Yam San, C., & Ek Ming, T. (2010). Unpacking the design process in design-based research. In *Proceedings of the 9th International Conference of the Learning Sciences* (Vol. 2). International Society of the Learning Science, Chicago, IL.

More, C. (2008). Digital stories targeting social skills for children with disabilities multidimensional learning. *Intervention in School and Clinic*, *43*(3), 168–177. doi:10.1177/1053451207312919

Odom, S. L., Brantlinger, E., Gersten, R., Horner, R., Thompson, B., & Harris, K. (2005). Research in special education: Scientific methods and evidence-based practices. *Exceptional Children*, *71*(2), 137–148.

Putnam, C., & Chong, L. (2008). Software and technologies designed for people with autism: What do users want? *Proceedings from Assets '08: The 10th International ACM SIGACCESS Conference on Computers and Accessibility*, Nova Scotia, Canada.

Rees, D. (2010). *Designing learning games for children with autism spectrum disorder. Considering media and technology when creating the game world.* Retrieved from http://diannereessdsuassignments.weebly.com/uploads/6/3/9/0/6390810/literature_review.pdf

Robin, B. (2006). The educational uses of digital storytelling. In C. Crawford et al. (Eds.), *Proceedings of Society for Information Technology and Teacher Education International Conference 2006* (pp. 709-716). Chesapeake, VA: AACE.

Sadik, A. (2008). Digital storytelling: A meaningful technology-integrated approach for engaged students learning. *Educational Technology Research and Development*, *56*, 487–506. doi:10.1007/s11423-008-9091-8

Sansosti, F. J., Powell-Smith, K. A., & Kincaid, D. (2004). A research synthesis of social story interventions for children with autism spectrum disorders. *Focus on Autism and Other Developmental Disabilities*, *19*(4), 194–204. doi:10.1177/10883576040190040101

Sarbin, T. R. (1986). *Narrative psychology: The storied nature of human conduct*. New York, NY: Praeger.

Tutt, R., Powell, S., & Thornton, M. (2006). Educational approaches in autism: What we know about what we do. *Educational Psychology in Practice*, *22*(1), 69–81. doi:10.1080/02667360500512452

van Gils, F. (2005). Potential applications of digital storytelling in education. In *3rd Twente Student Conference on IT, University of Twente, Faculty of Electrical Engineering, Mathematics and Compute Science*, Enschede, Netherlands.

Welton, E., Vakil, S., & Carasea, C. (2004). Strategies for increasing positive social interactions in children with autism: A case study. *Teaching Exceptional Children*, *37*, 40–46.

Witmer, B. G., & Singer, M. J. (1998). Measuring presence in virtual environments: A presence questionnaire. *Presence (Cambridge, Mass.)*, *7*(3), 225–240. doi:10.1162/105474698565686

Yuksel, P., Robin, B., & McNeil, S. (2011). Educational uses of digital storytelling around the world. In M. Koehler & P. Mishra (Eds.), *Proceedings of Society for Information Technology & Teacher Education International Conference 2011* (pp. 1264-1271). Chesapeake, VA: AACE.

## KEY TERMS AND DEFINITIONS

**Ability to Generalize:** The ability to apply something learned in the instructional setting to different situations in real life.

**Autism Spectrum Disorders:** A group of developmental disorders: autistic disorder, Asperger syndrome, and pervasive developmental disorders-not otherwise specified.

**Immersion (Sense of Presence):** "The subjective experience of being in one place or environment, even when one is physically situated in another" (Witmer & Singer, 1998, p. 225).

**Motivation:** "The direction, intensity, and persistence of attentional effort invested by the trainee toward training" (Ricci, Salas, & Cannon-Bowers, 1996, p. 297).

**Social Interaction:** "The ability to make oneself understood to another person, to use communication to achieve a common goal with another person, and the ability to behave in ways that demonstrate mutuality or joint work in conversation" (Tartaro & Cassell, 2007, p. 8).

**Story:** The "symbolized account of actions of human beings that has temporal dimension" (Sarbin, 1986, p. 3).

# Chapter 11
# Simulation Games as Interventions in the Promotion of Social Skills Development among Children with Autism Spectrum Disorders

**Carolyn Kinsell**
*Solers Research Group, USA*

**Boaventura DaCosta**
*Solers Research Group, USA*

**Angelique Nasah**
*Solers Research Group, USA*

## ABSTRACT

*It has been suggested that game technology can be successfully used to aid in social skills development among those with special needs. Based on the body of research available, such technology has been used in social skills development with children with Autism Spectrum Disorders (ASD). Furthermore, there is research to suggest that certain game technology, such as simulation-based games, can enhance learning and the retention of knowledge, which is of important benefit, given children with ASD show great difficulty in generalizing newly learned skills and knowledge from the instructional to the functional setting. However, at the time of this publication, very little empirical evidence exists that has specifically investigated the use of simulation-based games as interventions in the promotion of social skill development among children with ASD.*

DOI: 10.4018/978-1-4666-5015-2.ch011

## INTRODUCTION

This chapter presents the benefits and challenges in using game technology as an effective intervention in social skills development for children with ASD. Specifically, the characteristics of simulation-based games are presented that help make this technology particularly appealing in education, especially for children diagnosed with ASD. In addition to gaming and simulation, the pivotal storytelling component contributing to the successful development of such technology is explored in the context of instructional settings. Furthermore, a discussion on the importance of immersion and motivation is presented.

Although this chapter is introductory in nature, and only begins to scratch the surface as to the potential benefits and challenges of leveraging simulation-based games in the development of social skills for children with special needs, it is anticipated that this chapter will be of particular interest to researchers and practitioners who see potential in game technology as educational and training interventions. More importantly though, the information presented in this chapter is intended to serve as a catalyst, to spark interest and future research, which may provide insight and guidance into the use of simulation-based games in special education settings and how such interventions can help effectively promote the generalization of social skills among children with ASD.

To ensure scholarly rigor, the information presented in this chapter was compiled in a staged approach very similar to that found in primary research (Cooper, 1998). This chapter compiles the great majority of its content from substantive literature including books, academic journals and databases, and online journals. Considerable effort was made to ensure peer reviewed materials were foremost whilst researching and gathering content for this chapter. Although the great majority of the content within this chapter is directly based on information derived from such sources, other sources were used as well, including online articles. These sources were used mainly in a supplemental fashion befitting their academic stature, and are used mostly within the chapter to provide context regarding "practicing real world examples or an in-the-trenches view" of current happenings regarding the line of research.

## SIMULATION GAMES AS INTERVENTIONS IN SOCIAL SKILLS DEVELOPMENT

### Autism Spectrum Disorders

According to the Diagnostic and Statistical Manual of Mental Disorders (DSM), autism spectrum refers to a range of pervasive developmental disorders comprising autism, Asperger syndrome, and pervasive developmental disorder not otherwise specified. Childhood disintegrative disorder and Rett syndrome are sometimes included in autism spectrum disorders (ASD) discussions, although these two conditions are not considered to be part of the autism spectrum (Johnson & Myers, 2007). Children with ASD are afflicted to varied degrees (Chatzara, Karagiannidis, & Stamatis, 2012). However, those diagnosed are typically characterized by:

1. Impaired social interaction,
2. Difficulties communicating (verbal and non-verbal), and
3. Stereotyped and repetitive behaviors (Laushey & Heflin, 2000).

Specifically, children with ASD have trouble with everyday social situations not seen with neurotypical children. According to the DSM, children with ASD make little eye contact; they tend to pay little attention and fail to respond to others; they do not share their enjoyment and react atypically in response to the show of anger, affection, and other emotions (NIMH, 2011).

These children may also experience communication difficulties not seen with neurotypical children. Children with ASD, for instance, may fail or be slow to develop gestures, language, or use words or phrases that are unusual, out of context, or can only be understood by themselves or those close to them. Lastly, those who develop good language skills often have difficulty in back and forth conversations (NIMH, 2011).

Children with ASD may often show signs of repetitive (stereotyped) or unusual behavior, which may or may not be noticeable. These children have a tendency to focus excessively on objects or may become intensely preoccupied with a certain activity or task. Children with ASD are said to do best with everyday structure and routine to the extent that they may become extremely inflexible to any deviation from their daily schedule (NIMH, 2011).

So it should not come as a surprise that the components of everyday routine – structure, familiarity, and predictability – have been argued as necessary if an intervention is to be effective in helping children with ASD (Tutt, Powell, & Thornton, 2006). However, while such components are considered indispensable, there is no single intervention or treatment that is best for these children. Special education, the practice of providing individualized instruction to those with learning challenges, includes those who work on providing learning solutions for children with ASD. Essential to the special education approach for children with learning challenges and diagnoses such as ASD is to provide interventions specifically tailored to the needs of each child (Fenstermacher, Olympia, & Sheridan, 2006; Dishion, McCord, & Poulin, 1999).

## Game Technology in Education and Training

Interest among researchers and practitioners to use game technology in the instructional setting has been steadily mounting. Such interest has led to the investigation of how this technology can be used to target specific learning objectives (Jenkins & Squire, 2003; Squire, 2005). This growing interest should not come as a surprise. The increasing popularity of "video games" among school-aged adolescents dates back decades (e.g., Bowman, 1982; Chaffin, Maxwell, & Thompson, 1982; Kiesler, Sproull, & Eccles, 1983; Needham, 1983). Regrettably, the relationship between these games and education has been historically wrought with trepidation.

As long as anyone can remember, video games have been a social concern in both hemispheres (Kirsh, 2002; Schneider, Lang, Shin, & Bradley, 2004), with many researchers and practitioners focused on the psychosocial implications of these games, examining the relationships between video games and violence (Anderson & Bushman 2001; Bensley & Van Ewnwyk, 2001; Ellis, 1990; Griffiths, 1999). For the longest time, these concerns appeared to overshadow the educational benefits of video games within the literature. For instance, research has reported that video games can lead to real-life violence and aggression (Anderson & Bushman, 2001), manifest as violent thoughts or feelings (Anderson & Ford 1986; Calvert & Tan, 1994; Graybill, Kirsch, & Esselman, 1985), and impact aggressive behavior, affect, cognition, and arousal (Kirsh, 2002).

While such focus continues today, game technology has also been viewed in a much more positive light, as potentially motivating learning interventions. Namely, there are those who have taken to studying the effects this technology has on learners and its place in instructional design (Driskell & Dwyer, 1984; Bowman, 1982). For example, there is fairly early research that suggests game technology can increase the retention of embedded instructional subject matter (Dempsey, Lucassen, Gilley, & Rasmussen, 1993; Jacobs & Dempsey, 1993; Pierfy, 1977; Ricci, 1994; Ricci, Salas, & Cannon-Bowers, 1996). Thus today, the question is not so much as *can* game technology be used in learning, but instead *how*.

Historically speaking, game technology has been used to support drill-and-practice (Jonassen, 1988) instructional paradigms. This approach was used to teach basic skills (e.g., math and reading), which focused predominately on the retention of information through repetitive exercise (Mireille, 2005). It has been suggested that this technology is most effective when targeting very specific skills and knowledge (Griffiths, 2002).

Advancements in game technology however, have allowed researchers and practitioners to examine games beyond rote learning, and focus instead on high-order cognitive skills. That is to say, there is research to suggest that game technology may play a significant role in critical thinking, personal problem development, (Bowman, 1982; Chaffin, Maxwell, & Thompson, 1982; Trinkaus, 1983; Turkle, 1982), reasoning skills, and higher order thinking (Wood & Stewart, 1987). In fact, a good amount of information has emerged from the U.S. defense industry, in that the application of simulations in military training (Anton, 2009) to teach such higher order thinking and reasoning skills has shown great promise (Chatham, 2007; Ricci, Salas, & Cannon-Bowers, 1996).

Such findings make the prospect of game technology, specifically simulation-based games that hold characteristics typically not found in traditional games, appealing in not only helping neurotypical children, but children with special needs as well. In other words, traditional games, such as computer or video games and simulation-based games are not necessarily the same. And simulation-based games may, therefore, lend more naturally to the instructional setting.

## Simulation-Based Game Characteristics

The military application of simulation is best to describe the differences between traditional games, such as computer or video games, and simulation-based games. The defense industry has spent considerable time and resources in the study, development, and use of what has been customarily high-end "simulations" for training. Ricci, Salas, and Cannon-Bowers (1996) assert that simulations model "a process or mechanism relating task-relevant input changes to outcomes in a simplified reality that may not have a defined endpoint" (p. 296) and computer or video games as "competitive interactions bound by rules to achieve specified goals that are dependent on skill or knowledge and that often involve change and imaginary settings" (p. 296). The idea is simulations allow players to reach their own conclusions by exploring the relationships between their inputs and the resulting outputs in simulated environments that may closely resemble the real world.

Strictly speaking, simulations have been a means in which to model real-world environments or situations. Simulations are typically associated with a degree of fidelity, in that they can be loosely based on reality or closely model objects or situations found in the real-world (Prensky, 2001). From a military viewpoint, simulations have typically always striven to achieve the highest fidelity possible in the training of individuals and groups. Simulations can also offer a great deal of freedom in terms of exploration and may not necessarily follow a linear path of completion.

Video games, on the other hand, may model what appear to be real-world environments or situations, but there is no planned intent for knowledge and/or skills transfer. That is to say, they may be simulation-based, but the intent is purely entertainment. Furthermore, although computer and video games allow exploration of say territories or worlds, these game environments may not have any bearing on reality. Take for instance the massively multiplayer online role-playing game worlds of EverQuest® and World of Warcraft®. These are fantasy-themed virtual worlds that are visually realistic, but given their fantasy construction, have no interaction in the real-world.

This finding appears to be substantiated by a study commissioned by the British Education and Technology Agency, which found that simple simulation-based games were the most common type of entertainment-based game used in the classroom. They reported that more instances of games, such as SimCity® and RollerCoaster Tycoon®, were called out than any other genre of game (Kirriemuir & McFarlane, 2003). It is important to note that the majority of these low-cost alternative games, although commonly called "computer," "video," or "console" games, could also easily be classified as simulation-based because of how they are designed to operate (DaCosta, Nasah, Kinsell, & Seok, 2011). This distinction is important, in that it is this low-cost and commercially available simulation-based genre of game technology (referred to as "simulation games" from this point forward) that is of interest in the context of this chapter.

These low-cost and commercially available simulation games have made the distinction between video games and simulations unclear. A blurring of roles that has actually created opportunities for other fields, such as education (Kinsell, 2010). This is shown in the production of a number of commercially available and popular games that have and are being used in instructional settings, such as the SimCity® (Jenkins & Squire, 2003; Squire, 2005) and the Civilization® (Jenkins & Squire, 2003) series; or in military training settings, games such as America's Army® and Full Spectrum Warrior® (Roth, 2003; Schneider, et al., 2004). What this means is that even the military has begun to investigate the benefits of these low-cost alternatives, which we assert should be the focus of those investigating use of simulations and gaming with ASD learners.

A critical take-away regarding the points of view described in this chapter is that simulations have traditionally been able to offer greater fidelity and flexibility and typically have some pedagogical motive, whereas video games have been almost exclusively recreational. It is this ability for simulations to mimic, at least in part, the functional setting which allows for increased learning expectations (Herczeg, 2004; Kritzenberger, Winkler, & Herczeg, 2002). This is a key reason why simulation games have been so appealing in instructional and training settings.

We want to emphasize that the use of game technology requires upfront analysis in that the appropriate scope, focus, and context must be defined (Provenzo, 1991). This applies to computer or video games and simulations alike. Furthermore, these technologies are most useful when very specific content is targeted (Randall, Morris, Wetzel, & Whitehill, 1992). Part of that analysis involves what all games – technology-enabled or otherwise – have in common: A storytelling element. Take for instance the case study of Demarest's (2000) autistic son, who suffered from deficiencies in language and social skills and who also exhibited emotional challenges. Demarest reported that although her child was severely challenged in these areas, he excelled at computer game play, which Demarest attributed to the fact that game technologies provide visual patterns, speed development, and in the context of the current discussion, the element of story. (It should be pointed out that Demarest's findings were based on a single case study and anecdotal nature, thus methodologically in question. However, the findings are promising and help warrant further study.) Then there is Anton (2009), who presented the work of Tartaro and Cassell (2006) on the Authorable Virtual Peers program, which used language-based avatars to help children with ASD develop language and social skills through collaborative storytelling.

## Storytelling in Human Development and Game Technology

Some researchers have reported that humans have a natural inclination toward narratives and that story plays a very important role in human development. It also has been proposed that people automatically construct story lines so that they can make correlations between information (Sarbin, 1986). Story helps bring people together and provides another way at looking at the world (Laurel, 2004).

Another component of storytelling is the environment. Environment plays a significant role in that it creates a predisposition for stories as early as birth and that this predilection is developed because humans tend to organize everyday occurrences into mental templates or genetically embedded scripts, so that they can make better sense of situations, events, relationships and characters (Newman, 2005). Douglas and Haragadon (2000) refer to these mental templates as "schemas" that represent generic concepts and knowledge about the world that enable people to perceive, comprehend, perform, and act. In addition, it has been argued that certain types of scripts are common across all people and that these scripts have become universally accepted. Booker (2004) identifies basic scripts or archetypal plot types that have frequently appeared throughout history and have influenced everything from television formats to game designs. Some of the archetypal plot forms that are popular in game genres, for instance, include the hero's journey, origin myths, and ancestor myths.

There are several key components of narratives used in game technology that influence play. Mallon and Webb (2005) found that characterization and the manner of implementation significantly affect a players' engagement. Mallon and Webb also found that using social or psychological elements like trust and suspicion through the development of alliances between players make game play much more interactive. In addition, endings of narratives in game play are also important. Sgouros (2000) found that the endings of interactive stories, in which the player takes part as one of the characters and interacts with the rest of the cast to influence the development of the plot, motivates continued play and character (avatar) growth.

Using the social or psychological storytelling elements in game technology can significantly influence players' motivation for play. Newman (2005), for example, found a strong correlation between narrative predisposition and immersive tendencies. Newman discovered that people with high narrative predispositions gathered details about the environment, characters, and events and organized the information into narrative scripts to be used for future game play. In other words, players with high narrative predispositions become immersed, whereas those with lower narrative predispositions can become overloaded by the narrative details and can show a lower willingness to suspend belief and continue play.

Furthermore, the more fascinating and intriguing the story events and journey, the more players empathize with the characters. Schell (2005) found that upon entering the game experience, players' attention must be grabbed. If the experience is well constructed, interest will continue to rise until it reaches a climatic point when the player will be satisfied. An interesting storyline can, therefore, enhance play and motivate the player to continue playing. Furthermore, Schell discovered that uninteresting storylines can hinder players and discourage play. Games that use narratives that deviate from the storyline can also hinder motivation. It has been argued that continuity in story and allowing players to move about freely within the game environment also adds to the motivational level of the player which is vital in both promoting an immersive environment and facilitating learning.

## Computer and Game Technology Instructional Interventions

Individualized instruction, coupled with the need for structure, familiarity, and predictability, make computers a good intervention choice in social skills development because computer software can be individualized (Thompson et al., 2010) and computers can offer a predictable and organized environment that lacks particular stimuli, which can be difficult for children with ASD to manage (Chatzara, Karagiannidis, & Stamatis, 2012). One advantage of using computer gaming technology with ASD children is that these children find computers easy to use (Chatzara, Karagiannidis, & Stamatis, 2012) and can successfully interact with them (Demarest, 2000). Generally speaking, children with ASD are said to be drawn to computers (Anton, 2009; Heo, 2009; Tartaro & Cassell, 2006) for entertainment as well as for educational purposes (Heo, 2009). So the premise that computers and related game technology can be a positive influence in helping children with ASD improve their social skills is entirely fathomable (Barakova, Gillessen, & Feijs, 2009; Bernard-Optiz, Sriram, & Nakhoda-Sapuan, 2001; Gal et al., 2009).

Note that care should be exercised when using such technologies. Rees (2010), for instance, cautions that media and technology used with neurotypical children may not necessarily be appropriate for children with ASD, and that user preferences as well as the needs of the learner should govern the content and interaction parameters. This is particularly true with respect to the use of game technology. However, the integration of such technology into the instructional setting can be a challenge.

One of the biggest obstacles in using game technology (irrespective of platform and genre) is ensuring that these interactions are in line with learning objectives. Namely, game technology in learning or training involves more than just play. Granted, computer and video games can be engaging. They can be fun, interactive, aid in problem solving, and help facilitate user involvement, and provide structure (Prensky, 2001). They provide players with a means in which to explore, experience, practice, and improve skills (Piaget, 1962; Turkle, 1995; Vygotksy, 1978). What's more, few will argue that play isn't a vital component in child development. However, when used in the instructional setting, game technology must be coupled with context or guidance (Gee, 2005). More importantly, exploiting the features of game technology requires upfront analysis in that the appropriate scope, focus, and context must be defined (Provenzo, 1991). As it has been argued that computer and game technology are most effective when very specific content is targeted (Randall, Morris, Wetzel, & Whitehill, 1992); in fact, the more specific the content, the better potential for the transfer of learning. This transfer, or ability to generalize, is incredibly important in the context of assisting children with ASD.

## Generalization and Maintenance of Social Skill Development

The ultimate goal of instruction is for the learner to take what has been learned in the instructional setting to the functional setting. That is to say, the ability to generalize newly learned skills and knowledge to like tasks and different situations. Regrettably, such generalization can be problematic for children with ASD in that this ability does not necessarily occur naturally.

In working with children with ASD, generalization and maintenance must be consciously incorporated into the intervention. In doing so, the burden falls squarely on educators, parents, and those responsible for the growth of these children, because it must be assumed that these children may not be able to apply what they have learned outside the instructional setting (i.e., classroom). This is especially true with regard to social skills development, as children with ASD must be explicitly taught such skills. This is in contrast to neurotypical children, who usually develop these and similar skills naturally (Chatzara, Karagiannidis, & Stamatis, 2012). Thus, the ability to generalize newly learned social skills from one setting to another continues to be one of the biggest challenges (Haring, 1992) in the development of effective instruction to assist children with ASD.

## Simulation Games Can Enhance Learning and Retention of Knowledge

Simulation games may be an effective intervention in social skills development among children with ASD. There is research to suggest that this technology can enhance learning and the retention of knowledge as well as enhancing inductive reasoning, metacognitive analysis, and problem solving (Ricci, Salas, & Cannon-Bowers, 1996). Simulation games can contain a fidelity level of low, medium, or high and be effective. To contrast, low fidelity is an environment loosely based on reality or having a fantasy element, whereas high fidelity models reality as closely as possible (Prensky, 2001). Furthermore, this technology can be used to help motivate learners to reach their own conclusions through the exploration of relationships between inputs into the simulated environment and resulting outcomes (Ricci, Salas, & Cannon-Bowers, 1996).

As a consequence of these and other characteristics, simulation games have seen strong support as education and training alternatives to traditional instruction among researchers and practitioners in K-12, higher education, and military settings (DaCosta, Nasah, Kinsell, & Seok, 2011). More importantly, it has been argued that this technology should be considered in aiding those with special needs who otherwise would not be capable of obtaining the proper intervention when traditional instructional settings have been unsuccessful (Kinsell, 2010).

Storytelling has been described as the most commonly used traditional instructional approach in teaching literacy skills (Maier & Fisher, 2007) and may provide a number of benefits in the instructional setting (More, 2008) as well as to those with special needs (Anton, 2009); particularly when used as part of game technology. The use of story in this context therefore may show promise in helping promote social skills development in children with ASD.

The enjoyment of story may help immerse the player, resulting in greater involvement and engagement (Schneider, et al., 2004), both of which are important factors in the instructional setting. This immersive state is dependent on the player's ability, desire, and motivation to momentarily suspend belief (Brown, 1999; Witmer & Singer, 1998). Motivation therefore is critical in helping the player feel immersed in play. Some elements of game technology helpful in motivating neurotypical gamers may prove to be useful in engaging children with ASD during game play. These elements may also provide insight into the development and/or use of game technology interventions in order to better target learning objectives and promote generalization and maintenance from the perspective of children with ASD in social skills development.

## Importance of Immersion and Motivation

Game technology has the ability to immerse the player in another world, especially when the narrative structure aligns with the environment that affords the player opportunities to conduct behaviors, especially risky behaviors, which are either not found or impermissible in daily life (Bruner, 1986). However, as important as immersion is to this technology, a definition has yet to be agreed upon in the literature. Witmer and Singer (1998), for instance, define immersion as a psychological state characterized by a person perceiving to be enveloped by, included in, and interacting with, an environment that provides continuous experiences. Schell (2005) defines immersion as the state of being engaged by streaming stimuli. Douglas and Haragadon (2000) define immersion as being completely absorbed within the ebb and flow of a narrative schema. Finally, Brown and Cairns (2004) divide immersion into the three levels of – engagement, engrossment, and total immersion – where engagement is the lowest level of involvement with the game and total immersion the highest.

Although researchers disagree on a definition, there is some agreement as to how this immersive state can be achieved. Players can be so engrossed in game play that they reach what Eisenberg (1990) calls "jamming," which is the highest form of immersion. Jamming occurs when the player shows little effort during game play and exhibits a lack of self-consciousness in the surroundings or in sense of time. Csikszentmihalyi (1991) refers to jamming as a "flow" where players feel their game play is unlimited and extend their skills to deal with the challenges. In addition, as players become more deeply immersed, the intensity with which they play and familiarize themselves with the game characters increases. Dodsworth (1998) explains that as players get to know characters within the story, they can identify with the characters and develop psychological proximity. Namely, the players create a tendency to put themselves in the place of the characters and events.

To be successfully immersed, however, players must be motivated to do so. Motivation can be difficult to muster. Squire (2005), for instance, argues that the general introduction of computer or video games into the instructional setting may create as many motivational challenges as it solves. In his experience with studying and using Civilization®, Squire found that learners are not always immediately motivated to play these games as part of an overall educational paradigm. Such insight is important in that without motivation, the odds of successfully integrating game technology in the instructional setting can be significantly diminished.

There are several elements that help keep players motivated. For instance, Malone (1980) found that game technology should incorporate:

1. Optimal challenge;
2. Have appropriate goals and uncertain outcomes;
3. Provide clear, constructive, and encouraging feedback; and
4. Offer elements of curiosity and fantasy.

All factors are argued to be intrinsically motivating. Malone and Lepper (1987) found that intrinsically motivating games include:

1. A number of choices and
2. Give the players control over features of the game.

Rouse (2001) proposed that games must have:

1. A consistent environment,
2. A clear understanding of game boundaries,
3. A clear understanding of game rules,
4. Reasonable solutions,
5. Clear definition of goals,
6. Short term rewards,
7. Lack of distractions,
8. Challenge,
9. Achievable milestones,
10. Lack of repetition,
11. Ability to save game state, and
12. An interactive role.

Lastly, according to research from Garris, Ahlers, and Driskell (2002),

1. Fantasy,
2. Rules and goals,
3. Sensory stimuli,
4. Challenge,
5. Mystery, and
6. Control, motivate and promote continued play.

These elements paint a picture of game characteristics found across the literature that could be used to help motivate and engage players, but more importantly, could be used to engross learners (including ASD learners) and help facilitate the instructional setting by aligning game technology with overall pedagogy and learning objectives. However, even with motivation, when working with children with ASD, generalization and maintenance must be consciously incorporated into the intervention.

## Generalizing Social Skills from the Instructional to Functional Setting

Children with ASD are able to learn skills and knowledge in one situation or setting, but often have difficulty generalizing the same skills and knowledge when they have to be applied to different situations or settings. Namely, these children oftentimes cannot take what they have learned in a structured instructional setting and apply it to a similar natural functional setting without further explicit instruction. For instance, a child with ASD may learn to tie his or her shoe laces at home, but may have difficulty generalizing the skill and may not be able to tie the same shoe laces in a school or playground setting. This difficulty is usually not found with neurotypical children, in that the transfer of such a skill is entirely expected to occur naturally (Chatzara, Karagiannidis, & Stamatis, 2012).

Since generalization is not guaranteed or naturally occurring in children with ASD, it must be programmed into the intervention. Furthermore, maintenance must be planned so that the skills and knowledge are continuously and systematically strengthened over the long term. Otherwise the information can be lost. This programming and planning is, therefore, critical if the intervention is to meet the intended learning objectives. Such programming and planning can be difficult to incorporate into the intervention, particularly given that each child is different and the instruction must be tailored to the needs of each individual.

Be that as it may, Stokes and Baer (1977) identify methods, which are considered to be effective in the promotion of generalization. These are:

1. Train and hope,
2. Sequential modification,
3. Introduce to natural maintaining contingencies,
4. Train sufficient exemplars,
5. Train loosely,
6. Use indiscriminable contingencies,
7. Programming common stimuli,
8. Mediate generalization, and
9. Train "to generalize."

These methods provide a foundation in which to increase the likelihood of generalization. Stokes and Baer (1977) note that *train and hope* is considered the most frequently used method in the study of generalization. At the same time, the method can be argued to be the least successful. While social skills are likely to develop naturally in neurotypical children, as has been discussed thus far in this chapter, the same cannot be assumed for children with ASD. Consequently, better methodologies are needed that entail more than optimism.

For instance, it is advantageous to apply the same intervention across different settings, people, and situations. If the child is exhibiting difficulties both at home and in school with regard to certain social skills, the same intervention should be used by educators and parents alike in both settings to address the skills in question. According to Stokes and Baer (1977), such consistency across settings, or *sequential modification*, can greatly promote the generalization of skills.

Generalization is not enough, however. Maintenance must be planned for in the intervention. For the newly learned social skill to continue outside of the instructional setting, the learned skill must continuously make contact with the maintaining contingencies (Arnold-Saritepe, Phillips, Mudford, De Rozario, & Taylor, 2009). That is to say, there should be *natural maintaining contingencies* or rewards in the functional setting where the child will routinely practice their newly learned social skills.

Motivation is a huge factor in social skills development with children with ASD. Social skills may be foreign and perplexing to these children. Thus *natural contingencies* are needed to help maintain the newly acquired social skills. Such natural contingencies may be as simple as the child receiving a smile in response to the appropriate social behavior. So long as the reinforcement is strong enough, the learned skill is likely to continue in the functional setting.

Stokes and Baer (1977) also point out that it is advantageous to conduct the intervention in more than one setting. In other words, *train sufficient exemplars*. These settings should be added gradually one after the other until the desired social skill is acquired and is consistently generalized. The child, for instance, should be given the opportunity to practice the social skills with different people, in different situations, and in various contexts.

Moreover, the learning intervention should incorporate many different natural responses that exist in the functional settings. The intervention should afford for the natural opportunity to solve problems in the manner in which they would be solved in the functional setting. Understandably, this *train loosely* method to instruction can be a departure from the controlled and structured paradigms used in traditional instructional settings. However, such controlled settings may in fact be counterproductive, in that children with ASD may not be able to generalize what they have learned.

It has been established that natural occurring contingencies should be used whenever possible. However, such contingencies may be weak. Children with ASD must understand that they may not always receive the desired or appropriate response from others. As a result, *indiscriminable contingencies* should be programmed into the intervention and the child should not be rewarded each and every time the skill is appropriately used. Instead, only some responses should be rewarded. According to Stokes and Baer (1977), this intermittent reinforcement occurs through schedule thinning, and the resulting intermittent schedule is beneficial in that it helps with maintaining learned social skills in the functional setting for the long term.

*Programming common stimuli* is also of significant importance when developing interventions for social skills development. Namely, the instructional and functional setting should be examined for commonalities and differences. To maximize generalization, contingencies found in the functional settings should be incorporated into the instructional setting so that the instructional setting closely mirrors the functional setting as much as possible. Having an instructional setting that strongly resembles the functional setting can only help children with ASD in generalizing what they have learned.

It is also important *to mediate generalization*. Mediation stimuli should be used to ensure that the desired social skill is generalized to the functional setting (Arnold-Saritepe, Phillips, Mudford, De Rozario, & Taylor, 2009). For example, the child sets the goal for practicing a newly learned social skill and follows through with that skill in the functional setting. This act of goal setting is said to help promote generalization.

Finally, Stokes and Baer (1977) advocate the importance to *train to generalize*. In other words, reinforce generalization by asking children with ASD during the intervention to generalize.

From the perspective of simulation games, these methods may not only help in the selection and possible modding of games that have potential for helping children with ASD, but more importantly introduce a framework which aligns with overall pedagogy and learning objectives. For example, in train loosely, the simulation game would afford for the natural opportunity to solve problems in a similar if not the same way they would be tackled in the real-world. That is to say, the game would allow for the learner to practice in a simulated environment that allows for exploration, and attempts to account for real-world variables. Commonalities would also be accounted for to ensure the programming of common stimuli as much as possible. The simulation game would take, for instance, advantage of indiscriminable contingencies, in which the simulated environment would not always reward the learner, but instead would impose intermittent reinforcement as a way to acclimate the learner to the real-world.

As mentioned, the use of game technology (simulated or otherwise) requires upfront analysis in that the appropriate scope, focus, and context must be defined (Provenzo, 1991). These methods along with other factors discussed in this chapter may prove invaluable in such analysis.

## FUTURE RESEARCH DIRECTIONS

It has been suggested that game technology can be successfully used to aid in social skills development among those with special needs (Griffiths, 2002). In the context of this chapter, such technology has been used in social skills development for children and adolescents with ASD along with other developmental challenges (Demarest, 2000; Gaylord-Ross, Haring, Breen, & Pitts-Conway, 1984; Grandin, 2012; McElroy, 2011; Porter, 1995; Tartaro & Cassell, 2006), to include helping children with limited vocal speech acquisition (Horn, Jones, & Hamlett, 1991), disabilities in spatial ability development (Masendorf, 1993), problem-solving (Hollingsworth & Woodward, 1993), and mathematics (Okolo, 1992).

Another area warranting study is that of mobile gaming. The explosion of mobile devices, and consequently mobile games, has far reaching implications. In that such devices and games are so pervasive that they can be played anywhere and at any time. Such a medium might show promise in the context of generalization and maintenance. For example, mobile games may be a strong way to maintain consistency and help children transfer skills between home and school. Mobile games could also be used to delivery consistent rewards providing feedback wherever and whenever the child is demonstrating or practicing a skill. And that the anywhere-anytime nature of these games is of particular importance because this benefit could also be used to help promote the practice of skills in different settings, contexts, and with different individuals. Take for instance a mobile game that provides a way to practice social skills by incorporating a live actor in a virtual world, such as Second Life®. This would create a situation in which children with ASD are interacting with real people in safe and non-judgmental virtual social situations, without having to the face the repercussions or social fears that might accompany a live interaction.

## CONCLUSION

Regrettably, at the time of this publication, very little empirical evidence exists which has specifically investigated the use of simulation games with a story component as interventions in the promotion of social skill development among children with ASD. Much more research is needed; particularly given the cautionary tale by those, such as Rees (2010), who have proclaimed that media and technology used with neurotypical children may not necessarily be appropriate for those with ASD. Further study is needed to determine how best to use simulation games to help promote social skill development for children with ASD. As has been discussed in this chapter, there are many factors that must be taken into consideration when leveraging such technology. Also, learning how to use these factors together is imperative if game technologies, such as simulation games or story-based simulation games, are to be effective in helping children with ASD in social skills development.

Although this chapter only begins to scratch the surface as to the potential benefits and challenges of leveraging simulation games in helping children with special needs, the information provided herein is a call for researchers and practitioners who see potential in game technology, including simulation games as well as game integrating components, such as storytelling, to not only expand the investigation of such technology and its use in educational and training interventions, but also push for the specific investigation into how this technology presents greater possibilities in promoting the generalization of social skills among children with ASD and other disabling conditions. And in doing so, push for practical examples that can be shared with researchers and practitioners alike as to how simulation games can be used to help mitigate the many challenges experienced by these children.

## REFERENCES


Anderson, C. A., & Bushman, B. J. (2001). Effects of violent video games and aggressive behavior, aggressive cognition, aggressive affect, physiological arousal and prosocial behavior: A meta-analytic review of the scientific literature. *Psychological Science*, *12*(5), 353–359. doi:10.1111/1467-9280.00366 PMID:11554666

Anderson, C. A., & Ford, C. M. (1986). Affect of the game player: Short-term effects of highly and mildly aggressive video games. *Personality and Social Psychology Bulletin*, *12*(4), 290–402. doi:10.1177/0146167286124002

Anton, J. J. (2009). *The application of modeling and simulation to the behavioral deficit of autism*. Retrieved from http://ntrs.nasa.gov/archive/nasa/casi.ntrs.nasa.gov/20100012859_2010013740.pdf

Arnold-Saritepe, A. M., Phillips, K. J., Mudford, O. C., De Rozario, K. A., & Taylor, S. A. (2009). Generalization and maintenance. In J. L. Matson (Ed.), *Applied behavior analysis for children with Autism Spectrum Disorders* (pp. 207–223). New York: Springer. doi:10.1007/978-1-4419-0088-3_12

Barakova, E., Gillessen, J., & Feijs, L. (2009). Social training of autistic children with interactive intelligent agents. *Journal of Integrative Neuroscience*, *8*(1), 23–34. doi:10.1142/S0219635209002046 PMID:19412978

Bensley, L., & Van Ewnwyk, J. (2001). Video games and real-life aggression: A review of the literature. *The Journal of Adolescent Health*, *29*, 244–257. doi:10.1016/S1054-139X(01)00239-7 PMID:11587908

Bernard-Optiz, V., Sriram, N., & Nakhoda-Sapuan, S. (2001). Enhancing social problem solving in children with Autism and normal children through computer-assisted instruction. *Journal of Autism and Developmental Disorders*, *31*(4), 377–384. doi:10.1023/A:1010660502130 PMID:11569584

Booker, C. (2004). *The seven basic plots: Why we tell stories*. New York, NY: Continuum Books.

Bowman, R. F. (1982). A Pac-Man theory of motivation: Tactical implications for classroom instruction. *Educational Technology*, *22*(9), 14–17.

Brown, A. H. (1999). Simulated classrooms and artificial students: The potential effects of new technologies on teacher education. *Journal of Research on Computing in Education*, *32*(2), 307–318.

Brown, E., & Cairns, P. (2004). A grounded investigation of immersion in games. In *Proceedings of ACM Conference on Human Factors in Computing Systems*. ACM Press.

Bruner, J. (1986). *Actual minds, possible worlds*. Cambridge, MA: Harvard University Press.

Calvert, S. L., & Tan, S. (1994). Impact of virtual reality on young adults' physiological arousal and aggressive thoughts: Interaction versus observation. *Journal of Applied Developmental Psychology*, *15*(1), 125–139. doi:10.1016/0193-3973(94)90009-4

Chaffin, J. D., Maxwell, B., & Thompson, B. (1982). ARC-ED curriculum: The application of video game format to educational software. *Exceptional Children*, *49*, 173–178.

Chatham, R. E. (2007). Games for training. *Communications of the ACM*, *50*(7), 37–43. doi:10.1145/1272516.1272537

Chatzara, K., Karagiannidis, C., & Stamatis, D. (2012). *Structural learning through digital storytelling for people with autism*. Paper presented at the 8th Hellenic Conference on ICT in Education (HCICTE 2012). Volos, Greece.

Cooper, H. (1998). *Synthesizing research* (3rd ed., Vol. 2). Thousand Oaks, CA: Sage Publications.

Csikszentmihalyi, M. (1991). *Flow: The psychology of optimal experience*. New York: Harper Collins.

DaCosta, B., Nasah, A., Kinsell, C., & Seok, S. (2011). Digital propensity: An investigation of video game and information and communication technology practices. In P. Felicia (Ed.), *Handbook of research on improving learning and motivation through educational games: Multidisciplinary approaches* (pp. 1148–1173). Hershey, PA: IGI Global. doi:10.4018/978-1-60960-495-0.ch052

Demarest, K. (2000). *Video games - What are they good for?* Retrieved from http://www.lessontutor.com/kd3.html

Dempsey, J., Lucassen, B., Gilley, W., & Rasmussen, K. (1993). Since Malone's theory of intrinsically motivating instruction: What's the score in the gaming literature? *Journal of Educational Technology Systems*, *22*(2), 1973–1983. doi:10.2190/2TH7-5TXG-TAR7-T4V2

Dishion, T. J., McCord, J., & Poulin, F. (1999). When interventions harm: Peer groups and problem behavior. *The American Psychologist*, *54*(9), 755–764. doi:10.1037/0003-066X.54.9.755 PMID:10510665

Dodsworth, C. Jr. (1998). *Digital illusion*. New York: ACM Press.

Douglas, Y., & Haragadon, A. (2000). The pleasure principle: Immersion, engagement, flow. In *Proceedings of ACM Conference on Hypertext and Hypermedia*, (pp. 153-160). ACM.

Driskell, J. E., & Dwyer, D. J. (1984). Microcomputer videogame based training. *Educational Technology*, *24*(2), 11–15.

Eisenberg, E. (1990). Jamming: Transcendence through organization. *Communication Research*, *17*(2), 139–164. doi:10.1177/009365090017002001

Ellis, J. (1990). Computer games and aggressive behavior: A review of the literature. *Educational Technology*, *30*(2), 37–40.

Fenstermacher, K., Olympia, D., & Sheridan, S. M. (2006). Effectiveness of a computer-facilitated, interactive social skills training program for boys with attention deficit hyperactivity disorder. *School Psychology Quarterly*, *21*(2), 197–224. doi:10.1521/scpq.2006.21.2.197

Gal, E., Bauminger, N., Goren-Bar, D., Pianesi, F., Stock, O., & Zancanaro, M. et al. (2009). Enhancing social communication of children with high-functioning autism through a co-located interface. *Artificial Intelligence and Society*, *24*(1), 75–84.

Garris, R., Ahlers, R., & Driskell, J. E. (2002). Games, motivation, and learning: A research and practice model. *Simulation & Gaming*, *33*(4), 441–467. doi:10.1177/1046878102238607

Gaylord-Ross, R. J., Haring, T. G., Breen, C., & Pitts-Conway, V. (1984). The training and generalization of social interaction skills with autistic youth. *Journal of Applied Behavior Analysis*, *17*, 229. doi:10.1901/jaba.1984.17-229 PMID:6735954

Gee, J. P. (2005). What would a state of the art instructional video game look like?. *Innovate: Journal of Online Education, 1*(6).

Grandin, T. (2012). What's the big deal about video games? *Autism Asperger's Digest*. Retrieved from http://autismdigest.com/whats-the-big-deal-about-video-games/

Graybill, D., Kirsch, J. R., & Esselman, E. D. (1985). Effects of playing violent versus non-violent video games on the aggressive ideation of aggressive and nonaggressive children. *Child Study Journal*, *15*(3), 299–205.

Griffiths, M. D. (1999). Violent video games and aggression: A review of the literature. *Aggression and Violent Behavior*, *4*(2), 203–212. doi:10.1016/S1359-1789(97)00055-4

Griffiths, M. D. (2002). The educational benefits of videogames. *Education for Health*, *20*(3), 47–51.

Haring, T. G. (1992). The context of social competence: Relations, relationships, and generalization. In S. L. Odom, S. R. McConnell, & M. A. McEvoy (Eds.), *Social competence of young children with disabilities: Issues and strategies for intervention*. Baltimore, MD: Paul H Brooks Publishing Co.

Heo, M. (2009). Digital storytelling: An empirical study of the impact of digital storytelling on pre-service teachers' self efficacy and dispositions towards educational technology. *Journal of Educational Multimedia and Hypermedia*, *18*(4), 405–428.

Herczeg, M. (2004). *Experience design for computer-based learning systems: Learning with engagement and emotions*. Paper presented at the ED-MEDIA 2004 World Conference on Educational Multimedia, Hypermedia and Telecommunications. New York, NY.

Hollingsworth, M., & Woodward, J. (1993). Integrated learning: Explicit strategies and their role in problem solving instruction for students with learning disabilities. *Exceptional Children*, *59*, 444–445. PMID:8440301

Horn, E., Jones, H. A., & Hamlett, C. (1991). An investigation of the feasibility of a video game system for developing scanning and selection skills. *Journal for the Association for People with Severe Handicaps*, *16*, 108–115.

Jacobs, J. W., & Dempsey, J. V. (1993). Simulation and gaming: Fidelity, feedback, and motivation. In J. V. Dempsey, & G. C. Sales (Eds.), *Interactive instruction and feedback*. Englewood Cliffs, NJ: Educational Technology Publications.

Jenkins, H., & Squire, K. (2003). Understanding civilization (III). *Computer Games Magazine*. Retrieved from http://educationarcade.org

Johnson, C. P., & Myers, S. M. (2007). Identification and evaluation of children with autism spectrum disorders. *Pediatrics*, *120*(5), 1183–1215. doi:10.1542/peds.2007-2361 PMID:17967920

Jonassen, D. H. (1988). Integrating learning strategies into courseware to facilitate deeper processing. In D. H. Jonassen (Ed.), *Instructional designs for microcomputer courseware*. Hillsdale, NJ: Erlbaum.

Kiesler, S., Sproull, L., & Eccles, J. S. (1983). Second class citizens? *Psychology Today*, *17*(3), 41–48.

Kinsell, C. (2010). Investigating assistive technologies using computers to simulate basic curriculum for individuals with cognitive impairments. In S. Seok, E. Meyen, & B. DaCosta (Eds.), *Handbook of research on human cognition and assistive technology: Design, accessibility and transdisciplinary perspectives* (pp. 61–74). Hershey, PA: IGI Global. doi:10.4018/978-1-61520-817-3.ch004

Kirriemuir, J., & McFarlane, A. (2003). *Use of computer and video games in the classroom*. Paper presented at the Video games Research Conference. Utrecht, The Netherlands.

Kirsh, S. J. (2002). The effects of violent video games on adolescents: The overlooked influence of development. *Aggression and Violent Behavior*, *8*, 377–389. doi:10.1016/S1359-1789(02)00056-3

Kritzenberger, H., Winkler, T., & Herczeg, M. (2002). *Mixed reality environments as collaborative and constructive learning spaces for elementary school children.* Paper presented at the ED-Media 2002 World Conference on Educational Multimedia, Hypermedia and Telecommunications. Denver, CO.

Laurel, B. (2004). Narrative construction as play. *Interaction*, *11*, 73–74. doi:10.1145/1015530.1015568

Laushey, K. M., & Heflin, L. J. (2000). Enhancing social skills of kindergarten children with autism through the training of multiple peers as tutors. *Journal of Autism and Developmental Disorders*, *30*(3), 183–193. doi:10.1023/A:1005558101038 PMID:11055455

Maier, R. B., & Fisher, M. (2007). Strategies for digital storytelling via tabletop video: Building decision making skills in middle school students in marginalized communities. *Journal of Educational Technology Systems*, *35*(2), 175–192. doi:10.2190/5T21-43G4-4415-4MW5

Mallon, B., & Webb, B. (2005). Stand up and take your place: Identifying narrative elements in narrative adventure and role play games. *ACM Computers in Entertainment*, *3*(1), 1–19. doi:10.1145/1057270.1057285

Malone, T. (1980). *What makes things fun to learn? A study of intrinsically motivating computer games*. (Ph.D. dissertation). Stanford University, Palo Alto, CA.

Malone, T., & Lepper, M. (1987). Making learning fun: A taxonomy of intrinsic motivations of learning. In R. E. Snow & M. J. Farr (Eds.), Aptitude, learning, and instruction: Vol. 3: Connotative and affective process analysis (pp. 223-253). Hillsdale, NJ: Lawrence Erlbaum.

Masendorf, F. (1993). Training of learning disabled children's spatial abilities by computer games. *Zeitschrift fur Padagogische Psychologie*, *7*, 209–213.

McElroy, J. (2011). Asperger's expert recommends L.A. Noire as teaching tool. *Jostiq*. Retrieved from http://www.joystiq.com/2011/05/24/aspergers-expert-recommends-l-a-noire-as-teaching-tool/

Mireille, B. (2005). *Assessing the educational potential of video games through empirical research on their impact on cognitive and affective dimensions*. Retrieved from http://tecfa.unige.ch/perso/staf/rebetez/blog/wp-content/files/SNSFapplication-videogames-oct05.pdf

More, C. (2008). Digital stories targeting social skills for children with disabilities multidimensional learning. *Intervention in School and Clinic*, *43*(3), 168–177. doi:10.1177/1053451207312919

National Institute of Mental Health. (2011). *A parent's guide to autism spectrum disorder: What are the symptoms of ASD?* Retrieved from http://www.nimh.nih.gov/health/publications/a-parents-guide-to-autism-spectrum-disorder/what-are-the-symptoms-of-asd.shtml

Needham, N. R. (1983). The impact of video games on American youth. *Education Digest*, *48*, 40–42.

Newman, K. (2005). The case for the narrative brain. In *Proceedings of Second Australasia Conference on Interactive Entertainment* (pp. 145-149). Sydney, Australia: Australasia.

Okolo, C. (1992). The effect of computer-assisted instruction format and initial attitude on the arithmetic facts proficiency and continuing motivation of students with learning disabilities. *Exceptionality, 3*, 195–211. doi:10.1080/09362839209524815

Piaget, J. (1962). *Play, dreams and imitation in childhood*. New York, W.: Norton.

Pierfy, D. A. (1977). Comparative simulation game research: Stumbling blocks and stepping stones. *Simulation & Games, 8*(2), 255–268. doi:10.1177/003755007782006

Porter, D. B. (1995). Computer games: Paradigms of opportunity. *Behavior Research Methods, Instruments, & Computers, 27*(2), 229–234. doi:10.3758/BF03204737

Prensky, M. (2001). *Video game-based learning*. New York: McGraw-Hill.

Provenzo, E. F. (1991). *Video kids: Making sense of Nintendo*. Cambridge, MA: Harvard University Press.

Randall, J. M., Morris, B. A., Wetzel, C. D., & Whitehill, B. V. (1992). The effectiveness of games for educational purposes: A review of recent research. *Simulation & Gaming, 23*, 261–276. doi:10.1177/1046878192233001

Rees, D. (2010). *Designing learning games for children with autism spectrum disorder: Considering media and technology when creating the game world*. Retrieved from http://diannereessdsuassignments.weebly.com/uploads/6/3/9/0/6390810/literature_review.pdf

Ricci, K, E., Salas, E., & Cannon-Bowers, J. A. (1996). Do computer-based games facilitate knowledge acquisition and retention? *Military Psychology, 8*(4), 295–307. doi:10.1207/s15327876mp0804_3

Ricci, K. E. (1994). The use of computer-based videogames in knowledge acquisition and retention. *Journal of Interactive Instruction Development, 7*(1), 17–22.

Roth, P. (2003, May 16). America's Army is a big hit, and not just with civilians. *Wall Street Journal Online*. Retrieved from http://online.wsj.com/article/0,SB105285932212326700,00.html?mod=technology%5Ffeatured%5Fstories%5Fhs

Rouse, R. III. (2001). *Game design theory and practice*. Plano, TX: Wordware.

Sarbin, T. R. (1986). *Narrative psychology: The storied nature of human conduct*. New York: Praege.

Schell, J. (2005). Understanding entertainment: Story and game play are one. *ACM Computers in Entertainment, 3*(1), 1–19. doi:10.1145/1057270.1057284

Schneider, E. F., Lang, A., Shin, M., & Bradley, S. D. (2004). Death with a story: How story impacts emotional, motivational, and physiological responses to first-person shooter video games. *Human Communication Research, 30*(3), 361–375.

Sgouros, N. (2000). Using character motives to drive plot resolution in interactive stories. *Applied Intelligence, 12*, 239–249. doi:10.1023/A:1008323325555

Squire, K. (2005). Changing the game: What happens when video games enter the classroom?. *Innovate: Journal of Online Education, 1*(6).

Stokes, T. F., & Baer, D. M. (1977). An implicit technology of generalization. *Journal of Applied Behavior Analysis, 10*(2), 349–367. doi:10.1901/jaba.1977.10-349 PMID:16795561

Tartaro, A., & Cassell, J. (2006). *Authorable virtual peers for autism spectrum disorders*. Paper presented at the Combined Workshop on Language-Enabled Educational Technology and Development and Evaluation for Robust Spoken Dialogue Systems at the 11th European conference on Artificial Intelligence (ECA 106). Riva del Garda, Italy.

Thompson, D., Baranowski, T., Buday, R., Baranowski, J., Thompson, V., Jago, R., & Griffith, M. J. (2010). Serious video games for health: How behavioral science guided the development of a serious video game. *Simulation & Gaming*, *41*(4), 587–606. doi:10.1177/1046878108328087 PMID:20711522

Trinkaus, J. W. (1983). Arcade video games: An informal look. *Psychological Reports*, *52*, 586. doi:10.2466/pr0.1983.52.2.586

Turkle, S. (1982). The subjective computer: A study in the psychology of personal computation. *Social Studies of Science*, *12*, 173–205. doi:10.1177/030631282012002001

Turkle, S. (1995). *Life on the screen: Identify in the age of the internet*. New York: Simon & Schuster.

Tutt, R., Powell, S., & Thornton, M. (2006). Educational approaches in autism: What we know about what we do. *Educational Psychology in Practice*, *22*(1), 69–81. doi:10.1080/02667360500512452

Vygotksy, L. (1978). *Mind and society*. Cambridge, MA: MIT Press.

Witmer, B. G., & Singer, M. J. (1998). Measuring presence in virtual environments: A presence questionnaire. *Presence (Cambridge, Mass.)*, *7*(3), 225–240. doi:10.1162/105474698565686

Wood, L. E., & Stewart, P. W. (1987). Improvement of practical reasoning skills with a computer game. *Journal of Computer-Based Instruction*, *14*(2), 49–53.

## ADDITIONAL READING

Anton, J. J. (2009). *The application of modeling and simulation to the behavioral deficit of autism*. Retrieved from http://ntrs.nasa.gov/archive/nasa/casi.ntrs.nasa.gov/20100012859_2010013740.pdf

Arnold-Saritepe, A. M., Phillips, K. J., Mudford, O. C., De Rozario, K. A., & Taylor, S. A. (2009). Generalization and maintenance. In J. L. Matson (Ed.), Applied behavior analysis for children with Autism Spectrum Disorders (pp. 207-223). New York: Dordrecht Heidelberg London.

Barakova, E., Gillessen, J., & Feijs, L. (2009). Social training of autistic children with interactive intelligent agents. *Journal of Integrative Neuroscience*, *8*(1), 23–34. doi:10.1142/S0219635209002046 PMID:19412978

Bernard-Optiz, V., Sriram, N., & Nakhoda-Sapuan, S. (2001). Enhancing social problem solving in children with Autism and normal children through computer-assisted instruction. *Journal of Autism and Developmental Disorders*, *31*(4), 377–384. doi:10.1023/A:1010660502130 PMID:11569584

Booker, C. (2004). *The Seven Basic Plots: Why We Tell Stories*. New York, NY: Continuum Books.

Brown, E., & Cairns, P. (2004). A grounded investigation of immersion in games. *ACM Conference on Human Factors in Computing Systems*, CHI 2004, ACM Press, 1297-1300

Bruner, J. (1986). *Actual minds, possible worlds*. Cambridge: Harvard University Press.

Chatham, R. E. (2007). Games for training. *Communications of the ACM*, *50*(7), 37–43. doi:10.1145/1272516.1272537

Chatzara, K., Karagiannidis, C., & Stamatis, D. (2012, September). *Structural learning through digital storytelling for people with Autism*. Paper presented at the 8th Hellenic Conference on ICT in Education (HCICTE 2012). Volos, Greece.

Cloud, D. J., & Rainer, L. B. (1998). *Applied modeling and simulation: An integrated approach to development and operation*. New York: McGraw Hill.

Demarest, K. (2000). *Video games - What are they good for?* Retrieved from http://www.lessontutor.com/kd3.html

Dodsworth, C. Jr. (1998). *Digital Illusion. SIGGRAPH series*. New York: ACM Press.

Fenstermacher, K., Olympia, D., & Sheridan, S. M. (2006). Effectiveness of a computer-facilitated, interactive social skills training program for boys with attention deficit hyperactivity disorder. *School Psychology Quarterly*, *21*(2), 197–224. doi:10.1521/scpq.2006.21.2.197

Gal, E., Bauminger, N., Goren-Bar, D., Pianesi, F., Stock, O., & Zancanaro, M. et al. (2009). Enhancing social communication of children with high-functioning Autism through a co-located interface. *Artificial Intelligence and Society*, *24*(1), 75–84.

Garris, R., Ahlers, R., & Driskell, J. E. (2002). Games, motivation, and learning: A research and practice model. *Simulation & Gaming*, *33*(4), 441–467. doi:10.1177/1046878102238607

Gaylord-Ross, R. J., Haring, T. G., Breen, C., & Pitts-Conway, V. (1984). The training and generalization of social interaction skills with autistic youth. *Journal of Applied Behavior Analysis*, *17*, 229. doi:10.1901/jaba.1984.17-229 PMID:6735954

Griffiths, M. D. (2002). The educational benefits of videogames. *Education for Health*, *20*(3), 47–51.

Haring, T. G. (1992). The context of social competence: Relations, relationships, and generalization. In S. L. Odom, S. R. McConnell, & M. A. McEvoy (Eds.), *Social competence of young children with disabilities: Issues and strategies for intervention*. Baltimore: Paul H Brooks Publishing Co.

Jacobs, J. W., & Dempsey, J. V. (1993). Simulation and gaming: Fidelity, feedback, and motivation. In J. V. Dempsey, & G. C. Sales (Eds.), *Interactive instruction and feedback*. Englewood Hiils, NJ: Educational Technology Publications.

Johnson, C. P., & Myers, S. M. (2007). Identification and evaluation of children with autism spectrum disorders. *Pediatrics*, *120*(5), 1183–1215. doi:10.1542/peds.2007-2361 PMID:17967920

Kinsell, C. (2010). Investigating assistive technologies using computers to simulate basic curriculum for individuals with cognitive impairments. In S. Seok, E. Meyen, & B. DaCosta (Eds.), *Handbook of research on human cognition and assistive technology: Design, accessibility and transdisciplinary perspectives* (pp. 61–74). Hershey, PA: IGI Global. doi:10.4018/978-1-61520-817-3.ch004

Laurel, B. (2004). Narrative construction as play. *Interaction*, *11*, 73–74. doi:10.1145/1015530.1015568

Laushey, K. M., & Heflin, L. J. (2000). Enhancing social skills of kindergarten children with Autism through the training of multiple peers as tutors. *Journal of Autism and Developmental Disorders*, *30*(3), 183–193. doi:10.1023/A:1005558101038 PMID:11055455

Mallon, B., & Webb, B. (2005). Stand up and take your place: Identifying narrative elements in narrative adventure and role play games. *ACM Computers in Entertainment*, *3*(1), 1–19. doi:10.1145/1057270.1057285

Malone, T. (1980). *What makes things fun to learn? A study of intrinsically motivating computer games*. (Ph.D. dissertation, Stanford University, 1980). Dissertation Abstracts International, 65-03B, (UMI No. 3119783).

Malone, T., & Lepper, M. (1987). Making learning fun: A taxonomy of intrinsic motivations of learning. In R. E. Snow & M. J. Farr (Eds.), Aptitude, learning, and instruction: Vol. 3. Connotative and affective process analysis (pp. 223-253). Hillsdale, NJ: Lawrence Erlbaum.

Masendorf, F. (1993). Training of learning disabled children's spatial abilities by computer games. *Zeitschrift fur Padagogische Psychologie*, *7*, 209–213.

Mireille, B. (2005). *Assessing the educational potential of video games through empirical research on their impact on cognitive and affective dimensions*. Retrieved from http://tecfa.unige.ch/perso/staf/rebetez/blog/wp-content/files/SNSFapplication-videogames-oct05.pdf

More, C. (2008). Digital stories targeting social skills for children with disabilities multidimensional learning. *Intervention in School and Clinic*, *43*(3), 168–177. doi:10.1177/1053451207312919

National Institute of Mental Health. (2011). *A parent's guide to autism spectrum disorder: What are the symptoms of ASD?* Retrieved from http://www.nimh.nih.gov/health/publications/a-parents-guide-to-autism-spectrum-disorder/what-are-the-symptoms-of-asd.shtml

Okolo, C. (1992). The effect of computer-assisted instruction format and initial attitude on the arithmetic facts proficiency and continuing motivation of students with learning disabilities. *Exceptionality*, *3*, 195–211. doi:10.1080/09362839209524815

Piaget, J. (1962). *Play, dreams and imitation in childhood*. New York, W.: Norton.

Pierfy, D. A. (1977). Comparative simulation game research: Stumbling blocks and stepping stones. *Simulation & Games*, *8*(2), 255–268. doi:10.1177/003755007782006

Porter, D. B. (1995). Computer games: Paradigms of opportunity. *Behavior Research Methods, Instruments, & Computers*, *27*(2), 229–234. doi:10.3758/BF03204737

Randall, J. M., Morris, B. A., Wetzel, C. D., & Whitehill, B. V. (1992). The effectiveness of games for educational purposes: A review of recent research. *Simulation & Gaming*, *23*, 261–276. doi:10.1177/1046878192233001

Ricci, K, E., Salas, E., & Cannon-Bowers, J. A. (1996). Do computer-based games facilitate knowledge acquisition and retention? *Military Psychology*, *8*(4), 295–307. doi:10.1207/s15327876mp0804_3

Ricci, K. E. (1994). The use of computer-based videogames in knowledge acquisition and retention. *Journal of Interactive Instruction Development*, *7*(1), 17–22.

Sarbin, T. R. (1986). *Narrative Psychology: The Storied Nature of Human Conduct*. New York: Praege.

Squire, K. (2005). Changing the game: What happens when video games enter the classroom? *Innovate: Journal of Online Education*, *1*(6). Retrieved from http://www.innovateonline.info/index.php?view=article&id=82

Stokes, T. F., & Baer, D. M. (1977). An implicit technology of generalization. *Journal of Applied Behavior Analysis*, *10*(2), 349–367. doi:10.1901/jaba.1977.10-349 PMID:16795561

Tartaro, A., & Cassell, J. (2006). *Authorable virtual peers for autism spectrum disorders*. Paper presented at the Combined Workshop on Language-Enabled Educational Technology and Development and Evaluation for Robust Spoken Dialogue Systems at the 11th European conference on Artificial Intelligence (ECA 106), Riva del Garda, Italy.

Tartaro, A., & Cassell, J. (2007). Using virtual peer technology as an intervention for children with Autism. In J. Lazar (Ed.), *Universal Usability: Designing Computer Interfaces for Diverse User Populations*. West Sussex, England.

Thompson, D., Baranowski, T., Buday, R., Baranowski, J., Thompson, V., Jago, R., & Griffith, M. J. (2010). Serious video games for health: How behavioral science guided the development of a serious video game. *Simulation & Gaming*, *41*(4), 587–606. doi:10.1177/1046878108328087 PMID:20711522

Tutt, R., Powell, S., & Thornton, M. (2006). Educational approaches in Autism: What we know about what we do. *Educational Psychology in Practice*, *22*(1), 69–81. doi:10.1080/02667360500512452

Vygotksy, L. (1978). *Mind and society*. Cambridge, MA: MIT Press.

## KEY TERMS AND DEFINITIONS

**Generalization:** The ability to apply what has been learned in the instructional setting to the functional setting. Children with autism have difficulty applying what they have learned in different situations and settings.

**Immersion (Sense of Presence):** The ability to experience being in one environment, although one is physically located in a completely different environment (Witmer & Singer, 1998).

**Motivation:** The magnitude of attentional effort made toward a task, such as training or learning (Ricci, Salas, & Cannon-Bowers, 1996).

**Story:** The human account of symbolized actions that have temporal dimension (Sarbin, 1986).

**Transfer of Learning:** The process of applying what has been learned to new or similar situations, problems, or settings (Kinsell, 2010).

# Section 3
# Implementation, Assessment, and Evaluation

*Finally, section 3 focuses on the challenges in the implementation, assessment, and evaluation of Assistive Technology (AT) for those with disabilities of all ages, both in and out of the classroom. Namely, common barriers experienced by students with disabilities, as well as professionals and educators are discussed. More importantly, solutions are offered in mitigating such barriers by providing strategies and best practices.*

*In chapter 12, the author discusses the shifting and dynamic barriers that make the implementation of new media a challenge, while at the same time illuminating convergences between the goal of new media and AT. Solutions are presented, including some classroom protocols and a list of resources that can be used to evaluate new media as well as in the integration of new and old media as AT. Chapter 13 continues the discussion, with the authors focusing on identifying the unaddressed perspectives that impede technology implementation in diverse learning environments. Among other topics, the process by which educators can be supported in integrating technology tools into learning tasks is reviewed to include the presentation of a matrix that connects student-learning tasks with technology tools common to every classroom. In chapter 14, the author presents the challenges facing those who wish to effectively implement AT from the perspective of infants and toddlers. Along with discussing the importance of play through the presentation of research, practice-based suggestions are also offered. For instance, how to position an infant and toddler for play with the use of low- and high-tech AT adaptations in the home and preschool is discussed, along with providing examples of adaptations for toys.*

*In chapters 15, 16, and 17, barriers to implementing AT are further discussed, but are done so in the context of online learning. Chapter 15 serves as a catalyst in the facilitation of discussion between professionals in industry and academia in how to work together in what should be a symbiotic relationship in assisting those with disabilities in not only accessing a quality education but at the same time being prepared for meeting the employment needs and demands of the business community. Chapter 16 focuses exclusively on online learning, specifically distance learning courses, and the benefits they can provide to people with disabilities. Finally, Chapter 17 offers a checklist comprised of 15 factors and*

*157 items rooted in cognitive psychology, instructional design, computer science, but most importantly, human-computer interface study, which can be used to guide researchers and practitioners in assessing the usability and accessibility of website design. While in no way exhaustive, the checklist is meant to be viewed as a practical starting point that can be augmented to meet the specific needs of companies, organizations, and individuals in their website assessment efforts.*

# Chapter 12
# From Barriers to Beginnings: New Media as Assistive Technology

**Aubry Threlkeld**
*Harvard University, USA*

## ABSTRACT

*The ubiquity of new media in the lives of young people with high-incidence disabilities raises two important questions: how can new media be used as Assistive Technology (AT) and what can new media offer that other technologies may not? This chapter attempts to answer these questions by discussing the shifting and dynamic barriers to making this transition while also illuminating convergences between the goals of new media and AT. While this chapter explicitly concentrates on opportunities within the classroom, educators can also employ the guidelines provided herein generally in out-of-school contexts. Barriers to be discussed include electronic curb cuts and aggressive Internet filters. After discussing such barriers, solutions, including some classroom protocols and a list of resources, are shared to help educators evaluate new media as well as in the integration of new and old media as AT.*

## INTRODUCTION

There are at least half a dozen books, book chapters, and articles from the last ten years that predict advances in or the future of assistive technologies (AT) for people with disabilities in schools (Abbott, 2002; Birnbaum, 2005; Dove, 2012). In the world of AT, a future orientation exists in parallel to the push for cloud computing and new media generally in the technology sector. The term "new media" has become a buzzword to describe almost anything related to technology. Manovich (2001), for instance, describes it in terms of categories of technology that are commonly cited in the popular press, to include the Internet, websites, multimedia, video games, CD-ROMs an DVDs, and virtual reality. Schools from around the U.S. and other parts of the world continue to invest in technology and access. Many U.S. schools are

DOI: 10.4018/978-1-4666-5015-2.ch012

upgrading their infrastructure in order to support broadband and wireless speeds; they are introducing mobile technologies to include the integration and promotion of mobile applications (apps); and offering conferences that discuss how to use mobile tablet devices for instruction and remediation. While advancements such as these are encouraging, how can new media be seen as AT for students with high-incidence disabilities? Where and when does it work? And for what?

New media, because of its broad definition, is almost any technology where computers are the center of "production, distribution, and communication," including old media like television and film produced using digital means (Manovich, 2001). Although such a broad definition allows for the incorporation of many technologies, it also unfortunately fails to help teachers, and not to mention young people with high-incidence disabilities, fully grasp what is *new* about new media and whether such technology is even useful and usable in their specific contexts. Web-based technologies have enjoyed a long history of proclaiming inclusivity for people with disabilities while leaving them out. Debating competing definitions of the term "new media" is beyond the scope of this chapter. Instead, this chapter looks at new media with a critical approach to accessibility.

In the context of this focus, the use of new media as AT can lead to two positive outcomes: greater social connectivity and inclusion of people with disabilities and the possibility of higher educational attainment and improved life conditions (Bouck, Maeda, & Flanagan, 2012; Maor, Currie, & Drewry, 2011). New media also has the opportunity to increase the ease of differentiating within inclusive settings by providing different applications to different students and by suggesting unique combinations of applications and web-based social networks for students.

An obvious criticism of this approach is that providing technology at all is differentiating for students with high-incidence disabilities. For example, students with high incidence disabilities, especially those with language-based learning disabilities, typically have or need access to computers to complete their writing. Since many of these students have other co-morbid conditions, like attention deficit disorder (ADD) and attention deficit hyperactivity disorder (ADHD), access to a computer and word processing program may not be substantial enough to truly support independent learning. They may also need a distraction-free computer environment with timed tasks, to-do lists, schedules, and organizational tools as well. This becomes increasingly complex in inclusive classes because the adaptations and focus may not be intuitive for or acceptable to general educators because they go beyond the usual cognitive supports provided. New media solves this through applications like digital timers and distraction-free writing software that should be considered when aiding those with special needs in the inclusive classroom.

In this chapter, the reader is acquainted with common barriers to access along with new beginnings for special educators to think more creatively about the use of ubiquitous and well-liked media with their students. Specific examples of new media are presented which can be accessed across different platforms or devices, that are low-cost or free, complement older technologies, assist students without increasing stigma, and connect students with each other across able/disabled status.

## WHAT BARRIERS PREVENT NEW MEDIA FROM PROLIFERATING IN SCHOOLS?

### Unfamiliarity with New Media and Assistive Technologies

The sad reality is special educators and those responsible for AT oftentimes end up guessing at which technologies are appropriate or accessible to students in schools. Special educators rarely receive training on how to choose, assign, manage, or evaluate compensatory technologies; so they rely sometimes heavily on marketing material and online content, which almost always describes products as accessible and beneficial. In typical special education graduate coursework, novice teachers with little to no practical experience are at best acquainted with the possibilities available to students usually only through relevant frameworks for understanding accessibility.

Both lawyers and educators have called out that end-users, namely people with disabilities, should be more involved in the outcome of products, from engineering and design education, to research and design practices, as well as longer term policy development (Blanck, 2008), with the stern reminder that new technology is often not accessible at inception (Ellis & Kent, 2011). Some evidence suggests that organizations, like academic institutions, for instance, have already started recruiting people with disabilities to test website accessibility at the design phase, instead of waiting for a formal complaint to add accessibility features (Foley, 2011).

Given the challenges faced, how do we address unfamiliarity among special educators? Researchers have conducted some preliminary studies to help mitigate the challenges associated with the unfamiliarity of AT, by specifically using wikis and embedded video (Dreon & Dietrich, 2009) as well as webquests (Manning & Carpenter, 2008). Dreon and Dietrich's model (2009), for instance, used video of students working with assistive devices as well as wiki-generation among graduate students enrolled in instructional technology courses to address the misconception that AT was about the devices themselves rather than the students who used them. In their reporting of graduate students seeing implementation of AT plans as well as the evaluation of students with special needs, they have highlighted a key lesson of practice: that seeing practice is important for implementation of that practice.

One aspect of teacher preparation to use new media that appears be relatively absent from the discussion is how most pre-service teachers today are considered to be "digital natives," signifying that this generation has grown up with technology and uses it differently from earlier generations (Beck & Wade, 2004; Dede, 2005; Gee, 2003; Prensky, 2001). Lei (2009) has conducted preliminary research on how and when digital natives use technology and has concluded that while these individuals have more extensive experience with technology, the depth and systematic use of technology is often lacking. The work of Lei (2009), coupled with that of Dreon and Dietrich (2009), help suggest that Dreon and Dietrich's approach allows teachers to discover more about technology and its use, whereas a webquest alone actually may not help most pre-service teachers who are digital natives. Among organizers of graduate curriculum for pre-service special educators, more study is needed here as well to orient new teachers to systematic use of technology in classrooms in order to both aid instruction and assist students with high-incidence disabilities.

## Aggressive Internet Filters

Internet filters are a common barrier for schools intending to use new media with students. As more and more schools' infrastructure is upgraded to support broadband access, school districts are developing Internet filters and enforcing security policies to protect students from inappropriate, questionable, and lewd content. There is an overt emphasis on cyber-safety and preventing cyberbullying and a covert emphasis on preventing students from accessing pornography. According to a 2009 report released by the National Center for Educational Statistics (2011), approximately 6% of students, 12-18 years of age, reported having experienced being cyberbullied. Scholars and educators alike have postulated that because cyberbullying can follow students across spaces and terrorize them when they feel safe, cyberbullying has a more profound effect on students than the traditional bullying of the past. However, little empirical evidence supports this assumption (Bauman & Newman, 2013). Cyberbullying, while a problem, does not seem to match the solution.

Broad studies of the use of Internet filters in schools have reported serious over-blocking problems (Heins, Cho, & Feldman, 2006). Students trying to complete coursework in history or needing to access health information are reported to be commonly blocked. Further compounding the matter, Frechette (2005) describes how cyber-safety concerns have filtered out interactivity without filtering out predatory corporate messaging. More importantly, when interactivity is removed, filters prevent students with disabilities from the primary benefit of new media: connectivity.

Inevitably, these filters filter out some of the good with the bad, and it becomes the responsibility of special educators to seek out multiple websites or mirror websites to get around these filters. Instead of accessing wordpress.com, for instance, to create a class blog, teachers might have to use a mirror website like edublogs.org. Instead of using podcasts from ITunes®, students may have to use generic websites like Audacity®. Teachers in both of these cases are forced to communicate clearly with personnel at their district and regional levels to find out why and when certain websites are accessible and others are blocked. While these policies may be relaxed with time, they currently are the burden of teachers and are not easily remedied. Predicting which websites will be accessible daily may shift with the updates to the filter algorithms, mechanics, or school district policies. This forces teachers to plan flexibly, which leaves teachers who have less knowledge of technological options scrambling to be successful.

## Electronic Curb Cuts

Electronic curb cuts have been touted as ways in which accessibility features can promote access for all on the Web. Like curb cuts that were originally designed for people with mobility impairments, so too electronic curb cuts in the form of accessibility options can benefit not only the intended disabled group, but everyone else (Richards, 2001). For that reason, when mentioned, the term "electronic curb cuts" generally has a positive, if somewhat empty, connotation.

Regrettably, electronic curb cuts are as unpredictable as curb cuts. While curb cuts might be good for mothers with strollers and people in wheelchairs, they are notoriously difficult for the blind. So researchers in disability studies and new media have redefined the term to connote accessibility features that aid one person with a disability to the detriment of another (Ellis & Kent, 2011; Shakespeare, 2006). For example, YouTube™ enables students with learning disabilities to communicate with each other and complete multimedia projects in classrooms, but it may also prevent students who are hard of hearing or deaf from accessing their content without additional provisions (e.g., captions, sign language interpreters). This suggests that solutions involve prioritizing impairment, long a part of AT evaluation, instead of preaching solutions *for all*. Here, disability as categorical understanding can be replaced with specific understanding of individual needs and abilities.

The solutions to electronic curb cuts appear to be guided by not only universal design (UD) on the Web, but also by blending new media technologies with old, such as spellchecking on Facebook™ and captioning on YouTube™. This also may mean tailoring available options in programs, rather than leaving all options open all the time, to benefit students with ADD and ADHD. In these ways, students can increase embedded learning, which corresponds to general UD principles emphasizing flexibility (, thaThe Center for Universal Design, 1997). In this case, flexibility means creating opportunities to access information in more than one way. Teachers who show their students how to develop content with flexibility of use do two things simultaneously.

That is to say, they participate actively in social media while promoting access for many. In fact, teaching *all* students to design accessible content on the Web may be a means to accomplishing the original goals of accessibility on the Web.

## WHAT CAN EDUCATORS DO TO EVALUATE THE POTENTIAL OF NEW MEDIA AS ASSISTIVE TECHNOLOGY?

Now that some of the most common and difficult barriers to using new media as AT in schools has been discussed, some of the best practices for teachers who want to use new media as AT are highlighted. Many of these practices will be familiar for AT evaluators. They all, however, involve adapting and refining these practices for the demands of new media. By evaluating old technologies for use in new ways and reviewing accessibility features in professional publications for lists of new technological uses, teachers can be better prepared to implement new media as AT.

### Evaluate Existing Devices and How they Might be Used in New Ways (TAPE)

In terms of general access to new media, cost-effective approaches advanced by Bouck et al. (2012) include the guidelines – Transportable, Available, Practical, and Engaging (TAPE) – for repurposing older technologies. Some researchers may refer to this process as a technology audit. Essentially, Bouck et al. (2012) emphasized using what you have first, and then thinking about how you might use this technology in new ways.

*Transportable* is considered one of the features of new media technology. Increasingly, new media and web-based technologies are located within what is referred to as the "Cloud" and, therefore, accessible everywhere. For example, a student can use a mobile phone to produce a video for a class project, edit it on the same phone using a video editing app, and post it on YouTube™ where it can be shared with other students asynchronously. Furthermore, audio recording technologies abound, in both mobile apps and as part of larger software packages used on smart phones and tablet computers, these technologies can benefit in the writing process for students with language-based learning disabilities by allowing pre-writing and brainstorming in an alternate format.

*Available* refers to the access to the technology. Access within school websites must still be navigated with care since many schools have various Internet connection speeds (e.g., dial-up, DSL, cable, etc.) and may or may not have a limited number of computers, often outside of classrooms. Students may not have access to certain applications or websites, and these barriers need to be considered as well. Conducting an audit for what is available allows for teachers and AT evaluators to plan accordingly. Here, electronic curb cuts and Internet filters figure in.

New media technologies also need to be practical and engaging. With *practical*, Bouck et al. (2012) reference a genuine need for the technology not to be cumbersome or difficult for teachers to use. With *engaging*, they intend for the technology to motivate students and for teachers to want to use it. New media fits both of these paradigms easily because it is ubiquitous and often used by teachers and students alike. When using new media with older technologies, teachers should be especially careful of processing speeds and download times that may make a simple program or technology difficult, if not impossible to use.

These pragmatic approaches allow teachers to make the best of their current access to technology, instead of focusing only on what technology they need to purchase. Using and repurposing older technologies is not new to the AT community, but with the speed of technological progress, this skill has become increasingly important in educational environments where resources are often limited.

## Review Lists of Available Technologies for Accessibility and Use

One solution is to review the accessibility features of web-based technology for use by a special educator in the classroom from the perspectives of the website developers alongside third-party evaluators like AbilityNet™ (www.abilitynet.org.uk) or developers like the Center for Applied Special Technologies (CAST; www.cast.org). Teachers reading such reviews would be better equipped to appropriately select technologies for individual students and their particular needs in accordance with available resources.

Practitioner-focused journals regularly curate and describe newly available resources to teachers. However, only their membership and those educators who have access to academic libraries tend to benefit. At least two of these lists circulated for different purposes in 2011. These entail the Berkeley and Lindstrom's (2011) work on resources for struggling readers and Cumming's (2011) broad resource list of assistive and adaptive technology resources. Lists such as these have circulated for years in the professional and educational press, but have rarely shown how specific tools work with students with specific needs. They focus on either the disability without looking at the purpose for the technology or link to large, difficult to navigate websites. Remedying these challenges is not easy without knowing the specific needs of students and evaluating the technology to see if it best serves these students. While providing such a solution is out of the scope of this chapter, a general list to supplement those lists already in circulation has been compiled for the purposes of this discussion and is shown in Table 1.

While in no way all encompassing, Table 1 is designed to be a springboard for further discussions of appropriate technology use among students with high-incidence disabilities. Many of these new media solutions are also useful for students who do not have any disabilities what-

*Table 1. Low cost new media technologies for students with high incidence disabilities*

| Type of Technology | Use | Examples | Benefits |
|---|---|---|---|
| Social Networks | Video sharing for presentations, crowdsourcing questions, connecting to other communities, researching lived experiences, sharing reading recommendations | YouTube™, Facebook™, Goodreads™ | Relieves social isolation, connects to peer support networks for all students |
| Applications for Tablets and Mobile Devices | Notetaking software, digital timers, task lists, calendar tools for managing homework and due dates, flashcard use, audio to text, emotional awareness games, reading intervention | iHomework®, AlertNotes®, Dragon Dictation® | Easy to differentiate for teachers, students enjoy these devices, students with attention problems, students with organization problems |
| Blogging Tools | Extending discussions from class, independent research, developing arguments, generating questions about texts | Wordpress™, Livejournal™, edublogs.org | Students who struggle with stamina in writing, students with social phobias |
| Podcasting and Screencasting (audio and video) | Audio reflections on work, rehearsed readings of work instead of impromptu readings in class, screencasting class presentations | Audacity®, Sourceforge®, Screenr®, Prezi® | Students who struggle with handwriting, students who need help with spelling, students who have social phobias |
| Wikis | Concept development, vocabulary building | Wikispaces™ | Students with memory deficits, students with difficulty forming an understanding of abstract concepts |

soever and such technology can be integrated into general classroom easily by teachers with little to no technical expertise. Most of these websites will be familiar to students already and would require simple tailoring to classroom goals so that students can be more successful.

## CONCLUSION

Goggin and Newell (2003) probably best articulate the possibilities of new media in their conclusion to their book "Digital Disability":

*Will the promises accompanying new media be realized? In different accents and voices, we are ceaselessly promised that technology will deliver us from disability. Yet we would suggest not only that technology will never deliver society from the reality of disability, but that disability continues to be constructed through such technology. (p. 153)*

In the years that have followed, similar concerns to those of Goggin and Newell (2003) have been articulated (e.g., Ellis & Kent, 2012). And while no one can answer these concerns definitely, this chapter has attempted to show that simple and low-cost solutions *do* exist. Even the most simple and inexpensive of these solutions require awareness, creativity, training, and communication among stakeholders.

Therefore, it should not come as a surprise that more work by researchers and practitioners needs to be conducted in order to properly evaluate the effectiveness of blending and using these AT strategically with students with high-incidence disabilities. Unfortunately, the research literature on the matter is meager, and by and large, special educators continue to rely on literature and recommendations promoted by AT manufacturers and vendors. These challenges aside, educators still find themselves in a time of technological advancement, where trying a few low-cost technologies and strategies, may show huge advancements in inclusive education classrooms and where the stigma of difference can be managed by offering all students these resources.

## REFERENCES


Abbott, C. (Ed.). (2002). *Special educational needs and the internet: Issues for the inclusive classroom*. London, UK: Routledge. doi:10.4324/9780203400180

Bauman, S., & Newman, M. (2013). Testing assumptions about cyberbullying: Perceived distress associated with conventional and cyberbullying. *Psychology of Violence*, *3*(1), 27–38. doi:10.1037/a0029867

Beck, J. C., & Wade, M. (2004). *Got game: How the gamer generation is reshaping business forever*. Boston, MA: Harvard Business School Press.

Berkeley, S., & Lindstrom, J. H. (2011). Technology for the struggling reader: Free and easily accessible resources. *Teaching Exceptional Children*, *43*(4), 48–55.

Birnbaum, B. W. (2005). *Using assistive technologies for instructing students with disabilities: A survey of new resources*. Lewiston, NY: Edwin Mellon Press.

Blanck, P. (2008). Flattening the (inaccessible) cyberworld for people with disabilities. *Assistive Technology*, *20*, 175–180. doi:10.1080/10400435.2008.10131944 PMID:18939657

Bouck, E. C., Maeda, Y., & Flanagan, S. M. (2012). Assistive technology and students with high incidence disabilities: Understanding the relationship through the NLTS2. *Remedial and Special Education*, *33*(5), 298–208. doi:10.1177/0741932511401037

Bouck, E. C., Shurr, J. C., Tom, K., Jasper, A. D., Basette, L., Miller, B., & Flanagan, S. M. (2012). Fix it with TAPE: Repurposing technology to be assistive technology for students with high incidence disabilities. *Preventing School Failure*, *56*(2), 121–128. doi:10.1080/1045988X.2011.603396

Center for Universal Design. (1997). The principles of universal design. *The Center for Universal Design, NC State University*. Retrieved from www.ncsu.edu/www/ncsu/design/sod5/cud/about_ud/udprinciplestext.htm

Cummings, E. O. (2011). Assistive and adaptive technology resources. *Knowledge Quest*, *39*(3), 70–73.

Dede, C. (2005). Planning for neomillenial learning styles: Implications for investments in technology and faculty. *Educating the Net Generation Educause*. Retrieved from www.educause.edu/educatingthenetgen/

Dove, M. (2012). Advancements in assistive technology and AT laws for the disabled. *Delta Kappa Gamma Bulletin*, *78*(4), 23–29.

Dreon, O., & Dietrich, N. (2009). Turning lemons into lemonade: Teaching assistive technology through wikis and embedded video. *TechTrends*, *53*(1), 78–80. doi:10.1007/s11528-009-0241-6

Ellis, K., & Kent, M. (2011). *Disability and new media*. New York, NY: Routledge.

Foley, A. (2011). Exploring the design, development and use of websites through accessibility and usability studies. *Journal of Educational Multimedia and Hypermedia*, *20*(4), 361–385.

Frechette, J. (2005). Cyber-democracy or cyber hegemony? Exploring the political and economic structures of the internet as an alternative source of information. *Library Trends*, *53*(4), 555–575.

Gee, J. P. (2003). *What video games can teach us about literacy and learning*. New York: Palgrave-McMillan.

Goggin, G., & Newell, C. (2003). *Digital disability: The social construction of disability in new media*. Lanham, MD: Rowman & Littlefield Publishers.

Heins, M., Cho, C., & Feldman, A. (2006). *Internet filters: A public policy report*. Retrieved from http://www.fepproject.org/policyreports/filters2.pdf

Lei, J. (2009). Digital natives as pre-service teachers: What technology preparation is needed? *Journal of Computing in Teacher Education*, *25*(3), 87–97.

Manning, J. B., & Carpenter, L. B. (2008). Assistive technology webquest: Improving learning for pre-service teachers. *TechTrends*, *52*(6), 47–52. doi:10.1007/s11528-008-0217-y

Manovich, L. (2001). *The language of new media*. Cambridge, MA: MIT Press.

Maor, D., Currie, J., & Drewry, R. (2011). The effectiveness of assistive technologies for children with special needs: A review of research-based studies. *European Journal of Special Needs Education*, *26*(3), 283–298. doi:10.1080/08856257.2011.593821

National Center for Educational Statistics. (2011). *Indicators of school crime and safety: 2011*. Retrieved from http://nces.ed.gov/programs/crimeindicators/crimeindicators2011/ind_11.asp

Prensky, M. (2001). Digital natives, digital immigrants, part II: Do they really think differently? *Horizon*, *9*(6), 1–6. doi:10.1108/10748120110424843

Richards, P. L. (2001). *Review of the electronic curb-cut effect. H-Disability*. H-Net Reviews.

Shakespeare, T. (2006). *Disability rights and wrongs*. New York, NY: Routledge.

## ADDITIONAL READING

Beck, J. C., & Wade, M. (2006). *The kids are alright: How the gamer generation is changing the workplace*. Cambridge, MA: Harvard Business School Press.

CAST. (2011). *Universal Design for Learning Guidelines version 2.0*. Wakefield, MA: Author.

Dede, C. (2007). *Transforming Education for the 21st Century: New Pedagogies that Help All Students Attain Sophisticated Learning Outcomes*. Raleigh, NC: Friday Institute, North Carolina State University.

Dell, A. G., Newton, D. A., & Petroff, J. G. (2008). *Assistive technology in the classroom: Enhancing the school experiences of students with disabilities*. Upper Saddle River, NJ: Pearson/ Merrill Prentice Hall.

Harwell, J. M., & Jackson, R. W. (2008). *The complete learning disabilities handbook: Ready-to-use strategies & activities for teaching students with learning disabilities*. San Francisco, Calif: Jossey-Bass.

MacArthur, C. A., Ferretti, R. P., Okolo, C. M., & Cavalier, A. R. (2001). Technology applications for students with literacy problems: A critical review. *The Elementary School Journal, 101*(3), 273–301. doi:10.1086/499669

Prensky, M., & Thiagarajan, S. (2007). *Digital game-based learning*. St. Paul, MN: Paragon House Publishers.

## KEY TERMS AND DEFINITIONS

**Aggressive Internet Filters:** Technologies that filter access to websites used in public and institutional settings to prevent people for accessing lewd or questionable material.

**Electronic Curb Cuts:** A term describing accessibility features which aid one person with a disability to the detriment of another. Typically, electronic curb cuts are unintended consequences of efforts to promote accessibility.

**High-Incidence Disabilities:** Disabilities with a high prevalence in student populations, which typically include behavioral, communication, and learning disorders.

**New Media:** A generic term used to describe media that includes social networking, web-based and cloud-based applications, mobile technologies, etc.

# Chapter 13
# Teacher Education and Principles of Effective Assistive Technology Implementation

**Jennifer Courduff**
*Azusa Pacific University, USA*

**Amy Duncan**
*Claremont Graduate University, USA & California State University – San Bernardino, USA*

**Joanne Gilbreath**
*Azusa Pacific University, USA*

## ABSTRACT

*The effective implementation of Assistive Technology (AT) is transformative for teacher practice and student learning outcomes. Educators who embrace this effort are faced with a set of challenges that are not found in typical technology integration efforts. In order to deeply integrate technology into instruction and learning, a change in pedagogy is required. In this chapter, the focus is to identify the unaddressed perspectives that impede technology implementation in diverse learning environments. When this unique set of perspectives is addressed, strategies for effective practice can emerge. First, there is a discussion on special education law and AT. Next, foundations of AT and effective implementation strategies at the classroom level are discussed. The process by which teachers can be supported in integrating technology tools into learning tasks is reviewed. A matrix that connects student-learning tasks with technology tools common to every classroom is presented. The importance of making emotional connections and providing time to practice and share in an environment where failure is seen as an opportunity for growth is provided. Finally, systemic implementation issues and strategies for success are shared.*

DOI: 10.4018/978-1-4666-5015-2.ch013

## PROLOGUE

It is after school on Friday and a special education teacher is reading the individual education program (IEP) of Aaron, a student who will be entering her class on Monday. She reads that this student is included in the general education classroom for the majority of the day and requires an augmentative device to support communication. She knows that the previous device will remain with the previous district and there is little information about how it was used and its level of effectiveness with the student. It is becoming clear to this teacher that if this IEP is to be implemented she is not going to be able to do it alone. She will need to collaborate with a team of other professionals to make this plan a reality. She sighs. Where is she going to begin?

## INTRODUCTION

When educational teams begin to expand their instructional practice with the integration of AT, they realize that they are impacting a complex set of individuals in a system. Each has an area of expertise and responsibility that is essential to bringing the dream of what AT can do for a student to life in the classroom.

Teams making requests on behalf of students do not journey far down the road before realizing that there are issues that if not addressed will create roadblocks to accurate assessment, procurement of equipment and resources as well as implementation of AT and Augmentative and Alternative Communication/Assistive Augmentative Communication (AAC) for students. Acknowledging the need to build the bridges that will bring these individuals into a cohesive team is the catalyst for change that is most needed.

It should therefore not come as a surprise that the effective implementation of assistive technology (AT) is transformative for teacher practice and student learning outcomes. Educators who embrace this effort are faced with a set of challenges that are not found in typical technology integration efforts. In order to deeply integrate technology into instruction and learning, a change in pedagogy is required. In this chapter, the focus is to identify the unaddressed perspectives that impede technology implementation in diverse learning environments. When this unique set of perspectives is addressed, strategies for effective practice can emerge.

First, there will be a discussion on special education law and AT. Next, foundations of AT and effective implementation strategies at the classroom level will be discussed. The process by which teachers can be supported in integrating technology tools into learning tasks will be reviewed. A matrix that connects student-learning tasks with technology tools common to every classroom will be presented. The importance of making emotional connections and providing time to practice and share in an environment where failure is seen as an opportunity for growth will be provided. Finally, systemic implementation issues and strategies for success will also be shared.

## BACKGROUND

### Law and Assistive Technology

The Individuals with Disabilities Education Act (IDEA) ensures that students who have special needs receive early intervention and services that support learning in the least restrictive environment (Blackhurst, 2005). Although students with special needs are now integrated into mainstream school environments, technology tools may not be ubiquitously integrated into the teaching of these students. Technology has great potential for improving the lives of these students. In considering the use of technology in special education, it might be helpful to review the basic terminologies used within this population. Assistive technology is an umbrella term that encompasses any technology device, program, website, or other resource that enables students with special needs to have fair and appropriate access to curriculum and learning of content (Edyburn, Higgins, & Boone, 2005). By law, technology resources must include accessibility features that enable users to access programs and communicate regardless of disability (see http://idea.ed.gov/explore/home). Common accessibility features include screen readers, text-to-speech, and speech-to-text options. These are found within the general settings on any electronic device.

Assistive technology resources must be considered within the context of the IEP process for students with disabilities of any kind. Additionally, the Technology-Related Assistance for Individuals with Disabilities Act of 1988 (amendment 1990), requires that AT devices and services be considered through ongoing evaluation of student needs; selection, purchase, lease, or acquisition technology resources; design, customization, and maintenance of technology devices; and training and technical assistance of all stakeholders involved in the education of the student including, but not limited to, the student, teacher(s), support personnel, administration, and family members (Blackhurst, 2005).

Augmentative and Alternative Communication/Assistive Augmentative Communication technologies are specific devices or applications supporting communication that can improve levels of independence, interaction, behavior, and learning. Until very recently, AAC device options have been expensive and bulky. The evolution of mobile devices has changed this. Many applications have been released that enable AAC features on mobile devices at a relatively low cost.

Universal design for learning (UDL; Edyburn, 2010) was developed as a means to address the inaccessibility of curriculum for diverse learners. Universal design for learning is built upon a framework that uses:

1. Multiple means of representation to give learners various ways of acquiring information and knowledge;
2. Multiple means of expression to provide learners alternatives for demonstrating what they know; and
3. Multiple means of engagement, to tap into learners' interests, offer appropriate challenges, and increase motivation (Zabala, 2004).

Universal designs are developed to be flexible and to anticipate the need for alternatives, options, and adaptations based on individual learning needs (Rose, Hasselbring, Stahl, & Zabala, 2005). The underlying philosophy of UDL is to connect learners to content in ways that are cognitively and motivationally appropriate in supporting academic, social, behavioral, and physical goals. Universal design for learning should not be understood as AT. Rather, because of its flexibility, UDL can be combined with technology tools to effectively meet student-learning goals.

Sound teaching includes the use of technology and non-technological tools as appropriate in consideration of their natural fit to the learner and the curriculum being taught. In that light, it is important for university coursework to provide meaningful technology integration training in pre-service special education programs. This includes addressing teachers' perceptions about using technology in daily life and how this differs from integration within instructional practice. Both pre- and in-service teachers need to be provided with a structure for managing technology tools in ways that creatively address students' diverse needs as they complete curricular tasks. In that regard, the recommendations provided in this chapter are applicable to both pre-service and in-service coursework and implementation strategies.

## Foundations of Integration

Integration of technology into special education instructional practice should be viewed through two perspectives: access to information and access to learning. Universal design for learning places importance on access to curriculum in technology integration for students with special needs. Technologies should be integrated into instructional practice frequently and should be centered on specific, measurable student learning outcomes (Edyburn, 2009).

Successful implementation is a process that begins with a collaboratively developed IEP and is actualized through instruction. Technology resources noted in the AT section of the IEP should be integrated into daily curriculum. Assistive technologies should be chosen and re-evaluated using evidence-based practices such as the collection of ongoing assessment data. These resources should be used to remove barriers to a student's participation and performance. Scaffolded mentoring on the use of technology tools should be provided for students, teachers, families, and other support staff. Mentoring and collaboration through educator study groups could effectively move the process of implementation forward. Ongoing mentoring should include participation in a community of practice (Wenger, 1998) committed to using technology resources to connect the student to curriculum in meaningful ways. Additionally, equipment management and repair should be defined and assigned to appropriate and supportive district representatives. Most importantly, teachers must be proactively supported by and held accountable to site-level administration.

## Foundations of Student Access to Technology

Simply requiring an AT checkbox on an IEP does not mean that effective processes of assessment, procurement, and application has changed the level of technology integration for students with special needs. Rather, a complete change in the approach to training and implementation that focuses on core curriculum wherein technology resources are integrated based on specific student learning outcomes is needed. In other words, the focus should be on the student when determining the appropriate resources needed to access curriculum.

The SETT framework (Zabala & Carl, 2005) is a powerful tool for planning and implementing appropriate technology tools based on student learning needs. The framework stands for *Student – Environment – Task – Tool*. The first step of the SETT framework is to consider the *Student*. What are the physical, linguistic, or psychosocial issues that deter student access to curriculum? Has the student received testing or previous services? What are the student's strengths? What are the weak areas? Is there history or background that affects the student's ability to communicate or process information? Are there known medical issues?

The next step is to consider the learning *Environment*. What is the most appropriate placement for the student? Does the student have an instructional aide? What sort of physical or emotional supports might the student need to be successful?

The third step is to consider the learning *Tasks* that need support. What is the student's cognitive level? How might we best support access to the curriculum? As previously discussed, UDL principals should be considered. Simply put, UDL scaffolds content to meet student-learning abilities. Curriculum that is developed using UDL offers the same content, but scaffolded to meet a range of cognitive levels. Essentially, *Tasks* are specific learning goals that are developed and revised yearly by the IEP team.

The fourth step is to consider *Tools* that help the student gain access to the content in ways that authentically support learning needs. For example, mobile devices are becoming powerful solutions to address AT needs in some educational settings. Using mobile devices, students with mild to severe disabilities are able to access curriculum that is formatted specifically to bridge gaps between disability and content.

## Barriers to Successful Integration

There are several barriers to successful implementation of technology tools in learning. Barriers include:

1. Need for support from district Information Technology (IT) professionals,
2. Expense of AT/AAC and the impact on the district's budget,
3. Lack of time to explore new AT resources,
4. Development of supportive procedures that are used consistently throughout the educational setting,
5. Training needed for the educational team that ensures effective implementation of AT/AAC once it has arrived,
6. Maintenance and responsibility procedures needed for AT/AAC, and
7. The cultural barriers that exist between general and special education teachers.

Of all the barriers listed above, the cultural barrier is by far the most difficult to overcome within school level communities. Human experience and perception is a product of culture as well as a product of nature. To deny that culture is a grounding force is to deny that life is culturally based (Bruner, 1986; Brown & Duguid, 2002; Gardner, 2006). Understanding the culture of the teaching community is critical because what is valued by the culture is actualized within the group. Within the teaching community, there is a unique and not often recognized cultural divide between general education and special education teachers. Indeed, within the special education community, there is a cultural divide between special educators who teach one class of students from multiple grades and of varying disabilities (e.g., special day classes) and teachers who see small groups of students for shorter time periods over the course of a school day (e.g., resource specialist program classes). Within the resource specialist setting, the very structure of school day often impedes the use of technology within instruction. For example, many special educators who see students from the general education classroom have limited instructional time with each group of students and this time must be divided between general education curriculum and IEP goals. Technology is not integrated because there is just no time to think about it. Additionally, in many instances, teachers have indicated that although they thought technology was valuable to their professional activities, they did not think technology could help impact student learning or raise student achievement (Courduff, 2011a). Thus, teachers are burdened with an overwhelming number of professional responsibilities and personal bias that prevent openness to the power of integrating technology into learning.

Successful integration programs should not assume that teachers share similar belief systems regarding the value technology-integrated instruction. In fact, there is no consensus on how frequently technology should be used during an instructional day. Rather, technology integration means different things to different teachers. Generally, if there are 25 different classroom teachers, each teacher will have a different understanding of what classroom instruction should look like (Anderson & Anderson, 2005). These scenarios are based on such factors as experience, depth of subject matter knowledge, and sense of priority.

## Successful Integration Strategies at the Classroom Level

There are strategies that can be implemented that provide more support for successful integration of technology into teaching at the classroom level. A new matrix for technology integration has been developed from the synthesis of literature on technology integration in diverse instructional environments (Courduff, 2011a). In addition to using the matrix, it is critical that a sound mentoring program using a community of practice (CoP) model be in place (Wenger, 1998). The unique combination of using a matrix within the supportive environment of a CoP, and including UDL philosophies, has the potential to impact instructional practices. Simply stated, teachers learn to associate common tasks with appropriate technology tools through sharing and troubleshooting on an ongoing basis. Thus, teachers are empowered to learn to identify and integrate technology resources appropriately into student learning tasks.

The matrix was developed using common technology resources that are available, easily integrated into learning activities, adaptable to learner differences, (i.e., type of disability, learning space), adaptable to learning styles, adaptable to appropriate instructional delivery, interactive, and easily adapted in ways that remove physical or social barriers to participation (Courduff, 2011b). There are many things to consider when introducing teachers to a matrix for appropriate integration of technology tools. First, teachers must be aware that instructional practice should change when a student needs intervention. Currently, when an intervention is used, it is generally more of the same activity that did not work in the first place. More of the same type of instructional delivery is not better. Different instructional design, tools, and delivery are critical. Next, initial training in the use of a technology tool is not enough to support sustained integration. Teachers should be guided through four stages in using technology tools:

1. Introduction to the technology tool,
2. Instruction on how to use the tool,
3. Instruction on how to integrate the tool, and
4. Instruction on how to mange the tool with students.

Although the stages sound very simple, training generally stops at the second stage, how to use the tool. Introduction to the matrix should involve strategies that provide initial training on the technology tools and ongoing support to enable the transfer of knowledge to integration and management within instructional practice.

As previously discussed, knowledge sharing among special education teachers is a challenge due to the isolated nature of the job. This can be addressed using a CoP model. Training and ongoing support should be organized in a CoP and directly address matching technology tools with curriculum tasks so that students can accomplish IEP goals and progress toward academic achievement. The community should be scaffolded to meet the needs, skill levels, and learning style of all participants. Within the culture of special education opportunities to share ideas, troubleshoot, and create curricular connections are slim due to the isolated nature of the social structure. The situated nature of a CoP provides a forum for guiding these teachers through the process of integrating and managing technology during instruction. As teachers begin to integrate technology into specific student learning goals, mentors and administrators should point out the value of technology to learning the curriculum. Through group interaction, teachers can build knowledge based on prior experiences and collaborate on technology tool ideas for specific curriculum tasks. Teachers develop a shared goal of connecting all learning to professional duties and instructional practice. Finally, an evaluation plan should be developed to measure efficacy based on changes in instructional practice and student growth toward IEP goals (Courduff, 2011a; Desimone, 2009; Ertmer & Ottenbreit-Leftwhich, 2010).

Sadly, it is often a lack of guidance toward creativity and vision that hinders the process of matching technology tools with tasks more than limitations of the hardware and software. Special education teachers simply do not have a system in place where they can easily make meaningful adaptations integrating technology into instruction. In considering the use of the matrix within a CoP, the following questions should be addressed:

- Is there an evident match between the learner's strengths and needs, the teacher's instructional philosophy, the nature of the learning environment, the curriculum goals, and the technology tool selected for the task?

- What are the key features of the technology tool?
- Does the technology address the cognitive, metacognitive, and motivational needs of the learner?
- How does using the tool create a diverse/new learning activity for the student? Is this an activity using new strategies for instruction or it is just more of the same?
- Does the teacher have enough background knowledge and skills to integrate and manage the use of this tool in instruction?
- Does the student have enough background knowledge and skills to use this tool without much pre-teaching?
- Under what conditions will the student be able to use this technology tool in learning? Will it be available in the regular education classroom, in the special education classroom, and at home?
- Does the tool remove a physical, motivational, or academic barrier to student learning?

In this light, the matrices below use a set of widely applicable, generally acceptable technology resources to guide the development, delivery, and evaluation of AT services in daily teaching and learning activities. These matrices summarize current research in connecting curricular tasks with AT tools (Edyburn, Higgins, & Boone, 2005). The first matrix focuses on reading and writing tasks. The second matrix focuses on math, social studies, and science tasks (see Tables 1 and 2).

At the classroom level, the matrix provides a quick reminder of the technology tools that are available to meet various student-learning tasks. Through ongoing interaction and support in the CoP, teachers experience a safe place to troubleshoot, share ideas, celebrate successes, and learn from perceived or real failure. The community provides a place where the emotional side of learning is supported. Teachers learn to see failure as growth opportunities rather than as time to give up. The community understands deeply that we learn more from failure than we ever learn from success. In that light, the emotional part of learning is strengthened and supported because the fear of failure is alleviated. Rather, a culture that failing leads to learning emerges within the community.

How can this be supported on a systemic level? The next section provides ways to address the larger issues that, in the end, support technology integration at the classroom level.

## Assessment to Implementation: Partnering Strategies that Work

At the systems level, when educational teams begin to expand their instructional practice with the integration of AT, they realize that they are impacting a complex set of individuals in a system. Each has an area of expertise and responsibility that is essential to bringing the dream of what AT can do for a student to life in the classroom.

The following AT planning tables have been designed to support educational teams in identifying the core issues that they as educators may face. Each table includes an issue, perspectives to understand, options to explore, potential tools to use, and action plan steps to be considered. Tables 3 through 8 are intended to clarify the perspectives that are behind each area of need and guide the team in tools, procedures, and actions that can be transformative in addressing student needs.

## CONCLUSION

This chapter has provided a framework for implementing and supporting technology integration within diverse learning environments. As educational teams strive to provide effective AT supports for students, they are challenged to develop a new

*Table 1. Matrix of reading/writing task and appropriate assistive technology tools ©JCourduff (2011a)*

| Curriculum Tasks | Design Strategies | Hardware | Tools/Software |
|---|---|---|---|
| Reading | Universal design for learning: cognitive rescaling<br>Universal access: Architecture vs. curriculum (CAST) | Microsoft Office®<br>AlphaSmarts®<br>Fusion Writers®<br>iPod®/iPod touch®<br>PDA/Handhelds<br>Interactive whiteboard<br>Interactive dance mats (e.g., RM EasyTeach Dance-Mats®)<br>Student response systems<br>AAC devices | Text-to-speech (screen readers)<br>Word recognition<br>Hypertext<br>Animated graphics<br>Video<br>Supported digital texts<br>Digitized speech<br>Online tutorial programs (e.g., Study Island®, Rosetta Stone®)<br>ClickIt®<br>Typing software<br>Intellitalk®<br>Speech-to-text (e.g., WordQ®/SpeakQ®)<br>Graphic organizers (e.g., Inspiration®/Kidspiration®)<br>Accessibility websites: www.bookshare.org and www.shep-pardsoftware.com<br>Tutorial development (e.g., Jing®)<br>Start-to-finish books<br>iPod touch®/iPad® apps |
| Writing | Mainstream design: Visibility: user can determine options for advancing learning on a device intuitively<br>Conceptual model: device offers consistency of operations and feedback<br>Mapping: user can determine relationships between actions/results; controls/effects; what is visible/what is available on the system<br>Feedback: user receives full continuous feedback | Microsoft Office®<br>AlphaSmarts®<br>Fusion Writers®<br>iPod®/iPod touch®<br>PDA/Handhelds<br>Interactive whiteboard<br>RM EasyTeach DanceMats®<br>Student response systems<br>Digital camera<br>Microphone | Scaffolding<br>Concept mapping/Graphic organizers<br>Typing tutorials<br>Spell check/Custom vocabulary/Thesaurus<br>Voice recognition<br>Graphics/Picture support<br>Word prediction/Word counts<br>Auto summarize<br>Writing statistical analysis, Kincaid score<br><br>Frequency lists<br>Co-Writer®/Write OutLoud®<br>Study Island®<br>Typing software<br>Intellitalk®<br>WordQ®/SpeakQ®<br>iPod touch®/iPad® apps<br>Accessibility websites: www.readwritethink.org, www.iknowthat.org, and www.spellingcity.com |

way of thinking about the ways students can access curriculum as well as the resources that are needed for them to be successful. Opportunities for educators to examine resources, develop procedures for assessment, selection, and integration of AT must be developed so that the needed systemic change can occur. When such networking and resource development are in place, the AT supports are transformative for students and educators alike.

## EPILOGUE

The IEP Team is gathered for an annual review for Aaron. At last year's meeting Aaron's team was concerned about his limited ability to communicate and unsure about how to help him. Aaron's needs drove them to reach out, to make connections to those that had the expertise to help them provide an effective assessment, choose an AAC device that met his needs, understand how to program it and to integrate it into all dimensions of his day. They created a "village" of support that is needed to successfully provide AT for a student.

Today the educational team and Aaron's family will focus on all of the ways that Aaron's AAC device has allowed him to communicate with friends, to respond to classroom discussions, to share what he knows with his teachers and his family. Today, they will celebrate the many ways that Aaron's life has been transformed.

*Table 2. Matrix of math/social science task and appropriate assistive technology tools ©JCourduff (2011a)*

| Curriculum Tasks | Design Strategies | Hardware | Tools/Software |
|---|---|---|---|
| Math | Mainstream design:<br>Visibility: user can determine options for advancing learning on a device intuitively<br>Conceptual model: device offers consistency of operations and feedback<br>Mapping: user can determine relationships between actions/results; controls/effects; what is visible/what is available on the system<br>Feedback: user receives full continuous feedback | Microsoft Office®<br>Fusion Writers®<br>iPod®/iPod touch®<br>PDA/Handhelds<br>Interactive whiteboard<br>RM EasyTeach Dance-Mats®<br>Student response systems | Spreadsheets/Databases<br>Graphing calculators<br>Gaming software<br>Tutorial software<br>Contextualized math word problems through web-based learning environments<br>Math websites:<br>www.mathprojects.com,<br>http://www.ablenetinc.com/Curriculum/Equals-Mathematics-Program,<br>http://a4cwsn.com/tag/math/, and<br>www.minecraft.edu<br>Study Island®<br>iPod touch®/iPad® apps |
| Social Studies | Mainstream design: Visibility: user can determine options for advancing learning on a device intuitively<br>Conceptual model: device offers consistency of operations and feedback<br>Mapping: user can determine relationships between actions/results; controls/effects; what is visible/what is available on the system<br>Feedback: user receives full continuous feedback | Microsoft Office®<br>iPod®/iPod® touch<br>Interactive whiteboards<br>Digital camera<br>Microphone | Supported digital texts<br>Presentation tools<br>Spreadsheets/Databases<br>Virtual field trips<br>Virtual reality websites<br>Concept mapping/Graphic organizers<br>Research tutorials<br>Screen readers<br>Text-to-speech<br>Interactive simulation games (e.g., Oregon Trail®)<br>Inspiration®/Kidspiration®<br>iPod touch®/iPad® Apps<br>Social studies websites: www.besthistorysites.net and www.pbs.org/history |
| Science | Three-dimensional learning environments<br>Experiential learning<br>Social skills | High-end computer system<br>Interaction in both simulated and real worlds<br>Digital camera<br>Microphone | Virtual reality games<br>Screen readers<br>Text-to-speech<br>PDAs<br>iPod® touch/iPad® apps<br>Websites: www.enabling.org/grassroots |
| Social Skills | Three-dimensional learning environments<br>Experiential learning<br>Social skills | Microsoft Office®<br>Digital camera<br>Microphone | Social stories<br>Multi-user Domain, Object Oriented (MOO)/Multi User Domain (MUD)<br>Social skills websites |

*Table 3. IT Support*

| Issue | Perspectives to Understand | Options to Explore | Potential Tools to Use | Action Plan |
|---|---|---|---|---|
| Need for support from district IT professionals | "We have not been trained to understand the needs of students with disabilities."<br>"Our responsibilities need to focus on technology needs for an entire district."<br>"Because we don't fully understand the needs/dimensions for AT support, it is a challenge to be accountable for it."<br>"To be honest, special education is such a small group of teachers that their needs are less important in the grand scheme of things when you look at the needs of an entire district." | Engage the IT team in a dialog about what AT and AAC are<br>Listen to their issues and concerns with respect<br>Provide video of students using AT successfully<br>Stories are powerful tools<br>Engage the IT team in a dialog with leadership responsible for instruction to examine the "big picture" of technology for instruction<br>Identify webinars for viewing, and use those as a catalyst for discussion<br>Identify elements of AT that can benefit all students | The QIAT List Serve to support questions and to expand networking options<br>(i.e., Resources tab)<br>Webinars: www.atcoalition.org and http://www.assistivetechnology.net/<br>State resources for AT training and procedural guidelines<br>Universal Design for Learning Resources<br>(i.e., www.udlcenter.org) | Considering the perspectives that influence this issue, what might be the options and tools that hold the most potential for your team?<br>Identify:<br>the actions;<br>the persons responsible;<br>and the timeline |

*Table 4. Budget*

| Issue | Perspectives to Understand | Options to Explore | Potential Tools to Use | Action Plan |
|---|---|---|---|---|
| The expense of AT/AAC and the impact on the district's budget | "Assistive technology is expensive and we are already financially strapped."<br>"How can we justify spending such a significant amount of money on one student?"<br>"We don't know if this will work for this student. How can we say for sure that it is needed?" | Share the AT/AAC assessment process with district leadership. Link the assessment process to more effective choice making for students.<br>Support parents in utilizing their health insurance for AT (i.e., allowing it to belong to the student)<br>Develop materials to share that identify free and low-cost apps and other digital resources<br>Develop materials that identify supports within the operating systems of both Mac and PC that are free and low cost<br>Develop CoP to share and beta test apps for effectiveness. Publish the results.<br>Encourage the best practice of collaborative assessments that encourage empowerment among all members of the team<br>Share tutorials and YouTube™ videos of teachers using AT/AAC with students<br>Partner teachers to work together to provide support<br>Provide support in understanding that increasing the achievement scores of the special needs population of students increases the test scores of all | Apple iOS® 6 accessibility features exploring tools that exist currently in the operating system at no additional charge<br>Microsoft® accessibility features (i.e., http://www.microsoft.com/enable/education/)<br>Use apps for stages to make good decisions about apps (e.g., http://apps4stages.wikispaces.com/)<br>Resources lab found at the QIAT listserv<br>Investigate Adobe® tools that enhance accessibility<br>Utilize the SETT Framework (e.g., www.joyzabala.com)<br>Collaborative assessment tools (e.g., www.wati.org)<br>Utilize rental options that each AT/AAC company has available<br>Investigate state agencies and resources that may provide free loans of equipment<br>Utilize resources provided when students qualify for low incidence funding<br>30-day free trials available for most product lines | Considering the perspectives that influence this issue, what might be the options and tools that hold the most potential for your team?<br>Identify:<br>the actions;<br>the persons responsible;<br>and the timeline |

*Table 5. Time constraints*

| Issue | Perspectives to Understand | Options to Explore | Potential Tools to Use | Action Plan |
|---|---|---|---|---|
| Lack of time to explore new AT resources | "I don't have time to learn all of this new stuff!"<br>"To implement this well I really need time. Where can I fit that into my instructional day?"<br>"I have to know everything about something before I even think about using it." | Highlight teachers using AT/AAC tools and case studies of success<br>Publicize ways that technology impact behavior and engagement and learning<br>Focus district professional development on AT/AAC so that time is built into the instructional day<br>Develop CoP to facilitate interest and ease for implementation<br>Demonstrate connections to time and efficiency with tech tools so that teachers can see the time that is saved<br>Develop AT/AAC Teams<br>Celebrate and publicize success | Focus on iPad® apps<br>Look at tools and resources already (e.g., www.wati.org)<br>Explore opportunities for learning individually and in teams: www.iste.org, www.resna.org, www.cast.org, www.closingthegap.com/, and www.katsnet.org/ | Considering the perspectives that influence this issue, what might be the options and tools that hold the most potential for your team?<br>Identify:<br>the actions;<br>the persons responsible;<br>and the timeline |

*Table 6. Procedures*

| Issue | Perspectives to Understand | Options to Explore | Potential Tools to Use | Action Plan |
|---|---|---|---|---|
| Development of supportive procedures that are used consistently throughout the educational setting | "We already have so much paperwork! This adds on one more set of procedures!"<br>"I already have so many IEP meetings; I can't add anything more to the plate in trying to be compliant!" | Site/district procedures developed that support assessment, procurement and implementation of AT/AAC supports within the IEP process<br>Training opportunities provided for district and site level administration so that they can be familiar with legal and procedural guidelines<br>Provide emotional connections by sharing the impact of AT/AAC on students within the district | Research state and district websites for existing practices<br>Access procedural and assessment documents (e.g., www.wati.org) | Considering the perspectives that influence this issue, what might be the options and tools that hold the most potential for your team?<br>Identify:<br>the actions;<br>the persons responsible;<br>and the timeline |

*Table 7. Training and support*

| Issue | Perspectives to Understand | Options to Explore | Potential Tools to Use | Action Plan |
|---|---|---|---|---|
| Training needed for the educational team that ensures effective implementation of AT/AAC once it has arrived | "This looks like a great recommendation for this student, but I don't know how to program it!"<br>"I am not sure when/how to use this during the instructional day!"<br>"This speech generating device looks so complex, I am intimidated to even turn it on"<br>"I am not familiar with this communication app. How do I find out how to use it?" | Tutorials that are available on commercial websites that provide training<br>YouTube™ videos that share tutorial and implementation for each speech generating device (SGD)<br>Consultation time scheduled with representative of the manufacturer of the SGD for training | Identify implementation process (e.g., www.joyzabala.com) | Considering the perspectives that influence this issue, what might be the options and tools that hold the most potential for your team?<br>Identify:<br>the actions;<br>the persons responsible;<br>and the timeline |

*Table 8. Maintenance*

| Issue | Perspectives to Understand | Options to Explore | Potential Tools to Use | Action Plan |
|---|---|---|---|---|
| Maintenance and responsibility procedures needed for AT/AAC | "Who is responsible for programming this device?"<br>"Can this device go back and forth to the child's home?"<br>"Who is responsible for repairs?" | Design a responsibility matrix that is consistently used within the educational setting<br>Ensure that there is a discussion regarding roles and responsibilities at the IEP meeting | Please see: www.wati.org and www.resna.org | Considering the perspectives that influence this issue, what might be the options and tools that hold the most potential for your team?<br>Identify:<br>the actions;<br>the persons responsible;<br>and the timeline |

## REFERENCES

Anderson, K., & Anderson, C. L. (2005). Integrating technology in standards-based instruction. In D. Edyburn, K. Higgins, & R. Boone (Eds.), *Handbook of special education technology research and practice* (pp. 521–544). Whitefish Bay, WI: Knowledge by Design.

Blackhurst, A. (2005). Historical perspectives about technology applications for people with disabilities. In D. Edyburn, K. Higgins, & R. Boone (Eds.), *Handbook of special education technology research and practice* (pp. 3–29). Whitefish Bay, WI: Knowledge by Design.

Brown, J., & Duguid, P. (2002). *The social life of information*. New York, NY: Harvard Business School Press.

Bruner, J. (1986). *Actual minds, possible worlds*. Boston, MA: The President and Fellows of Harvard College.

Center for Applied Special Technology. (2010). CAST: 25 years of innovation. *CAST*. Retreived from http://www.cast.org/index.html

Courduff, J. (2011a). *Technology integration in the resource specialist environment*. (Unpublished doctoral dissertation). Walden University, Minneapolis, MN.

Courduff, J. (2011b). One size never fits all: Tech integration for special needs. *Learning and Leading with Technology*, *38*(8), 16–19.

Desimone, L. M. (2009). Improving impact studies of teachers' professional development: Toward better conceptualizations and measures. *Educational Researcher*, *38*(3), 181–199. doi:10.3102/0013189X08331140

Edyburn, D. (2009). Using research to inform practice. *Special Education Technology Practice*, *11*(5), 21–29.

Edyburn, D. (2010). Would you recognize universal design for learning if you saw it? Ten propositions for new directions for the second decade of UDL. *Learning Disability Quarterly*, *33*, 33–41.

Edyburn, D., Higgins, K., & Boone, R. (2005). *Handbook of special education technology research and practice*. Whitefish Bay, WI: Knowledge by Design.

Ertmer, P., & Ottenbreit-Leftwich, A. T. (2010). Teacher technology change: How knowledge, confidence, culture, and beliefs intersect. *Journal of Research on Technology in Education*, *42*(3), 255–284.

Gardner, H. (2006). *Changing minds: The art and science of changing our own and other people's minds*. Boston, MA: Harvard Business School Press.

Jackson, R. (2005). Curriculum access for students with low-incidence disabilities. *Eugene*. Retreived from http://www.cast.org/policy/ncac/index.html

Kotter, J. P. (1996). *Leading change*. Cambridge, MA: Harvard Business School Press.

Lave, J., & Wenger, E. (1991). *Situated learning: Legitimate peripheral participation*. New York, NY: Cambridge University Press. doi:10.1017/CBO9780511815355

Maddux, C. (2009). *Research highlights in technology and teacher education 2009*. Chesapeake, VA: Society for Information Technology & Teacher Education.

Marzano, R., Pickering, D., & Pollock, J. (2001). *Classroom instruction that works*. Alexandria, VA: Association for Supervision and Curriculum Development.

Rose, D., Hasselbring, T. S., Stahl, S., & Zabala, J. (2005). Assistive technology and universal design for learning: Two sides of the same coin. In D. Edyburn, K. Higgins, & R. Boone (Eds.), *Handbook of special education technology research and practice* (pp. 507–518). Whitefish Bay, WI: Knowledge by Design.

Smaldino, S. E., Lowther, D. L., & Russell, J. D. (2008). *Instructional technology and media for learning* (9th ed.). Upper Saddle River, NJ: Pearson Merril Prentice Hall.

Technology-Related Assistance for Individuals with Disabilities Act 1988, Pub. L. 100-407, Sec. 2, 102 Stat. 1044 (1988) (amendment 1990).

Wenger, E. (1998). *Communities of practice: learning, meaning, and identity*. New York, NY: Cambridge University Press. doi:10.1017/CBO9780511803932

Zabala, J. (2004). Quality indicators for assistive technology services in school settings. *Journal of Special Education Technology*, *15*, 25–36.

Zabala, J., & Carl, D. F. (2005). Quality indicators for assistive technology services in schools. In D. Edyburn, K. Higgins, & R. Boone (Eds.), *Handbook of special education technology research and practice* (pp. 179–208). Whitefish Bay, WI: Knowledge by Design.

## KEY TERMS AND DEFINITIONS

**Assistive Technology (AT):** Any mechanical, electronic, computer-based, non-electronic, or non-computer-based instructional materials, strategies, or services that people with disabilities can use to assist in the learning process, assist in accessibility to resources, develop competence and success in the workplace, or enhance and improve quality of life (Blackhurst, 2005).

**Center for Applied Special Technology (CAST):** Organization that supports and actively promotes UDL to create and expand learning opportunities for individuals who are exceptional (Center for applied special technology, 2010).

**Community of Practice (CoP):** A group that is formed with the purpose of collective learning within a shared area or goal (Lave & Wenger, 1991).

**Culture:** Implicit and explicit behavioral and procedural norms found within an established group of people (Kotter, 1996).

**Curriculum:** Student interaction with instructional content, materials, resources, and evaluation of educational objectives (Marzano, Pickering, & Pollock, 2001).

**Diverse Learners:** Students who are exceptional or students who come from cultural or linguistic backgrounds, that are different from the mainstream school population (Edyburn, Higgins, & Boone, 2005).

**Individuals with Disabilities Education Act (IDEA):** Federal law that supports state and local educational systems in meeting the needs of all persons with disabilities and their families. Specifically, IDEA guarantees the right of all children with disabilities to a free and appropriate education in the least restrictive environment (Edyburn, Higgins, & Boone, 2005).

**Instruction:** Actions and efforts intended to stimulate learning by the deliberate arrangement of information, environment, and experience in ways that help learners achieve knowledge, skills, or other changes in capability (Smaldino, Lowther, & Russell, 2008).

**Quality Indicators for Assistive Technology (QIAT):** Eight areas of focus when considering and implementing appropriate and effective AT. Quality indicators for AT include quality indicators of the development and delivery of AT services (Zabala, 2004).

**Students with Special Needs:** Students who exhibit deficiencies including visual, physical, hearing, behavior/social impairments, and learning disabilities. Gifted students are also considered to be exceptional. This term is used interchangeably with "students with special needs" or "special needs students" (Edyburn, Higgins, & Boone, 2005).

**Technology Integration:** The use of technology resources in daily teaching and learning activities within a school. This includes using technology for professional duties and in the management of student information. Technology integration is achieved when the use of technology is embedded naturally and is appropriately applied to curriculum tasks in ways that enhance student learning (Maddux, 2009).

**Technology Tools:** Technology-related electronic hardware and software resources used for professional, personal, and instructional duties (Maddux, 2009).

**Universal Design for Learning (UDL):** A framework developed to provide flexible teaching approaches and student access to curriculum. The focus is on advocacy for accommodation and universal access of digital content through: (a) multiple means of representation, (b) multiple means of expression, and (c) multiple means of engagement (Jackson, 2005).

## APPENDIX

The following provides a list of additional resources in order to learn more about the information presented in this chapter:

**AT Coalition:** http://atcoalition.org/
**CAST (Center for Applied Special Technology):** http://www.cast.org/
**CEC (Council for Exceptional Children):** http://www.cec.sped.org/
**ISTE (International Society for Technology in Education):** https://www.iste.org/
**JSET (Journal of Special Education Technology):** http://www.tamcec.org/jset/
**NATRI (National Assistive Technology Research Institute):** http://natri.uky.edu/index.html
**NCAC (National Center on Accessing the General Curriculum):** http://4.17.143.133/ncac/
**SEIMC (Special Education Instructional Materials Center):** http://www.cesa11.k12.wi.us/home/special-education/seimc---special-education-instructional-media-center
**SETSIG (Special Education Technology Special Interest Group):** http://www.iste.org/connect/special-interest-groups/setsig
**SETT (Student – Environment – Task – Tool) framework:** http://www.joyzabala.com/Home.php
**TAM (Technology and Media):** http://www.tamcec.org/
**QIAT Listserv (Quality Indicators for Assistive Technology Network):** http://indicators.knowbility.org/

# Chapter 14
# Engaging in Play through Assistive Technology:
## Closing Gaps in Research and Practice for Infants and Toddlers with Disabilities

**Fiona S. Baker**
*Emirates College for Advanced Education, UAE*

## ABSTRACT

*The importance of play for all infants and toddlers should not be underestimated. However, owing to barriers and tensions in Assistive Technology (AT) in early intervention, opportunities are often limited for infants and toddlers with special needs to play, and where early intervention exists, it is slow to develop with AT. This chapter first discusses the importance of play and then draws attention to some issues and tensions that limit play and AT in early intervention for infants and toddlers with special needs. It then discusses how crucial it is to explore the potential of play for infants and toddlers with disabilities and gives research and practice-based suggestions to enact the spirit of the law: the Individuals with Disabilities Act (IDEA): Part C – Early Intervention program for infants and toddlers using AT. It concludes with some thoughts for the future of AT through research, early intervention play-based practices, and on-going education and development of early intervention providers and parents of infants and toddlers with special needs.*

DOI: 10.4018/978-1-4666-5015-2.ch014

## INTRODUCTION

As early as infancy and toddlerhood, children may be identified as being at risk for cognitive, social-emotional and physical difficulties. Some have inherited disabilities, and others may be born preterm leading to special needs such as intellectual disabilities, cerebral palsy, and hearing or vision loss. Such infants and toddlers may be slower in developing their functional and learning abilities and may be eligible for early intervention services in their natural environments: home and child care. In the U.S., the Individuals with Disabilities Act (IDEA): Part C – Early Intervention program for infants and toddlers, was designed to provide a broad array of services to children with special needs, from birth through three years of age, and their families. Anyone who has a concern about an infant or toddler's development may make a referral for Early Intervention services. A team, including parents, draw up an Individual Family Service Plan (IFSP) which is a document designed to identify supports and strategies for achieving outcomes that will enhance a child's academic, communication, developmental and functional needs. The Department for Children and Families Agency of Human Services in Vermont, for example, reported that in 2013, there were approximately 20,000 children from birth to three eligible for Early Intervention services statewide. Based on estimated prevalence, approximately 3% (or 600 children) may be eligible for early intervention services. Of this population, approximately 400 infants and toddlers are receiving early intervention services statewide (2% of the birth to three population). Assistive technology (AT) provision is dependent on services and AT use is reported on IFSPs for only a small percentage of infants and toddlers which, as Wilcox, Guimond, Campbell, and Weintraub Moore (2006) suggest, means that services should improve. A comparison of the Office of Special Education Programs Annual Reports to Congress from 1998 to 2002 indicated that AT is consistently listed as a service for only approximately 4% of infants and toddlers nationally (U.S. Department of Education, 2012). Additionally, there are infants and toddlers who have delays not severe enough to be eligible for early intervention services, yet would benefit from AT. Even if the AT device is used for only a brief period of time; it may give an infant or toddler the extra support they need to develop and use skills on their own which are essential to early childhood play. Regrettably, many infants and toddlers do not experience AT as an option.

### The Purpose of this Chapter

The purpose of this chapter is to discuss the importance of play for infants and toddlers, including those with special needs. It discusses how AT can help those infants and toddlers with special needs experience the benefits of play by making important adaptations to the infant and toddler's natural environment accessible; explains how to position an infant and toddler for play with the use of low- and high-tech AT adaptations in the home and preschool, and gives examples of adaptations for toys. It makes suggestions for some easily applied practical solutions for providers and parents to demystify AT use and discusses some of the tensions that currently limit the provision of AT and services for infants and toddlers. This chapter ends by explaining where efforts should be made to provide more opportunities for children with special needs to enjoy and learn through play in natural settings.

It is anticipated that this chapter will bring current issues and tensions into focus and stimulate further research and debate. Most importantly though, it will contribute to the future of play for infants and toddlers with special needs by providing the impetus for those involved in early intervention to work toward enacting the spirit of the law in AT practice for infants and toddlers with special needs, especially for the development of pedagogical play-based practices.

## BACKGROUND

### The Importance of Play in Early Childhood

Play is the main preoccupation in early childhood (Parham & Primeau, 1997). Children explore their natural environment through play and as Rogers (2011) states, "there is a substantial well-documented empirical and theoretical research literature to support the view that play is a highly significant activity in human experience and development" (p. 9). As children interact with objects and materials, they start to establish relationships with an understanding of control and causality which means that they repeat and modify their actions. Children communicate as they explore and mimic activities in the real world within their social environment (Vygotsky, 1978). Children are playful if they are intrinsically motivated, internally controlled, free to suspend reality, and able to set and maintain a play frame (Bundy, 1997).

For early learners, play is self-initiated, self-directed and flexible in a way not found in the development and refinement of a specific skill. From birth, children learn how to solve problems, make decisions, persevere, and interact with people and objects in their environment. The benefits of play are numerous across all of the domains of development and Piaget (1962) theorized that play and cognitive skills are inseparable. Play has been associated with emotional, social, communication, and physical/motor development. For infants and toddlers, play is the primary mode of learning about how objects work and play develops the skills of learning as they interact with people in their world. According to Vygotsky (1978), when a child is engaging in play he is functioning close to his optimal developmental level. Successful play interactions and environmental control "lays the foundations for crucial life skills such as empathy, problem solving and imagination" (Rogers, 2011, p.9).

Indeed, the concept of learning through play has a long and established history and tradition in educational contexts stemming from the work of successive pioneer educators and enacted in innovative pedagogical practices of, for instance, Reggio Emilia in Northern Italy and Te Whariki in New Zealand. The Reggio Approach derives its name from its place of origin, Reggio Emilia, a city located in Emilia Romagna in Northern Italy. Shortly after World War II, Loris Malaguzzi, a young teacher and the founder of this unique system, joined forces with the parents of this region to provide childcare for young children. Te Whāriki is the curriculum framework for the Early Childhood Education (ECE) sector in New Zealand. It covers the education and care of children from birth to school age and is used by most New Zealand ECE services to guide children's learning opportunities. The literal meaning of Te Whāriki is 'the woven mat.' Early Childhood Education services use the curriculum's principles and strands to weave a learning programme for children. A child's strengths and interests, all the things they learn as part of their family, and the service's learning opportunities are all woven together to contribute to a child's unique learning story where learning is responsive to the needs, passions, and interests of children. These curricula are characterized by many features advocated by contemporary research on young children, including real-life problem-solving among peers, with numerous opportunities for creative thinking, playfulness and exploration which may derive directly from teacher observations of children's spontaneous play and exploration. For a toddler with a disability, such child-centred pedagogical practices characterized by spontaneous play are as equally desirable as for any other child, yet few may experience such opportunities. In accessing such opportunities, AT can play an important role.

## Play for Children with Disabilities

A variety or combination of special needs can affect an infant or toddler's ability to play. This means that often an infant or toddler with a special need requires assistance to play with the degree of severity of the disability from mild to profound, requiring different degrees of assistance. Irrespective of the severity of disability though, all children have some capacity to engage in play and with adaptations and interventions, these infants and toddlers can be helped to experience a range of play activities on a par with their fellow peers.

What tends to happen though is that natural play for infants and toddlers with disabilities is diminished or absent. This is because it is replaced by therapies and/or special instruction which concentrate on the development of a skill. Indeed, many medical and therapeutic interventions for children with disabilities do not incorporate play. When play is limited, the ability to learn and develop the skills and attitudes of accomplishment associated with play is diminished. Disability then, tends to limit the infant and toddler's innate drive to play with interventions rarely designed to develop a child's ability to play. With an emphasis on skill development, play and playfulness become lost. While therapists use toys as therapeutic tools, the focus tends to be on what the child cannot do rather than what the child can do, as is fostered in spontaneous creative play.

In essence, there should be a combination of both therapy and play for infants and toddlers with special needs. It is crucial that methods be identified which can augment existing play abilities or compensate for limitations caused by disabilities. In play, the focus is on supporting success rather than remediating for disability and the focus is on what toys are interesting to the child rather than what toys work to remediate for disability. Play is important for all children, including those with cognitive delay; a population who may be thought of as being disinterested in play.

Play repertories may be more limited and play incidences may occur less frequently for children with developmental disabilities. Play for infants and toddlers with physical disabilities, for example, has been described as being more solitary with the amount of time spent in play less frequent. For some, there is play deprivation and the specific type of play deficits may be related to the type and severity of the disability. When play is too difficult for a child, it will negatively impact on social and cognitive development. Frustration will ensue when toys are too difficult to operate, and so play may become an obstacle to learning rather than a facilitator of the learning process. It is, therefore, imperative that early intervention providers and parents develop their awareness of how to nurture the development of an infant or toddler with a disability through play.

Research has shown that parents of young children may find play interactions with children with disabilities more challenging than with non-disabled children. Freeman and Kasari's study (2013) demonstrated that parents of autistic children found it more difficult to match or increase the level of play of their child compared to parents with typically developing children. Without positive play intervention though, children with disabilities may develop learned helplessness that can lead to indifference and apathy from as young as two years of age (Langley, 1990) as infants and toddlers are waiting for parents to initiate interactions (Van Tatenhove, 1987). Through positive play interactions, children develop pro-social skills and "construct their own understanding of a concept" (Bredekamp & Copple, 1997, p. 114). Children with disabilities however, are often frustrated by a lack of success when their every effort to explore the world, and to manipulate playthings and toys, or communicate is unsuccessful. Consequently, the child fails to develop cause and effect skills and choice making, which can lead to the development of passivity and dependency on others (Sullivan & Lewis, 2000) with the potential for apathy and lack of interest. It is crucial therefore, that adults facilitate positive play interactions for infants and toddlers with special needs through the use of a variety of strategies and adaptations.

## Making Play Accessible

### The Environment, Child Positioning for Play, and Adapted Toys and Materials

The environment for play should be accessible for infants and toddlers with special needs and lighting and noise levels should be adjusted to the individual. Especially important are modifications of space and an accessible location for toddlers using wheelchairs and other mobility aids. Assistive technology positioning items can help infants and toddlers with disabilities as they often have difficulty in changing and maintaining different positions when they play. Infants born with cerebral palsy, Down syndrome, or other disabilities may have motor difficulties and very low muscle tone which may result in an inability to support oneself to be in a position to play. Using a supportive Boppy® pillow may allow a young child to be more upright to observe his or her world and interact in play. An infant with very high muscle tone may be unable to reach out efficiently to interact with his or her environment. The positions a child can use greatly impact their quality of play, such as a sitting opposed to a lying position. A child's head can be propped up using a horse-shoe shaped pillow which provides support in a range of positions and rolled towels, pillow, or stuffed animals placed under the head, neck, and knees are also valuable. A soothing bouncer seat or a three stage reclining seat assists a child in a semi-reclined position. To lie on the side, items designed for sleeping can be used to support a side lying position for play. These may be commercially made or can consist of rolled towels, pillows, and couch cushions which can be used in front of and behind a child for side support. Lying on the tummy is a good developmental position for a child as it strengthens the muscles in their neck, back, shoulders, and hips, but the infant or toddler needs to be positioned using wedges under the child's chest. In a sitting position, the child can see and interact with the environment. Again, these are commercially made for safety and allow the child security. With an accompanying lock on tray, the child will have front support which can free up the child's hands for play. In the same way, the standing position is beneficial as infants and toddlers can see and interact with their environment. Such AT can provide swivels and positioning items that allow the individual to move, bounce, and/or turn in place. Everyday materials such as cardboard boxes, car seat head positioners, towels, pillows, and cylinders can also be used as positioning options for infants and toddlers.

Infants and toddlers may need assistance in moving to explore their environments which is a critical component of play. Assistive devices are available that encourage and support children to move. These are commercial walkers, rocking and riding toys, and climbing and sliding equipment, and well-designed swings. Switches, adapted battery-operated toys, and interfaces make it possible for children to turn a toy on and off with a movement of a body part against a switch. Single switch use can also be applied to motorized scooters, which give the child the opportunity to move through space independently at a young age. Adapted computer peripherals and appropriate software for infants and toddlers, can also be adapted. A single switch which reduces control to a single key, or the use of a touch window, may be the most appropriate input device for this population. Some communication devices can act as a switch interface to include a message which is heard when the toy is activated. This strategy can be used to enhance opportunities for pretend play for young learners with disabilities.

When an infant with a disability grows into toddlerhood, a simple box easel can allow participation in creative activities like painting and drawing by moving paper to a vertical surface. By adding binder clips to an easel, the toddler may find a book to be more engaging to explore than one that lies flat on a table. A carpet square can become a play mat for a child. Cars and blocks can also be safely attached to the carpet so they won't roll away when played with.

The use of a well-placed switch (i.e., a device attached to a toy that allows the child to interact in play when pressed) makes the toy accessible to a toddler who may not otherwise be able to make the toy move or make noise. To build an interaction with electronic toys, children can begin with highly reactive toys that provide immediate and intense reaction when touched (Mistrett, Lane, & Goetz, 2000). AblePlay.org (2009), for instance, has a comprehensive list of switch accessible toys that are available. A switch may also allow the infant to activate a mobile or play music to self-soothe.

## Restrictions to Assistive Technology Use

Assistive technologies range from low-tech toys with simple switches to expansive high-tech systems capable of managing complex environments. Assistive technology can increase young children's options and facilitate their physical and social inclusion in various settings (Judge & Lahm, 1998). When used thoughtfully, AT can empower young children, increasing their independence and supporting their inclusion in play with their peers. Assistive technology can, for example, be used as a tool to augment sensory input and reduce distractions. It can provide support for cognitive processing or enhancing memory and recalls and it promotes children's learning and development by allowing them to more effectively participate in activities and routines in their natural environments (Langone, Malone, & Kinsley, 1999; Mistrett, Lane, & Ruffino, 2005).

Although using AT with infants and toddlers holds much promise, it is often overlooked. Assistive technology devices remain underutilized and poorly integrated into IEPs for young children with disabilities (Dugan, Cambell, & Wilcox, 2006; Lesar, 1998). In the U.S., annual state child count reports identify a surprisingly small and consistently stable percentage of infants and toddlers who have AT listed on their IFSPs (Wilcox, Bacon, & Campbell, 2004). In 1999, for example, states documented AT on only 3.8% of IFSPs for infants and toddlers served through Part C of IDEA and similarly, only 4.4% of IFSPs 4 years earlier. Data from the National Early Intervention Longitudinal Study (NEILS, 2001) appear to help substantiate such findings. While examining a nationally representative sample of 2,820 children in early intervention, NEILS found that 4% of the records listed AT. Illustrating that utilization remains low in early intervention (Lesar, 1998; Mistrett, Hale, Gruner, Sunshine, & McInerney, 2001).

## Barriers That Limit Assistive Technology Use for Play

There are several barriers and tensions that may account for limited AT use in early intervention (Lahm & Sizemore, 2002; Lesar, 1998; Mistrett, 2001a). Tensions that exist are the dichotomy between therapy and play; family and provider beliefs about using AT, funding issues, the availability of AT devices, a lack of providers trained in the use of AT devices, and attitudinal barriers (e.g., negative images or a fear of technology). Scarce use of AT may also be attributed to the relative newness of AT with infants and toddlers (Lesar, 1998; Mistrett, 2001a) and a lack of research examining the selection, use, and efficacy with this population of children (Campbell, Milbourne, Dugan, & Wilcox, 2006; Mistrett, Milbourne, Dugan, & Wilcox, 2001). Some of these barriers and tensions will now be further examined.

## Therapy and Play

Supporting infants and toddlers in play and playful experiences through the use of both low-tech and high-tech AT is important for the developing child. It is critical to realize that the child needs a combination of skills-based therapeutic work and play-based learning. Assistive technology allows for comfort and can broaden the scope for the infant and toddler to play. The notion is that infants and toddlers with disabilities should not be restricted in their provision and ability to play, but rather should be given every opportunity to do so through adaptive and enabling technologies. There are many simple adaptations that can be made to get the most out of play even for novices, so parents and teachers should be involved in workshops and other training type events so that they can learn how to work with these adaptations and develop them.

In therapy, the first use of *play* is as a distracter. A therapist may use the child's motivation to interact with a toy as a way to position him longer on his stomach or to shift weight from side to side.

Sensory and cognitive skills are targeted during focused skills development. For instance, toys are provided that encourage a child to use both hands to manipulate an object, or play which is designed to strengthen "bilateral hand coordination" which can then be used in higher level play activities. The goal is to increase the quality and quantity of the play interactions.

Interventions focused on facilitating playfulness emphasize the quality of a child's play with the child guiding play to incorporate motor, sensory, language, creative and cognitive skills in a holistic manner, without focusing on any specific goal or skills.

While all three approaches on play are important, it is the third perspective which is so often ignored for infants and toddlers with special needs. Assistive technology is a solution that can be leveraged to help to begin to address barriers that exist by affording the child the opportunity to initiate and sustain playful activity within the stages of play development from sensory through to pretend play, creative expression and literacy development.

## Family Beliefs

Sometimes parents and educators are reluctant to begin to use an AT device as they may believe it will discourage their child from learning important skills. Research has shown that the opposite may be true, as using AT devices may encourage a child to increase communication efforts and skills. Indeed, as Alliance Action (2006) reports, the earlier the child is taught to use an AT device, the more easily the child will learn to accept and use it. Although concerns have been expressed that AT use in early childhood may mean that children do not develop to the best of their capability as they become reliant on the technology or that it may slow them down in their learning, research has not shown this to be true.

Instead, AT opens up opportunities for a child with special needs to play in early childhood. Assistive technology has the potential to open up play options to the child and parents which means the child has opportunities to learn. Through the use of different levels of technology, ranging from wheelchairs to infrared control units, children with disabilities are able to access physical environments and technological devices such as computers and interactive videos. Toys can be adapted through switches and adaptations so children can activate them when their manual dexterity is severely limited, thus enabling them to participate with their peers with typical development. Augmentative communication materials and devices allow young children who cannot speak to communicate with the world around them. These devices can be simple such as pointing at a photo on a picture board, or they can be more complicated, such as pressing message buttons on a device that activates pre-recorded messages such as "I'm thirsty."

## Provider Beliefs and Training

Providers may be concerned that a very young child's use of AT will inhibit an infant or toddler's skills development (Cress & Marvin, 2003; Romski & Sevick, 2005) such as, speech and mobility. Some may also hold the view that AT necessitates expense which leads to a parent or provider ensuring that a particular device is needed (Judge & Parette, 1998). The AT may not be well-matched with the child leading to disuse or abandonment (Judge, 2002; Parette & Angelo, 1996; Philips & Zhao, 1993). Providers may believe that there are few resources to support the selection and use of AT. Funding, availability of trial devices, and support for maintenance and use in natural environments may be of particular concern (Judge, 2002; Lesar, 1998). In Lahm and Sizemore's (2002) study, for example, providers felt it was important to act as an interdisciplinary team. However, none of the 15 respondents identified the family and child as part of the team. Nearly all of the providers indicated that funding was an important consideration in decision making. Although the Lahm and Sizemore study had methodological concerns, such as it focusing on providers serving infants and toddlers, and a small sample size, the findings are still worthy of attention.

Unfortunately, beyond this study there is remarkably little data about the use of AT in early intervention practices. Lesar (1998) found that among 62 early childhood special education teachers, speech-language pathologists, administrators, and other related providers, that most respondents reported they either had no knowledge of were at a novice level. A significant concern for all participants was support for using AT, including on-site assistance, training in device use, training in how to teach a child to use a device, and technical support for families. Other areas of concern were family involvement in AT decision making, funding for AT, and access to devices. Lahm and Sizemore (2002) examined 15 early intervention providers who met state requirements for provision of AT services in early intervention. They rated child goals and family and environmental demands as the most important factors to consider when making decisions about AT. All stated how important it was to work as a member of an interdisciplinary team. Nearly all providers indicated that funding was an important consideration in decision making.

Lack of awareness and lack of training for service providers continue to be barriers to use of AT for early learners (Judge, Floyd, & Jeffs, 2008). For this reason, early intervention providers may not inform families of its potential in promoting and supporting development and learning (Lane & Mistrett, 1996; McInerney, Osher, & Kane, 1997; Romski, Sevik, & Forrest, 2001). Sawyer, Milbourne, Dugan, and Campbell (2005) reported that a reason for underutilization of AT with infants and toddlers may be limited knowledge of parents and providers and a lack of training to provide them with the knowledge required. A primary research question of the Tots n Tech Research Institute has been to identify the current methods in which early intervention providers and families of infants and toddlers learn about AT. The results of these related research studies indicate the need for increased training and reference material which focuses on AT for the infant/toddler population.

Optimistically though, Wilcox, Guimond, Campbell, and Weintraub Moore (2006) found that providers have a relatively broad view of technology that encompasses high-tech and low-tech. They also found that training makes a difference in many areas concerning AT practices in early intervention. Providers with more training focused on AT in early intervention reported greater use of AT and a greater sensitivity to important factors to consider in AT decision-making, including enhancing children's participation in daily activities and routines. Irrespective of training, providers appeared aware of the importance of AT in facilitating children's participation in activities and in promoting family interactions. In addition, providers viewed parental attitudes and children's environments as important factors in making decisions about AT. This suggests that providers recognize the potential that AT brings in terms of increasing children's ability to be included in everyday activities and routines. Finally, providers tended to disagree with many of the reasons that have been identified as barriers to AT use in early intervention.

Providers have been found to believe that a child should demonstrate assumed pre-requisites before they are ready to use AT (Romski, Sevik, & Forrest, 2001; Romski & Sevick, 2005), or that the AT is too difficult for the child, and therefore, it is easier to simply do things for the child (Cress & Marvin, 2003; Mistrett, 2001b).

MacArthur (2001) studied early childhood teachers and found that to be successful, teachers need opportunities to discuss their beliefs about technology and its relationship with pedagogy. Stoner, Parette, Watts, Wojcik, and Fogal (2008) found that teacher input was critical to developing effective approaches for the integration of AT into the preschool curricula. To encourage professional development teachers suggested the use of stipends to support teacher professional development (PD) through a range of approaches and to provide continuous learning opportunities for teachers. One strategy found to hold particular promise was AT user groups which required one person who has expertise and is the facilitator to hold sessions with a small group of people who express interest in cooperating.

## Low-Tech and High-Tech Assistive Technology and its Benefits for Play

Research has shown positive outcomes associated with the use of AT by infants and toddlers with special needs and has documented several ways in which AT can enable infants and toddlers to perform functional skills such as playing with toys across various contexts, thereby providing evidence in support of using AT to facilitate very young children's participation in their natural environments and to enable infants and toddlers to perform functional skills (Mistrett, Hale, Gruner, Sunshine, & McInerney, 2001; Sullivan & Lewis, 2000). Studies undertaken in the child's natural environment (Benedict, Lee, Marrujo, & Farel, 1999; Judge, 2002; Langone, Malone, & Kinsely, 1999) all point to the participation of children in activities and routines and in everyday settings facilitated by AT. It should therefore, be included as part of early intervention under IDEA. Assistive technology services may include teaching a child or family how to use a device, providing consultations on the environment, or offering provision of technical expertise for device programming or modification.

## Demystifying Assistive Technology Use for Parents through Low-Tech Assistive Technology

There are a number of low-tech AT adaptations that can be used to enhance play which are inexpensive and work to create an environment to meet play outcomes for infants and toddlers, where children are in a position to initiate playful interaction. These are positioning options for children which include materials to ensure the comfort and safety of children in getting ready to play, and supports that encourage movement, such as rolling to walking. Included are adaptations to toys available for purchase on the market which make them easier to access or to activate. Low-tech AT also includes the use of positioning items that make it easier for the child to sit or lay on his tummy or back, thus allowing the child to be able to reach toys. Furthermore, it also includes the use of specially adapted toys and appropriate switches and interfaces, and the use of communication aids, which can be used to enhance playful interaction. Toys that are engaging may be linked to an overhead gym to bring the toy closer to the child's hands or feet, or Velcro could be attached to the bottom of the toy to secure it to a surface so it doesn't move out of reach. Toys and play materials are vital elements of the play environment with strategies to use them in enhancing playfulness.

Parents should recognize that very often low-tech devices are extremely useful, affordable, and versatile. However, it is important to understand that parents need time to explore, be creative, and know where to purchase adapted toys and materials. First, commercial, off-the-shelf play materials can be selected by identifying the toy's features that appeal to the child and can be adapted to make them easier to use. Each infant and toddler has his/her own preferences but a toy can be evaluated for its sensory interaction which includes sound, visual appearance, and touch. Toys can also be assessed for their access, addressing questions such as, "How is it activated?" "How can it be positioned?" "How does it handle?" and "How can its knobs and parts be adapted?" For their physical characteristics, a toy can also be assessed for its size, construction, stability and versatility. Commercial toys can be adapted for their positioning and access. Attachers are materials that are used to bring the item closer to the infant or toddler and can be made from simple materials, such as, elastic to give a pulling effect, shoelaces, or snap straps. These can be anchors to the toy with the child simply pulling on the links to retrieve it. Extenders are materials that can be used to build up access features of the toy. Where buttons are too small, this feature can be extended using foam, Popsicle sticks, or larger knobs from kitchen stores which will make puzzles easier to complete. Clay can also be used to make a knob larger or a key longer, for example. Stabilizers are materials that support play by preventing a toy from moving out of the child's reach or vision. Often toys need less adaptation if they can stay in one place. Stabilizers can be used to hold a toy in place or connect a communication device to it. To stabilize a toy, non-slip materials can be used such as Velcro and carpet squares can all improve stability of an item. Magnets may also be useful in stabilising a toy on a metal sheet surface. Bed trays with tilt tops can be used as floor tables and covered with carpet squares for a more stable play environment. Any materials that contain toys and prevent them from moving too far away from a child – items such as hula-hoops, box tops, or planter bases – help a child to control his immediate play environment.

## FUTURE RESEARCH DIRECTIONS

Assistive technology research for infants and toddlers is still in its formative years. Research is needed to better understand how young children use and learn with AT as they play, and also to better understand the short- and long-term effects. The established body of research and literature on the positive effects of AT does not adequately inform early intervention providers. As AT becomes more readily available for infants and toddlers, new research is needed on what young learners are able to do and how these tools can be integrated successfully into the natural environment to promote play-based experiences. Research-based evidence about what constitutes quality AT for play-based learning is needed to guide policy and inform practice, and to ensure that AT is used in effective, supportive, engaging, and appropriate ways in infant and toddler play-based programs in natural settings.

It is a team effort to enhance future efforts for AT in early intervention. Libraries should have access to facilities and special lending libraries for mothers of young children with disabilities where parents can borrow toys with switches, computer software and other devices, or parents may choose to purchase a device directly for their child. Parents should be fully aware and involved in this endeavour. Issues of equity and access remain unresolved for device use. Early childhood providers have an opportunity to provide leadership in assuring equitable access to AT tools for the children, parents, and families in their care. When early intervention providers appropriately integrate AT, equity and access are addressed by providing opportunities for all children to participate and learn, including those with special needs (Hasselbring & Glaser, 2000). Research and awareness of the value of AT need to be shared with policy makers who are interested in issues of access and equity for children, and parents and families within the framework of developmentally appropriate practice (NAEYC, 2009), to support learning goals for individual children in child care settings.

To make informed decisions on the intentional use of AT in ways that support a child's play-based learning and development, early intervention providers need information and resources on the nature of these technologies and the implications of their use with children along with responsive interactions between adults and children which are essential for early brain development and cognitive, social, emotional, physical, and linguistic development. Professional judgement is required to determine if and when a specific use of AT is appropriate and the provider role is essential in making certain that thoughtful planning, careful implementation, reflection, and evaluation, all guide decision-making about how to introduce and integrate any form of technology into the child's experience to promote positive experiences for the child (NAEYC, 2009).

Early intervention providers and parents must take time to train, evaluate, and select AT, and observe the child as he/she uses them. So they must be willing to learn about and become familiar with the various options and make appropriate adaptations, being intentional in the choices they make. Early intervention providers have always had a responsibility to support parents and families by sharing knowledge about child development and learning. Assistive technology tools offer new opportunities to build relationships, maintain ongoing communication, exchange information, and share online resources with parents and families. There is also the responsibility of providers to model appropriate effective and positive uses of AT in play for families. For this to happen, professional development courses would need to integrate understandings of AT, and workshops should be available for parents and families.

There is a desperate need to educate parents and families on the delivery of services. As there are many tensions that surround AT use in early intervention which are not research-based, greater awareness is needed in the professional population of the value of AT and its potential benefits, if it is to be demystified. The findings of Wilcox, Bacon, and Campbell (2006) identify areas of AT practices in early intervention that should be strengthened. Only 18% of providers considered themselves to be well trained, or having a lot of knowledge about AT for infants and toddlers with disabilities. The providers viewed facilitation of developmental skills as very important to AT decision-making, a situation which may mean that AT efforts are more focused on skill sets than on promoting participation in natural environments. Additional research is required to understand the complexities surrounding AT in early intervention, as well as the best ways to promote young children's full participation. A fuller understanding of the factors that may influence, promote, or hinder the use of AT in early intervention practices is required.

Judge, Floyd, and Jeffs (2008) suggest that the use of an AT toolkit approach that anticipates the learning, language, motor, and sensory needs of young children that would give immediate access to meaningful experiences and allow young children to participate in play, should be considered. Judge (2006) found, in a survey of early childhood teachers, that devices teachers required were low-tech items that should be included in a toolkit. By demystifying AT and giving parents and families solutions they can implement right away, there is greater hope for infants and toddlers to play. When parents and early intervention providers are creative, AT is by no means expensive and restricted in use for some children. For painting, for example, using a natural sponge may be easier to grasp than a paintbrush. If the child cannot hold a paintbrush or marker, a ruler with a Velcro handle can be secured on the child's arm. Brushes and markers can then be attached to the ruler. Assistive technology is responsible for providing the child access to self-initiated playful learning experiences to develop in all of the domains of development in much the same way as for any other child. Assistive technology sets aside the need for a focus on individual skills to develop through therapy as a prerequisite to play, potentially increasing participation in playful learning and greater joy and access to learning in general.

More commercially adapted toys for children with disabilities should emerge on the market created with the knowledge of AT experts. Adaptations and adjustment accessories should be available to purchase alongside a toy in every major toy store. Such an addition would help parents to make their own purchasing decisions when an expert or teacher is not available and would mean that adapted toys can simply be purchased at a regular rather than a specialized store. More support should develop for parents and early intervention providers whose professional development opportunities should include in-depth, hands-on use of AT for infants and toddlers accompanied by on-going support and access to the latest AT tools for play, as they enter the market.

To improve and enhance AT use, providers need positive examples of how toys and the play environment has been adapted, selected, used and integrated, and evaluated successfully in natural environments. Assistive technology providers also need education in play-based pedagogies and practices of play. Research is also needed to support evidence-based practice for the effective and appropriate uses of AT as tools for learning and development in early childhood settings. It is anticipated that as more is learned and newer advances are made in AT, more opportunities will be possible for infants and toddlers with disabilities to participate in early childhood play, so providers and parents should be continually updated.

## CONCLUSION

New connections need to be made between AT, research, and play in natural early intervention settings. To be effective advocates for play, practitioners and parents alike, need comprehensive and sophisticated understandings of how play can be enabled by AT in natural settings which is grounded in research in natural contexts. Providers need to grapple with the notion that some children may not respond favourably to play in the first instance and may find toys frustrating, so it is worth balancing advocacy with some healthy scepticism that acknowledges there may be a challenge in enabling and encouraging play-based activity for some infants and toddlers with special needs. However, all children can play and should experience play, so it is critically important to continue to stimulate thought on this topic amongst professionals and parents. It is anticipated that this chapter will continue to motivate research, debate, and practice, to close the gaps in play experiences for infants and toddlers with special needs by enacting the spirit of the law for what has been an often overlooked phenomenon.

## REFERENCES


AblePlay.org. (2009). *AblePlay: Play products for children with special needs*. Retrieved from http://www.ableplay.org/

Alliance Action. (2006). *Information sheets: Assistive technology for infants, toddlers, and young children with disabilities*. Retrieved from http://www.parentcenternetwork.org/assets/files/national/all7.pdf

Benedict, R. E., Lee, J. P., Marrujo, S. K., & Farel, A. M. (1999). Assistive devices as an early childhood intervention: Evaluating outcomes. *Technology and Disability*, *11*(1/2), 79–90.

Bredekamp, S., & Copple, C. (Eds.). (1997). *Developmentally appropriate practice in early childhood programs*. Washington, DC: NAEYC.

Bundy, A. C. (1997). Play and playfulness: What to look for. In L. D. Parham, & L. S. Fazio (Eds.), *Play in occupational therapy for children* (pp. 52–66). St. Louis, MO: Mosby.

Campbell, P. H., Milbourne, S., Dugan, L. M., & Wilcox, M. J. (2006). A review of evidence on practices for teaching young children to use assistive technology devices. *Topics in Early Childhood Special Education*, *26*(1), 3–13. doi: 10.1177/02711214060260010101

Cress, C. J., & Marvin, C. A. (2003). Common questions about AAC services in early intervention. *Augmentative and Alternative Communication*, *19*, 254–272. doi:10.1080/0743461031000 1598242

Dugan, L. M., Campbell, P. H., & Wilcox, M. J. (2006). Making decisions about assistive technology with infants and toddlers. *Topics in Early Childhood Special Education*, *26*(1), 25–32. doi :10.1177/02711214060260010301

Freeman, S., & Kasari, C. (2013). Parent-child interaction in autism: Characteristics of play. *Autism*, *17*(2), 147–161. doi:10.1177/1362361312469269 PMID:23382513

Hasselbring, T. S., & Glaser, C. H. W. (2000). Use of computer technology to help students with special needs: The future of children. *Children and Computer Technology*, *10*, 102–123.

Judge, S. (2002). Family-centred assistive technology assessment and intervention practices for early intervention. *Infants and Young Children*, *15*(1), 60–68. doi:10.1097/00001163-200207000-00009

Judge, S. (2006). Constructing an assistive technology toolkit for young children: Views from the field. *Journal of Special Education Technology*, *21*(4), 17–24.

Judge, S. L., Floyd, K., & Jeffs, T. (2008). Using an assistive technology toolkit to promote inclusion. *Early Childhood Education Journal*, *36*(2), 121–126. doi:10.1007/s10643-008-0257-0

Judge, S. L., & Lahm, E. A. (1998). Assistive technology applications for play, mobility, communication, and learning for young children with disabilities. In S. L. Judge, & H. P. Parette (Eds.), *Assistive technology for young children with disabilities: A guide to family-centred services* (pp. 16–44). Cambridge, MA: Brookline.

Judge, S. L., & Parette, H. P. (Eds.). (1998). *Assistive technology for young children with disabilities: A guide to providing family-centered services*. Cambridge, MA: Brookline.

Lahm, E. A., & Sizemore, L. (2002). Factors that influence assistive technology decision-making. *Journal of Special Education Technology*, *17*(1), 15–26.

Lane, S., & Mistrett, S. (1996). Play and assistive technology issues for infants and young children with disabilities: A preliminary examination. *Focus on Autism and Other Developmental Disabilities*, *11*(2), 96–104. doi:10.1177/108835769601100205

Langley, M. (1990). A developmental approach to the use of toys for facilitation of environmental control. *Physical & Occupational Therapy in Pediatrics*, *10*(2), 69–91. doi:10.1080/J006v10n02_04

Langone, J., Malone, D. M., & Kinsley, T. (1999). Technology solutions for young children with developmental concerns. *Infants and Young Children*, *11*(4), 65–78. doi:10.1097/00001163-199904000-00011

Lesar, S. (1998). Use of assistive technology with young children with disabilities: Current status and training needs. *Journal of Early Intervention*, *21*(2), 146–159. doi:10.1177/105381519802100207

MacArthur, C. A. (2001). Technology implementation in special education. In J. Woodward, & L. Cuban (Eds.), *Technology, curriculum and professional development: Adapting schools to meet the needs of students with disabilities* (pp. 115–120). Thousand Oaks, CA: Corwin.

McInerney, M., Osher, D., & Kane, M. (1997). *Improving the availability and use of technology for children with disabilities*. Washington, DC: Chesapeake Institute of the American Institutes for Research.

Mistrett, S. G. (2001a). *Synthesis on the use of assistive technology with infants and toddlers (birth through age two)* (Contract No. HS97017002, Task Order No. 14). Washington, DC: U.S. Department of Education, Office of Special Education Programs, Division of Research to Practice.

Mistrett, S. G. (2001b). *Let's play! Project final report (Final report to OSERS, No. H024B50051)*. Buffalo, NY: OSERS.

Mistrett, S. G., Hale, M. M., Gruner, A., Sunshine, C., & McInerney, M. (2001). *Synthesis on the use of assistive technology with infants and toddlers with disabilities (birth–two)*. Washington, DC: American Institutes of Research.

Mistrett, S. G., Lane, S., & Goetz, A. (2000). *A professional's guide to assisting families in creating play environments for children with disabilities*. Buffalo, NY: State University of New York at Buffalo, Center for Assistive Technology.

Mistrett, S. G., Lane, S. J., & Ruffino, A. G. (2005). Growing and learning through technology: Birth to five. In D. Edyburn, K. Higgins, & R. Boone (Eds.), *Handbook of special education technology researchand practice* (pp. 273–307). Whitefish Bay, WI: Knowledge by Design.

NAEYC. (2009). *Developmentally appropriate practice in early childhood programs serving children from birth through age 8: A position statement of the national association for the education of young children*. Retrieved from http://www.naeyc.org/files/naeyc/file/positions/PSDAP.pdf

National Early Intervention Longitudinal Study (NEILS). (2001). Services received by families and children in early intervention. In *Proceedings of the 23rd Annual Report to Congress on Implementation of IDEA* (pp. 1–69). Washington, DC: U.S. Department of Education.

Parette, H. P., & Angelo, D. H. (1996). Augmentative and alternative communication impact on families: Trends and future directions. *The Journal of Special Education*, *30*, 77–98. doi:10.1177/002246699603000105

Parham, L. D., & Primeau, L. A. (1997). *Play and occupational therapy for children*. St. Louis, MO: Mosby.

Phillips, B., & Zhao, H. (1993). Predictors of assistive technology abandonment. *Assistive Technology*, *5*(1), 36–45. doi:10.1080/10400435.1993.10132205 PMID:10171664

Piaget, J. (1962). *Play, dreams, and imitation in childhood*. New York: Norton.

Rogers, S. (Ed.). (2011). *Rethinking play and pedagogy: Contexts, concepts and cultures*. London: Routledge.

Romski, M., & Sevick, R. (2005). Augmentative communication and early intervention: Myths and realities. *Infants and Young Children*, *18*(3), 174–185. doi:10.1097/00001163-200507000-00002

Romski, M. A., Sevik, R. A., & Forrest, S. (2001). Assistive technology and augmentative communication in early childhood inclusion. In M. J. Guralnick (Ed.), *Early childhood inclusion: Focus on change* (pp. 465–479). Baltimore, MD: Paul H. Brookes Publishing Co., Inc.

Sawyer, B., Milbourne, S., Dugan, L., & Campbell, P. (2005). *Report of assistive technology training for providers and families of children in early intervention*. Retrieved from http://tnt.asu.edu/files/ATtrainingbrief2-8-05.pdf

Stoner, J. B., Parette, H. P., Watts, E. H., Wojcik, B. W., & Fogal, T. (2008). Preschool teacher perceptions of assistive technology and professional development responses. *Education and Training in Developmental Disabilities*, *43*(1), 77–91.

Sullivan, M., & Lewis, M. (2000). Assistive technology for the very young: Creating responsive environments. *Infants and Young Children*, *12*(4), 34–52. doi:10.1097/00001163-200012040-00009

U.S. Department of Education. (2012). *Office of special education programs*. Retrieved from http://www2.ed.gov/about/offices/list/osers/osep/index.html?src=mr

Van Tatenhove, G. M. (1987). Teaching power through augmentative communication: Guidelines for early intervention. *Journal of Childhood Communication Disorders*, *10*, 185–199. doi:10.1177/152574018701000207

Vygotsky, L. (1978). Interaction between learning and development. In T. M. Cole (Ed.), *From mind and society* (pp. 79–91). Cambridge, MA: Harvard University Press.

Wilcox, M., Bacon, C., & Campbell, P. (2004). *National survey of parents and providers using AT in early intervention*. Retrieved from http://tnt.asu.edu

Wilcox, M., Guimond, A., Campbell, P., & Weintraub Moore, H. (2006). Assistive technology for infants and toddlers with disabilities: Provider perspectives regarding use, decision-making practices, and resources. *Topics in Early Childhood Special Education*, *26*(1), 33–50. doi:10.1177/02711214060260010401

## ADDITIONAL READING

AblePlay.org. (2009). *AblePlay: Play products for children with special needs*. Retrieved from http://www.ableplay.org/

Judge, S. (2002). Family-centred assistive technology assessment and intervention practices for early intervention. *Infants and Young Children*, *15*(1), 60–68. doi:10.1097/00001163-200207000-00009

Mistrett, S. G. (2001a). *Synthesis on the use of assistive technology with infants and toddlers (birth through age two)* (Contract No. HS97017002, Task Order No. 14). Washington, DC: U.S. Department of Education, Office of Special Education Programs, Division of Research to Practice.

Mistrett, S. G. (2001b). Let's Play! Project final report. (Final report to OSERS, No. H024B50051). Buffalo, New York.

NAEYC. (2009). *Developmentally appropriate practice in early childhood programs serving children from birth through age 8. A position statement of the National Association for the Education of Young Children*. Retrieved from http://www.naeyc.org/files/naeyc/file/positions/PSDAP.pdf adopted 2009

Wilcox, M., Bacon, C., & Campbell, P. (2004). *National survey of parents and providers using AT in early intervention.* Retrieved from Tots-n-Tech Research Institute website: http://tnt.asu.edu

Wilcox, M., Guimond, A., Campbell, P., & Weintraub Moore, H. (2006). Assistive technology for infants and toddlers with disabilities: Provider perspectives regarding use, decision-making practices, and resources. *Topics in Early Childhood Special Education*, *26*(1), 33–50. doi:10.1177/02711214060260010401

# Chapter 15
# Creating Protective Barriers for Students with Disabilities in E-Learning Environments

**Bob Barrett**
*American Public University, USA*

## ABSTRACT

*As corporations and organizations continue to make strides in employing people with disabilities, in part, as an act of social responsibility, other entities have started to realize the need and value of this untapped human resource. Studies have shown that employees with disabilities have low turnover rates, low absenteeism, and high motivation to prove themselves. In today's workplace, many organizations will need to rethink their employment practices in order to compete for employees from the current, shrinking workforce. Thus, these employers are now looking towards academic institutions for well-qualified candidates. The key question here is whether academic institutions and educators are prepared to enable, educate, protect, and motivate learners with and without disabilities for changes in the workforce. One way that academia is helping to break down barriers to education is through the incorporation of online learning, or "e-learning." Whereas barriers to education for people with disabilities have traditionally taken the form of architectural and attitudinal impediments, e-learning may help mitigate such barriers, equalizing the learning environment for all students.*

DOI: 10.4018/978-1-4666-5015-2.ch015

## INTRODUCTION

*Disability used to signal the end of active life. Now it is a common characteristic of a normal lifespan. Sooner or later it will occur in the lives of most people, surely in the life of every family (Dart, 1996, p. 5).*

It has been estimated that as many as 650 million people from around the world are disabled, approximately 10 percent of the world's total population (Disabled World, 2013). Although such a figure is alarming, regrettably, societies in general have had a long history of attitudes, biases, and prejudices towards anyone who has looked, acted, or behaved differently than the social norm. This has resulted in barriers in the form of difficulties endured in securing permanent employment and obstacles in obtaining a quality education for people with sickness or disabilities. Fortunately, in the past few decades, such barriers have been eroding. Particularly in countries such as the U.S., which has enacted legislation, to include the Americans with Disabilities Act of 1990 (ADA), advocating for the legal rights of those with disabilities to have the same opportunities as those without disabilities. Much more needs to be done, however, from organizations to individuals, if people with disabilities are to be given the same opportunities as everyone else.

To understand the barriers and need for organizational and individual change, it is first important to understand the overall picture of the U.S. workforce. Historically speaking, it can be seen that this workforce has been narrowly focused toward able-bodied individuals. One of the key elements driving this has been choice. Employers may have certain attitudes and biases toward certain group of individuals, creating a predisposition to not hire certain groups of people, such as those with disabilities. Such bias could be founded on negative attitudes, misinformation about certain disabilities, or perhaps nothing more than a personal dislike of individuals not similar to their *ideal* current workforce employee. These biases, predispositions, and prejudices are attitudes which have a pervasive negative influence in the minds of coworkers, managers, and executives. Fortunately, there has been an equal amount of opposition from various organizations, groups, and society in general. In fact, there has been a growing movement towards more social responsibility than ever before. Unfortunately, for people with disabilities, this has been a very slow movement on their behalf.

Not surprisingly, when speaking from the perspective of the corporate entity, many organizations have traditionally worked inside a vacuum focused almost exclusively on profits. One of the leading federal mandates for facilitating change in organizations has been the ADA. Disappointingly, while the role of business to implement the ADA has been a critical component to its success, at the same time, business has been slow in the implementation process. That is, while the ADA addresses the areas of employment, education, transportation, and telecommunications, and as mandated, requires organizations to change employment practices and equalize the hiring process for people with disabilities, implementation has been longer with some organizations than others. This is in part due to the fact that organizations hold different perspectives, views, and overall objectives, shaped by the values and assumptions held by their organization's culture; values and assumptions that need to be changed.

Opportunely, organizations have started to realize that there is a need to change or modify their culture to reflect new policies, practices, and procedures in the treatment and view of people with disabilities. As Brutoco (1993) states, "because business is fully internationalized, it is the only institution with the resources and structure to serve as a catalyst for the broader planetary evolution that is underway" (p. 6). Therefore, organizations have a major role in making changes internationally, especially for the employment of people with disabilities. Such organizations are quickly realizing that policies, practices, and procedures alone are not enough, and changes must also occur in their local community and society in general (Boyett & Boyett, 1995) to include support from academic institutions.

That is, the relationship between academic institutions and business is reciprocal. Academic institutions play a critical role in aiding business in regard to job shortages, by producing curriculum, for example, that focuses on relevant skills and knowledge that employers need. While academic institutions have been seen to place particular emphasis on helping students based on socio-economic status or other factors, such as race, these institutions also need to place importance in helping students with disabilities. Namely, as more students with disabilities focus on obtaining high education, there is a growing movement toward online education in lieu of the physical classroom. However, such a transition always creates some level of apprehension, along with a certain amount of anxiety. It is therefore important for online education professionals to focus on the needs of these learners, and in the process, perhaps start to change some of their own values and assumptions about people with disabilities.

### The Purpose of this Chapter

This chapter focuses on what this author argues are two of the most disparaging barriers facing people with disabilities: difficulties endured in securing permanent employment and obstacles in obtaining a quality education. In presenting barriers to employment, the significance of culture is discussed. This includes a discussion on the values and assumptions held by organizations, and the societal changes that must occur if people with disabilities are to be given the same equal opportunities toward employment as those without disabilities are given. In presenting the barriers to education, the important role that academic institutions play in preparing people with disabilities for the workforce is discussed. This discussion is followed by the challenges facing not only disabled learners, but the challenges facing educational professionals in today's technologically rich online learning environment. This chapter ends with a discussion in the creation of strategies to eroding the barriers commonly found in course design and how to empower students with disabilities with strategic tools.

Although this chapter touches upon, what this author believes are barriers facing people with disabilities in regard to today's professional workplace and academic setting, this chapter should in no way be considered definitive. But instead, a catalyst in the facilitation of discussion between professionals in industry and academia in how to work together in what should be a symbiotic relationship in assisting those with disabilities in not only accessing a quality education, but at the same time, being prepared for meeting the employment needs and demands of the business community.

## BARRIERS TO EMPLOYMENT

### The Importance of Culture

Schein (1992) noted that values and assumptions held by organizations can be changed only when the entity makes new and explicit changes to facilitate such change. It should be noted here that organizational culture can sometimes help or hinder change. Defined as the behaviors learned from other members of a society as to how they should perceive, think, and feel about events (Schein, 1985; Schein, 1992), one way of facilitating a change in an organization is the hiring of individuals who are not acclimated to the current culture. Schein further goes on to note that "one simply cannot understand organizational phenomena without considering culture as both a cause and as a way of explaining such phenomena" (p. 311).

It should then not come as a surprise that an organization's culture can play a major role in recruitment and hiring practices. For example, such practices could be explained as a cause in the context of whether or not they recruit and hire people with disabilities. Whereas, many organizations may claim that they are a diverse and equal opportunity organization (in terms of hiring employees of different ethnic backgrounds, gender, etc.), they may not be as eager to consider people with disabilities. This can also be found in the field of education, but instead with regard to changes to educational offerings, such as online courses, for example. Fortunately, as mentioned earlier in this chapter, such barriers are slowly eroding.

Goodenough (1971) stated that culture is comprised of "standards for deciding what is, standards for deciding what can be, standards for deciding how one feels about it, standards for deciding what to do about it, and standards for deciding how to go about doing it" (pp. 21-22). While each culture may be different, many of them use their standards as a way of believing what is right and wrong, as well as just and unjust. Culture is a set of learned behaviors in a society, which is passed onto others in its group. Although culture is somewhat regimented, it can be changed through the introduction of new ideas or from others. However, some changes are very slow to occur, such as the acceptance of disability as being a cause of one or more physical or mental factors, rather than being labeled as a punishment for evil doing (i.e., religious/cultural beliefs are sometimes still upheld in some cultures). New employees or people from outside the organization can help to change an organization's culture. Thus, the key element is whether the organization wants to change and how it goes about such a change. Change may be a slow process, but an organization needs to consider its world view and compare it with its internal and external environment; and the role and function of its internal and external stakeholders can impact many of their daily operations, for the long term.

## Changing Values and Assumptions

Organizations tend to hire those who already have similar organizational values, and sometimes, company image (Champy, 1995; Hofstede, 1980). This demonstrates a narrowly focused world view by some organizations, and such a view is in danger with the enactment and enforcement of federal mandates that oppose such practices; potentially causing a challenge to such organizational norms. Organizations will need to *unlearn* some of their values and assumptions, and in the process, attempt to learn new ones (Hedberg, 1981). This type of change or movement may be slow to occur due to many factors. Weisbord (1992), for instance, stated that organizations change when they have a compelling business reason to do so. Whatever circumstances exist, such as the passage of a federal mandate, exposure to a social problem, or the presenting of a potential public relations situation, the final decision for most organizations, as previously mentioned, is an economic one. The *bottom line* figure is the key fighting point for any organization in the decision-making process. Organizations will be faced today with the decision of how they will respond to the implementation of the ADA. However, even 20 years later, some organizations are still not fully compliant with the ADA, which have resulted in numerous ADA compliance cases with the Equal Employment Opportunity Commission (EEOC).

Grand, Bernier, & Strohmer (1982) stated that research literature over the past 35 years revealed that "non-disabled persons' attitudes toward the disabled are primarily negative and result in societal prejudice against and rejection of disabled persons" (p. 165). Consequently, these attitudes toward people with disabilities consist of an assortment of social restrictions and possibly affect self-esteem (Roessler & Bolton, 1978). Festinger (1954) stated that social comparison theory posits that people will behave more favorably to others who are more like them. However, people with disabilities have banded together and developed their own sense of identity in their form of culture.

Disability culture consists of a sense of shared history, world view, and strategies for surviving in society. Unique communication, evolving language and symbols, and disability humor are other facets of disability culture (Gill, 1995). Although over 1,000 different types of disability impairments have been identified (Hall & Hall, 1994), the one element of bonding for people with disabilities has been their form of culture. Disability culture has provided a sense of meaning for people with disabilities in coping with everyday life in a society designed for the *able-bodied* person. Thus, we have two competing cultures in mind here: the organizational culture and disability culture. This leads one to wonder if the two can meet at some point and become truly integrated.

### The Promotion of Social Change

One of the major challenges for people with disabilities has been to educate the public about their abilities and potential in the workplace. Senge (1990) noted that within this community there is a commitment for truth. He also stated that it is not a search for truth, but rather, "a relentless willingness to root out the ways we limit or deceive ourselves from seeing what is, and to continually challenge our theories of why things are the way they are" (p. 141). Historically, once an employee suffered a bad accident or disability, the employee's productive years were considered finished by society. Not all countries have various laws for protection in case of certain life events, but the U.S. does consider age, pregnancy, and medical conditions as some type of job protection. As social responsibility started to grow in the U.S., the development of day care and treatment centers, as opposed to institutions, began to appear. Organizations started to look toward the stakeholders inside and outside of their organization. They began to take notice of the concerns of society and how society controlled organizations in general. The key point to take away here from the discussion is that organizations began to take note that changes were taking place both in marketplace and the world, and these organizations needed to ensure that they were aligned and making similar changes in order to become compliant and socially responsible.

Barrett (1999) conducted the first academic study on best disability employment practices in the U.S., based on the EEOC study on this same topic (EEOC, 1992). He found the following similar elements, as discussed by Senge (1990) to be important in instituting best disability employment practices:

1. Top leader commitment,
2. Key internal person,
3. Education/training and development, and
4. Shared understandings/partnerships of stakeholders.

It is important to note that his study could also be applied to education, especially online learning, in terms of academics working with various stakeholders and business in learning more about what is needed in the workplace, rather than tell the workplace what they should need. While this has been a paradigm that has slowly eroded away over the years, the stigma of disability is still prevalent in some educational institutions today.

## BARRIERS IN EDUCATION

Due to barriers encountered in their lives, people with disabilities have long been underrepresented in the educational system and the workplace. Even though organizations and companies have made strides in employing workers with disabilities as an act of social responsibility, other entities have started to realize the need and value of this untapped human resource (Thakker, 1997). Research has shown that employees with disabilities have low turnover rates, low absenteeism, and high motivation to prove themselves (Fersh & Thomas, 1993). Thus, organizations need to rethink their employment strategies and practices in order to compete for employees from the current, shrinking workforce. While the workforce has become smaller due to the retirement of the Baby Boom generation, for instance, there has been a growing need for a more educated workforce to operate the growing amount of technology being introduced.

## The Role of Academic Institutions

Over the past several decades, many employers have relied on the assistance of academic institutions to help provide them with well-qualified job candidates. However, it should be reexamined as to whether today's academic institutions are capable of enabling, educating, and motivating all learners for the many changes in the workforce. Also, are academic institutions able to set themselves apart from others in their industry by making radical changes that demonstrate that they practice what they preach? In other words, if they are going to enroll students with disabilities, will they hire people with disabilities to serve as role models and start to replace barriers in learning environments, replacing them with more proactive and responsible learning systems?

Generally, most academic approaches have been centered on the mastery of course content knowledge (teacher-centered instruction). However, not everyone learns in the same way. Thus, educators need to utilize different teaching techniques, strategies, and tools in the teaching process so that they can help all students acquire, understand, and apply learning gained from course content. This leads to a larger question as to whether or not online learning, otherwise referred to in this chapter as "e-learning," can fill this void in helping to focus on the learning style and skills needed by learners. This is especially the case for students with disabilities. Or can it be assumed that e-learning is nothing more than just a passing trend.

Without a doubt, there are obstacles or barriers in education that prevent students with disabilities from succeeding in face-to-face learning environments, especially in certain courses. This is where e-learning can play a significant role. That is, e-learning can create protective barriers for educating students with disabilities. It is also helpful in eroding antiquated barriers to learning that have stifled and restricted educational opportunities for many people with disabilities. Most obviously, e-learning eliminates the physical barriers hampering those with disabilities from attending traditional brick and mortar academic institutions.

## Identification of Educational Barriers

For many centuries only the strongest of students and those from affluent families were educated. Eventually, society did change, but the education of students with disabilities has been slow to keep up (Almazan & Quirk, 2002). In the U.S., the introduction of students with disabilities in the public school system helped to break down some barriers, but not all (Almazan & Quirk, 2002). While some barriers were attitudinal, others for students with disabilities were in the form of architectural ones. Consequently, physical classrooms have not always been conducive to learning for these students.

Prior to the passage of the ADA, many public and private offices, buildings and schools, were not accessible for people with disabilities. In terms of academic institutions, some of the architectural barriers were the layout of classrooms, restroom access, and entry to buildings (Alleghany Community College of Maryland, n.d.). For example, students with disabilities may have problems with one or more of the following barriers in the classroom or educational institution as a whole: (a) parking space (i.e., lack of proper disability parking space availability), (b) lack of ramps or elevators for building access, and (c) lack of proper handicap accessible rooms and bathrooms (e.g., doorways may not accommodate some wheelchairs).

To help academic institutions, the Open University (2006) has suggested such institutions remember the 4 A's: (a) Physical *access* as well as access to the curriculum, (b) *awareness* of the needs of people with disabilities and the barriers they may experience, (c) *acceptance* that you may need to do things differently, and (d) *appreciation* of the effects of hidden difficulties, such as pain, tiredness and emotional stress. While educational institutions need to remember each of these areas, very little emphasis has been placed on them by many of these schools, unless a specific need like financial aid, state rules/laws, or a lawsuit has caused a movement towards better acceptance and implementation. Some of the ways that academic institutions have shown a movement towards compliance and implementation of changes in the approach to education for all students is changing their teacher training courses/programs, as well as the course design and strategies used for teaching. These can be barriers in themselves, however.

For instance, educators could be argued as being a barrier in the learning environment. The mixing of students with professional educators with limited or no education or training in the teaching of students with disabilities is yet another problem. Thus, many disability and education groups (e.g., Association on Higher Education and Disability, National Association of the Deaf, National Federation for the Blind, etc.) have lobbied for change in the instruction of professional educators teaching all types of students. Fortunately, in the U.S., the passage of the ADA changed many factors affecting the lives of people with disabilities. In particular, it mandated that in the field of education, changes had to be made to accommodate the needs and rights of people with disabilities. This included disability classifications not only related to:

1. Mobility and dexterity challenges, but also
2. Visual impairment,
3. Deafness and hearing impairment,
4. Mental health challenges, and
5. Various learning disabilities.

Given the diversity of disabilities that professional educators must account for in the general classroom, there has been a growing interest and push for the use of e-learning that has seemed to offer more for students with disabilities than the traditional brick and mortar classroom. This not only makes the role of the professional educator more important than ever, but also increases the number of challenges facing these educators.

## Challenges Facing Educators in Today's Online Learning Environment

During the past twenty years since the passages of the ADA, even more changes in the field of education are being seen, especially in the classroom. This is alongside the many technological improvements and changes to learning in general. Professional educators and staff have begun to see instructional methods moving from the paper-based realm to that of the computer screen. The role and function of these educators has changed with the introduction and placement of personal computers in the classroom. Even as more technology appears in the educational environment, educational institutions are finding out that these computers hold many different qualities and benefits. For example, with computers come massive storage capacity, easier software for learners to be able to better navigate, computer skills building at earlier and earlier ages, and easier adaptation of course materials to the digital environment.

While there have been many technological advances, schools systems still have to face other problems due to poor planning and constraining budgets. Historically, the number of computers has been limited in the classroom; which has been seen as having an impact on the learning process. In addition to budgetary problems, sometimes there has been limited use of software licenses due to the amount of budgetary restrictions, which intern has resulted in limited access for users. In addition, limited training for teachers has impacted how many students have received quality technological instruction. Furthermore, not all technology is fully accessible for students with disabilities. And as a result of this limitation, not all educational professionals have been trained to teach students with certain types of disabilities. Finally, to the chagrin of professional educators, staff, and academic institutions, not all students are going to embrace e-learning.

These challenges aside, e-learning can offer more opportunities for accessibility and usability than other learning environments for students with disabilities. For example, visual learners are able to benefit from software applications in PowerPoint® and Flash® multimedia technology. Auditory learners could benefit from online classrooms with auditory lectures, podcasts for students, as well as live chats. From a blended-approach perspective, some online programs offer both auditory lectures, as well as PowerPoint® slide presentations. Also, live chats (both auditory and visual; i.e., Elluminate®, Horizon Wimba®) offer more opportunities for a variety of learners.

Examples such as these illustrate the potential of e-learning. However, these examples also bring up an important question for consideration: how can we train educators to become more accessible with technology and help bridge the learning gap for new online learners, especially students with disabilities with assistive technology needs? While there are many facets in answering such a question, first and foremost, educators need to be motivated to become more computer literate and have the desire and drive to use more technology in the classroom. Professional educators also need to be shown how to use various types of technology to achieve learning objectives in the online learning environment. With this, educators need to be helped to learn different ways, approaches, techniques, and strategies to help motivate students with disabilities to use these new technologies. While not all educators have formally prepared to work with students with disabilities, the use of technology can be quite helpful in this educational venture.

## Creating Strategies to Erode Barriers in Course Design

As online schools, programs, and courses have increased, not all professional educators have input into the design and development of their curriculum. Zhu, Payette, and DeZure (2006) wrote about several areas of consideration when one is creating an online course:

1. Course content,
2. Delivery of instruction,
3. Communication and interaction,
4. Student time spent on learning tasks, and
5. Assessment of student learning.

While the course content may remain the same, the delivery of instruction may be given in either synchronous or asynchronous learning formats. Instead of a live chat discussion in a physical classroom, the discussion/dialogue could be done in a chat session, a forum discussion thread, and/or video session. Each student's participation in the online course could depend on the learning format, as designed. Finally, selected assessment activities of student learning can be done in terms of live chats, forum discussion threads, assignments, quizzes/exams, and/or projects.

In order to consider such items within a course design, one needs to look at key areas to incorporate each of these items. That is, while course development and design are key elements to the online learning experience, the teaching strategies, tools, and techniques used by the professional educator can be equally important. Since each environment is unique, as well as the learners in it, the educator needs to assess their online environment and determine if changes are necessary for a course to help all learners or to continue with the said course design. While not all educators may be as flexible in their teaching methodologies, they should consider the possible effect on their classroom and learners if modifications and/or adjustments are required to their curriculum.

The creativity and innovative ways of teaching must also continue to change as new technologies are introduced. Professional educators and instructional designers need to enhance and modify their online programs. While many educators will agree that learning concepts, principles, and theories are necessary in establishing a good foundation of learning in any course, this may not be enough to reach all of the learning needs of today's online learners. While these educators may have a challenging position of motivating and keeping the attention of young learners, we can also see the same problem with adult learners. Despite the learning environment, motivation is a key element that all educators must continuously work on at times. The online instructor may face challenges in motivating and keeping the attention of learners when there are issues of differences in generational learning, time zone challenges, technology skills, and perceptions of course value.

This leads to the last discussion of this chapter: how can students with disabilities be empowered with the use of various strategic tools. Traditionally, this group of students has always been limited in what they could use in the learning environment, perhaps using the same type of tools given to all students. However, this has been traditionally argued to not be effective and has not worked in the past.

### Empowering Students with Disabilities with Strategic Tools

While many various disability-related concerns have been considered, how technology has helped to deter from the barriers in the traditional brick and mortar classroom setting to perhaps less evasive environment in the online learning realm should be considered. It should be realized that these new technologies have been helping to create a new type of barrier, which is more protective and accessible for all types of students. Thus, it should be realized that e-learning is not only a strategic tool for all types of adult learners, but it also offers a good platform for educating a variety of students, faculty, and administrators in the areas of diversity awareness and accommodation. Specifically, e-learning can be used to help educate all users, as well as serving as a training tool to illustrate how societal views are changing or need to change. That is e-learning:

1. Is a technological tool, as well as a tool for learning and socialization,
2. Can be used to educate not just one group of learners, but many others,
3. Can help to promote "diversity awareness,"
4. Can help to accommodate learners with disabilities and accommodate the needs of instructors and educational institutions, and probably most importantly in the context of this chapter as well as in its summary,
5. E-learning as a strategic tool can benefit both business and education.

## CONCLUSION

Historically, students with disabilities have not always been a part of mainstream learning in a global or international context. In fact, in the U.S., it was not until the 1970s that changes took place to help students with disabilities. Even as the ADA went into effect, problems in the learning environment for many were (and still are) reported. With technological advancements, online learning has grown in popularity and support. Even so, this new mode of learning has not completely mitigated the challenges in helping those with disabilities; as there is still a general deficiency in educator training, course design, and usability/accessibility. While society may not see all barriers impacting people with disabilities erode in the new millennium, the building of better protective barriers can be focused on for people with disabilities in the forms of employment and education.

In conclusion, this chapter has focused on what this author argues are two of the most disparaging barriers facing people with disabilities. The relationship between academic institutions and business is give-and-take. That is, academic institutions play a critical role in supporting business in regard to job shortages, by producing curriculum, for example, that focuses on relevant skills and knowledge that employers need. Although this chapter should in no way be considered definitive, it is hoped that it will serve as a catalyst in the facilitation of discussion between professionals in industry and academia in how to work together in what should be a symbiotic relationship in assisting those with disabilities in not only accessing a quality education, but at the same time, being prepared in meeting the employment needs of the business community.

## REFERENCES


Alleghany Community College of Maryland. (n.d.). *Assistant students with disabilities: A faculty & staff guide book*. Retrieved from http://www.allegany.edu/Documents/Helping%20You%20Succeed/studdisability_faculty.pdf

Almazan, S., & Quirk, C. (2002). *Historical and legal perspectives: Court cases, federal law and educational practices related to the education of students with disabilities*. Retrieved from http://www.mcie.org/docs/publications/Historical_LegalPerspectives.doc

*Americans with Disabilities Act, 42 U.S.C., Sections 12101-12213*. (1990). Retrieved from http://www.eeoc.gov/laws/statutes/ada.cfm

Barrett, B. (1999). *Best disability employment practices: A case study*. (Doctoral Dissertation). George Washington University, Washington, DC.

Boyett, J. H., & Boyett, J. T. (1995). *Beyond workplace 2000: Essential strategies for the new American corporation*. New York: Dutton.

Brutoco, R. (1993). *Introduction: What is the new paradigm in business? The new paradigm in business: Emerging strategies for leadership and organizational change*. New York: G. P. Putnam & Sons.

Champy, J. (1995). *Reengineering management: The mandate for new leadership*. New York: HarperCollins.

Dart, J. (1996, July 26). *Achieving independence: The challenge for the 21st century*. Washington, DC: National Council on Disability.

Disabled World. (2013). *World facts and statistics and disabilities and disability issues*. Retrieved from http://www.disabled-world.com/disability/statistics/

Fersh, D., & Thomas, P. W. (1993). *Complying with the Americans with disabilities act: A guidebook for management with people with disabilities*. Westport, CT: Quorum Books.

Festinger, L. (1954). A theory of social comparison processes. *Human Relations*, *7*, 117–140. doi:10.1177/001872675400700202

Gill, C. (1995). A psychological view of disability culture. *Disability Studies Quarterly*, *15*(4), 16–19.

Goodenough, W. (1971). *Culture, language & society*. Reading, MA: Addison-Wesley.

Grand, S. A., Bernier, J. E., & Strohmer, D. C. (1982). Attitudes toward disabled persons as a function of social context and specific disability. *Rehabilitation Psychology*, *27*(3), 165–173. doi:10.1037/h0090966

Hall, F. S., & Hall, E. L. (1994). The ADA: Going beyond the law. *The Academy of Management Executive*, *8*(1), 17–26.

Hedberg, B. (1981). *Handbook of organizational design: How organizations learn and unlearn*. Stockholm: Arbetslivscentrum.

Hofstede, G. (1980). *Culture consequences: International differences in work-related values*. Beverly Hills, CA: Sage.

Open University. (2006). *Making your teaching inclusive*. Retrieved from http://www.open.ac.uk/inclusiveteaching/pages/inclusive-teaching/barriers-to-learning.php

Roessler, R., & Bolton, B. (1978). *Psychosocial adjustment to disability*. Baltimore, MD: University Park Press.

Schein, E. H. (1985). *Organizational culture and leadership*. San Francisco, CA: Jossey-Bass.

Schein, E. H. (1992). *Organizational culture and leadership*. San Francisco, CA: Jossey-Bass.

Senge, P. M. (1990). *The fifth discipline: The art and practice of the learning organization*. New York: Doubleday.

Thakker, D. (1997). *Employers and the Americans with disabilities act: Factors influencing manager adherence with the ADA, with special reference to individuals with psychiatric disabilities*. Dissertations Abstracts International. (University Microfilms No. 9727300).

Weisbord, M. R. (1992). *Discovering common ground*. San Francisco, CA: Berrett-Koehler Publishers Inc.

Zhu, E., Payette, P., & DeZure, D. (2006). *An introduction to teaching online*. Ann Arbor, MI: University of Michigan.

## ADDITIONAL READING

Chin, R., & Benne, K. D. (1969). General strategies for effecting changes in human systems. In W. G. Bennis (Ed.), *The planning of change*. New York, NY: Holt, Rinehart and Winston.

Erickson, W. A., & Lee, C. G. (2010). *Disability statistics in the United States*. Ithaca, NY: Cornell University Rehabilitation Research and Training Center.

Fitz-enz, J. (1997). The truth about best practices: What they are and how to apply them. *Human Resource Management*, *36*(1), 97–103. doi:10.1002/(SICI)1099-050X(199721)36:1<97::AID-HRM16>3.0.CO;2-B

Johnston, W. B. (1987). *Workforce 2000: Work and workers for the twenty-first century*. Indianapolis: Hudson Institute.

Oblinger, D., & Ruby, L. (2004, January). *Accessible technology, Opening doors for disabled students*. Retrieved from http://www.nacubo.org/x2074.xml

Preece, J. (2000). *Online communities: Designing usability, supporting sociability*. Chichester: Wiley.

Schein, E. H. (1984). Coming to a new awareness of organizational culture. *Sloan Management Review*, *25*, 3–16.

# Chapter 16
# Assistive Technology and Distance Learning:
## Making Content Accessible

**Kathleen Bastedo**
*University of Central Florida, USA*

**Jessica Vargas**
*Rollins College, USA*

## ABSTRACT

*For those with disabilities, distance-learning courses can provide access to a world that was once inaccessible. Online learning becomes a possibility and for many a gateway to contributing to the world around them. However, there are many points to consider when ensuring accessibility in distance-learning courses. By exploring the current research and trends, this chapter reviews learning management systems, learner interaction styles and tools, and methods to design accessible course materials. It provides the educator with not only a working vocabulary but also with strategies and implementation methods for ensuring accessible content in online learning.*

## INTRODUCTION

Distance learning has been in existence for almost 150 years (Phillips, 1998), but it has never changed as quickly as it has over the last 20 years. The advent of the Internet, the availability of learning management systems (LMS), the variety and ease in use of all types of media (e.g., audio, video, social media), and the changing face of today's learners are all reasons for these developments. This chapter explores these changes as well as the latest trends in distance learning, the differences between online learning modalities among the K-12 and the higher education environments, and how the needs of all students, including students with disabilities, can be met online today and in the future.

DOI: 10.4018/978-1-4666-5015-2.ch016

## Objectives

The objectives of this chapter are:

- Investigate the types of interactions in distance learning
- Identify the distance learner and their technological needs
- Distinguish between two classifications of LMS (i.e., open vs. closed or proprietary)
- Recognize features of learning management systems that incorporate accessible design
- Identify the laws related to accessibility of distance learning materials in K-12 and higher education
- Apply accessibility best practices to the creation of distance learning course materials

## DISTANCE LEARNING

### Historical Overview

As mentioned, distance learning has changed. Correspondence courses, which have been around since the late 1800s (Phillips, 1998), were perhaps the first noted distance learning courses available. Communication between instructors and students was slow and materials were transmitted using the United States Postal Service. With the advent of the Internet, communication between online learners and instructors occurs at lightning speed. Instructors are no longer restricted to the physical classroom; they can pursue academic ventures while delivering a class literally a world away. Likewise, students who lead busy lives can attend classes and advance their careers at times that are convenient for them. The very nature of this modality has transformed how instructors teach and how students learn.

In addition, educational institutions began to invest in distance learning in order to reach a larger demographic that could no longer be accommodated at a physical site (e.g., lack of physical classroom space). Other students soon found reasons to sign on as well. Non-traditional students who were unable to pursue a degree in the face-to-face setting (e.g., individuals working full-time, single-parents) were afforded the opportunity to do so online. Student choices towards instruction expanded because of the availability of these types of courses, and eventually non-traditional students began taking online education as a matter of convenience (Moskal, Dziuban, Upchurch, Hartman, & Truman, 2006). Due to student demand, many institutions began to offer more online courses. As new technologies became embedded into American culture, students began to expect instructors to incorporate technologies into the classroom and deliver more courses online. As the number of these courses increased, the number of students taking these courses also began to rise. According to the 2010 Sloan Survey of Online Learning conducted by the Sloan Consortium, "in fall 2009, colleges—including public, nonprofit private, and for-profit private institutions—reported that one million more students were enrolled in at least one Web-based course, bringing the total number of online students to 5.6 million" (as cited in Kaya, 2010, p. 1) from the previous year. Demographics have also changed to reflect that most traditional students now take some form of distance education study (Zatynski, 2013).

### Distance Learning and Disabilities

This leads to a discussion about students with disabilities and education. Prior to 1970, it was difficult if not impossible for many students with disabilities to attend public school, never mind institutions of higher education. In response to this situation, Congress first passed the Education for All Handicapped Children Act (later known as the Individuals with Disabilities Education Act of 1990 or IDEA) in the mid-1970s to ensure that students with disabilities would have access to a free and appropriate public education or FAPE (National Dissemination Center for Children with Disabilities, 2012; Special Education News, 2013). With this law in effect, more students with disabilities began to attend K-12 schools. Provision of transitional services from K-12 to institutions of higher education in the 1997 amendments to IDEA, along with Section 504 of the Rehabilitation Act (U.S. Department of Labor, 2011), and the ADA, helped to increase the number of these students applying to institutions of higher education (U.S. Department of Justice, 2009; U. S. Government Accountability Office, 2009). Given the combination of these factors along with the proliferation of online course offerings, it is not surprising that institutions have reported an increase in the number of students with disabilities not only attending institutions of higher education, but taking online courses as well. In 1999, the U.S. Department of Education's National Center for Education Statistics (NCES) reported that "the numbers of students with disabilities transitioning from high school to higher education is expected to increase even more in the decades to come because of increased implementation of federal laws" (Justesen, Stage, & de la Teja, 2013). The strength of these laws together is intended to ensure that all students with disabilities have the right to the same educational opportunities as the rest of their peers.

The benefits to taking distance education courses for students with disabilities are similar to their peers without disabilities such as the increased flexibility and convenience online courses provide. Learning from home provides many of these students with the ability to work in familiar surroundings and function with the equipment and support systems they already have in place, especially if they are physically unable to attend school (Woods, Maiden, & Brandes, 2011). Due to these reasons, distance learning appeals to students with or without disabilities.

## Distance Learning Defined

Distance learning is a method of instruction where the student does not always have to be present in the physical classroom in order to interact with the instructor. Some or all course content can be delivered over the Internet using an LMS. The LMS provides instructors an area to place their course materials online and for students to receive that instruction while interacting with other students and/or the instructor. Distance learning utilizes two modes of learning: synchronous and asynchronous. Synchronous course components require instructors and students to be at their computers at the same time (e.g., an online chat). Instructors can also provide learning activities, quizzes, discussions, etc. that students can access at various times independently or asynchronously (e.g., discussion board interactions).

In higher education there are generally two types of classes designed for distance learning: fully online courses and blended courses. For fully online courses, all course materials (e.g., assignments, interactions, assessments, grades) are provided and submitted via the online environment (e.g., LMS) without a face-to-face component. There is no specific face-to-face time as everyone meets virtually in the designated online environment, though some courses may require minimal face-to-face requirements (e.g., attendance at proctored examinations).

The second mode of distance learning courses common in higher education is called a blended course (also known as a hybrid or mixed-mode course), which consists of both face-to-face and online class components. At the University of Central Florida, where online classes have existed since 1996, students not only succeed better in a blended format, but also both faculty and students alike preferred the blended method over either fully-online or fully face-to-face classes (Moskal et al., 2006). It is up to the instructor's discretion which components are completed online and which components are completed in the face-to-face environment.

## Distance Learning in the K-12 Setting

Although distance learning has existed in higher education longer than in the K-12 environment (U.S. Department of Education, 2010), online courses and programs have been increasing rapidly at the K-12 level (Barth, Hull, & St. Andre, 2012). Even though the idea of distance learning in the K-12 environment may seem unfamiliar or new to some, the following provides a list of reasons why online learning has been emerging in this environment:

- **Creation of a virtual learning environment:** for students who may not have the opportunity to take a course due to the lack of the availability of a trained local instructor or the lack of class availability or for students who have a medical condition or a physical disability that prevents them from attending class.
- **Access to higher-level credited courses:** for those students who have the capability to advance further while still taking classes in the K-12 environment.
- **Increased access to education for non-traditional students:** for students who may have left schooling for a variety of reasons (e.g., dropouts, juvenile delinquency).

Currently, most K-12 environments offer face-to-face courses and online courses. Blended learning in K-12 is when a student takes a combination of both face-to-face classes and fully online courses during the school year. Reduced seat time, while common in the higher education setting, is not typically a component of blended learning in the K-12 setting.

In higher education, the same instructor teaches both components in the face-to-face and in the online environment for both blended and fully online courses. In most cases the onus of designing these courses falls largely to the instructor teaching these courses. In order to meet the educational needs of faculty members slated to teach online, many institutions offer professional development programs while other institutions expect faculty to learn on their own. Course content usually remains the intellectual property of the instructor who created the course, though there are exceptions to this practice.

In the K-12 environment, however, online courses are often created and delivered by for-profit, third-party vendors. These instructors are generally not affiliated with the school system that the student attends. Also, vendors have the ability to purchase courses from other vendors (Staker & Horn, 2012). In fact, there is a movement by some K-12 institutions that include a clause for students to take an online course as a graduation requirement. For example, beginning with the 2011-2012 school year, high school students in the Florida Public School system are required to successfully complete one online course during high school before they graduate (Online Sunshine, 2012).

Despite all the complexities facing the institutional implementation of these courses, today's instructor must also consider how to accommodate the various learners in his/her classroom. In a traditional face-to-face classroom environment, instructors have multiple avenues in place, such as the Individualized Education Plan (IEP) at the K-12 level and the institution's disability services office in higher education, to assist students with disabilities. However, as more and more digital materials are added to courses, instructors are less equipped to ensure that students with disabilities are able to access this type of content. Fortunately, growing trends in distance learning and accessibility can be applied to meet the needs of students with disabilities and professionals online.

## Quality Control of Online Courses

This discussion also raises the salient question: How does one control the quality of online courses? In the K-12 environment this has become a point of concern with more research necessary to fully answer the question (U.S. Department of Education, 2010). In higher education, one organization has been working towards that goal for well over 10 years. Although it's not the purpose of this chapter to instruct how to build and design distance learning courses from scratch, becoming familiar with the Quality Matters Program (2013; http://www.qualitymatters.org/) will assist instructors in doing so. The Quality Matters Rubric© contains several accessibility-related topics that are used to evaluate the design of a course in addition to covering many other content areas. There are also many other rubrics that are available for free online, but care should be taken to review these rubrics to make sure accessibility is addressed. With this push towards online instruction, it can be safely assumed that distance learning courses are here to stay. However, it is up to individuals on the forefront to make sure online content remains accessible to students with disabilities.

## Differences Between Face-to-Face and Online Course Components

Learning management systems have become synonymous with distance learning courses because most courses today are embedded into one of these systems for several reasons. For example, they help keep the course organized, track student data, and provide the tools to help students interact with the instructor and each other. Prior to delving into the discussion about the accessibility of LMS, the primary differences between face-to-face and online course components are outlined.

*Time:* Within the face-to-face environment, class meetings and learning opportunities are constrained by the physical space and time designations placed on a course. It is difficult to replicate or provide the information for those students who miss instruction in the face-to-face setting. In the online environment, the information has been provided in a digital format so students can easily locate the information within the course when they need to and have the option of viewing the information at their own convenience within a given period of time.

*Location:* Face-to-face classes require a dedicated physical space, which may limit the growth of a university or college due to space constraints. Turning to online has meant that faculty and students do not require a physical learning space and thus classes are not limited to a set date, time, or place. Class meetings generally occur completely inside an LMS. Online classes also appeal to students with mobility concerns (e.g., lack of transportation or have a difficult time maneuvering across large campuses). Undergraduate data shows that "students with mobility disabilities enrolled in a distance education course more often than students with no disabilities (26 percent compared with 20 percent)…" (Radford & Weko, 2011, p. 3).

*Discussion:* Regardless of modality, meaningful class discussion that includes everyone's participation is difficult to engender. In-class discussions must occur within a designated class time so that students and instructors can interact and learn from each other but it's rare that all students are able to participate given classroom time constraints. It can be especially difficult for someone with learning disabilities or speech difficulties to formulate an answer in this setting. Discussion in the online environment generally takes place over a much longer period of time providing students with the time they need to better formulate an answer.

*Assessments:* It is generally easier to provide proctored exams in a face-to-face environment because instructors have the opportunity to monitor students in person, within a specific setting. When moving assessments into the online environment, there is a heightened concern for cheating. The following are a few strategies developed to help combat cheating in the online environment:

1. Not using the same exam over and over,
2. Shuffling the order of the questions (Harmon, Lambrinos, & Buffolino, 2010),
3. Include higher level types of questions, and
4. When feasible, assign an authentic assessment such as a project, an essay, or a research paper (Olt, 2002; Watson & Sottile, 2010).

*Community:* The opportunity to build a learning community is available in both mediums. So despite the concern that the online modality is considered to be less personal, instructors find that students who may not ordinarily speak up in class find the online modality space as an opportunity to contribute. In many cases, instructors report that they often feel they know their online students better than students they only see in the face-to-face environment.

## LEARNING MANAGEMENT SYSTEMS CLASSIFICATION

### Enterprise vs. Open-Source Systems

Over the years, distance learning systems have been created to house online course tools and materials. Generally termed a "learning management system," they are also called "course management systems" or "virtual learning environments." They are available from a variety of vendors and not surprisingly, supplying these systems has become a multi-billion dollar industry. These tools allow educators to:

1. Deliver content,
2. Manage assessments,
3. Provide materials for students to download,
4. Integrate other learning technologies,
5. Create opportunities for online learning activities,
6. Encourage communication exchanges between instructors and students, and
7. Disseminate grades to users.

These systems can be proprietary (closed source) or open source. Proprietary systems mean that the public does not have access to the source code that is used to run the program (e.g., Blackboard Learn®). Open source means the code is available to the public who has the ability to customize, change, or adjust the code as they need. The trend is toward LMS that are cloud-based, offer open-source code access, customer support, and a fee for use (e.g., Canvas®, D2L®). Even though a system may be open source, depending on the sophistication of the LMS, it is not always better to be responsible for updating the code. It may be better for the institution to pay for the product vendor to host the system and let the vendor update the code as well. The information in Table 1, though by far not an exhaustive list, includes the LMS (and related information) that are most often used in distance learning in both the higher education and the K-12 environments.

Many of these vendors are aware of the limitations of their systems and work continually with their user base to improve the system experience. Whichever system institutions choose, it's best to maintain a close working relationship with the respective product vendor. Most of the vendors will address accessibility issues as they arise and several have won awards related to accessibility. Desire-2-Learn®, for example, has been awarded the Gold Level NFB-NVA Certification by the National Federation of the Blind twice (Desire-2-Learn, 2013). However, some components of an LMS may not be accessible and seeking accessibility is always an ongoing process especially as new tools are added to the systems. In addition, most LMS also offer a free option to use their system to try it out to conduct a pilot study so testing can occur before purchasing or investing time, energy, or money in such a product.

*Table 1. LMS comparison list*

| LMS | Description | Benefits | Challenges |
|---|---|---|---|
| Blackboard Learn® (http://www.blackboard.com/) | Blackboard™, founded in 1997, has the largest user base to date (usage has been adopted by over 60 countries), but has been seeing a steady decrease over the last few years with the availability of new systems (Chung, Pasquini, & Koh, 2013). It is a proprietary (closed source) system that can be self-hosted by the institution or hosted by the company. Institutions pay according to the number of licenses determined by user enrollments. | Can support institutions with a large amount of users | Currently the most expensive of LMS available to implement<br><br>Features available according to pricing structure |
| Desire2Learn® (http://www.desire2learn.com/) | Desire2Learn®, founded in 1999, is an open source, cloud-based learning system. The institution pays for its use, but its open source ability allows end users to help customize its features as necessary. | Full customization options from system-wide to course level<br><br>Can support institutions with a large amount of users | Customization options can be overwhelming for those with limited experience |
| Canvas® (http://www.instructure.com/) | A relative newcomer, Canvas®, founded in 2008 by Instructure, Inc.™, is an open source, cloud-based system. The LMS can be self-hosted for free and the institution using the system can update the code or the institution can pay the company to host it for them and to make updates. It also incorporates Web 2.0 functionality and tools. | Ease of use for faculty and students<br><br>Works best for smaller institutions<br><br>Content creation is simple based on Web 2.0 technologies<br><br>Newest modifications go to cloud-based customers first | Customization occurs on a system level rather than course level<br><br>Third-party tool integration can mean commonly used features go down with minimal available support to fix those items |
| Moodle® (https://moodle.org/) | Moodle®, founded in 2002 by Martin Dougiamas (Moodle, 2012), is a free, open source, self-hosted LMS. It has enjoyed widespread adoption of its tool mostly in the international markets. | Cost is minimal to implement<br><br>Works best for smaller institutions (Smith, 2011)<br><br>Maintains a large community base of programmers dedicated to its continual improvement | Lack of human resource capabilities |
| Sakai® (http://www.sakaiproject.org/) | Sakai®, developed by a group of colleges and universities in 2004 (Unicorn, n.d.), is a free, open source LMS used for teaching, research, and collaboration in what is called a Collaboration and Learning Environment. It can be self-hosted for free or an institution can pay a service for hosting purposes. Since one of its goals is for use in research, the system contains a system-wide wiki, mailing list distribution, archiving and a rich site summary or an RSS reader. Yet it contains many of the same features available in other LMS (Sakai Project, n. d.). | Cost is minimal to implement<br>Maintains a large community base of programmers dedicated to its continual improvement | Complicated programming language makes it difficult to manage and implement<br><br>Lack of human resource capabilities |

## INTERACTIONS IN DISTANCE LEARNING

As distance learning began to evolve and options of LMS became available, there were concerns related to the type of interaction available in the online classroom. Critics worried that with correspondence courses, students were only self-directed learners who missed the opportunity to reflect and to reconstruct their knowledge when confronted with multiple viewpoints. This lack of interaction was often cited as a barrier to distance learning (Parker, 1999). Improvements in technologies over the years have improved the quality of interactions in distance learning. There are five types of interactions that instructors can incorporate into the curriculum. The first three are the most common types of interactions, while the last two interactions listed have evolved along with distance learning and the Internet.

- **Learner to instructor:** The most common interaction, this requires that interactions occur between the instructor and the learner and vice versa.
- **Learner to learner:** Regardless of instructor intent, students will inevitably interact with each other. These interactions become more meaningful with guidance from the instructor.
- **Learner to content:** Learners interact with the content either by reconstructing its meaning or working with problems that allow students to further engage with the content.
- **Learner to tools:** Learners engage with the tools selected for the classroom curriculum and learning opportunities. There are a wide variety of tools available ranging from Web 2.0 technologies to hardware and software.
- **Learner to environment:** The learner engages with the environment via different classroom modalities (e.g., face-to-face classroom, blended/hybrid, and fully online), which dictates how the students will engage in the classroom.

### Distance Learning Tools for Interaction

There are a variety of tools that assist in facilitating interaction in distance learning. These tools have been classified into two categories: asynchronous and synchronous technologies and are defined as follows:

- **Asynchronous technologies:** These technologies have an anytime, anywhere component that allows a variety of learners to engage in the online environment at various times. They have the greatest capabilities for breaking down learning barriers as they allow the user to access online course content at their own convenience. These tools include email, discussion boards, social networking sites, Google Drive™, wikis, and other online collaborative methods (e.g., e-portfolios, audio/videos).
- **Synchronous Technologies:** These technologies provide learners the opportunity to engage during a set date and time. The strength to these technologies is that interactions occur simultaneously and questions/answers can be delivered within the construct of the activity. Furthermore, these technologies solidify learning communities quickly by having students engage with each other and the instructor (e.g., chat, video or web conferencing, and live podcasts).

After all this discussion about interactions in distance learning and the tools that facilitate those interactions, it may be difficult to decide when and which tool to incorporate into an online course. Table 2 identifies the type of interaction, the available tools, and the benefits to teaching

*Table 2. Matching interactions with the tool*

| Type of Interaction | Asynchronous Tools | Synchronous Tools | Value of Teaching | Value of Learning |
|---|---|---|---|---|
| Learner to instructor | Discussion board<br>Email<br>Course Calendar<br>Rubrics<br>Announcements | Videoconferencing tools (e.g., Skype™, Adobe™, Connect®, Collaborate®, Google Hangouts™)<br>Live Chat/Instant Messaging | Provides "written" documentation of communications.<br><br>Identifies potential need for intervention. | Enables students the opportunity to engage with the instructor. |
| Learner to learner | Discussion board<br>Email<br>Text<br>Peer Review | In-class peer review<br>Live Chat/Instant messaging<br>Videoconferencing tools<br>Group projects | Provides opportunities for virtual coaching and peer mentoring.<br>Creates a learning community. | Encourages peer sharing of information and experiences. |
| Learner to content | Rubrics<br>Games<br>HTML pages<br>YouTube™<br>Weblinks<br>Podcast<br>PowerPoint® | Live-streaming lecture (e.g., lecture capture, webinars)<br>Videoconferencing tools<br>PowerPoint® | Solicits understanding from learners on a specific topic | Provides information that is integral in student learning of class material. |
| Learner to tools | Blogs<br>Wikis<br>ePortfolio | Paper-based assignments | Aggregates student learning in one centralized location. | Allows for student-generated content.<br><br>Students are allowed an opportunity to demonstrate learning in a tangible format, which maximizes retention. |
| Learner to environment | LMS<br>Social networking applications (e.g., Twitter™, LinkedIn™, Facebook™, etc.) | Videoconferencing tools<br>Face-to-face classroom time | Allows learning to occur in a structured environment. | Creates opportunity for students to learn within a community. |

and learning. Because many of these tools overlap, choose the interactions and tools that best meet the need of the learning objective.

## ACCESSIBILITY AND ASSISTANCE TECHNOLOGY FOR STUDENT LEARNING

Access is providing the flexibility to accommodate the user's needs and preferences. The following is a list of users who need various types of access to the Internet and online course materials. Namely, students with:

1. Visual impairments,
2. Hearing impairments,
3. Learning disabilities,
4. Mental disabilities,
5. English as a second language,
6. Physical impairments and
7. Slow connection speeds.

At the K-12 level, an IEP must be completed on an annual basis for qualified students. It is the IEP team's responsibility to determine how the student will access the curriculum and if any assistive technology (AT) is needed based on the student's goals. In higher education, there is no

IEP available to students; therefore, students must learn to become self-advocates and meet with the institution's student disability office as needed. There are typically a few accessible computers stations scattered across campuses and at the institution's student disabilities office, but these stations are generally designed and may not meet the specific needs of each individual student with disabilities.

Students with disabilities who complete high school and move onto higher education are often faced with an additional set of challenges. Some students will be reluctant to report their disability for fear of non-acceptance by other students. Some students may be unable to develop the necessary self-advocacy skills in order to become successful on their own. In other cases, some faculty perceive students as trying to abuse the system to obtain unnecessary accommodations related to homework and test taking. Students who are not officially diagnosed with a disability may not be eligible to receive services from the institution's disabilities office (Justesen et al., 2013). These are just some of the obstacles students with disabilities attending higher education will face on their own.

## Four Components of Access

In addition to self-advocacy skills, students will also need access to the following four components of access in order to help them be successful when taking distance learning courses. They are computer access, browser access, access to the tools located within the LMS, and online course material accessibility. The following information provides a breakdown of these components.

### Computer Access

Computer accessibility also varies depending on the student's type of disability. Students with visual impairments may require screen enlargement programs so they can read the print on a screen. For web pages, it is easy to enlarge the text on a browser page by pressing the control and the plus key on a PC running Windows® and the command and the plus key on an Apple Macintosh®. Further evaluation by trained professionals may be necessary to accommodate other visual impairments. For a student who is blind, screen reading software such as JAWS® for Windows® may be required.

Accommodating students with hearing impairments can be a daunting task due to the increase in the availability and ease of use of media tools. A transcript makes it easier for the instructor to film a video or record an audio clip; and it also provides the basis for captioning, which is required by law to assist students with hearing impairments. Captioning also helps students who are speakers of English as a second language and for students who work in noisy or quiet (e.g., library) environments.

Learning keyboarding skills at the K-12 level is critical for students to be successful at the college level. For some students with disabilities computer access may be the only way they can make significant contributions to classroom or homework activities. Proficiency using the computer and the Internet (e.g., e-mail, search tools, creating/viewing web pages, using social media, and media in general) are skills today's students need to succeed in a competitive work force. For students with physical disabilities, alternate access may be required. Assistive equipment can range from an adapted mouse, an alternate or an onscreen keyboard, special scanning software, or a specialized switch that can be activated using various body parts (e.g., hand, finger, head, or foot). The AT used on campus may be unfamiliar to a student who requires access so training may also be needed.

### Web Browser Access

A web browser or browser is a software application that provides users with the ability to access, view, and retrieve materials on the Internet. Some of the common browsers include Mozilla Firefox®, Microsoft Internet Explorer®, Safari®

by Apple™, and Google Chrome™. In order for individuals with disabilities to be able to use the same materials, browsers must be equipped with accessibility features. Most browsers have these features built-in, such as: the ability to adjust the size of the text (zoom in or out), the ability to change the color or improve color contrast, and access to keyboard shortcuts.

### Learning Management Systems

The last component that needs to be evaluated for accessibility in the online learning environment is the LMS that is being used by the institution. In most cases users do not have a say as to which LMS will be supported by the institution. However, it is still the responsibility of the institution to ensure LMS accessibility to its students.

Unfortunately, when some LMS are being created, developers do not always consider accessibility during the design phase. For instance, the discussion tool can be difficult for a blind student to access or for those who have a learning disability to follow the flow of a particular discussion. Likewise, chat tools tend to be overall inherently inaccessible for students who are blind. In both cases, it may be necessary to change the assignment interaction strategy to one that is accessible (e.g., use the email tool instead), until the tool is retrofitted for accessibility by the LMS, or until another accessible tool is found and can be used in the meantime. Assessment tools are generally accessible and most LMS provide a way to extend time to one or more students as needed. There continues to be improvements in these areas, but institutions need to be diligent and maintain an open line of communication with the LMS, in order to address issues as they arise.

### Course Page Accessibility

When it comes to the creation of accessible online course materials, it is the responsibility of the institution (both the K-12 and higher education levels) and the instructor to provide these materials in accessible formats. In many cases instructors are not aware of the strategies or techniques that should be used to assist students to easily read or access online materials. Some things to consider before creating content are: style elements such as color and background as well as date format, layout, and organization of course pages, which all play an important part in making digital content accessible. If course materials are located outside of an LMS, for example on a college or department website, then these pages must be accessible as well. There are a variety of tools (some of the most common tools are listed in Table 3) to ascertain whether or not the content created is accessible. One great tool for reviewing web accessibility of content is WAVE (see http://wave.webaim.org/for details), a free evaluation tool for checking HTML files. Use this tool and others similar to it to check the accessibility of all web pages.

It is becoming not only easier to add multimedia components to course materials, but it is also easier to add multimedia components to assessments. Therefore, keep in mind that the instructor is responsible for making these components accessible as well. For example, any images that are added to assessments must have alt text, audio portions must include text transcripts, and videos must have captions. There is a multitude of resources available on the Internet designed for this purpose; however, if the instructor is not sure where to begin, Table 3 contains a list of concepts and best practices in order to get started.

## RESOURCES FOR ACCESSIBILITY IN DISTANCE LEARNING

Gaining access to professional organizations can also help the instructor keep current with how AT is evolving in the distance-learning medium. Table 4 contains many online resources and several helpful organizations. There are also more resources located in the *Additional Readings* section of this chapter.

*Table 3. Best practices for accessibility*

| Concept | What to Do |
|---|---|
| Formatting Text | Avoid using small font sizes. |
| | Use fonts that are basic, simple, and easily read on a computer screen (e.g., sans-serif fonts). |
| | Use a limited number of font styles. Most web developers will only recommend 2-3 fonts per page of onscreen content. |
| | Only underline text when it is a link. Use bold for emphasis instead. |
| | Use headings to show topics and subtopics within the content. |
| | Use WebAim Color Contrast Checker (http://webaim.org/resources/contrastchecker/) to ensure high contrast between the text and the background (e.g., avoid using dark blue text on a black background). |
| | Avoid using only color to denote importance (e.g., using red text, color blind students will see grey instead, which depending on contrast may or may not be helpful.) |
| File Formatting | Use standard file extensions that work for all Windows®, Macintosh®, and Linux® users, including mobile technologies. |
| | PDFs should be scanned in as Optical Character Recognition (OCR) so it is read as text and not an image. |
| | Use the built-in Microsoft PowerPoint® Accessibility Checker to verify PowerPoint® presentations are accessible (http://office.microsoft.com/en-us/powerpoint-help/check-for-accessibility-issues-HA010369192.aspx) |
| Graphics Usage | Provide a text description for images included on the page. |
| | Use an alt tag, which provides the opportunity to offer a short description in the HTML code (http://teach.ucf.edu/resources/document-formatting-guidelines/images/#about). |
| | If an alt tag does not provide enough characters to describe a picture, then use a long description in the HTML code. |
| | For the technically savvy, you can incorporate a span class using CSS and HTML to hide the text from the page visually. However, a screen reader will read the *hidden* content. The class' attribute would look like this:<br>.hidden {position: absolute; left: -9999px;} |
| Audio/Video Usage | Provide users with either open or closed captioning. Open captioning is when captions are on all of the time and there is no ability to turn them off. Closed captioning allows the user control of turning the captions on and off.<br>Search for video that has closed captioning. |
| | Ask companies to add closed captioning to their video products. |
| | If the instructor does not have copyright permission to add captions, provide a video transcript. |
| | Provide scene descriptions so that someone unable to see the content may know what's occurring onscreen. |

## TRENDS IN DISTANCE LEARNING

As distance learning continues to evolve so do the trends that will influence its future. Some of the most current trends in distance learning, such as mobile devices, HTML5 used in web and mobile application development, Massive Open Online Courses (MOOCs), and the proliferation of companies offering adaptive learning options, are discussed below.

### Mobile Devices

The increased use of mobile devices by both students and instructors, especially in higher education, is affecting user's access in positive ways. These devices are portable, personalized with data and settings, and allow free or relatively inexpensive applications, especially those related to traditional AT, to be incorporated into the device quickly and easily. Preferred applications for those

*Table 4. Online resources*

| Title | URL | Description |
|---|---|---|
| Accessibility Tips Page | http://teach.ucf.edu/resources/accessibility-tips/ | This page is designed to help individuals create or modify online course components so they are accessible. |
| Access Technology Higher Education (ATHEN) | http://www.athenpro.org/ | Access Technology Higher Education Network focuses on accessible learning technology in higher education. |
| Association on Higher Education and Disability (AHEAD)® | http://www.ahead.org | A professional association dedicated to ensuring that all individuals with disabilities have access to postsecondary education. |
| Assistive Technology Industry Association (ATIA) | http://www.atia.org/i4a/pages/index.cfm?pageid=1 | A not-for-profit organization of those involved with manufacturing, selling and providing technology-based assistive devices and services. |
| Blended Learning Toolkit | http://blended.online.ucf.edu/ | A free resource created by the University of Central Florida and the American Association of State Colleges and Universities; it provides best practices, models and research related to blended learning. |
| California University System, Chico | http://www.csuchico.edu/roi/the_rubric.shtml | This rubric includes six domains that can be used to evaluate online course instruction. |
| Center for Applied Special Technology (CAST) | http://www.cast.org | A non-profit organization that works to provide learning opportunities and practical applications of accessibility. |
| Center on Disabilities at California State University (C-SUN) | http://www.csun.edu/cod/conference/ | Provides an avenue for practitioners to share knowledge and best practices in the field of AT. |
| Closing the Gap (CTG) | http://www.closingthegap.com/ | Provides resources and training opportunities through the publishing of its magazine. |
| Equal Access to Software and Information (EASI) | http://people.rit.edu/easi/itd.htm | Home of the free, Information Technology and Disabilities E-Journal. |
| Educause | http://www.educause.edu/ | A non-profit organization that promotes the use of information technology to advance higher education. |
| Faculty Focus | http://www.facultyfocus.com/ | Provides effective teaching strategies for face-to-face and online teaching. |
| FETC | http://fetc.org/ | An organization that explores integration of technology and teaching strategies for K-12 and higher education through its annual conference. |
| IDC | http://www.idc.com | Use the search terms, "Education" and "IT" and you can track future trends. |
| National Federation for the Blind | https://nfb.org/ | Advocating for blind individuals, the organization's goal is to educate everyone with how to accommodate those who are blind by providing training, education and technology. |
| Quality Matters Program | https://www.qualitymatters.org/ | A program created to assist faculty with designing a quality online program. |

who require AT are generally built in HTML5 and tend to be more naturally accessible for users, but not always. Each device or application must be evaluated on its own merits and it should not be assumed that it is accessible. Some of these devices have built-in hardware features that are also inherently accessibility features (e.g., GPS, speech-to-text, text-to-speech navigation). With these types of features now within the mainstream culture, technology improves faster as more individuals have the ability to test it. Furthermore, it has been noted that mobile devices' counterpart, desktops and laptops, have been experiencing a marked decline. According to the market research firm, IDC, "...smart phones and tablets carried the 'smart connected device' category to new highs, topping one billion units worldwide" (Nagel, 2013, p. 1). This means that certain devices are becoming more accessible especially when professionals and instructors know how to utilize these technologies.

## HTML5

Currently an increase in the use of HTML5 marks some exciting changes in terms of design and previously inaccessible materials like those using Adobe Flash®. In particular, HTML5 along with Accessible Rich Internet Applications (ARIA) will contribute extensively to the future appearance of the Web, its ease of use, and overall accessibility for individuals with disabilities. HTML5 focuses on creating accessible multimedia by turning the browser into a media player. What's particularly interesting is that Google™ decided in August 2011 to no longer support legacy browsers in order to be able to create enriched media applications using HTML5 (Panchapakesan, 2011). A larger question looms regarding when HTML5 will see full implementation. In the meantime, HTML5 promises to make content consistent without requiring multiple plugins. The intent of ARIA is to increase the overall web accessibility for screen reader users. It identifies the areas of a web page to the screen reader user and explains what is being *seen* (e.g., the navigation, title, or content). These two technologies lend hope that media will become even more heavily integrated while making access universal to all, which is the principle mission of Universal Design for Learning (UDL). But with these two exciting developments, there's still much to be done in making content user-friendly and media enriched.

## Massively Open Online Courses

Another trend in online learning provides access to anyone. Deriving its title from the gaming realm (i.e., "Massively Multiplayer Online Games"), Massively Open Online Courses, or MOOCs have seen a marked increase in availability on the Web. These courses invite users from anywhere in the world to participate in learning a particular topic regardless of their institution affiliation. Evolving from sites such as MIT's OpenCourseWare, where information was provided, but the teaching component was missing, MOOCs boast anywhere from 250 to thousands of users and today's MOOCs generally provide student-to-instructor interaction. A downside to taking one of these classes is the high levels of attrition rates; yet, the benefit to taking one can be far reaching. Most allow individuals the ability to access material for free, though some require students to purchase a textbook. Also, there is a large variety of courses available from some very credible institutions (e.g., Stanford). Individuals that successfully complete a MOOC may be able to apply this information towards promotions or other comparable rewards at their place of employment. Since college credit is generally not provided with the completion of a MOOC, a badge is sometimes awarded to indicate some level of proficiency or completion. As James Marshall Crotty (2012) of Forbes online magazine stated, "they are a free or low-cost way in which job-seekers can demonstrate hyper-specialized competency in lieu of, or as an adjunct to, a certificate or diploma" (p. 1). Some educational experts see MOOCs as an area of disruptive innovations, meaning "technology takes root in areas of nonconsumption – where the alternative is nothing at all" (Horn & Staker, 2011, p. 1). In many cases, MOOCs provide higher education courses to those who could not otherwise afford to do so.

No matter where MOOCs lead higher education, these courses should be created with accessibility in mind. When the institution falls under the premise of the Rehabilitation Act of 1973 or the ADA or both, any content including audio or video components will need to be adapted for accessibility as appropriate (Anastopoulus & Baer, 2013).

## Flipped Classrooms

Another learning trend that bears discussing is what has been labeled, the "Flipped Classroom" (Goodwin & Miller, 2013). Based on the first tier of Bloom's Taxonomy of Learning (Kahn, 2012), this pedagogical style insists that mastery of information occurs in the online mode. According to this teaching premise, instructors provide basic knowledge and comprehension tasks online prior to the face-to-face meeting of the course. This is typically accomplished by taping a lecture and placing it into an online environment. In theory, watching the instructor's lecture prepares students to handle kinesthetic tasks in the classroom to further enrich learning. Originally designed to provide classroom information for students who were absent from class (Tucker, 2012), the flipped classroom optimizes the classroom-learning environment by ensuring that students are provided with material to review at their own pace with the ability to re-examine material as needed. This frees up the instructor to use classroom time to reinforce learning or tackle harder-to-grasp concepts. In the K-12 learning environment, taped lectures are provided online, there is commonly no decrease in the face-to-face learning time as there is in higher education (e.g., blended or hybrid courses). The idea is for the taped lectures to replace the assigned homework, and homework activities are discussed in the face-to-face setting. Care should be taken when implementing the use of taped lectures, and they should be used in conjunction with discussions and other types of activities whether online or in the face-to-face environment. Any taped lectures placed into an online environment will require captioning to accommodate students with hearing impairments. This is where lessons learned in the face-to-face and online environment become increasingly important for those who are aware of accessibility concerns.

## Adaptive Learning

"Adaptive learning," also referred to as "computer-based learning" or "intelligent tutoring," is one last trend worthy of discussion. It is a concept based on the premise from the 1970s that predicted how computers would be used to create programs to provide interactive teaching opportunities for students (Dunn, 2012). Originally cost prohibitive, advances in computer technology, decreased overall computer costs, and advances in research in the area of student algorithm models has once again brought adaptive learning to the forefront (National Institute of Standards & Technology, 2005). It is being promoted as a way to provide students with a personalized learning environment. Many companies creating materials for adaptive learning provide personalized programs that *learn* how the student is progressing, which automatically increases or decreases the difficulty of the content and testing materials being provided. Adaptive learning collects detailed analytics and in some cases provides the flexibility to adapt student feedback within the courseware. Claims by companies piloting these products include better student retention, higher student satisfaction rates, and overall higher student scores. Other benefits to adaptive learning products may include a lower cost to students, single sign-on through the LMS, and the application of UDL in the design of the course materials (e.g., videos include captioning options). Distance learning has become the perfect medium for this concept and has the ability to meet the needs of today's diverse learners.

## CONCLUSION

The focus of this chapter covered the history and definition of distance learning, types of distance learning interactions, and accessibility of online courses. Several trends affecting course delivery have also been discussed. Though many of the current issues related to managing and delivering distance learning were reviewed, there is still more work to be done in terms of ensuring access of online materials. This chapter has been designed to help guide instructors in creating accessible course materials for distance learning, understanding the landscape of today's learner, becoming familiar with the various types of LMS, and combating issues that could arise when these practices are not implemented. There have been dramatic improvements over the years by combining the developer's visions for new and improved technology and the end user experience.

Most of these trends support the overall status quo of education and some are purported to improve ease of access and learning outcomes. Who knows what other new developments and technologies are on the horizon. Keeping in mind that some technologies are considered as disruptive innovation, George Mehaffey, Vice President for Academic Leadership and Change at the American Association of State Colleges and Universities (2012), cautions those in education to learn to welcome and embrace change and "never be satisfied with the status quo" even though "following these rules will be more difficult" because "disruption happens most often to the unprepared." Accessibility will have to evolve as these new trends and disruptive technologies come to the forefront of education.

## REFERENCES

Anastopoulus, N., & Baer, A. M. (2013). When opening doors to education, institutions must ensure that people with disabilities have equal access. *The New England Journal of Higher Education*. Retrieved from http://www.nebhe.org/thejournal/moocs-when-opening-the-door-to-education-institutions-must-ensure-that-participants-with-disabilities-have-equal-access/

Barth, P., Hull, J., & St. Andre, R. (2012). Searching for the reality of virtual schools. *The Center for Public Education*. Retrieved from http://www.centerforpubliceducation.org/Main-Menu/Organizing-a-school/Searching-for-the-reality-of-virtual-schools-at-a-glance/Searching-for-the-reality-of-virtual-schools-full-report.pdf

Chung, C., Pasquini, L., & Koh, C. (2013). Web-based learning management system considerations for higher education. *Learning and Performance Quarterly, 1*(4).

Crotty, J. M. (2012). Why get a pricey diploma when a bleepin' badge will do? *Forbes*. Retrieved from http://www.forbes.com/sites/jamesmarshallcrotty/2012/01/26/the-end-of-the-diploma-as-we-know-it/

Desire2Learn. (2013). *Innovations and awards*. Retrieved from http://www.desire2learn.com/about/awards/

Dunn, J. (2012). How adaptive learning technology is being used in online courses. *Edudemic*. Retrieved from http://www.edudemic.com/2012/03/how-adaptive-learning-technology-is-being-used-in-online-courses/

Goodwin, B., & Miller, K. (2013). Evidence on flipped classrooms is still coming in. *Educational Leadership, 70*(6), 78–80.

Harmon, O., Lambrinos, L., & Buffolino, J. (2010). Assessment design and cheating risk in online instruction. *Online Journal of Distance Learning Administration*, *8*(3).

Horn, M. B., & Staker, H. (2011). *The rise of K-12 blended learning*. Retrieved from http://www.innosightinstitute.org/innosight/wp-content/uploads/2011/01/The-Rise-of-K-12-Blended-Learning.pdf

Justesen, T. R., Stage, F. K., & de la Teja, M. H. (2013). College students with disabilities – Accommodating, special learning needs. *Online Educational Encyclopedia: Classroom Management – Creating a Learning Environment to Association for Science Education (ASE)*. Retrieved from http://education.stateuniversity.com/pages/1865/College-Students-with-Disabilities.html

Kahn, R. L. (2012). A taxonomy for choosing, evaluating, and integrating in-the-cloud resources in a university environment. *Journal of Educational Technology Systems*, *41*(2), 171–181. doi:10.2190/ET.41.2.e

Kaya, T. (2010). Enrollment in online courses at the highest rate ever. *The Chronicle of Higher Education*. Retrieved from http://chronicle.com/blogs/wiredcampus/enrollment-in-online-courses-increases-at-the-highest-rate-ever/28204

Mehaffy, G. L. (2012). Challenge and change. *Educause Review Online*. Retrieved from http://www.educause.edu/ero/article/challenge-and-change

Moodle. (2012). *Moodle headquarters*. Retrieved from http://moodle.com/hq/

Moskal, P., Dziuban, C. D., Upchurch, R., Hartman, J., & Truman, B. (2006). Assessing online learning: What one university learned about student success, persistence, and satisfaction. Peer review: Emerging trends and key debates in undergraduate education. *Learning & Technology*, *8*(4), 26–29.

Nagel, D. (2013). Smart connected devices hit record levels even as PCs decline. *Campus Technology*. Retrieved from http://campustechnology.com/articles/2013/03/27/smart-connected-devices-hit-record-levels-even-as-pcs-decline.aspx

National Dissemination Center for Children with Disabilities. (2012). *IDEA – The individuals with disabilities act*. Retrieved from http://nichy.org/laws/idea

National Institute on Standards and Technology. (2005). ATP focused program: Adaptive learning systems. *Advanced Technology Program*. Retrieved from http://www.atp.nist.gov/focus/als.htm

Olt, M. (2002). Ethics and distance education: Strategies for minimizing academic dishonesty in online assessment. *Capella University*. Retrieved from http://www.westga.edu/~distance/ojdla/fall53/olt53.html

Online Sunshine. (2012). *The 2012 Florida statutes: Title XLVIII, chapter 1003*. Retrieved from http://leg.state.fl.us/statutes/index.cfm?App_mode=Display_Statute&Search_String=&URL=1000-1099/1003/Sections/1003.428.html

Panchapakesan, V. (2011). Our plans to support modern browsers across Google apps. *Google: Official Enterprise Blog*. Retrieved from http://googleenterprise.blogspot.com/2011/06/our-plans-to-support-modern-browsers.html

Parker, A. (1999). Interaction in distance education: The critical conversation. *AACE Journal*, *1*(12), 13–17.

Phillips, V. (1998). Virtual classrooms, real education. *Nation's Business*, *86*(5), 47–51.

Quality Matters Program. (2013). *Quality matters program: A national benchmark for online course design*. Retrieved from https://www.qualitymatters.org/

Radford, A. W., & Weko, T. (2011). Learning at a distance: Undergraduate enrollment in distance education courses and degree programs (PDF). *National Center for Education Statistics*. Retrieved from http://nces.ed.gov/pubs2012/2012154.pdf

Sakai Project. (n.d.). *About sakai*. Retrieved from http://www.sakaiproject.org/about-sakai

Smith, K. (2011). Butler LMS evaluation executive summary. *The LMS Project*. Retrieved from http://blogs.butler.edu/lms/files/2011/08/executive-summary.pdf

Special Education News. (2013). *EHA: Education for all handicapped children act*. Retrieved from http://www.specialednews.com/special-education-dictionary/eha---education-for-all-handicapped-children-act.htm

Staker, H., & Horn, M. B. (2012). *Classifying K-12 blended learning*. Retrieved from http://www.innosightinstitute.org/innosight/wp-content/uploads/2011/01/The-Rise-of-K-12-Blended-Learning.pdf

Tucker, B. (2012). The flipped classroom: Online instruction at home frees class time for learning. *Education Next*. Retrieved from http://educationnext.org/the-flipped-classroom

U. S. Government Accountability Office. (2009). Higher education and disability: Education needs a coordinated approach to improve its assistance to schools in supporting students. *United States Government Accountability Office*. Retrieved from http://www.gao.gov/new.items/d1033.pdf

Unicorn. (n.d.). *Sakai collaboration and learning environment*. Retrieved from http://www.unicon.net/opensource/sakai

U.S. Department of Education. (2010). *Understanding the implications of online learning for educational productivity*. Retrieved from http://www2.ed.gov/about/offices/list/os/technology/implications-online-learning.pdf

U.S. Department of Justice. (2009). *A guide to disability rights laws*. Retrieved from http://www.ada.gov/cguide.htm#anchor62335

U.S. Department of Labor. OSAM. (2011). *Section 504, rehabilitation Act of 1973*. Retrieved from http://www.dol.gov/oasam/regs/statutes/sec504.htm

Watson, G., & Sottile, J. (2010). Cheating in the digital age: Do students cheat more in online courses? *Online Journal of Distance Learning Administration*, *13*(1).

Woods, M., Maiden, J., & Brandes, J. (2011). An exploration and the representation of students with disabilities in distance education. *Online Journal of Distance Learning Administration*, *19*(5).

Zatynski, M. (2013). Calling for success: Online retention rates get boost from personal outreach. *ESSelect*. Retrieved from http://www.educationsector.org/sites/default/files/publications/ESS_ECore_1.pdf

## ADDITIONAL READING

Access, I. T. (2013). *The National Center on Accessible Information Technology in Education. What is the difference between open and closed captioning?* Retrieved from http://www.washington.edu/accessit/articles?50

Burgstahler, S. (2003). The role of technology in preparing youth with disabilities for postsecondary education and employment. *Journal of Special Education Technology*, *18*(4), 7–19.

Educause. (2013). 7 things you should know about. *Educause*. Retrieved from http://www.educause.edu/research-and-publications/7-things-you-should-know-about

Kelly, R. (Ed.). (2013). Synchronous and asynchronous learning tools: 15 strategies for engaging online students using real-time chat, threaded discussions and blogs. *Faculty Focus*. Retrieved from http://www.facultyfocus.com/free-reports/synchronous-and-asynchronous-learning-tools-strategies-for-engaging-online-students/

Moskal, P., Dziuban, C., & Hartman, J. (2013). Blended learning: A dangerous idea? *The Internet and Higher Education*, *18*, 15–23. Retrieved from http://www.sciencedirect.com/science/article/pii/S109675161200084X doi:10.1016/j.iheduc.2012.12.001

Vai, M., & Sosulski, K. (2011). *Essentials of online course design: A standards-based guide*. New York, NY: Routledge.

W3C Math home. (2011). *What is MathML?* Retrieved from http://www.w3.org/Math/

## KEY TERMS AND DEFINITIONS

**Accessible Rich Internet Applications (ARIA):** Improves the way screen readers read information on the Internet to the user, thereby increasing overall web accessibility for screen reader users.

**Cloud-Based:** When digital information/data is stored somewhere on the Internet for someone else.

**Hypertext Markup Language v5 (HTML5):** The latest revision of HTML, the coding language that is used to present formatted content on the Internet.

**Individuals with Disabilities Education Act (IDEA):** As amended in 2004, this federal law is designed to make sure students with disabilities receive the following services: early intervention, special education, and any other related services.

**Individualized Education Plan (IEP):** Is a plan developed by a team of specialists assigned to a student with disabilities in the K-12 environment. The IEP has input by the parents and possibly the student. The plan must contain student objectives and it must be reviewed and updated each year by law (i.e., IDEA).

**Job Access with Speech (JAWS®):** A software program, called a screen reader, developed for personal computers that helps individuals who are blind or visually impaired read what is on the computer screen.

**Proprietary Software:** Also called closed source, refers to source code that is not open to the public, but instead must be changed, modified, or updated by the owner (business).

**Screen Reader:** Generic term for software that "reads" information presented on a computer screen to individuals who have a disability, such as a visual impairment or a learning disability.

**Self-Hosted:** Housing a software program or system (e.g., an LMS) in a special physical location or on specific hardware that is housed at the institution.

# Chapter 17
# A 15 Factor and 157 Item Checklist for Assessing Website Usability and Accessibility

**Carolyn Kinsell**
*Solers Research Group, USA*

**Boaventura DaCosta**
*Solers Research Group, USA*

## ABSTRACT

*Website assessment is still a very much ill-defined practice, conducted by some and largely ignored by most. Instruments to help assess and measure the usability of websites are vital in ensuring that websites not only meet their intended purpose but are also usable and accessible. This chapter presents a checklist comprised of 15 factors and 157 items matured over years that are rooted in cognitive psychology, instructional design, computer science, but most importantly, human-computer interface study, which can be used to guide researchers and practitioners in assessing the usability and accessibility of website design.*

## INTRODUCTION

Although academic researchers have long advocated the importance of assessing the effectiveness of websites (Law, Qi, & Buhalis, 2010), with numerous approaches published (Law & Bai, 2006; Tullis & Stetson, 2004; e.g., Evans & King, 1999; Lu & Yeung, 1998; Stern, 2002; Stout, 1997), and efforts made to help improve the overall quality of websites (Law & Bai, 2006), website assessment is still a very much ill-defined practice, conducted by some and largely ignored by most. Even defining terms, such as "website usability" (Corry, Frick, & Hansen, 1997) and "website evaluation" (Law, Qi, & Buhalis, 2010), have shown to be troublesome, with no globally accepted definition for either. In spite of this, website assessment continues to be

DOI: 10.4018/978-1-4666-5015-2.ch017

a topic of interest to academic researchers and industry practitioners (Law, Qi, & Buhalis, 2010).

According to Chiew and Salim (2003), usability is one of the major factors that can be used to measure website success. The development of instruments to help assess and measure the usability of websites is, therefore, vital (Chiew & Salim, 2003) in that such instruments could be used to help researchers and practitioners design and develop websites that not only meet their intended purpose, but are also usable and accessible. This is an important distinction. Websites must not only be easy to use, but they must also be accessible by visitors, some of which may have special needs. Take for instance amendments, such as Section 508 of the Rehabilitation Act of 1973, which mandates that those with disabilities are afforded the same access to information as those without disabilities (The Rehabilitation Act Amendments, 2013).

This chapter presents a checklist comprised of items matured over a number of years rooted in cognitive psychology, instructional design, computer science, but most importantly, human-computer interface study, which can be used to guide software and web developers, instructional designers, and human factors professionals in assessing the usability and accessibility of website design. While many of us, who may have already internalized the material presented in this chapter based on years of Internet usage, feel that we *know* good website design when we see it; or *feel* good design when we interact with it, website assessment is still a very much ill-defined practice. Although the checklist provided in this chapter should in no way be considered exhaustive, it should be viewed as a practical starting point which can be augmented to meet the specific needs of companies, organizations, and individuals in their website assessment efforts.

## WEB USABILITY AND ACCESSIBLITY CHECKLIST

The checklist presented in this chapter is comprised of 15 factors and 157 items deemed important in website design and development that should be assessed in terms of usability and accessibility. Specifically, these factors include:

1. Browser support, add-ons, plug-ins, and extensions (Table 1);
2. Domain and URLs (Table 2);
3. Website performance (Table 3);
4. Trademarks, logos, and associated information (Table 4);
5. Advertisements and pop-ups (Table 5);
6. Navigation (Table 6);
7. Searching (Table 7);
8. Online help (Table 8);
9. Web page layout and content organization (Table 9);
10. Language use (Table 10);
11. Graphics, figures, and tables (Table 11);
12. Text formatting (Table 12);
13. Video and audio (Table 13);
14. User interface and behavior (Table 14); and
15. Authentication and error handling (Table 15).

The checklist design is functional. Each item is individually assessed. A "pass," "NA," or "fail" mark can be given and comments can be added that may, for instance, include the rationale for the mark or provide specific instruction as to what should be done to the website to address the item in question. Finally, each item contains a brief explanation, providing further detail and clarification.

*Table 1. Website usability and accessibility checklist: Browser support, add-ons, plug-ins, and extensions*

| Item | Pass | NA | Fail | Comments |
|---|---|---|---|---|
| 1. All web browsers are supported; otherwise browser requirements are clearly displayed and easily found and accessible? | | | | *Comments:* |
| *Explanation:* With the number of major web browsers available on the market today that follow the World Wide Web Consortium (W3C) specifications, it has become easier to ensure that websites are cross-browser compatible. However, conducting tests to verify that the website and respective functionality does in fact work as expected is advisable. If compatibility issues are found with certain browsers, or the website is only supported by certain browsers, such information should be clearly displayed on the website. Ideally, the website should identify the visitor's browser and automatically warn them that they are using an incompatible browser or a browser with known compatibility issues. If the compatibility issues are severe enough, the visitor may be prevented from accessing the website altogether, until such time that they install a compatible browser or upgrade to a supported version. | | | | |
| 2. Only necessary web add-ons, plug-ins, and extensions are required and/or used? | | | | *Comments:* |
| *Explanation:* Unneeded and/or nice-to-have web add-ons, plug-ins, and extensions should be avoided whenever possible. Exceptions include special readers or plug-ins to help those with special needs. If such assistive components are used, they should comply with the requirements of Section 508 paragraphs §1194.21(a)-(l) of the Rehabilitation Act of 1973, which mandates that those with disabilities are afforded the same access to information as those without disabilities (The Rehabilitation Act Amendments, 2013). | | | | |
| 3. Multimedia add-ons, plug-ins, and extensions (e.g., Flash®) are used sparingly? | | | | *Comments:* |
| *Explanation:* Multimedia add-ons, plug-ins, and extensions can be resource intensive. Too much can lead to crippling performance issues, degrading the visitor's experience and usability. Such components should be used sparingly or limited to those components that are typically (pre-) installed with the browser. | | | | |
| 4. The website visitor is notified if web add-ons, plug-ins, and extensions (e.g., Flash®) are required? | | | | *Comments:* |
| *Explanation:* If add-ons, plug-ins, and extensions are required (*see item 2*), the visitor should be notified that such components need to be installed. Simple and concise instructions should be provided as to how to accomplish this. Ideally, the website should automatically identify which components are missing from the visitor's browser and offer to install them. | | | | |
| 5. The opening of third-party web pages within the same browser is avoided? | | | | *Comments:* |
| *Explanation:* Third-party web pages and documents (e.g., PDF) should always be opened in a new browser tab or in a different browser window altogether. Such resources *should never be opened* within the same browser window being used by the current website. | | | | |
| 6. A warning message is displayed if the visitor is about to be redirected away from the website to a third-party website or page? | | | | *Comments:* |
| *Explanation:* If the visitor must be redirected away from the current website to a third-party website or page (*see item 5*), the visitor should first be warned of the redirect. This is especially important if the content of the third-party website or page or the security of the third-party cannot be verified or controlled. In fact, the visitor should be given the option as to whether or not they wish to be redirected (*see item 7*). | | | | |
| 7. The visitor is given the opportunity to grant or deny the request to be redirected to a third-party website or web page? | | | | *Comments:* |
| *Explanation:* If the visitor must be redirected away from the current website to a third-party website or page (*see item 6*), the visitor should first be given the option as to whether or not they wish to proceed. This is especially important if the content of the third-party website or page or the security of the third-party cannot be verified or controlled. | | | | |

*Table 2. Website usability and accessibility checklist: Domain and URLs*

| Item | Pass | NA | Fail | Comments |
|---|---|---|---|---|
| 8. The website operates under a professional, appropriate, and non-offensive name? | | | | *Comments:* |
| *Explanation:* The domain name and uniform resource locator (URL) selected for the website should be professional, appropriate for the purpose of the website, and non-offensive. The name, logo, and other identifying information of the website should also be professional, appropriate, and non-offensive. While such a concern should be mute, sometimes a good intentioned website, company, or organization name does not necessarily translate well into a URL. | | | | |
| 9. The appropriate domain type is used (e.g.,.com,.net,.org,.gov,. edu)? | | | | *Comments:* |
| *Explanation:* The domain type should be appropriate given the purpose of the website. For instance, a commercial website more than likely would be best suited using a .”com” domain, whereas an educational institution should be using an .”edu.” It would be inappropriate, for example, for a commercial company to use an .”org,” whereas such a domain would be appropriate for a foundation or well-known or well-established organization. | | | | |
| 10. Alternate spelling, abbreviation, or common misspelling domain names are used? | | | | *Comments:* |
| *Explanation:* Unfortunately, it has become common practice for third-parties to acquire domain names that are very similar to well-established or popular domains. In many cases, these alternative URLs comprise common misspellings, hyphenations, abbreviations, or alternate domain types. These alternate third-party websites may hyperlink to inappropriate content or content that is counter-productive to the legitimate website in question. It may, therefore, be of value to acquire such alternate domain names to ensure that the legitimate website owner(s) have control of these alternate domains. Incurring the registration costs of these domains may be much less expensive in the long term than the legal costs that may arise resulting from malicious or unwanted third-party alternate websites. | | | | |
| 11. Alternate domains redirect to single authorized website? | | | | *Comments:* |
| *Explanation:* Alternate websites (*see item 10*) should always automatically redirect the visitor to the primary website domain. In other words, the website should only operate under a single domain. | | | | |
| 12. Alternate spelling, abbreviation, or common misspelled domain names are checked for improper or illegal redirect to a third-party website? | | | | *Comments:* |
| *Explanation:* Unfortunately, it has become common practice for third-parties to acquire domain names that are very similar to well-established or popular domains (*see item 10*). Before acquiring a domain name for the website, company, or organization in question, first check for domain names that use alternate spellings or abbreviations of the domain to be acquired. Better to do the detective work now than be surprised later. | | | | |
| 13. HTTPS and HTTP appropriately used based on purpose and content of website? | | | | *Comments:* |
| *Explanation:* The differences between hypertext transfer protocol *secure* (HTTPS) and HTTP are pretty much now well known among website visitors. Many associate secure sockets layer (SSL) with banking, financial, e-commerce, and other websites that store or transmit personal information. So much so that visitors may not frequent a website because they feel that the website is not secure. Consequently, always ensure that HTTPS is used if the purpose of the website warrants it. | | | | |
| 14. The URL is meaningful and user-friendly (within reason)? | | | | *Comments:* |
| *Explanation:* The more meaningful and user-friendly the URL, the more likely the visitor will remember the website. The URL should as closely as possible match the company or organization name. Also be sure to avoid underscores, hyphens, or other characters that normally do not appear in the company or organization name. Such special characters may lead to misspellings and the possible inadvertent redirection to third-party websites (*see item 10*). | | | | |

*Table 3. Website usability and accessibility checklist: Website performance*

| Item | Pass | NA | Fail | Comments |
|---|---|---|---|---|
| 15. Overall website load times are reasonable? | | | | *Comments:* |
| *Explanation:* Make sure the overall website load times are reasonable. If the load times are too long, visitors may not frequent the website. Keep in mind that not everyone may have a high-speed broadband Internet connection (e.g., Cable). Some visitors may still be restricted to slower broadband connections such as DSL, or perhaps even yet use dial-up as their means to access the Internet. | | | | |
| 16. The "Home" web page loads within 5 seconds? | | | | *Comments:* |
| *Explanation:* The "Home" web page may be the first thing the visitor sees (exception may be a "Login" web page). This main page should load within a reasonable amount of time. In fact, depending on the nature of the website and the degree of multimedia used, 5 seconds may be too long. | | | | |
| 17. Web page sizes are restricted to 50KB to accommodate slow and non-broadband (e.g., Dial-up) Internet connections? | | | | *Comments:* |
| *Explanation:* Keep in mind that not everyone may have a high speed broadband Internet connection (e.g., Cable). Some visitors may still be restricted to slower broadband connections such as DSL (*see item 15*), or perhaps even yet use dial-up as their means to access the Internet. Web pages should be kept as small as possible. | | | | |
| 18. All graphics are optimized for display size and download considerations? | | | | *Comments:* |
| *Explanation:* Keep in mind that not everyone may have a high-speed broadband Internet connection (e.g., Cable). Some visitors may still be restricted to slower broadband connections such as DSL (*see item 15*), or perhaps even yet use dial-up as their means to access the Internet. In the same way that web pages should be kept as small as possible (*see item 17*), so should the KB weight of the graphics. That is, the graphics can still be large in dimension and hold the required quality, but can be compressed JPEGs, for instance, to accommodate slower broadband connections. There are numerous tutorials available on the Internet today on graphic optimization for the Web. | | | | |
| 19. Overall website feedback is timely? | | | | *Comments:* |
| *Explanation:* Results and feedback provided by the website should occur in a timely fashion. Findings that take too long to load may discourage the visitor from frequenting the website. | | | | |
| 20. Any action can be canceled? | | | | *Comments:* |
| *Explanation:* The visitor should be able to cancel any, and all actions or processes started either by the visitor or by the website. Furthermore, the action or process should stop in a reasonable period of time. | | | | |
| 21. Web pages display correctly under different screen resolutions? | | | | *Comments:* |
| *Explanation:* The VGA screen resolution of 640 x 480 is probably gone forever, replaced by the more than likely lowest XGA screen resolution of 1024 x 768. Modern operating systems and monitors, however, can now support (and recommend) high definition resolutions in excess of 1366 x 768. The website and respective web pages should display correctly under different resolutions. Particularly, the most popular screen resolutions worldwide. | | | | |

*Table 4. Website usability and accessibility checklist: Trademarks, Logos, and Associated Information*

| Item | Pass | NA | Fail | Comments: |
|---|---|---|---|---|
| 22. The website, company, or organization logo is predominately displayed? | | | | *Comments:* |
| *Explanation:* The website, company, or organization logo should be predominately displayed. Typically placed on the "Home" web page, the logo should be easy to find and identify, but most importantly, strategically placed so that it makes a presence, while at the same time not interfering with the navigation or usability of the website. | | | | |
| 23. The website, company, or organization logo is reasonably sized? | | | | *Comments:* |
| *Explanation:* The website, company, or organization logo should be strategically placed so that it does not interfere with the navigation or usability of the website (*see item 22*). This includes ensuring that the logo is reasonably sized. | | | | |
| 24. Tagline makes website, company, or organization purpose clear? | | | | *Comments:* |
| *Explanation:* The tagline should contribute to understanding the website, company, or organization. Otherwise, if it befuddles the visitor, consider whether or not it should be displayed on the website at all. | | | | |
| 25. The website, company, or organization logo is a hyperlink to the current website "Home" web page? | | | | *Comments:* |
| *Explanation:* It has become common practice to hyperlink the website, company, or organization logo to the website. While this has been seen by some as redundant, in that the visitor is already in the website, such a recursive (as it has been described) hyperlink may allow the visitor to be quickly redirected to the "Home" web page of the website from a different area of the website. | | | | |
| 26. The website, company, or organization information is grouped together on an "About Us" web page hyperlinked from the "Home" web page? | | | | *Comments:* |
| *Explanation:* It has become common practice for information about the website, company, or organization to be displayed on a separate "About Us" web page that is typically hyperlinked from the "Home" web page. | | | | |
| 27. The website, company, or organization information is well written and gives a clear and concise overview of the mission, products, services, and/or values? | | | | *Comments:* |
| *Explanation:* The information about the website, company, or organization found on the "About Us" web page (*see item 27*), should be a well-written, clear, and concise overview of the mission, products, services, and/or values related to the website. | | | | |
| 28. The website, company, or organization contact information is grouped together on a "Contact Us" web page hyperlinked from the "Home" web page? | | | | *Comments:* |
| *Explanation:* It has become common practice for contact information about the website, company, or organization to be displayed on a separate "Contact Us" web page that is typically hyperlinked from the "Home" web page. | | | | |
| 29. The publication of private information in public areas of the website is avoided? | | | | *Comments:* |
| *Explanation:* The placement of private or sensitive information in public or non-restricted areas of the website should be avoided. Such information should be placed in areas of the website that are adequately protected with, secured by, or require the use of a user name and password in addition to using additional security, such as SSL (*see item 13*). | | | | |

*continued on following page*

*Table 4. Continued*

| 30. If personal information is collected from visitors, a "Privacy Policy" web page is hyperlinked from the "Home" web page? | Pass | NA | Fail | *Comments:* |
|---|---|---|---|---|
| *Explanation:* If the website collects or stores personal information about visitors, the website, company, or organization privacy policy should be clearly displayed on a "Privacy Policy" page hyperlinked from the "Home" page. | | | | |
| 31. A "Terms of Use" web page is hyperlinked from the "Home" web page? | Pass | NA | Fail | *Comments:* |
| *Explanation:* The rights of the website owner, company, or organization as well as the rights of the visitor should be clearly spelled out on a "Terms of Use" web page that is hyperlinked from the "Home" web page. | | | | |
| 32. Copyright information about the website, company, organization, content, products, or services, can be found on or hyperlinked from the "Home" web page? | Pass | NA | Fail | *Comments:* |
| *Explanation:* Copyright or trademark information about the website, company, or organization content, products, or services, can be found on or hyperlinked from the "Home" web page. A separate web page is typically used if the copyright or trademark content spans a page or more, otherwise, if a single copyright statement is required, such a statement is typically found at the bottom of every web page in the website. | | | | |

*Table 5. Website usability and accessibility checklist: Advertisements and pop-ups*

| 33. All advertisements are unobtrusive? | Pass | NA | Fail | *Comments:* |
|---|---|---|---|---|
| *Explanation:* If advertisements must be placed on the website, banners and other types of commonly used website advertisements should be unobtrusive and not interfere with the website content or usability. | | | | |
| 34. The use of pop-ups is avoided? | Pass | NA | Fail | *Comments:* |
| *Explanation:* Pop-ups have become such a nuisance that most modern browsers (e.g., Microsoft Internet Explorer®, Firefox®) have built-in pop-up blockers. Given this negative stigma coupled with the fact that most pop-ups are nowadays automatically blocked, the practice of using such pop-ups should be avoided. | | | | |
| 35. The use of splash screens is avoided (unless, for example, the website has material inappropriate for minors)? | Pass | NA | Fail | *Comments:* |
| *Explanation:* Splash screens should be avoided. The exception is when websites contain inappropriate material or material that should not be viewed by certain age groups such as minors. The most commonly provided example typically given is that of websites that use splash screen to warn visitors of inappropriate content or adult content found on the website. In some instances, such a splash screen may force the visitor to verify his or her age prior to entering the website. | | | | |
| 36. Advertisements are only found on the periphery of the website? | Pass | NA | Fail | *Comments:* |
| *Explanation:* If advertisements must be placed on the website, such banners and other types of commonly used website advertisements should be unobtrusive and not interfere with the website content or usability (*see item 33*). Consequently, such advertisements should be placed on the periphery of the website. | | | | |

*continued on following page*

*Table 5. Continued*

| 37. Advertisement banners are preferably located at the top of the website? | Pass | NA | Fail | *Comments:* |
|---|---|---|---|---|
| *Explanation:* If advertisements must be placed on the website, banners and other types of commonly used website advertisements should be unobtrusive and not interfere with the website content or usability (*see item 33*). Consequently, such advertisements should be placed on the periphery of the website (*see item 37*). Specifically, at the top or near the top of the website. | | | | |
| 38. Advertisements which are found outside periphery of the website are labeled as such? | Pass | NA | Fail | *Comments:* |
| *Explanation:* If advertisements must be placed on the website, banners and other types of commonly used website advertisements should be unobtrusive and not interfere with the website content or usability (*see item 33*). Consequently, such advertisements should be placed on the periphery of the website (*see item 37*). Specifically, at the top or near the top of the website. However, if advertisements must be placed outside the periphery of the website, they should be clearly identified as such. Otherwise, such advertisements may be inadvertently confused with the website content. | | | | |
| 39. Advertisements have value to the visitor? | Pass | NA | Fail | *Comments:* |
| *Explanation:* If advertisements must be placed on the website, they should be of value to the visitor and should not hyperlink to vendors selling products or services not appropriate for the website audience. | | | | |
| 40. Advertisements are from reputable vendors selling legal products and services? | Pass | NA | Fail | *Comments:* |
| *Explanation:* If advertisements must be placed on the website, they should be of value to the visitor and should not hyperlink to vendors selling illegal or inappropriate products or services. In other words, the owner(s) of the website in question should only agree to advertisements that they themselves would stand behind, support, and defend. | | | | |

*Table 6. Website usability and accessibility checklist: Navigation*

| 41. The main navigation is easily identifiable? | Pass | NA | Fail | *Comments:* |
|---|---|---|---|---|
| *Explanation:* While there are typically standard conventions that have emerged throughout the history of website development with regard to the look and feel of navigation, website navigation continues to be a matter of artistic challenge for many in incorporating such navigation into the overall theme of a website. With this said, navigation for websites should be easy to identify irrespective of their overall look and feel. | | | | |
| 42. The navigation is located in a desirable place on the website? | Pass | NA | Fail | *Comments:* |
| *Explanation:* While there are typically standard conventions that have emerged throughout the history of website development with regard to the look and feel of navigation, website navigation continues to be a matter of artistic challenge for many in incorporating such navigation into the overall theme of a website. With this said, navigation for websites should be easy to locate irrespective of their overall look and feel. | | | | |
| 43. The navigation is simple and intuitive? | Pass | NA | Fail | *Comments:* |

*continued on following page*

*Table 6. Continued*

| Item | Pass | NA | Fail | Comments |
|---|---|---|---|---|
| *Explanation:* While there are typically standard conventions that have emerged throughout the history of website development with regard to the look and feel of navigation, website navigation continues to be a matter of artistic challenge for many in incorporating such navigation into the overall theme of a website. With this said, navigation for websites should be intuitive and easy to use irrespective of their overall look and feel. | | | | |
| 44. The navigation design is consistent? | Pass | NA | Fail | *Comments:* |
| *Explanation:* While there are typically standard conventions that have emerged throughout the history of website development with regard to the look and feel of navigation, website navigation continues to be a matter of artistic challenge for many in incorporating such navigation into the overall theme of a website. With this said, navigation for websites should be consistent from web page to web page irrespective of their overall look and feel. That is, the navigation should have the same look and feel throughout an entire website. | | | | |
| 45. The navigation does not traverse more than three levels? | Pass | NA | Fail | *Comments:* |
| *Explanation:* Depending on the complexity of a website, visitors can get easily lost. Website layout and overall design should ensure that no more than three levels of nesting are required in which to traverse a website. | | | | |
| 46. The navigation does not include unnecessary levels? | Pass | NA | Fail | *Comments:* |
| *Explanation:* Depending on the complexity of a website, visitors can get easily lost. Website layout and overall design should ensure that no more than three levels of nesting are required in which to traverse a website (*see item 46*). This also means that the website navigation does not include unnecessary levels. | | | | |
| 47. The major parts of the website are accessible from the "Home" web page? | Pass | NA | Fail | *Comments:* |
| *Explanation:* Website layout and overall design should ensure that all major areas of a website can be easily accessible within one to three levels (*see item 45*) using the navigation. | | | | |
| 48. Breadcrumbs are used to help the visitor identify the current location within the website? | Pass | NA | Fail | *Comments:* |
| *Explanation:* Depending on the complexity of a website, visitors can get easily lost. Breadcrumbs should help the visitor identify where they are currently within a website. Breadcrumbs also help the visitor over time understand the overall layout and design of the website, making navigation and the access of content easier with each subsequent visit. | | | | |
| 49. The navigation control (e.g., buttons, hyperlinks) labels are clear and concise? | Pass | NA | Fail | *Comments:* |
| *Explanation:* While there are typically standard conventions that have emerged throughout the history of website development with regard to the look and feel of navigation, website navigation continues to be a matter of artistic challenge for many in incorporating such navigation into the overall theme of a website. Navigation controls (e.g., buttons, hyperlinks) found on websites should be properly labeled with clear and concise language. | | | | |
| 50. Icons used as navigation controls are representative of their function (e.g., e-commerce order system looks like a shopping cart)? | Pass | NA | Fail | *Comments:* |

*continued on following page*

*Table 6. Continued*

| | | | | |
|---|---|---|---|---|
| *Explanation:* If icons are used as navigation controls, these icons should be representative of their respective functions. All icons used should be easily identified as to their function or purpose. Take for instance an e-commerce order system that is typically represented as a shopping cart, a "Home" web page icon represented as a house, or an icon used for searching the website represented as a magnifying glass. Such examples depict symbols that are universally recognized and need little to no explanation as to their intended purpose. | | | | |
| 51. The navigation controls are easy to identify? | Pass | NA | Fail | *Comments:* |
| | | | | |
| *Explanation:* In the same way that icons should be representative of their respective functions (*see item 50*), the same can be said about all navigation controls used on a website. All navigation controls should be easy to identify as to their intended purpose. | | | | |
| 52. The navigation control to the "Home" web page can be found on every web page? | Pass | NA | Fail | *Comments:* |
| | | | | |
| *Explanation:* The "Home" web page is typically the heart of a website, serving as a central hub to all other areas of a website. Consequently, the navigation should provide a means in which to access the "Home" web page from anywhere within the website. | | | | |
| 53. A recursive hyperlink on the "Home" web page is avoided? | Pass | NA | Fail | *Comments:* |
| | | | | |
| *Explanation:* If the visitor is on the "Home" web page of the website, the navigation control for the page should be disabled, grayed out, or not hyperlinked. In other words, the visitor should not be able to recursively hyperlink to the same page he or she is already on. | | | | |
| 54. The number of navigation controls on each web page is reasonable? | Pass | NA | Fail | *Comments:* |
| | | | | |
| *Explanation:* Sometimes less is more. An overly complicated or detailed navigation comprising too many controls can clutter a website and dumbfound visitors in a counterproductive way. It is therefore recommended that the number of navigation controls found on each web page of a website is reasonable for the website layout and design. | | | | |
| 55. Groups of navigation controls are of the same type (e.g., buttons, hyperlinks)? | Pass | NA | Fail | *Comments:* |
| | | | | |
| *Explanation:* In much the same way that the navigation should be consistent – having the same look and feel throughout the entire website (*see item 44*) – logically grouped navigation controls should be of the same type. If the main navigation is comprised of hyperlinks, all main navigation controls should be comprised of hyperlinks. Inconsistently intermingling hyperlinks with buttons and icons, for instance, may be too much for the visitor and degrade from the overall appeal and usability of the website. | | | | |
| 56. The navigation has redundancy (e.g., graphics are also represented with text hyperlinks)? | Pass | NA | Fail | *Comments:* |
| | | | | |
| *Explanation:* Consideration should be taken in implementing redundancy into the navigation to ensure all visitors can successfully navigate the website. For those with special needs, this may include, for instance, text hyperlinks in addition to graphical hyperlinks. While both types of navigation controls may be difficult to implement due to website real-estate issues, layout and design considerations, or may seem contradictory to items found in this checklist (e.g., *item 55*), an effort should be made to ensure that all visitors can properly navigate the website. | | | | |
| 57. The browser "Back" and "Forward" buttons are enabled? | Pass | NA | Fail | *Comments:* |
| | | | | |

*continued on following page*

*Table 6. Continued*

| | | | | |
|---|---|---|---|---|
| *Explanation:* The use of the "Back" and "Forward" navigation buttons found in web browsers has become second nature. These buttons allow users to navigate between websites stored in cache or history or even within the websites themselves. Thus, these buttons should be kept enabled by the website. While this typically is not an issue for the majority of websites, there are those which go to great lengths to disable such functionality to prevent the visitor from using these buttons as a means in which to navigate the website itself opposed to using the built-in navigation controls found in the website. Consideration should be made to ensure that the website navigation design takes these "Back" and "Forward" navigation buttons into consideration and does not exclude them. | | | | |
| 58. A "Site map" web page is readily available and easily accessible? | Pass | NA | Fail | *Comments:* |
| *Explanation:* In the same way that the "Home" web page is typically the heart of a website, serving as a central hub to all other areas of a website (*see item 52*), the same can be said about the "Site map" web page. This web page typically provides the visitor with an overview of the entire website, offering a quick and easy way in which to access any area of a website. This "Site map" web page, should therefore, be easy to access. | | | | |
| 59. Colors used for visited and unvisited hyperlinks are easily seen and decipherable? | Pass | NA | Fail | *Comments:* |
| *Explanation:* When using colors to separate visited from unvisited hyperlinks, the colors should be distinct enough that they are easily distinguishable from one another. This is particularly important for those visitors who may have difficulty in discerning colors. | | | | |
| 60. The use of generic instructions (e.g., "Click here") is avoided? | Pass | NA | Fail | *Comments:* |
| *Explanation:* The use of generic instructions, such as "Click here," should be avoided. While such statements have become commonplace, actual content should be hyperlinked instead of generic statements. The majority of visitors do not need these instructions and know when something should be clicked. | | | | |
| 61. The use of generic hyperlinks (e.g., "More…") is avoided? | Pass | NA | Fail | *Comments:* |
| *Explanation:* The use of generic hyperlinks, such as "More..." should be avoided. While such statements have become commonplace, actual content should be hyperlinked instead of generic statements. The majority of visitors do not need these instructions and know when something should be clicked. | | | | |

*Table 7. Website usability and accessibility checklist: Searching*

| | | | | |
|---|---|---|---|---|
| 62. An easy-to-use and simple search feature is available? | Pass | NA | Fail | *Comments:* |
| *Explanation:* The search feature on the website should be easy-to-use. To best accomplish this, the search feature should be simple. | | | | |
| 63. The search feature is easy to access? | Pass | NA | Fail | *Comments:* |
| *Explanation:* The search feature on the website should be easy to access. | | | | |
| 64. The search feature is found on every web page? | Pass | NA | Fail | *Comments:* |
| *Explanation:* The search feature on the website should be easy to access (*see item 63*), and consequently, should be available throughout the entire website from every web page. | | | | |

*continued on following page*

*Table 7. Continued*

| 65. The search feature is found in upper right hand corner of the website? | Pass | NA | Fail | *Comments:* |
|---|---|---|---|---|
| | | | | |
| *Explanation:* The search feature on the website should be easy to access (*see item 63*), and is typically found in the upper right hand corner of the website. If the design of the website warrants a different location, ensure that it is consistently placed. | | | | |
| 66. The heading used to label the search feature is avoided, instead a "Search" button or icon is found to the right of the search text box? | Pass | NA | Fail | *Comments:* |
| | | | | |
| *Explanation:* The search feature on the website should be easy to use. To best accomplish this, the search feature should be simple (*see item 62*). Website search features today are usually comprised of a text box for data entry and a search icon or button to the right of the text box. | | | | |
| 67. The search text box is long enough to hold most entered search criteria (25-30 characters)? | Pass | NA | Fail | *Comments:* |
| | | | | |
| *Explanation:* The search text box should be long enough to hold most of the entered search criteria. Typically 25-30 characters are considered a long enough text box. The text box does not have to show the entire text at once as it behaves like a scrolling line. | | | | |
| 68. The search feature crawls the entire website instead of offering a "Search the Web" feature? | Pass | NA | Fail | *Comments:* |
| | | | | |
| *Explanation:* It has become common practice for websites to provide a search feature that not only crawls the website but the Web as well. Many websites, for instance, can crawl themselves as well as the Web using Google™. Search engines such as Google™ and Bing® are easily accessible. Search features, should therefore, crawl websites and their content and leave the crawling of the Web to those who can do it best. | | | | |
| 69. An advanced search and tips information is offered on a separate web page? | Pass | NA | Fail | *Comments:* |
| | | | | |
| *Explanation:* The search feature on the website should be easy-to-use. To best accomplish this, the search feature should be simple (*see item 62*). Website search features today are usually comprised of a text box for data entry and a search icon or button to the right of the text box (*see item 66*). However, the search feature may provide advanced search capabilities that may not be intuitive or may require some explanation. If this is the case, this advanced search or tips information should be displayed on a separate web page that is hyperlinked from the search feature. | | | | |

*Table 8. Website usability and accessibility checklist: Online help*

| 70. Online help and/or instructions are available? | Pass | NA | Fail | *Comments:* |
|---|---|---|---|---|
| | | | | |
| *Explanation:* While the layout and design of websites should be simple, easy to navigate, and intuitive, online help and/or instructions for specific aspects or features of the website may be needed. | | | | |
| 71. Online help and/or instructions are easily accessible from the "Home" web page? | Pass | NA | Fail | *Comments:* |
| | | | | |
| *Explanation:* While the layout and design of websites should be simple, easy to navigate, and intuitive, online help and/or instructions for specific aspects or features of the website may be needed (*see item 70*). Such online help and/or instructions should be easily accessible from anywhere within the website, specifically the "Home" web page. | | | | |
| 72. Comments, questions, and/or issues can be easily reported? | Pass | NA | Fail | *Comments:* |
| | | | | |
| *Explanation:* The website should provide the visitor with an easy way in which to submit comments, questions, and/or issues. This might be as simple as providing an email address, or more complex, such as providing the visitor with a form in which to submit their correspondence. | | | | |

*continued on following page*

*Table 9. Website usability and accessibility checklist: Web page layout and content organization*

| Item | Pass | NA | Fail | Comments |
|---|---|---|---|---|
| 73. The page layout is simple and not over-designed? | | | | *Comments:* |
| *Explanation:* The website layout should be simple and not over-designed. Sometimes the best designs are the simplest. | | | | |
| 74. Frames are avoided? | | | | *Comments:* |
| *Explanation:* Once upon a time, frames were incredibly popular in websites. Frames, however, were overly used, to the extent that they caused challenges with browsers, printing, and searching, to name a few. (Did you ever have a web page with frames open in a frame of an existing web page?) Today, it is recommended that frames are used sparingly if at all. | | | | |
| 75. The "Home" web page can be digested within 5-10 seconds? | | | | *Comments:* |
| *Explanation:* The website layout should be simple and not over-designed. Sometimes the best designs are the simplest (*see item 73*). One of the ways to check this is to see if the "Home" web page can be easily digested in approximately 5 to 10 seconds. | | | | |
| 76. The website reflects the visitor's workflow? | | | | *Comments:* |
| *Explanation:* The website layout and design should take into consideration how the visitor would naturally navigate and use the website based on its intended purpose. | | | | |
| 77. Critical web page elements are displayed first "above the fold?" | | | | *Comments:* |
| *Explanation:* "Above the fold" is considered the portion of the website that is visible to the visitor without having to scroll either vertically or horizontally. The most critical elements of web pages should be displayed first above this fold. | | | | |
| 78. White space is sufficient (i.e., adequate spacing between text and graphics; a contrast ratio of at least 4.5:1 is followed)? | | | | *Comments:* |
| *Explanation:* The website layout should be simple and not over-designed. Sometimes the best designs are the simplest (*see item 73*). The appropriate amount of white space can help with this simplicity. To ensure the right amount of white space, adequate spacing between text and graphics, for example, should follow a contrast ratio of at least 4.5:1. | | | | |
| 79. The most important content is displayed from left to right and from top to bottom? | | | | *Comments:* |
| *Explanation:* "Above the fold" is considered the portion of the website that is visible to the visitor without having to scroll either vertically or horizontally. The most critical elements of web pages should be displayed first above this fold (*see item 77*). Along with this, content is displayed from left to right and from top to bottom. Keep in mind though that this item may not apply in some instances, such as in cultures in which the written word is not read from left to write and/or from top to bottom. | | | | |
| 80. The content is less than 2/3 a screen length wide? | | | | *Comments:* |
| *Explanation:* The argument that content should be less than 2/3 a screen length wide is a matter of debate. However, following this rule ensures that the website remains clean and readable. Keep in mind thought that this may be difficult to achieve based on the visitor's screen resolution. | | | | |

*continued on following page*

*Table 9. Continued*

| Item | Pass | NA | Fail | Comments |
|---|---|---|---|---|
| 81. Text across web pages is organized by columns (because side-to-side text is hard to read)? | | | | *Comments:* |
| *Explanation:* In the same way that content less than 2/3 a screen length wide ensures that the website remains clean and readable (*see item 80*), so does organizing text across web pages by columns. | | | | |
| 82. There is good text-to-background contrast? | | | | *Comments:* |
| *Explanation:* The website layout should be simple and not over-designed. Sometimes the best designs are the simplest (*see item 73*). Part of this is ensuring that there is good text-to-background contrast. Too similar of colors may cause readability issues of the content. | | | | |
| 83. The forced use of horizontal and vertical scrolling is avoided? | | | | *Comments:* |
| *Explanation:* "Above the fold" is considered the portion of the website that is visible to the visitor without having to scroll either vertically or horizontally. The most critical elements of web pages should be displayed first above this fold (*see item 77*). An effort should also be made to ensure that the visitor is not forced to use horizontal and vertical scrolling in order to successfully use the website. | | | | |
| 84. When appropriate, short paragraphs, bulleted lists, and headings are used? | | | | *Comments:* |
| *Explanation:* The website layout should be simple and not over-designed. Sometimes the best designs are the simplest (*see item 73*). In addition to using the 2/3 rule and columns, when appropriate, short paragraphs, bulleted lists, and headings are used when displaying text. | | | | |
| 85. The website layout accommodates novice to expert visitors? | | | | *Comments:* |
| *Explanation:* The website layout should be simple and not over-designed. Sometimes the best designs are the simplest (*see item 73*). Such simple layouts and designs can accommodate novice to expert visitors. | | | | |
| 86. The most frequently used text is available directly from the "Home" web page? | | | | *Comments:* |
| *Explanation:* "Above the fold" is considered the portion of the website that is visible to the visitor without having to scroll either vertically or horizontally. The most critical elements of web pages should be displayed first above this fold (*see item 77*). With this the most frequently used text should be available directly from the "Home" web page. | | | | |
| 87. Window titles begin with information-carrying words (e.g., the website, company, or organization name)? | | | | *Comments:* |
| *Explanation:* Windows titles should begin with information-carrying words. Examples include the website, company, or organization name. | | | | |
| 88. The top-level domain name (e.g.,.com) is avoided in the window titles, unless it is part of the website, company, or organization name? | | | | *Comments:* |
| *Explanation:* Windows titles should begin with information-carrying words. Examples include the website, company, or organization name (*see item 87*). Since real-estate is scarce, the top-level domain name should be avoided in windows titles. The domain can be found in the URL if it is needed. | | | | |
| 89. Window titles are no more than 8 words or 64 characters? | | | | *Comments:* |

*continued on following page*

*Table 9. Continued*

| | | | | |
|---|---|---|---|---|
| *Explanation:* Windows titles should be kept short and concise. No more than 8 words or 64 characters should be used. | | | | |
| 90. Content represented by color is also conveyed using text, markup, graphics, or other means? | Pass | NA | Fail | *Comments:* |
| | | | | |
| *Explanation:* Content should not be solely represented by color, but instead should also be conveyed using text, markup, graphics, or other means. This is particularly important for those visitors who may have difficulty in discerning colors (*see item 59*). | | | | |

*Table 10. Website usability and accessibility checklist: Language use*

| | | | | |
|---|---|---|---|---|
| 91. Language is appropriate based on the website purpose? | Pass | NA | Fail | *Comments:* |
| | | | | |
| *Explanation:* Care should be taken to ensure that the appropriate language is used based on the intended purpose of the website. If for instance, the website is intended to be used by adolescents, the language should be written for this target audience and at the appropriate grade level. It goes without saying that profanity or other explicit language should always be avoided. Not only will such language potentially offend visitors, but may also become counterproductive with regard to the website's search engine ranking. | | | | |
| 92. The language is plain? | Pass | NA | Fail | *Comments:* |
| | | | | |
| *Explanation:* Care should be taken to ensure that the appropriate language is used based on the intended purpose of the website. If for instance, the website is intended to be used by adolescents, the language should be written for this target audience and at the appropriate grade level (*see item 91*). And with this, the language should be kept simple, to the point, and plain. The use of extravagant or uncommon language should be avoided. | | | | |
| 93. The use of jargon is avoided? | Pass | NA | Fail | *Comments:* |
| | | | | |
| *Explanation:* Language found on the website should be kept simple, to the point, and plain. The use of extravagant or uncommon language should be avoided (*see item 92*). This includes avoiding jargon or slang that may be regional and not necessarily understood by the national or international community. Ultimately, the language should be appropriate based on the website purpose (*see item 91*). | | | | |
| 94. Wordiness is avoided? | Pass | NA | Fail | *Comments:* |
| | | | | |
| *Explanation:* Language found on the website should be kept simple, to the point, and plain. The use of extravagant or uncommon language should be avoided (*see item 92*). Avoid long-windedness and keep things to the point. Keep in mind that web pages, such as "Home," should be digestible within 5-10 seconds and wordiness will be counterproductive in meeting this goal (*see item 75*). | | | | |
| 95. The use of redundant language is avoided? | Pass | NA | Fail | *Comments:* |
| | | | | |
| *Explanation:* Language found on the website should be kept simple, to the point, and plain. The use of extravagant or uncommon language should be avoided (*see item 92*). This includes the use of redundant language. | | | | |
| 96. The same word or phrase is used consistently to describe an item? | Pass | NA | Fail | *Comments:* |
| | | | | |

*continued on following page*

*Table 10. Continued*

| | | | | |
|---|---|---|---|---|
| *Explanation:* While the use of redundant language should be avoided (*see item 95*), items or concepts described within the website should be consistent. Avoid using different language or terminology to identify or describe the same items or concepts. Doing so will do nothing but burden the visitor with unnecessary cognitive load. Keep it simple; keep it consistent. | | | | |
| 97. Only imperative language (e.g., "Enter") is used for mandatory tasks? | Pass | NA | Fail | *Comments:* |
| *Explanation:* Language found on the website should be kept simple, to the point, and plain. The use of extravagant or uncommon language should be avoided (*see item 92*). Consequently, only imperative language (e.g., "Enter") should be used when speaking to mandatory tasks. | | | | |
| 98. Unfamiliar terms are defined? | Pass | NA | Fail | *Comments:* |
| *Explanation:* Language found on the website should be kept simple, to the point, and plain. The use of extravagant or uncommon language should be avoided (*see item 92*). However, if uncommon language must be used, it should be properly defined for the visitor's understanding. | | | | |
| 99. Abbreviations, initials, and acronyms are spelled out followed immediately by the abbreviation in the first instance? | Pass | NA | Fail | *Comments:* |
| *Explanation:* Abbreviations, initials, and acronyms should be spelled out followed immediately by the abbreviation in the first instance. This is simply good practice to help those unfamiliar with such nomenclature in understanding these terms. | | | | |
| 100. Terminology is consistent with general web usage? | Pass | NA | Fail | *Comments:* |
| *Explanation:* Use terminology that is consistent with general web usage. Visitors today are well-versed with common household type web verbiage. Take advantage of this commonplace understanding and use terms that do not require follow-up explanation (*see item 98*). Language found on the website should be kept simple, to the point, and plain (*see item 92*). | | | | |
| 101. Capitalization is consistent? | Pass | NA | Fail | *Comments:* |
| *Explanation:* In the same way that the same word or phrase should be used consistently to describe an item or concept (*see item 96*), the same holds true for capitalization. Be consistent. | | | | |
| 102. The use of all capitalization is avoided? | Pass | NA | Fail | *Comments:* |
| *Explanation:* All capitalization of word/words is seen today in email, instant messaging, and texting circles as YELLING!, expressing strong emotion, or strong emphasis. Not to mention all caps is difficult to read. Unless the situation warrants the use of all capitalization (e.g., headings), avoid it. | | | | |
| 103. The inappropriate use of space and punctuation is avoided? | Pass | NA | Fail | *Comments:* |
| *Explanation:* In the same way that capitalization should be consistent (*see item 101*), the proper use of spacing and punctuation should be followed. The inappropriate or strange use of spacing and punctuation, even for artistic purposes, may be counterproductive and may do nothing more than make the website hard to digest (*see item 75*). | | | | |
| 104. The use of exclamation points is avoided? | Pass | NA | Fail | *Comments:* |

*continued on following page*

*Table 10. Continued*

| | Pass | NA | Fail | Comments |
|---|---|---|---|---|
| *Explanation:* In the same way that all capitalization should be avoided because it is seen today in email, instant messaging, and texting circles as yelling, expressing strong emotion, or strong emphasis (*see item 102*), the use of exclamation points should also be avoided. | | | | |
| 105. The website is free from typos, spelling or grammatical errors? | | | | *Comments:* |
| *Explanation:* Have a professional editor review the website content. One of the most embarrassing experiences in web development and hosting is to have a visitor point out (*see item 72*) typos, spelling, or grammatical errors on the website. Even worse, visitors may not be so kind, and such errors may come to light as part of third-party reviews. | | | | |

*Table 11. Website usability and accessibility checklist: Graphics, figures, and tables*

| | Pass | NA | Fail | Comments |
|---|---|---|---|---|
| 106. All graphics depict content and do not solely decorate the website? | | | | *Comments:* |
| *Explanation:* Microsoft PowerPoint® brought on an age of including graphics and photos to fill empty space. Use graphics when they depict content and convey information. Avoid graphics for the sole purpose of filling empty space or in decorating the website. This is not to say that graphics should not be used in the overall layout and design of the website. However, graphics which are not part of the look and feel of the website that do not contribute to the depiction of value-added information should be avoided. Typically, the "filling in" with graphics is a symptom of bigger issues…such as layout choice or the lack of content. | | | | |
| 107. Graphics and photos with unclear meaning are appropriately labeled? | | | | *Comments:* |
| *Explanation:* Graphics and photos should be clear in their meaning. Graphics and photos that are unclear in their meaning should be appropriately labeled for the visitor's benefit. | | | | |
| 108. The use of watermark graphics (i.e., images with text on top of them) is avoided? | | | | *Comments:* |
| *Explanation:* Unless the website must depict graphics that include watermarks (e.g., professional photographer and stocking photography websites), such practice should be avoided. | | | | |
| 109. The use of unnecessary animations is avoided (e.g., GIFs, marquees)? | | | | *Comments:* |
| *Explanation:* PowerPoint® brought on an age of including graphics and photos to fill empty space (*see item 106*). This included the use of animated GIFs. The practice also became popular at the end of the twentieth century with websites typically depicting animated GIFs to represent everything from "under construction" messages (e.g., remember the construction worker on a jack hammer GIF?) to rows of dancing smiley faces to help divide sections of text on a single web page or to separate different ideas. The practice of using animated GIFs is rarely used today and should be avoided. | | | | |
| 110. Critical elements of the website (e.g., website, company, or organization logo, tagline, etc.) are not animated? | | | | *Comments:* |
| *Explanation:* In the same way that animated GIFs (*see item 109*) should be avoided, so should the practice of animating the website, company, or organization logo. There are exceptions to this of course. Advertisements are probably the most commonly cited example (*see items 33-40*). | | | | |

*continued on following page*

*Table 11. Continued*

| 111. All graphics have appropriate descriptions and ALT tags? | Pass | NA | Fail | *Comments:* |
|---|---|---|---|---|
| | | | | |
| *Explanation:*<br>All graphics should have appropriate descriptions and ALT tags. This is especially important with regard to graphics and photos with unclear meaning (*see item 107*). | | | | |
| 112. All figures, diagrams, and charts are appropriately summarized? | Pass | NA | Fail | *Comments:* |
| | | | | |
| *Explanation:*<br>When using figures, diagrams, and charts, ensure that they are appropriately summarized either in the text or in a respective label. There are exceptions to this of course. Particularly when the figures, diagrams, or charts are simple, clear, and self-explanatory. | | | | |
| 113. All graphics are of good quality (not pixilated, dithered, stretched, scanned, or too dark)? | Pass | NA | Fail | *Comments:* |
| | | | | |
| *Explanation:*<br>If using graphics, ensure they are of good quality. Graphics that are pixilated, dithered, and stretched do nothing but make the website appear amateurish. Furthermore, avoid graphics that are scanned from other sources, such as printed documents, or which are so dark, they cannot be read. | | | | |
| 114. The use of blinking or floating graphics is avoided? | Pass | NA | Fail | *Comments:* |
| | | | | |
| *Explanation:*<br>In the same way that animated GIFs and marquees should be avoided (*see item 109*), the same holds true to blinking, floating, or other animated or motion graphics that deter from the usability of the website. | | | | |
| 115. The use of "under construction" graphics is avoided? | Pass | NA | Fail | *Comments:* |
| | | | | |
| *Explanation:*<br>Avoid the use of "under construction" graphics (*see item 109*). These will do nothing more than date the website. | | | | |
| 116. Tables are uncluttered and cells are padded? | Pass | NA | Fail | *Comments:* |
| | | | | |
| *Explanation:*<br>If tables must be used, make sure they are clean, easy to read, and the cells are well padded so that the content does not come across as cluttered. | | | | |

*Table 12. Website usability and accessibility checklist: Text formatting*

| 117. The use of blinking text is avoided? | Pass | NA | Fail | *Comments:* |
|---|---|---|---|---|
| | | | | |
| *Explanation:*<br>In the same way that the use of blinking graphics should be avoided (*see item 114*), so should the use of blinking text. | | | | |
| 118. Bolded text is used for emphasis, but sparingly? | Pass | NA | Fail | *Comments:* |
| | | | | |
| *Explanation:*<br>The use of bolded text should be used sparingly and only for emphasis and formatting matters, such as headings. | | | | |
| 119. Italic text is used for emphasis, but sparingly? | Pass | NA | Fail | *Comments:* |
| | | | | |

*continued on following page*

*Table 12. Continued*

| Item | Pass | NA | Fail | Comments |
|---|---|---|---|---|
| *Explanation:* The use of italic text should be used sparingly and only for emphasis and formatting matters, such as headings. | | | | |
| 120. Underlined text is avoided and only used for navigational hyperlinks? | Pass | NA | Fail | *Comments:* |
| *Explanation:* The use of underlined text should be strictly avoided if the text is not intended to be hyperlinked. Underlying text in websites will confound the visitor and may lead to frustrations. | | | | |
| 121. Font size is readable? | Pass | NA | Fail | *Comments:* |
| *Explanation:* Most modern web browsers allow visitors to change the text size between a number of predefined sizes (e.g., smallest, smaller, medium, larger, and largest). Even so, changing the text size using such a browser-based feature may inadvertently distort the website. Font size should therefore be taken into consideration in the website layout and design to ensure that the font is easily readable to all visitors, to include those who may be visually impaired. | | | | |
| 122. The use of font styles is kept to a minimum? | Pass | NA | Fail | *Comments:* |
| *Explanation:* The website layout should be simple and not over-designed. Sometimes the best designs are the simplest (*see item 73*). With this said, font styles should be kept to a minimum. If at all possible, use a single font style, and at most, keep to 2 to 3 complementing font styles. | | | | |
| 123. A sans serif font is used? | Pass | NA | Fail | *Comments:* |
| *Explanation:* The website layout should be simple and not over-designed. Sometimes the best designs are the simplest (*see item 73*). So, in the same way that font styles should be kept to a minimum, when choosing a font style, use sans serif. | | | | |
| 124. Resizable fonts are used? | Pass | NA | Fail | *Comments:* |
| *Explanation:* Most modern web browsers allow visitors to change the text size between a number of predefined sizes (e.g., smallest, smaller, medium, larger, and largest). Even so, changing the text size using such a browser feature may inadvertently distort the website (*see item 121*), particularly when non-resizable fonts are used. Whenever possible, resizable fonts should be used. | | | | |
| 125. Colored text is used for emphasis, but sparingly? | Pass | NA | Fail | *Comments:* |
| *Explanation:* Great care should be taken when using colored text on websites. Such colored text can be inadvertently misunderstood for hyperlinks and/or can be difficult to disseminate. As a result, colored text should only be used for emphasis, but sparingly. | | | | |
| 126. Text is left justified? | Pass | NA | Fail | *Comments:* |
| *Explanation:* Text that is centered, align right, or fully-justified may be difficult to read. Most text found in textbooks is left justified. Whenever possible, align text left. Keep in mind though that this item may not apply in some instances, such as in cultures in which the written word is not read from left to write and/or from top to bottom. | | | | |
| 127. A print page feature is offered and all content prints okay? | Pass | NA | Fail | *Comments:* |

*continued on following page*

*Table 12. Continued*

| | | | | |
|---|---|---|---|---|
| *Explanation:* Modern web browsers support the printing of web pages. However, this built-in browser feature does not necessarily always work as expected. Thus, it is best to offer a built-in website feature that can properly print content within the website. For instance, websites that offer mapping services (e.g., MapQuest™, Google Maps™) typically have such a built-in print capability. | | | | |
| 128. Standard abbreviations are used (e.g., EST, AM, PM)? | Pass | NA | Fail | *Comments:* |
| *Explanation:* Standard abbreviations should be used (e.g., EST, AM, PM). Particularly those abbreviations that are universally known. | | | | |
| 129. If automated content is used, can it be easily started, paused, and stopped? | Pass | NA | Fail | *Comments:* |
| *Explanation:* If automated content is used, the visitor should be able to easily start, pause, and stop the content. The most common example is video. However, other content, such as Interactive Multimedia Instruction (IMI), should also provide such ability. | | | | |

*Table 13. Website usability and accessibility checklist: Video and audio*

| | | | | |
|---|---|---|---|---|
| 130. Video is optimized for download or easy streaming? | Pass | NA | Fail | *Comments:* |
| *Explanation:* Multimedia add-ons, plug-ins, and extensions can be resource intensive (*see item 3*). This is especially the case for multimedia, such as video. Whenever possible, video found on websites should be optimized for download and easy streaming to support different Internet connection speeds. | | | | |
| 131. Open and closed captions are available for all video found on website? | Pass | NA | Fail | *Comments:* |
| *Explanation:* To assist those with special needs, both open and closed captions should be available for all video found on the website. | | | | |
| 132. Full text transcripts can be easily downloaded for all video found on website? | Pass | NA | Fail | *Comments:* |
| *Explanation:* Along with making open and closed captions available for all video found on the website (*see item 131*), full text transcripts should also be made available for easy download. Keep in mind that although this item has been included in this checklist to assist visitors with special needs, rarely is this item practiced. | | | | |
| 133. Full text transcripts can be easily downloaded for all prerecorded audio? | Pass | NA | Fail | *Comments:* |
| *Explanation:* In addition to having full text transcripts of all video found on the website (*see item 133*), full text transcripts should also be available of all prerecorded audio. Keep in mind that although this item has been included in this checklist to assist visitors with special needs, rarely is this item practiced. | | | | |
| 134. Exit options are available for streaming videos? | Pass | NA | Fail | *Comments:* |
| *Explanation:* The visitor should have the capability to exit streaming video in a timely manner. | | | | |
| 135. The use of background music is avoided? | Pass | NA | Fail | *Comments:* |

*continued on following page*

*Table 13. Continued*

| | | | | |
|---|---|---|---|---|
| *Explanation:* The practice of incorporating background music (e.g., MIDI files) became popular at the end of the twentieth century. It was not uncommon to have music play in the background while visiting a website. Leave this practice in the twentieth century and unless such music is absolutely necessary, avoid the use of background music altogether. | | | | |
| 136. The use of background sounds is avoided? | Pass | NA | Fail | *Comments:* |
| | | | | |
| *Explanation:* The practice of incorporating background music (e.g., MIDI files) became popular at the end of the twentieth century (*see item 135*). It was not uncommon to have music play in the background while visiting a website. While this practice should be left in the twentieth century, so should the use of background sounds. Unless such sounds are absolutely necessary, avoid the use of background sound altogether. | | | | |

*Table 14. Website usability and accessibility checklist: User interface and behavior*

| | | | | |
|---|---|---|---|---|
| 137. User interface is intuitive and easy to use? | Pass | NA | Fail | *Comments:* |
| | | | | |
| *Explanation:* The website layout should be simple and not over-designed. Sometimes the best designs are the simplest (*see item 73*). This means that the user interface needs to be intuitive and easy to use. | | | | |
| 138. Required fields are clearly marked? | Pass | NA | Fail | *Comments:* |
| | | | | |
| *Explanation:* It is common practice to mark those fields on a web page that require data entry. Typically, these fields are marked with an asterisk (*). Other designators can be used as well. For instance, the field label could be distinguished with a different color, such as red. | | | | |
| 139. Formatted fields are appropriately masked (e.g., telephone number)? | Pass | NA | Fail | *Comments:* |
| | | | | |
| *Explanation:* Formatted fields should be appropriately masked. Examples of fields include telephone number, social security number, date and time, and zip code. | | | | |
| 140. The "Submit" button is always found on the left and the "Cancel" button is always found to the right? | Pass | NA | Fail | *Comments:* |
| | | | | |
| *Explanation:* On data entry web pages, the "Submit" button is always found on the left, whereas the "Cancel" button is always found on the right. | | | | |
| 141. A confirmation message is always offered before the submittal of data? | Pass | NA | Fail | *Comments:* |
| | | | | |
| *Explanation:* A confirmation message should always be displayed before a data entry form is submitted. The visitor should also be given the option as to whether or not they wish to submit the form. | | | | |
| 142. Data is always validated in the client web browser before submittal? | Pass | NA | Fail | *Comments:* |
| | | | | |
| *Explanation:* Data entered into forms should always be validated in the client web browser before submittal. This allows the data in the fields to be validated before being sent to the website, company, or organization server(s) for processing, thus saving on unnecessary network "round trips." | | | | |

*continued on following page*

*Table 14. Continued*

| 143. Data entry forms retain data when returning from another web page? | Pass | NA | Fail | *Comments:* |
|---|---|---|---|---|
| *Explanation:* Data entry forms that have not yet been submitted should retain data when returning from another web page. Otherwise, the visitor will be forced to re-enter the data. This can lead to frustration and the customer canceling the entry altogether. | | | | |

*Table 15. Website usability and accessibility checklist: Authentication and error handling*

| 144. There is a method for the visitor to retrieve their forgotten user name and/or password? | Pass | NA | Fail | *Comments:* |
|---|---|---|---|---|
| *Explanation:* The website should provide the visitor with a way in which to retrieve their forgotten user name and/or password. This typically entails the visitor entering their user name, for instance, with the website emailing the password or a link to reset the password to the email address on file for the account in question. | | | | |
| 145. There a single login or single sign-on for all restricted areas of the website? | Pass | NA | Fail | *Comments:* |
| *Explanation:* If authentication is required for all or a portion of the website, the visitor should only have to login once. That is, single sign-on should be practiced. | | | | |
| 146. The need for repetitive login is avoided? | Pass | NA | Fail | *Comments:* |
| *Explanation:* If authentication is required for all or a portion of the website, the visitor should only have to login once (*see item 145*), and this login should remain persistent so long as the visitors' actions on the website do not become idle resulting in a timeout. | | | | |
| 147. A public web page is available to the visitor? | Pass | NA | Fail | *Comments:* |
| *Explanation:* If authentication is required for all or a portion of the website, a public web page should be available to the visitor. Even if the web page simply instructs the visitor to login. | | | | |
| 148. The website has custom error web pages? | Pass | NA | Fail | *Comments:* |
| *Explanation:* In the event of an error – either due to activity within the website or activity resulting from third-parties, such as an Internet Service Provider (ISP) – custom error messages should be used that are user-friendly and easy to understand. | | | | |
| 149. The website is free of broken hyperlinks? | Pass | NA | Fail | *Comments:* |
| *Explanation:* A methodology should be adopted to ensure that broken hyperlinks are checked regularly and either remapped or removed altogether. | | | | |
| 150. Error messages are clearly visible? | Pass | NA | Fail | *Comments:* |
| *Explanation:* In the event of an error, custom error messages should be used that are user-friendly and easy to understand (*see item 148*). In addition, the error message should be clearly visible and easy to find. | | | | |

*continued on following page*

*Table 15. Continued*

| 151. Errors are not displayed unnecessarily? | Pass | NA | Fail | *Comments:* |
|---|---|---|---|---|
| | | | | |
| *Explanation:* Care should be taken to ensure that error messages are not displayed haphazardly. | | | | |
| 152. Error messages are in plain language? | Pass | NA | Fail | *Comments:* |
| | | | | |
| *Explanation:* In the event of an error, custom error messages should be used that are user-friendly and easy to understand (*see item 148*). The error messages themselves should be expressed in plain language. | | | | |
| 153. Error messages do not include exclamation points? | Pass | NA | Fail | *Comments:* |
| | | | | |
| *Explanation:* In the same way that the use of exclamation points should be avoided in the text (*see item 104*), the same holds true for this punctuation in error messages. | | | | |
| 154. Error messages do not blame the visitor? | Pass | NA | Fail | *Comments:* |
| | | | | |
| *Explanation:* In line with avoiding the use of exclamation points in error messages (*see item 153*), error messages should not blame the visitor for the reason behind the error. | | | | |
| 155. Error messages describe what action is required of the visitor? | Pass | NA | Fail | *Comments:* |
| | | | | |
| *Explanation:* The error message should do more than simply display what has happened, but instead instruct the visitor in what action(s) (if any) need to take place. | | | | |
| 156. Error messages provide a way to exit the error or return to a working state of the website before the error occurred? | Pass | NA | Fail | *Comments:* |
| | | | | |
| *Explanation:* The visitor should be given a way in which to return to the website to a state before the error happened. This may not always be possible; however, such considerations should be made. | | | | |
| 157. Error messages provide contact details or a way in which to request assistance? | Pass | NA | Fail | *Comments:* |
| | | | | |
| *Explanation:* The error message should do more than simply display what has happened, but instead instruct the visitor in what action (if any) need to take place (*see item 155*). This includes providing contact details or instructions in how the visitor can request assistance. | | | | |

*Table 16. Additional resources*

| Resource | URL | Description |
|---|---|---|
| Section508.gov | https://www.section508.gov/ | Offers resources for understanding and implementing Section 508. |
| Usability.gov | http://www.usability.gov/ | Described as the one-stop source for user experience best practices and strategies, the websites offers government resources on website usability and user-centered designs. |
| W3C Web Content Accessibility Guidelines (WCAG) 2.0 | http://www.w3.org/TR/WCAG20 | Guidelines covering a broad range of recommendations for making Web content more accessible. |
| W3C Web Accessibility Initiative (WAI) | http://www.w3.org/WAI/ | Provides strategies, guidelines, and resources to make the Web accessible to people with disabilities. |

## ADDITIONAL RESOURCES

In Table 16 are additional resources that may prove useful in the assessment of website usability and accessibility.

## REFERENCES

Chiew, T. K., & Salim, S. S. (2003). Webuse: Website usability evaluation tool. *Malaysian Journal of Computer Science*, *16*(1), 47–57.

Corry, M. D., Frick, T. W., & Hansen, L. (1997). User-centered design and usability testing of a web site: An illustrative case study. *Educational Technology Research and Development*, *45*(4), 65–76. doi:10.1007/BF02299683

Evans, J. R., & King, V. E. (1999). Business-to-business marketing and the world wide web: Planning, managing, and assessing websites. *Industrial Marketing Management*, *28*(4), 343–358. doi:10.1016/S0019-8501(98)00013-3

Law, R., & Bai, B. (2006). Website development and evaluations in tourism: A retrospective analysis. In M. Hitz, M. Sigala, & J. Murphy (Eds.), *Information and communication technologies in tourism* (pp. 1–12). New York: Springer-Wien. doi:10.1007/3-211-32710-X_1

Law, R., Qi, S., & Buhalis, D. (2010). Progress in tourism management: A review of website evaluation in tourism research. *Tourism Management*, *31*, 297–313. doi:10.1016/j.tourman.2009.11.007

Lu, M., & Yeung, W. L. (1998). A framework for effective commercial web application development. *Electronic Networking Applications and Policy*, *8*(2), 166–173. doi:10.1108/10662249810211638

Rehabilitation Act Amendments. (2013). *Section 508*. Retrieved from http://www.access-board.gov/sec508/guide/act.htm

Stern, J. (2002). *Web metrics: Proven methods for measuring web site success*. New York, NY: Wiley Publishing.

Stout, R. (1997). *Web site stats: Tracking hits and analyzing traffic*. Berkeley, CA: Osborne/McGraw-Hill.

Symantec. (2013). *Introduction to SSL*. Retrieved from https://www.symantec.com/page.jsp?id=how-ssl-works

TechTerms.com. (2013). *DSL*. Retrieved from http://www.techterms.com/definition/dsl

Tullis, T. S., & Stetson, J. N. (2004). *A comparison of questionnaires for assessing website usability*. Retrieved from http://home.comcast.net/~tomtullis/publications/UPA2004TullisStetson.pdf

W3C. (2003). *HTTP - Hypertext transfer protocol*. Retrieved from http://www.w3.org/Protocols/

W3C. (2012). *About W3C*. Retrieved from http://www.w3.org/Consortium/

W3C. (2013). *Uniform resource locators*. Retrieved from http://www.w3.org/Addressing/URL/Overview.html

## KEY TERMS AND DEFINITIONS

**Digital Subscriber Line (DSL):** The medium for transferring information via the Internet using regular phone lines (TechTerms.com, 2013).

**Hypertext Transfer Protocol (HTTP):** A protocol which defines how information should be formatted, transmitted, and processed via the Internet (W3C, 2003).

**Interactive Multimedia Instruction (IMI):** The blending of interactivity, multimedia, and sound instructional design (pedagogy) in the creation of effective digital instruction.

**Internet Service Provider (ISP):** A company or organization that provides Internet services to include access.

**Secure Sockets Layer (SSL):** A secure protocol used to manage the security of information transmitted via the Internet (Symantec, 2013).

**World Wide Web Consortium (W3C):** An international community comprised of member organizations, staff, and public support in the development of Web standards (W3C, 2012).

**Uniform Resource Locator (URL):** Otherwise known as a web or Internet address (e.g., http://www.solersresearchgroup.com) comprising a string of characters using a standardized naming convention that represents a unique identifier to resources on the World Wide Web (W3C, 2013).

# Compilation of References

(1988). Technology-Related Assistance for Individuals with Disabilities Act of 1988 (Tech Act). *Public Law*, 100–407.

Abbott, C. (Ed.). (2002). *Special educational needs and the internet: Issues for the inclusive classroom*. London, UK: Routledge. doi:10.4324/9780203400180

Abedi, J., Lord, C., Hofstetter, C., & Baker, E. (2000). Impact of accommodation strategies on English language learners' test performance. *Educational Measurement: Issues and Practice*, *19*(3), 16–26. doi:10.1111/j.1745-3992.2000.tb00034.x

AblePlay.org. (2009). *AblePlay: Play products for children with special needs*. Retrieved from http://www.ableplay.org/

Agran, M., Blanchard, C., & Wehmeyer, M. (2000). Promoting transition goals and self-directed learning model of instruction. *Education and Training in Mental Retardation and Developmental Disabilities*, *35*, 351–364.

Agran, M., Blanchard, C., Wehmeyer, M., & Hughes, C. (2002). Increasing the problem-solving skills of students with developmental disabilities participating in general education. *Remedial and Special Education*, *23*(5), 279–288. doi:10.1177/07419325020230050301

Agran, M., Wehmeyer, M. L., Cavin, M., & Palmer, S. (2008). Promoting student active classroom participation skills through instruction to promote self-regulated learning and self-determination. *Career Development for Exceptional Individuals*, *31*(2), 106–114. doi:10.1177/0885728808317656

Albanese, M. A., & Mitchell, S. (1993). Problem based learning: A review of literature on its outcomes and implementation issues. *Medicine*, *68*(1), 52–81. PMID:8447896

Aleven, V., & Koedinger, K. (2002). An effective metacognitive strategy: Learning by doing and explaining with a computer-based cognitive tutor. *Cognitive Science*, *26*(2), 147–181. doi:10.1207/s15516709cog2602_1

Alleghany Community College of Maryland. (n.d.). *Assistant students with disabilities: A faculty & staff guide book*. Retrieved from http://www.allegany.edu/Documents/Helping%20You%20Succeed/studdisability_faculty.pdf

Alliance Action. (2006). *Information sheets: Assistive technology for infants, toddlers, and young children with disabilities*. Retrieved from http://www.parentcenternetwork.org/assets/files/national/all7.pdf

Almazan, S., & Quirk, C. (2002). *Historical and legal perspectives: Court cases, federal law and educational practices related to the education of students with disabilities*. Retrieved from http://www.mcie.org/docs/publications/Historical_LegalPerspectives.doc

American Psychological Association. (2002). Ethical principles of psychologists and code of conduct. *APA Online*. Retrieved from http://www.apa.org/ethics/code/code-1992.aspx

*Americans with Disabilities Act, 42 U.S.C., Sections 12101-12213*. (1990). Retrieved from http://www.eeoc.gov/laws/statutes/ada.cfm

Anastopoulus, N., & Baer, A. M. (2013). When opening doors to education, institutions must ensure that people with disabilities have equal access. *The New England Journal of Higher Education*. Retrieved from http://www.nebhe.org/thejournal/moocs-when-opening-the-door-to-education-institutions-must-ensure-that-participants-with-disabilities-have-equal-access/

Anderson, N. (2009). US 20th in broadband penetration, trails S. Korea, Estonia. *ARS*. Retrieved from http://arstechnica.com/tech-policy/news/2009/06/us-20th-in-broadband-penetration-trails-s-korea-estonia.ars

Anderson, C. A., & Bushman, B. J. (2001). Effects of violent video games and aggressive behavior, aggressive cognition, aggressive affect, physiological arousal and prosocial behavior: A meta-analytic review of the scientific literature. *Psychological Science*, *12*(5), 353–359. doi:10.1111/1467-9280.00366 PMID:11554666

Anderson, C. A., & Ford, C. M. (1986). Affect of the game player: Short-term effects of highly and mildly aggressive video games. *Personality and Social Psychology Bulletin*, *12*(4), 290–402. doi:10.1177/0146167286124002

Anderson-Inman, L., & Horney, M. A. (1998). Transforming text for at-risk readers. In D. Reinking, L. Labbo, M. McKenna, & R. Kieffler (Eds.), *Handbook of literacy and technology: Transformations in a post-typographical world* (pp. 15–44). Mahwah, NJ: Lawrence Erlbaum Associates.

Anderson, K., & Anderson, C. L. (2005). Integrating technology in standards-based instruction. In D. Edyburn, K. Higgins, & R. Boone (Eds.), *Handbook of special education technology research and practice* (pp. 521–544). Whitefish Bay, WI: Knowledge by Design.

Anderson, T., & Shattuck, J. (2012). Design-based research: A decade of progress in education research? *Educational Research*, *41*(1), 16–25.

Anton, J. J. (2009). *The application of modeling and simulation to the behavioral deficit of autism*. Retrieved from http://ntrs.nasa.gov/archive/nasa/casi.ntrs.nasa.gov/20100012859_2010013740.pdf

Arnold-Saritepe, A. M., Phillips, K. J., Mudford, O. C., De Rozario, K. A., & Taylor, S. A. (2009). Generalization and maintenance. In J. L. Matson (Ed.), *Applied behavior analysis for children with Autism Spectrum Disorders* (pp. 207–223). New York: Springer. doi:10.1007/978-1-4419-0088-3_12

Assistivetech.net. (2013). *National public website on assistive technology: State tech ACT projects*. Retrieved from http://assistivetech.net/webresources/stateTechAct-Projects.php

Azevedo, R., & Cromley, J. G. (2004). Does training on self-regulated learning facilitate students' learning with hypermedia? *Journal of Educational Psychology*, *96*(3), 523–535. doi:10.1037/0022-0663.96.3.523

Azevedo, R., Cromley, J. G., Winters, F. I., Moos, D. C., & Greene, J. A. (2006). Using computers as metacognitive tools to foster students' self-regulated learning. *Technology, Instruction, Cognition, and Learning Journal*, *3*, 97–104.

Balajthy, E. (2005). Text-to-speech software for struggling readers. *Reading Online*, *8*(4), 1–9.

Bannan, B. (2007). The integrative learning design framework: An illustrated example from the domain of instructional technology. In T. Plomp, & N. Nieveen (Eds.), *An introduction to educational research* (pp. 53–73). Dordrecht, The Netherlands: SLO.

Barakova, E., Gillessen, J., & Feijs, L. (2009). Social training of autistic children with interactive intelligent agents. *Journal of Integrative Neuroscience*, *8*(1), 23–34. doi:10.1142/S0219635209002046 PMID:19412978

Barrett, B. (1999). *Best disability employment practices: A case study*. (Doctoral Dissertation). George Washington University, Washington, DC.

Barrows, H. (1986). A taxonomy of problem-based learning methods. *Medical Education*, *20*(6), 481–486. doi:10.1111/j.1365-2923.1986.tb01386.x PMID:3796328

Barth, P., Hull, J., & St. Andre, R. (2012). Searching for the reality of virtual schools. *The Center for Public Education*. Retrieved from http://www.centerforpubliceducation.org/Main-Menu/Organizing-a-school/Searching-for-the-reality-of-virtual-schools-at-a-glance/Searching-for-the-reality-of-virtual-schools-full-report.pdf

Batorowicz, B., Missiuna, C. A., & Pollock, N. A. (2012). Technology supporting written productivity in children with learning disabilities: A critical review. *Canadian Journal of Occupational Therapy*, *79*(4), 211–224. doi:10.2182/cjot.2012.79.4.3 PMID:23210371

Bauman, S., & Newman, M. (2013). Testing assumptions about cyberbullying: Perceived distress associated with conventional and cyberbullying. *Psychology of Violence*, *3*(1), 27–38. doi:10.1037/a0029867

Beck, R. J. (2009). *What are learning objects?* Milwaukee, WI: University of Wisconsin-Milwaukee, Center for International Education. Retrieved from http://www4.uwm.edu/cie/learning_objects.cfm?gid=56

Beck, J. C., & Wade, M. (2004). *Got game: How the gamer generation is reshaping business forever*. Boston, MA: Harvard Business School Press.

Beigel, A. R. (2000). Assistive technology assessment: More than the device. *Intervention in School and Clinic, 35*(4), 237–243. doi:10.1177/105345120003500407

Benedict, R. E., Lee, J. P., Marrujo, S. K., & Farel, A. M. (1999). Assistive devices as an early childhood intervention: Evaluating outcomes. *Technology and Disability, 11*(1/2), 79–90.

Bennett, S., Maton, K., & Kervin, L. (2008). The digital natives debate: A critical review of the evidence. *British Journal of Educational Technology, 39*(5), 775–786. doi:10.1111/j.1467-8535.2007.00793.x

Bensley, L., & Van Ewnwyk, J. (2001). Video games and real-life aggression: A review of the literature. *The Journal of Adolescent Health, 29*, 244–257. doi:10.1016/S1054-139X(01)00239-7 PMID:11587908

Berkeley, S., & Lindstrom, J. H. (2011). Technology for the struggling reader: Free and easily accessible resources. *Teaching Exceptional Children, 43*(4), 48–55.

Bernard-Optiz, V., Sriram, N., & Nakhoda-Sapuan, S. (2001). Enhancing social problem solving in children with autism and normal children through computer-assisted instruction. *Journal of Autism and Developmental Disorders, 31*(4), 377–384. doi:10.1023/A:1010660502130 PMID:11569584

Berninger, V., Richards, T., Stock, P., Abbott, R., Trivedi, P., Altemeier, L., & Hayes, J. R. (2008, Summer). From idea generation to idea expression in written composition: Expressing thought in language by hand. *British Journal of Educational Psychology: Monograph.*

Berninger, V. (2009). Highlights of programmatic, interdisciplinary research on writing. *Learning Disabilities Research & Practice, 24*, 68–79. doi:10.1111/j.1540-5826.2009.00281.x PMID:19644563

Betsy, P., & Hongxin, Z. (1993). Predictors of assistive technology abandonment. *Assistive Technology, 5*(1), 36–45. doi:10.1080/10400435.1993.10132205 PMID:10171664

Bettelheim, B. (1976). *The uses of enchantment: The meaning and importance of fairy tales*. New York, NY: Knopf.

Birnbaum, B. W. (2005). *Using assistive technologies for instructing students with disabilities: A survey of new resources*. Lewiston, NY: Edwin Mellon Press.

Blackhurst, A. (2005). Historical perspectives about technology applications for people with disabilities. In D. Edyburn, K. Higgins, & R. Boone (Eds.), *Handbook of special education technology research and practice* (pp. 3–29). Whitefish Bay, WI: Knowledge by Design.

Blanck, P. (2008). Flattening the (inaccessible) cyberworld for people with disabilities. *Assistive Technology, 20*, 175–180. doi:10.1080/10400435.2008.10131944 PMID:18939657

Blecher, S., & Jaffee, K. (1998). *Weaving in the arts: Widening the learning circle*. Portsmouth, NH: Heinemann.

Booker, C. (2004). *The seven basic plots: Why we tell stories*. New York, NY: Continuum Books.

Borgh, K., & Dickson, W. (1992). The effects on children are writing of adding speech synthesis to a word processor. *Journal of Research in Computing in Education, 24*(4), 533–544.

Bouck, E. C., Maeda, Y., & Flanagan, S. M. (2012). Assistive technology and students with high incidence disabilities: Understanding the relationship through the NLTS2. *Remedial and Special Education, 33*(5), 298–208. doi:10.1177/0741932511401037

Bouck, E. C., Shurr, J. C., Tom, K., Jasper, A. D., Basette, L., Miller, B., & Flanagan, S. M. (2012). Fix it with TAPE: Repurposing technology to be assistive technology for students with high incidence disabilities. *Preventing School Failure, 56*(2), 121–128. doi:10.1080/1045988X.2011.603396

Bowman, R. F. (1982). A Pac-Man theory of motivation: Tactical implications for classroom instruction. *Educational Technology, 22*(9), 14–17.

Boyett, J. H., & Boyett, J. T. (1995). *Beyond workplace 2000: Essential strategies for the new American corporation*. New York: Dutton.

Bransford, J. D., Brown, A. L., & Cocking, R. R. (Eds.). (2000). How people learn: Brain, mind, experience, and school: Expanded ed. Washington, DC: National Academies Press.

Bredekamp, S., & Copple, C. (Eds.). (1997). *Developmentally appropriate practice in early childhood programs*. Washington, DC: NAEYC.

Brill, M. T. (1994). *Keys to parenting the child with autism* (2nd ed.). Hauppauge, NJ: Barron's Educational Series, Inc.

Brinckerhoff, L., & Banerjee, M. (2011). Brochure on college students with learning disabilities. *Association on Higher Education and Disability (AHEAD)*. Retrieved from http://www.ahead.org/

Brown, E., & Cairns, P. (2004). A grounded investigation of immersion in games. In *Proceedings of ACM Conference on Human Factors in Computing Systems*. ACM Press.

Brown, A. (1992). Design experiments: Theoretical and methodological challenges in creating complex interventions in classroom settings. *Journal of the Learning Sciences*, *2*(2), 141–178. doi:10.1207/s15327809jls0202_2

Brown, A. H. (1999). Simulated classrooms and artificial students: The potential effects of new technologies on teacher education. *Journal of Research on Computing in Education*, *32*(2), 307–318.

Brown, J., & Duguid, P. (2002). *The social life of information*. New York, NY: Harvard Business School Press.

Brown, M. (2005). Access granted: Achieving technological equity in the 21st century. In D. Edyburn, K. Higgins, & R. Boone (Eds.), *Handbook of special education technology research and practice* (pp. 105–118). Whitefish Bay, WI: Knowledge by Design.

Brown, S., & Vaughan, C. (2009). *Play: How it shapes the brain, opens the imagination, and invigorates the soul*. New York, NY: Avery.

Bruner, J. (1986). *Actual minds, possible worlds*. Cambridge, MA: Harvard University Press.

Bruner, J. (1990). *Acts of meaning: Four lectures on mind and culture*. Cambridge, MA: Harvard University Press.

Brutoco, R. (1993). *Introduction: What is the new paradigm in business? The new paradigm in business: Emerging strategies for leadership and organizational change*. New York: G. P. Putnam & Sons.

Bryant, B. R., Ok, M. W., Kang, E. Y., Kim, M. K., Lang, R., Bryant, D. P., & Pfannestiel, K. (2013). A multidimensional comparison of mathematics interventions for 4th grade students with learning disabilities. *Journal of Special Education Technology*.

Bryant, B., Seok, S., & Bryant, D. (2010). Assistive technology solutions for individuals with learning problems: Conducting assessments using the functional evaluation for assistive technology (FEAT). In S. Seok, E. Meyen, & B. DaCosta (Eds.), *Handbook of research on human cognition and assistive technology: Design, accessibility and transdisciplinary perspectives* (pp. 264–284). Hershey, PA: IGI Global. doi:10.4018/978-1-61520-817-3.ch018

Bryant, D. P., & Bryant, B. R. (2011). *Assistive technology for people with disabilities* (2nd ed.). Boston: Allyn & Bacon/Pearson.

Bryant, D. P., Bryant, B. R., & Ok, M. W. (2013). *Assistive technology for students with learning disabilities*. New York: Springer Publishing.

Bryant, D. P., Smith, D. D., & Bryant, B. R. (2008). *Teaching students with special needs in inclusive classrooms*. Boston: Allyn and Bacon.

Bundy, A. C. (1997). Play and playfulness: What to look for. In L. D. Parham, & L. S. Fazio (Eds.), *Play in occupational therapy for children* (pp. 52–66). St. Louis, MO: Mosby.

Burgess, B. (2012). A new way to think about assistive technology. *The bookshare blog*. Retrieved from http://blog.bookshare.org/2012/03/08/a-new-way-to-think-about-assistive-technology/

Burgess, J. E. (2006). Hearing ordinary voices: Cultural studies, vernacular creativity and digital storytelling. *Continuum: Journal of Media and Cultural Studies*, *20*(2), 201–214. doi:10.1080/10304310600641737

Burton, D. (2006). Reading by hand: A review of the Kurzweil-national federation of the blind reader. *Access World*. Retrieved from http://www.afb.org/afbpress/pub.asp?DocID=aw070604

Butler, D. (2008). Promoting authentic inquiry in the sciences: Challenges faced in redefining university students' scientific epistemology. *Inquiry in Education: Overcoming Barriers to Successful Implementation*, *2*, 301–324.

Byrne, B. M. (2001). Structural equation modeling with AMOS, EQS, and LISREL: Comparative approaches to testing for the factorial validity of a measuring instrument. *International Journal of Testing*, *1*(1), 55–86. doi:10.1207/S15327574IJT0101_4

Byrne, B. M. (2010). *Structural equation modeling with AMOS: Basic concepts, applications, and programming* (2nd ed.). New York, NY: Routledge.

Calkins, L. M. (1986). *The art of teaching writing*. Portsmouth, NH: Heinemann.

Calvert, S. L., & Tan, S. (1994). Impact of virtual reality on young adults' physiological arousal and aggressive thoughts: Interaction versus observation. *Journal of Applied Developmental Psychology*, *15*(1), 125–139. doi:10.1016/0193-3973(94)90009-4

Camp, G. (1996). *Problem based learning: A paradigm shift or a passing fad?* Retrieved from http://www.med-ed-online.org/f0000003.htm

Campbell, P. H., Milbourne, S., Dugan, L. M., & Wilcox, M. J. (2006). A review of evidence on practices for teaching young children to use assistive technology devices. *Topics in Early Childhood Special Education*, *26*(1), 3–13. doi:10.1177/02711214060260010101

Carter, E., & Kennedy, C. (2006). Promoting access to the general curriculum using peer support strategies. *Research and Practice for Persons with Severe Disabilities*, *31*, 284–292.

CAST. (2012). *About UDL*. Retrieved from http://www.cast.org/udl/

CAST. (2012a). *About CAST: Staff: David H. Rose*. Retrieved from http://www.cast.org/about/staff/drose.html

CAST. (2012b). *About UDL: What is universal design for learning?* Retrieved from http://www.cast.org/udl

Center for Applied Special Technology (CAST). (2013). *UDL book builder*. Retrieved from http://bookbuilder.cast.org

Center for Applied Special Technology. (2010). CAST: 25 years of innovation. *CAST*. Retreived from http://www.cast.org/index.html

Center for Universal Design. (1997). The principles of universal design. *The Center for Universal Design, NC State University*. Retrieved from www.ncsu.edu/www/ncsu/design/sod5/cud/about_ud/udprinciplestext.htm

Center for Universal Design. (2010). *Ronald L. Mace*. Retrieved from http://www.ncsu.edu/project/design-projects/udi/center-for-universal-design/ron-mace

Chaffin, J. D., Maxwell, B., & Thompson, B. (1982). ARC-ED curriculum: The application of video game format to educational software. *Exceptional Children*, *49*, 173–178.

Champy, J. (1995). *Reengineering management: The mandate for new leadership*. New York: HarperCollins.

Chatham, R. E. (2007). Games for training. *Communications of the ACM*, *50*(7), 37–43. doi:10.1145/1272516.1272537

Chatzara, K., Karagiannidis, C., & Stamatis, D. (2012, September). *Structural learning through digital storytelling for people with autism*. Paper presented at the 8th Hellenic Conference on ICT in Education (HCICTE 2012). Volos, Greece.

Chiang, H., & Jacob, K. (2009). Effect of computer-based instruction on students' self-perception and functional task performance. *Disability and Rehabilitation. Assistive Technology*, *4*(2), 106–118. doi:10.1080/17483100802613693 PMID:19253099

Chiang, H., & Liu, C. (2011). Evaluation of the benefits of assistive reading software: Perceptions of high school students with learning disabilities. *Assistive Technology*, *23*(4), 199–204. doi:10.1080/10400435.2011.614673 PMID:22256668

Chiew, T. K., & Salim, S. S. (2003). Webuse: Website usability evaluation tool. *Malaysian Journal of Computer Science*, *16*(1), 47–57.

Choi, I., Land, S. M., & Turgeon, A. J. (2005). Scaffolding peer-questioning strategies to facilitate metacognition during online small group discussion. *Instructional Science*, *33*, 483–511. doi:10.1007/s11251-005-1277-4

Chung, C., Pasquini, L., & Koh, C. (2013). Web-based learning management system considerations for higher education. *Learning and Performance Quarterly*, *1*(4).

Clay, M. (1993). *Reading recovery in English and other languages*. Paper presented at the West Coast Literacy Conference. Palm Springs, CA.

Collins, A. (1992). Toward a design science of education. In E. Scanlon, & T. O'Shea (Eds.), *New directions in educational technology* (pp. 15–22). New York, NY: Springer-Verlag. doi:10.1007/978-3-642-77750-9_2

Common Core State Standards. (2012). *Implementing the common core state standards*. Retrieved from http://www.corestandards.org/

Cone Inc. in collaboration with AMP Agency. (2006). *The 2006 Cone millennial cause study: The millennial generation: Pro-social and empowered to change the world.* Retrieved from http://www.greenbook.org/Content/AMP/Cause_AMPlified.pdf

Conole, G., Laat, M. D., Dillon, T., & Darby, J. (2006). JISC LXP student experiences of technologies: Final report. *Joint Information Systems Committee*. Retrieved from http://www.jisc.ac.uk/media/documents/programmes/elearningpedagogy/lxpprojectfinalreportdec06.pdf

Consortium for Citizens with Disabilities. (2013). *Protection and advocacy for assistive technology*. Retrieved from http://www.c-c-d.org/task_forces/tech_telecom/ATprotectadvoch.htm

Consumer Union. (2001). *Lessons from 1996 telecommunications act: Deregulation before meaningful competition spells consumer disaster*. Retrieved from http://www.consumersunion.org/telecom/lessondc201.htm

Cooper, H. (1998). *Synthesizing research* (3rd ed., Vol. 2). Thousand Oaks, CA: Sage Publications.

Cornell University Law School. (2013). *47 USC § 613 - Video programming accessibility*. Retrieved from http://www.law.cornell.edu/uscode/text/47/613

Corry, M. D., Frick, T. W., & Hansen, L. (1997). User-centered design and usability testing of a web site: An illustrative case study. *Educational Technology Research and Development*, *45*(4), 65–76. doi:10.1007/BF02299683

Cote, D. (2007). Problem-based learning software for students with disabilities. *Intervention in School and Clinic*, *43*(29), 29–37. doi:10.1177/10534512070430010401

Council for Exceptional Children (CEC). (2005). Universal design for learning: A guide for teachers and education professionals. Arlington, VA: Pearson: Merrill Prentice Hall.

Courduff, J. (2011a). *Technology integration in the resource specialist environment*. (Unpublished doctoral dissertation). Walden University, Minneapolis, MN.

Courduff, J. (2011b). One size never fits all: Tech integration for special needs. *Learning and Leading with Technology*, *38*(8), 16–19.

Cress, C. J., & Marvin, C. A. (2003). Common questions about AAC services in early intervention. *Augmentative and Alternative Communication*, *19*, 254–272. doi:10.1080/07434610310001598242

Crotty, J. M. (2012). Why get a pricey diploma when a bleepin' badge will do? *Forbes*. Retrieved from http://www.forbes.com/sites/jamesmarshallcrotty/2012/01/26/the-end-of-the-diploma-as-we-know-it/

Csikszentmihalyi, M. (1991). *Flow: The psychology of optimal experience*. New York: Harper Collins.

Cummings, E. O. (2011). Assistive and adaptive technology resources. *Knowledge Quest*, *39*(3), 70–73.

Cummins, J. (2000). *Language, power and pedagogy: Bilingual children in the crossfire*. Clevedon, UK: Multilingual Matters.

D'Silva, R. (2005). *Promoting reading skills of young adult EAL learners through voice recognition software*. (Masters dissertation). University of British Columbia, Vancouver, Canada.

DaCosta, B., Kinsell, C., & Nasah, A. (2013). Millennials are digital natives? An investigation into digital propensity and age. In Information Resources Management Association (Ed.), Digital literacy: Concepts, methodologies, tools, and applications (Vol. 1, pp. 103-119). Hershey, PA: IGI Global.

DaCosta, B., Nasah, A., Kinsell, C., & Seok, S. (2011). Digital propensity: An investigation of video game and information and communication technology practices. In P. Felicia (Ed.), *Handbook of research on improving learning and motivation through educational games: Multidisciplinary approaches* (pp. 1148–1173). Hershey, PA: IGI Global. doi:10.4018/978-1-60960-495-0.ch052

DaCosta, B., & Seok, S. (2010). Managing cognitive load in the design of assistive technology for those with learning disabilities. In S. Seok, E. Meyen, & B. DaCosta (Eds.), *Handbook of research on human cognition and assistive technology: Design, accessibility and transdisciplinary perspectives* (pp. 21–42). Hershey, PA: IGI Global. doi:10.4018/978-1-61520-817-3.ch002

DaCosta, B., & Seok, S. (2010a). Human cognition in the design of assistive technology for those with learning disabilities. In S. Seok, E. Meyen, & B. DaCosta (Eds.), *Handbook of research on human cognition and assistive technology: Design, accessibility and transdisciplinary perspectives* (pp. 1–20). Hershey, PA: IGI Global. doi:10.4018/978-1-61520-817-3.ch001

DaCosta, B., & Seok, S. (2010c). Multimedia design of assistive technology for those with learning disabilities. In S. Seok, E. Meyen, & B. DaCosta (Eds.), *Handbook of research on human cognition and assistive technology: Design, accessibility and transdisciplinary perspectives* (pp. 43–60). Hershey, PA: IGI Global. doi:10.4018/978-1-61520-817-3.ch003

Daley, B. J., Shaw, C. R., Balistrieri, T., Glasenapp, K., & Piacentine, L. (1999). Conceptual maps: A strategy to teach and evaluate critical thinking. *The Journal of Nursing Education*, *38*, 42–47. PMID:9921788

Danko-McGhee, K., & Slutsky, R. (2007). *Impact of early art experiences on literacy development*. Reston, VA: National Art Education Association.

Dart, J. (1996, July 26). *Achieving independence: The challenge for the 21st century*. Washington, DC: National Council on Disability.

Davis, J. A. (1971). *Elementary survey analysis*. Englewood, NJ: Prentice Hall.

Dede, C. (2005). Planning for neomillenial learning styles: Implications for investments in technology and faculty. *Educating the Net Generation Educause*. Retrieved from www.educause.edu/educatingthenetgen/

Demarest, K. (2000). *Video games - What are they good for?* Retrieved from http://www.lessontutor.com/kd3.html

Dempsey, J., Lucassen, B., Gilley, W., & Rasmussen, K. (1993). Since Malone's theory of intrinsically motivating instruction: What's the score in the gaming literature? *Journal of Educational Technology Systems*, *22*(2), 1973–1983. doi:10.2190/2TH7-5TXG-TAR7-T4V2

Deno, S. L. (2003). Developments in curriculum-based measurement. *The Journal of Special Education*, *37*(3), 184–192. doi:10.1177/00224669030370030801

Des Marchais, J. E. (1999). A Delphi technique to identify and evaluate criteria for construction of PBL problems. *Medical Education*, *33*, 504–508. doi:10.1046/j.1365-2923.1999.00377.x PMID:10354334

Desimone, L. M. (2009). Improving impact studies of teachers' professional development: Toward better conceptualizations and measures. *Educational Researcher*, *38*(3), 181–199. doi:10.3102/0013189X08331140

Desire2Learn. (2013). *Innovations and awards*. Retrieved from http://www.desire2learn.com/about/awards/

DIBELS. (2013). *Dynamic indicators of basic early literacy skills*. Eugene, OR: University of Oregon. Retrieved from https://dibels.uoregon.edu/

Disabled World. (2013). *World facts and statistics and disabilities and disability issues*. Retrieved from http://www.disabled-world.com/disability/statistics/

Dishion, T. J., McCord, J., & Poulin, F. (1999). When interventions harm: Peer groups and problem behavior. *The American Psychologist*, *54*(9), 755–764. doi:10.1037/0003-066X.54.9.755 PMID:10510665

Dodsworth, C. Jr. (1998). *Digital illusion*. New York: ACM Press.

Donovan, C. A., & Smolkin, L. B. (2006). Children's understanding of genre and writing development. In C. A. MacArthur, S. Graham, & J. Fitzgerald (Eds.), *Handbook of writing instruction* (pp. 131–143). New York: The Guilford Press.

Douglas, Y., & Haragadon, A. (2000). The pleasure principle: Immersion, engagement, flow. In *Proceedings of ACM Conference on Hypertext and Hypermedia*, (pp. 153-160). ACM.

Dove, M. (2012). Advancements in assistive technology and AT laws for the disabled. *Delta Kappa Gamma Bulletin*, *78*(4), 23–29.

Drent, M., & Meelissen, M. (2008). Which factors obstruct or stimulate teacher educators to use ICT innovatively? *Computers & Education*, *51*, 187–199. doi:10.1016/j.compedu.2007.05.001

Dreon, O., & Dietrich, N. (2009). Turning lemons into lemonade: Teaching assistive technology through wikis and embedded video. *TechTrends*, *53*(1), 78–80. doi:10.1007/s11528-009-0241-6

Drezek, J. (2007). *Adult ESOL reading comprehension and text-to-speech software*. (Masters dissertation). University of Texas, Arlington, TX. Retrieved from dspace.uta.edu/bitstream/handle/10106/23/umi-uta-1661.pdf?sequence=1

Driskell, J. E., & Dwyer, D. J. (1984). Microcomputer videogame based training. *Educational Technology*, *24*(2), 11–15.

Dugan, L. M., Campbell, P. H., & Wilcox, M. J. (2006). Making decisions about assistive technology with infants and toddlers. *Topics in Early Childhood Special Education*, *26*(1), 25–32. doi:10.1177/02711214060260010301

Dunlap, G., & Bunton-Pierce, M. (1999). *Autism and autism spectrum disorder (ASD)* (Accession No. ED436068). Washington, DC: Office of Special Education and Rehabilitative Services (Ed.). Retrieved from http://search.ebscohost.com

Dunn, J. (2012). How adaptive learning technology is being used in online courses. *Edudemic*. Retrieved from http://www.edudemic.com/2012/03/how-adaptive-learning-technology-is-being-used-in-online-courses/

Dunn, M. W. (2013b). *Using art media during pre-writing: Helping students with dysgraphia manage idea generation before encoding text*. Manuscript submitted for publication.

Dunn, M. W. (2013c). *Students at-risk of having dysgraphia: Applying assistive technology tools to help with pre-writing*. Manuscript under review.

Dunn, M. W. (2012). Response to intervention: Employing a mnemonic strategy with art media to help struggling writers. *Journal of International Education and Leadership*, *2*(3), 1–12.

Dunn, M. W. (2013a). Comparing two story-writing mnemonic strategies: A randomized control trial study. *International Journal of Special Education*.

Dunn, M., & Finley, S. (2008). Thirsty thinkers: A workshop for artists and writers. *Journal of Reading Education*, *33*(2), 28–36.

Ebner, I. (2004). *Abandonment of assistive technology*. Retrieved from http://www.florida-ese.org/atcomp/_PDF/MATR%20Abandon%20of%20Assistive%20Technology.pdf

ed.gov. (n.d.). *Building the legacy: IDEA2004*. Retrieved from http://idea.ed.gov/

Education Quality and Accountability Office. (2013). *Ontario student achievement: EQAO's provincial elementary school report: Results of the 2011-2012 assessments of reading, writing and mathematics, primary division (grades 1-3) and junior division (grades 4-6)*. Retrieved from http://www.eqao.com/ProvincialReport/ProvincialReport.aspx?Lang=E&yr=12&cat=e

Educreations. (2012). *Educreations*. Retrieved from http://www.educreations.com

Edyburn, D. (2009). Using research to inform practice. *Special Education Technology Practice*, *11*(5), 21–29.

Edyburn, D. L. (2010). Would you recognize universal design for learning if you saw it? Ten propositions for new directions for the second decade of UDL. *Learning Disability Quarterly*, *33*(1), 33–41.

Edyburn, D., Higgins, K., & Boone, R. (2005). *Handbook of special education technology research and practice*. Whitefish Bay, WI: Knowledge by Design.

Eisenberg, A. R. (1985). Learning to describe past experiences in conversation. *Discourse Processes*, *8*, 177–208. doi:10.1080/01638538509544613

Eisenberg, E. (1990). Jamming: Transcendence through organization. *Communication Research*, *17*(2), 139–164. doi:10.1177/009365090017002001

Eisner, E. (1994). *Cognition and curriculum reconsidered*. New York: Teachers College Press.

Electronic and Information Technology Accessibility Standards. (2000). *Section 508*. Retrieved from http://www.access-board.gov/sec508/standards.htm

Elkind, J. (1998). *Computer reading machines for poor readers*. Los Angeles, CA: Lexia Institute.

Elkind, J., Black, M., & Murray, C. (1996). Computer-based compensation of adult reading disabilities. *Annals of Dyslexia*, *46*, 159–186. doi:10.1007/BF02648175

Elkind, J., Cohen, K., & Murray, C. (1993). Using computer-based readers to improve reading comprehension of students with dyslexia. *Annals of Dyslexia*, *43*, 238–259. doi:10.1007/BF02928184

Ellis, J. (1990). Computer games and aggressive behavior: A review of the literature. *Educational Technology*, *30*(2), 37–40.

Ellis, K., & Kent, M. (2011). *Disability and new media*. New York, NY: Routledge.

Elrod, G. F., Coleman, A. M., & Medley, M. B. (2005). The use of problem-based learning in rural special education preservice training programs. *Rural Special Education Quarterly*, *24*(2), 28–32.

Engel, J. (1991). Not just a method but a way of learning. In D. Bould, & G. Felletti (Eds.), *The challenge of problem-based learning* (pp. 21–31). New York, NY: St. Martin's Press.

Ernst, K. (1993). *Picture learning*. Portsmouth, NH: Heinemann.

Ertmer, P. A., Lehman, J., Park, S. H., Cramer, J., & Grove, K. (2003, June). Barriers to teachers' adoption and use of technology in the problem-based learning. In *Proceedings of Association for the Advancement of Computing in Education (AACE) Society for Information Technology and Teacher Education (SITE) International Conference,* (pp. 1761-1766). Washington, DC: AACE.

Ertmer, P., & Ottenbreit-Leftwich, A. T. (2010). Teacher technology change: How knowledge, confidence, culture, and beliefs intersect. *Journal of Research on Technology in Education*, *42*(3), 255–284.

Evans, J. R., & King, V. E. (1999). Business-to-business marketing and the world wide web: Planning, managing, and assessing websites. *Industrial Marketing Management*, *28*(4), 343–358. doi:10.1016/S0019-8501(98)00013-3

Federal Communications Commission. (2011a). *Guide: Closed captioning*. Retrieved from http://www.fcc.gov/guides/closed-captioning

Federal Communications Commission. (2011b). *Guide: Speech-to-speech relay service*. Retrieved from http://www.fcc.gov/guides/speech-speech-relay-service

Federal Communications Commission. (2011c). *Telecommunications act of 1996*. Retrieved from http://transition.fcc.gov/telecom.html

Federal Interagency Forum on Child and Family Statistics. (2000). *America's children: Key national indicators of well-being*. Washington, DC: Federal Interagency Forum on Child and Family Statistics.

Fenstermacher, K., Olympia, D., & Sheridan, S. M. (2006). Effectiveness of a computer-facilitated, interactive social skills training program for boys with attention deficit hyperactivity disorder. *School Psychology Quarterly*, *21*(2), 197–224. doi:10.1521/scpq.2006.21.2.197

Fersh, D., & Thomas, P. W. (1993). *Complying with the Americans with disabilities act: A guidebook for management with people with disabilities*. Westport, CT: Quorum Books.

Festinger, L. (1954). A theory of social comparison processes. *Human Relations*, *7*, 117–140. doi:10.1177/001872675400700202

Fitzgerald, J. (1995). English-as-a-second-language reading instruction in the United States: A research review. *Journal of Reading Behavior*, *27*(2), 115–152.

Fivush, R. (1994). Constructing narrative, emotion, and self in parent-child conversations about the past. In U. Neisser, & R. Fivush (Eds.), *The remembering self: Construction and accuracy in the self-narrative* (pp. 136–157). Cambridge, UK: Cambridge University Press. doi:10.1017/CBO9780511752858.009

Florida Bar. (2012, March). *E-fillings musts be ADA compliant*. Retrieved from http://www.floridabar.org/DIVCOM/JN/jnnews01.nsf/Articles/5ED3206D77DA1280852579AA004E0B17

Foley, A. (2011). Exploring the design, development and use of websites through accessibility and usability studies. *Journal of Educational Multimedia and Hypermedia*, *20*(4), 361–385.

Fombonne, E. (2003). Epidemiological surveys of autism and other pervasive developmental disorders: An update. *Journal of Autism and Developmental Disorders*, *33*(4), 365–382. doi:10.1023/A:1025054610557 PMID:12959416

Fraser, C. (2007). Reading rate in L1 Mandarin Chinese and L2 English across five reading tasks. *Modern Language Journal*, *91*(3), 372–394. doi:10.1111/j.1540-4781.2007.00587.x

Frechette, J. (2005). Cyber-democracy or cyber hegemony? Exploring the political and economic structures of the internet as an alternative source of information. *Library Trends*, *53*(4), 555–575.

Freeman, S., & Kasari, C. (2013). Parent-child interaction in autism: Characteristics of play. *Autism*, *17*(2), 147–161. doi:10.1177/1362361312469269 PMID:23382513

Friend, M. (2008a). *Co-teach! A handbook for creating and sustaining successful classroom partnerships in inclusive schools*. Greensboro, NC: MFI.

Friend, M. (2008b). Co-teaching: A simple solution that isn't simple after all. *Journal of Curriculum and Instruction*, *2*(2), 9–19. doi:10.3776/joci.2008.v2n2p9-19

Gal, E., Bauminger, N., Goren-Bar, D., Pianesi, F., Stock, O., & Zancanaro, M. et al. (2009). Enhancing social communication of children with high-functioning autism through a co-located interface. *Artificial Intelligence and Society*, *24*(1), 75–84.

Gardner, H. (2006). *Changing minds: The art and science of changing our own and other people's minds*. Boston, MA: Harvard Business School Press.

Gardner, R. C. (1983). *Frames of mind: The theory of multiple intelligences*. New York: Basic Books.

Garris, R., Ahlers, R., & Driskell, J. E. (2002). Games, motivation, and learning: A research and practice model. *Simulation & Gaming*, *33*(4), 441–467. doi:10.1177/1046878102238607

Gaylord-Ross, R. J., Haring, T. G., Breen, C., & Pitts-Conway, V. (1984). The training and generalization of social interaction skills with autistic youth. *Journal of Applied Behavior Analysis*, *17*, 229. doi:10.1901/jaba.1984.17-229 PMID:6735954

Gee, J. P. (2005). What would a state of the art instructional video game look like?. *Innovate: Journal of Online Education, 1*(6).

Gee, J. P. (2003). *What video games can teach us about literacy and learning*. New York: Palgrave-McMillan.

Gijbels, D., Dochy, F., Van den Bossche, P., & Segers, M. (2005). Effects of problem-based learning: A meta-analysis from the angle of assessment. *Review of Educational Research*, *75*, 27–61. doi:10.3102/00346543075001027

Gilbert, J. N., & Driscoll, P. M. (2002). Collaborative knowledge building: A case study. *Educational Technology Research and Development*, *50*(1), 59–79. doi:10.1007/BF02504961

Gill, C. (1995). A psychological view of disability culture. *Disability Studies Quarterly*, *15*(4), 16–19.

Go track. (2012). *H.R. 4227 (112th), workforce investment act of 2012*. Retrieved from http://www.govtrack.us/congress/bills/112/hr4227#overview

Goggin, G., & Newell, C. (2003). *Digital disability: The social construction of disability in new media*. Lanham, MD: Rowman & Littlefield Publishers.

Goodenough, W. (1971). *Culture, language & society*. Reading, MA: Addison-Wesley.

Goodwin, B., & Miller, K. (2013). Evidence on flipped classrooms is still coming in. *Educational Leadership*, *70*(6), 78–80.

GPII. (2011). *Raising the floor*. Retrieved from http://www.gpii.net

Graham, R., & Warnie, R. (2012). Levelling the playing field: Assistive technology, special education, and a Canadian perspective. *American International Journal of Contemporary Research*, *1*(2), 6–15.

Graham, S., & Harris, K. R. (1989). A component analysis of cognitive strategy instruction: Effects on learning disabled students' compositions and self-efficacy. *Journal of Educational Psychology*, *81*, 353–361. doi:10.1037/0022-0663.81.3.353

Graham, S., & Harris, K. R. (2003). Students with learning disabilities and the process of writing: A meta-analysis of SRSD studies. In H. L. Swanson, K. R. Harris, & S. Graham (Eds.), *Handbook of learning disabilities* (pp. 323–344). New York: The Guilford Press.

Graham, S., & Harris, K. R. (2005). *Writing better: Effective strategies for teaching students with learning difficulties*. Baltimore, MD: Paul H. Brookes Publishing Co.

Graham, S., Harris, K. R., & Mason, L. (2005). Improving the writing performance, knowledge, and motivation of struggling young writers: The effects of self-regulated strategy development. *Contemporary Educational Psychology*, *30*, 207–241. doi:10.1016/j.cedpsych.2004.08.001

Graham, S., & Perin, D. (2007). A meta-analysis of writing instruction for adolescent students. *Journal of Educational Psychology*, *99*, 445–476. doi:10.1037/0022-0663.99.3.445

Grandin, T. (2012). What's the big deal about video games? *Autism Asperger's Digest*. Retrieved from http://autismdigest.com/whats-the-big-deal-about-video-games/

Grand, S. A., Bernier, J. E., & Strohmer, D. C. (1982). Attitudes toward disabled persons as a function of social context and specific disability. *Rehabilitation Psychology*, *27*(3), 165–173. doi:10.1037/h0090966

Graves, D. (1983). *Writing: Teachers & children at work*. Portsmouth, NH: Heinemann.

Graybill, D., Kirsch, J. R., & Esselman, E. D. (1985). Effects of playing violent versus nonviolent video games on the aggressive ideation of aggressive and nonaggressive children. *Child Study Journal*, *15*(3), 299–205.

Gray, C. A., & Garand, J. D. (1993). Social stories: Improving responses of students with autism with accurate social information. *Focus on Autistic Behavior*, *8*(1), 1–10.

Griffiths, M. D. (1999). Violent video games and aggression: A review of the literature. *Aggression and Violent Behavior*, *4*(2), 203–212. doi:10.1016/S1359-1789(97)00055-4

Griffiths, M. D. (2002). The educational benefits of videogames. *Education for Health*, *20*(3), 47–51.

Guo, R. X., Dobson, T., & Petrina, S. (2008). Digital natives, digital immigrants: An analysis of age and ICT competency in teacher education. *Journal of Educational Computing Research*, *38*(3), 235–254. doi:10.2190/EC.38.3.a

Hall, F. S., & Hall, E. L. (1994). The ADA: Going beyond the law. *The Academy of Management Executive*, *8*(1), 17–26.

Hamilton, P. (2012). Mobile devices as powerful assistive technology for all. *Supporting universal access and universal design for learning*. Retrieved from http://paulhami.edublogs.org/2012/05/17/mobile-devices-as-powerful-assistive-technology-for-all/

Haring, T. G. (1992). The context of social competence: Relations, relationships, and generalization. In S. L. Odom, S. R. McConnell, & M. A. McEvoy (Eds.), *Social competence of young children with disabilities: Issues and strategies for intervention* (pp. 307–320). Baltimore, MD: Paul H Brookes Publishing Co.

Harmon, O., Lambrinos, L., & Buffolino, J. (2010). Assessment design and cheating risk in online instruction. *Online Journal of Distance Learning Administration*, *8*(3).

Harris, K. R., Graham, S., & Mason, L. (2006). Improving the writing, knowledge, and motivation of struggling young writers: Effects of self-regulated strategy development with and without peer support. *American Educational Research Journal*, *43*, 295–340. doi:10.3102/00028312043002295

Harris, K. R., Graham, S., Mason, L., & Friedlander, B. (2008). *Powerful writing strategies for all students*. Baltimore, MD: Brookes.

Harris, K., & Graham, S. (1985). Improving learning disabled students' composition skills: Self-control strategy training. *Learning Disability Quarterly*, *8*(1), 27–36. doi:10.2307/1510905

Hasselbring, T. S., & Glaser, C. H. W. (2000). Use of computer technology to help students with special needs: The future of children. *Children and Computer Technology*, *10*, 102–123.

Hayes, J. R., & Flower, L. S. (1980). Identifying the organization of writing processes. In L. W. Gregg, & E. R. Steinbert (Eds.), *Cognitive processes in writing* (pp. 3–30). Hillsdale, NJ: Lawrence Erlbaum Associates.

Hedberg, B. (1981). *Handbook of organizational design: How organizations learn and unlearn*. Stockholm: Arbetslivscentrum.

Heins, M., Cho, C., & Feldman, A. (2006). *Internet filters: A public policy report*. Retrieved from http://www.fepproject.org/policyreports/filters2.pdf

Heo, M. (2009). Digital storytelling: An empirical study of the impact of digital storytelling on pre-service teachers' self efficacy and dispositions towards educational technology. *Journal of Educational Multimedia and Hypermedia*, *18*(4), 405–428.

Heo, M. (2009). Digital storytelling: An empirical study of the impact of digital storytelling on pre-service teachers' self-efficacy and dispositions towards educational technology. *Journal of Educational Multimedia and Hypermedia*, *18*(4), 405–428.

Herczeg, M. (2004). *Experience design for computer-based learning systems: Learning with engagement and emotions*. Paper presented at the ED-MEDIA 2004 World Conference on Educational Multimedia, Hypermedia and Telecommunications. New York, NY.

Hernandez, A. (2003). *Making content instruction accessible for English language learners: Reaching the highest level of English*. Retrieved from http://www.reading.org

Higgins, E. L., & Raskind, M. H. (2005). The compensatory effectiveness of the Quicktionary Reading Pen II on the reading comprehension of students with learning disabilities. *Journal of Special Education Technology*, *20*(1), 31–40.

Hmelo-Silver, C. E. (2004). Problem-based learning: What and how do students learn? *Educational Psychology Review*, *16*, 235–266. doi:10.1023/B:EDPR.0000034022.16470.f3

Hodapp, J. B., & Rachow, C. (2010). Impact of text-to-speech software on access to print: A longitudinal study. In S. Seok, E. L. Meyen, & B. DaCosta (Eds.), *Human cognition and assistive technology: Design, accessibility, and transdisciplinary perspectives* (pp. 199–219). Hershey, PA: IGI Global. doi:10.4018/978-1-61520-817-3.ch014

Hofstede, G. (1980). *Culture consequences: International differences in work-related values*. Beverly Hills, CA: Sage.

Hollingsworth, M., & Woodward, J. (1993). Integrated learning: Explicit strategies and their role in problem solving instruction for students with learning disabilities. *Exceptional Children*, *59*, 444–445. PMID:8440301

Hoover, E. (2009, October 11). The millennial muddle: How stereotyping students became a thriving industry and a bundle of contradictions. *The Chronicle of Higher Education*. Retrieved from http://chronicle.com/article/The-Millennial-Muddle-How/48772/

Horn, M. B., & Staker, H. (2011). *The rise of K-12 blended learning*. Retrieved from http://www.innosightinstitute.org/innosight/wp-content/uploads/2011/01/The-Rise-of-K-12-Blended-Learning.pdf

Horn, E., Jones, H. A., & Hamlett, C. (1991). An investigation of the feasibility of a video game system for developing scanning and selection skills. *Journal for the Association for People with Severe Handicaps*, *16*, 108–115.

Howe, N., & Strauss, W. (2000). *Millennials rising: The next great generation*. New York, NY: Vintage Books.

Hurwitz, A., & Day, M. (2001). *Children and their art: Methods for the elementary school*. Belmont, CA: Wadsworth Group/Thomson Learning.

Hutinger, P. L. (1996). Computer applications in programs for young children with disabilities: Recurring themes. *Focus on Autism and Other Developmental Disabilities*, *11*(2), 105–114. doi:10.1177/108835769601100206

IDEIA. (2004). *Individuals with disabilities education improvement act of 2004*. Pub. L. No. 108-446, 118 Stat. 2647.

Individuals with Disabilities Education Improvement Act of 2004. Pub. L. No. 108-446.

Inspiration Software Inc. (2013). *Kidspiration*. Retrieved from http://www.inspiration.com/Kidspiration

International Business Machines. (1991). *Technology and persons with disabilities*. Atlanta, GA: IBM Support Programs.

Jackson, R. (2005). Curriculum access for students with low-incidence disabilities. *Eugene*. Retreived from http://www.cast.org/policy/ncac/index.html

Jacobs, A. E. J. P., Dolmans, D. H. J. M., Wolfhagen, I. H. A. P., & Scherpbier, A. J. J. A. (2003). Validation of a short questionnaire to assess the degree of complexity and structuredness of PBL problems. *Medical Education*, *37*, 1001–1007. doi:10.1046/j.1365-2923.2003.01630.x PMID:14629413

Jacobs, J. W., & Dempsey, J. V. (1993). Simulation and gaming: Fidelity, feedback, and motivation. In J. V. Dempsey, & G. C. Sales (Eds.), *Interactive instruction and feedback*. Englewood Cliffs, NJ: Educational Technology Publications.

Jenkins, H., & Squire, K. (2003). Understanding civilization (III). *Computer Games Magazine*. Retrieved from http://educationarcade.org

Johnson, C. P., & Myers, S. M. (2007). Identification and evaluation of children with autism spectrum disorders. *Pediatrics*, *120*(5), 1183–1215. doi:10.1542/peds.2007-2361 PMID:17967920

Johnston, S. S., & Evans, J. (2005). Considering response efficiency as a strategy to prevent assistive technology abandonment. *Journal of Special Education Technology*, *20*(3), 45–50.

Jonassen, D. H. (1988). Integrating learning strategies into courseware to facilitate deeper processing. In D. H. Jonassen (Ed.), *Instructional designs for microcomputer courseware*. Hillsdale, NJ: Erlbaum.

Jonassen, D. H. (1996). *Handbook of research for educational communications and technology*. New York: Macmillan.

Jonassen, D., Howland, J., Moore, J., & Marra, R. (2003). *Learning to solve problems with technology: A constructivist perspective* (2nd ed.). Upper Saddle River, NJ: Merrill Prentice Hall.

Judge, S. (2002). Family-centered assistive technology assessment and intervention practices for early intervention. *Infants and Young Children*, *15*(1), 60–68. doi:10.1097/00001163-200207000-00009

Judge, S. (2006). Constructing an assistive technology toolkit for young children: Views from the field. *Journal of Special Education Technology*, *21*(4), 17–24.

Judge, S. L., Floyd, K., & Jeffs, T. (2008). Using an assistive technology toolkit to promote inclusion. *Early Childhood Education Journal*, *36*(2), 121–126. doi:10.1007/s10643-008-0257-0

Judge, S. L., & Lahm, E. A. (1998). Assistive technology applications for play, mobility, communication, and learning for young children with disabilities. In S. L. Judge, & H. P. Parette (Eds.), *Assistive technology for young children with disabilities: A guide to family-centred services* (pp. 16–44). Cambridge, MA: Brookline.

Judge, S. L., & Parette, H. P. (Eds.). (1998). *Assistive technology for young children with disabilities: A guide to providing family-centered services*. Cambridge, MA: Brookline.

Justesen, T. R., Stage, F. K., & de la Teja, M. H. (2013). College students with disabilities – Accommodating, special learning needs. *Online Educational Encyclopedia: Classroom Management – Creating a Learning Environment to Association for Science Education (ASE).* Retrieved from http://education.stateuniversity.com/pages/1865/College-Students-with-Disabilities.html

Kahn, R. L. (2012). A taxonomy for choosing, evaluating, and integrating in-the-cloud resources in a university environment. *Journal of Educational Technology Systems, 41*(2), 171–181. doi:10.2190/ET.41.2.e

Kanitkar, A. S., Ochoa, T. A., & Handel, M. L. (n.d.). *Kurzweil: A computer-supported reading tool for students with learning.* Retrieved from http://www.kurzweiledu.com/files/kurzweil-white-paper-report-from-indiana-university.pdf

Karmarkar, A. M., Dicianno, B., Graham, J. E., Cooper, R., Kelleher, A., & Cooper, R. A. (2012). Factors associated with provision of wheelchairs in older adults. *Assistive Technology, 24*(3), 155–167. doi:10.1080/10400435.2012.659795 PMID:23033733

Katahira, J. (2012). *Note writing in the primary classroom.* Retrieved from http://www.readwritethink.org/classroom-resources/lesson-plans/note-writing-primary-classroom-285.html

Kaya, T. (2010). Enrollment in online courses at the highest rate ever. *The Chronicle of Higher Education.* Retrieved from http://chronicle.com/blogs/wiredcampus/enrollment-in-online-courses-increases-at-the-highest-rate-ever/28204

Keen, A. (2007). *The cult of the amateur: How today's Internet is killing our culture.* London, UK: Broadway Business.

Kennedy, C. H. (2005). *Single-case designs for educational research.* Boston: Allyn and Bacon.

Kennedy, G., Krause, K.-L., Judd, T., Churchward, A., & Gray, K. (2008). First year students' experiences with technology: Are they really digital natives? *Australasian Journal of Educational Technology, 24*(1), 108–122.

Kiesler, S., Sproull, L., & Eccles, J. S. (1983). Second class citizens? *Psychology Today, 17*(3), 41–48.

Kim, A., Vaughn, S., Klingner, J. K., Woodruff, A. L., Reutebuch, C. K., & Kouzekanani, K. (2006). Improving the reading comprehension of middle school students with disabilities through computer-assisted collaborative strategic reading. *Remedial and Special Education, 27,* 235–249. doi:10.1177/07419325060270040401

Kinsell, C. (2010). Investigating assistive technologies using computers to simulate basic curriculum for individuals with cognitive impairments. In S. Seok, E. Meyen, & B. DaCosta (Eds.), *Handbook of research on human cognition and assistive technology: Design, accessibility and transdisciplinary perspectives* (pp. 61–74). Hershey, PA: IGI Global. doi:10.4018/978-1-61520-817-3.ch004

Kirby, D., & Kuykendall, C. (1991). *Mind matters: Teaching for thinking.* Portsmouth, NH: Boynton/Cook.

Kirriemuir, J., & McFarlane, A. (2003). *Use of computer and video games in the classroom.* Paper presented at the Video games Research Conference. Utrecht, The Netherlands.

Kirsh, S. J. (2002). The effects of violent video games on adolescents: The overlooked influence of development. *Aggression and Violent Behavior, 8,* 377–389. doi:10.1016/S1359-1789(02)00056-3

Kitao, K., Kitao, S. K., Headrick Miller, J., Carpenter, J. W., & Rinner, C. (1995). *Culture and communication.* Kyoto, Japan: Yamaguchi Shoten.

Kitao, K., Yoshida, S., & Yoshida, H. (1986). Daigakusei no eigo dokkairyoku no mondaiten--Gotou noruikei to genin. *Chubu Chiku Eigo Kyoiku Gakkai Kiyo, 15,* 8–13.

Klassen, R. M., & Welton, C. (2009). Self-efficacy and procrastination in the writing of students with learning disabilities. In G. A. Troia (Ed.), *Instruction and assessment for struggling writers* (pp. 51–74). New York: The Guilford Press.

Klepsch, M., & Logie, L. (1982). *Children draw and tell: An introduction to the projective uses of children's human figure drawings.* New York: Brunner/Mazel Publishers.

Klingner, J. K., Artiles, A., & Méndez Barletta, L. (2006). English language learners who struggle with reading: Language acquisition or LD? *Journal of Learning Disabilities, 39*(2), 108–128. doi:10.1177/00222194060390020101 PMID:16583792

Knight, W. (2012). Where speech recognition is going. *MIT Technology Review*. Retrieved from http://www.technologyreview.com/news/427793/where-speech-recognition-is-going/

Knox, C., & Anderson-Inman, L. (2001). Migrant ESL high school students succeed using networked laptops. *Learning and Leading with Technology*, *28*(5), 1–53.

Kotter, J. P. (1996). *Leading change*. Cambridge, MA: Harvard Business School Press.

Kritzenberger, H., Winkler, T., & Herczeg, M. (2002). *Mixed reality environments as collaborative and constructive learning spaces for elementary school children.* Paper presented at the ED-Media 2002 World Conference on Educational Multimedia, Hypermedia and Telecommunications. Denver, CO.

Kuhn, D. (2000). Metacognitive development. *Current Directions in Psychological Science*, *9*(5), 178–181. doi:10.1111/1467-8721.00088

Kuhne, G. W., & Quigley, A. B. (1997). Understanding and using action research in practice settings. In A. B. Quigley, & G. W. Kuhne (Eds.), *Creating practical knowledge: Posing problems, solving problems, and improving daily practice* (pp. 23–40). San Francisco, CA: Jossey-Bass. doi:10.1002/ace.7302

Kulla-Abbott, T., & Polman, J. L. (2008). Engaging student voice and fulfilling curriculum goals with digital storytelling. *Technology, Humanities. Education & Narrative*, *5*, 38–60.

Kvavik, R. B., Caruso, J. B., & Morgan, G. (2004). *ECAR study of students and information technology, 2004: Convenience, connection, and control.* Retrieved from http://net.educause.edu/ir/library/pdf/ers0405/rs/ers0405w.pdf

Lahm, E. A., & Sizemore, L. (2002). Factors that influence assistive technology decision-making. *Journal of Special Education Technology*, *17*(1), 15–26.

Lamb, P. (2010). Hidden opportunity: Mobile reading solutions for the blind. *Educational technology debate exploring ICT and learning in developing countries.* Retrieved from https://edutechdebate.org/assistive-technology/mobile-reading-solutions-for-the-blind/

Lambe, J. (2007). Student teachers, special educational needs and inclusion education: Reviewing the potential for problem based e-learning pedagogy to support practice. *Journal of Education for Teaching*, *33*(3), 359–377. doi:10.1080/02607470701450551

Lane, S., & Mistrett, S. (1996). Play and assistive technology issues for infants and young children with disabilities: A preliminary examination. *Focus on Autism and Other Developmental Disabilities*, *11*(2), 96–104. doi:10.1177/108835769601100205

Langley, M. (1990). A developmental approach to the use of toys for facilitation of environmental control. *Physical & Occupational Therapy in Pediatrics*, *10*(2), 69–91. doi:10.1080/J006v10n02_04

Langone, J., Malone, D. M., & Kinsley, T. (1999). Technology solutions for young children with developmental concerns. *Infants and Young Children*, *11*(4), 65–78. doi:10.1097/00001163-199904000-00011

Laurel, B. (1993). *Computers and theatre*. Reading, MA: Addison-Wesley.

Laurel, B. (2004). Narrative construction as play. *Interaction*, *11*, 73–74. doi:10.1145/1015530.1015568

Laushey, K. M., & Heflin, L. J. (2000). Enhancing social skills of kindergarten children with autism through the training of multiple peers as tutors. *Journal of Autism and Developmental Disorders*, *30*(3), 183–193. doi:10.1023/A:1005558101038 PMID:11055455

Lave, J., & Wenger, E. (1991). *Situated learning: Legitimate peripheral participation.* New York, NY: Cambridge University Press. doi:10.1017/CBO9780511815355

Law, R., & Bai, B. (2006). Website development and evaluations in tourism: A retrospective analysis. In M. Hitz, M. Sigala, & J. Murphy (Eds.), *Information and communication technologies in tourism* (pp. 1–12). New York: Springer-Wien. doi:10.1007/3-211-32710-X_1

Law, R., Qi, S., & Buhalis, D. (2010). Progress in tourism management: A review of website evaluation in tourism research. *Tourism Management*, *31*, 297–313. doi:10.1016/j.tourman.2009.11.007

Lazear, D. (1991). *Seven ways of knowing: Teaching for multiple intelligences*. Retrieved from http://pss.uvm:edu/pss162/learningstyles.html

Lehman, J. F. (1998). *A feature-based comparison of software preferences in typically developing children versus children with autism spectrum disorders*. Retrieved from http://www.cs.cmu.edu/~jef/survey.html

Lei, J. (2009). Digital natives as pre-service teachers: What technology preparation is needed? *Journal of Computing in Teacher Education*, *25*(3), 87–97.

Lenz, K. B., & Deshler, D. D. (2004). *Teaching content to all*. Boston, MA: Pearson.

Lepper, M. R., & Chabay, R. W. (1985). Intrinsic motivation and instruction: Conflicting views on the role of motivational processes in computer-based education. *Educational Psychologist*, *20*, 217–231. doi:10.1207/s15326985ep2004_6

Lesar, S. (1998). Use of assistive technology with young children with disabilities: Current status and training needs. *Journal of Early Intervention*, *21*(2), 146–159. doi:10.1177/105381519802100207

Leung, B. P. (1996). Quality assessment practices in a diverse society. *Teaching Exceptional Children*, *28*(3), 42–45.

Leven, B., Hibbard, K., & Rock, T. (2002). Using problem-based learning as a tool for learning to teach students with special needs. *Teacher Education and Special Education*, *25*, 278–290. doi:10.1177/088840640202500307

Lewandowski, L., & Montali, J. (1996). Bimodal reading: Benefits of a talking computer for average and less skilled readers. *Journal of Learning Disabilities*, *29*, 271–279. doi:10.1177/002221949602900305 PMID:8732888

Li, L. (2007). Digital storytelling: Bridging traditional and digital literacy's. In T. Bastiaens & S. Carliner (Eds.), *Proceedings of World Conference on E-Learning in Corporate, Government, Healthcare, and Higher Education 2007* (pp. 6201-6206). Chesapeake, VA: AACE.

Livingstone, S., & Bober, M. (2004). Taking up online opportunities? Children's use of the internet for education, communication and participation. *E-learning*, *1*(3), 395–419. doi:10.2304/elea.2004.1.3.5

Losh, M., & Capps, L. (2003). Narrative ability in high-functioning children with autism or Asperger's Syndrome. *Journal of Autism and Developmental Disorders*, *33*(3), 239–251. doi:10.1023/A:1024446215446 PMID:12908827

Lovett, M. C. (2002). Problem-solving. In D. Medin (Ed.), *Stevens' handbook of experimental psychology: Memory and cognitive processes* (3rd ed., pp. 317–326). New York, NY: Wiley. doi:10.1002/0471214426.pas0208

Lu, M., & Yeung, W. L. (1998). A framework for effective commercial web application development. *Electronic Networking Applications and Policy*, *8*(2), 166–173. doi:10.1108/10662249810211638

MacArthur, C. A. (2001). Technology implementation in special education. In J. Woodward, & L. Cuban (Eds.), *Technology, curriculum and professional development: Adapting schools to meet the needs of students with disabilities* (pp. 115–120). Thousand Oaks, CA: Corwin.

MacArthur, C. A., Graham, S., Haynes, J. B., & DeLaPaz, S. (1996). Spelling checkers and students with learning disabilities: Performance comparisons and impact on spelling. *Special Education Technology*, *30*(1), 35–57. doi:10.1177/002246699603000103

MacArthur, C., & Philippakos, Z. (2010). Instruction in a strategy for compare-contrast writing. *Exceptional Children*, *76*(4), 438–456.

Madar, K. (2012). Text messaging provide deaf with new means of communication. *The Daily Times*. Retrieved from http://www.daily-times.com/ci_20245436/text-messages-provide-deaf-new-means-communication

Maddux, C. (2009). *Research highlights in technology and teacher education 2009*. Chesapeake, VA: Society for Information Technology & Teacher Education.

Maier, R. B., & Fisher, M. (2007). Strategies for digital storytelling via tabletop video: Building decision making skills in middle school students in marginalized communities. *Journal of Educational Technology Systems*, *35*(2), 175–192. doi:10.2190/5T21-43G4-4415-4MW5

Malinowski, B. (1923). The problem of meaning in primitive language. In C. K. Ogden, & I. A. Richards (Eds.), *The meaning of meaning* (pp. 146–152). London: Routledge.

Mallon, B., & Webb, B. (2005). Stand up and take your place: Identifying narrative elements in narrative adventure and role play games. *ACM Computers in Entertainment*, *3*(1), 1–19. doi:10.1145/1057270.1057285

Malone, T. (1980). *What makes things fun to learn? A study of intrinsically motivating computer games*. (Ph.D. dissertation). Stanford University, Palo Alto, CA.

Malone, T., & Lepper, M. (1987). Making learning fun: A taxonomy of intrinsic motivations of learning. In R. E. Snow & M. J. Farr (Eds.), Aptitude, learning, and instruction: Vol. 3: Connotative and affective process analysis (pp. 223-253). Hillsdale, NJ: Lawrence Erlbaum.

Manning, J. B., & Carpenter, L. B. (2008). Assistive technology webquest: Improving learning for pre-service teachers. *TechTrends*, *52*(6), 47–52. doi:10.1007/s11528-008-0217-y

Manovich, L. (2001). *The language of new media*. Cambridge, MA: MIT Press.

Maor, D., Currie, J., & Drewry, R. (2011). The effectiveness of assistive technologies for children with special needs: A review of research-based studies. *European Journal of Special Needs Education*, *26*(3), 283–298. doi:10.1080/08856257.2011.593821

Margaryan, A., & Littlejohn, A. (2008). *Are digital natives a myth or reality? Students' use of technologies for learning*. Unpublished manuscript.

Margolis, L., & Goodman, S. (1999). *Assistive technology services for students: What are these?* Washington, DC: Assistive Technology Funding & System Change Project.

Marzano, R., Pickering, D., & Pollock, J. (2001). *Classroom instruction that works*. Alexandria, VA: Association for Supervision and Curriculum Development.

Masendorf, F. (1993). Training of learning disabled children's spatial abilities by computer games. *Zeitschrift fur Padagogische Psychologie*, *7*, 209–213.

Mason, L. H., Kubina, R. M., & Taft, R. J. (2011). Developing quick writing skills of middle school students with disabilities. *The Journal of Special Education*, *44*(4), 205–220. doi:10.1177/0022466909350780

Masrtropieri, M., & Scruggs, T. (2002). *Effective instruction for special education*. Austin, TX: Pro-Ed.

Maxcy, S. J. (2003). Pragmatic threads in mixed methods research in the social sciences: The search for multiple modes of inquiry and the end of the philosophy of formalism. In A. Tashakkori, & C. Teddlike (Eds.), *Handbook of mixed methods in social and behavioral research* (pp. 51–89). Thousand Oaks, CA: Sage.

Maxwell, J. A. (2004). Reemergent scientism, postmodernism, and dialogue across differences. *Qualitative Inquiry*, *10*(1), 35–41. doi:10.1177/1077800403259492

Mayer, R. E., & Wittrock, M. C. (2006). Problem-solving. In P. Alexander, & P. Winne (Eds.), *Handbook of educational psychology* (2nd ed., pp. 287–303). Hill Side, NJ: Erlbaum.

McElroy, J. (2011). Asperger's expert recommends L.A. Noire as teaching tool. *Jostiq*. Retrieved from http://www.joystiq.com/2011/05/24/aspergers-expert-recommends-l-a-noire-as-teaching-tool/

McInerney, M., Osher, D., & Kane, M. (1997). *Improving the availability and use of technology for children with disabilities*. Washington, DC: Chesapeake Institute of the American Institutes for Research.

McKeon, M. (2006). *Carl D. Perkins career and technical education improvement act of 2006, conference report*. Retrieved from http://www.gpo.gov/fdsys/pkg/CRPT-109hrpt597/pdf/CRPT-109hrpt597.pdf

McMurtrie, B. (2012, November). China continues to drive foreign-student growth in the United States. *The Chronicle of Higher Education*. Retrieved from http://chronicle.com/article/China-Continues-to-Drive/135700/

McWilliam, E. L. (2002). Against professional development. *Educational Philosophy and Theory*, *34*(3), 289–300. doi:10.1080/00131850220150246

Meadows, D. (2003). Digital storytelling: Research-based practice in new media. *Visual Communication*, *2*, 189–193. doi:10.1177/1470357203002002004

Mehaffy, G. L. (2012). Challenge and change. *Educause Review Online*. Retrieved from http://www.educause.edu/ero/article/challenge-and-change

Mesibov, G. B., Shea, V., & Schopler, E. (2004). *The TEACCH approach to autism spectrum disorders*. New York, NY: Kluwer Academic/Plenum Publishers. doi:10.1007/978-0-306-48647-0

Microsoft Accessibility. (2012). *Microsoft accessibility*. Retrieved from http://www.microsoft.com/enable/products/windows7/

Mills, D. (2006). *Problem based learning*. Retrieved from http://www.c-sap.bham.ac.uk/resources/project_reports/ShowOverview.asp?id=4

Mingfong, J., Yam San, C., & Ek Ming, T. (2010). Unpacking the design process in design-based research. In *Proceedings of the 9th International Conference of the Learning Sciences* (Vol. 2). Chicago: International Society of the Learning Science.

Mireille, B. (2005). *Assessing the educational potential of video games through empirical research on their impact on cognitive and affective dimensions*. Retrieved from http://tecfa.unige.ch/perso/staf/rebetez/blog/wp-content/files/SNSFapplication-videogames-oct05.pdf

Mistrett, S. G. (2001a). *Synthesis on the use of assistive technology with infants and toddlers (birth through age two)* (Contract No. HS97017002, Task Order No. 14). Washington, DC: U.S. Department of Education, Office of Special Education Programs, Division of Research to Practice.

Mistrett, S. G. (2001b). *Let's play! Project final report (Final report to OSERS, No. H024B50051)*. Buffalo, NY: OSERS.

Mistrett, S. G., Hale, M. M., Gruner, A., Sunshine, C., & McInerney, M. (2001). *Synthesis on the use of assistive technology with infants and toddlers with disabilities (birth–two)*. Washington, DC: American Institutes of Research.

Mistrett, S. G., Lane, S. J., & Ruffino, A. G. (2005). Growing and learning through technology: Birth to five. In D. Edyburn, K. Higgins, & R. Boone (Eds.), *Handbook of special education technology researchand practice* (pp. 273–307). Whitefish Bay, WI: Knowledge by Design.

Mistrett, S. G., Lane, S., & Goetz, A. (2000). *A professional's guide to assisting families in creating play environments for children with disabilities*. Buffalo, NY: State University of New York at Buffalo, Center for Assistive Technology.

Mithaug, D. E., Wehmeyer, M., Agran, M., Martin, J. E., & Palmer, S. (1998). The self-determined learning model of teaching: Engaging students to solve their learning problems. In M. Wehmeyer, & D. J. Sands (Eds.), *Making it happen: Student involvement in educational planning* (pp. 299–328). Baltimore, MD: Paul H. Brookes.

Mok, C. K. F., Whitehill, T. L., & Dodd, B. J. (2008). Problem-based learning, critical thinking and concept mapping in speech-language pathology education: A review. *International Journal of Speech-Language Pathology*, *10*(6), 438–448. doi:10.1080/17549500802277492 PMID:20840023

Monereo, C. (2004). The virtual construction of the mind: The role of educational psychology. *Interactive Educational Multimedia*, *9*, 32–47.

Moodle. (2012). *Moodle headquarters*. Retrieved from http://moodle.com/hq/

More, C. (2008). Digital stories targeting social skills for children with disabilities multidimensional learning. *Intervention in School and Clinic*, *43*(3), 168–177. doi:10.1177/1053451207312919

Morris, C. S., Handcock, P. A., & Shirkey, E, C. (2004). Motivational effects of adding context relevant stress in PC-based game training. *Military Psychology*, *16*(2), 135–147. doi:10.1207/S15327876MP1602_4

Moskal, P., Dziuban, C. D., Upchurch, R., Hartman, J., & Truman, B. (2006). Assessing online learning: What one university learned about student success, persistence, and satisfaction. Peer review: Emerging trends and key debates in undergraduate education. *Learning & Technology*, *8*(4), 26–29.

Moss, P. (2001). *Art and learning disabilities*. Retrieved from http://www.ldonline.org/article/5628/

NAEYC. (2009). *Developmentally appropriate practice in early childhood programs serving children from birth through age 8: A position statement of the national association for the education of young children*. Retrieved from http://www.naeyc.org/files/naeyc/file/positions/PSDAP.pdf

Nagel, D. (2013). Smart connected devices hit record levels even as PCs decline. *Campus Technology*. Retrieved from http://campustechnology.com/articles/2013/03/27/smart-connected-devices-hit-record-levels-even-as-pcs-decline.aspx

Nasah, A., DaCosta, B., Kinsell, C., & Seok, S. (2010). The digital literacy debate: An investigation of digital propensity and information and communication technology. *Educational Technology Research and Development*, *58*(5), 531–555. doi:10.1007/s11423-010-9151-8

National Assessment of Educational Progress. (2012). *NAEP writing assessment*. Retrieved from http://nces.ed.gov/nationsreportcard/writing/

National Association of the Deaf. (2013). *Hearing aid compatible telephones*. Retrieved from http://www.nad.org/issues/telephone-and-relay-services/hearing-aid-compatible-telephones

National Center for Educational Statistics. (2011). *Indicators of school crime and safety: 2011*. Retrieved from http://nces.ed.gov/programs/crimeindicators/crimeindicators2011/ind_11.asp

National Center for Learning Disabilities. (2011). *Learning disabilities and the arts*. Retrieved from http://www.ncld.org/in-the-home/parenting-issues/play-enrichment-aamp-holidays/learning-disabilities-and-the-arts

National Center on Universal Design for Learning. (2010). *UDL guidelines*. Retrieved from http://www.udlcenter.org/aboutudl/udlguidelines

National Center on Universal Design for Learning. (2011a). *National center for universal design on learning*. Retrieved from http://www.udlcenter.org/aboutudl/udlguidelines

National Center on Universal Design for Learning. (2011b). References to UDL in public policy, 2010. *UDL Bill – Maryland, 2010*. Retrieved from http://www.udlcenter.org/advocacy/referencestoUDL

National Dissemination Center for Children with Disabilities. (2012). *Assistive technology act*. Retrieved from http://nichcy.org/laws/ata

National Dissemination Center for Children with Disabilities. (2012). *IDEA – The individuals with disabilities act*. Retrieved from http://nichy.org/laws/idea

National Early Intervention Longitudinal Study (NEILS). (2001). Services received by families and children in early intervention. In *Proceedings of the 23rd Annual Report to Congress on Implementation of IDEA* (pp. 1–69). Washington, DC: U.S. Department of Education.

National Institute of Mental Health. (2011). *A parent's guide to autism spectrum disorder: What are the symptoms of ASD?* Retrieved from http://www.nimh.nih.gov/health/publications/a-parents-guide-to-autism-spectrum-disorder/what-are-the-symptoms-of-asd.shtml

National Institute on Standards and Technology. (2005). ATP focused program: Adaptive learning systems. *Advanced Technology Program*. Retrieved from http://www.atp.nist.gov/focus/als.htm

National Joint Committee on Learning Disabilities (Ed.). (1994). *Collective perspectives on issues affecting learning disabilities*. Austin, TX: PRO-ED.

Needham, N. R. (1983). The impact of video games on American youth. *Education Digest*, *48*, 40–42.

Newman, K. (2005). The case for the narrative brain. In *Proceedings of Second Australasia Conference on Interactive Entertainment* (pp. 145-149). Sydney, Australia: Australasia.

Nolan, J. (2006). The influence of ASCII on the construction of internet-based knowledge. In J. Weiss, J. Nolan, J. Hunsinger, & P. Trifonas (Eds.), *International handbook of virtual learning environments* (pp. 207–220). Dordrecht, The Netherlands: Springer. doi:10.1007/978-1-4020-3803-7_7

Norman, D. K. (2008). *Predicting the performance of interpreting instruction based on digital propensity index score in text and graphic formats*. (Unpublished dissertation). University of Central Florida, Orlando, FL.

Norman, G. R., & Schmidt, H. G. (1992). The psychological basis of problem-based learning: A review of the evidence. *Academic Medicine*, *67*(9), 557–565. doi:10.1097/00001888-199209000-00002 PMID:1520409

North Carolina State University (NCSU). (2008). About the center: Ronald L. Mace. *The Center for Universal Design*. Retrieved from http://www.ncsu.edu/www/ncsu/design/sod5/cud/about_us/usronmace.htm

Novak, J. D., & Gowin, D. B. (1984). *Learning how to learn*. Cambridge, UK: Cambridge University Press. doi:10.1017/CBO9781139173469

Ochoa, T. A., & Robinson, J. M. (2005). Revisiting group consensus: Collaborative learning dynamics during a problem-based learning activity in education. *Teacher Education and Special Education*, *28*(1), 10–20. doi:10.1177/088840640502800102

Odom, S. L., Brantlinger, E., Gersten, R., Horner, R., Thompson, B., & Harris, K. (2005). Research in special education: Scientific methods and evidence-based practices. *Exceptional Children*, *71*(2), 137–148.

Okolo, C. (1992). The effect of computer-assisted instruction format and initial attitude on the arithmetic facts proficiency and continuing motivation of students with learning disabilities. *Exceptionality*, *3*, 195–211. doi:10.1080/09362839209524815

Olshansky, B. (1994). Making writing a work of art: Image-making within the writing process. *Language Arts*, *71*, 350–357.

Olt, M. (2002). Ethics and distance education: Strategies for minimizing academic dishonesty in online assessment. *Capella University*. Retrieved from http://www.westga.edu/~distance/ojdla/fall53/olt53.html

Online Sunshine. (2012). *The 2012 Florida statutes: Title XLVIII, chapter 1003*. Retrieved from http://leg.state.fl.us/statutes/index.cfm?App_mode=Display_Statute&Search_String=&URL=1000-1099/1003/Sections/1003.428.html

Open University. (2006). *Making your teaching inclusive*. Retrieved from http://www.open.ac.uk/inclusiveteaching/pages/inclusive-teaching/barriers-to-learning.php

Palfrey, J., & Gasser, U. (2008). *Born digital: Understanding the first generation of digital natives*. New York, NY: Basic Books.

Palmer, S., Wehmeyer, M. L., Gipson, K., & Agran, M. (2004). Promoting access to the general curriculum for students with intellectual disabilities by teaching self-determination skills. *Exceptional Children*, *70*, 427–439.

Panchapakesan, V. (2011). Our plans to support modern browsers across Google apps. *Google: Official Enterprise Blog*. Retrieved from http://googleenterprise.blogspot.com/2011/06/our-plans-to-support-modern-browsers.html

Parette, H. P., & Angelo, D. H. (1996). Augmentative and alternative communication impact on families: Trends and future directions. *The Journal of Special Education*, *30*, 77–98. doi:10.1177/002246699603000105

Parham, L. D., & Primeau, L. A. (1997). *Play and occupational therapy for children*. St. Louis, MO: Mosby.

Parker, A. (1999). Interaction in distance education: The critical conversation. *AACE Journal*, *1*(12), 13–17.

Park, S. H., & Ertmer, P. A. (2008). Examining barriers in technology-enhanced problem-based learning: Using a performance support systems approach. *British Journal of Educational Technology*, *39*(4), 631–643. doi:10.1111/j.1467-8535.2008.00858.x

Parr, M. (2011). *The voice of text-to-speech technology: One possible solution for struggling readers, what works?* Retrieved from http://www.edu.gov.on.ca/eng/literacynumeracy/inspire/research/whatWorks.html

Partnership for 21st Century Skills. (2004). *Framework for 21st century skills*. Retrieved from http://www.21stcenturyskills.org

Pedersen, E. (1995). Storytelling and the art of teaching. *English Teaching Forum*, *33*(1).

Phillips, V. (1998). Virtual classrooms, real education. *Nation's Business*, *86*(5), 47–51.

Piaget, J. (1962). *Play, dreams and imitation in childhood*. New York, W.: Norton.

Piaget, J. (1962). *Play, dreams, and imitation in childhood*. New York: Norton.

Pierfy, D. A. (1977). Comparative simulation game research: Stumbling blocks and stepping stones. *Simulation & Games*, *8*(2), 255–268. doi:10.1177/003755007782006

Pivec, M., & Pivec, P. (2008). *Games in schools: Executive summary*. Retrieved from http://www.paulpivec.com/Games_in_Schools.pdf

Plainlanguage.gov. (2011). *Federal plain language guidelines*. Retrieved from http://www.plainlanguage.gov/howto/guidelines/bigdoc/fullbigdoc.pdf

Porter, D. B. (1995). Computer games: Paradigms of opportunity. *Behavior Research Methods, Instruments, & Computers*, *27*(2), 229–234. doi:10.3758/BF03204737

Prensky, M. (2001). *Video game-based learning*. New York: McGraw-Hill.

Prensky, M. (2001a). Digital natives, digital immigrants. *Horizon*, *9*, 1–6.

Prensky, M. (2001b). Digital natives, digital immigrants, part II: Do they really think differently? *Horizon*, *9*, 1–6.

Prior, M. (2003). Is there an increase in the prevalence of autism spectrum disorders? *Journal of Paediatrics and Child Health*, *39*(2), 81–82. doi:10.1046/j.1440-1754.2003.00097.x PMID:12603792

Provenzo, E. F. (1991). *Video kids: Making sense of Nintendo*. Cambridge, MA: Harvard University Press.

Public Law 101-336. (1990). *Public law 101-336 – July 26, 1990*. Retrieved from http://www.brockport.edu/~govdoc/SocPol/pl1013a.pdf

Putnam, C., & Chong, L. (2008). Software and technologies designed for people with autism: What do users want? In *Proceedings from Assets '08: The 10th International ACM SIGACCESS Conference on Computers and Accessibility*. Nova Scotia, Canada: ACM.

Quality Matters Program. (2013). *Quality matters program: A national benchmark for online course design*. Retrieved from https://www.qualitymatters.org/

Radford, A. W., & Weko, T. (2011). Learning at a distance: Undergraduate enrollment in distance education courses and degree programs (PDF). *National Center for Education Statistics*. Retrieved from http://nces.ed.gov/pubs2012/2012154.pdf

Ramirez, S. (1986). The effects of Suggestopedia in teaching English vocabulary to Spanish dominant Chicano third graders. *The Elementary School Journal*, *86*, 325–333. doi:10.1086/461453

Randel, J. M., Morris, B. A., Wetzel, C. D., & Whitehill, B. V. (1992). The effectiveness of games for educational purposes: A review of recent research. *Simulation & Gaming*, *23*(3), 261–276. doi:10.1177/1046878192233001

Rao, S. M., & Gagie, B. (2006). Learning through seeing and doing: Visual supports for children with autism. *Teaching Exceptional Children*, *38*(6), 26–33.

Rappolt-Schlichtmann, G., Daley, S., & Rose, L. T. (2012). *A research reader in universal design for learning*. Cambridge, MA: Harvard Education Press.

Raskind, M., & Bryant, B. R. (2002). *Functional evaluation for assistive technology*. Austin, TX: Psycho-Educational Services.

Ravitz, J. (2008). *Project-based learning as a catalyst*. Paper presented at the annual meeting of the American Educational Research Association. New York, NY.

Raymond, E. B. (2008). *Learners with mild disabilities: A characteristics approach* (3rd ed.). San Francisco, CA: Pearson.

Recker, K., & Kalluri, S. (2009). The impact of new technology on phone use. *Hearing Review*, *16*(3), 16–20.

Rees, D. (2010). *Designing learning games for children with autism spectrum disorder: Considering media and technology when creating the game world*. Retrieved from http://diannereessdsuassignments.weebly.com/uploads/6/3/9/0/6390810/literature_review.pdf

Rehabilitation Act Amendments. (2013). *Section 508*. Retrieved from http://www.access-board.gov/sec508/guide/act.htm

Reid, R., & Lienemann, T. (2006). *Strategy instruction for students with learning disabilities*. New York: The Gilford Press.

Reinking, D., & Bradley, B. A. (2008). *Formative and design experiments*. New York, NY: Teachers College Press.

Rhodes, L. K. (1993). *Literacy assessment: A handbook of instruments*. Portsmouth, NH: Heinemann.

Ricci, K, E., Salas, E., & Cannon-Bowers, J. A. (1996). Do computer-based games facilitate knowledge acquisition and retention? *Military Psychology*, *8*(4), 295–307. doi:10.1207/s15327876mp0804_3

Ricci, K. E. (1994). The use of computer-based videogames in knowledge acquisition and retention. *Journal of Interactive Instruction Development*, *7*(1), 17–22.

Richards, P. L. (2001). *Review of the electronic curb-cut effect. H-Disability*. H-Net Reviews.

Rinehart, N. J., Bellgrove, M. A., Tonge, B. J., Brereton, A. V., Howells-Rankin, D., & Bradshaw, J. L. (2006). An examination of movement kinematics in young people with high-functioning autism and Asperger's disorder: Further evidence for a motor planning deficit. *Journal of Autism and Developmental Disorders*, *36*(6), 757–767. doi:10.1007/s10803-006-0118-x PMID:16865551

Roberts, D. F., Foehr, U. G., & Rideout, V. (2005). *Generation M: Media in the lives of 8-18 year-olds*. Retrieved from http://www.kff.org/entmedia/upload/Generation-M-Media-in-the-Lives-of-8-18-Year-olds-Report.pdf

Roberts, K. D., Park, H. J., Brown, S., & Cook, B. (2011). Universal design for instruction in postsecondary education: A systematic review of empirically based articles. *Journal of Postsecondary Education and Disability*, *24*(1), 5–15.

Robin, B. (2006). The educational uses of digital storytelling. In C. Crawford et al. (Eds.), *Proceedings of Society for Information Technology and Teacher Education International Conference 2006* (pp. 709-716). Chesapeake, VA: AACE.

Roessler, R., & Bolton, B. (1978). *Psychosocial adjustment to disability*. Baltimore, MD: University Park Press.

Rogers, S. (Ed.). (2011). *Rethinking play and pedagogy: Contexts, concepts and cultures*. London: Routledge.

Romski, M. A., Sevik, R. A., & Forrest, S. (2001). Assistive technology and augmentative communication in early childhood inclusion. In M. J. Guralnick (Ed.), *Early childhood inclusion: Focus on change* (pp. 465–479). Baltimore, MD: Paul H. Brookes Publishing Co., Inc.

Romski, M., & Sevick, R. (2005). Augmentative communication and early intervention: Myths and realities. *Infants and Young Children*, *18*(3), 174–185. doi:10.1097/00001163-200507000-00002

Root, C. (1994). *A guide to learning disabilities for the ESL classroom practitioner*. Retrieved from http://www.ldonline.org/article/8765/

Rose, D. H., Harbour, W. S., Johnston, C. S., Daley, S. G., & Abarbanell, L. (2006). Universal design for learning in postsecondary education: Reflections on principles and their application. *Journal of Postsecondary Education and Disability*, *19*(2), 135–151.

Rose, D. H., & Meyer, A. (2002). *Teaching every student in the digital age: Universal design for learning*. Alexandria, VA: Association for Supervision & Curriculum Development.

Rose, D. H., & Meyer, A. (Eds.). (2006). *A practical reader in universal design for learning*. Cambridge, MA: Harvard Education Press.

Rose, D., Hasselbring, T. S., Stahl, S., & Zabala, J. (2005). Assistive technology and universal design for learning: Two sides of the same coin. In D. Edyburn, K. Higgins, & R. Boone (Eds.), *Handbook of special education technology research and practice* (pp. 507–518). Whitefish Bay, WI: Knowledge by Design.

Roth, P. (2003, May 16). America's Army is a big hit, and not just with civilians. *Wall Street Journal Online*. Retrieved from http://online.wsj.com/article/0,SB105285932212326700,00.html?mod=technology%5Ffeatured%5Fstories%5Fhs

Rouse, R. III. (2001). *Game design theory and practice*. Plano, TX: Wordware.

Rowlands, I., Nicholas, D., Williams, P., Huntington, P., Fieldhouse, M., & Gunter, B. et al. (2008). The Google generation: The information behaviour of the researcher of the future. *Aslib Proceedings*, *60*(4), 290–310. doi:10.1108/00012530810887953

Ruiz-de-Velasco, J., Fix, M., & Clewell, B. (2000, December). *Overlooked and underserved: Immigrant students in U.S. secondary schools*. Washington, DC: The Urban Institute.

Runco, M. A. (2003). *Critical creative processes*. Creskill, NJ: Hampton Press.

Saddler, B., Behforooz, B., & Asaro, K. (2008). The effects of sentence-combining instruction on the writing of fourth-grade students with writing difficulties. *The Journal of Special Education*, *42*(2), 79–90. doi:10.1177/0022466907310371

Saddler, B., Moran, S., Graham, S., & Harris, K. R. (2004). Preventing writing difficulties: The effects of planning strategy instruction on the writing performance of struggling writers. *Exceptionality*, *12*, 13–17. doi:10.1207/s15327035ex1201_2

Sadik, A. (2008). Digital storytelling: A meaningful technology-integrated approach for engaged students learning. *Educational Technology Research and Development*, *56*, 487–506. doi:10.1007/s11423-008-9091-8

Safer, M. (2007, May 25). The millennials are coming. *60 Minutes*. Retrieved from http://www.cbsnews.com/stories/2007/11/08/60minutes/main3475200.shtml

Sage, S. M. (2000). A natural fit: Problem-based learning and technology standards. *Learning and Leading with Technology*, *28*(1), 6–12.

Sailor, W., & Skrtic, T. M. (2009). Policy. In T. M. Skrtic, C. M. Gary, & E. M. Horn (Eds.), *Taking stock of special education policy & practice: A retrospective commentary* (pp. 409–422). Denver, CO: Love Publishing Company.

Sakai Project. (n.d.). *About sakai*. Retrieved from http://www.sakaiproject.org/about-sakai

Salend, S. J. (2005). Creating inclusive classrooms: Effective and reflective practices for all students (5th ed.). Columbus, OH: Pearson: Merrill/Prentice Hall.

Sansosti, F. J., Powell-Smith, K. A., & Kincaid, D. (2004). A research synthesis of social story interventions for children with autism spectrum disorders. *Focus on Autism and Other Developmental Disabilities*, *19*(4), 194–204. doi:10.1177/10883576040190040101

Sarbin, T. R. (1986). *Narrative psychology: The storied nature of human conduct*. New York, NY: Praege.

Savoie, J. M., & Hughes, A. S. (1994). Problem-based learning as classroom solution. *Educational Leadership*, *52*(3), 54–60.

Sawyer, B., Milbourne, S., Dugan, L., & Campbell, P. (2005). *Report of assistive technology training for providers and families of children in early intervention*. Retrieved from http://tnt.asu.edu/files/ATtrainingbrief2-8-05.pdf

Schein, E. H. (1985). *Organizational culture and leadership*. San Francisco, CA: Jossey-Bass.

Schell, J. (2005). Understanding entertainment: Story and game play are one. *ACM Computers in Entertainment*, *3*(1), 1–19. doi:10.1145/1057270.1057284

Scherer, M. J., & Craddock, G. (2002). Matching person and technology (MPT) assessment process. *Technology and Disability*, *14*, 125–131.

Schmidt, H. G. (1999). *Testing a causal model of problem-based learning*. Paper presented at the annual meeting of the American Educational Research Association. Montreal, Canada.

Schneider, E. F., Lang, A., Shin, M., & Bradley, S. D. (2004). Death with a story: How story impacts emotional, motivational, and physiological responses to first-person shooter video games. *Human Communication Research*, *30*(3), 361–375.

Schreiber, J. B., Nora, A., Stage, F. K., Barlow, E. A., & King, J. (2006). Reporting structural equation modeling and confirmatory factor analysis results: A review. *The Journal of Educational Research*, *99*(6), 323–337. doi:10.3200/JOER.99.6.323-338

Scruggs, T., & Mastropieri, M. (1990). The case for mnemonic instruction: From laboratory research to classroom applications. *The Journal of Special Education*, *24*(1), 7–32. doi:10.1177/002246699002400102

Selwyn, N. (2009). *The digital native - Myth and reality*. Paper presented at the CILIP (Chartered Institute of Library and Information Professionals) London Seminar Series. London, UK. Retrieved from http://www.scribd.com/doc/9775892/Digital-Native

Senge, P. M. (1990). *The fifth discipline: The art and practice of the learning organization*. New York: Doubleday.

Seok, S. (2007a). Item validation of online postsecondary courses: Rating the proximity between similarity and dissimilarity among item pairs (validation study series I – multidimensional scaling). *Educational Technology Research and Development*, *57*(5), 665–684. doi:10.1007/s11423-007-9072-3

Seok, S. (2007b). Standards, accreditations, benchmarks in distance education. *Quarterly Review of Distance Education*, *8*(4), 387–398.

Seok, S. (2008a). Teaching aspects of e-learning. *International Journal on E-Learning*, *7*(4), 725–741.

Seok, S. (2008b). Maximizing web accessibility through user-centered interface design. In C. Calero, C. C. Munoz, A. M. Moraga, & P. Mario (Eds.), *Handbook of research on web information systems quality* (pp. 206–219). Hershey, PA: IGI Global. doi:10.4018/978-1-59904-847-5.ch012

Seok, S., & DaCosta, B. (2013). Development and standardization of an assistive technology questionnaire using factor analyses: Eight factors consisting of 67 items related to assistive technology practices. *Assistive Technology*. doi:10.1080/10400435.2013.778917

Seok, S., Meyen, E., & DaCosta, B. (Eds.). (2010). *Handbook of research on human cognition and assistive technology: Design, accessibility and transdisciplinary perspectives*. Hershey, PA: IGI Global. doi:10.4018/978-1-61520-817-3

Seo, Y., & Bryant, D. (2012). Multimedia CAI program for students with mathematical difficulties. *Remedial and Special Education*, *33*(4), 217–225. doi:10.1177/0741932510383322

Sgouros, N. (2000). Using character motives to drive plot resolution in interactive stories. *Applied Intelligence*, *12*, 239–249. doi:10.1023/A:1008323325555

Shakespeare, T. (2006). *Disability rights and wrongs*. New York, NY: Routledge.

Shanahan, T. (2006). Relations among oral language, reading, and writing development. In C. A. MacArthur, S. Graham, & J. Fitzgerald (Eds.), *Handbook of writing instruction* (pp. 171–183). New York: The Guilford Press.

Shane, H. C., & Albert, P. D. (2008). Electronic screen media for persons with autism spectrum disorders: Results of a survey. *Journal of Autism and Developmental Disorders*, *38*(8), 1499–1508. doi:10.1007/s10803-007-0527-5 PMID:18293074

Shaw, S. Madaus, J., & Dukes, L. (2010). Preparing students with disabilities for college success: A practical guide for transition planning. Baltimore, MD: Brookes.

Shaywitz, S. (2003). *Overcoming dyslexia: A new and complete science-based program for reading problems at any level*. New York: Knopf.

Short, D., & Echevarria, J. (1999). *The sheltered instructional observation protocol*. Washington, DC: Center for Applied Linguistics.

ShowMe. (2012). *Showme*. Retrieved from http://www.showme.com

Silió, M., & Barbetta, P. (2010). The effects of word prediction and text-to-speech technologies on the narrative writing skills of Hispanic students with specific learning disabilities. *Journal of Special Education Technology*, *25*(4), 17–32.

Slavin, R., & Cheung, A. (2003). *Effective programs for English language learners: A best-evidence synthesis*. Baltimore, MD: Johns Hopkins University, CRESPAR.

Slotznick, B., Hershberger, D., & Higginbotham, J. (2009). *Point-and-chat instant messaging software for augmentative/alternative communications users*. Retrieved from http://www.nationaltechcenter.org/documents/point_and_chat_final_report.pdf

Slotznick, B. (2010). Point-and-Chat®: Instant messaging for AAC users. In S. Seok, E. Meyen, & B. DaCosta (Eds.), *Handbook of research on human cognition and assistive technology: Design, accessibility and transdisciplinary perspectives* (pp. 169–175). Hershey, PA: IGI Global. doi:10.4018/978-1-61520-817-3.ch011

Smaldino, S. E., Lowther, D. L., & Russell, J. D. (2008). *Instructional technology and media for learning* (9th ed.). Upper Saddle River, NJ: Pearson Merril Prentice Hall.

Smith, K. (2011). Butler LMS evaluation executive summary. *The LMS Project*. Retrieved from http://blogs.butler.edu/lms/files/2011/08/executive-summary.pdf

Soppe, M., Schmidt, H. G., & Bruysten, R. (2005). Influence of problem familiarity on learning in a problem-based course. *Instructional Science*, *33*, 271–281. doi:10.1007/s11251-004-7688-9

Sorrell, C., Bell, S., & McCallum, R. (2007). Reading rate and comprehension as a function of computerized versus traditional presentation mode: A preliminary study. *Journal of Special Education Technology*, *22*(1), 1–12.

Sousa, D. A., & Tomlinson, C. A. (2011). *Differentiation and the brain: How neuroscience supports the learner-friendly classroom*. Bloomington, IN: Solution Tree Press.

Special Education News. (2013). *EHA: Education for all handicapped children act*. Retrieved from http://www.specialednews.com/special-education-dictionary/eha---education-for-all-handicapped-children-act.htm

Squire, K. (2005). Changing the game: What happens when video games enter the classroom?. *Innovate: Journal of Online Education, 1*(6).

Staker, H., & Horn, M. B. (2012). *Classifying K-12 blended learning*. Retrieved from http://www.innosightinstitute.org/innosight/wp-content/uploads/2011/01/The-Rise-of-K-12-Blended-Learning.pdf

Steinberg, E. R. (1977). Cognition and learner control: A literature review. *Journal of Computer-Based Instruction, 16*(4), 117–121.

Steinberg, E. R., Baskin, A. B., & Hofer, L. (1986). Organizational/memory tools: A technique for improving problem solving skills. *Journal of Educational Computing Research, 2*(2), 169–187. doi:10.2190/QNF3-NM3V-FRTE-17B3

Stern, J. (2002). *Web metrics: Proven methods for measuring web site success*. New York, NY: Wiley Publishing.

Stokes, T. F., & Baer, D. M. (1977). An implicit technology of generalization. *Journal of Applied Behavior Analysis, 10*(2), 349–367. doi:10.1901/jaba.1977.10-349 PMID:16795561

Stoner, J. B., Parette, H. P., Watts, E. H., Wojcik, B. W., & Fogal, T. (2008). Preschool teacher perceptions of assistive technology and professional development responses. *Education and Training in Developmental Disabilities, 43*(1), 77–91.

Stout, R. (1997). *Web site stats: Tracking hits and analyzing traffic*. Berkeley, CA: Osborne/McGraw-Hill.

Student, P. O. L. L. (2010). Research dispels millennial theories: Millennials appear more like than different from their parents' generation. *The CollegeBoard*. Retrieved from http://professionals.collegeboard.com/data-reports-research/trends/studentpoll/millennial

Sullivan, M., & Lewis, M. (2000). Assistive technology for the very young: Creating responsive environments. *Infants and Young Children, 12*(4), 34–52. doi:10.1097/00001163-200012040-00009

Symantec. (2013). *Introduction to SSL*. Retrieved from https://www.symantec.com/page.jsp?id=how-ssl-works

Tapscott, D. (1998). *Growing up digital: The rise of the net generation*. New York, NY: McGraw-Hill Companies.

Tartaro, A., & Cassell, J. (2006). *Authorable virtual peers for autism spectrum disorders*. Paper presented at the Combined Workshop on Language-Enabled Educational Technology and Development and Evaluation for Robust Spoken Dialogue Systems at the 11th European conference on Artificial Intelligence (ECA 106). Riva del Garda, Italy.

Tartaro, A., & Cassell, J. (2007). Using virtual peer technology as an intervention for children with autism. In J. Lazar (Ed.), *Universal Usability: Designing Computer Interfaces for Diverse User Populations* (pp. 231–262). West Sussex, UK: Academic Press.

Taylor, A. (2005). What employers look for: The skills debate and the fit with youth perceptions. *Journal of Education and Work, 18*, 201–218. doi:10.1080/13639080500085984

Technology-Related Assistance for Individuals with Disabilities Act 1988, Pub. L. 100-407, Sec. 2, 102 Stat. 1044 (1988) (amendment 1990).

Technology-Related Assistance for People with Disabilities. (1988). Catalog No. 850. (senate rpt. 100-438). Washington, DC: U.S. Government Printing Office.

TechSmith. (2013). *ScreenChomp*. Retrieved from http://www.techsmith.com/labs.html

TechTerms.com. (2013). *DSL*. Retrieved from http://www.techterms.com/definition/dsl

Television Decoder Circuitry. (1990). *Public law 101-431 – Oct. 15, 1990*. Retrieved from http://transition.fcc.gov/Bureaus/OSEC/library/legislative_histories/1395.pdf

Thakker, D. (1997). *Employers and the Americans with disabilities act: Factors influencing manager adherence with the ADA, with special reference to individuals with psychiatric disabilities*. Dissertations Abstracts International. (University Microfilms No. 9727300).

Thevenot, B. (2012, February). Most community college students never graduate. *The Texas Tribune*. Retrieved from http://www.texastribune.org/texas-education/higher-education/most-community-college-students-never-graduate/

Thomas, E. (1996). *Overview of the telecommunications act of 1996: Pros and cons for municipal provision of fiber optic utilities*. Retrieved from http://www.mrsc.org/subjects/legal/telecomm/thomas.aspx

Thompson, D., Baranowski, T., Buday, R., Baranowski, J., Thompson, V., Jago, R., & Griffith, M. J. (2010). Serious video games for health: How behavioral science guided the development of a serious video game. *Simulation & Gaming*, *41*(4), 587–606. doi:10.1177/1046878108328087 PMID:20711522

Traweek, D. (1993). *Teacher and learner variables in early literacy instruction: Treatment, evaluation and ethnographic studies*. (Ph.D. Dissertation). University of Washington, Seattle, WA.

Trinkaus, J. W. (1983). Arcade video games: An informal look. *Psychological Reports*, *52*, 586. doi:10.2466/pr0.1983.52.2.586

Troia, G. A. (Ed.). (2009). *Instruction and assessment for struggling writers*. New York: The Guilford Press.

Tsou, W., Wang, W., & Tzeng, Y. (2006). Applying a multimedia storytelling website in foreign language learning. *Computers & Education*, *47*, 17–28. doi:10.1016/j.compedu.2004.08.013

Tucker, B. (2012). The flipped classroom: Online instruction at home frees class time for learning. *Education Next*. Retrieved from http://educationnext.org/the-flipped-classroom

Tullis, T. S., & Stetson, J. N. (2004). *A comparison of questionnaires for assessing website usability*. Retrieved from http://home.comcast.net/~tomtullis/publications/UPA2004TullisStetson.pdf

Turkle, S. (1982). The subjective computer: A study in the psychology of personal computation. *Social Studies of Science*, *12*, 173–205. doi:10.1177/030631282012002001

Turkle, S. (1995). *Life on the screen: Identify in the age of the internet*. New York: Simon & Schuster.

Turnbull, A., Turnbull, R., & Wehmeyer, M. L. (2007). Exceptional lives: Special education in today's schools (5th ed.). Columbus, OH: Pearson: Merrill/Prentice Hall.

Tutt, R., Powell, S., & Thornton, M. (2006). Educational approaches in autism: What we know about what we do. *Educational Psychology in Practice*, *22*(1), 69–81. doi:10.1080/02667360500512452

Twyman, T., & Tindal, G. (2006). Using a computer-adapted conceptually based history text to increase comprehension and problem-solving skills of students with disabilities. *Journal of Special Education Technology*, *21*(2), 5–16.

U. S. Government Accountability Office. (2009). Higher education and disability: Education needs a coordinated approach to improve its assistance to schools in supporting students. *United States Government Accountability Office*. Retrieved from http://www.gao.gov/new.items/d1033.pdf

U.S. Department of Education, Office of Special Education Programs. (n.d.). *IDEA data*. Retrieved from http://www.ideadata.org

U.S. Department of Education. (2002).. . *Public Law*, 107–110. Retrieved from http://www.ed.gov

U.S. Department of Education. (2003). *Carl D. Perkins career and technical education act of 2006*. Retrieved from http://www2.ed.gov/offices/OVAE/CTE/legis.html

U.S. Department of Education. (2004a). *Assistive technology act of 1998 as amended in 2004*. Retrieved from http://www.gpo.gov/fdsys/pkg/PLAW-108publ364/html/PLAW-108publ364.htm

U.S. Department of Education. (2004b). *Individuals with disabilities education act, section 602(35)*. Retrieved from http://idea.ed.gov/explore/view/p/%2Croot%2Cstatute%2CI%2CA%2C602%2C

U.S. Department of Education. (2006). *34 CFR parts 300 and 301, assistance to states for the education of children with disabilities and preschool grants for children with disabilities, final rule*. Retrieved from http://idea.ed.gov/download/finalregulations.html

U.S. Department of Education. (2008). *Higher education opportunity act - 2008, public law 110-315*. Retrieved from http://www.gpo.gov/fdsys/pkg/PLAW-110publ315/html/PLAW-110publ315.htm

U.S. Department of Education. (2010). *Free appropriate public education for students with disabilities: Requirements under section 504 of the rehabilitation act of 1973*. Retrieved from http://www2.ed.gov/about/offices/list/ocr/docs/edlite-FAPE504.html

U.S. Department of Education. (2010). *Understanding the implications of online learning for educational productivity*. Retrieved from http://www2.ed.gov/about/offices/list/os/technology/implications-online-learning.pdf

U.S. Department of Education. (2012). *Office of special education programs*. Retrieved from http://www2.ed.gov/about/offices/list/osers/osep/index.html?src=mr

U.S. Department of Education. (2013a). *Building the legacy: IDEA 2004*. Retrieved from http://idea.ed.gov/

U.S. Department of Education. (2013b). *Carl D. Perkins career and technical education act of 2006*. Retrieved from http://www2.ed.gov/policy/sectech/leg/perkins/index.html

U.S. Department of Education. (2013c). *Office of special education and rehabilitation services: Thirty-five years of progress in educating children with disabilities through IDEA*. Retrieved from http://www2.ed.gov/about/offices/list/osers/idea35/history/index.html

U.S. Department of Education. (n.d.). *No child left behind: Elementary and secondary education act (ESEA)*. Retrieved from http://www2.ed.gov/nclb/landing.jhtml

U.S. Department of Housing and Urban Development. (2013). *Adoption of final guidelines*. Retrieved from http://portal.hud.gov/hudportal/HUD?src=/program_offices/fair_housing_equal_opp/disabilities/fhguidelines/fhefha1

U.S. Department of Justice. (2009). *A guide to disability rights laws*. Retrieved from http://www.ada.gov/cguide.htm#anchor62335

U.S. Department of Justice. Americans with Disabilities Act. (2013). *ADA home page: Information and technical assistance on the Americans with disability act*. Retrieved from http://www.ada.gov/

U.S. Department of Labor. Employment and Training Administration. (2010). *The plain English version of the workforce investment act of 1998*. Retrieved from http://www.doleta.gov/usworkforce/wia/Runningtext.cfm

U.S. Department of Labor. OSAM. (2011). *Section 504, rehabilitation Act of 1973*. Retrieved from http://www.dol.gov/oasam/regs/statutes/sec504.htm

U.S. Government Printing Office. (1996). *Telecommunications act, public law 104-104*. Retrieved from http://www.gpo.gov/fdsys/pkg/PLAW-104publ104/html/PLAW-104publ104.htm

Unicorn. (n.d.). *Sakai collaboration and learning environment*. Retrieved from http://www.unicon.net/opensource/sakai

Uzuntiryake, E., & Geban, O. (2005). Effect of conceptual change approach accompanied with concept mapping on understanding of solution concepts. *Instructional Science*, *33*, 311–339. doi:10.1007/s11251-005-2812-z

Valkanova, Y., & Watts, M. (2007). Digital story telling in a science classroom: Reflective self-learning (RSL) in action. *Early Child Development and Care*, *177*(6-7), 793–807. doi:10.1080/03004430701437252

Van Berkel, H., & Schmidt, H. G. (2001). Motivation to commit oneself as a determinant of achievement in problem-based learning. *Higher Education*, *40*, 231–242. doi:10.1023/A:1004022116365

Van den Bossche, P., Gijselaers, W., Segers, M., & Kirschner, P. A. (2006). Social and cognitive factors driving teamwork in collaborative learning environments: Team learning beliefs & behaviors. *Small Group Research*, *37*(5), 490–521. doi:10.1177/1046496406292938

van Gils, F. (2005). Potential applications of digital storytelling in education. In *Proceedings of 3rd Twente Student Conference on IT*. Enschede, The Netherlands: University of Twente.

Van Tatenhove, G. M. (1987). Teaching power through augmentative communication: Guidelines for early intervention. *Journal of Childhood Communication Disorders*, *10*, 185–199. doi:10.1177/152574018701000207

Vaughn, S., Bos, C. S., & Schumm, J. S. (2007). *Teaching students who are exceptional, diverse, and at risk in the general education classroom*. Boston, MA: Allyn & Bacon.

Vygotksy, L. (1978). *Mind and society*. Cambridge, MA: MIT Press.

Vygotsky, L. (1978). Interaction between learning and development. In T. M. Cole (Ed.), *From mind and society* (pp. 79–91). Cambridge, MA: Harvard University Press.

Vygotsky, L. (1986). *Thought and language*. Cambridge, MA: The MIT Press.

W3C. (2003). *HTTP - Hypertext transfer protocol*. Retrieved from http://www.w3.org/Protocols/

W3C. (2012). *About W3C*. Retrieved from http://www.w3.org/Consortium/

W3C. (2013). *Uniform resource locators*. Retrieved from http://www.w3.org/Addressing/URL/Overview.html

Watson, G., & Sottile, J. (2010). Cheating in the digital age: Do students cheat more in online courses? *Online Journal of Distance Learning Administration, 13*(1).

Webb, B. J., Miller, S. P., Pierce, T. B., Strawser, S., & Jones, W. P. (2004). Effects of social skill instruction for high-functioning adolescents with autism spectrum disorders. *Focus on Autism and Other Developmental Disabilities, 19*(1), 53–62. doi:10.1177/10883576040190010701

Wehmeyer, M. L. (1999). Assistive technology and students with mental retardation: Utilization and barriers. *Journal of Special Education Technology, 12*(1), 48–58.

Wehmeyer, M. L., Abery, B., Mithaug, D. E., & Stancliffee, R. J. (2003). *Theory in self-determination: Foundations for educational practice*. Springfield, IL: Thomas.

Wehmeyer, M. L., & Palmer, S. B. (2003). Adult outcomes for students with cognitive disabilities three years after high school: The impact of self-determination. *Education and Training in Developmental Disabilities, 38*, 131–144.

Wehmeyer, M. L., Palmer, S. B., Agran, M., Mithaug, D. E., & Martin, J. (2000). Promoting causal agency: The self-determined learning model of instruction. *Exceptional Children, 66*, 439–453.

Wehmeyer, M. L., & Schwartz, M. (1997). Self-determination and positive adult outcomes: A follow-up study of youth with mental retardation or learning disabilities. *Exceptional Children, 63*, 245–255.

Weil, F., & Pascal, M. (1990). The place of verbal games in the framework of in-patient group psychotherapy with adolescents. *Journal of Group Psychotherapy, Psychodrama and Sociometry, 43*(3), 128–138.

Weisbord, M. R. (1992). *Discovering common ground*. San Francisco, CA: Berrett-Koehler Publishers Inc.

Welton, E., Vakil, S., & Carasea, C. (2004). Strategies for increasing positive social interactions in children with autism: A case study. *Teaching Exceptional Children, 37*, 40–46.

Wenger, E. (1998). *Communities of practice: learning, meaning, and identity*. New York, NY: Cambridge University Press. doi:10.1017/CBO9780511803932

Wertsch, J. V. (1997). *Vygotsky and the formation of the mind*. Cambridge, MA: Harvard University Press.

Whitney, L. (2011). Smartphones to dominate PCs in Gartner forecast. *CNET News*. Retrieved from http://news.cnet.com/8301-1001_3-10434760-92.html

Wilcox, M., Bacon, C., & Campbell, P. (2004). *National survey of parents and providers using AT in early intervention*. Retrieved from http://tnt.asu.edu

Wilcox, S., & Peyton, J. K. (1999). American sign language as a foreign language. *ERIC Clearinghouse on Language and Linguistics Digest* (EDO-FL-89-01). (ERIC Document Reproduction Service No. ED309651).

Wilcox, M., Guimond, A., Campbell, P., & Weintraub Moore, H. (2006). Assistive technology for infants and toddlers with disabilities: Provider perspectives regarding use, decision-making practices, and resources. *Topics in Early Childhood Special Education, 26*(1), 33–50. doi:10.1177/02711214060260010401

Williams, D., Hemstreet, S., Liu, M., & Smith, V. (1998). Examining how middle school students use problem-based learning software. In T. Ottmann & I. Tomek (Eds.), *Proceedings of ED-MEDIA/ED-TELECOM 98,* (pp. 1550-1556). Charlottesville, VA: Association for the Advancement of Computing in Education.

Williams, M. D., Burden, R. L., & Lanvers, U. (2002). French is the language of love and stuff: Student perceptions of issues related to motivation in learning a foreign language. *British Educational Research Journal, 28*(4), 503–528. doi:10.1080/0141192022000005805

Wise, B. K., Olson, R. K., Ring, J., & Johnson, M. C. (1997). Interactive computer support for improving phonological skills in remedial reading. In J. Metsala, & L. Ehri (Eds.), *Word recognition in beginning literacy*. Mahwah, NJ: Lawrence Erlbaum Inc.

Witmer, B. G., & Singer, M. J. (1998). Measuring presence in virtual environments: A presence questionnaire. *Presence (Cambridge, Mass.)*, *7*(3), 225–240. doi:10.1162/105474698565686

Wolfram Research, Inc. (2012). *Wolfram MathWord: Venn diagram*. Retrieved from http://mathworld.wolfram.com/VennDiagram.html

Wood, J. W. (2006). *Teaching students in inclusive settings: Adapting and accommodating instruction* (5th ed.). Upper Saddle River, NJ: Pearson/Merrill Prentice Hall.

Wood, L. E., & Stewart, P. W. (1987). Improvement of practical reasoning skills with a computer game. *Journal of Computer-Based Instruction*, *14*(2), 49–53.

Woods, M., Maiden, J., & Brandes, J. (2011). An exploration and the representation of students with disabilities in distance education. *Online Journal of Distance Learning Administration*, *19*(5).

Xueqin, J. (2011, November). Selecting the right Chinese students. *The Chronicle of Higher education*. Retrieved from http://chronicle.com/article/Selecting-the-Right-Chinese/129621/

Yuksel, P., Robin, B., & McNeil, S. (2011). Educational uses of digital storytelling around the world. In M. Koehler & P. Mishra (Eds.), *Proceedings of Society for Information Technology & Teacher Education International Conference 2011* (pp. 1264-1271). Chesapeake, VA: AACE.

Zabala, J. S. (2000). Setting the stage for success: Building success through effective selection and use of assistive technology systems. *LD Online*. Retrieved from http://www.ldonline.org/article/5874/

Zabala, J. (2004). Quality indicators for assistive technology services in school settings. *Journal of Special Education Technology*, *15*, 25–36.

Zabala, J., & Carl, D. F. (2005). Quality indicators for assistive technology services in schools. In D. Edyburn, K. Higgins, & R. Boone (Eds.), *Handbook of special education technology research and practice* (pp. 179–208). Whitefish Bay, WI: Knowledge by Design.

Zatynski, M. (2013). Calling for success: Online retention rates get boost from personal outreach. *ESSelect*. Retrieved from http://www.educationsector.org/sites/default/files/publications/ESS_ECore_1.pdf

Zehler, A. M., Fleischman, H. L., Hopstock, P. J., Stephenson, T. G., Pendzick, M. L., & Sapru, S. (2003). Descriptive study of services to LEP students and LEP students with disabilities: Vol. I. *Research report*. Arlington, VA: Development Associates, Inc.

Zhu, E., Payette, P., & DeZure, D. (2006). *An introduction to teaching online*. Ann Arbor, MI: University of Michigan.

Zull, J. E. (2011). *From brain to mind: Using neuroscience to guide change in education*. Sterling, VA: Stylus Publishing, LLC.

# About the Contributors

**Boaventura DaCosta** is a research fellow with Solers Research Group. He holds a Ph.D. in Education: Instructional Technology, an M.A. in Instructional Technology/Media: Instructional Systems, and a B.S. in Computers Science from the University of Central Florida. His research interests include topics in assistive technology; cognitive psychology, to include cognitive load reduction, decision making, problem solving, and transfer; Information and Communication Technology (ICT); and serious games. He has authored and co-authored peer reviewed articles published in scholarly journals; books and peer reviewed chapters; and papers, presented at technical conferences and workshops. Published topics have included massively multiplayer online game addiction and high engagement, digital propensity and ICT, and various foci in modeling and simulation. Complimenting his research, Dr. DaCosta has almost 20 years of professional software development life cycle experience in multi-tier proprietary and open source software solutions in the commercial and government training sectors.

**Soonhwa Seok** is a research professor in special education at Korea University, where she teaches special education courses to service students. Dr. Seok holds interests in assistive technology with applications for students with special needs, focusing on developmental and learning disabilities. Most recently, she has examined special education teachers' priority for students with developmental disabilities in their curriculum with assistive technology application. Her main research focus is assistive technology evaluation, to include functional evaluation, and supporting intensity scales implementing assistive technology for students with disabilities. She is also interested in the application of mobile technology for students with developmental disabilities. In her research, she has used advanced statistical applications using validation approaches, including factor analysis and multidimensional scaling. She has also actively served as a peer reviewer for conference proposals, presented on Web accessibility and game addiction, and published articles on special education technology and information and communication technology in general curriculum.

* * *

**Fiona S. Baker** is an assistant professor of education studies at Emirates College for Advanced Education in Abu Dhabi, United Arab Emirates. She has lectured and supervised teachers in special education primary and early childhood preparation on programs in Europe, the U.S., and the U.A.E. She has published on topics of special education, assistive technology, Teaching English to Speakers of Other Languages (TESOL), bilingualism, early childhood care and education, and teacher development. She is currently conducting research in kindergarten classrooms exploring cultural perspectives on the meaning of play.

**Bob Barrett** holds an Ed.D. in the field of Human Resource Development from George Washington University, Washington, D.C. Dr. Barrett has been teaching at American Public University for the past 10 years, actively teaching online for the past 12 years. He is an adjunct instructor with other online programs, as well as a course developer and online teacher and trainer. His research interests include online learning, disability, teacher training, knowledge management, and intellectual capital. His specialization has been concentrated on human and intellectual capital, as well as knowledge management in the context of human resource management and human resource development. He has worked in both the private and public sectors, and has spoken extensively at various international conferences in Europe, South America, and Asia.

**Kathleen Bastedo** received a B.S. in Occupational Therapy from Utica College in 1982 and has worked in occupational therapy for over 20 years, including 10 years specializing in the area of assistive technology. She earned a M.Ed. in Curriculum and Instruction from the University of South Florida in 1997 and has been working as an instructional designer at the University of Central Florida (UCF) since 2006. She facilitates faculty with the design and delivery of online courses, and has created and taught online for the UCF College of Education in the area of assistive technology. Her area of specialization includes Universal Design for Learning and the accessibility of online course materials. Kathleen has presented on these topics at a variety of conferences including Sloan-C (both the Online Learning Conference and the Blended Learning Conference and Workshop), the Educause Learning Initiative, and the Assistive Technology Industry Association (ATIA) annual conference.

**Brian R. Bryant**, Ph.D., lives and works in Austin, Texas. Brian taught in the Maine public schools as a K-8 and high school special education teacher before moving to Austin, Texas, to pursue his doctorate in special education. After graduating from the University of Texas (UT) at Austin, Brian served as the Research Director for Pro-Ed Publishing Company for 10 years, during which time he taught at UT and also taught as visiting professor at the University of Louisville, Pacific Lutheran University, and the University of Hawaii. He currently holds the title of Research Professor and Fellow with the Meadows Center for Preventing Educational Risk. He has over 100 publications, including articles, books, chapters in books, and tests. Brian has also given over 100 presentations across the U.S. and internationally. His current research interests are in the areas of mathematics and reading learning disabilities and support needs of individuals with intellectual and developmental disabilities, along with their applications for assistive technology.

**Jennifer Courduff**, Ph.D., is an assistant professor at Azusa Pacific University where she develops and teaches courses in the Master of Arts: Digital Teaching and Learning program. Dr. Courduff is an active member of the International Society for Technology in Education (ISTE) and chair of the special education SigML subcommittee. Her research and presentations focus on technology integration within diverse learning environments and mobile learning.

**Amy Duncan** is devoted to quality services for students with special needs through professional development, consultation and coaching in instructional methodology, positive behavior supports, inclusive practice, and assistive technology for teachers and families. In her role as Program Specialist with the West End Special Education Local Plan Area (WESELPA) in San Bernardino County, Amy co-created a community of practice for assistive technology that included practitioners within 11 districts, designers of the assistive technology strand within the Computer Using Educator's Conference. She is also responsible for the co-development of the Assistive Technology Certificate Program for the WESELPA. Amy holds a B.A. from the University of California at Santa Barbara and an M.A. in Special Education from the California State University, Los Angeles. She is currently an adjunct faculty member at Claremont Graduate University and California State University San Bernardino in their graduate programs preparing special education teachers for their future work with students.

**Michael Dunn** was an elementary/middle school teacher in the Toronto (Ontario, Canada) area for 11 years, 6 of which were as a special education consultant teacher in inclusion classrooms. He completed his Ph.D. at Indiana University Bloomington in 2005 and currently is an associate professor of special education and literacy at the Vancouver campus of Washington State University. His research interests include developing strategies that help struggling readers and writers as well as response to intervention.

**Joanne Gilbreath** is a professor of education for the Master of Arts: Digital Teaching and Learning program at Azusa Pacific University. The program prepares new teachers in regular and special education to embed technology tools and resources into the classroom. Dr. Gilbreath is an active member of the International Society for Technology in Education (ISTE) and regularly presents on topics such as teaching and learning in the digital age, and educational leadership in the changing education environment. She has also presented on accreditation and accountability for the National Council for Accreditation of Teacher Education (NCATE) and other accrediting bodies.

**Sukun Jin** is a professor in the Department of Education at Konkuk University, Seoul, South Korea, as well as the Director of the Institute of Educational Research at the same university. Since he earned his Ph.D. at Purdue University, he has been committed to educational research focused on students with special needs to include gifted students and students with autism. Dr. Jin is currently conducting a research project that is focused on mobile application use and its benefits to these students.

**Woo Kim** has over 30 years of professional experience as a special education teacher and is currently the principal of Ja Hae Special School in Suwon, South Korea. His main focus of research is inclusion and students with intellectual disabilities. As a special educator, he has contributed to research on inclusion, the application of mobile technology, to include iPad use in the context of special education, and smart learning. He is considered by many as one of the leaders in special education in South Korea.

**Carolyn Kinsell** has more than 20 years of experience in the education and training sectors. Her background includes extensive work as a human performance technologist. She is considered a subject matter expert in instructional design and has extensive experience in the administration and conduct of both technical and soft-skill training programs. Her work on the application of training includes both commercial and government sectors. Dr. Kinsell has worked closely with all branches of the military to include the Army, as well as cryptologists and intelligence specialists throughout the Navy and Marines. Commercial clients include the public school system in Florida, the automobile industry, and telecommunication companies.

**Angelique Nasah** is an experienced Human Performance Improvement (HPI) professional who endeavors to provide energetic and compelling leadership where the goal is to offer innovative solutions to the performance challenges facing organizations. She is interested in front end analysis, design, development, summative evaluation stages of the HPI process, as well as with instructional technology program administration and faculty technology training and curricular integration. Dr. Nasah has worked in the education and training sector for more than 20 years and has experience in secondary and higher education, the commercial sector, as well as defense training.

**Min Wook Ok**, M.Ed., is a doctoral student in the Department of Special Education in the College of Education at the University of Texas at Austin and the manager of the College of Education's Assistive and Instructional Technology Lab. Her focused research interests include the use of technology to enhance academic learning and the lives of students with disabilities, and supporting teacher preparation to integrate technology effectively in classroom instruction.

**Kavita Rao** is an assistant professor in the Department of Special Education of the College of Education at the University of Hawai'i at Mānoa. Her research areas include technology for children with disabilities, online learning for non-traditional students, application of universal design for learning, and technology-related educational strategies for English language learners and immigrant students. Kavita teaches undergraduate and graduate level courses on assistive and educational technologies and courses on instructional strategies in the special education department. She has worked with state education agencies and schools in Hawaii, Guam, American Samoa, Commonwealth of the Northern Marianas Islands, Palau, Republic of the Marshall Islands, and the Federated States of Micronesia, conducting professional development training to help teachers integrate technology into curriculum.

**Benjamin Slotznick**, J.D., Ph.D., is a lawyer, inventor and software developer, with broad research and entrepreneurial experience. He is president, founder, and principal of Point-and-Read, Inc. In the assistive technology field, Dr. Slotznick is the inventor of phatic assistive and Augmentative Communications (AAC) interfaces (patent pending) and several other Point-and-Read™ technologies (patented and patent pending). He is a member of the Assistive Technology Industry Association and has served on several of its committees. He has presented on assistive technology at national conferences, including the American Association on Intellectual and Developmental Disabilities (AAIDD; formerly AAMR), Closing the Gap, Assistive Technology Industry Association (ATIA), and California State University at Northridge (CSUN). In a prior academic setting, he conducted laboratory and theoretical studies of small-group decision making and published articles in peer reviewed journals on game theory.

**James Stachowiak** holds the role of Associate Director of the Iowa Center for Assistive Technology Education and Research (ICATER) in the College of Education at the University of Iowa. James has a B.S.E. in Industrial and Operations Engineering and an M.S.E. in Biomedical Engineering from the University of Michigan. James is a member of the Rehabilitation Engineering and Assistive Technology Society of North America (RESNA) and is a RESNA certified Assistive Technology Professional. James has also served as the chair of RESNA's Education Committee and Educator's Professional Specialty Group. He has presented several presentations on providing AT training to pre-service teachers at conferences such as RESNA, Closing the Gap, Assistive Technology Industry Association (ATIA), and Regional and National Dyslexia Conferences.

**Aubry D. Threlkeld** is an advanced doctoral candidate in Human Development and Education at the Harvard Graduate School of Education. He holds an M.S. in Education from Mercy College in New York and a B.A. from Middlebury College in Vermont. His interests range from disability studies, queer studies, assistive technologies, and critical psychology to program evaluation and reading intervention. He specializes in qualitative approaches to talk and text. His current research centers on a small group of high school students who advocate for other students with learning disabilities. In the last 13 years, he has been a special educator, teacher trainer, lecturer, grassroots activist, and consultant.

**Jessica Vargas** is currently an instructional technologist at Rollins College. She has over 11 years of experience in designing and developing higher level learning distance education courses, which she has accumulated through professional advancement in positions such as programmer, tech support assistant, graphic designer, system administrator, and instructional designer. Jessica has also presented since 2004 at a variety of conferences for Educause, ELI (formerly NLI), and American Association of State Colleges and Universities (AASCU) regarding the "Millennial Generations" learning styles as well for Educause, Sloan-C, and the Distance Teaching and Learning Conference regarding accessibility, universal design and copyright. She earned a M.A. in Instructional Technology from the University of Central Florida in 2009.

# Index

## M



## N



## O



## P



## Q



## R



## S



## T



## U



## V



## W